# ADRIANUS SARAVIA

(c. 1532-1613)

# STUDIES IN THE HISTORY
# OF
# CHRISTIAN THOUGHT

EDITED BY

HEIKO A. OBERMAN, Tübingen

IN COOPERATION WITH

HENRY CHADWICK, Oxford
EDWARD A. DOWEY, Princeton, N.J.
JAROSLAV PELIKAN, New Haven, Conn.
BRIAN TIERNEY, Ithaca, N.Y.
E. DAVID WILLIS, Princeton, N.J.

VOLUME XXI

**WILLEM NIJENHUIS**

ADRIANUS SARAVIA
(c. 1532-1613)

LEIDEN
E. J. BRILL
1980

# ADRIANUS SARAVIA

## (c. 1532-1613)

*Dutch Calvinist, first Reformed defender of the English episcopal Church order on the basis of the ius divinum*

BY

WILLEM NIJENHUIS

LEIDEN

E. J. BRILL

1980

Published with financial support from the Netherlands Organization for the Advancement of Pure Research (Z.W.O.)

92
Sa7ln

8101155

ISBN   90 04 06194 0

PRINTED IN THE NETHERLANDS

"Unus Deus, unus Dominus Jesus Christus,
una Ecclesia, unum Baptisma, unum Ministerium".
H. Saravia, *Defensio tractationis De diversis ministrorum Evangelii gradibus,* 32

"Sine sacrorum ministro non potest esse respublica".
*Ibid.,* 39 seq.

"Cavendum imprimis ne qui homines fanaticos vitare vult, ipse fanaticus fiat".
UBA. Ms. B. 69; Doc. XLVII

# CONTENTS

SECOND PART

# THEOLOGY

# PREFACE

"Saravia still lacks the biography which he certainly merits" (*NNBW*, IX, 938), declared the Dutch historian, A. A. van Schelven, 45 years ago and nothing has happened since to remedy this state of affairs. All we have are a few scattered articles not based on original research. The reason for the reluctance to undertake such research is obvious enough for, in the course of a long life, Saravia lived in very different parts of the world and set his hand to a wide variety of tasks. If we are accurately to fill in the hitherto fragmentary and partly unreliable picture of this Dutch Englishman's life, we must follow him on his lengthy travels and search many archives, predominantly in the Netherlands and England but also in France and present-day Belgium. The author of this study has made a start and has gathered some material without, however, making any pretence at supplying what is necessary for a biography in the true sense of the word. Information about Saravia, especially about the first 27 years of his life, is still too scarce for this. Where ecclesiastical and civil archives contain richer material, as for example for the period 1582-1587, our account has become correspondingly more detailed. On the other hand, the biographical information for the period 1588-1595, in which Saravia wrote his most important works, is pretty scanty. All of which has meant that this study is somewhat unequally proportioned. The same applies to the impression left by Saravia's theology. In his most important works he confines himself almost exclusively to two subjects, first, church government and church order, and, secondly, forms of civil government and their powers and the relationship between church and state. Meanwhile Dutch, English and French archives probably conceal material that would serve to throw into sharper relief the picture of the man whose life and work we here portray. If this study inspires others to follow up the search then the author will have achieved one important goal which he has pursued with this publication.

In spite of the limitations just mentioned we have thought this inquiry worth undertaking and that for three reasons. As a theologian, the author is fascinated by the fact that the man who is the subject of this book, a con- \ nced Dutch Calvinist who served the Reformed church in his native land for many years, became the first in England to defend episcopal church order by an appeal not only to tradition but to the "ius divinum" and this without in any way denying his doctrinal convictions. At the same time as rejecting the Calvinist Puritan "new presbyter" (N. Sykes, *Old Priest and New Presbyter*) Saravia created a "new bishop", that is to say a figure whose office could be founded on the "ius divinum" every bit as much as could that of the Reformed elder. This theory was new to the Church of

England in whose post-Reformation foundation of the episcopate practical considerations had hitherto outweighed the theoretical.

Secondly, there is the ecumenical importance of the subject. The debate between Beza and Saravia about the ministry and structure of the church, presbyterian or episcopal, continues to our own day. To some extent it dominates discussion on Church unity in various parts of the world. Is Calvinism reconciliable with episcopacy? Is the figure of the ''episcopus in presbyterio'' conceivable? Must Reformed Christians reject on principle any more than local ecclesiastical office? Must Anglicans deny on principle the legitimacy of non-episcopal ordination? These questions have a historical background, springing as they do from sixteenth century England and Scotland. An enquiry such as the present one can go some way towards modifying the difference in the opposing points of view just outlined by shedding light on their historical origins. Calvinist though he was, Saravia opted for a hierarchical episcopal church structure, appealing frequently to the Genevan reformer. Episcopalian though he was, he never denied the validity or lawfulness of presbyterian ordination. Why must churches, which in the sixteenth century, despite different structures prized the maintenance of intercommunion, remain divided in the twentieth century? It seems to us that, even if he cannot accept Saravia's ecclesiological views, the ecumenist nonetheless has something to learn from him.

As a historian the author has been struck during this investigation by Saravia's role as liaison officer between the Netherlands and England: in the early sixties, the period of severe persecution, primarily in the ecclesiastical field, in the eighties predominantly in the political. After William of Orange's death, at the time when the revolt of the Low Countries, steadily suppressed by military pressure in the South, continued vigorously in the North, Saravia took part in the attempts to interest the English Queen in supplying political and military aid to the young republic. To be sure, as a cleric and university professor, he could not play a leading role on the stage of Anglo-Dutch relations, but an enquiry into his activities, prompted as they were by strong anglophile sentiments, brings to light many interesting details of this history.

It must be stressed that this study is purely historical and in no sense dogmatic. Its aim is to outline Saravia's life and his opinions in their historical context. Any assessment from the view-point of biblical or dogmatic theology has deliberately been left to others. Beside the autobiographical references scattered throughout the corpus of Saravia's published works, his correspondence is important for obtaining insight into his life and theological development. Hence a number of letters together with two of his memoranda (Document Nos. XXXIII and XXXIX) are included in the third part. 32 of the 49 documents presented here have never been published before. There are two reasons for giving sources which have already appeared in print. In the first place, some of the earlier editions, especially that of John Strype's, required some correction. Secondly, it is convenient for the reader to have reproduced in one place all the material under consideration; at any rate, all that is known at present, since there is sure to be more hidden away in the archives.

This work could not have been written without the cooperation of numerous colleagues and learned institutions who at various moments in the research rendered invaluable service to the author both with written informations and advices and with personal assistance. As far as Great Britain is concerned, we are indebted to the Rev. W. A. Pembroke (Breaston), Mr Alastair Duke (Southampton), Prof. K. W. Swart and Prof. Geoffrey F. Nuttall (London). In the first stage of the enquiry Mr. Alain Dufour (Geneva) aided the author with useful advice. He is also obliged for informations to his colleagues J. N. Bakhuizen van den Brink, J. van den Berg (Leiden) who, just as his colleague G. H. M. Posthumus Meyjes, read through the manuscript of this study, and C. van der Woude (Leeuwarden) as well as to Prof. J. Rott (Strasburg), Dr. G. Moreau (Liège) and Dr. J. Lenselink (Dordrecht). Dr. F. F. Blok (University of Amsterdam) never refused an appeal for the solution of linguistic problems involving Latin texts.

In numerous English libraries and archives we received helpful and expert guidance in the discovery and examination of the material here considered. The writer was greatly encouraged by the interest shown by the council of the Dutch Church, Austin Friars, London. He is further obliged to Miss Anne M. Oakley, archivist of the Cathedral Archives and Library, Canterbury, who always made it easy for him to work in that historic place. The staffs of the Manuscript Departments of the University Library, Cambridge, the City Library, Gloucester, the civil and ecclesiastical archives on the Island of Guernsey, the County Record Office, Lichfield, the British Library, London, the Greater London Record Office, Guild Hall Library and Lambeth Palace Library were all very helpful. Special mention is due to the Public Record Office where, besides many others, Mr. John Walford in the Search Department went to considerable trouble to solve a problem of biographical detail. Thanks are also due to Mr. N. H. MacMichael, Keeper of the Muniments of Westminster Abbey and to the staffs of the Kent Council Archives (Maidstone), the Bodleian Library (Oxford) and the archives of Worcester Cathedral. As historian of the town and its neighbourhood, Mr. F. H. Clayton (Lichfield) interested himself in Saravia's residence in Tatenhill.

In France, M. Marcel Boutte (Hesdin) made possible our research in the municipal library of Saravia's birthplace and the same is true for St. Omer of the custodian of the Bibliothèque Municipale in that town. The staffs of the Manuscript Departments of the Bibliothèque Nationale and the Library of the Sorbonne (Paris) have given as ready help as have those of the Belgisch Rijksarchief (Brussels) and the Stadsarchief of Ghent in Belgium.

In the Netherlands we are first of all indebted to Her Majesty the Queen for permission to consult the Koninklijk Huisarchief (The Hague). In his own country, the author had every assistance from the Manuscript Departments of the University of Amsterdam, the Free University and the Universities of Leiden and Utrecht, from those in charge of the Municipal archives of Delft, Dordrecht, Leiden and Utrecht where some archives of the local church communities are kept, and also from the archivist of the Dutch Reformed Church and the Manuscript Department of the Gemeentebibliotheek in Rotterdam. Special mentions must be made of the trouble taken by the staff of the Koninklijke Bibliotheek (The Hague) during the years of this enquiry and to the consideration and expertise with which Miss R. Damstra of the Central Catalogue has time and again helped us.

During our research we have been able to make grateful use of H. J. Witkam's edition of *De dagelijkse zaken van de Leidse Universiteit van 1581 tot 1596,* 10 vls; Leiden 1969-1975 in which Saravia's name appears so frequently.

We acknowledge with gratitude the opportunity given us during the academic year 1974-5 to devote ourselves uninterruptedly to academic work in an international community of scholars at N.I.A.S. (Netherlands Institute for Advanced Studies in the Humanities and Social Studies) at Wassenaar and thus to work out the results of our research.

The writer wishes to express his grateful thanks to Z.W.O. (Netherlands Organization for the Advancement of Pure Research) who made it possible for him to make several journeys for research in England and France and to publish the results of his undertaking in this book. In his expressions of appreciation he naturally includes the translator, the Rev. Dr. J. E. Platt (Oxford). The author wants also to express his appreciation for the reception of this study into the series *Studies in the History of Christian Thought.*

We must now add a brief word about technicalities. In the notes and bibliography we have followed the rules of the Nederlands Historisch Genootschap (E. H. Kossmann and C.B. Wels, ed. *Aanwijzingen voor tekstbewerking en annotaties,* Utrecht, 1971). Quotations in the footnotes are given in the original text (Dutch, French or Latin) since this can contribute to a better understanding. For references to the works of Saravia included in the *Tractatus,* we adopt the pagination used in that collection.

In the documents we have not aimed at a uniformity in the orthography which is not present in the text itself. Only, for the sake of greater general ease in reading, has j been altered to i, the v used as a vowel to u and, vice versa, the consonant u to v. From the same consideration in some places the spelling has been corrected and the punctuation modernized. Abbreviation marks in the original texts have been altered by completing the words and where abbreviations, which were current in the sixteenth century, are likely to be unclear to the modern reader we have written them out in full.

Finally, the continental reader is alerted to two chronological peculiarities of English documents in this period. The Julian calendar was in use until 1 January 1752 which, during the time dealt with here, resulted in a difference of ten days (vetus stilus; old style). The calendar year began on 25 March (Annunciation of the Virgin Mary), almost three months later than on the continent (stilus Angliae; mos anglicanus).

Groningen, Easter 1979                              Willem Nijenhuis

# ABBREVIATIONS

| | |
|---|---|
| *DGM* | H. Saravia, *De diversis gradibus ministrorum Evangelii*. References are to the edition in *DTT*. |
| *DT* | H. Saravia, *Defensio tractatus de diversis ministrorum gradibus*. References are to the edition in *DTT*. |
| *DTT* | H. Saravia, *Diversi tractatus theologici*. |
| *ETB* | H. Saravia, *Examen tractatus D. Bezae de triplici episcoporum genere*. References are to the edition in *DTT*. |
| *IA* | H. Saravia, *De imperandi authoritate et christiana obedientia*. References are to the edition in *DTT*. |
| *RG* | H. Saravia, *Responsio ad convitia quaedam Gretseri Iesuitae*. References are to the edition in *DTT*. |
| *SE* | H. Saravia, *De sacra eucharistia tractatus*. G. A. Denison, ed. |
| *VV* | H. Saravia, *Venerabili viro, mihi multum dilecto et observando fratri*. References are to the edition in *DTT*. |
| | |
| *A* | *Archief voor kerkelijke geschiedenis, inzonderheid in Nederland,* 1829-1840. |
| *AC* | H. Hardenberg, *Het archief van curatoren der Leidsche universiteit.* |
| *AGN* | *Algemene geschiedenis der Nederlanden.* |
| *ANK* | *Archief voor Nederlandsche kerkgeschiedenis,* 1885-1899. |
| *ARG* | *Archiv für Reformationsgeschichte.* |
| *ASF* | H. Hardenberg, *De archieven van senaat en faculteiten benevens het archief van de academische vierschaar der Leidsche universiteit.* |
| *BBHS* | C. Read, *Bibliography of British History Stuart Period.* |
| *BBHT* | C. Read, *Bibliography of British History Tudor Period.* |
| *BHEW* | *Bulletin de la commission de l'histoire des Églises Wallonnes.* |
| BL | British Library, London: |
| | Add.Ms.    Additional Manuscripts. |
| | LM.    Lansdowne Manuscripts. |
| | CM.    Cotton Manuscripts. |
| *BMHG* | *Bijdragen en Mededelingen van het Historisch Genootschap.* |
| *BN* | *Bibliographie nationale.* |
| BodL | Bodleian Library, Oxford. |
| Brandt, *Reformatie* | G. Brandt, *Historie der Reformatie.* |
| *BSHPB* | *Bulletin de la Société d'histoire du Protestantisme Belge.* |
| *BSHPF* | *Bulletin de la société de l'histoire du protestantisme français.* |
| *BWPGN* | *Biografisch Woordenboek van Protestantsche godgeleerden in Nederland.* |
| Burman, *Sylloges* | *Sylloges epistolarum a viris illustribus scriptarum*. Tomi quinque, collecti et digesti per Petrum Burmannum (Leiden, 1727) I. |
| Cardwell, *Annals* | E. Cardwell, ed. *Documentary Annals of the Reformed Church of England.* |
| Cardwell, *History of Conferences* | E. Cardwell, ed. *A History of Conferences . . . connected with the Revision of the Book of Common Prayer.* |
| Cardwell, *Synodalia* | E. Cardwell, ed. *A Collection of Articles of Religion.* |
| *CChrSL* | *Corpus Christianorum. Series Latina.* |
| CC | Canterbury Cathedral: |
| | CA 1   Chapter Acts 1581-1607. |

|  |  |
|---|---|
| | CA 2 Chapter Acts 1608-1628. |
| | TA Treasurer's Accounts. |
| | FCR French Church Records (Actes du consistoire de l'église wallonne de Canterbury 1595-1599). |
| *CH* | *Church History.* |
| *CO* | *Ioannis Calvini Opera.* |
| *CR* | *Corpus Reformatorum.* |
| *CSPD* | *Calendar of State Papers. Domestic Series.* |
| *CSPF* | *Calendar of State Papers. Foreign Series.* |
| Coornhert, *Werken* | Dieryck Volkertsz. Coornhert, *Wercken.* |
| *DNB* | *Dictionary of National Biography.* |
| *EE* | *Praestantium ac eruditorum virorum epistolae ecclesiasticae et theologicae.* Ed. tertia. |
| Fuller, *Church History* | Th. Fuller, *The Church History of Britain.* |
| GAD | Gemeentearchief Delft (City Archives: Archives Reformed Church Delft). |
| GADO | Gemeentearchief Dordrecht (City Archives: Archives Reformed Church Dordrecht). |
| GAL | Gemeentearchief Leiden (City Archives) |
| GAU | Gemeentearchief Utrecht (City Archives). |
| GDB | GAL, Gerechtsdagboek A 1. |
| GDR | Gloucester Diocesan Records. |
| GHL | Guild Hall Library, London. L 19.22: Dutch Church Austin Friars. |
| Groen, *Archives* | G. Groen van Prinsterer, ed. *Archives ou correspondance de la maison d'Orange-Nassau,* 1. série. |
| Hessels, *ELBA* | J. W. Hessels, ed. *Ecclesiae Londino-Batavae Archivum.* |
| Hooyer, *Kerkordeningen* | C. Hooyer, ed. *Oude kerkordeningen der Nederlandsche Hervormde gemeenten (1563-1638).* |
| Janssen, *Kerkhervorming Vlaanderen* | H. Q. Janssen, *De kerkhervorming in Vlaanderen.* |
| *Inv. Lipse* | A. Gerlo and H. D. L. Vervliet, ed. *Inventaire de la correspondance de Juste Lipse.* |
| *JEH* | *The Journal of Ecclesiastical History.* |
| Jewel, *Works* | *The Works of John Jewel.* Parker Society, ed. |
| *KA* | *Kerkhistorisch Archief,* 1857-1866. |
| KAO | Kent Archives Office, Maidstone: |
| | DRC.R8 Rochester Episcopalis Register, V (1543-1637). |
| | DRA.Ai.8 Induction mandates Lewisham. |
| | PRC.32/42 fols. 153-155. Saravia's Last Will. |
| | PRC.27/2/67. Inventory of Saravia's goods. |
| KB | GAL: Boek des Kerkenraets. Archives Reformed Church. Nr. 001. |
| KHA | Koninklijk Huisarchief, The Hague. (Archives of the Royal House). |
| LC | GAL: Premier livre du consistoire de l'église wallonne de Leyden 1584-1611. |
| *Liturgies of Edward VI* | *Two Liturgies in the Reign of King Edward VI.* Parker Society, ed. |
| LP | Lambeth Palace Library, London. |
| *LSW* | *Livre synodal des églises wallonnes des Pays-Bas,* I. |
| Molhuysen, *Bronnen* | P. C. Molhuysen, ed. *Bronnen tot de geschiedenis der Leidsche universiteit.* |

| | |
|---|---|
| *NA* | *Nieuw Archief voor kerkelijke geschiedenis,* 1852-1854. |
| *Ned. A.* | *Nederlands Archief voor kerkelijke geschiedenis,* 1841-1849. |
| *Ned.AK.* | *Nederlands Archief voor kerkgeschiedenis.* |
| Le Neve, *Fasti,* III | J. Le Neve, ed. *Fasti Ecclesiae Anglicanae 1541-1857,* III, M. Horn, ed. 1974. |
| Le Neve-Hardy, *Fasti* | J. Le Neve, *Fasti Ecclesiae Anglicanae.* T. D. Hardy, ed. 1854. |
| *NNBW* | *Nieuw Nederlandsch Biografisch Woordenboek.* |
| *NTT* | *Nederlands Theologisch Tijdschrift.* |
| *PG* | J. P. Migne, ed. *Patrologiae cursus completus. Series graeca.* |
| *PHS* | *Publications of the Huguenot Society of London.* |
| *PL* | J. P. Migne, ed. *Patrologiae cursus completus. Series latina.* |
| PRO | Public Record Office, London: |
| | SP   State Papers. |
| | PR   Patent Rolls. |
| *ProHS* | *Proceedings of the Huguenot Society of London.* |
| RA | Rijksarchief. The Hague. (Public Record Office). |
| Reitsma, *Acta.* | J. Reitsma and S. D. van Veen, ed. *Acta der provinciale en particuliere synoden in de Noordelijke Nederlanden.* |
| *RGG* | *Die Religion in Geschichte und Gegenwart,* 3rd. ed. |
| Rogge, *Brieven Wtenbogaert* | *Brieven en onuitgegeven stukken van Johannes Wtenbogaert,* H. C. Rogge, ed. |
| *RStH* | *Resolutiën van de Staten van Holland.* |
| Rutgers, *Acta* | *Acta van de Nederlandsche synoden der zestiende eeuw.* F. L. Rutgers, ed. |
| *SJT* | *Scottish Journal of Theology.* |
| *St. B.* | *Studiën en bijdragen op het gebied der historische theologie.* |
| *STC* | *Short-title Catalogue 1475-1640,* II. 2nd ed. |
| Strype, *Annals* | J. Strype, *Annals of the Reformation.* |
| Strype, *Parker* | J. Strype, *The Life and Acts of Archbishop Parker.* |
| Strype, *Whitgift* | J. Strype, *The Life and Acts of John Whitgift.* |
| UBA | Amsterdam, Universiteitsbibliotheek (University Library). |
| UBL | Leiden, Universiteitsbibliotheek (University Library). |
| WA | Westminster Abbey: |
| | CA   Chapter Acts. |
| | TA   Treasurer's Accounts. |
| | SA   Steward's Accounts. |
| Witkam, *Dagelijkse zaken* | H. J. Witkam, *De dagelijkse zaken van de Leidse universiteit. 1581 tot 1596,* 10 vls. with intr. privately published. Leiden, 1969-1975. |
| Wtenbogaert, *Kerckelicke Historie* | J. Wtenbogaert, *De Kerckelicke Historie,* 1647. |

FIRST PART

# LIFE AND WORK

# CHAPTER ONE

# PREPARATION (c. 1532-1578)

### 1. HESDIN AND SAINT-OMER (c. 1532-1557)

Very little is known about the first 25 years of Adrianus Saravia's life. Even the year of his birth is not entirely certain. According to the inscription on his tombstone in Canterbury Cathedral, he was in his 82nd year on 15 January 1613[1] (1612 stilo Angliae). Assuming that the autobiographical reference in the last edition of his *Defensio Tractationis,* "Ago iam annum 77",[2] was written in 1609, then we can perhaps conclude that Saravia was born in the first half of January 1532.

There is no doubt about his place of birth: Hesdin in Artois.[3] Thus he was a Netherlander, "natione belga", as the memorial inscription in Canterbury Cathedral records. For the rest of his days Saravia never forgot that the Netherlands was his father land. On the title page of his *De Gradibus,* 22 years after he had acquired English nationality, he still styled himself "Hadrianus Saravia Belga".[4] He habitually spoke of Dutch Calvinists as "our people"[5] and of their churches as "our churches".[6] His father Christopher, however, was a native Spaniard who for reasons unknown had settled in Hesdin. He married Elizabeth Boulanger.[7] At this point the archives of present-day Hesdin can help us no further since they contain no material about Vieil-Hesdin where Saravia was born and which was demolished by order of Charles V in August 1553.

His name can be spelt in a seemingly countless variety of ways. In the members' register of the Dutch Church in London (Austin Friars) he appears as Adrianus Saravis or Saravi.[8] In the minutes of that church he is

---

[1] J. M. Cowper, *Memorial Inscriptions of the Cathedral Church of Canterbury* (Canterbury, 1897) 212.

[2] *DT,* 39.

[3] In the members' register of the Dutch Church in London (Austin Friars) his name appears in the year 1561 as "Adrianus Saravis (in another copy: Saravi) van Hesdin". *Returns of Aliens dwelling in the City and Suburbs of London from the Reign of Henry VIII to that of James I,* R. E. G. and E. F. Kirk, ed. (3 vols., Aberdeen, 1900-1908) I, 278.

[4] *DGM,* title-page.

[5] *DT,* Preface to the reader, 2.

[6] *Ibid.,* Prologus, and 3.

[7] H. Q. Janssen, *De kerkhervorming te Brugge* (2 vols., Rotterdam, 1856) II, 286; *Troubles religieux du XVIe siècle dans la Flandre maritime,* Éd. de Coussemaker, ed. (4 vols., Brugge, 1877) I, 340. About Saravia's parents, see p. 40, notes 268 and 269.

[8] Note 3.

called Adrianus a Saravia[9] or Adrianus Soravius.[10] The form Moravius[11] is doubtless due to a mistake. As author of the pamphlet *Een hertgrondighe Begheerte* (1568), he called himself Adrianus Zaraphya.[12] In Hessels' *Archivum,* after the commonest forms, Adrianus Saravia[13] and de Saravia,[14] we come across, Seravia,[15] Saravius,[16] Serravius,[17] Seraphius,[18] Seravius,[19] and Serravia.[20] He customarily signed French letters as Adrien de Saravia.[21] Twice he called himself Adrian van Saravia.[22] He also signed himself as a Saravia with the Christian name Adrianus[23] or Hadrianus.[24] In England he signed other documents and accounts as Hadrian Saravia,[25] de Saravia[26] or de Sarravia.[27] In his Will he is called Hadrianus de Saravia.[28]

At some stage the youthful Adrian entered the religious life. From information provided by Jean Ballin, a monk of the Cistercian abbey of Clairmarais near Saint-Omer, in his *Naamreeks der valse profeten,* we know that Saravia had been a Franciscan friar (Cordelier) in the community at Saint-Omer and that he had quitted it on his conversion to the Reformation.[29] However, it is not unlikely that he had already previously been a friar at Hesdin. This latter town was a cultural centre of the province. Among other things it housed the first printing and publishing office in Artois[30] and it possessed numerous religious foundations[31] including,

---

[9] *Kerkeraadsprotocollen der Nederduitsche vluchtelingen-kerken te Londen 1560-1563,* A. A. van Schelven, ed. (Amsterdam, 1921) 285.

[10] *Ibid.,* 235, 267 f., 395.

[11] *Ibid.,* 201.

[12] *Hertgrondighe Begheerte* (For bibliographical details see p. 28 f.) D4v.

[13] Hessels, *ELBA,* II, Nr. 223, 5.

[14] *Ibid.,* Nr. 162, 1.

[15] *Ibid.,* Nr. 160, 2.

[16] *Ibid.,* III, Nr. 535, 1.

[17] *Ibid.,* Nr. 533, 6.

[18] *Ibid.,* Nr. 571, note 1.

[19] *Ibid.,* Nr. 1373, 1.

[20] *Ibid.,* Nr. 1671, 3.

[21] PRO.SP. 83/17, fol. 10; 83/23, fol. 235r; Doc. IV and VIII; Amsterdam. Library of the Free University; Department of manuscripts, Bos Collection, catalogue Nr. 63. The author thanks Prof. J. van den Berg (Leiden) for drawing his attention to this manuscript.

[22] GAD, Nr. 160; Ancient Archives Synod. Neth. Ref. Church, I, 20, fol. 12; Doc. XXII, XXIII and XXIV.

[23] GAD, Nr. 112; Doc. XXXIV.

[24] BodL. Ms. Tanner 79, fol. 148; Doc. XXXVII.

[25] WA. TA. 1601, Nr. 33655.

[26] *Ibid.* 1607, Nr. 33660.

[27] *Ibid.* 1605 and 1606, Nrs. 33658, 33659.

[28] PRC. 32/42, fol. 153r; Doc. L.

[29] Janssen, *Kerkhervorming Brugge,* II, 286.

[30] B. Danvin, *Vicissitudes, heur et malheur du Vieil-Hesdin* (Saint-Pol, 1866) 199.

[31] P. Meunier, *Histoire d'Hesdin,* I: *La paroisse. Depuis la fondation de la ville en 1554 jusqu'à la révolution française* (Montreuil-sur-Mer, 1896) 5.

from 1294, a Franciscan community.[32] Hesdin, together with Thérouanne, was one of the towns which suffered most from the decades of
conflict between Habsburg and Valois. When Charles V captured it in
1553, it changed hands for the eighth time in 75 years.[33] As the miseries of
its uncertain lot had been largely due to the difficulty of defending it, the
Emperor had the old town demolished and rebuilt 5 kilometres to the
north west on the Canche at the spot where Le Maisnil was situated. The
new, present-day, Hesdin was easier to defend and it was not until 1639
that it finally passed into French possession. The demolition of Vieil-
Hesdin in 1553 was very thorough. Even in 1690 it still numbered no
more than 50 inhabitants.[34] Only two nunneries were allowed to stay. All
the rest of the religious were forced to find a home elsewhere. It is
reasonable to suppose that Saravia was among the Franciscans who were
received into the house of the Cordeliers in Saint-Omer. A lot of people
and property moved from the ill-fated Hesdin to Saint-Omer which thus
profited from the ruin of its neighbour, as it did also from that of
Thérouanne destroyed by imperial troops two months previously.[35] Cordeliers from Saint-Omer continued to preach in Hesdin.[36]

Saint-Omer takes its name from Audomarus, the third Bishop of
Thérouanne, who founded a Benedictine community on land granted him
in 648. One of the two friends who accompanied him from Luxeuil and
who arrived with him, Saint-Bertin, shortly afterwards founded the
famous abbey named after him. After a visit on the occasion of his investiture as Count of Artois in 1520, Charles V had the town fortified. In
1548 Philip II came to the town for the same purpose, accompanied by his
father and by Granvelle, then still Bishop of Arras. In the fifties Saint-
Omer, which the emperor had made an arsenal, continued to escape the
fate of Hesdin and Thérouanne, though it was seriously threatened by the
French in 1555 and 1558.[37]

Saint-Omer, which in 1559 took the place of Thérouanne as a cathedral
town, was an important ecclesiastical centre. It housed many religious
communities, among them that of the Cordeliers[38] of which brother
Adrian was a member. Their first home, which had lain outside the town,
had been demolished in 1477, once again for military reasons. In its place
they had been allocated a site within the walls. An extension of the

---

[32] *Ibid.*, 7.

[33] Ch. de la Charie, *Hesdin. Ses origines, ses monuments, ses promenades* (Hesdin, s.a.) 9.

[34] Danvin, *Vicissitudes*, 256.

[35] *Ibid.*, 294.

[36] De Coussemaker, *Troubles religieux*, IV, 58.

[37] J. Derheims, *Histoire de la ville de Saint-Omer* (St. Omer, 1843) 315-324.

[38] Saint-Omer Bibliothèque publique, Ms. Nr. 809: *Les Annales de la ville de St. Omer et
l'établissement des maisons religieuses*, I: *jusq'en l'an 1554;* G. Coolen, "Fragment d'obituaire et
réforme des Cordeliers de St. Omer", *Bulletin de la Société Académique des Antiquaires de la
Morinie*, XX (1963) 375.

buildings was begun in 1493 and the conventual church was completed in 1502.[39] In the years 1408 and 1409 the community played an important part in the dispute between the Observants and the Conventualists. The quarrel had ended in the victory of the former party.[40] Later in the fifteenth century close relations grew up between the house at Saint-Omer and the first Observant community in the North Netherlands, that of Gouda. In 1439 the first friars from Saint-Omer entered the Franciscan house at Gouda. Soon afterwards they were withdrawn from the jurisdiction of the Minister Provincial and placed under their own Vicar Provincial to form the nucleus of a separate congregation of Observants.[41]

It is well known that the Observants took an active part in combatting the Reformation.[42] At Saint-Omer special mention should be made of Pierre Leroy, lector in Theology, Provincial of the order in Flanders in 1549 and again in 1561, Maria of Hungary's confessor, who was to the fore in opposing Baius' teaching.[43] The repeated presence of the Inquisition in the town in the pre-Reformation period is further indication that already in the Middle Ages heterodox elements were to be found amongst its population and in the surrounding area.[44]

It is evident from the relations which Erasmus maintained with the clergy of the town that Humanism had left its mark there.[45] During his stay at Saint-Omer from the autumn of 1501 to the summer of 1502, first as guest of the prior of the abbey of Saint-Bertin and then at the neighbouring castle of Courtebourne, Erasmus got to know the Guardian of the Franciscan community, Jean Vitrier, who most probably inspired him to publish his *Enchiridion.*[46] Erasmus greatly admired Vitrier who as early as 1498 had been condemned by the Sorbonne for his persistent promotion of monastic reform and his opposition to the prevailing systems of indulgences and veneration of saints; views expressed, amongst other oc-

---

[39] Derheims, *Histoire de Saint-Omer,* 594 f.

[40] P. Gratien, "Le grand schisme et la réforme des Cordeliers à Saint-Omer (1408-1409). Notes et documents", *Franciscana,* V (1922) 5-15, 143-180.

[41] R. R. Post, *Kerkgeschiedenis van Nederland in de Middeleeuwen* (2 vols., Utrecht/Antwerp, 1957) II, 154 f.; A. G. Jongkees, *Staat en kerk in Holland en Zeeland onder de Bourgondische hertogen 1425-1477* (Groningen/Batavia, 1942) 254.

[42] P. Gaudentius, *Bedeutung und Verdienste des Franziskaner-Ordens im Kampfe gegen den Protestantismus,* I (Bozen, 1880) 92-133.

[43] P. F. Servais Dirks, *Histoire littéraire et bibliographique des Frères Mineurs de l'Observance de St. François en Belgique et dans les Pays-Bas* (Antwerp, 1885) 72-78.

[44] *Corpus Documentorum Inquisitions,* P. Fredericq, ed. (5 vols., Ghent, 1889-1906) I, 299; II, 118; III, 21, 139 f. 154.

[45] *Opus Epistolarum Erasmi* P. S., H. M. Allen and H. W. Garrod, ed. (11 vols., Oxford, 1906-1947) I, Nrs. 162-164, 166-170.

[46] J. Huizinga, *Verzamelde Werken* (9 vols., Haarlem, 1948-1953) VI, 49 f.; A. Renaudet, "Erasme, sa vie et son œuvre jusqu'en 1517 d'après sa correspondance", *Revue historique,* III (1912) 253-255; Id., *Préréforme et Humanisme* (Paris, 1953) 426-428, 700; Id., *Erasme, sa pensée religieuse et son action d'après sa correspondance (1518-1521)* (Paris, 1926) 29 f.

casions, in his preaching at Tournai in that same year.[47] The Dutchman ranked the Franciscan guardian with John Colet[48] and, in a detailed letter to Luther's subsequent supporter, Justus Jonas of Erfurt, he provided biographical sketches of the two men he so highly regarded.[49] From these we learn that Vitrier was an admirer of Origen and an opponent both of Scholasticism and of all outwardly ritualistic religion. In his efforts for the recovery of biblical thought and a more spiritual religion he appealed above all to Paul whose epistles he knew by heart. Evidently Erasmus often heard Vitrier preach at Saint-Omer and was greatly impressed by the latter's biblical theology.

As the Reformation spread throughout Germany, heretical movements also emerged in Artois. In November, 1534 the magistrates of Hesdin, Saint-Omer and several other towns received an order from the governess of the Netherlands, Maria of Hungary, to be on their guard against "Anabaptists and others who have dissented from our faith".[50] Calvinism spread in the forties and struggled not only with Rome but also with the Anabaptists and especially with the spiritual Libertines who, according to Calvin's tract *Contre la secte phantastique et furieuse des Libertins* (1545),[51] had a great appeal. If we may believe the reformer then, along with Quintin Thiery, a certain Antoine Pocquet had made disciples of at least 4,000 people in Hainault and Artois.[52] Again, when this same Pocquet had sought refuge at the court of Navarre, the reformer warned Jeanne d'Albret against this "the most pernicious and abominable sect the world has ever seen".[53]

Saravia thus spent his youth at the centre of one of the political and military cockpits of Europe where religious opinions and ecclesiastical parties clashed violently with each other. Naturally the happenings of the outside world were known and discussed within the walls of the community. It was probably at this period that the Franciscan friar acquired the hatred and dread of Anabaptists, Spiritualists and all their harmful works which characterized his whole life. At first he remained true to the old faith. According to an autobiographical note he lived and studied for a time in Paris. He recalled, "that there I saw and heard learned theologians of all orders and yet, so far as human opinion could judge, there were none so

---

[47] G. Moreau, *Histoire du Protestantisme à Tournai jusqu'à la veille de la Révolution des Pays-Bas* (Paris, 1962) 53; *Corpus Documentorum Inquisitionis*, I, 490-492; A. Renaudet, "Paris de 1494 à 1517", in: *Courants religieux et Humanisme à la fin du XVIe siècle. Colloque de Strasbourg 9-11 mai 1975* (Paris, 1959) 21.

[48] A. Godin, *Spiritualité franciscaine en Flandre au XVIe siècle. L'homéliaire de Jean Vitrier* (Geneva, 1971) 12 f. and passim.

[49] *Opus Epistolarum Erasmi*, IV, 507-527.

[50] Moreau, *Histoire du Protestantisme à Tournai*, 83.

[51] *CO*, VII, 145-248.

[52] *Ibid.*, 161, 163.

[53] *Ibid.*, XII, 64-68.

incompetent and uneducated that, setting aside knowledge of the true Gospel, we cannot find equally unlearned preachers and ministers in our own ranks".[54] Thus he rated the standard of theological scholarship and teaching in Paris as highly as that of Protestant institutions. The great difference, so he wrote forty years later, had been the lack of the Gospel faith. Yet, after his conversion to the Reformation, he never allowed himself to be led into a sterile antipapalism. We are unable to ascertain exactly when and for how long he studied in Paris; the registers of the Sorbonne make no mention of his name.

## 2. CONVERSION TO THE REFORMATION (1557-1558)

Jacques Taffin, who had a hand in Saravia's quitting of the cloister, was one of the five sons, all of whom were converted to the Reformation, of Denis Taffin, seigneur de la Prée, a prominent burgher of Tournai and "receveur" of the Estates there.[55] Jacques was himself "receveur général" of Cassel and Bois de Nieppe between Hazebrouck and Merville, about 30 kilometres south-east of Saint-Omer. He was in close touch with his brother Nicholas, "conseiller pensionnaire" of Tournai and one of the leading Protestants of that town.[56] Both brothers were together charged with assisting the heretical movement. In January 1562, Jacques was transferred as a prisoner to the Gravensteen at Ghent and accused of having attended a sermon of Guido de Brès and of having aided the friar Adrian Saravia in his flight from the convent of Saint-Omer.[57] A certain François, a native of neighbouring Wallon-Cappel and Guardian of the community at Biez in Artois, figured as prosecution witness in the second of these charges. He was prevented from coming to Ghent to appear in person before the Council of Flanders and he wrote down his testimony and sent it to the inquisitors. He mentioned the rumour, "publica vox . . . et fama", according to which Taffin had caused Saravia to leave his order and had further helped him with 100 guilders.[58] Also of interest is the evidence of a certain Frans Spronckhoef, probably a servant, who had lived for more than 36 years in Taffin's castle. He too cited the rumour of Taffin's involvement with "a brother Adrian, friar of Saint-Omer who has fled" and named the above-mentioned François as the source of his information. Speaking from his own experience, he reported that about Candlemas, 2nd February, "shortly before his flight", Saravia had preached at the castle, but he had heard the latter say nothing contrary to

---

[54] *DT,* 39.

[55] Moreau, *Histoire du Protestantisme à Tournai,* 149.

[56] *Ibid.,* 345.

[57] De Coussemaker, *Troubles religieux,* IV, 59 f.; J. Decavele, *De dageraad van de Reformatie in Vlaanderen (1520-1565)* (2 vols., Brussels, 1975) I, 427.

[58] RA. Brussels. Papiers d'Etat, Nr. 27, 4.

the Catholic faith. According to Spronckhoef, this appearance of Saravia as preacher was not all unusual since passing religious often preached, especially at Christmas and Lent. Saravia sometimes spent the night at the castle, sometimes at the inn and now and then was invited to a meal by the governor of the castle, Lieutenant Stapele. Spronckhoef could not corroborate the Franciscans' charge that Adrian would sometimes stay with Taffin for a fortnight. He at least could recall nothing of this and he thought that such an occurrence would not have remained hidden from the castle guard.[59] This last remark sounds like a prevarication. That Saravia was a familiar and welcome guest at Taffin's castle emerges even more clearly from the evidence of the defence witness than from that of the witness for the prosecution.

In his written defence against the charges Taffin admitted having given money to Saravia but not more than three daalders, two from the castle coffers and one "par dévotion". The receveur promised the Council that he would never do anything like this again. As regards Saravia's flight from the cloister, Taffin reported that Adrian had already considered this step four years previously in consultation with German captains garrisoned in Saint-Omer who encouraged him with books from their native country. Finally, as defence against the suspicion aroused by brother François, he pleaded his customary hospitality towards "toutes gens de Religion et deglise", who were always welcome at his table.[60]

It is established that, during Philip II's war against France, Saravia did indeed come into contact with Germans who favoured the Reformation. As appears from a later autobiographical reference he was thoroughly familiar with the Habsburg army[61] in which three princes from the House of Braunschweig and two counts of Schwartzburg and Schaumburg served as field officers.[62] Jacques Taffins's account was thus based on the facts of the matter, but that he and his relations had themselves also played a part in Saravia's conversion to Protestantism and his flight from the convent emerges from the latter's later statement that he was "very deeply indebted" to the Taffins "for important and well founded reasons".[63] It is apparent from the records of the trial referred to above that the Franciscan friar got to know Protestant beliefs in both their Lutheran and Calvinist forms. The literature which he obtained from the Germans would most

---

[59] *Ibid.*, 8, 9.

[60] *Ibid.*, 5.

[61] During his time in Guernsey he contrasted the disorder in the Channel Islands with the order in the Spanish King's army. "Ego militiam nunquam sum secutus; tamen longe diversum ordinem memini vidisse cum in castris Philippi Regis tum in urbibus militum presidio munitis...". Saravia to William Cecil, 26 February, 1565/66. PRO.SP. 15/12, fol. 100r; Doc. I.

[62] K. Brandi, *Deutsche Geschichte im Zeitalter der Reformation und Gegenreformation* (repr. Darmstadt, 1960) 326.

[63] Hessels, *ELBA*, II, Nr. 232; III, Nr. 1059; Doc. XVIII.

probably have consisted primarily of Lutheran writings. Throughout his life he repeatedly showed his regard for Lutheranism by declaring his approval of the Augsburg Confession. He became acquainted with Reformed Christianity at Jacques Taffin's home and it was this tradition in which he was to live for the next thirty years without, however, evincing any antagonism to Lutheranism. If we accept that Saravia's four year association with German officers began after his removal from Hesdin to Saint-Omer in the late summer of 1553, then it seems likely that his conversion to Protestantism and his flight from the convent were completed by the end of 1557. These actions were the outcome of serious deliberation and a prolonged period of development. After the process had come to fruition we once more lose track of him for a time.

### 3.  AMONG THE DUTCH IN LONDON AND FLANDERS (1559-1563)

Saravia may possibly have spent some time inconspicuously in the Churches "under the cross" in the South Netherlands. On 17 November 1558 Queen Mary Tudor died in England to be followed on the same day by the Roman Catholic Archbishop of Canterbury, Reginald Pole. On 23 November Elizabeth arrived in London where she was crowned on 15 January 1559. Immediately the news of Mary's death reached the continent the so-called Marian exiles began to return home in great numbers,[64] to be followed shortly afterwards by Dutch and French Protestants who, the positions now reversed, took the opportunity to flee the persecutions in their own countries.[65] According to the memorial inscription in Canterbury Cathedral Saravia crossed to England early in 1559.[66] However, so strong were his ties with his co-religionists in the South Netherlands that early in the summer of that same year we once more encounter the well-travelled young man in the Netherlands. On 6 July 1559 he was in Ghent to witness Philip II's entry into the town. Years later he still talked of the pomp and circumstance with which the King surrounded himself on that occasion.[67]

---

[64] J. E. Neale, *Queen Elizabeth I* (repr. pb. Harmondsworth, 1973) 63.

[65] J. Lindeboom, *Austin Friars. Geschiedenis van de Nederlandse Hervormde Gemeente te Londen 1550-1950* (The Hague, 1950) 29 f.

[66] "Angliam petiit sub initium regni Beatae memoriae Elizabethae". Cowper, *Memorial Inscriptions,* 3.

[67] "J'ay veu par cy devant comment et avec quelle magnificence le Roy Philippe fut reçeu, ...lequel tenoit une Majeste si tres grande, que iamais il ne donne aucune signification davoir pour aggreable les hommes qu'on luy faisoit". Saravia to Walsingham, 3 September, 1582. PRO.SP. 83/17. Nr. 5; Doc. IV. The occasion referred to is; "Den VIen July quam de coninck van Spangen Philips, hertoghe van Bourgoignen, grave van Vlaenderen, binnen deze zyne stede van Ghendt met schoonen state van vele edele machtighe princhen ende princessen", *Memorieboek der Stad Ghent van 't jaer 1301 tot 1795.* Publ. Maatsch. v. Vlaamse Biblioph., II, 15(4 vols., Ghent, 1852-1861) II, 303 f.

In 1561 Saravia married Catherine d'Allez, a native of Saint-Omer, whose father had been put to death for his Protestant beliefs.[68] The marriage lasted almost 45 years[69] and one son and an unknown number of daughters were born.[70] On 22 June 1561 Saravia joined the Dutch Church in London. From the description "iuvenis studiosus"[71] added to his name we gather that he was a student, but we do not know where or for how long. There is no evidence that he studied at Oxford. His wife Catherine, who did not understand Dutch, would surely have been a member of the Walloon refugees' church in London. He, for his part was, as we have noted, enrolled in the members' register of the Dutch speaking church.[72] By a charter of King Edward VI, dated 24 July 1550, the Dutch, both French speaking Walloons and Dutch speakers, had been granted the use of the well known church of the Augustinian order, Austin Friars.[73] The "templum Jesu", which was destroyed by German bombing in 1940 and rebuilt after the Second World War, still serves as a place of worship for Dutch Protestants in London. The Walloons, on the other hand, quickly moved and, on 16 October 1550 went to the Church of St. Anthony's Hospital in Threadneedle Street.[74]

At the beginning of the fifties the Dutch in and around London must have numbered between 3000 and 3500 of whom between 1000 and 2000 belonged to the congregation of Austin Friars.[75] Following their tragic flight at the start of Mary's reign in 1553[76] they enjoyed a rapid and vigorous recovery under Elizabeth. The number of refugees fluctuated according to the political and military situation in their home land. In the mid-sixties about 4000 Dutchmen lived in London. After Alva's arrival in the Netherlands in 1567 the numbers rose to 6000 just before the end of the decade only to drop again in the seventies with the changed military

---

[68] Janssen, *Kerkhervorming Brugge*, II, 286; De Coussemaker, *Troubles religieux*, 340.

[69] Cathérine died on 1 February, 1605/06 "anno a nuptiis 45". Cowper, *Memorial Inscriptions*, 212.

[70] Saravia referred to his children in the plural. PRO.SP. 15/12, fol. 155r; Doc. II. On 30 July, 1589 Lipsius commisserated with him on the loss of his "unicus filius". Inv. Lipse (88) 08. 30; Doc XXXV. On 2 September, 1588 Pierre de Villiers wished to be remembered only to his son; GAD, Nr. 160; Doc. XXIX. Had the daughter(s) predeceased him?

[71] *Returns of Aliens*, 273.

[72] *Ibid.*, 278; GHL.L. 19.92. Ms. 7402/2.

[73] For the Dutch Churches and refugees in England, see Ch. A. Rahlenbeck, "Les réfugiés belges du seizième siècle en Angleterre", *Revue trimestrielle*, XII (1865) 3-48; Id., "Quelques notes sur les réformés flamands et wallons de 16e siècle refugiés en Angleterre", *PHS*, IV (1891-1893) 22-44; A. A. van Schelven, *De Nederduitsche vluchtelingenkerken der XVIe eeuw in Engeland en Duitsland en hunne beteekenis voor de Reformatie in de Nederlanden* (The Hague, 1909) 57-113, 131, 208; Lindeboom, *Austin Friars;* N. Schilling, *Niederländische Exulanten im 16. Jahrhundert. Ihre Stellung im Sozialgefüge und im religiösen Leben deutscher und englischer Städte* (Gütersloh, 1972) 45-51, 135-151, 155-157.

[74] Van Schelven, *Vluchtelingenkerken*, 71.

[75] Lindeboom, *Austin Friars*, 32.

[76] Van Schelven, *Vluchtelingenkerken*, 104-113.

situation in Holland. The fall of Antwerp in 1585 meant a great flood of refugees and, in consequence, the number of Dutch in London mounted to 10000. At the close of the century this figure again gradually declined but at the start of the Stuart period it was certainly not less than 5000.[77] Besides a striking proportion of intellectuals, the Dutch church had among its members many craftsmen, especially weavers. The number of merchants and big businessmen joining it rose with the increase in immigration from the South Netherlands.[78] Edward VI's charter[79] said that, as a Christian prince, the King acknowledged his obligation to admit to his country those persecuted and exiled for their religion. It appears from his diary that, in helping fugitive Calvinists, he had a second aim namely "for avoiding of all sects of Anabaptists and such like".[80] He was here expressing a concern which constantly occupied the political and ecclesiastical authorities in England: they wanted at all costs to remain free of the Anabaptists whose revolutionary menace they feared. The Dutch congregation which, in Edward's reign enjoyed a measure of independence under its superintendent, Jan Laski (Johannes a Lasco), was placed by Elizabeth under the supervision of the Bishop of London, Edmund Grindal. This gave rise to an interesting state of affairs whereby the episcopal Church of England admitted a church of the Reformed confession and presbyterian church order which was akin to the Puritans and could count on their sympathy.[81] This situation sometimes led to tensions especially since the Dutch found themselves restricted in their freedom to organize their church according to their own principles. Thus, for example, they did not obtain permission to divide the Church into Classes,[82] an extremely sensitive point of difference between the Church of England and presbyterian Puritans.[83]

From the acta of the Church council it is evident that young Adrian, who was later to emerge as the ardent defender of episcopal church government against the presbyterian, was at this period an influential member of the Reformed congregation of Austin Friars. On 26 May, 1561 he asked for letters credential for a proposed visit to Flanders. The request was in complete accord with the conduct of the Dutch in London who gave help in money and manpower on an impressive scale to their co-

---

[77] Schilling, *Exulanten*, 45, 175.

[78] *Ibid.*, 45 f.

[79] Hessels, *ELBA*, III, Nr. 14.

[80] Lindeboom, *Austin Friars*, 9.

[81] P. Collinson, "The Elizabethan Puritans and the Foreign Reformed Churches in London," *PHS*, XX (1958-1964) 528-555. The church order of the Dutch Church in: Marten Micron, *De christlicke ordinancien der Nederlantscher ghemeinten te London (1554)*, W. F. Dankbaar, ed. The Hague, 1956.

[82] Lindeboom, *Austin Friars*, 31.

[83] P. Collinson, *The Elizabethan Puritan Movement* (London, 1967) 106, 177 f., 226, 333-345.

religionists in their native land. The church council agreed to Adrian's request, although it stated its preference for his continuing to serve the London Church as a member of the consistory. The young man was warned of the dangers involved in the journey and he was asked not to leave before first giving an exposition of Scripture.[84] Saravia met this request, preaching on the Epistle of Jude on 29 May[85] and continuing on 7 August.[86] Between these two dates he paid a brief visit to the South Netherlands on which he reported to the Church council on 17 July, when he mentioned the progress of Protestantism in Middelburg.[87]

We know about this visit to the Netherlands because it is documented, but it certainly was not the only one. The well travelled man, who up to 1588 crossed the North Sea many times, would in this period also certainly have paid many visits to the Netherlands from English territory. In the same year Saravia's name again appeared several times in the acta of the Dutch Church. On 11 September 1561 the consistory determined that he and two other members of the church should, after consultation with the minister Petrus Delenus, again expound a scriptural passage. Curiously enough, although he had already been known to the consistory for a considerable time, he was still reckoned among those "who have recently appeared here".[88] In November Adrian became the centre of a theological dispute. The point at issue concerned the "omnipresence of the divine being or essence", "ubiquitas divinae essentiae", a subject which would concern him again fifty years later during the controversies over Vorstius' appointment to Leiden.[89] On 16 November the question came up in the consistory which postponed discussion of it,[90] as it did also on 20 November.[91] On Sunday, 23 November the members of the consistory agreed together on the formula: "that God is alike complete in Himself and is the perfect plenitude, in this sense that He is omnipresent, excluded from nothing neither confined by anything".[92] The background to the dispute is not clear from the few references in the consistory's acta, but probably Saravia feared an attack from some quarter on the Church's tradition concerning God's omnipresence. His orthodoxy was evidently

---

[84] *Kerkeraadsprotocollen,* 201.

[85] *Ibid.,* 202.

[86] *Ibid.,* 235.

[87] "Adrianus Moravia reversus Londinum refert magnam accensam Middelburgi lucem". *Ibid.,* 229. Despite the fact that the acta mentions Flandria—"Adrianus Saravius ex Flandria reversus" is written in the margin—the present writer is less certain than A. A. van Schelven, *NNBW,* IX, 934, that this refers not to Middelburg in Zeeland, but to the small town of the same name about 10 miles north east of Bruges.

[88] *Kerkeraadsprotocollen,* 247 f.

[89] p. 190-192.

[90] *Kerkeraadsprotocollen,* 266.

[91] *Ibid.,* 267.

[92] *Ibid.,* 268.

fully recognized. Moreover, he enjoyed the complete confidence of the Walloons as well as of the Dutch preachers. The proof of this is to be seen in the entry of 22 January 1562 about a discussion between the ministers of the Dutch and Walloon congregations over the above-mentioned departure of the Frenchman, Nicholas des Gallars and the possible choice of Saravia as his successor.[93] Des Gallars, a supporter of Calvin and a participant in the Colloquy of Poissy in September 1561,[94] had already three weeks earlier informed the Genevan reformer of his desire to leave London and to see the young Adrian Saravia appointed as his successor. He wrote to him on 31 December 1561: "I have found a very learned and, as it seems to me, a wise man to put in my place. His name is Adrianus Saravius, a native of Hesdin, who commands the Dutch tongue as well as the French. He has already spent a considerable time with us so he can receive good testimony of his conduct. And he has already begun to please the faithful with his sound doctrine."[95] Nothing at that time came of des Gallars' plan to leave London and so the question of his succession also lapsed. From his letter to Calvin it appears that Saravia was known for his command of Dutch as well as French. The latter must have remained on good terms with des Gallars. Saravia discussed fundamental questions concerning the order and government of the Church with him and later held, wrongly in fact, that the Frenchman shared his views.[96]

It was 6 April 1563 before Saravia's name was again mentioned in the acta of the Dutch Church. On that date des Gallars, who was still in London—he was to leave in the summer of that year—, announced that he had received a request from the Walloon church in Antwerp to nominate a suitable minister for them because it was rumoured that Adrian Saravia intended leaving.[97] It appears from this that, at the beginning of 1562, shortly after 22 January, after three years in London[98] during which he was a member of the Dutch Church at Austin Friars,[99] he went to Antwerp to enter the service of the Walloon congregation in that city. A modern historian saw in his presence there an example of Anglo-French influence which boded ill for the peace of that region: "that foreigners plotted against our government is undeniable".[100] If Saravia's efforts in connec-

[93] *Ibid.*, 285 f.; cf. Ph. Denis, *Les églises d'étrangers à Londres jusqu'à la mort de Calvin* (Mémoire Université de Liège, 1973-1974) 40, 84.

[94] For Des Gallars see: Haag, *La France protestante* (2nd ed., 6 vols., Paris, 1877-1888) V, 298-305.

[95] *CO*, XIX, 226.

[96] *DT*, 113 f.

[97] *Ibid.*, 395.

[98] This may be concluded from his report: "... totos tres annos habitaverim in Anglia". Saravia to William Cecil, 26 Feb. 1565. PRO.SP. 15/12, fol. 99; Doc. I.

[99] His name does not appear in the acta of the Walloon congregation, *Actes du consistoire de l'église française de Threadneedle Street, Londres,* I: *1560-1565, PHS,* XXXVIII, but these are only extant for the periods June 1560-September 1561 and April 1564-December 1565.

[100] Fl. Prims, *Geschiedenis van Antwerpen* (29 vols., Brussels, 1927-1949) VIII, 51.

tion with the Dutch Confession of Faith are to be considered subversive activities of this sort, then he is certainly guilty of the charge. It appears from information provided by himself in a letter which, in extreme old age, he wrote[101] to Johannes Wtenbogaert, the leader of the Dutch Remonstrants, that during his time in Antwerp he did not engage only in the building up and expansion of the Reformed churches strictly forbidden by the authorities, founding, for example, the Walloon church in Brussels; this in cooperation with Jean, Lord of Toulouse, brother of Marnix of St. Aldegonde. But in addition, having already had a hand in its creation, he strove to make the Dutch Confession of Faith, the *Confessio Belgica,* known to Orange and the high nobility. Because the account of the origins of the Confession still presents historical problems for us,[102] it is important to go further into the part which, as appears from his own disclosures and in the opinion of later writers, Adrian Saravia played in it.

In the above mentioned letter Saravia relates the following to Wtenbogaert; "I was at that time minister of the French Church in Antwerp and I had copies of the Confession presented to the Prince of Orange and to the Count of Egmont. A brother of my wife's was gentleman in waiting to Count Louis. He introduced me to his master so that the latter could become acquainted with me and so that I could give him copies of the recently printed Confession for circulation amongst the rest of the nobles". Saravia thus took a part in the early stages of the relations between the small, persecuted Reformed churches in the South Netherlands and the nobility, relations which in the course of the sixties were to become very important in the birth of the Dutch Revolt. Again, in this connection, Saravia's significant announcement that the Walloon church in Brussels consisted "of court officials and several French speaking burghers", fits in. With this information the author of the letter wanted to demonstrate to Wtenbogaert, an advocate of the government's authority in church affairs, that such authority had been recognized by the Reformed from the beginning. As proof of this he also cited the letter to the Spanish King with which the *Confessio Belgica* opens. In this period William of Orange's line on religious matters was still unclear, as witness the events surrounding his marriage to Anne of Saxony on 25 August 1561.[103] Saravia used his personal relations and family connections to draw the attention of the prince, his brother Louis and the nobility to the cause of the persecuted. Then, just as fifty years later, he shared their faith and regarded their Confession as an authoritative exposition of the Scriptures.

[101] *EE,* Nr. 181; Doc. XLVI.

[102] The best edition of the text together with an introduction in which the latest results of historical research are digested is to be found in: *De Nederlandse Belijdenisgeschriften in authentieke teksten met inleiding en tekstvergelijkingen,* J. N. Bakhuizen van den Brink, ed. (2nd ed., Amsterdam, 1976) 1-27, 59-146. For an account of the relevant literature see the notes in the introduction to this edition.

[103] A. A. van Schelven, *Willem van Oranje* (Amsterdam, 1948) 69-75.

The events described here could have taken place soon after his move to Antwerp, in February or March 1562. It is hard to determine which edition Saravia meant when he wrote about the "recently printed Confession". The latter was published twice in both 1561 and 1562.[104] L. A. van Langeraad, the authoritative biographer of Guido de Brès incorrectly assigned these events to 1566, probably because he was not aware of the acta of the Dutch Church Council in London and therefore wrongly supposed that Saravia spent the whole of 1562 in that city.[105] In addition, the letter to Wtenbogaert contains further important information on the *Confessio Belgica,* namely about Saravia's own contributions to its formulation. He wrote "I own to being one of the first authors of the Confession, as was Herman Moded. I do not know if any others besides myself are still alive. The Confession was first drawn up in the French language by the servant of Christ and martyr, Guido de Brès. But before it was published he showed it to the ministers of God's Word whom he could contact for them to add or subtract anything if they had objections". Again, 35 years later in his Church History, Wtenbogaert quoted these two passages from Saravia's letter, apparently from memory, running them together thus, "I have seen and read an autograph letter of D. Adrianus Saravia, sometime Professor of Theology at Leiden, in which he said that the same Confession had been drawn up by only three or four ministers of whom he was one, that in it they had for the most part followed the French Confession, also that he, Saravia, was at that time himself employed to deliver it to the Lords, the Prince of Orange and the Count of Egmont (in whose courts he had friends) so that it could be communicated further".[106] The information about following the pattern of the French *Confession de Foy* is not in Saravia's letter but it fits in well with the facts as is well enough known.[107] The words "three or four ministers" provide a correct interpretation of the letter if we may think of them as de Brès, Moded and Saravia with perhaps another, fourth, theologian. Van Langeraad has critically examined various traditions about the names of contributors to the drafting of the Confession, particularly those of Thysius and Schoock, and has pointed out the errors in their accounts.[108] He lays great stress on Guido de Brès' personal authorship, "in all quiet and secrecy at Doornik, whilst

[104] *Nederlandse Belijdenisgeschriften,* 13 f.

[105] L. A. van Langeraad, *Guido de Brès. Zijn leven en werken* (Zierikzee, 1884) 141 f. See also [J. N. Paquot,] *Mémoires pour servir à l'histoire des dix-sept provinces des Pays-Bas, de la principauté de Liège, et de quelques contrées voisines* (3 vols., Louvain, 1765-1770) II, 534; Prims, *Geschiedenis van Antwerpen,* VIII, 51. A disputing of van Langeraad's theory by H. G. Kleyn, "Adrianus Saravia en de Confessio Belgica", *Kerkelijke Courant,* 7 March 1896.

[106] [J. Wtenbogaert,] *De kerckelicke Historie* (5 vols. s.l., 1647) III, 7.

[107] J. N. Bakhuizen van den Brink, "La Confession de Foi des Églises Réformées de France de 1559 et la Confession des Pays-Bas de 1561", in: *Ecclesia,* II (The Hague, 1966) 309-335.

[108] Van Langeraad, *Guido de Bray,* 97-118.

he would have communicated his intention only to a few of his most trusted friends''. He considers it just as self-evident ''that de Brès, after completing his work, should submit it for approval to a few ministers whom he knew and that the heads of the congregation at Antwerp particularly should have sanctioned it again''.[109]

The correctness of this supposition emerges from the acta of the Church councils of the Walloon and Dutch churches in London dated 6 and 9 April 1561. They mention a request from the Church of Antwerp for advice about the publication of the Confession. The latter church having evidently first authorized the document,[110] wanted to print it and to address it, together with an accompanying petition, to the city government. What did the Dutch churches in London think of this plan? In their joint assembly the latter considered it too dangerous and instructed des Gallars to consult the Bishop of London on the matter.[111] On this occasion des Gallars and his close friend Saravia, future minister of Antwerp, would undoubtedly have deliberated together about the Confession.[112] Perhaps the opinion which the Frenchman expressed on this occasion became the source of the report that spread here and there that he was one of the Confession's authors.[113]

As for Saravia we ought now to focus attention on the source which informs us, that already long before he was involved with the communication of the Confession at Antwerp in 1562 and also before he had given his opinion about its possible publication in the spring of 1561—to our mind these two facts are beyond dispute—he had been concerned with these articles of faith. We are referring to the report of the theologian, rhetorician and historian, Martinus Schoock, a follower of Voetius, in his *Liber de bonis vulgo ecclesiasticis dictis* (1651).[114] This runs as follows, ''Various writers differ in the accounts they give as to which men were primarily responsible for the formulation of this as the generally agreed standard of orthodoxy as far as the Netherlands is concerned. For my part, I have learned from reliable documents, which ought certainly at some time with God's help to be published, that things happened thus. Already in 1559 that very godly man Guido de Brès (indeed, as we saw before, he sealed the Gospel truth with his blood), largely because the raving Anabaptists were being

---

[109] *Ibid.*, 118.

[110] Moreau, *Histoire du Protestantisme à Tournai*, 156 f.

[111] *Actes Threadneedle Street*, 38.

[112] This disproves the view maintained by Th. van Oppenraay that Saravia would only have been concerned with the Dutch translation of the Confession. See: *La doctrine de la prédestination dans l'église réformée des Pays-Bas depuis l'origine jusqu'au synode national de Dordrecht en 1618 et 1619* (Louvain, 1906) 25.

[113] Van Langeraad, *Guido de Bray*, 111 ff. Cf. Ch. Paillard, ''Les grands prêches calvinistes de Valenciennes'', *BSHPB*, XXVI (1877) 122.

[114] Martini Schoockii Ultratraiectini *De bonis vulgo ecclesiasticis dictis...* (Groningen, 1651) 519-521.

classed with the true believers by the inquisitors, began to compile some
articles of orthodox unity. Afterwards he first showed these to Adrianus
Saravia who was just about to travel to Geneva and through his offices
they were submitted to Calvin and other theologians towards the end of
that year. But because the articles had been written by the author in
French (since for most Netherlanders this was either the colloquial
language or was at least familiar), they got Saravia to take the advice to the
author and the rest of the Dutch ministers to concur rather with the French
fathers in the Confession which had recently been drawn up at the first
Synod of Paris on 19 May of that same year. Returning to the Netherlands
shortly afterwards, Saravia communicated the advice of Calvin and his
colleagues to the author both verbally and by a letter which he brought
with him from the Genevans. De Brès kept the articles to himself until
1561. Then, on the advice of Godfried van Wingen whom we mentioned
before,[115] he sent them to the church of Emden. (This was contrary to the
wish of Saravia who contended that the Genevans ought again to be consulted)''. After this, according to Schoock, numerous other theologians
were consulted: Petrus Dathenus and Caspar van der Heyden in Franken-
thal (The Palatinate), Valérand Poullain (Frankfurt), unnamed ministers
of the Dutch congregation in London and the following ministers of the
Walloon congregation there: Nicholas des Gallars, Pierre Cousin and
Petrus Alexander.

According to this report Saravia had already in 1559 been acquainted
with the contents of the Confession by de Brès and had submitted the latter
to Calvin and his colleagues in Geneva. Van Langeraad, rightly holding
that Schoock had taken a number of incorrect details from Thysius,
disputed the reliability of this report of Saravia's journey to Geneva and
this for four particular reasons. In the first place, he considered the information about Saravia, which des Gallars felt he had to supply in his letter
of 31 December 1561, proof that at the end of that year this young
theologian was as yet unknown to the reformer. But if Saravia really had
been in Geneva in 1559, does it follow that Calvin would have known
him? Secondly, van Langeraad thought it improbable that the Genevans
would have advised rejection exclusively on the grounds of the French
language in which the Confession was formulated. Thirdly, he considered
it significant that there is no trace of Saravia's visit to Geneva in the archives there; this was according to information provided for van
Langeraad by the archivist Th. A. Dufour.[116] The correctness of this
information and the inaccuracy of that supplied to H. Q. Janssen by Ch.
Rahlenbeck, according to which Saravia's name often appears in the archives of Geneva,[117] became evident to the author of this study during his

---

[115] For van Wingen see: *NNBW*, III, 1433-1437.

[116] Van Langeraad, *Guido de Bray*, 150, n.l.

[117] Janssen, *Kerkhervorming in Vlaanderen*, I, 200, n.l.

own researches into the Genevan archives. Moreover, this was confirmed for him from another quarter.[118] Finally, de Brès' biographer thought that it would have been incompatible with the authority Calvin bore for the author of the Confession, if the latter had flouted his master's advice by going ahead with its publication.[119]

This entire line of reasoning appears unconvincing to us. It is quite conceivable that, if Saravia's visit to Geneva had taken place, no record of it would be found in the archives and even that Calvin would not have known of it. There was little interest in the Netherlands in the Geneva of that period. Calvin himself had scant respect for the Dutch and for what he termed "the barbarism of that people".[120] Saravia was still young and unknown and could well have been received by one or more ministers. The city was crowded with refugees from abroad and the visit of a young inexperienced Dutchman would certainly have been nothing to make a fuss about. The advice not to proceed with the publication of the Confession and to subscribe to the French *Confession de Foy* sounds extremely credible. The continuing publication of new Reformed Confessions was not as a rule advocated in Geneva. Calvin was particularly unhappy about confessions which were the work of individual theologians. He had originally also indicated his reservations about the publication of the *Confession de Foy*,[121] while they had nevertheless gone ahead with this in France. After his death his successor, Beza appeared similarly averse to any increase by the Dutch in the number of Reformed Confessions.[122] Consequently Schoock's account of Geneva's advice sounds credible whilst van Langeraad's counter arguments seem untenable.

All this is not to say that we can confidently accept Schoock's report of Saravia's journey to Geneva as true. The most important reason for doubting it remains the complete lack of even the slightest reference to any such journey in Saravia's own works. Although again and again he appeared to be very well versed in church life at Geneva and with the church order there which he later rejected, his accounts of these give no hint at all of any personal encounter with the Genevan theologians themselves. Consequently, as regards this aspect of the history of the *Confessio Belgica*'s emergence, we have as yet to make do with conjecture. It is credible that

---

[118] On 22 July 1974 J. N. Bakhuizen van den Brink, Leiden, informed the author that Mr. P. Fränkel of the Institute d'Histoire de la Réformation and his assistants "have looked everywhere where it was possible that a trace of Saravia might be found, in the records of both Church and State. Absolutely nothing has been found... The result remains completely negative... Van Langeraad was right in this, though not in his arguments".

[119] Van Langeraad, *Guido de Bray,* 97-107.

[120] Calvin to Bullinger, 1 Oct. 1560; *CO,* XVIII, 205.

[121] J. Pannier, *Les origines de la Confession de Foi et de la Discipline des églises réformées de France* (Paris, 1936) 90 f.

[122] Th. de Bèze, *Correspondance,* recueillie par H. Aubert; publiée par H. Meylan, A. Dufour, C. Chimelli et M. Turchetti (vol. I-  ; Geneva, 1960-  ) VI, 145; VII, 32 f.

Saravia was well acquainted with Guido de Brès plans at a very early stage. There is not the slightest foundation for van Langeraad's surmise that the young Franciscan fled to Germany after his conversion to Protestantism.[123] On the contrary, it is much more probable that, until his flight to England, he lived in the South Netherlands. Again, afterwards he returned to his native land on various occasions. As we have already mentioned, in July 1559 he stayed in Ghent. His parents settled in this city and continued to live there until, because of the unsettled conditions in that place, their son Adrian took them into his family in Guernsey.[124] It is plausible that through Jacques Taffin he came into contact with the latter's brother, Nicholas, town clerk of Tournai, and that this ardent disciple of the Calvinist religion introduced him to Guido de Brès. But Saravia could have met the author of the *Confessio Belgica* in Valenciennes, Lille or Antwerp, which the latter regularly visited after settling in Tournai,[125] or elsewhere in Flanders or Artois, and at such an encounter have been told by de Brès of the Confession's preparation.

In 1566 Saravia was once again involved in the fortunes of the Dutch Confession of Faith. At that time he was living in the Channel Islands, on Guernsey. From there he was invited and took part in the Synod which was held at Antwerp in May 1566[126] and of which we possess information from Franciscus Junius' autobiographical references.[127] The text of the Confession authorized by this Synod came from the printers at Geneva on the 23 July.[128] After Saravia, in company with Junius, Pérégrin de la Grange and Moded, had once more submitted the text at Antwerp,[129] he and they made their way to St. Trond in the diocese of Liège where the assembled nobility were preparing the organization of their revolt against Spain.[130] Here the representatives of the consistories expressed the willingness of the oppressed Calvinists to support the uprising. Saravia must have still been in the Netherlands when the iconoclasm began in August. From the manner in which he later expressed his abhorrence of this event,[131] it may be concluded that he observed the popular fury at close quarters. Probably it was these incidents which led him to take his parents with him from Ghent on his return to Guernsey.

---

[123] Van Langeraad, *Guido de Bray*, 99.

[124] Saravia to William Cecil, 31 Jan. 1566/67. PRO.SP. 15/12, fol. 155r; Doc. II.

[125] Moreau, *Histoire du Protestantisme à Tournai*, 149 f., 345.

[126] Schoockius, *De bonis ecclesiasticis*, 521; "... Antwerpiae occulto synodus, cur et ipse Philippus Marnixius interfuit, et ad quam vocatus quoque erat Zaravia...". Schoockius wrongly refers to 1565 instead of 1566.

[127] *D. Francisci Junii Opuscula Theologica Selecta*, A. Kuyperus, ed. (Amsterdam, 1882) 26.

[128] *Nederlandse Belijdenisgeschriften*, 18.

[129] W. Cuno, *Franciscus Junius der Ältere, Professor der Theologie und Pastor (1545-1602). Sein Leben und Wirken, seine Schriften und Briefe* (Amsterdam/Leipzig/Basel, 1891) 30.

[130] Van Langeraad, *Guido de Bray*, 138; van Schelven, *Willem van Oranje*, 117.

[131] p. 26, 254, 257.

#### 4. HEADMASTER OF ELIZABETH COLLEGE, GUERNSEY (1563-1568)

Nothing is known of the relations between Saravia and the English ec-clesiastical authorities before 1563. That he had got to know persons of in-fluence during his stay in London and had found obliging patrons amongst them may be concluded from his appointment as Headmaster of Elizabeth College in the Channel Island of Guernsey.[132] The school was founded in September 1563.[133] Its financial basis was provided by the value of the possessions, confiscated in 1537, of the Franciscan house dissolved by Henry VIII. In the regulations for the new educational establishment, dated 27 September 1563, the official name was assigned: School of Queen Elizabeth. A statue of the Queen was placed over the en-trance. The rent of 80 quarters of wheat was conferred on the master as in-come. If the latter neglected his duties as prescribed in the regulations, he was to be admonished by the dean. In the event of three unheeded warn-ings or if the master had been guilty of crime or immorality, then he was to be dismissed. These stipulations appear somewhat comic in the light of Saravia's harsh opinion of the moral life of the island's population. Prayer for the Queen was one of the obligations of pupils and parents.[134]

The religious situation in the Channel Islands was rather complicated.[135] After the Reformation the Roman Catholic Bishop of Coutances (Normandy) continued to assert his claim to ecclesiastical authority over the islands. At the same time as this issue was a bone of con-tention between Coutances and Winchester, many Calvinist fugitives from France sought refuge there. They maintained relations with Calvin and the Church of Geneva. At the close of 1559 the latter sent Nicholas Baudouin with warm recommendations as the first Calvinist minister of Guernsey.[136] The churches in the Channel Islands acquired a Calvinist character from the powerful influx of these French refugees. On 22 June 1564 their presbyterian organization was complete and the first synod met on Guernsey.[137] The Queen who was herself averse to Calvinist-

---

[132] The slipshod article by G. F. Hodges, "Adrian Saravia Headmaster of Elizabeth College," in: W. Rolleston, ed. *Société Guernesiaise. Reports and Transactions,* XII (1933) 57-72, is academically worthless.

[133] W. E. de Faye, "Huguenots in the Channel Islands," *ProHS,* XIX (1952-1958), 2, 39.

[134] J. Duncan, *The History of Guernsey* (London, 1841) 331.

[135] For the following see: F. de Schickler, *Les églises du refuge en Angleterre* (3 vols., Paris, 1892) II, 367 f.

[136] Calvin to Guillaume Beauvoir, 26 Dec. 1559; Rémond Chauvet to Guillaume Beauvoir, 26 Dec. 1559. For the text of Calvin's letter see: *Lettres de Calvin.* J. Bonnet, ed. (2 vols., Paris, 1854) II, 251-253. Bonnet's notes on the addressee and the date of the letter are corrected by A. Maulvault, "La Réforme à Guernesey. Observation sur une des lettres françaises de Calvin," *BSHPF,* XVII (1868) 254-256, where the text of Chauvet's letter is also given.

[137] For the history of the Reformation in the Channel Islands, see: M. Lelièvre, "La Réforme dans les îles de la Manche", *BSHPF,* XXXIV (1885) 4-18, 52-68, 97-109, 145-163; de Schickler, *Églises du refuge.* II, 363-483.

Presbyterian influences in England, surprisingly allowed the Channel
Islands a church order in accordance with that of the church of Geneva
and the Walloon refugees' church in London.[138] It is true that an Order of
Council of 1565 confined this permission to the two capitals, St. Helier
and St. Peter Port: the other parishes had to follow the order of the Church
of England. However this rule was not observed. An Order of Council of
1568 definitely placed the church in the Channel Islands under the
authority of Robert Horne who had been Bishop of Winchester since
1561.[139] He was a Marian exile,[140] who had no sympathy with the Puritan
radicalism after his return,[141] but had some understanding of certain
liturgical desires of the Puritans.[142] The bishop followed a course that was
more opportunist and pragmatic than principled. He was prepared to
overcome his scruples about the aforementioned liturgical vestments so as
to avoid his dismissal from office and replacement by a prelate with
Roman Catholic sympathies.[143] It is self-evident that a bishop who allowed
his policy to be promoted so little by convictions of principle undertook
nothing to make himself unpopular with the Calvinists in the remote
Channel Islands.[144] That, prior to 1568, Horne did not concern himself at
all with this part of the world, appears from his Register. The Channel
Islands are mentioned here for the first time on 14 June 1569.[145]

If we may assume that Saravia arrived in Guernsey at the same time as
the foundation of Elizabeth College at the end of September 1563, then he
was present at the completion of the presbyterian church order in the
Channel Islands and probably contributed to it. Later, when as a defender
of episcopal church government, he opposed Presbyterianism, he recalled
that this exceptional arrangement of a local presbyterian church order
united to a national episcopal church had only been possible thanks to the
obliging consent of the Bishop of Winchester and under his authority.
That this bishop scarcely concerned himself with the entire affair, he
naturally ommitted to mention. In the letter which he wrote to the
ministers of the Channel Islands towards the end of his life, in any event
after the autumn of 1610,[146] he exhorted them to return to obedience to the

---

[138] *Ibid.*, 375 f.

[139] John le Neve, *Fasti Ecclesiae Anglicanae 1541-1857*, III: *Canterbury, Rochester and Winchester Dioceses*, J. M. Horn, ed. (London, 1974) 80.

[140] Chr. Garrett, *The Marian Exiles* (repr. Cambridge, 1966) 188 ff.

[141] N. Sykes, *Old Priest and New Presbyter.* Cambridge, 1957.

[142] P. Collinson, *The Elizabethan Puritan Movement* (London, 1967) 73 f.

[143] Horne to R. Gualter, 17 July 1565. *The Zurich Letters* (2 vols., Cambridge, 1842-1844) I, 142; M. M. Knappen, *Tudor Puritanism* (Chicago/London, 1970³) 204 f.

[144] A. J. Eagleston, "The Quarrel between the Ministers and the Civil Power, 1581-5", *Société guernésiaise. Reports and Transactions,* XII, 480, which mistakenly gives Horne the Christian name, Richard, and incorrectly assigns him to "the Puritan wing of the Church".

[145] Hampshire Record Office Winchester. Bp. Horne's Register, fol. 66v, 67r.

[146] Namely after he had published his *Examen Tractatus de Episcopatuum Triplici Genere* in the autumn of 1610 to which he refers in the letter: *Clavi Trabales; or Nailes fastened by some Great*

bishop. Quite distinct from the anti-presbyterian tenor of the detailed letter, are the autobiographical references bearing on this important
period.[147] They shed light upon the far from flourishing state of the churches in the Channel Islands in the sixties. Saravia wrote: "All the favour
we then obtained was through the Bishops means, and without them I dare
confidently assure you, that you will obtain nothing of what you look for.
In the beginning there was no other Reformation in the Islands then that
common throughout the whole Kingdome of England. The Priests which a
little before had sung Mass, became suddenly Protestants; but yet not one
of them was appointed to preach the word of God. They were but ignorant
blockheads, continuing still in heart and affection Papists, and enemies to
the Gospel. Now such as were sincerely affected to the Gospel, prevailed so
far as they obtained Ministers, with whom the Priests could not agree:
they retained their service, and the ministers preached, and had the exercise of Religion asunder, following the order of the churches of France. In
those beginnings at the pursuit of Mr. John After, Dean, I was sent by my
Lords of the Councell to the Islands, as well in regard of the School that
was newly erected, as to be a minister there". At this time the Roman
Catholic priests retained their liturgical functions. However, because they
were incapable of preaching and pastoral duties owing to their lack of learning, these activities were taken over by ministers "following the order of
the Churches of France". Both found a place under the authority of the
Bishop of Winchester who, together with the Dean, John After, permitted
the two capitals, St. Peter Port (Guernsey) and St. Helier (Jersey), a
church order at variance with that of the Church of England. This,
however, remained confined to the two above-mentioned local congregations. According to Saravia the introduction of classes and synods had
taken place outside the bishop's jurisdiction.[148] Such a church order might
be acceptable for the French and Dutch: "they have laws from their
Soveraigns, and particular places for themselves,[149] but all that you doe is
contrary to the laws and ordinance of the king your soveraign".[150] The
many ministers who were not appointed by the bishop cannot be regarded
as "true and lawfull ministers", but rather as "excommunicants and
schismaticks".[151] The letter then concludes; "When your Governors shall
have a liking to the English Reformation, then will they make you leave
the French Reformation".[152] It is well to remember that this criticism was

---

Masters of Assemblyes. Confirming the Kings Supremacy, the Subjects Duty, Church Government by
Bishops ...Nic. Bernard, ed. (London, 1661) 144.

[147] "A Letter of Dr. Hadrianus Saravia to the Ministers of the Isle of Garnsay; written in
French and translated into English", in: Clavi Trabales, 137-146.

[148] Ibid., 139.

[149] The reference is to relevant stipulations in the Edict of Nantes (1598).

[150] Clavi Trabales, 140.

[151] Ibid., 142 f.

[152] Ibid., 144.

expressed after the autumn of 1610, more than forty years after Saravia had left the Channel Islands. During his stay there he gave no sign of any such fundamental rejection of the Calvinist church order. Again in 1587, in his last year as professor at Leiden, he was to offer to return to the Islands,[153] an offer which in fact says more about his growing dislike of the circumstances in the Dutch church and state at that period than about his love for the Channel Islands of whose people he had an extremely unfavourable opinion.

In a detailed letter to the Queen's secretary, William Cecil,[154] he complained bitterly about their untrustworthiness. They were not very particular about the truth in the ruling assembly. People went little to church and behaved irreverently during services. Disturbances of the peace were frequent occurrences. So small was the number of those favouring Protestantism that the progress of the Reformation depended on three or four people. This complaint sounds somewhat exaggerated if we take into account that the French Huguenots who had sought refuge in the islands would scarcely have been lukewarm in the practice of religion. Saravia further drew a picture of disorder and lawlessness on the island. He held the local authorities responsible for this and in his view they were hostile to the Reformation. The population was idle and stupid. For example, it was too lazy to avail itself of the natural means to hand and, by construction of a proper harbour, to do something towards increasing its prosperity. In his letter Saravia showed his concern at the government's carelessness in the matter of defence. The islands, which were of great strategic importance to England, lay completely open to French attacks. Yet the military authorities occupied themselves in threatening the faithful "whom as a term of abuse they call Huguenots" rather than in the defence of their territory. These and similar alarming reports would have been based on experiences during the last six months of the war between France and England which had ended in April, 1564.

Least of all was the headmaster enthusiastic about the College. The promised salary had still not been paid to him. The desire for education scarcely existed amongst the island's inhabitants. They sent no more than ten pupils to the school. The rest of the pupils were of English nationality. The writer of the letter himself longed for English citizenship. He would prefer to live in England in the most reduced of circumstances than to continue living on Guernsey at three times the salary. The manner in which he finally solicits the interest of the Queen's Secretary leads one to suspect that the obtaining of English nationality was an important aim in the writing of the letter. Saravia made the same desire known to the captain of Guernsey, Francis Chamberlain. On 24 September 1566 the latter

---

[153]  De Schickler, Églises du refuge, II, 438, n. 2.
[154]  Saravia to William Cecil, 26 Feb. 1565/66. PRO.SP. 15/12, fol. 99 f.; Doc. I.

informed William Cecil that Saravia "would be much pleased to be
naturalised, and is worthy that favour", and added meaningly "and of a
much better reward, which I will not fail to consider". Furthermore,
Chamberlain was in a position to report that the headmaster of Elizabeth
College, who had given a home to his parents, "his father a Spaniard, and
his mother of Artois", was anxious to consult the Secretary about a
dispensation from his duties because of "the alteration of times in
Flanders". The captain requested Cecil to induce Saravia to stay in
Guernsey. It was considered difficult to replace him because of his "virtue
in instructing youth" and "setting forth sound doctrine".[155]

## 5. ADVENTURES IN THE NETHERLANDS (1568-1571)

Saravia, however, wanted to leave Guernsey. During his earlier mentioned visit to Antwerp and St. Trond (summer 1566) the churches in the
South Netherlands probably tried to prevail on him to return, but his experiences were such that he preferred England to his native land. The outcome of the meeting with the nobility at St. Trond on 15 July, in which he
had taken part with Franciscus Junius, Pérégrin de la Grange and Moded,
had been disappointing as regards church affairs. To be sure plans had
been drawn up for an armed revolt against Philip II. The Reformed consistories were to provide financial support for this. Yet, on the other hand,
the Calvinists were asked, pending the outcome of the nobility's petition
presented earlier on 5 April to the Governess, Margaret of Parma, at
Brussels, to suspend their "hedge sermons" (open-air services) for the
time being. Amongst other things, this petition requested a meeting of the
States General in order to provide a legal means for resolving the religious
problems which were so clearly not being solved by inquisition and harsh
edicts. However, the Reformed did not want to wait any longer to obtain
the right to practise their religion freely. The nobility was powerless to
check the irresistible upsurge which burst out emotionally and violently in
the iconoclasm. This began in Poperinge on 14 August, the same day on
which a Calvinist was burned at the stake in Antwerp.[156] On August 15 it
was the turn of the neighbourhood of Ypres, on 18 August, Oudenaarde.
The images were smashed in Antwerp on the 20th, at Ghent and Amsterdam on the 22nd and later in Leiden, Delft, Utrecht and the far North of
the country.[157] How furiously the authorities reacted is apparent from a
new execution on 4 September at Antwerp in which a Calvinist, who had

---

[155] *CSPD. Add. 1566-1579*, 17.

[156] *De Kroniek van Godevaert van Haecht over de troebelen van 1565 tot 1574 te Antwerpen en elders.*
R. van Roosbroeck, ed. (2 vols., Antwerp, 1929-1930) II, 35.

[157] P. Geyl, *Geschiedenis van de Nederlandse Stam* (unfinished, 3 vols., Amsterdam/Antwerp,
1948-1959) I, 200-208; *AGN*, IV, 337-345; O. J. de Jong, *Beeldenstorm in de Nederlanden.*
Groningen, 1964.

already been imprisoned for a year, was beheaded.[158] These events made
such an impression on Saravia that they permanently influenced his thinking about the relationship between church and state. The reform of the
Church, so he was later to argue, ought to be the concern of the government, in this case of the nobility. Where the common people took the law
into their own hands by violent action, the Reformation was doomed to
failure as, to his mind, the further history of the South Netherlands
demonstrated.

A few months after his return to Guernsey Saravia wrote to Cecil that
he had not acceded to the Dutch request that he rejoin the Flemish
Church. According to his not very convincing explanation, his departure
would be taken as proof of his ingratitude towards the church of the Channel Islands. The real motive for his refusal to return to the Netherlands
was his repugnance to the disturbance in that area. He was not inclined to
expose his parents, whom he had just brought over from Ghent, his family
and himself to the dangers of what he called "this unquiet age". Once
more, this time more plainly, he asked that he might receive English
citizenship.[159] His request was granted a year later. On 10 February 1568
Adrianus Saravia was naturalized as an Englishman.[160]

In the same year it became apparent that his naturalization in no way
meant that he had renounced his native land. Between 11 April and 21
July, with three poorly co-ordinated military actions at different places on
Dutch soil, Orange had vainly tried to support the opposition to the Duke
of Alva who had been conducting a veritable reign of terror for a year. He
did indeed manage to penetrate the territory of Liège as far as Tongres
and St. Trond, but Alva's harsh preventive measures in the towns and ac-
complished strategic tactics and the disorder in Orange's own expensive
army led the expedition to fail miserably.[161] On this occasion, in the same
way as Franciscus Junius,[162] Saravia served the prince as an army
chaplain.[163] It is true that he himself never made any mention of the campaign in contrast to Junius who, in his autobiographical notes, went into

[158] Van Haecht, *Kroniek*, II, 42.

[159] Saravia to William Cecil, 31 January 1566/67. PRO.SP. 15/12, fol. 55r; Doc. II.

[160] *Letters of Denization and Acts of Naturalisation for Aliens in England 1509-1603. PubHS*, VIII
(1893) 77: "*De Saravia*, Adrian, from the dominions of Philip, king of Spain. 10 Feb., 1568
(*Pat.*, 10 Eliz., p. 5, m. 32)".

[161] *AGN*, V, 18 f.; Geyl, *Geschiedenis van de Nederlandse stam*, I, 218 f.; Van Schelven,
*Willem van Oranje*, 149-160; J. W. Berkelbach van der Sprenkel, *Oranje en de vestiging van de
Nederlandse staat* (2nd ed., Amsterdam, 1960) 68 ff.

[162] J. Reitsma, *Franciscus Junius. Een levensbeeld uit den eersten tijd der kerkhervorming* (Groningen, 1864) 92 f.; Cuno, *Junius*, 43 f.; B. A. Venemans, *Franciscus Junius en zijn Eirenicum de
pace ecclesiae catholicae* (Leiden, s.a.) 28 f.

[163] See e.g. R. C. Bakhuizen van den Brink, *Studiën en Schetsen over de vaderlandsche
geschiedenis en letteren* (5 vols., 1863-1913) I, 316; A. A. van Schelven, "Adrianus Saravia",
in: *NNBW*, IX, 935; id., *Willem van Oranje*, 155; J. Meyhoffer, "Adrien Saravia", *BSHPB*,
II, 2 (1921) 70.

detail about his experiences on this "wretched campaign, than which I think there was never in our time one more ill-fated".[164] Nonetheless his presence in Orange's forces is clearly enough documented by his reference at the end of the pamphlet he wrote for this occasion: "Composed by me, Adrianus Zaraphya, minister of the Divine Word, with the noble Prince of Orange, dated 1568, the 21 September".[165]

The pamphlet is rare and little known.[166] For example, the historian P. Bor does not mention it amongst the tracts published between 1564 and 1568.[167] A copy of the original edition is to be found in the library of the Walloon Church, nowadays housed in the Walloon Hospice in Amsterdam.[168] The work belongs to the stream of pamphlets to which the revolt gave rise.[169] There was a need to strengthen morale particularly in the extremely critical phase of Orange's military ventures at the beginning of the autumn of 1568. Following a number of pamphlets which Orange had earlier had published[170] and two weeks before his crossing of the Maas, Saravia's work appeared. It numbered 32 octavo pages and its title-page read, *A heartfelt desire of the noble, very long-suffering, high-born Prince of Orange, together with all his Christian, noble, pious allies, a desire of all men, of whatever condition or quality they are, who love and fear the Lord and who also have a fondness for the welfare of our gracious, high born King Philip of Spain and the Netherlands together also that Imperial Realm; which lands, under the pretext of protection, one named Duke of Alva, now seeks to spoil and wholly to ruin. In whose heart, concealed lies an unspeakably bloodthirsty tyranny which he will accomplish so far as he gains the mastery, so will you find this small book is true.*

The vignette consists of the arms of Charles V with the motto: "Plus Oultre". 2 Thess. 5: "Prove all things, hold fast that which is good". On the reverse side: "Psalm LXVIII and XLIIII. But God thou art our King, through thy might we shall defeat our enemies and in Thy name will we tread them under that rise up against us. For I will not trust in my bow or sword, but Thou, God, art our refuge and strength, a help in great need, therefore will we not fear although the earth fall in and the mountains collapse in the middle of the sea; yea although the sea rage and gather into a

---

[164] Junius, *Opuscula*, 32 f.

[165] HB, D4r. Cf. Ph. M. Crew, *Calvinist Preaching and Iconoclasm in the Netherlands 1544-1569* (Cambridge/London/New York/Melbourne, 1978) 117.

[166] J. K. van der Wulp, ed. *Catalogus van de tractaten, pamfletten, enz. over de geschiedenis van Nederland, aanwezig in de bibliotheek van Isaac Meulman* (3 vols., Amsterdam, 1866-1868) I, 31, Nr. 190; new edition in: M. G. Schenk, ed. *Verantwoordinge, Verklaringhe ende Waerschouwinghe mitsgaders eene Hertgrondighe Begheerte des edelen, lancmoedighen ende hooghgeboren Princen van Oraengien* (Amsterdam, 1933) 129-155.

[167] P. Bor, *Oorspronck, begin en vervolgh der Nederlandsche oorlogen* (9 vols., Amsterdam, 1679-1684) I, 180.

[168] *Catalogue de la Bibliothèque Wallonne déposée à Leide*, 2e suppl. (Leiden, 1865) 5.

[169] P. A. M. Geurts, *De Nederlandse opstand in de pamfletten 1566-1584*, Nijmegen, 1956.

[170] Schenk, *Verantwoordinge*, 18-20.

heap, so will I put my trust in my Lord, for I called upon Thee in need and Thou heardest me".[171] Vignette: the arms of William of Orange. "2 Thess. 5. Prove all things, hold fast that which is good".[172]

The pamphlet's title and its opening, in which the prince is presented speaking,[173] deliberately create the impression that the revolt of the Dutch was directed against the Duke of Alva, not against the Spanish King. On the contrary, they sought the welfare of the "gracious" (title-page) and "noble" (opening) "high-born" King Philip. This representation of affairs, quite at odds with historical reality, was maintained until the abjuration of Philip in 1581. Direct attacks on him were therefore unsuitable in a dissertation of this tenor. Indirectly, however, he was impugned, namely by comparing him with his father; a tactic which is often met with in the pamphlets of this period. The line taken was that Charles V was guided more than his son by a concern for the welfare of the whole nation. Just as he had allowed the Religious Peace of Augsburg in Germany, so, in the Netherlands also, unlike Philip, he would have known how to guarantee peace and quiet by wise statesmanship. We encounter this version of affairs current in the pamphlets[174] in Saravia's *Heartfelt Desire*. It is no accident that Charles V's arms stand out on the title page. The writer of the pamphlet supposed: "that the noble, high-born Emperor Charles the Fifth of blessed memory had never dared or wanted to do such things"[175] as Alva did. Saravia's pamphlet was directed above all against this governor's cruelties. He was acquainted with the contents of a "small book" in which the prince had recently explained the purpose of his struggle.[176] The reference was to the *Admonition of the Prince of Orange to the inhabitants and subjects of the Netherlands,*[177] which Orange was said to have written himself. Much shorter than Saravia's work, this is more of a political pamphlet with references to the rights and privileges of the land[178] and accusations not only against Granvelle and Alva but also against the Spanish sovereign himself whose house wielded a "rule and dominion" over the land which had for its goal "to govern and tyrannize it according to their desire in the same manner that they do elsewhere".[179]

Saravia's work, on the other hand, is ruled much more by religious motives. It was in the main a call to prayer and conversion. For, as it was noted at the beginning, the prince and his allies drew the sword "by the in-

---

[171] See: Ps. 44:5, 6, 7 and Ps. 46:2, 3.
[172] *HB*, Alv.
[173] *Ibid.*, A2r.
[174] Geurts, *Nederlandse opstand*, 158 f.
[175] *HB*, B3v.
[176] *Ibid.*, A2r.
[177] Schenk, *Verantwoordinge*, 117-128.
[178] *Ibid.*, 120 f.
[179] *Ibid.*, 121.

spiration of God's Holy Spirit".[180] Victory was only attainable by God's power.[181] It was observed that the prince never went to bed at night without praying God for Alva's conversion,[182] a somewhat curious observation to be offered in a justification of an armed revolt.[183] It sounded equally conflicting when, in a pamphlet intended to strengthen military morale, the wish was expressed that people should pray for the prince "that he might win victory and defeat his enemy without much bloodshed". This was he, once again, "into whose heart it came . . . by the inspiration of God's Holy Spirit".[184] In a remarkable mixture of piety and foreboding Saravia prophesied that a period of severe bloodshed was in store. God alone could prevent the prince's victory from being exacted at so great a price.[185] Still more confusing sounds the appeal: "Therefore my dear brothers in the Lord, love your enemies from the bottom of your hearts, so Christ has loved us who were his enemies: otherwise indeed your prayer is utterly loathsome to God".[186] Can the army chaplain's paradoxical position be put into words more clearly?

The struggle was conducted, so Saravia wrote, "for the protection and welfare of the noble, high-born Philip, King of Spain, our lawful Sovereign of the Netherlands, and also for the praise of God's name".[187] They considered themselves pledged to the struggle because of the obligation they had entered into towards the King at the Joyous Entry.[188] In this way the rising acquired a constitutional appearance: it was not a revolt against the role of the lawful sovereign. The author was very well aware that the well armed Alva held a clear military ascendency, but he comforted his reader by referring to dozens of examples from the Bible which declared that victory lay not in the multitude of horses or soldiers but in God's power. "All human help is vain without God. Vana salus hominum: but wise is he who puts his faith in God".[189]

The pamphlet's title expressed the desire of Orange and his allies, "that all men would pray for them unceasingly with a firm faith and heart that Almighty God would protect them from treachery by His power and also grant them fortune, prosperity and victory over their enemy, whom he could never satisfy by any peaceful means".[190] The enemy was Alva for

---

[180] *HB*, A2r.
[181] *Ibid.*, A2v.
[182] *Ibid.*, C1v.
[183] Bakhuizen van den Brink, *Studiën en kritieken*, I, 317.
[184] *HB*, A2v.
[185] *Ibid.*, A3r.
[186] *Ibid.*, A3v, 4r.
[187] *Ibid.*, C1r.
[188] *Ibid.*, B4v.
[189] *Ibid.*, C3v.
[190] *Ibid.*, D3r.

whose conversion prayer must above all be made.[191] Saravia voiced William of Orange's political and military views in the form of an edifying tract which had the character of a sermon, a call for prayer, faith, conversion and the readiness to accept suffering. In this he identified the affliction which conduct of the war brought to the population with the bearing of Christ's cross.[192]

For this pamphlet's author the revolt had broken out in the first place "religionis causae". Its aim was the ousting of tyranny "so that the dispersed Christians might enter their native country and that the lands might be restored to their first freedom to the glory of God".[193] This displays the Calvinist ideal which along with the political and economic motives became increasingly a driving force in the Dutch revolt. Later, in 1593, Saravia was to expand his constitutional ideas systematically and in detail.[194] This defence of absolute monarchy displayed no fundamental alteration from the first of his works. In 1568 there was no question for Saravia that anyone other than "the high born prince and his allies", that is to say: the high nobility, possessed the right to rebel. According to this interpretation, the rising was not directed against the Spanish monarch, but was intended to protect him. The Dutch revolt held Alva as the "tyrant".

The historian P. J. Blok supposed that there were characteristics to be found in the *Heartfelt Desire* similar to those of *Wilhelmus van Nassau,* which was later, and is still today, sung as the Dutch national anthem. There is still uncertainty about both the origins and the authorship of this song.[195] The theory of Marnix van St. Aldegonde's authorship has as much support[196] as it does opposition.[197] Blok saw the following similarities between

---

[191] *Ibid.,* D3v.

[192] *Ibid.,* D2v f.

[193] *Ibid.,* A2v.

[194] p. 244-255.

[195] "Whoever reads through the publications on the Wilhelmus of the last hundred years—and there are indeed some 80 of them—is overwhelmed by the number of opinions, convictions and views about the exposition of the text, the interpretation of its meaning, the elucidation of the historical and religious backgrounds. In short, after a 100 years of study of the Wilhelmus, the Dutch people still do not know when and where the song was composed and who was its author; they still do not know what it says in it and what it refers to, what sort of song it is and how it was composed", thus S. J. Lenselink, "Het Wilhelmus, een andere interpretatie," *De Nieuwe Taalgids,* LVIII (1964) 140; cf. H. Bruch, *Slaat op den trommele. Het Wilhelmus en de Geuzenliederen* (Leiden, 1971) 90-92.

[196] E. g. A. A. van Schelven, *Marnix van Sint Aldegonde* (Utrecht, 1939) 65-72; S. J. Lenselink, "De dichter van het Wilhelmus," *Levende talen,* Nr. 146 (Oct. 1948) 147-151; id., 'Marnix en het Wilhelmus", *Tijdschrift voor Nederlandse Taal- en Letterkunde,* LXVII (1950) 241-263.

[197] K. Heeroma, " 't Sal hier haest zijn ghedaen," *Verslagen en Mededelingen van de Koninklijke Vlaamse Academie voor Taal- en Letterkunde.* New Series (Ghent, 1970) 526-542; J. and A. Romein, *Erflaters van onze beschaving. Nederlandse gestalten uit zes eeuwen* (9th imp., Amsterdam, 1971) 143.

Saravia's pamphlet and the "Wilhelmus". In both the Spanish King is spoken of with respect as the rightful sovereign. "The King of Spain have I always honoured" proclaims the first verse of the "Wilhelmus". In the last verse the song puts a profession of loyalty to the King into Orange's mouth. Like Saravia's pamphlet it calls for prayer, day and night, (verses 3 and 13) and avows faith in God (verse 6). Although these agreements are undeniably present, it is open to question whether they are sufficient for the otherwise tentative suggestion proposed by Blok that Saravia was perhaps the author of the "Wilhelmus".[198] The ideas mentioned here are in complete accord with the common picture of the pamphlet literature of this period: the revolt as a struggle not against the monarch but against his false servants;[199] to him indeed are ascribed all the virtues proper to a king which were already set before him by the example of his father, Charles V.[200] It goes without saying that he is to be honoured. Again the contrast between lawful kingship and tyranny is very familiar in this type of literature.[201] The attribution of the pastoral function of the prince to William of Orange, borrowed from the Old Testament, which we find in the "Wilhelmus", is only apparently in conflict with the fidelity to the Spanish monarch mentioned earlier. It needs to be investigated whether this myth making about Orange is characteristic of the pamphlets in this period[202] rather than only of the "Wilhelmus" and whether it is similar to Saravia's esteem for the function of the prince as the representative of the lawful authority.[203] Setting aside all these difficult questions, it is to be noted that if Saravia really were to have been the author of the later Dutch national anthem, then this would be his only known poetic work. All in all Blok's hypothesis about the authorship of the "Wilhelmus" does not convince us. All of which does not alter the fact that the pamphlet a *Heartfelt Desire* clearly demonstrates Saravia's excellent command of the Dutch language. Moreover it bears powerful witness to his great admiration for Orange and to his sense of responsibility for political developments in his native land.

After the failure of Orange's military venture we again lose sight of Saravia for a time. Did he return once more to Guernsey to resume his work at the College? It is not out of the question, but we cannot be certain about this because the archives of church and school relating to this period have been lost.

---

[198] P. J. Blok, "Aanteekeningen over 'de Zwijger' en over het Wilhelmus," *Bijdragen voor Vaderlandsche Geschiedenis en Oudheidkunde.* 4th series, VIII (1910) 443-447.

[199] Geurts, *Nederlandse opstand,* 158.

[200] *Ibid.,* 159.

[201] *Ibid.,* 192-195.

[202] In his study Geurts devotes attention only to the negative myth-making of opponents, *ibid.,* 183-186, but not to the positive by supporters.

[203] p. 254.

Saravia's surname appears in Southampton for the first time on 3 July 1569. According to the registers of the Walloon refugees' church there his parents were admitted to the Lord's Supper on that date.[204] On 1 January 1570 the same is recorded of "la femme de monsieur mestre Adrien Saravia et sa servante".[205] It must therefore be presumed that the members of Saravia's household: his parents, wife, children and servants settled in this seaport town on the south coast of England in the latter half of 1569. The servants were apparently chosen from the Walloons because this was the language spoken by the mistress of the house. On 3 July 1575, Colette Cartret[206] and on 6 October 1577, Clemence Arthurs,[207] both described as "servante a M. adrien Saravia", were admitted to the Lord's Supper in the Walloon Church.

But where was the head of the family at this time? Horlocke, his predecessor as Headmaster of King Edward VI School, first left the town at the end of 1571 after his appointment as Rector of Exton.[208] Saravia could not therefore have taken up his post as the latter's successor earlier than the end of 1571 or the beginning of 1572. The town archives contain very little material about him.[209] The first reliable mention of his presence and office in Southampton is the report of the admission to the Lord's Supper on 6 April 1572 of two of his pupils, Nichollas Effard and Nichollas Carryé.[210] Did Saravia first have another, less important educational post? Among the many foreigners in the town there were several schoolmasters,[211] a sign of the share that, in view also of the shortage of native English teachers, foreigners had in education in sixteenth century England.[212] It is therefore not unlikely that, prior to his appointment as Headmaster of King Edward VI School, Saravia had first engaged in a lesser educational role.

Even if this supposition is correct then it is nevertheless certain that he also spent some time in the Netherlands at the beginning of the seventies. A remarkable report in the acta of the consistory of the Walloon Church in London points in this direction. On 26 November 1572 a request from Saravia came up for discussion, a request to help him "to receive payment

---

[204] *Registre de l'église wallonne de Southampton*, H. M. Godfray, ed. *PubHS*, IV, 3.

[205] *Ibid.*, 5.

[206] *Ibid.*, 11.

[207] *Ibid.*, 13.

[208] Ch. Fr. Russell, *A History of King Edward VI School* (priv. pr., s.l., 1940) 28.

[209] The author is grateful to the City Archivist, Miss S. D. Thomson, for her helpfulness in providing information.

[210] *Registre*, 7.

[211] Russell, *King Edward VI School*, 39.

[212] F. Watson, "Notes and Materials on Religious Refugees in their Relations to Education in England before the Revocation of the Edict of Nantes, 1685," *ProHS*, IX (1909) 299-475; W. M. Jones, "Foreign Teachers in Sixteenth Century England," *The Historian*, XXI (1958/1959) 162-175.

from those of Flushing for the services he had performed in the said place''. The consistory decided to advise him to ask the church of Flushing for an official notice of discharge containing the permission for his departure from there. Why did Adrian address such a request to the Walloons in London? The answer lies in the second part of his question to the consistory, namely in what way would he be of most service to the church in London.[213] This offer does not in any way mean that, in less than a year, the Headmaster of King Edward VI School, Southampton, was considering leaving his post. It only shows that, in whatever part of England he might live and work, he always strove to maintain close relations with London. We shall see later that to this end he was to take up a number of minor offices in the capital. That Saravia should address a problem about a Zeeland congregation not to the Dutch but to the Walloon congregation shows how deeply the French speakers managed to involve themselves in the course of affairs in the whole of the Netherlands. We shall encounter many more examples of this.

Meanwhile it is clear that Saravia worked for a time as a minister in Flushing. When exactly this happened we cannot determine with any certainty, but we must think in terms of 1570 and 1571. In this period, under Alva's reign of terror and despite the persecutions which claimed numerous victims, secret meetings were held on the island of Walcheren at which sermons were preached and the sacraments administered.[214] Indeed long before the coming of ''the iron duke'' preaching had been secretly conducted in Flushing[215] and elsewhere in Zeeland by men who supported themselves by manual work. In this province as everywhere in the South Netherlands the importance of the Dutch refugees' churches in England for the progress of the Reformation in their native land became evident. Geleyn d'Hoorne,[216] who had carried out the trade of a cabinet-maker in London, worked in this way from 1559 to 1567, principally in Middelburg and Flushing,[217] remaining in correspondence with the Dutch church in London during this stay.[218] On August 1562 he appeared in the consistory with the request that he might be released from his service in Flushing. The consistory deferred a decision on this request at that time.[219] Over a year before, in May 1561, the weaver, Erasmus Top, had also been sent as

---

[213] *Actes du Consistoire de l'Église Française de Threadneedle Street, Londres*, II: *1571-1577*, A. M. Oakley, ed. *PubHs*, XLVIII (London, 1969) 96.

[214] J. W. te Water, *Kort verhaal der Reformatie van Zeeland* (Middelburg, 1766) 146 ff.

[215] J. H. van Dale, "Geheime verkondiging der hervormde leer te Vlissingen, ten jare 1558," in: H. Q. Janssen and J. H. van Dale, ed., *Bijdragen tot de Oudheidkunde en Geschiedenis inzonderheid van Zeeuwsch-Vlaanderen*, I (1856) 353.

[216] *NNBW*, IV, 782 f.

[217] Decavele, *Dageraad der Reformatie*, I, 406.

[218] *Kerkeraadsprotocollen*, 200 f., 229, 236, 263.

[219] *Ibid.*, 349.

a minister to Flushing.[220] On 25 July 1563 a request came from Flushing for a minister "who is to be an artisan and a bachelor".[221] This was probably prompted less by a desire for ministers, who by origin and occupation would be close to the common people, than by the possibility that these workmen, by their inclusion in the ordinary industrial processes, would be less easily discovered by the judicial authorities.[222] Still more important, however, was the fact that these men did not need to be paid for their ministry since they carried this out as part-time voluntary work. It appears from Saravia's question to the Walloon consistory in London, that a change came about in this situation the moment that, in a town like Flushing, the call went out for better educated ministers who, however, had no technical skills by which they could support themselves.

Apparently, after the great military turnabout in April 1572 when indeed they had received freedom for Reformed public worship yet had a severe shortage of ministers,[223] the church at Flushing intended to assert the rights of the man who had served them in the dangerous days of persecution, although there had then naturally been no question of an institutionalized church life and of the legalized appointment to and dismissal from office which this involved. On 22 January 1572 the Walloon consistory in London did at least write to Flushing asking them either to reappoint Saravia or to discharge him honourably.[224] Thereafter Saravia's name appears once more in the proceedings of the consistory, on 10 June 1574. They had lent him twelve pounds which he evidently repaid. It was decided to put the money back into the church chest, this is to be distinguished from the diaconal chest whose contents were earmarked for the poor.[225]

## 6.  HEADMASTER OF KING EDWARD VI SCHOOL, SOUTHAMPTON (1572-1578)

Possibly Saravia borrowed the above-mentioned amount from the Walloons in London because he was in very needy circumstances in Flushing. Evidently he was in a position to make repayment when his financial status at Southampton, which was also not initially rosy, was improved especially by the letting of lodgings to pupils. From the pettycustom books it appears that from Michaelmas 1571 the headmaster no

---

[220] *Ibid.*, 191.

[221] *Ibid.*, 436.

[222] Decavele, *Dageraad der Reformatie*, I, 406.

[223] From April to September 1572 preaching was still conducted by unknown ministers at odd times in houses: the Roman Catholics were provisionally allowed to retain their churches. The first official Reformed service took place on 28 September 1572. *Ibid.* 164 f.

[224] *Actes Threadneedle Street*, 102.

[225] *Ibid.*, 140.

longer had to pay the usher out of his own salary. From that date he was paid a salary of £13-6s-8d per year and Saravia enjoyed this income up to his leaving in 1578. In 1571/72 the usher was paid a salary of £6-13s-4d which was raised to £10 from 1573/74. After his departure the head-master's salary was also increased and his successor Guydo Dobbyns or Dobin received £20 per year.[226] Furthermore mention is made in the Mayor's town accounts of two payments to Saravia, namely in 1576 "to Mr. Adrian for his charges and paies in his tragedie, by consent XXs" and in 1577, "Paid for IV yardes of broade cloth for a gowne for Mr. Adrian Saravia the Schoolmaster at IXs the yarde . . . XXXVIs".[227] The first reimbursement concerned expenses incurred in connection with an annual theatrical performance by the pupils for the Earl of Southampton's household.[228]

Saravia enjoyed great prestige as headmaster. His pupils later spoke of him with profound respect. One of these pupils, the philologist and Hebraist, Nicholas Fuller ( ± 1557-1626),[229] honoured Horlocke and Saravia as those who had taught him Latin and Greek.[230] Robert Ashley (1565-1641),[231] a polyglot noted for his translations of multifarious works from French, Spanish and Italian, also studied at Southampton when Saravia was headmaster there. Together with sixteen to twenty other pupils he lived in lodgings with him. In his autobiography, extant in manuscript in the British Library, he later recorded the following reminiscences of this. "I was taken by my mother, together with my younger brother of six years of age, to Southampton School, which was well-known both because of the place itself and because of its headmaster . . . Sixteen or twenty young fellows of noble rank were being brought up there in the house of the master, Adrian Saravia, a Belgian, whose wife and family habitually used the French language. We used to talk French at ordinary times in the house, just as if we were living in France, the rule being that if any one was caught using his native language while indoors he had to wear a dunce's cap at meal times in the dining-room, and continued to do so until he would pass it on to somebody else who had been caught in the same offence".[232] In medieval England French was the language of political and legal intercourse just as Latin was the language of the learned. At the end of the middle ages both languages

---

[226] *The Third Book of Remembrance of Southampton 1514-1602.* A. L. Merson, ed. III: *1573-1589* (Southampton, 1965) 103.

[227] J. Silvester Davies, *History of Southampton* (Southampton, 1833) 312; Russell, *King Edward VI School,* 39.

[228] *Ibid.,* n.l.

[229] *DNB,* XX, 131 f.

[230] Russell, *King Edward VI School,* 39 f., 338.

[231] *DNB,* II, 172.

[232] Cit. Russell, *King Edward VI School,* 40, 116, 343.

were likewise still taught in the Inns of Court.[233] In the sixteenth century
French also continued to have an important part in education in the higher
social circles, especially for students who were destined for a political or
diplomatic career.[234] Thus what went on in Saravia's house in this respect
was not so remarkable as the historian of King Edward VI School makes
out.[235] The court and the nobility made frequent use of private tutors.
This concurs with Ashley's report that the pupils whom Saravia had in his
home were of noble birth. What could be more self-evident than the learned headmaster's offer to acquaint these young men in such a sound educational fashion with his native language which was essential for their future
careers? Moreover the income produced by the lodging and instruction of
the boarders would not have been unwelcome to him.

The historian of King Edward VI School describes Saravia as "by far
the most famous headmaster the school ever had".[236] Under his leadership
the institution experienced a period of prosperity. It turned out many men
who served their nation in a variety of positions in society. Besides the two
referred to earlier, mention must be made of Edward Reynolds, who also
lived in Saravia's house and, although an Englishman, became a member
of the Walloon Church in Southampton.[237] As secretary of the Earl of
Essex he became a man of great influence.[238] The poet Joshua Sylvester
(1563-1618)[239] was one of Saravia's pupils from 1573 to 1576. In a poem
he later spoke of Southampton as "Thy [that is the Earl of Southampton's]
Town (where my Saravia taught)". He expressed his regret that he had
only been able to study for three years in that town and the great admiration he had for his teacher, in a *Funeral Elegie* on the occasion of the death
of Saravia's second wife, Margaretha Wyts. After her husband's death she
married Sylvester's friend, Dr. Robert Hill, but died in child-birth on 29
June 1615. After describing her virtues, Sylvester wrote further:

"Such shee was a Wife
To (my) Saravia; to whose reverend name
Mine owes the honour of du-Bartas' fame[240] . . .
From th' ample Cisterns of his sea of skill,
Suckt I (my Succour) my short shallow Rill:

---

[233] J. Simon, *Education and Society in Tudor England* (Cambridge, 1967) 18 f., 53.

[234] K. Lambley, *The Teaching and Cultivation of the French Language in England during Tudor
and Stuart Times*. Manchester, 1920.

[235] Russell, *King Edward VI School*, 40.

[236] *Ibid.*, 28.

[237] *Registre Southampton*, 13: "edouart Reinnoulx, J. f., Angelois, demeurant Chez M.
adrien".

[238] Russell, *King Edward VI School*, 56 f.

[239] *DNB*, LV, 260-265.

[240] Sylvester translated into English the work of the Huguenot Guillaume de Saluste,
seigneur du Bartas (1544-1590).

The little All I can and all I could
In three poor years, at three times three years old".[241]

On a few occasions while Saravia was in charge of the school in Southampton pupils came from other places of education. Francis Markham (1565-1627),[242] second son of Sir Robert Markham of Cotham, twice high sheriff of Nottinghamshire and a confidant of Queen Elizabeth, tells in his autobiography how he broke off his education in Winchester under the then schoolmaster, the later Bishop Bilson, in order to receive instruction from Saravia. The moment the latter left for the Low Countries, Markham also quitted Southampton.[243] His military career later brought him to the Netherlands at least three times. It is evident from these examples that Saravia managed to raise the standard of education at the school to such a degree that many men of rank decided to entrust their sons to his guidance.

From his arrival in Southampton Saravia was in close touch with the Walloon refugees' church, founded in 1567.[244] Sometimes he and Wallerand Thevelin are reckoned together as the first two ministers of the congregation,[245] sometimes he is regarded as the second after Thevelin.[246] However, in view of his demanding educational work it is hard to believe that he had much time to spare for a full pastoral office. According to the church registers, Thevelin, who died on 13 September 1584,[247] carried out his official duties at least until 1580.[248] Saravia could well have been described as "minister" because he assisted where necessary in preaching and pastoral care in the church which rapidly expanded after its foundation. Besides French immigrants from the Channel Islands and several Englishmen, it also had amongst its members Dutchmen who had fled the Low Countries after Alva's arrival. They gave Southampton, whose port had somewhat fallen into decay, a new impetus as a centre of the wool trade. Most of them would doubtless have originated from the French speaking Netherlands.

In Southampton people were very closely concerned with the fluctuating fortunes of the persecuted Reformed Churches in France and the Netherlands. Of the long list of fast days called for on the occasion of striking events in the French religious wars and the Dutch revolt, —there

---

[241] Cit. Russell, *King Edward VI School*, 70 f.

[242] *DNB*, XXXVI, 165.

[243] *Ibid.*, 91, 339.

[244] On the history of this church: W. J. C. Moens, "The Walloon Settlement and the French Church at Southampton," *ProHS*, III (1888-1889) 51-76.

[245] *Ibid.*, 76.

[246] Silvester Davies, *History of Southampton*, 422; J. W. de Grave, "Notes on the Register of the Walloon Church of Southampton and on the Churches of the Channel Islands," *ProHS*, V (1894-1896) 136.

[247] *Registre Southampton*, 104.

[248] *Ibid.*, 87.

were thirteen of them during Saravia's residence in the town[249]—it seems
that William of Orange's military operations, his appointment as
Stadholder, the liberation and defence of Holland and Zeeland, the struggle for the South Netherlands, were observed with prayer and penance by
the Walloons in Southampton. The French speakers were united with the
Dutch speaking refugees in their desire of freedom for the proclamation of
the Gospel in both countries. As regards the Netherlands, however,
another sort of aid was expected of them, namely financial support for the
conduct of the war. On 31 October 1573 William of Orange wrote on this
matter to Saravia the only letter of the prince to his former army chaplain
at present known.[250] Orange was well aware, "that the Protestant Dutchmen who fled to England, far from being few and needy, were richly blessed in their exile".[251] In May 1573 he sent Lieven Calwaert (Livinus or
Levinus Calvart), who himself had lived for a time as a refugee in
England, working in 1569 as a minister amongst the Dutch in Norwich,[252]
and who was therefore well acquainted with the refugees' life, to London
with a letter which included a request for financial support for the conduct
of the war.[253] However, the amount collected was, according to the prince,
far less than what was required for the war. He therefore repeated his request on 31 October of the same year in a large number of letters to the
French, Dutch and Italian churches in England, amongst others.[254] Their
tone is rather severe: the refugees have for long not made the contribution
which, thanks to their prosperity, they were in a position to do. A monthly
sum of one thousand crowns might reasonably be expected of the said
three churches. The letter to Saravia was sent at the same time as these letters. The headmaster had pledged Calvart, who had evidently called on
him, that he would lose no opportunity of furthering the Dutch cause.
Orange thanked Saravia for his help and urged him to see to it that the
money collected by Dutch refugees in Sandwich be sent immediately to the
Netherlands. The prince would assuredly later show his gratitude for the
service rendered to the Dutch cause. Saravia was further to see to the col-
lections in Southampton itself as well as those among the French in San-
down and Rye, which the last time had managed only ten pounds between
them all. We do not know how Saravia discharged the task committed to
him by Orange. Meanwhile it seems from the collection amongst the
French speaking refugees that their solidarity with the warring Dutch was
presumed as a matter of course.

[249] *Ibid.,* 125 f.
[250] *KHA,* 11, XIV, I, 12, fol. 358; Doc. III. The author is grateful to Prof. K. W. Swart, Department of History, University College, London, who drew his attention to this letter.
[251] Te Water, *Reformatie van Zeeland,* 156.
[252] *NNBW,* IV, 392 f.
[253] Hessels, *ELBA,* II, Nrs. 87, 90, 112-116, 118, 119, 123, 125, 126.
[254] *Ibid.,* Nrs. 129, 129a; III, Nr. 167.

The Dutch in London continued to regard Saravia as one of them during his residence in Southampton.[255] For his part he valued the continuance of relations with the Dutch churches. They tried repeatedly throughout this period to get him as a minister in the North Netherlands. On Thursday, 12 March 1573 he was summoned to the consistory at Austin Friars and was asked whether he was prepared to accept a call to Dordrecht.[256] Three days later he returned a negative reply. The most important reason for his decision was the lack of a French-speaking church in Dordrecht which meant that his wife would have no opportunity to hear the preaching of the Gospel.[257] This was not the only request from Dordrecht. They had already twice before asked the London church to send ministers. According to a relevant letter of 29 August 1572[258] Bartholdus Wilhelmi had already been sent from England for that purpose.[259] On 28 January 1573 a request was again sent to the Dutch Church in London, prompted by the growth of the Dordrecht congregation and the overburdening of the available ministers.[260] This time they expressly asked that Georgius Sylvanius (Wybo, Wybotius)[261] be sent, but he chose to remain a minister in London.

Three years later, on 23 April 1576, the consistory of Dordrecht decided once again to make an attempt to get Saravia to join the Reformed church in that town; this time in company with Ysbrandus Trabius (Ysbrand Balck),[262] who was then minister in the Dutch church at Sandwich[263] and whom we shall meet again later in Leiden.[264] Again the growth of the congregation made necessary an increase in the number of ministers. Olevianus and Dathenus were also called to Dordrecht at the end of the same year but the consistory had as little to show for their attempts in the Palatinate as they did in England.[265] It is not known why in 1576, Saravia still did not yet want to move to the Netherlands nor whether on this occa-

---

[255] De Schickler, Églises du refuge, II, 377, n. 2.

[256] GHL, Ms. 9397/5, fol. 15v. There is nothing to be found about this invitation in the acts of the Reformed Church in Dordrecht. For the period 1572-21 March 1574 (they were first recorded after this last date) they are very brief and cover only 3½ pages.

[257] Ibid.

[258] Hessels, ELBA, III, Nr. 205.

[259] G. D. J. Schotel, Kerkelijk Dordrecht. Eene bijdrage tot de geschiedenis der Vaderlandsche Hervormde kerk (2 vols., Utrecht, 1841-1845) I, 89-95.

[260] Hessels, ELBA, III, Nr. 220.

[261] NNBW, III, 1494-1497.

[262] GADo, Nr. 10. 10, fol. 11r: "Is besloten by den Ouderlingen ende Diaconen in deser tyt in bijwesen sommiger ouderlingen en diakenen die te vooren gedient hebben, oick sommiger broederen als Cornelis van Beveren, Michiel sijn broeder, Reinier van Eest, Wijnant Fransen, M. Jacob Pauwels, dat Ysbrandus [Trabius] met Saravia wt Engellant tot desen kercken dienst soude beroepen worden".

[263] NNBW, I, 227-230; BWPGN, I, 301-309; van Schelven, Vluchtelingenkerken, 180.

[264] p. 56 f.

[265] Schotel, Kerkelijk Dordrecht, I, 120.

sion also the Austin Friars consistory was an intermediary.[266] For more than two years he still continued his work at the school in Southampton.

In the summer of 1578 he resigned as headmaster[267] in order to cross the North Sea with his wife and children. His father had already died long before on 20 November 1572.[268] His mother, who stayed behind in England, died at the end of the year in which she had had to take her final leave of her son.[269] Flanders, not Holland,[270] was the object of his journey. In itself this was somewhat remarkable because in doing so he went to a Dutch-speaking area. True, he had, during his second stay in England, kept up contact with the Dutch-speaking church in London—the Walloon and Dutch churches in this period were not yet so distinct from each other as later[271]—but for all that, such personal encounters as the one in London in 1573 would not have been frequent occurrences. Again, although the Walloon congregation in Southampton had several Dutch-speaking members yet Saravia would scarcely have spoken Dutch in that town. When the question of a return to Flanders was first mooted in the summer of 1577, he initially raised the objection "that his capacity for service would not as yet be great since in 17 years had not had much to do with the Dutch people". This excuse was not plausible because, at any rate in his contact with the Dutch between 1559 and 1563 and in the Flushing period he had surely spoken their language very regularly. To this excuse he added the expectation that, after a few months practical experience of the Dutch tongue, he would again fully master it.[272]

---

[266] GHL. Ms. 7397 for the most part omits the period 1575-1578.

[267] *Third Book of Remembrance,* 103.

[268] *Registre Southampton,* 101: "1572... 21 Nov. Christofle de Saravia, espaignol De Nation, ob. 20. Nov.".

[269] *Ibid.,* 102: "1578... 29 Déc. Elizabeth Boulengier, vesve de Christofle de Saravia, ob. 28 Déc.".

[270] By Holland we here mean the territory of the two present-day provinces of North and South Holland. This is to be distinguished from the Netherlands, by which, in the period here described, we understand an area more or less covered by the present-day Benelux.

[271] Lindeboom, *Austin Friars,* 96-102: de Villiers was paid by both congregations to teach Latin to their theologians and to those of the Italian Church. *WMV,* III; 1, 90; C. Boer, *Hofpredikers van Prins Willem van Oranje* (The Hague, 1952) 54. After its expansion the Walloon congregation received permission, "het heyligh Avontmael maendelijcks the celebreren in de tempel der Duytschen, Jesus tempel ghenoemt", *WMV,* III; 1, 92.

[272] Hessels, *ELBA,* II, Nr. 162.

# CHAPTER TWO

# MINISTER AND PROFESSOR IN THE NETHERLANDS (1578-1587)

## 1. MINISTER IN GHENT (1578-1582)

The first mention of the possibility that Adrianus Saravia might join a congregation in the South Netherlands came in a letter from the classis of Walcheren to the Dutch congregation in London, dated 13 June 1577. Ghent and Antwerp were particularly named in this letter.[1] In this period Calvinism gave powerful evidence of its growth in the southern provinces and the need for ministers increased.[2] In 1576 the Pacification of Ghent granted the Calvinists freedom to preach and for a short time Ghent became one of the most important Calvinist centres. As in Antwerp, this is to be seen in the desire for an increase in the number of ministers.[3] At first objections arose to the importation of ministers from England. Would it not be better to call ministers who had been expelled from the Palatinate after the death of the Elector Frederick III?[4] The financial means necessary for the maintenance of ministers were limited.[5]

Nevertheless Saravia's name cropped up again and again amongst those considered for an invitation to the South Netherlands. He was extolled for his "godliness, erudition not only in God's Word but also in speaking, peacebleness and capability".[6] He was considered especially suitable because of his command of both Dutch and French.[7] Jacobus Regius, who had himself come over to Ghent from London,[8] very much hoped to get Saravia as his Dutch speaking colleague. The congregation expanded vigorously. He feared "the French will work hard to alienate him [Saravia] from our [Dutchspeaking] people".[9] When Regius wrote this on 13 June 1578, he knew that two months before they had also wanted

[1] Hessels, *ELBA*, II, Nr. 160.
[2] Janssen, *Kerkherv. Vlaanderen*, I, 27 f.
[3] Hessels, *ELBA*, II, Nr. 169; III, Nrs. 513, 535, 543, 544, 568, 569, 571; A. L. E. Verheyden, *De Hervorming in de Zuidelijke Nederlanden in de XVIe eeuw* (Brussels, 1949) 113 f.
[4] Hessels, *ELBA*, III, Nrs. 513, 535. In consequence of the Lutheran restoration carried out by the Elector Ludwig VI, who succeeded his Reformed father Frederik III in 1576, about 500 Reformed ministers and teachers had to surrender office.
[5] *Ibid.*, Nr. 535.
[6] *Ibid.*
[7] *Ibid.*, Nr. 544.
[8] Janssen, *Kerkherv. Vlaanderen*, I, 199 f.
[9] Hessels, *ELBA*, II, Nr. 169.

Saravia at Oudenaarde on account of his knowledge of both languages.[10] Furthermore we learn from letters sent to the Dutch congregation in London by Petrus Dathenus, written at Kortrijk on 22 July 1578,[11] and from the consistory of the Reformed congregation of the same town, dated a day later,[12] that they also invited this much prized minister;[13] a reference which is confirmed by Ruytink.[14] The call was confirmed by the meeting of the classis at Poperinge on 27 August.[15]

There was no lack of attempts to keep Saravia in England. The Dutch refugee congregations overseas, to which the Flemish sister churches had appealed so urgently, also saw from this the need to fill their own vacancies. Thus the Dutch congregation at Colchester, who had lent their minister, Theodorus van den Berge, asked to receive Saravia in his place.[16] Yet London's answer to the Walcheren classis in the summer of 1577 had already indicated that his departure for the Netherlands must be reckoned with sooner or later. However, as we observed, the learned man thought more modestly of his fluency in the Dutch language than those who wanted to appoint him. Other problems which had to be faced were the size of his family, his obligations towards a number of English noblemen whose children's education he had undertaken, and, as regards material concerns, the uncertain prospects in the Netherlands which were in glaring contrast to the established position he had built up in England.[17] As we shall frequently see in what follows, the financial benefits always played an important part in Saravia's acceptance and discharge of a job.

Nonetheless he again crossed the North Sea. This must have happened at the beginning of the autumn of 1578. At the time of this arrival in the Netherlands the political situation there was very uncertain. The Spanish governor, King Philip II's half-brother, Don John, died at the beginning of October. He was succeeded by Alexander Farnese, Duke of Parma, and son of the former governess, Margaret (1559-1567). Parma was a man of great military and diplomatic ability. One of the first results of his appearance on the scene was the conclusion of the Union of Arras (6 January 1579) in which the Walloon provinces, Artois, Hainault and Douai joined together under the authority of the King of Spain. The North reacted quickly by concluding the Union of Utrecht (23 January 1579) between Gelderland and Utrecht, which was presently also joined by Holland,

---

[10] Hessels, *ELBA*, III, Nr. 544.

[11] *Ibid.*, Nr. 568. Cf. Th. Ruys Jr., *Petrus Dathenus* (Utrecht, 1919) 136 f.

[12] Hessels, *ELBA*, III, Nr. 569.

[13] In his letter Dathenus gave a description of the tumultuous crowd at the Calvinist preaching: in spite of the lack of ministers and uncertainty about the day and hour of the services more than 1000 people used to take part in the meetings.

[14] *WMV*, III; 1, 133.

[15] Hessels, *ELBA*, III, Nr. 571, n. 1.

[16] *Ibid.*, Nr. 570.

[17] Hessels, *ELBA*, II, Nr. 162.

Zeeland and other provinces including Flanders and Brabant. Orange's ideal of the unity of the Netherlands and the recovery of religious peace had definitely failed. The Union of Utrecht, in which Calvinism was the predominant religion and which was to abjure Philip II in 1581, stood in opposition to the Catholic Union of Arras which was reconciled with the Spanish King. Although the fortunes of war continually altered, Flanders and with it Ghent came under increasing military pressure from Parma. The expansion of Calvinism in these areas, accompanied alas by fanatical expressions of intolerance against the Roman Catholics, proved to be a temporary phenomenon. One after another, Dunkirk (1583), Ypres, Bruges (1584) and the Netherlands' richest city, Antwerp (17 August 1585) fell into Parma's hands.

Saravia had difficulty over the above-mentioned call to Kortrijk. On 7 August 1578 he consulted the consistory of the Dutch church in London, which still evidently had great authority for him even though he had already moved for many years in French speaking circles. He explained that he was indeed prepared to accept the call but complained about the lack of a Walloon congregation at Kortrijk which meant that his wife, his mother and his son who understood no Dutch, would not be able to participate in worship. The consistory found this a serious argument and decided that Saravia should delay his departure. They wanted to send an answer to Kortrijk after first considering the matter.[18] Three days later it was decided that Saravia should go, not to Kortrijk, but to Ghent and then that they should write to Dathenus and Regius about the affair.[19] The "journey of D. Adrianus Saravia to Gent and Kortrijk" came up for discussion again in the consistory's meeting of 4 September. He was given letters of introduction. At his request, half of his yearly salary of £30, the same as that of ministers in London, was reserved for his wife who apparently remained behind in England for the time being. He received a further £2 to be spent in Ghent on travelling expenses.[20] Both the earnest deliberation over Saravia's departure for the Netherlands and the financial support that he received, add further to the abundant proofs of the great importance which the Dutch church in London had for its sisters in the Netherlands.

It is thus improbable that Saravia, as indeed it has been asserted,[21] would have been minister of the Reformed congregation in Kortrijk. As

---

[18] GHL. Ms 7397/5, fol. 33r.

[19] *Ibid.*, fol. 34r.

[20] *Ibid.*, fol. 37r. The two payments to Saravia are to be found recorded in the congregation's accounts. GHL. Ms 7396/1, fol. 95. We may reasonably conclude from the fact that no mention is afterwards made of any payment to Mrs. Saravia, that she quickly followed her husband to the Netherlands.

[21] H. Q. Janssen, *Bescheiden aangaande de kerkhervorming in Vlaanderen*, in: *WMV*, III; 3, 59; Id., *Kerkherv. Vlaanderen*, I, 275; J. Meyhoffer, "Adrien Saravia", *BSHPB*, II, 2 (1921) 71, n. 2; *BN*, XXL, 394.

Jean Ballin mentioned in his "List of False Prophets", Saravia may have preached Calvin's doctrine in that town[22]—probably whilst passing through—but his stay there can only have been very brief. In October 1580 he was living in Ghent.[23]

Ghent played an important part in the history of Calvinism at this period.[24] In September 1577 the town had received back its former privileges, deprived it by the Emperor Charles V. It was once more provided with the fortifications which the emperor had dismantled. Many Calvinist refugees returned. These were not prepared to take any account at all of the Pacification of Ghent concluded in 1576. In July 1578 the conduct of Roman Catholic public worship was forbidden. This course of action was naturally completely at odds with the ideals and strategies of Orange, who on 10 July laid before the States his "Religious Peace", also sometimes called a second Pacification of Ghent. Whilst Bruges was disposed, in the spirit of this project, to allow some freedom to the Roman Catholic religion, the intolerant Calvinists of Ghent, led by the fanatical Petrus Dathenus,[25] would not own any sort of religious freedom whatever. Furthermore, even after Orange had tried to win acceptance for his ideas in Ghent by repeated personal visits, even after Dathenus had fled to the Palatinate in August 1579 and the intolerant Calvinist magistrate Jan van Hembyze had left the town, religious freedom in Ghent remained an unattainable ideal. The pressure of the Reformed ministers made life in the town impossible[26] for an advocate of toleration such as Pieter de Zuttere.[27] Saravia's name is not mentioned in connection with the struggle. Although dislike of Rome, especially of the Roman efforts for domination, formed a constant undertone in his theology throughout his life, it may be taken that he disapproved of the strivings of such men as Dathenus and van Hembyze and that he was sympathetic to Orange's policy. Belonging himself to the moderates' party, he later attributed the loss of the South Netherlands for the Reformation to the fanaticism of the zealots.

On 6 October 1578 a Reformed theological high school, the beginnings of a university, was opened. Jacobus Kimedoncius became professor there. The authorities, greatly interested in this institution, entrusted several citizens with its supervision. Saravia was one of these inspectors

---

[22] Janssen, *Kerkhervorming Brugge,* II, 286.

[23] J. W. te Water, *Historie der Hervormde Kerke en doorluchtige schoole te Gent* (Utrecht, 1794) 61.

[24] For developments in Ghent: A. Despretz, "De instauratie der Gentse Calvinistische Republiek (1577-1579)," *Handelingen der Maatschappij voor Geschiedenis en Oudheidkunde te Gent,* N.R., XVII (1963) 119-229.

[25] For his part in the conflicts in Ghent, see: Th. Ruys, *Petrus Dathenus* (Utrecht, 1919) 140-157.

[26] P. Fredericq, *Note sur l'université calviniste de Gand (1578-1584)* (Ghent, 1878) 8 f.

[27] Chr. Sepp, *Drie Evangeliedienaren uit den tijd der Hervorming* (Leiden, 1879) 85-104.

from 8 October 1580.[28] This indicates that by this time he had already acquired a position of authority in the town and thus had probably already been there for some time.

Saravia did not himself take part in education at Ghent,[29] but he did contribute in other ways to its cultural life. He supported the work of the chamber of rhetoric which made use of his proficiency in both French and Dutch in the production of its plays: he translated plays into French and corrected other people's translations.[30] As minister Saravia was attached to St. Salvatorkerk,[31] in company with Pieter Haechman.[32] He took his part in the work of the ecclesiastical province of Flanders and in the Ghent classis. On 8 March 1582 the provincial synod of the Flemish churches met at Ghent and Adrian Saravia appeared as the chairman of the assembly.[33] He clearly enjoyed the confidence of the presbyterian Calvinists and played his part in a church structure to which he was later to entertain grave objections. Together with the assessor and the secretary of this provincial synod, he was instructed to urge the magistrates that the religious goods confiscated by the local authority should be appropriated for the benefit of the Reformed church.[34] The issue of the employment of religious goods was to occupy him continually. Later he was even to write a tract "de bonis ecclesiasticis", that in the North Netherlands would repeatedly serve to bring the desires of the Reformed church on this matter to the attention of the authorities.[35]

During the last months of his residence in Ghent the situation became ever more critical owing to the military threat from Parma. On 3 September 1582 Saravia wrote an account to Walsingham of Anjou's and Oranges's stay in the town. The investiture of Anjou, who was extremely

---

[28] *Ibid.*, 5.

[29] In the town accounts of Ghent his name appears only amongst the ministers. See: A. van der Haeghen, "Bijdragen tot de geschiedenis der Hervormde Kerk te Gent, gedurende de jaren 1578-1584. Bloeitijd der Gentsche Reformatie", *BMHG*, XII (1889) 182-280.

In a letter of 14 July 1582 the Arnhem minister Johannes Fontanus recommended Ghent to Count John of Nassau as a place of education for the latter's two youngest children, because scholarship flourished, many famous teachers were there, French was widely used and also because "Adrianus, E. G. voriger diener und junger Herren alter schulmeister daselbst wonet". Groen, *Archives*, VIII, 115. Even if this were to refer to Saravia—which we doubt—then at the most it points to the possibility of private tuition. There is nothing to indicate a University position for Saravia.

[30] E. de Busscher, *Recherches sur les peintres et sculpteurs à Grand aux XVIe, XVIIe et XVIIIe siecles* (Ghent, 1866) 216, 218.

[31] Van der Haeghen, "Bijdragen", 204, 207, 212.

[32] In 1581, at the request of the church itself, the ministers' work was organised by the local authorities so that each town church was served by two ministers, a verger, a precentor and a sick-visitor. Fredericq, *Note*, 7.

[33] Janssen, *Kerkherv. Vlaanderen*, II, 70.

[34] *Ibid.*

[35] Reitsma, *Acta*, II, 220, 271, 300.

amiable, took place without much outward display in contrast to the pomp
and circumstance with which Philip II had had himself surrounded in
1559. However, the circumstances then obtaining were not conducive to a
day of revelry. Shortly before, as Saravia reported, relying on the rumours
of the matter, an attempt had been made on Anjou and Orange at
Bruges.[36] Parma's troops had launched an attack on Ghent at the end of
August.[37] From the town wall, Anjou and Orange had seen how this was
beaten off. Saravia did not neglect to mention the gallant conduct of
English troops on this occasion.[38] In October 1582, shortly before
Saravia's departure for the North Netherlands, Doornik asked him to take
part as a god-father at the baptism of the son of the minister Michel de la
Forest.[39] As appears from a receipt signed by him on 17 November 1582,
his tenure of office at Ghent ended on that date.[40]

## 2.   THE MOVE TO LEIDEN (1582)

After a stay of over four years in the South Netherlands Saravia left for
safer parts at the end of 1582. He moved to Leiden, the Holland town
which in 1574 withstood a Spanish siege for more than four months and
which still celebrates its relief on 3 October each year. On the proposal of
Prince William of Orange, the States of Holland had quickly decided to
reward the town for its courageous resistance with a university which was
opened on 8 February 1575. It was no simple matter, in this turbulent
period in which the result of the struggle against Spain was not nearly
determined, to fill the necessary professorial chairs properly. Yet they succeeded in attracting distinguished scholars there. Among such we may
mention the humanist, Justus Lipsius, professor at Louvain until 1578,
and the French jurist, Hugo Donellus, who exchanged his chair at
Heidelberg for one at Leiden in 1579. In 1582 they secured from Vienna
the botanist, Rembertus Dodonaeus, author of the *Book of Spices,* who unfortunately died three years later. After some time Lipsius was succeeded
by the French Huguenot, Josephus Justus Scaliger.[41]

As Orange had put it, the university must serve "as a firm stay and support of the freedom and lawful good government of the nation, not only in
matters of religion, but also in those which pertain to the common civic
welfare . . .".[42] The first Dutch institution for higher education was thus

---

[36] L. van der Essen, *Alexandre Farnèse. Prince de Parma. Gouverneur général des Pays-Bas
(1545-1592)* (5 vols., Brussels, 1933-1937) III, 85 f.
[37] *Ibid.,* 94-96.
[38] SP, 83/17, fol. 10; Doc. IV.
[39] De Schickler, *Églises du refuge,* III, 372.
[40] Van der Haeghen, "Bijdragen", 212.
[41] J. J. Woltjer, *De Leidse Universiteit in verleden en heden* (Leiden, 1965) 3 f.
[42] Molhuysen, *Bronnen,* I, 1 f.

intended as an intellectual centre of the Reformation and a bulwark of political freedom—"praesidium libertatis" proclaims its title of honour. With its great interest in classical studies it bore a markedly humanist character.[43] This presented no problem for the Calvinist theologians who saw their faculty— which otherwise had very few students at the outset—tacitly accorded pride of place. What was more difficult for them to accept was the fact that the Leiden magistrates allowed the church no say in university business. The rector magnificus was appointed by the stadholder or his representative. The appointment of professors, the fixing of the curriculum, textbooks and salaries was the business of the curators in consultation with the rector, the assessors and the town magistrates. There was no question of professors signing the Reformed confession of faith. Only the theological students had to declare under oath that they would not follow any strange doctrine. Despite all efforts on the side of the Reformed Church to unite church and university more closely together on the pattern of Geneva, there was no altering this situation. Thus the life of the university was one of the areas where the tensions between church and secular authority, in which the history of Leiden in the last quarter of the sixteenth century abounded, came clearly to light.[44]

These tensions were occasioned by the same municipal government which, brooking no church interference in the affairs of the university, conversely strove itself for influence in the internal business of the Reformed church, especially in the matter of the calling of ministers and the appointment of other members of the consistory. The Leiden administration comprised capable, self-confident and, in part, learned regents. Burgomasters and town clerks developed into the real political leaders of the town. As was the case with members of the town council, they did not confine themselves exclusively to local interests but in increasing measure engaged in national affairs as well.[45] These same men regarded it as a matter of course that their supervision extended over the church and because they themselves belonged to the moderate current in Calvinism, that influenced by Erasmianism, they thought they must use their authority to minimize and to suppress doctrinal disputes in the Reformed Church. Above all the town clerk, Jan van Hout, who was also secretary to the curators of the university, was a sure guarantee of the secular authority's control of this place of education.

Saravia came to Leiden more than a year after 22 July 1581 when the

---

[43] Woltjer, *Universiteit*, 9 f. For Leiden as an international university, the methods and building up of its system of instruction, see: H. Wansink, *Politieke wetenschappen aan de Leidse Universiteit 1575- ± 1650* (Utrecht, 1975) 3-61.

[44] W. F. Dankbaar, "De stichting van de Leidsche Universiteit en de eerste decennia van haar bestaan", in: *Hoogtepunten uit het Nederlandsche Calvinisme in de zestiende eeuw* (Haarlem, 1946) 126-161.

[45] P. J. Blok, *Geschiedenis eener Hollandsche stad* (4 vols., The Hague, 1910-1918) III, 75 f.

States General had renounced King Philip II and in the midst of the complications caused by the French King Henry III's brother, the Duke of Anjou, to whom the sovereignty over the Netherlands had been committed. Saravia had worked four years in Ghent where the Frenchman had had himself recognized as Count of Flanders. However, when in January 1583 Anjou with his French troops made a vain attempt to take control of Antwerp (the so-called French Fury), Saravia had already been living in Leiden for months. When Antwerp fell into Parma's hands in 1585, many Calvinists emigrated from the South Netherlands to the North. There they strengthened the radically-Calvinist element of the population. Their arrival caused a new stiffening of the opposition between the consistory of the Reformed church and the municipal government in Leiden. The consistory strove for freedom for the church to order its internal affairs itself and to deal drastically with dissentient teaching. The magistrates, on the other hand, wanted as much influence for themselves as possible in the internal business of the church and believed in a measure of toleration with regard to differing doctrinal opinions. The opposition had already for long engaged the more earnestly-minded. One of the chief characters in the drawn-out conflict was the minister Caspar Coolhaes, upholder of the local government's authority over the church in line, among others, with the Swiss Rodolphus Gualterus, one of whose works he translated. Coolhaes held dissident views on some points of doctrine and liturgy.[46] Already in 1578 the dispute over the appointment of elders and deacons had become so acute that, for a time, two consistories had come into open opposition against each other. The Leiden magistrates dismissed Coolhaes' Calvinist colleague, Pieter Cornelisz. After Orange had vainly sought to mediate, Coolhaes was at long last suspended by the States of Holland, but the municipal government continued to support him and allowed him to go on preaching. He also went on expressing his opinions in writing. In October 1580 a compromise was reached by an external arbitral decision, the so called Arbitral Accord. The division in the consistory was healed, Pieter Cornelisz returned to Leiden and Coolhaes had to undertake to submit his writings to the judgement of a synod.

The particular synod at Rotterdam (25 April-3 May 1581) occupied itself with the dispute.[47] The national synod of Middelburg (30 May-21 June 1581) rejected his writing and constrained the particular synod of South Holland to take measures "of excommunication gradatim, si perstat in inobedientia".[48] Finally it was the provincial synod of Holland at Haarlem which excommunicated Coolhaes on 25 March 1582.[49] The

---

[46] H. C. Rogge, *Caspar Janszoon Coolhaes. De voorlooper van Arminius en der Remonstranten* 2 vols. Amsterdam, 1856-1858; *NNBW*, I, 632-636.

[47] Reitsma, *Acta*, II, 198 f.

[48] Rutgers, *Acta*, 363.

[49] Reitsma, *Acta*, 114-117.

latter did not then cease his publishing activities and he was supported by
the fanatical minister Peter Hackius who was also the cause of much com-
motion in Leiden.

The controversy over the powers of the secular authority in church
affairs, especially in the calling of ministers, was such that, until the synod
of Dordrecht, the Reformed church did not succeed in arriving at a church
order which was acceptable to both church and government. The church
continued unwaveringly to start from the fundamental Calvinist vision
which upheld its complete freedom with regard to the state and which bar-
red any interferance from secular authority. The States, on the other
hand, so they usually declared, did not want to risk following liberation
from Roman Catholicism by falling under a new Protestant tyranny based
on a church order according to pure Calvinistic principles.

The complications outlined above were not without their influence upon
the life of the university. For example, the behaviour of the magistrates
towards the consistories of the Dutch and Walloon congregations and the
university caused the Calvinist Lambert Daneau to leave for Ghent.[50]
Although all these problems did not appear to make an office in church or
university especially attractive, there must have been compensating advantages for Saravia which turned the scale in his eventual decision. Thus
one of the first benefits was the fact that the position of a town in Holland
like Leiden was externally, that is to say from the military angle, more
secure than that of Ghent where the continuing survival of the Protestant
churches and the life of Protestant Christians was increasingly threatened
by the turn of events in the war. Despite all internal tensions, Leiden yet
offered the possibility to work in a measure of peace. Moreover, life in a
university town had many inviting aspects for a scholar, such as the
possibility of making international contacts and the material advantages
attached to enrolling in the university's registers. One of the especially interesting features for Saravia was the fact that Leiden was a centre of
Anglo-Dutch cultural relations.[51] In all probability these were the considerations which decided him to move to the North Netherlands. From
November 1582 to the summer of 1584 he was to serve the church and
afterwards, until November 1587, the university.

### 3.  MINISTER IN LEIDEN (1582-1584)

Saravia's move to Leiden was initiated by a conversation which two
Leiden magistrates had held with him at Ghent and which was followed by
consultation with the Prince of Orange. Among other things it was hoped

---

[50] O. Fatio, *Nihil pulchrius ordine. Contribution a l'étude de l'établissement de la discipline ecclésiastique aux Pays-Bas. Ou Lambert Daneau aux Pays-Bas (1581-1583)* Leiden, 1971.

[51] J. A. van Dorsten, *Poets, Patrons and Professors. Sir Philip Sydney, Daniel Rogers and the Leiden Humanists.* Leiden, 1962.

that his appointment would bring about a settlement of the earlier mentioned quarrel in Leiden.[52] Orange, for whom this disunity had long been a thorn in the flesh,[53] evidently had the fullest confidence in his former army chaplain in this respect. The conversation with the prince probably took place during the latter's visit to Ghent in August 1582 to which we have already referred.[54]

In the conversation at Antwerp, at which was present the then court chaplain to the prince, Jean Taffin, who had also been involved in the Leiden disputes about Coolhaes,[55] the following conditions were stipulated. After his acceptance of this call and for so long as there was still no final decision taken on church order there, Saravia was to abide by that concluded in the Arbitral Accord of 1580.[56] Once a church order had been accepted then it naturally must be adhered to. If Hackius or others were to resist this they were to be dismissed. It was agreed that Saravia should preach in both Dutch and French. In this way he was to take part in an arrangement arrived at eighteen months previously, by which there was to be a Dutch and French service held in the university, the first as an early service at 6.30, the second at 8.00 a.m. and "that for the French service a bell shall be rung which is to be hung in the tower for the purpose and that the deacons of the congregation shall gather there the alms of the congregation".[57] This French service began on Sunday 26 March 1581. According to the wording of the announcement three days before, the profitable and the pleasant were in this way united, "that all those who wish to practise the said French language, may attend the said service and in so doing, may together increase and advance in the knowledge of God and of His Holy Word as well as of the said language".[58]

It was certainly not to be expected that Ghent would readily part with its

---

[52] Jean Taffin to Arent Cornelisz., 27 October 1582. *WMV*, III; 5, 207.

[53] Jean Taffin to Arent Cornelisz., 17 July 1581. *WMV*, III; 5, 195; 19 June 1582. *WMV*, III; 5, 201 f.

[54] p. 45 f.

[55] Boer, *Hofpredikers*, 88 f.

[56] In this agreement, eventually accepted by all parties on 29 October 1580, it was decided that a new consistory should be chosen before 21 February 1581, in this manner: six elders and deacons from the old and the same number from the new consistory were to be submitted to the magistrates. After they had been approved by two thirds of the latter they were to be presented to the congregation and elected by it. Thus the consistory had henceforward to propose as many new candidates for office to the secular authority as was necessary for the latter to approve two thirds of them. The magistrates moreover obtained the right to be represented at each meeting of the consistory by two deputies, who were to be members of the congregation, without the right to vote or to preside and bound to silence. In this way political commissioners made their entry into the Leiden consistory.

[57] GDB, fol. 134v; 23 March 1581.

[58] GAL. Afleesingboek der Stadt Leyden, E, fol. 118; N. C. Kist, "Het allereerste begin der Fransche Evangelie-prediking en der Waalse gemeente te Leiden in 1581," *Ned. A.*, VII (1847) 309-313.

minister. Hence Saravia obtained a letter from the prince to the church and magistrates of the South Netherlands town in support of the Leiden request. Before his move to Leiden was a certainty, new difficulties arose there: Coolhaes' party tried their utmost to have his excommunication withdrawn.[59] Long before the conversation in question at Antwerp, Saravia must have been acquainted with the complications in Leiden. He would have heard about it from Jacobus Regius, the minister loaned to Ghent by the Dutch congregation in London, who as one of the eight arbiters—peculiarly enough, one of the few chosen by Coolhaes—had assisted in the preparation of the Arbitral Accord.[60] Lambert Daneau, who settled in Ghent in May 1582,[61] certainly fully acquainted Saravia with his experiences in Leiden. Saravia was thus prepared for what awaited him in that town. He was indeed to discover quite another consequence of the Arbitral Accord; for he had to try, with the help of others, to pay off the debts incurred in the procedure by the Church congregation.[62] At the particular synod at Amsterdam on 3 May 1583 two members of the Leiden consistory appeared with a letter from Saravia ''and sought help from the community for the defraying of some expenses which they had had in respect of the Leiden magistrates, namely the expenses which had been incurred in the making of the compromise''.[63]

Daneau and Saravia worked together in Ghent for less than six months. Although Saravia later reported having discussed problems of church government with his French contemporary and colleague, yet he must have wanted to pass over their relationship. Why otherwise should Daneau long after Saravia's departure, accuse him in insulting terms of overindulgence in eating and drinking? The latter defended himself. In Ghent Daneau was able himself to observe how soberly he lived, and he had not altered his way of life since then: ''Lust for food and drink is foreign to me, as everyone knows. Furthermore I do not eat dainty foodstuffs. My table is simple. I prefer eating olives and carrots to meat. Cabbages, beets, salads, endives, beans and peas are for me the delicacies with which I fill my stomach''.[64] This statement of the case is wholly in accord with the picture of Saravia's sobriety and especially his frugality which we encounter again and again.

Ghent let Saravia go. At the beginning of November 1582 he became minister in Leiden at an annual stipend of 400 guilders payable from the 1 November 1582, plus a housing allowance equal to that of Hackius, ''in

---

[59] Jean Taffin to Arent Cornelisz., 27 October 1582; *WMV*, III; 5, 207 f.

[60] J. Hania, *Wernerus Helmichius* (Utrecht, 1895) 133 f.

[61] Fatio, *Nihil pulchrius*, 92.

[62] The total costs amounted to 900 guilders. Although the consistory had in fact spent only 200 guilders of this, it had to pay half, 450 guilders.

[63] Reitsma, *Acta*, I, 118.

[64] *RG*, 349.

order to prevent any emulation'', namely 50 guilders.[65] He was to receive extra payment for his university preaching.[66] Because of these services he counted as an extraordinary professor.[67] His removal costs were also reimbursed.[68] In 1584 at his request Saravia received an increase in his housing allowance: this was then fixed as 72 guilders a year, this in connection with the possession of a more expensive house, namely Adriaen Jansz's dwelling on the Steenschuur,[69] after he had first lived on the Oosterlingenplaats[70] and there had also been mention of a move to the Faliede Begijnhof.[71] In any event his income was far above the 300 guilders minimum fixed by the States of Holland for town ministers, and higher than most of his colleagues in other towns with the exception of Dordrecht.[72] The fact that his accommodation and the determining of the amount of his housing allowance repeatedly gave Saravia occasion to apply to the local authority confirms the suspicion that he was very far from indifferent to the material benefits of the post he had assumed.[73] On 18 March 1586 the curators of the university decided that Petrus Bailly, the writing-master from Antwerp, must quit his house in the Begijnhof for the sake of Saravia.[74] So under the pretext of saving the latter and his col-

---

[65] GDB, fol. 202v, 22 March 1583; GDB, fol. 207r, 14 April 1583.

[66] GAL, le Stadsdienaarsaanneemboek, fol. 88, records that ''die vanden Gerechte den voorn. Saravia mitsdezen ooc beloven hier en buyten te doen betalen van zodanige diensten als hij (behalven den voors. dienst des Woorts) de universiteyt dezer stede Theologiam extraordinarie profiterende doen zal ten goetduncken der heren [curators and burgermasters].''

[67] So in the list of names for 1583/1584. Witkam, *Dag. Zaken*, V, 47.

[68] These costs are specified GDB, fol. 202v. in the margin, 22 March 1583. ''Noch betaelt Mr. Adriaen de Saravia die meede bijde Magistraet van Leijden tot die bedieninge des Woordts al daer voor 400 ponden int jaer is angenomen, voor een halff jaer wedden hem verschenen zedert den eersten Novembris 82 totten lesten Aprilis 83 daer aen volgende. Incluijs die somme van 200 ponden. Ende noch voor een halff jaer huijshuyre verschenen totten lesten Aprilis voirs. 15£ maeckende tsaemen 215£. Daerom al hijer in Wuijtgeeff die voorschreven somme van 215£''. So GAL, *Reeckeninghe Lodewijcx van Treslongue Rentmeester over die Capittels van Hogelande goederen tot Leijden voor den jare 1582;* Kerk. Arch. Nr. 1208, fol. 120r; ''Item ende noch den zelffden Saravia betaeldt achter volgende zeeckere ordonn. des Magistraets van Leijden voor zijn reijscosten bij hem met zijn familie op herwerts compste wuijtgeleijt die somme van 69 pond 17 sh. Daer van al hijer 69£ 17 sh.'', *Reeck. 1582*, fol. 120v. The same amounts were paid in 1583, *Reeck. 1583*, fol. 143v, 144r. For 1584 a sum of £116 and 13 sh. is accounted for over the period from 1 May to 15 August ''deszelven jaers 1584 dat hij den voors. dyenst heeft verlaten, gereeckent teeghens 400 ponden in tjaer''. *Reeck. 1584*, fol. 138.

[69] GDB, fol. 270r; 13 March 1584.

[70] GAL, Vroedschapsboek KL, fol. 147v.

[71] GDB, fol. 206v; 14 April 1583.

[72] G. Groenhuis, *De Predikanten. De sociale positie van de gereformeerde predikanten in de Republiek der Verenigde Nederlanden voor ± 1700* (Groningen, 1977) 137 f.

[73] GDB, fol. 311r; 1 November 1584. For the last period of his ministry, from 1 May to 15 August 1584, he still received 21 guilders' housing allowance.

[74] GDB, fol. 404v; 18 March 1586; ''Pr. Baillys huys opten hof. Es geresolveert Pr. Bailly de bewooninge van 't huys opten Hof op te zeggen jegens meye, ooc de gage onder 't

league, Hackius, from searching for a suitable dwelling, Saravia came to live in the place which had earlier been intended for him.[75] The Begijns remaining in Leiden had been left in possession of their house for life. However, the empty dwellings in the Begijnhof were let out at a reasonable price by regents appointed by the magistrates to professors and other members of the university community.[76] Saravia had then to pay an annual rent of 80 guilders.[77] On his hurried departure from the town in 1587 it was to emerge that he was not too scrupulous in meeting his financial obligations.

According to the agreement made at Antwerp, Saravia had, on his arrival in Leiden, to sign the Arbitral Accord and promise to abide by it "provisionally", that is to say until the introduction of a church order. Objections were raised by some to this stipulation and also to the promise he made "to instruct the congregation in the doctrine received in the churches of Holland". The objectors were probably supporters of Caspar Coolhaes who, condemned by the national synod of Middelburg in 1581 and excommunicated by the provincial synod of Haarlem on 25 March 1582, was yet allowed by the Leiden magistrates to receive his salary. He would have nothing to do with a church order or subscription to the confession. On 14 April 1583 Burgomaster Warmont and magistrate Heemskerk consulted with Saravia about this. As regards the first objection it was considered how the introduction of the church order could be hastened. Nothing was altered in the second condition. The subscription to the confession was indeed in accordance with a letter from the prince to the States.[78] From all this it is evident enough that, from the outset, Saravia was drawn into the Leiden disputes.

Already during the discussions at Antwerp it had been taken into account that difficulties would arise between Saravia and Hackius.[79] At the

behagen vande Curateurs, ende dat 't huys zal werden verhuyrt aen den Heere rector Saravia, voor de bewooninge ende 't geryf van den welcken ende van andere naer hem 't zelve huys bequaem gemaect ende bereyt zal werden by advis van Baersdorp, Cortevelt, de Haes ende Merwen, gesamentlicken ende 't merendeel van hem, die ooc mitten zelven nopende de huyr als van somme ende tijt zullen accorderen, wel verstaende dat de voorn. Saravia de penn[ingen] tot de reparatie van noode, zal verschieten tot mindernisse vande huyr." Witkam, *Dag. zaken,* IV, 164. See also GDB, fol. 428r; 4 June 1586.

[75] GDB, fol. 206v; 14 April 1583.

[76] Frans van Mieris, *Beschrijving der stad Leyden* (Leiden, 1762), I, 150.

[77] GDB, fol. 428r; 4 June 1586; fol. 430v; 12 June 1586.

[78] GDB, fol. 207r; 14 April 1583.

[79] Hackius, who earlier had moved "amongst the musicians in the chapel and in the Court of the emperor", and was afterwards chaplain to Gerrit de Jonge van Haarlem's company garrisoning Wachtendonk, had been a failure in 1579 as "regent of the 'pedagogie' ", the "college for poor students" in Leiden. He revealed himself as a supporter of Caspar Coolhaes and helped the latter with a translation of a "extract from Gualterus" which, as we shall see, was greatly to concern Saravia. After much opposition from the consistory he became minister at Leiden on 29 October 1581. As A. A. van Schelven remarked, the Trojan horse came in with him. *NNBW,* VI, 661.

start, however, the latter kept quiet. After it became known that the invitation had been extended to Saravia he had praised his future colleague to the skies.[80] Initially the two ministers were able to work together reasonably. Both preached each Sunday according to a rota fixed for the purpose, in which Saravia's French services were also included.[81] They also co-operated well in pastoral work. Saravia certainly bestowed the necessary care on the members of the congregation entrusted to him. Several reports of this have come down to us. Saravia's signature appears in a letter to the Dutch congregation in London, dated 17 December 1582, containing a report about a certain Petrus Lambertus, a pupil at Leiden university who came from there. The advice was given to bring the young man back to London and to let him learn a trade or else set him to study under stricter discipline.[82] Was discipline in Leiden not strong enough to hold the unruly in check? Hackius and Saravia tried to get "an old miserable, decrepit man" taken into the home for the aged, "where he might serve by reading and perhaps expounding God's Word to the poor members". They joined together in getting a young Englishman a place at the university or the town school. They tried to squeeze a rise of 100 guilders for each elder from the municipal government. However, the latter made it known that there were insufficient means for this.[83]

The work expanded and before long the need arose there for more ministers. On 14 July 1583 a request from Hackius and Saravia that a third minister be called was sympathetically discussed by the municipal authorities. But the appointment of extra help "for the visitation and consolation of the sick members of the home for the aged" was refused because the magistrates considered that this was the task of the elders.[84]

Shortly before this the municipal authority of Ghent tried to get Saravia to return as minister. However, he refused the request or "at least put it off till a more suitable time", as Jean Taffin wrote to Arent Cornelisz on 6 June 1583.[85] Meanwhile, it is definitely established that he was in Ghent at

---

[80] Joh. Kuchlinus to Arent Cornelisz., 30 October 1582; *WMV*, III; 5, 256.

[81] "... is geresolveert dat op Zondag toekomende dewelke wezen zal den 18en Novembris Hackius prediken zal 's morgens ten 7 uyren in de Vrouwenkerk, Saravia ten half acht uyren in de Pieterskerk in Franchois, Hackius ten 9 uyren in dezelfde kerc, Saravia ten 2 uyren ten hogelande in 't duitsch en dat op Zondags daeraenvolgende Saravia weder predicken zal 's morgens ten 9 uyren in de Pieterskerk in 't duitsch, dezelve ten een uyren naermiddag in de voorz. Pieterskerk in Franchois, Hackius ten 2 ure ten hoogelande, alles preciselicken op ten voorz. uren te beginnen ende dat zij zulxs van weec tot weeck als voren veranderen zullen en dit alles bij provisie en gedurende zoo lange tot anderssins ten dienste vande kerke ende tot stichtinge vande gemeente zal zijn gestatueerd". GDB, fol. 122r; 16 November 1582. Some of the archival material reffered to here and later was published by L. A. van Langeraad, "Adrianus Saravia te Leiden", *Kerkelijke Courant,* 20 February (No. 8) 1897.

[82] Hessels, *ELBA,* III, Nr. 830.

[83] GDB, fol. 201v, 202r; 17 March 1583.

[84] GDB, fol. 220v; 14 July 1583.

[85] *WMV,* III; 5, 215.

the end of August and the beginning of September and there met the prince.[86] Did he make use of Ghent's offer in trying to secure a pay rise in Leiden? Taffin asked the prince for an increase and the latter wrote to the Leiden magistrates about it.[87] A month earlier Taffin had also discussed the matter with Villiers who had championed Saravia's interests before the prince, thinking that this had to be effected by external pressure. All these activities were aimed at "depriving Saravia of any inducement to leave the place and his office". His departure would mean a great blow to the churches.[88] Anyway it appears that, yet again, the financial aspects of the matter played a part.

At the end of 1583 or the beginning of 1584, not very long after the request for an increase in the number of ministers, Mattheus Platevoet came to Leiden from Hondschoote in Flanders.[89] In the autumn of 1584 Christiaan van de Wouwer came from Dordrecht where he had been since 1582.[90] Although these two are recorded together with Saravia and Hackius as ministers in Leiden in 1584 at the beginning of the consistory book of the Reformed congregation,[91] van de Wouwer is rather to be seen as Saravia's successor, that is when he had become professor at the university.

At the end of the year 1584 the municipal authority agreed to loan Hackius for two months to Medemblik. He had to promise to return to Leiden after the expiry of the term. The consistory objected and asked the magistrates through van de Wouwer and Saravia, who had by then ceased to be minister, not to agree to the North Holland's congregation's request to take Hackius from them temporarily or permanently.[92] Already on 5 December a letter was written asking Hackius to return as quickly as possible.[93] Six days later he came back to Leiden,[94] not so much because of this request but because this turbulent man had contrived to cause difficulties in the shortest possible time in Medemblik so that his stay there was no longer possible. It appears from the minutes of the Leiden consistory that Hackius, supported by the magistrates, had come into conflict with the consistory in Medemblik as also with the governor of the Northern Quarter, Diederik Sonoy who in many respects, especially in his at-

---

[86] p. 46, n. 38.

[87] *WMV*, III; 5, 217.

[88] *Ibid.*

[89] Janssen, *Kerkherv. Vlaanderen*, I, 245. According to A. A. van Schelven, *NNBW*, IV, 1084, he was still in Dunkirk on 16 July 1583 when it was captured by Parma.

[90] Schotel, *Kerkelijk Dordrecht*, I, 193-196. "Dus Saravia en Timan Jacopsz [elder] sullen ordonantie voor Christianum aen mijn Heeren solliciteren". KB, fol. 3r; 18 November 1584.

[91] KB, title page.

[92] KB, fol. 2r; 7 November 1584. fol. 3r; 15 November 1584.

[93] KB, fol. 3v; 5 December 1584.

[94] KB, fol. 3v; 11 December 1584.

titude towards the States of Holland, was very independently minded. A deputy from the States was summoned in the Leiden consistory, apparently to elucidate Hackius' position.[95] The latter had obviously proved himself also in Medemblik to be an upholder of the secular authority's interference in church affairs. The matter continued to occupy the Leiden consistory for months. This still upheld Hackius, not only when he himself called his position into question,[96] but also when he repeatedly compromised the congregation by his defiant behaviour in the pulpit.[97] The consistory proceeded cautiously, not wishing to provoke the secular authority needlessly.

During these complications Saravia was already a professor. His name no longer appears in the consistory book amongst the ministers serving the congregation in 1585. More curiously, however, he is mentioned again amongst such in 1586, and that as "Dns Rector Saravia".[98] It appears from this, that the office of professor in theology presumed a much more direct involvement in church affairs at this time than was the case later. As he interfered in 1584 in the problems surrounding Hackius, so he continued up to his departure in 1587 to be involved in church developments and in the work of the consistory. He preached regularly. On one Saturday in June 1586 he apologized for a delay in finishing a report intended for Leicester: he had to preach twice the next day.[99] When the minister Ysbrand Trabius, who originally had only wanted to come for six months on trial[100] and who was first permanently called on 18 March 1586,[101] raised difficulties about the complete discharge of his official duties, amongst others, of sick-visiting, an account of his advanced age and ill health, Saravia voluntarily offered to take the early services on a Sunday for him, if he was not there himself,[102] a not unreasonable condition! Probably it

---

[95] KB, fol. 7v; 23 February 1585.

[96] KB, fol. 4r; 22 December 1584.

[97] KB, fol. 4v; 23 December 1584: Antonis de Droghe heard Peter de Voghel say, in the inn amongst many witnesses, that Hackius was a false teacher. The said de Voghel maintained that he had not said this but that Hackius was of the same opinion as Coolhaes and that "the latter has done much dishonour to our Religion" and was a heretic and false teacher. See also KB, fol. 5r-7r; 11 January, 18 January, 25 January, 27 January, 3 February, 6 February, 10 February 1585. On 18 January Willem de Huse brought up objections against Hackius' preaching. He defended himself to everyone's satisfaction and "parted" from Hackius "in love and friendship".

[98] KB, title page.

[99] Saravia to John James, June 1586. GHL. MS. 7428/7, fol. 1027; Hessels, *ELBA*, II, Nr. 223; III, Nr. 1027.

[100] KB, fol. 11r; 26 September 1585.

[101] KB, fol. 14v; 18 March 1586.

[102] In his absence this duty was to be performed by Christiaan van de Wouwer. KB, fol. 16r; 8 April 1586. On the other hand, on 7 April 1587, Trabius, "dus noch inde stede wesende", was asked if he would speak in his place on the following Sunday, that is 13 April. Probably this referred to one of the early services already mentioned. KB, fol. 36v.

was on account of his physical infirmity that Trabius, together with Hackius and Saravia appealed to the magistrates to enable, at least provisionally, for the task to be carried out by the sick visitors.[103] In 1586 the Leiden consistory consulted by letter with the consistories of Amsterdam and Schiedam on the relationship between church and secular authority. Plancius and the consistory of Amsterdam agreed with the Leiden consistory's standpoint; the consistory of Schiedam and its minister, Petrus Taurinus were somewhat non-committal.[104] The consistory asked Saravia to act as host on this occasion,[105] most probably because he also gave advice on this matter. His advice was also called for on several occasions in the subsequent difficulties with Hackius, for example, in the denial of the validity of depositions of two witnesses summoned by Hackius.[106]

Furthermore Saravia acted as the liaison officer between the Dutch and Walloon congregations. He had to ask the Walloons, in the name of the Dutch consistory to uphold the agreement not to allow any Dutch speakers who were members of the Dutch congregation at their celebrations of the Lord's Supper.[107] When the Walloon minister, Lucas Trelcat was absent for two Sundays because he had to attend the Walloon synod at Flushing on 13 April, the Walloons asked permission from the Dutch consistory to allow Saravia to conduct the services in their church.[108] The request was granted. Apart from small unimportant frictions, such as that over the limitations concerning the celebration of the Lord's Supper, the relationship between the two consistories does not seem to have led to any difficulties. On 23 March 1586 at a meeting, at which Lucas Trelcat and the elder Wilhelmus Espel were present as representatives of the Walloon consistory, it was decided to hold a united meeting of the consistories once a month. This was in accord with proposals made to this effect at the meeting of the Walloon classis of Holland and Zeeland in Amsterdam on 19 March,[109] adopted by the national synod at The Hague (20 June to 1 August 1586).[110] That the Walloons were kept informed of the latest problems arising over Hackius,[111] points to the existence of more than formal relations between the two churches.

### 4.   Relations with the Walloons

Considering the role that he played amongst the Dutch and French speakers both in England and in the South Netherlands it is not surprising

---

[103] KB, fol. 12v; 20 January 1586.
[104] KB, fol. 13r; 4 February 1586.
[105] KB, fol. 14r; 24 February 1586.
[106] KB, fol. 28v; 5 November 1586.
[107] KB, fol. 25r; 21 October 1586.
[108] KB, fol. 36v; 31 March 1587.
[109] LSW, 114.
[110] Rutgers, Acta, 554.
[111] KB, fol. 26r; 25 October 1586.

that Saravia also maintained good relations with the Walloon congregation in Leiden. The latter owed its permanent foundation to the great crowd of refugees caused by the unfavourable course of the war in the South Netherlands. In 1584, as we saw,[112] Ypres and Bruges, amongst others, were lost to Parma. The entire Walloon consistory of Bruges with its minister, Jacques de la Dréve, fled to Leiden.[113] Among the refugees was Adolf van Meetkerke, president of the Council of Flanders who had become a Protestant in 1580. As an advocate of English help in the struggle against Spain[114] he was in 1587, like Saravia, to get into great difficulties and be forced to leave the Netherlands.

During the political period which favoured them in their native land, these refugees had acted extremely fiercely. On their arrival in the North Netherlands they were as little disposed to stand aside from the conflicts, as was to appear in Leiden especially during the Leicester disturbances. They were quickly seen by the government as disturbing elements who were too inclined to meddle in the ecclesiastical and political affairs of the nation.[115] On 12 October 1584 the States of Holland directed the municipal governments that no ministers from Ghent or Bruges should be accepted or allowed to preach without their consent.[116]

At Leiden already on 8 June 1583 "a request was made to those of the government of the town of Leiden by various merchants of the Walloon or French nation that they might be allowed to take on a French minister at their own expense who would teach and preach God's Word to them twice a week besides on Sundays on such various days as would in no way interfere with the church service here". The request was granted by the magistrates. The minister chosen might preach and administer the sacraments in the Vrouwenkerk on the days appointed.[117] Some conditions were made. The first of these was "for the maintenance with the church here of all good truth and so that they behave as one church, that not only the ministers, elders and deacons as well as the other members of both sides be free to communicate at the Lord's Supper both here and there, if they know the language, but that they in the aforesaid Walloon church shall admit to the aforesaid communion of the Lord's Supper none other than those speaking the Walloon or French language". No more

---

[112] p. 48.,

[113] Janssen, *Kerkhervorming Brugge,* I, 268.

[114] *Ibid.,* II, 237; *NNBW,* IV, 963-965.

[115] Brandt, *Reformatie,* I, 712, 718, 730.

[116] *RStH 1584,* 625; 12 October. Here and later the quotations are from the old series. In 1597 C. P. Hooft was to ask the magistrates of Amsterdam to ban foreigners from taking part in the government of city or church and was later to repeat this frequently. Brandt, *Reformatie,* I, 818 f; R. B. Evenhuis, *Ook dat was Amsterdam* (5 vols., Amsterdam, 1965-1978) I, 181, 207.

[117] GDB, fol. 233; 8 June 1584.

were French speaking members of the Dutch congregation, who were bar-
red from communion in their own congregation because of dissension or
schism, admitted to the Lord's table with the Walloons. From time to time
both these stipulations ought to be clearly announced before the celebration of the Lord's Supper. The minister had first to sign the Arbitral
Accord and account must also be taken of this in the choice of elders and
deacons. The deaconal care for the poor was to be carried out in common:
two Walloon deacons were assigned as assistants to the almoner; there was
to be a common poor chest, the proceeds of which were to be shared
amongst all the poor of the town. Finally the condition was made that the
minister should not concern himself with political matters, "which if he
presumes to do or if there arises any dispute, dissension or schism (for they
are united) between this church and the Walloon, wether the aforesaid
minister has given any cause for this or not, those of the Magistracy at the
time shall be able, straightway and without any counter argument from
anyone be they of churches, consistories, classes, synods or others,
whosoever they may be, to remove the minister and to discontinue the services immediately".[118] With this, the permanent foundation of the
Walloon congregation in Leiden was a fact.[119] Indeed in the years prior to
this the professors Guillaume Feugeray and Lambert Daneau had preached in French. In 1581, after many difficulties, Daneau had even managed
to form a consistory which was for a time tolerated by the magistrates. But
this was not recognized because the rules of the Arbitral Accord obtaining
for the Dutch congregation had not been observed by the Walloons in their
election of office holders. There was therefore no question of the official
institution of a form of church government. The Walloon congregation in
Leiden was thus also unrepresented at the Walloon synod in 1581 and
1582; they were not even mentioned in the acta of these synods.[120]

It appears from the consistory book of the Walloon congregation that
the first meeting of the consistory was held on 16 September 1584, the
same Sunday on which the election of four elders and four deacons took
place[121], "Monsr. de Saravia professeur en théologie et ministre de la
parolle de Dieu" was present.[122] The latter was naturally not a minister of

---

[118] *Ibid.*

[119] On the initial period: N. C. Kist, "Het allereerste begin der Fransche Evangelie-
prediking en der Waalsche gemeente te Leiden, in 1581", *Ned. A,* VII (1847) 309-313; W.
N. Du Rieu, "Lambert Daneau à Leyde. Fondation de la communauté wallonne à Leyde le
26 mars 1581," *BHEW,* I, 69-90; G. K. Fockema Andreae, "Uit de geschiedenis van de
Waals-Hervormde Kerk te Leiden," *Leids Jaarboekje,* XLVII (1955) 108-130, inaccurate on
Saravia; Fatio, *Nihil pulchrius.*

[120] Du Rieu, "Lambert Daneau," 81, 84 f.

[121] LC, fol. 1.

[122] LC, fol. 3; 16 September 1584. It is evident from a letter written by Lambert Daneau
to A. Cornelisz and published by Fatio, *Nihil pulchrius,* 147 f., that, as soon as they knew of
Saravia's coming to Leiden, the Walloons counted on his help. In this it says: "Ille est

the congregation, as indeed no more was de la Dréve,[123] but he had made himself useful as a liaison between the Dutch and Walloon congregations. From the way in which he had held to the latter.[124] Saravia had also acquired a trusted position outside Leiden. He appeared as chairman of the classical assembly of the Walloon congregations of Walcheren and Holland (Leiden, 29 October 1584). On the instructions of this meeting he had to address himself to the consistory of the congregation at Sluis and to the governor of that town as well as to the Walloon ministers of Walcheren on the matter of the incorrect procedure followed in the call of Chrestien du Bloq in that congregation, "in order that such disorder might be corrected".[125] In the synod at Antwerp (3 and 4 October 1584) it was decided to ask Saravia's opinion about the progress of a student named Jean Pekereau.[126] This opinion was evidently favourable for the young man was allowed to continue his studies. He was entrusted to Saravia's care[127] along with the other students, Jaspar Usile, subsequently the Walloon minister in Dordrecht,[128] and Daniel de Nielles who was later to serve the Walloon congregation at Middelburg.[129]

---

Saravia, qui a Leydensibus ad professionem theologicam evocatus hinc atque ad Ecclesiam Gallicam instaurandam, tibi, quemadmodum spero, saltem de domine non est ignotus". Are we to conclude from the words "ad professionem theologicam evocatus" that from the beginning Saravia reckoned on obtaining a university post?

[123] Du Rieu, "Lambert Daneau", 89.

[124] He was only in Leiden "par provision". LC, fol. 7; 4 November 1584. Already before he fled to the North Netherlands with a part of his Bruges congregation, he had given rise to dispute. There a charge of unchastity was brought against him. This was probably already dealt with at the synod of the Walloon churches at Antwerp on 15 March 1584. Janssen, Kerkhervorming Brugge, I, 267 f. It came up for discussion again at the classical assembly of the Walloon congregations of Zeeland and Holland on 29 October 1584 at Leiden where Saravia was chairman. The accused was declared innocent. LSW, 109. At this synod the representatives from Leiden were asked whether they wished to retain de la Dréve as minister or whether they preferred someone else. The unanimous opinion of the Leiden deputation was: someone else. The choice was left to the classical assembly. Saravia received instructions to assemble the members of the congregation, to exhort them to peace and quiet and to ask them in the name of the synod, in view of the growing numbers of members of the congregation, "de choisir tel ministre qu'ils trouveront convenier à la crainte de Dieu, et leur sera par ledit Saravia faict declaration de ceux qui seront en liberté d'estre esleus". LSW, 108 f. And so it happened, but the congregation decided otherwise. On 8 November 49 votes out of 78 were cast for de la Dréve, an absolute majority. Philippe de la Motte received 27 and Chrestien de la Queullerie 2. LC, fol. 8. He was removed from Leiden by the classical assembly at Middelburg (5 and 6 April 1585) and appears to have gone to Ostend. His place at Leiden was taken by Lucas Trelcat. LSW, 110.

[125] LSW, 109.

[126] LSW, 107.

[127] LSW, 111. Cf. G. H. M. Posthumus Meyjes, "Le collège wallon," in: Th. H. Lunsingh Scheurleer and G. H. M. Posthumus Meyjes, ed. Leiden University in the seventeenth Century. An Exchange of Learning (Leiden, 1975) 132, n. 33.

[128] LSW, 131, 138.

[129] LSW, 107, 172.

Despite the fact that Saravia was not a member of the consistory of the Walloon congregation, his name frequently appears in the acta. The possibility of his presence was taken into account at the drawing up of the agenda for the meeting.[130] If he could not be present, then they called to consult him at home.[131] The business he undertook at the behest of the consistory was often of a pastoral nature. So, as though he were the minister of the congregation, he had, with one of the elders, to admonish a member of the congregation for his behaviour.[132] He had to issue a testimonial for his colleague de la Dréve on the latter's departure.[133] He was consulted about an alteration in the preaching rota.[134] He was concerned in matrimonial difficulties between members of the congregation.[135] Madame Saravia was once involved in a dispute with a certain Potteau[136] who was found guilty in the matter and consequently excluded from the Lord's Supper.[137] A consultation was held at Saravia's home by the elder des Mestres and the minister Moreau over sending Daniel de Nielle to Frankfurt and thence to Geneva in accordance with a decision of the Walloon synod.[138] On 20 June 1585 the same elder was instructed, in consultation with Saravia, to approach the magistrates about the minister's stipend.[139] Apparently not much headway was made for two months later it was resolved that des Mestres with deacon Hespel and Saravia should make a personal request to the municipal authorities "to have some support for the minister of this town".[140] Three weeks later Saravia again received the consistory's request via des Mestres, "examine how the authorities have arranged the minister's payment".[141] Thus he evidently acted as liaison between the Walloon consistory and the magistrates. Whether the request made to him and the jurist, Donellus, at the consistory's meeting on 19 September to attend, "pour adviser etc", had something to do with this question, is not clear.[142] Saravia was apparently not present at this meeting for the acta mentions the decision that des Mestres should ask him to accompany him to the magistrates to discuss with them matters concerning the synod. This referred to the synod which was meeting in Leiden at that moment (18-20 September 1585). We can

---

[130] LC, fol. 5; 25 September 1584.
[131] LC, fol. 6; 14 October 1584.
[132] LC, fol. 20; 21 January 1585.
[133] LC, fol. 26; 27 June 1585.
[134] LC, fol. 26; 20 June 1585.
[135] LC, fol. 30; 7 November 1585; fol. 51; 20 August 1587.
[136] LC, fol. 27; 11 July 1585.
[137] LC, fol. 27; 13 July 1585.
[138] LSW, 111; LC, fol. 30; 26 September 1585.
[139] LC, fol. 26; 20 June 1585.
[140] LC, fol. 28; 22 August 1585.
[141] LC, fol. 29; 12 September 1585.
[142] LC, fol. 29; 12 September 1585.

only guess at what subject was considered so urgent that it had to be discussed immediately with the municipal authorities. Had it anything to do with the consistory's decision of the week before: "It will be discussed after the synod whether it is convenient to catechize in the church and whether it will be necessary to have a schoolmaster"?[143]

The most frequent mention of Saravia's name in the consistory's acta relate to the years 1584 and 1585. After that he is only named sporadically.[144] This is not to say that he then entirely ceased to concern himself any more with the life of the Walloon congregation. On the contrary, both consistories expected advice from the professors from time to time. Thus the acta of the consistory of the Dutch congregation for the 21 February 1586 record that they be requested to be present at the meeting on 10 March next.[145] We have already seen[146] that Saravia had to act between both congregations in the question of the Walloon communion service, as also his continuing concern with the business of Hackius.[147] When in April 1587 a letter from the Walloon congregation concerning a request for information about a certain Janneken Brunij, a divorced woman who wished to be admitted to the congregation, came up for discussion at the Dutch consistory, Saravia undertook to answer the letter.[148] There is an interesting report, that on 21 April 1587, the Dutch consistory dealt with Saravia's request for a letter of transfer, prompted by the fact that "he had ended his ministry at this church long ago". This request is remarkable because the question of the issue of a letter of transfer could only arise on leaving for another congregation.[149] Did Saravia already forsee in the spring of 1587 that his departure was imminent and that this could well happen so hurriedly that there would be no more opportunity to make a formal request for a letter of transfer? In any event the consistory abided by this rule: the letter of transfer would be issued as soon as the applicant planned to leave the town.[150]

5. PROFESSOR AND RECTOR MAGNIFICUS OF THE UNIVERSITY (1584-1587)

Saravia had already many contacts with the university before his appointment as professor in ordinary. He preached to the students, among whom was his son. We find in the Album Studiosorum that "Thomas de Saravia, Anglus", who intended studying philosophy, was registered on

---

[143] LC, fol. 29; 12 September 1585.
[144] LC, fol. 51; 20 August 1587. Concerns advice on a matrimonial problem.
[145] KB, fol. 13v; 21 February 1586.
[146] p. 57.
[147] p. 57.
[148] KB, fol. 37r, 14 April 1587.
[149] Rutgers, Acta, 138, 241 f.
[150] KB, fol. 38r; 21 April 1587.

23 November, 1582, a short time after the family had settled in Leiden. Saravia's own registration took place on 16 February 1583.[151] This matriculation was not at all strange at a time in which the members of the university, resident in the town, or graduates from elsewhere belonged to a group of so-called "viri honorati". They all matriculated, if not entirely then very probably with due regard, for the privileges attached which included, amongst others, freedom from taxes and excises.[152] Already before his appointment as professor in ordinary Saravia had served as assessor to the rector.[153] He was appointed by the curators on 12 May 1584.[154] At the same time Hubertus Sturmius was granted his release at his own request.[155] Saravia had also been involved in the controversies surrounding Sturmius and in the attempts to find him a place as a minister elsewhere.[156]

Probably he thought over his acceptance of the appointment for some time. In any event, he wanted first to make a short visit to England "to arrange some of his private business", as he himself put it. The request is further evidence that, during his stay in the Netherlands, Saravia remained in close touch with England. The burgomasters, however, wanted to be sure in the meantime that the notable and much esteemed theologian was actually linked with their town. Thus they insisted that the appointment should be settled before the requested journey.[157]

Are we to see in this projected visit further evidence that Saravia was already considering a permanent return to England? In any event he objected to his appointment for a long time. Finally the firm appointment was made only on 13 August 1584. In this it was agreed that Saravia would still continue to preach for the Reformed congregation at Leiden for

---

[151] *Album Studiosorum Academiae Lugduno Batavae 1575-1875.* G. du Rieu, ed. (Hagae Comitis, 1875) 13. The census list for 1582 recorded "Adrianus Saravia Gandensis, Theol. st." under householders and presumably added to it later, "Thomas Saravia, bij Saravia zijn [left blank]." In the lists from 1583 Thomas is living at his father's. Adrianus is listed among the professores extraordinarii in 1583/1584. Witkam, *Dag. zaken,* V, 47.

[152] P. C. Molhuysen, "De voorrechten der Leidsche universiteit," *Mededelingen der Koninklijke Academie van Wetenschappen,* afd. Letterkunde, 58, B (Amsterdam, 1924) I, 32.

[153] Molhuysen, *Bronnen,* I, 38; Witkam, *Dag. zaken,* I, 44.

[154] "D. Adrianus Saravia professor theologie, begonst den 12en meye 84 ende es verlaten den 5en novembris 87," *AC* 19, fol. 15v. Witkam, *Dag. zaken,* IV, 185.

[155] Molhuysen, I, 40.

[156] Already in the autumn of 1582 Sturmius had tried to get away from Leiden. The consistory of Dordrecht did not accede to his efforts to be called as minister there because he was suspected of unorthodoxy after his recommendation by Hermannus Herberts. *WMV,* III; 2, 217. Shortly after Saravia had arrived in Leiden, the other Dordrecht minister, Hendrik van den Corput, expressed the hope, in a letter to Arent Cornelisz., that Saravia would be able to do something for Sturmius and that Cornelisz. might be able to bring about a meeting between the two men so that "Sturmius might be helped to the ministry of the Word". *WMV,* III; 2, 226.

[157] GAL, *Missivenboeck A,* fol. 46. Witkam, *Dag. zaken,* V, 48.

six to eight weeks until the vacancy was filled.[158] His salary was fixed at
600 guilders a year. Each Sunday he had to preach in Latin ''for the further exercise and instruction of the students''.[159] The minister's stipend
and house rent were paid him until 15 August.[160]

The question of his successor as minister came up for discussion in the
States of Holland as early as August. From the resolution of 4 August 1584
it appears that Petrus Gille (Gillius) was to proceed in consultation with
Leiden ''so that the place be filled there of Saravia who was again to be
employed as Professor of Theology''.[161] On the instructions of the consistory and secular authorities in Leiden, Saravia himself had fallen in
with the request that Gillius should choose not The Hague, with which he
was also having discussions, but Leiden, ''since it was proper that the
great congregation of Leiden and the students be provided with a capable
person''.[162] Indeed the States asked Gillius, ''would he go to the aforesaid
Leiden, since the aforesaid Saravia will only be allowed henceforth to act
as Professor of Theology''.[163] However their effort was in vain. Christiaan
van de Wouwer became Saravia's successor.[164]

Initially Saravia enjoyed great respect in the university. On 8 February
1585, scarcely six months after taking up academic office, he became Rector Magnificus.[165] And this term was extended the following year.[166] In
1587 he was assessor under the rectorate of his friend, Justus Lipsius.[167] As
had already been decided during his first period of office,[168] his second
term as rector was ushered in with a feast held at his house.[169] This meal
was in place of the solemn rectoral feast which was not held in 1586, officially at least, because as the acta of the senate record, Leicester was to
make a visit to the town at the same time. Were the official rectoral feast to
proceed, then they would be obliged to invite the Governor as well and the
meal would then entail too great an expense.[170] Hollanders are thrifty folk
and it was war time.

---

[158] *AC*, 18, fol. 156v; 157r; 13 August 1584. Witkam, *Dag. zaken*, V, 49.

[159] *AC*, 18, fol. 156v; 13 August 1584. Witkam, *Dag. zaken*, V, 48.

[160] Reeckeninghe 1584, fol. 138.

[161] *RStH 1584*, 459.

[162] *Ibid.*

[163] *RStH 1584*, 462 f.

[164] Molhuysen, *Bronnen*, I, 41.

[165] *Ibid.*, 43.

[166] *Ibid.*, 43. On this occasion the nomination went from the burgermasters to Leicester
coupled with a warm recommendation for the granting of Saravia's rectorate.

[167] *Ibid.*, 48. After the senate had nominated him for the rectorate before Lipsius and
Beyma. *AC*, 18, fol. 183. The burgermasters protested against this that the nomination had
been made a day too late. Molhuysen, *Bronnen*, I, 47.

[168] *Ibid.*, 42.

[169] *Ibid.*, 43.

[170] *Ibid.*, 42. In 1579 the rectoral feast was held on 9 February at the university's expense
''conciliandae benevolentiae Magistratus''! The curators and burgermasters dined at the

Since there was no question at this time of a systematic classification and structure of theological discipline and education, it is difficult to distinguish the teaching responsibilities of the various professors. Actually scriptural exposition was the only subject taught. Saravia's predecessor, Hubertus Sturmius, had taught Hebrew in Ghent[171] and would perhaps have also done so in Leiden. Although it is nowhere expressly mentioned, it is not improbable that, at any rate in the beginning, Saravia taught Hebrew and the exposition of the Old Testament. Because he considered the knowledge of Hebrew of the utmost importance, he strove for an expansion of tuition in it. It was on his proposal[172] that Franciscus Raphelengius was appointed professor in Hebrew on 20 June 1586.[173] It is recorded that Raphelengius, originally "extra-ordinarius",[174] then appointed professor in ordinary on 8 February 1587,[175] began his lectures at ten o'clock in the morning. It was decided that Lipsius "should return to nine o'clock" and that Saravia would lecture at two in the afternoon.[176] It is not known what he taught in 1586. We are better acquainted with the subjects of the theological lectures in the first year for which we have at our disposal a "series lectionum" drawn up on 1 October 1587. In the mornings at eight o'clock Raphelengius expounded the minor Prophets and the Aramaic portion of Daniel, at nine o'clock Saravia did the same for the Epistle to the Hebrews. At two in the afternoon St. Matthew's Gospel was expounded by Lucas Trelcatius and at four o'clock, Isaiah by Carolus Gallus.[177]

---

'convivium publicum'. The expenses amounted to about ƒ 28. The magistrates presented sixteen jars of wine. *Ibid.*, 7 f. A year later the States were asked to grant the rector a higher allowance, partly as a salary increase, partly "ad convivia publica aliasque honestas sumptus". *Ibid.*, 13. In 1581 the 'solemne convivium academicum' was also held on 9 February. The curator Janus Doeza and five of the magistrates dined. The municipal government again provided sixteen jars of wine. *Ibid.*, 17. The resolutions of the curators record: "zijn gecommitteert omme die vande Univ. te vereeren opte maeltijt, de Schout, Heemskerck, Brouwer, Baersdorp, Noorde, Hout ende dat men die vande Univ. van statswegen zal beschencken met 8 statskannen." *Ibid.*, 25. Again a year later, on 10 February 1583, they did themselves particularly well. Then the meal cost ƒ 30 more than the ƒ 38 which had been previously agreed with the hostess. The rector had to cover the deficit out of the students' matriculation fees paid to him. The university was to reimburse his expenses on his laying down his office. On this occasion Heurnius squeezed ƒ 31 from his own pocket and a daalder for the girls who had prepared the meal. In order to compensate the hostess they dined at the same place on the last day of the same month and on this occasion paid a guilder per head. *Ibid.*, 35. The curators were to undertake the expenses of the annual rectoral feast from 1588. *Ibid.*, 50.

[171] *Ibid.*, 10.
[172] *Ibid.*, Appendices, 124.
[173] *Ibid.*, 46.
[174] *Ibid.*, 44.
[175] *Ibid.*, 47, 50.
[176] *Ibid.*, 44.
[177] *Ibid.*, Appendices, 157 f. Gallus had his temporary post of professor extraordinary extended by six months after Saravia's flight in November 1587. Witkam, *Dag. zaken*, I, 195,

During his three years of academic activity Saravia formed a clear idea of the fundamental and practical issues in education. On 6 May 1586 in the Senate in the presence of the curators and burgomasters a paper was considered, written in Latin in his own hand, "which he had not previously discussed with the professors" as it was somewhat critical. On this occasion the rector was admonished that if he wished to have important matters concerning the university dealt with, he must beforehand secure the agreement of the professors and burgomasters and not pursue his own course without consultation. At this time more symptoms were already to be observed of a growing estrangement between Saravia and both his colleagues and the university administration. The curators held the rector responsible for the declining number of students. His answer, in which the loss of Brabant and Flanders and the foundation of a rival university at Franeker (1585) were cited as causes, did not satisfy them. They thought another reason must be assigned: the frequent absence of some professors for days, weeks or even months was very prejudicial to education. Added to this, in Saravia's case, was the fact that he frequented Leicester's court in Utrecht to discuss university matters without the knowledge of the curators and burgomasters. Indeed rumour had it that he even tried to get the university moved to Utrecht. So seriously did they take this rumour that they delegated two of their number, Dousa and Buys, to Leicester to prevent this move.[178] Saravia paid little attention to the curator's admonitions. He was again absent at the promotions on 25 and 27 June. On the first occasion, as it was expressly noted in the acta of the Senate, he had gone to Utrecht. It was decided that henceforward at promotions half the sum due to the rector from the promovendus must be paid to the pro-rector.[179]

Meanwhile at the meeting in question on 6 May the rector gave the curators and burgomasters an exposition and explanation of his views in the light of his paper, translated into Dutch by Vulcanius.[180] In this it was first of all recalled that the study of theology had been one of the most important reasons for the foundation of the university. "So it is nevertheless that the study of theology itself does not and cannot progress on its own without the knowledge of languages". On the basis of this principle Saravia argued for the appointment of a professor in Hebrew. For the teaching of Greek indeed they had at their disposal "one professor who

---

203. He then got the lecture time assigned to the latter, 2 p.m. Witkam, *Dag. zaken*, III, 44. Previously it was known to Saravia and "some others" of Leicester's party that no one attended the lectures of the old man who was retained only out of respect for his advanced age. Witkam, *Dag. zaken*, III, 117.

[178] Molhuysen, *Bronnen*, I, 45 f.; Witkam, *Dag. zaken*, V, 50 f., 113. On plans for transferring the university to Utrecht: G. W. Kernkamp, *De Utrechtsche Universiteit 1636-1936* (3 vols., Utrecht, 1936) I, 29-32.

[179] Molhuysen, *Bronnen*, I, 44.

[180] *Ibid.*, Appendices, 124 f.; Witkam, *Dag. zaken*, II, 180; V, 50.

can sufficiently satisfy the students and lovers of this language''. This was a reference to Bonaventura Vulcanius, secretary to the Senate and professor in classical languages. "We are deficient in the Hebrew language'', so Saravia continued. "For Snellius' knowledge can only extend to the instructing and teaching of the rudiments and principles of the language, but it is not proper to expect him to go beyond that". Probably not, for among the many disciplines which this learned man had studied: mathematics, medicine, philosophy, Greek and Latin, Hebrew assumed a modest position. He only taught it temporarily. His actual teaching assignment at Leiden was mathematics, cosmography and astronomy.[181] But "the University has need of a Professor of Hebrew, who asked about grave and doubtful expositions of Holy Scripture urging the Hebrew text, and can make sure and well founded answer to it". As we have already learned, Saravia successfully proposed that Raphelengius be appointed for this.

However, there was no point in providing the faculty with professors if the students were lacking. The latter was unfortunately the case. "There are at present few there who undertake the study of theology and those who are students of it are nothing but poor and despised men who can expect no honour".

Here the rector struck a note that was frequently to be heard later in his treatises: the right of the holders of ecclesiastical office to a good salary and to due respect in a Christian society. According to Saravia, some young men did indeed want to study theology but their parents held them back and refused to pay the cost of their studies. He now proposed that two or three thousand guilders be set aside so that some more pupils could be maintained in this way.[182]

Another reason for the lack of students lay in the bad name which the university had acquired because of the ecclesiastical disputes in Leiden. People preferred to send their children to another university, "yet it would be much more useful for the church if those who were provided as the churches' future ministers were not sent so far out of sight, but that they should stay and be trained on the spot where proper supervision might be exercised over their conduct and their progress in studying". Proposal: Let the States of Holland recall to Leiden all those who have gone to study elsewhere and let study at another university remain limited to exceptional cases for which the university's permission was required.

Saravia touched a sore point when he inquired about the original act of

---

[181] Molhuysen, *Bronnen, I;* Appendices, *158.*

[182] It is not to be thought that the number of theological students was large in the period described here. In the same year the national synod in The Hague was to invite Leicester's attention in a remonstrance to the sad fact that only five or six theological students had matriculated there, whilst the university had been founded precisely with an eye to theological study. The governor was asked to seek advice on this matter from Saravia, Donellus and Lipsius. Rutgers, *Acta,* 639-642.

foundation of the university. Each year indeed some privileges were read out in public, "but the original instruments did not appear". If no original articles were yet drawn up this ought to be done. They should be kept in the university so that any one at any time could acquaint himself with them. Moreover, the steward who paid the professors their salaries was not employed by the university but by the States, whilst the privileges and donations talked expressly of the treasurer of the university, "and yet there is no need of a treasurer to keep accounts there, for there is no income or capital". True, the university was sometimes put to considerable expense in connection with the reception of distinguished guests or on account of aid to the destitute. The rector asked that, as was the custom in the university of Franeker, an annual sum be put aside for these purposes.

Whilst, in a marginal note of 8 August 1586, the curators and burgomasters agreed to the wishes of the senate on most points—four days after the above mentioned meeting Saravia's piece was adopted by the senate in an almost identical document[183]—their reaction to the last requirement was sharply negative. Naturally there were original "letters of foundation and institution drawn up in proper form", from copies of which the annual reading was made. These were kept in the municipal archives, not only because they were better protected from the effects of fire and accident there, but also because the university was granted to the town of Leiden, "as a reward for its great and unprecedented loyalty and constancy". But there was yet a third reason: "It is proper that the original instruments themselves remain in the custody of the town so that they may be an aid against those who (so common rumour runs) scheme to transfer and remove the university to Utrecht, with which also the honourable rector is accused (although they believe in his innocence), therefore, in order to prevent all occasion of suspicion, nothing at all ought to be done to remove the original instruments from the town of Leyden".[184] We see in this answer how strained Saravia's situation had become at this time.

Some time before, on 3 June 1586, the magistrates of Leiden had addressed a detailed remonstrance to Leicester, together with copies of the foundation and institution, so that the latter could satisfy himself of the great historical importance of the founding of the university at Leiden and would understand "that therefore the aforementioned members of the Tribunal of the university there hold and esteem it not only as costly and precious but more as their sole and finest pearl and that they would rather let him take everything than be deprived of it". Leicester answered this with the promise that the establishment of the university in Leiden would always be respected.[185] However, a few months later they were evidently

---

[183] Molhuysen, *Bronnen,* I; Appendices, 126-132.

[184] *Ibid.,* Appendices, 131 f.

[185] *Ibid.,* Appendices, 132-134.

still not easy about it. Whilst, in the magistrates' remonstrance in June, there was no mention of any names and only general talk of men who attempted to delude the governor that the Leiden town council itself, because of inexperience in and therefore of embarrassment at the management of a university, preferred to be rid of it, in the marginal note of 8 August "the honourable rector" is mentioned in so many words, albeit with the mitigating addition, "although they believe in his innocence". In the course of the years there was an ever widening rift developing between Saravia and the consistory on the one side and the municipal government and its representatives amongst the curators of the university on the other. The rector's anglophilia and his contacts with Leicester naturally did nothing to help the situation.

The curators let it be known that, as regards some of Saravia's proposals, these matters were exclusively their concern in which the professors must not interfere: financial administration, the improvement in the study of philosophy and the supervision of the teaching of schoolmasters.

It is apparent from what has been outlined that Saravia pursued his ecclesiastical and political activities after his appointment as professor without regarding the restriction which, since Daneau's departure in 1582, was set out at every installation of new professors: "that he shall not involve himself either in the ecclesiastical nor civic affairs of this town nor of the nation in such a way as might give rise to any dispute or dissension, but shall concern himself only with his professorial duties".[186]

Because, despite this restriction, there is a clear continuity in Saravia's actions in the political affairs of church and state in the period in which he was a minister and during the discharge of his university work, we can treat this behaviour between 1582 and 1587 as a whole. In what follows we shall devote attention to his views on ecclesiastical goods, his importance as adviser of the churches, especially in several disputes and in the preparation of the church order, his involvement in the disputes surrounding Coolhaes and Coornhert and his political opinions which came to light in his relations with England in general and with Leicester in particular.

## 6. ADVISER TO THE CHURCHES

### a. *Ecclesiastical goods*

Saravia rapidly acquired great prestige outside Leiden. He received requests for advice from various ecclesiastical assemblies. Thus the question of ecclesiastical goods came up for discussion on 7 June 1583 at the particular synod of South Holland in The Hague. The synod decided to send a remonstrance to the States on the right use of these goods. It was

---

[186] *Ibid.*, 48.

understood that Saravia had written something on this subject. He was
therefore asked to undertake the writing of the remonstrance, in which
it must be stated, "we declare that we have nothing to do with the
abominable abuses which have occurred in this respect, and that the overthrow and destruction of the churches be prevented". By abuses they
meant the expropriation of the goods of the medieval church in such a way
that the proceeds went for the benefit of the government and not of the
Reformed Church.[187] Saravia let the synod have a short piece and expounded it in the assembly, whereupon the latter resolved to send a
remonstrance to Orange himself.[188] Three years later Saravia's work came
up for discussion again at the particular synod in Rotterdam (2 June 1586)
which decided to ask the author to send the document to the state delegates
at the forthcoming national synod at The Hague "so that they might read
it and order things in accordance with it".[189] Again, after the national
synod, the discourse continued to be used as the starting point for discussion of this topic.[190]

It is not hard to guess what Saravia wrote about ecclesiastical goods. In
the introduction of his *De diversis ministrorum evangelii gradibus* he wrote a letter to the ministers in the Netherlands. He referred to what he called the
plunder of ecclesiastical goods thus "as if it would be a sin for the church
to have any possessions under a Christian government and as if the principal heresy of the Roman church lay in its wealth. What remains is under
the control of the burgomasters and city fathers (whose religion you
know) . . . . It is said that the ministers ought to be poor . . . . If I had remained with you I would have adjured the States about this . . . . They
have no right at all to church goods".[191] He was to devote many pages to
the issue in this book, arguing that what was given for the church's use
ought to continue for its intended purpose.[192]

For the rest, it is curious that when, four years later, a good opportunity
arose to bring the question of church goods to the attention of the States,
Saravia was silent on the matter. On 6 May 1587 the States of Holland
determined to summon some ministers before a commission of their
deputies and those of the courts to warn them not to interfere in politics in
their preaching and to show the necessary respect for the authorities.[193]

---

[187] Reitsma, *Acta,* II, 220. By an edict of February 1573, the States of Holland had
appointed that the revenue from those goods brought under the control of the secular
authorities were to be allocated for the support of ministers, other church officers and
schoolmasters. The States however had the proceeds of monastic properties.

[188] *Ibid.,* 271.

[189] *Ibid.*

[190] The particular synod of South Holland at Delft (24 August 1587) asked the author to
send it to them. The ministers of Leiden supported this request. *Ibid.,* II, 300.

[191] *DGM,* 2r.

[192] *Ibid.,* 57 f.

[193] *RStH* 1587, 767.

The interview in question took place in the Court in The Hague on 14 and 15 May.[194] Saravia took part along with twelve ministers whose spokesman was Hendrik van den Corput. They seized the opportunity to express all their grievances against the government (uncooperative attitude towards the church order; toleration of the public performance of the Roman Catholic religion; ministers' low stipends; the poor church attendance of individual members of the government etc.) and they repeated their demands in a memorandum. Precisely because this emerged as a lengthy document,[195] it is striking that there should be no sign of Saravia's wishes in the matter of church goods.

The particular synod of The Hague instructed Martinus Lydius, minister at Amsterdam, to conclude the business "concerning the university of Leiden". It is not clear what precisely this meant, but it may well have had to do with the relations between church and university. Now Daneau had left for Ghent Saravia would have been involved in this discussion. He apparently had the same views as the former.[196]

Saravia's judgement was also valued in questions of a moral nature (communion discipline). Thus, for example, he advised about the exclusion from the Lord's Supper of a man who, according to church rules, had married unlawfully.[197]

### b. *Doctrinal Controversies*

Amongst other doctrinal disputes in which Saravia engaged at the request of church assemblies was that involving Hieronymus Hortensius, a minister at The Hague and the one occasioned by the preaching of Herman Herberts which took place at Gouda. Afterwards we must devote a separate section to considering his disputation with D. V. Coornhert.

As for Hortensius,[198] church assemblies were occupied for many years on the question of his orthodoxy. Although he repeatedly declared himself to be in accord with Reformed doctrine, yet he was suspected of heterodoxy, namely Roman Catholic views on good works. In his defence he issued a memorandum in 1582, intended for "his brothers of the Reformed religion who held him in suspicion".[199] The following year he was suspected by the Court of Holland of having been involved in an attack against the state. One consequence of his behaviour was to divide the

---

[194] P. C. Hooft, *Nederlandtsche Histoorien* (Amsterdam, 1642) 245-247; Bor, *Oorspronck, begin en vervolgh* (Amsterdam, 1680) 975-981; Brandt, *Reformatie*, I, 724-727.

[195] Bor, *Oorspronck,* 977-979.

[196] Reitsma, *Acta,* II, 227.

[197] *Ibid.,* 231.

[198] For Hortensius see *BWPG*, IV, 316-322; *NNBW,* VIII, 853-855; Brandt, *Reformatie,* I, 702 f.; J. Smit, "De vestiging van het Protestantisme in Den Haag en zijn eerste Voorgangers," *Ned. AK,* XIX (1926) 205-264.

[199] P. Bor, *Historie der Nederlandtsche Oorloghen* (Amsterdam, 1670), 2nd part, 511-515.

Reformed congregation in The Hague into two parties, the Johannites, so named after Hortensius' fellow minister and opponent, Jan Pieterszoon,[200] and his own supporters, the Jeronymites. His dismissal by the classis was later revoked. The matter had already cropped up at the particular synod of South Holland at Rotterdam (25 April 1581)[201] and came up for more detailed discussion at that of The Hague (June 1583).[202] Here Saravia was brought into the affair. The synod determined to examine Hortensius on the questions of free will and predestination, justification and sanctification and it asked Saravia to carry out this examination in the presence of some of the synod's members. The accused objected at first to the procedure but later agreed and was even allowed to choose the members of the synod before whom the enquiry would take place.[203] The result turned out to be in his favour. The day after the conversation Saravia informed the synod that the minister from The Hague must be considered orthodox with respect to freewill, justification, sanctification, the keeping of the law, predestination and good works, "but that he cannot understand or believe or preach the doctrine of eternal reprobation as it is understood in the churches of this land, that God had ordained anyone to eternal damnation etc., desiring that we should bear with him in this, which we did".[204] This remarkable verdict meant that on Saravia's authority a minister was allowed to retain his office despite an undeniable difference in an area of the doctrine which was soon to play a great part in the doctrinal disputes of the nation. Although a reconciliation was effected at the synod between two ministers from The Hague, sealed by Hortensius' signing of the Confession,[205], yet he was later once more to figure in their discussions because of rumours of unsound doctrine and conduct.[206]

At the same synod Saravia became involved with the problems concerning Herman Herberts who, in the spring of 1582 had, after many disputes, left Dordrecht for Gouda.[207] In his unwillingness to use the Heidelberg Catechism and to acknowledge the binding authority of that manual and of the Confession and in his teaching that the Christian could attain perfection on earth, he could be likened to Coornhert.[208] Herberts had

---

[200] J. Smit, *Den Haag in den geuzentijd* (s.l., 1922) 308 f.

[201] Reitsma, *Acta,* II, 207.

[202] *Ibid.,* 230, 232-242, 244-248, 250-257, 260.

[203] *Ibid.,* 255.

[204] *Ibid.,* 257.

[205] *Ibid.,* 260 f.

[206] *Ibid.,* 272 f., 395 f.

[207] Schotel, *Kerkelijk Dordrecht,* I, 125-144; C. A. Tukker, *De Classis Dordrecht van 1573 tot 1609* (Leiden, 1965) 52-56.

[208] W. Nijenhuis, "Coornhert and the Heidelberg Catechism. Moment in the struggle between Humanism and Reformation," in: *Ecclesia Reformata. Studies on the Reformation* (Leiden, 1972) 188-206.

been summoned to the synod but had not appeared. Four ministers, Adamus Pillichius (or Billigius) of 's-Gravezande, Casper Swerinck-huysen of Rotterdam, and a certain Pieter Jansz[209] and Saravia represen-ting the Leiden classis, were instructed to explore the situation in Dor-drecht and Gouda and to restore peace in the congregations, especially in Dordrecht.[210] It appears from a report on the subsequent attempts at a mediation delivered in the particular synod of South Holland at Rotter-dam on 2 June 1586—almost three years later, so long did this question drag on—that the mission met with little success. Herberts, backed in his attitude by the magistrates at Gouda, also refused to appear at this assembly. A report was given of a conversation at Gouda between four men chosen by Herberts himself, namely Bastingius of Dordrecht, Helmichius of Utrecht, Donteclock of Delft and Saravia. These gentlemen had come home with nothing achieved from the meeting from which the ministers of Gouda had had to be excluded.[211] Herberts had caused a par-ticularly great stir[212] with a book on Roman 2:28.[213] There was no quieting the matter, not least because the classis of Gouda would not yet recognize the author as a member so long as he had not received a letter of transfer from Dordrecht.[214] The dispute came up for discussion again at the national synod in The Hague in 1586. Here Saravia was invited to report "in the matter of Hermannus Herberts and others" and to stay at the meeting after delivering this in order "to assist in the matter as the oc-casion shall demand".[215] The Leiden professor was present there without the right to vote.[216]

This time the accused did appear, accompanied by some members of the consistory and some of the magistrates of Gouda. In their presence and also in that of the president and assessor of the synod, Kimedoncius and Arent Cornelisz, he had a conversation with Saravia and Bastingius. It is reported in the acta that Herberts "entered into communication with D. Adrianus Saravia, assisted by several other gentlemen and brothers". It is clear that it was Saravia who really conducted the conversation. Was it due to him that the meeting had such a surprising outcome? Herberts gave a written explanation of the more obscure points in the work of his that had caused so much offence, on justification, the perfection of the faithful, letter and spirit, predestination, amongst others. He declared

---

[209] Is this a slip of the pen for Simon Jansz, minister at Dirksland, who represented the classis of Brielle at the synod? Reitsma, *Acta,* II, 218.

[210] *Ibid.,* 258.

[211] *Ibid.,* 266-268.

[212] Schotel, *Kerkelijk Dordrecht,* I, 136 f.

[213] *Corte verclaringe over de woorden Pauli geschreven totten Romeynen Cap. 2 vers 28: Want dat en is geen Jode, die wtwendich een Jode is.*

[214] Reitsma, *Acta,* 268.

[215] Rutgers, *Acta,* 534.

[216] *Ibid.,* 537 f.

himself ready to sign the confession provided that in article 16, dealing with predestination, he was allowed to understand that God was not the cause of sin. He would also accept that Catechism if he might understand the morally objectionable answer 114, also contested by Coornhert, "that even the holiest of men have only a small beginning of obedience to the law in this life", as referring to the perfect holiness in eternal life. He promised to have an explanation published of a number of points in his book and to submit this explanation beforehand to the judgement of Leiden University, Bastingius, Helmichius and Saravia, who was named separately, a promise which Herberts did not fulfill[217] as he did neither his undertaking to preach the Heidelberg Catechism at the Sunday afternoon service.[218] He pleaded guilty to the utterances with which he had injured his brothers and further promised to live in concord with them. Thus the acta in question were signed by Herberts and all the participants in the conversation.[219]

There is a striking similarity between the (provisional) result of the dispute with Herman Herberts and the decision over Hortensius. In both cases those accused of heterodoxy were accepted once more after a consultation in which Saravia had taken the largest part. That this last was indeed the case became apparent during the particular synod of South Holland at Schiedam (30 August 1588). Herberts had to defend himself because he had not adhered to the agreement by which he was to make satisfaction about his writing. He pleaded that he had never received the points which he had to explain and which he was to have received from Saravia.[220] The truth of this excuse could naturally not be ascertained since Saravia had left for England long before.

It frequently happened that, after his departure, his name was still referred to by people who had had dealings with him in one way or another. One such was Frank Willemsz, who was quite remarkably, minister at Hoogmade without being a member of the church[221] and who was unwilling for this situation to be altered.[222] At the particular synod of South Holland in The Hague (22 October 1591) it was reported that he had never been examined, "other than that, at an earlier date, he merely talked to Saravia and that, if he had been examined by the Leiden classis, they would have found him incompetent. He had never appeared in the classis nor had he ever been at the Lord's Supper until 8 or 14 days ago, nor could they find any church form or order in him". By examining some of its members the synod came to the conclusion "that Franco Willemsz did

---

[217] Reitsma, *Acta,* 318.

[218] J. Triglandius, *Kerkelycke Geschiedenissen* (Leiden, 1650) 219.

[219] On the procedure in the synod of The Hague: [J. Wtenbogaert], *De Kerkelicke Historie* (5 vols., s.l., 1647) III, 58; Triglandius, *Kerk. Gesch.,* 217-219; Brandt, *Reformatie,* I, 715 f.

[220] Reitsma, *Acta,* II, 318-320.

[221] *Ibid.,* 367.

[222] *Ibid.,* 381.

not manage to give any account of his beliefs and that he was even wholly uninstructed in God's holy commandments and in the teaching of the Law and the Gospel''.[223] He had therefore to leave his ministry in Hoogmade. But at the particular synod of South Holland a year later (2 November 1592) the sentence on Willemsz was much milder: he was pious in conduct and managed to expound the Sunday gospels reasonably in preaching at Hoogmade which he had evidently continued. He himself said that he had at that time been instituted to his ministry in the presence of the classis of Leiden by Saravia and the Leiden minister, Ysbrand Trabius (Balckius, Balk).[224] The truth of this explanation was borne out by the delegates of the Leiden classis. Here again we encounter an accused person who had been maintained in his ministry through Saravia's offices.

It is apparent from Saravia's conduct in doctrinal controversies in his own country that he had a less legalistic view of the confession and subscription to it than was to be the case in the seventeenth century. Much later, in his famous letter to Wtenbogaert on 13 April 1612, he wrote that the drawing up of the Confession had not been intended as the publication of a canon of faith. On the contrary, it was held that the validity of belief must be proved from Scripture. He himself felt no need of alternatives in the Confession. But if others raised objections, they ought to be listened to and instructed out of God's Word. Anyone who was prepared to be instructed ought not to be counted as an unbeliever. Saravia was thinking of what is nowadays called a "hierarchia veritatum". "Not all articles [of faith] carry the same weight. There are some amongst them of which it must be said that if people differ from them then still they ought not to be expelled from the church". This was also his opinion of the Genevan Confession and the Heidelberg Catechism. Moreover, he added that one of these manuals even had an aberrant view on Christ's descent into hell.[225] In the light of this utterance Saravia's conduct towards such men as Hortensius and Herberts is readily explained. What is more important: this standpoint found support from others and in the eighties could still tip the balance in the resolving of church disputes. Whoever agreed with the Confession, could be and continue to be a minister in the Reformed church although he believed as little as Hortensius in reprobation from eternity and though with Herberts he had a more habitual view of sanctifying grace than the Heidelberg Catechism.

## c. *The dispute over the church order*

At the national synod in The Hague, other topics came up for discussion in which Saravia had become involved during the course of the years:

---

[223] *Ibid.*, 395.
[224] *Ibid.*, 462.
[225] *EE*, Nr. 181; Doc. XLVI.

the realization of the church order, the disputes at Leiden occasioned by
Caspar Coolhaes' behaviour and also in this connection the dispute
between the Leiden congregation and the provincial synod of Holland.
Finally a decision was sought on the publication of the disputation held in
1583 at The Hague between Coornhert and Saravia.

The church order was the most important item on the synod's agenda.
As an ardent supporter of Leicester, the great protector of the Calvinists in
the Netherlands, Saravia agreed with the acceptance of the church order.
This agreement held especially for the controversial point of the relationship between the Reformed Church and the government, although the
synod at The Hague was much more accommodating towards the government on this score than the national synod of Middelburg (1581) had
been.[226]

Although Saravia was consistent in the controversies concerning the
church order yet his attitude was marked by a degree of reserve. When he
came to the Netherlands, much was expected of him as an ally in the struggle for a reformed church order, but when at his request,[227] van den Corput had read a letter from Saravia dated 15 December 1582, sent on by
Arent Cornelisz, he lamented; "Of the church order about which I had expressly written to Saravia in order to know his opinion on it, Saravia does
not write to you in the letter; nevertheless I do not think that he is refusing
to communicate it".[228] It is indeed surprising that Saravia kept van den
Corput waiting so long for an answer[229] and that when he did eventually
write he made not the slightest mention of the church order.[230]

In 1583 the States of Holland drew up a church order[231] "without", as
Trigland wrote, "any church officers or theologians".[232] In the particular
synods of North Holland (May 1583) and of South Holland (June/July
1583) amongst others, earnest objections were raised to this turn of
events.[233] They saw in this plan a serious curtailment of the church's
freedom and independence in the appointment of office holders and the

---

[226] Approval of the minister's call by the secular authority (art. 4) without the condition
that the latter had to be member of the Reformed religion; to accept a call elsewhere the
minister needed not only the consent of his classis but also that of the magistrates in the consistory (art. 34); the involvement of the state in the preparation of a national synod (art. 44);
no abolition of evening prayers without the decision of the secular authority (art. 57).
Hooyer, *Kerkordeningen,* 259.

[227] GAD, Nr. 112; Doc. V.

[228] *WMV,* III; 2, 233.

[229] "Ick hebben van Saravia noch geen antwoirt op mijnen brief", writes van den Corput
to Arent Cornelisz, 23 December 1582. *WMV,* III; 2, 230.

[230] "Van de kerkenordeninge maect hij geen mentie", writes van den Corput to Arent
Cornelisz, 2 February 1583. *WMV,* III; 2, 236.

[231] Hooyer, *Kerkordeningen,* 233-246.

[232] Triglandius, *Kerk. Gesch.,* 172.

[233] Reitsma, *Acta,* I, 122; II, 250.

exercise of discipline. Orange was inclined to press for a provisional acceptance of the plan. Jean Taffin tried to change the prince's mind and asked de Villiers also to use his influence to this end.[234]

On the earlier mentioned journey back from Ghent, Saravia told Taffin at Antwerp that he would probably attend the particular synod of South Holland which was to be held in The Hague from 7 June to 5 July 1583. The prince had given him a letter to the States of Holland in which he urged the addition to the proposed church order that the magistrates who would take part in the selection of ministers must be practising members of the pure religion.[235] This condition naturally did little or nothing to alter what was unacceptable to the church—the plan's fixed principle of the state's right to appointment. Taffin, however did not identify the bearer of the letter with its author and its contents, but trusted that Saravia would defend the Church's position in the synod.[236]

Saravia did indeed attend various sittings of the synod at its request and "in his private capacity", as the acta record.[237] The Leiden Classis was officially represented by Saravia's colleague, Hackius, and by the minister of Rijnsburg, Andreas Hagius, who presided over the assembly.[238] We do not know whether Saravia gave any advice on the church order or whether such an advice had any influence on the synod. All his life he defended the church's freedom vis à vis the state in the exercise of discipline. Although he would have had no serious objections to the views of Taffin, Cornelisz and the other Dutch Calvinists on the procedure to be followed in the appointment of office holders, yet in general he ascribed more authority to the state over the church than did his colleagues. Moreover it is the question whether in general he was able to agree with the structure of the young Reformed Church. Perhaps, without giving any open expression to them he already harboured objections to the principle on which all parties agreed and which was expressed in every plan for a church order including the 1583 one of the States of Holland.[239] The principle which supplied one of the foundations of Reformed church law, was that of the equality of all office holders, ministers, elders and deacons, the principle also of the equality of all congregations and of a church government by assemblies of the said three offices without any bearers of more or less monarchical authority. So far as is known, during his time in the Netherlands, Saravia never let out anything about this in writing or at any assembly. However, it is hardly conceivable that the opinions, which three years later he was to embody in his *De diversis gradibus* and with which he was to usher in a new

---

[234] Boer, *Hofpredikers,* 93 f.

[235] Jean Taffin to Arent Cornelisz, 3 June 1583. *WMV,* III; 5, 215.

[236] *Ibid.,* 216.

[237] Reitsma, *Acta,* II, 225.

[238] *Ibid.,* 218.

[239] Art. 42. Hooyer, *Kerkordeningen,* 243.

stage in the thinking on the bishop's office in England by frankly basing
this office on the ius divinum, were completely foreign to him in the period
described here. We may believe him when he later wrote that he was occupied with them already during his residence in the Netherlands.

It was said of Saravia that he was "more English than French, Flemish
or Dutch".[240] He was a great admirer of the Church of England. Already,
a short time after his conversion to Protestantism, an episcopal organization had some attraction for him. Whilst he was still living in London, he
discussed with Nicolas des Gallars, the French minister whom he greatly
respected, what he called "hunc meum scrupulum de episcopis et
presbyteris".[241] His preference for an episcopal church government must
have been strengthened during his stay in the Netherlands. This may be
gathered from several autobiographical remarks in his treatises. Writing
about the hindrances he had experienced in the discharge of his office in
the churches of Flanders and Holland, he disclosed: "Often in these
twenty-six years [the period from 1561 to 1587] I explained what I felt
about the order of bishops in private conversation with friends", to which
he added "although not everywhere and with everyone". As he said, he
wanted to avoid the ruin which had befallen others who had expressed
themselves in this spirit. In a conversation at which Saravia had not
himself been present, de Villiers had said that he was not such an opponent of episcopal authority. Some people had later complained about this
to Saravia. They had accused de Villiers of episcopal ambitions and showed their concern for the preservation of the equality of ministers in the
Walloon churches. What must he answer? Although he agreed with de
Villiers he dared not defend his views lest he also be suspected of aspiring
to episcopal authority.[242] Whether this was the real reason for his silence,
we must leave undecided, but probably episcopal church order did
seriously occupy him during his time in the Netherlands. He attended
classical assemblies and synods at which he longed for the "perpetuus
episcopus" who from the nature of his office possessed "authoritas" and
"magna reverentia" to a degree which the temporary president of a
Reformed church assembly could never acquire.[243] He also remarked in a
synod meeting that he had no objection against the principle of the equality of all ministers and deacons but that he would not approve it until those
who believed in this principle, also put equality into practice.[244] But,
according to Saravia, this they failed to do. "Ambitio" and "dominatio"
ruled amongst "the present-day ministers of the church with their equality
no less than with the earlier patriarchs . . . . I have lived with brother

---

[240] Van Dorsten, *Poets*, 128.
[241] *DGM*, 113.
[242] *Ibid.*, 7r.
[243] *ETB*, T2, 76.
[244] *DT*, 53.

ministers of the Gospel and to the best of my ability I have observed equality as well as anyone else. In the meantime this did not compel me to blind my observation of men's characters. I must honestly say that I perceived a greater modesty in bishops and archbishops than among some fellow ministers of equal rank to me. The craving for equality has led to most people in general taking no account of age, learning and experience, so that recently a young man, on his admission to the body of ministers, ventured to put himself on a par, not to say to set himself above, those who could have been his father, and this without feeling the slightest shame at his transgression of the law of nature''.[245] Just like the English ambassador, Carleton, before and during the synod of Dort in 1618 and 1619,[246] Saravia blamed much of the turbulent situation in church and state in the Netherlands on the ministers' ambition for power which in his opinion was inherent in the Calvinist presbyterian church government. He even blamed them for the failure of the Reformation in the South Netherlands. ''If we had behaved ourselves moderately in the year 1577 in Belgium,[247] as became Christians, then the preaching would have persisted undiminished there'',[248] so wrote Saravia in a remarkable underestimation of the military factors which brought an end to the Reformation's freedom in the South Netherlands.

In the long letter to the ministers of the Netherlands at the beginning of his *De diversis gradibus*, Saravia devoted much attention to what he called the plunder of church goods. He called the unlawful seizing of church goods by the state sacrilege. The proceeds of these possessions ought rather to be allocated for the study of divinity, for seminaries and for pensions for retired ministers. If he had stayed in Holland he would have adjured the States to put an end to the disastrous situation which was rousing God's vengeance on the nation. He did not want to take up this matter too hastily after Orange's death and the arrival of Leicester, in case he gave the impression that he was acting under the latter's influence. At the time he had discussed the subject with the ministers and with some magistrates but, as he conceded, not so freely as he was now writing about it in his treatise. Those who had only recently been won to the Reformation might perhaps be lost and he himself did not wish to appear to be full of ambition and avarice.[249] This all sounds very reasonable. But we cannot forget that Saravia himself repeatedly pleaded with the Leiden council for an improvement in ministers' stipends, that material factors led him in 1583 to

---

[245] *Ibid.,* 313.

[246] W. Nijenhuis, ''The controversy between Presbyterianism and Episcopalianism surrounding and during the Synod of Dordrecht 1618-1619,'' in: *Ecclesia Reformata,* 218 f.

[247] Saravia is evidently alluding here to the reckless behaviour of men such as Petrus Dathenus.

[248] *ETB,* aaaz.

[249] *DGM,* A 4v, 5r.

consider for a moment leaving the town and that these considerations always carried great weight for him.

We get the impression that the particular practical objections which Saravia held against the church government in the Netherlands were the rivalry and ambition of the ministers despite professed equality and the disorder due to the lack of an authoritative monarchical church leadership. He swiftly developed his main objections later, first in his *De diversis gradibus*. "I recognise that I have now progressed far further in my convictions than when I lived there in Holland", he wrote in the earlier mentioned letter to the Dutch ministers.[250] According to his own account he had only raised his objections to the circumstances in that country in a limited circle. It was probably these objections which led to his reserve when his opinion was sought on the church order.

However, Saravia was in no doubt when the church's freedom vis à vis the state in the exercise of discipline was at stake. In the same open letter to the Dutch ministers he rounded on those who supposed that the whole discipline of morals had been handed over to the magistrates and that only the bare preaching of God's Word and administration of the Gospel sacraments belonged to the ministers' task.[251] On the contrary Saravia wrote: "When matters are properly ordered in both church and state, the Christian magistrate ought not to be accorded primacy in the church of Christ, just as the church's ministers ought not in a Christian state".[252] It was the first part of the fundamental statement especially which, during his stay in the Netherlands, made Saravia unhesitatingly take sides with the church in the conflict with Coolhaes.

### d. *Conflict with Coolhaes*

As we have noted, the disputes around Coolhaes were an important reason for Saravia's call to Leiden. In that year Coolhaes had been excommunicated by the provincial synod at Haarlem on 25 March.[253] In a *Sendtbrief* he had protested against his condemnation by the national synod at Middelburg (1581). The Leiden magistrates contested the condemnation and defended the rights of the secular authority with respect to the church in a *Remonstrantie* written by Coornhert and signed by the town clerk Jan van Hout. Also in 1582 Coolhaes published a translation of parts of a sermon by Zwingli's son-in-law and Erastus' supporter,[254] Rudolph Walter (Rodolphus Gualterus), which argued for the proper rights of the state in the matter of church discipline. Although the magistrates did not have the

---

[250] *Ibid.*, A5r.

[251] *Ibid.*

[252] *Ibid.*

[253] Reitsma, *Acta*, I, 116.

[254] R. Wesel-Roth, *Thomas Erastus. Ein Beitrag zur Geschichte der reformierten Kirche und zur Lehre von der Staatssouveränität* (Lahr/Baden, 1954), passim.

slightest objection to Coolhaes' views, they were displeased at the printing
of Gualterus' work. Therefore they decided on 14 December 1582 to prevent its publication. The sheriff was instructed accordingly.[255] The harm
of new quarrels was considered greater than the advantage of Coolhaes'
support for the authority. The town government abided by its decision
even when Coolhaes lodged a complaint on the grounds of the loss he suffered by the publication-ban. He was asked to submit an account of his
losses and they would be settled.[256]

Soon after his arrival in Leiden Saravia was involved in the dispute. On
15 December 1582 he wrote to Arent Cornelisz about what he called: a
new evil that Satan was contriving against the church. Caspar was
endeavouring to disturb the modest beginnings of peace by the publication
of a booklet which contained nothing of himself apart from a letter and in
which he had made himself the mouthpiece of Gualterus' opinions.
Hackius and Saravia, accompanied by two elders, visited Coolhaes on 14
December and adjured him to give more heed to the peace of the church
than to his own desire for vengeance. Saravia fancied he understood
Coolhaes' intention, namely to set the two ministers, Hackius and
himself, against each other in their differences of opinion and to make
himself more agreeable by concealing his far more serious heresy. The
visitors did not manage to change Coolhaes' mind. Saravia now decided to
bring the matter personally to the magistrates for they had forbidden
Coolhaes to undertake or publish anything new. He promised to let his
Delft colleague know the authority's answer. He asked him to send on his
subsequent letters to van den Corput. He had not yet had an opportunity
to reply to the latter's questions on the matter of the church order.[257] On
29 December van den Corput acknowledged the receipt of Saravia's letter
as well as a letter from Franciscus Junius with an article against Gualterus.
As far as the "extract from Gualtero" itself was concerned, Hackius had
informed van den Corput that this was written and translated with a view
to publication. He would give up the latter scheme and consult with
Saravia about it. Very justly van den Corput concluded that Coolhaes had
indeed played a major part in the affair but that he had been strongly supported by Hackius: "so they are hand and glove". Indeed Hackius and a
third unnamed person had eaten with Coolhaes, something which ought
not to have happened.[258] The situation was also naturally very unpleasant
for Saravia personally: his closest colleague, Hackius, was playing a
double role in the dispute. On February 26, 1583 (stilo veteri) Helmichius
wrote to Arent Cornelisz from Utrecht, having heard that Coolhaes had

---

[255] GDB, fol. 186r; 14 December 1582.
[256] GDB, fol. 187r; 27 December 1582.
[257] GAD, Nr. 112. Cf. p. 76.
[258] WMV, III; 2, 231 f.

prepared an article against the synod of Middelburg's verdict but that Saravia had hindered this plan. The writer of the letter rejoiced at this, but he thought: "If Hackius carries on so insolently, although he will cause trouble for a pretty long time, he will undoubtedly be brought down by his own madness. When his powers are broken as the snow melts before the sun, he will eventually be worsted for the thoughtfulness and honesty shown him by Saravia, either to repent or, like the man who incites him [Coolhaes], be declared suspended from his office".[259] It can be seen which role Saravia was destined for by the Reformed ministers,—that of the powerful opponent of Coolhaes, Hackius and the local government of Leiden. This meant that he was already very quickly playing another part than that for which Orange had cast him, which we may recall was that of the man who, by his personal prestige, was to bring the Leiden quarrels to an end.[260] Instead of this he himself became increasingly involved in the dispute. This went so far that the consistory asked the magistrates to get the professor Holmannus, Daneau's successor, "to act as an arbiter or mediator to examine what has been discussed in writing between Coolhaes and Saravia in the hope of thus promoting the peace of the churches".[261] Holmannus who soon after his arrival in Leiden had acquired the name of being doctrinally unsound[262] and who "considering his poor reputation" was not expected to last long in the town,[263] refused the task, appealing to the promise made on his entry into office not to interfere in municipal and church disputes.[264]

Saravia continued to be involved with the struggle even after his appointment as professor. The consistory tried continually but in vain to get the magistrates to act against the formidable pamphleteer. Thus on 18 October 1584 Saravia and Christiaan van de Wouwer handed over "a certain

---

[259] WMV, III; 4, 37.

[260] It is certain that he undertook nothing at the particular synod of South Holland in The Hague (June 1583) where the Coolhaes matter came up for discussion. Hackius appeared there with the elder Joris Andriesz, as Coolhaes' advocate. On material and procedural grounds they contested the legality of the latter's condemnation in Middelburg and excommunication at Haarlem as well as the defence of the excommunication published in the name of the provincial synod, Cort eenvoudich ende warachtich verhael. H. C. Rogge, Coolhaes, I, 242 f. The synod declared itself incompetent to pass judgement on the Haarlem decisions, which were personally defended by A. Cornelisz. The possibility was raised of a ruling by impartial arbiters. Saravia attended the meeting "in zijn privé naem" when Hackius and Andriesz had returned to Leiden and had not complied with the request to appear again at the synod. Reitsma, Acta, II, 224 f.

[261] GDB, fol. 217r; 16 June 1583.

[262] On 5 December 1582 H. van den Corput wrote about this to Arent Cornelisz and suggested that Saravia should be sure to keep him and the consistory informed as necessary. WMV, III; 2, 226.

[263] H. van den Corput to Arent Cornelisz, 2 February 1583. Ibid., 236. For Holmannus: BWPG, IV, 176-178.

[264] GDB, fol. 217r; 16 June 1583.

article by Caspar Coolhaes—addressed to the ministers of God's Word
and elders of the church of Christ in Leyden'', seven full pages in length.
The magistrates naturally had no intention of doing anything about it but
they expressed themselves ready to cooperate if the ministers "knew of
some means and had a sure hope of uniting Caspar Coolhaes with the
church''.[265] A few weeks later the consistory decided that Saravia and the
elder Pieter Bloec should ask Coolhaes for a duplicate copy of "his complaint recently delivered to the consistory so that it could be proceeded
with as is necessary''.[266] At the end of the year came the troubles with
Hackius in Medemblik which we described earlier.[267] After his return the
latter revealed himself increasingly as a partisan of Coolhaes and an ardent
supporter of the state's authority in the church and thus an opponent of
the independent exercise of church discipline. On 25 January 1585
Saravia wrote to Arent Cornelisz that Hackius had preached "against the
discipline" and "that on the following Sunday Christianus [van de
Wouwer] had preached the opposite of what Hackius had preached''. The
magistrates had intimated that, apart from the Compromise of 1580, the
doctrine and order of the church in Leiden ought not to differ from that of
other churches. Saravia left no doubt as to his own position: "I have said
to some of Hackius' friends who are of the council and the burgomasters
that if he inveighs against the church discipline any more, I will take sides
against him''.[268] As if he had not already taken sides long ago'! Instead of
stopping his ranting, however, Hackius expressed himself even more
fiercely in the pulpit. He boasted in the consistory of having said in the
pulpit "that, like Popery, the synod had smallpox''.[269] The long drawn
out conflict ended in Hackius' suspension on 5 November 1586.[270]

It must be noted that the attitude towards England and Leicester also
played a part in this controversy. This is apparent in the reasons for
Hackius' suspension. He was "suspended for his false and seditious
teaching both against the English and against the churches''.[271] It appears
from the transactions of the consistory that the events of October 1587
were already casting their shadows far in advance. On 22 May 1586
Hackius claimed in the consistory that the town pensionary, Paulus Buys,
had declared about the magistrates "that they would in time oppose the
synod and the intentions of his excellency [Leicester]''. At this Christiaan
van de Wouwer had warned: do not let his excellency know. He could
come and take the town. But Hackius had said defiantly "they resisted the

---

[265] GDB, fol. 310; 19 October 1584.
[266] KB, fol. 3r; 25 November 1584.
[267] p. 55 f.
[268] GAD, Nr. 112.
[269] KB, fol. 18v; 22 May 1586. See also KB, fol. 19v; 27 May 1586.
[270] KB, fol. 29.
[271] KB, fol. 26v, 27r; 28 October 1586.

Spaniard and the French, they were also ready to resist the Englishman even though not one stone was left upon another".[272] Hackius further boasted of having said in the pulpit "Rather the Spanish Inquisition than the Genevan Discipline and my masters applauded and would so again should the occasion arrise".[273] These and similar threats were indications of the tensions which were to break out a year later. They make us aware how church disputes in the Netherlands and the development of international political and military relations were closely bound up with each other. We also get an impression of the proud self-assurance with which a Holland town fancied it could play its part in the whole affair.

Saravia was not directly involved in this course of events but his name was mentioned in it. The magistrates who, just as with Coolhaes, continued to pay Hackius' salary after his dismissal, were accused by the consistory of insulting remarks about the English governor. The latter was said to have "expelled Prof. de Saravia from the town". This remark might well have been to do with Saravia's frequent absence in connection with his political activities.

Finally Saravia was again concerned with the formal dispute in church law between the Leiden congregation and the provincial synod of Holland. The Leideners considered that this body was not competent to decide on an excommunication.[274] Leiden had not been consulted in the decision, representatives of its congregation had been absent because the magistrates had forbidden them to attend the synod in Haarlem.[275] The only sign of life from the church of Leiden had consisted in "a small letter [written by Petrus Hackius] sent to the synod late in the evening just before the excommunication".[276] As chairman of an arbitral committee Saravia tried to mediate between the parties.[277] The matter came up for detailed discussion at the national synod at The Hague (1586) where finally a reconciliation took place between Coolhaes and the synod: the excommunicant was once more received as a member of the church.[278]

In that year Coolhaes and Hackius exchanged roles. Now the indefatigable Coolhaes, whose excommunication had been lifted, agitated on behalf of the suspended Hackius.[279] After he had first got his wife to

---

[272] KB, fol. 18v; 192; 22 May 1586.

[273] *Ibid.*

[274] Although they held opposite views on the material side of this affair, Hackius and van de Wouwer together represented the Leiden congregation in defending in the national synod at The Hague its formal objection in church law against the procedure. Rutgers, *Acta,* 538, 565 f.

[275] Reitsma, *Acta,* I, 97.

[276] Rutgers, *Acta,* 578.

[277] *Ibid.,* 565 f.

[278] *Ibid.,* 588 f.

[279] KB, fol. 33v; 22 February 1587.

present a letter of accusations in the consistory,[280] but had repeatedly
refused to come there himself to answer for this,[281] yet declaring himself
ready for a meeting in his own house or in another private dwelling, the
meeting of the consistory appointed the house of the rector magnificus of
the university, Saravia, for the purpose.[282] Here on 20 March in an
amicable and fraternal conversation, Coolhaes admitted his guilt: he had
written the letter in haste without having been properly informed. He
wanted henceforward to live in unity with the consistory. They parted on
good terms. The surroundings of Saravia's home had evidently had a
calming effect on the emotions.[283]

### e. *Disputation with Coornhert*

On 8 November 1582,[284] at about the same time that Saravia came to
the North Netherlands, Coornhert's *Proeve van de Heidelbergse Catechismus*[285]
was published. Immediately the wish was expressed on the church's side,
"that someone from among the ministers of Holland would answer
Coornhert's dung with briefly outlined reasons and arguments so as to
check him somewhat".[286] It emerges from two important documents in
the archives of the Reformed congregation in Delft that Saravia was quickly involved in the opposition to Coornhert. The first is a memorandum
from Arent Cornelisz to the burgomaster of Haarlem, Nicolaas van der
Laan, dated 10 February 1583, which does not indeed mention Saravia's
name but which alludes to him in the suggestion that the States be requested to put Coornhert's work into the hands of the "doctors and professors in theology at Leiden"[287] to be examined, Coornhert's deviations
from Scripture summed up in propositions and, if he abides by his asser-
tions, to summon him to justify himself against the Leiden theologians in
the presence of delegates from the States.[288] The next day the States made
a decision. The book had to be given for examination to Reinier
Donteclock, minister at Delft, and Coornhert's subsequent reply as well as

---

[280] KB, fol. 33v; 3 March 1587.

[281] KB, fol. 34r; 35r; 5 and 17 March 1587.

[282] KB, fol. 35r; 17 March 1587.

[283] KB, fol. 35v; 20 March 1587.

[284] B. Becker, *Bronnen tot de kennis van het leven en de werken van D. V. Coornhert* (The Hague,
1928) 86. For Coornhert: B. Becker, "Coornhert, de 16de-eeuwsche apostel der volmaakbaarheid", *Ned. AK* (1926) 59-84; H. Bonger, *De motivering van de godsdienstvrijheid bij
Dirck Volckertszoon Coornhert* Arnhem, s.a. with an extensive bibliography; Id., *Leven en werk
van Dirk Volckertsz Coornhert* Amsterdam, 1978.

[285] *Proeve van de Heydelbergsche Catechismo, omme te verstaen Of die voortghecomen is uyte Godtlijcke
Schrift, dan wt het menschelijcke vernuft. Wt gheghecen tot allemans oordeel ende waerschouwinghe door
D. V. Coornhert* in: *Werken*, II, 223-236; III, 465-478.

[286] H. van den Corput to A. Cornelisz, 5 December 1582. *WMV*, III; 2, 227.

[287] At this time Saravia did not yet belong to the second category.

[288] GAD, Nr. 80.

the rejoinder of the examiners were to be printed. The magistrates of Haarlem were instructed to prevent the printing and distribution of the work.[289] The second, more detailed document is a petition, signed by Saravia, Cornelisz and Reinier Donteclock, directed to the States of Holland, in which a summary of Coornhert's attack on the catechism is given. Appended to the piece is a copy of a remonstrance written by the Delft ministers in answer to Coornhert's booklet. The States were asked to declare on some occasion in its assembly its responsibility for the doctrine of the Catechism.[290] This petition was written probably in August 1583, for the reception of the document is mentioned in the resolutions of the States on 26 August.[291]

Beforehand, on 11 June in the particular synod of South Holland at The Hague, Cornelisz had already reported on the measures he and Donteclock had taken against Coornhert's tract. Everything there depended on Saravia and the synod only dealt with the matter once he had arrived. On 30 June it was reported that the States had ordained "that D. Saravia and one of the ministers of Delft should extract certain theses from the said books which were found to be in conflict with the truth of God's Word taught in our churches so that this being demonstrated to the States they may themselves deal with the aforesaid Coornhert for his conversion or rebuttal, but so far this has not happened. It was therefore the request of those of Delft that, by the wish and ordination of the synod, D. Saravia and (so the synod thought proper) the ministers of Delft should first take this in hand without undertaking to make any written defence against Coornhert's books which would be an endless task". The meeting at which Coornhert had to defend himself was to be open to all the ministers of South Holland so that they might be instructed on any point of doctrine in which they held a variant opinion. Should the States not deal with the matter then the Provincial Council of Holland was to be approached.[292] However the States did act. They decided that "Coornhert ought to be heard before the States or its representatives and those of the Council at the same time as the ministers on what the same Coornhert has published in some books to the great contempt of Christ's congregation and God's Holy Word and doctrine".[293]

Coornhert himself had from the outset pressed for a disputation with the ministers in the presence of the States.[294] On 30 August he was informed of the decision.[295] The majority of the towns responded favourably to the

---

[289] *RStH 1583*, 35.
[290] GAD, Nr. 80.
[291] *RStH 1583.*
[292] Reitsma, *Acta*, II, 256 f.
[293] *RStH 1583*, 374 f.
[294] Coornhert, *Werken*, III, 431-432c.
[295] *RStH 1583*, 327.

request to assign representatives to attend the disputation.[296] On 10 October the States notified the burgomasters and magistrates of the towns of their decision to hear Coornhert and the ministers in The Hague. Deputies from the nobility and the towns were requested to be present on 24 October. A request also went out from the States to Saravia, Cornelisz and Donteclock, "on the 24 of this month, to appear then at the Inn in The Hague and to begin work the next day".[297]

The disputation began on 27 October at 8 o'clock in the morning[298] in the chamber of the Upper Council in the hearing of six members of that council, one member of the Court of Holland, and eight members of the States of whom six represented the towns.[299] The recorder A. Genieten appeared as notularius for the States as did Jan Wolf for Saravia and Govert van Rijswijck for Coornhert.[300] On each occasion Cornelisz would read out the article from Coornhert's *Proeve* which was to be disputed. The only spokesman for the ministers was Saravia[301] "with whom we the undersigned were unworthily associated", as the ministers of Delft wrote later.[302] Both in the oath of the disputants and that of the notularies the promise had been taken to keep the proceedings completely secret and not to divulge any part directly or indirectly.[303]

The disputation was interrupted on 3 November because Coornhert was called back to Haarlem because of his wife's serious illness. It was resumed on 28 November and finally concluded on 1 December. The publishers of Coornhert's works later declared "that this public disputation or conference was very amicably and reasonably conducted".[304] Cornelisz and Donteclock had been assigned to Saravia as assistants, as Coornhert later scoffingly remarked, to note down everything and "to prompt and to help him consider". He said the same also of a large number of ministers who sat behind Saravia during the disputation and who "quite openly" supported him when he needed it.[305]

We can deal briefly with the disputation itself[306] which lasted in all for eight days—there was no meeting on Sunday, 30 October. We are not to

---

[296] Becker, *Bronnen*, 86-90.

[297] *RStH 1583*, 469 f.

[298] Coornhert, *Werken*, III, 435c. J. H. de St[oppelaar], "De Leydsche Magistraat, Dirk Volkertszoon Coornhert en professor Adrianus Saravia. Een theologisch dispuut in de zestiende eeuw," *Leidsche Studenten-almanak*, (1851)135-170; On the disputation: H. Bonger, *Leven en werk van D. V. Coornhert* (Amsterdam, 1978) 111-118.

[299] *Ibid.*, 436a.

[300] *Ibid.*, 436c.

[301] *Ibid.*, 435d.

[302] *Wederlegginghe eens boecxkens... Ghedaen bij eenighe Dienaren der Kercke Christi tot Delff* Delft, 1585.

[303] Coornhert, *Werken*, III, 436ab.

[304] *Ibid.*, 430.

[305] *Ibid.*, 449a.

[306] Note 208.

think so much of what we nowadays call "a dialogue". The other side's propositions were attacked from positions of unshakable prejudice. The listeners must have been wearied by the endless repetitions. "The people listened in silence", says one of Coornhert's letters.[307] Coornhert complained that he was continually interrupted by Saravia and taxed with "a multitude of lengthy texts".[308] After he had returned from Haarlem on 27 November,[309] he did not get a word in; Saravia spoke for four days without a pause.

The real point of the controversy turned on the doctrine of justification by imputation which Saravia defended and Coornhert attacked. Against imputed righteousness the humanist opposed what he called actual righteousness. This was the habitual and perfect righteousness which is given us already in this life by Christ's grace. Christian love, a small thing in the beginning, grows daily "until the time that it will have come to the highest level of perfection which has been prescribed for us in God's Law".[310] Whoever is "truly, not falsely or imputatively" restored by Christ's blood, is no longer sick, "sin and doubt have left him". He dies according to the flesh and is brought to life in the spirit "in truth, not by imputation".[311] "If Christ is not to have died and suffered in vain this must happen in everyone".[312]

Against this Saravia replied with the answer 62 of the Heidelberg Catechism, that even our best works in this life are imperfect "The works of the faithful, which they do out of faith in Christ with a childlike affection towards God their Heavenly Father, are not examined according to the vigour and strictness of the Law, but according to the gracious acceptance of God's good pleasure in Christ, and as if they are accounted holy and perfect in him".[313] He argued, "that the faithful will receive perfect salvation from all sins, not here in this life, but hereafter in the other life where they look for a new heaven and a new earth, according to God's promise, where they will live in righteousness".[314]

To summarize we can say that Coornhert defended a doctrine of habitual and perfectionist justification whilst Saravia voiced the forensic and eschatological view of the doctrine. The disputation marked a point in the eternal struggle between Humanism and Reformation. The doctrine of justification defended by Saravia can indeed be called that of the Reformation in general. However, from the fact that he was not led into antino-

---

[307] Coornhert, *Werken,* III, 449c.
[308] *Ibid.,* 449c.
[309] *Ibid.,* 461c.
[310] *Ibid.,* 439b.
[311] *Ibid.,* 447b.
[312] *Ibid.,* 447c.
[313] *Ibid.,* 444c.
[314] *Ibid.,* 452b.

mianism by his opponent's moralism and perfectionism, but yet gave a clear exposition of the importance of the Law,[315] shows how deeply rooted his thinking was in the tradition of Calvinist doctrine. After Saravia had gone on speaking for four days, the States had had enough. They broke up the conference and directed the participants to exchange their further arguments in writing.[316] They delivered no verdict. The government's representatives had already declared beforehand that they were to be no judges in the matter itself but only in the following of the proceedings.[317]

Saravia also had an active part initially in the subsequent developments. Again some letters preserved in the archives of the Reformed congregation at Delft bear witness to this. On 27 December 1583 almost four weeks after the conclusion of the disputation, he wrote from The Hague that the method of rebuttal and rejoinder did not seem to him advisable because the articles would become increasingly voluminous. He himself had begun a systematic rejoinder to Coornhert's arguments and promised to send what he had written within a day or two so that Cornelisz and Donteclock could continue it. But he was not minded to alter anything in what he had written nor to put his name to a declaration in which not all Coornhert's arguments had been answered. If the two ministers were willing to help him in this he would be grateful to them. "Otherwise God will help me".[318] Despite the invitation to cooperation Saravia's letter gives the impression that he really preferred to handle the matter himself. This impression is reinforced by a letter of 27 December 1583 which is recognizable as Donteclock's handwriting. It is probably a reply by return to Saravia's letter. From this it emerges that the writer was with Saravia in The Hague at the time in order to ask the States for Coornhert's rejoinder. This had already been delivered to Saravia who had promised to come to Delft in a few days for consultation. To their surprise, however, he had changed his mind. Apparently he had no need of this consultation and wanted rather to deal with the matter on his own. Why? After all the States had committed it to the three of them. Let him indeed finish the work alone. But then it would have been better that he had also received the commission on his own; they could have been saved a great deal of trouble. But again if Saravia were to write the said discourse alone then his piece ought still to be compared with the text of the disputation itself. He had indeed done the talking alone in The Hague, but their names also appeared in the acta.

---

[315] "...Wij antwoorden daar op dat de Wet gegeven is, eerst omme dat wy daar uyt ons selven souden leeren kennen, en daar na ons toevlucht genomen hebbende tot Christum, hebben onszelven bevonden so onvolmaackt, dat wy nyet machtig en zijn het minste jota vande Wet te volbrengen, vanden vloeck der selver verlost souden werden, ende voorts ons leven daar na aan te stellen". *Ibid.*, 444a.

[316] *Ibid.*, 461d.

[317] *Ibid.*, 435d.

[318] GAD, Nr. 80; Doc. VI.

Moreover, Coornhert would object to a rejoinder from Saravia alone. Had he not boasted during the disputation that he had to be able to take on the three theologians on his own?[319] It appears from this long letter, written in an indignant tone, that there was no lack of personal ambition in the business on the part either of Saravia or the Delft ministers.

On 15 March 1585 Saravia wrote to Cornelisz that many people wanted the text of the disputation at The Hague to be published. The Leiden consistory was probably included among the many such. Saravia repeated that Coornhert had asked permission from the Leiden magistrates to be allowed to move to Leiden to spend the rest of his life "in literarum otio". He had promised to refrain from writing at least provided he was not compelled to defend himself by the writings of opponents. It was anticipated that the magistrates would seek the professors' advice.[320]

It emerges from a letter of Saravia's, written on 22 April, that the two ministers continued to complain that he did not inform them of his actions—he had evidently been in The Hague again. This time he apologized; he had expected that Wolf, his secretary at the disputation, had informed them. He further reported that Coornhert had also tried to involve Justus Lipsius in the dispute. He had asked the latter for a permission to translate his work *De Constantia*. Lipsius had replied that his book had appeared in public and that therefore anyone was at liberty to translate it. Coornhert had then answered him that he took exception to some passages in Lipsius' work. He therefore wanted to delay his translation until he had first had an opportunity to talk to the author about several points. Lipsius had rejoindered that his work had in general been well received but that he was naturally in favour of improvements. In a third letter Coornhert had then specified his objections to the work in question. These applied to Lipsius' views on God's providence and free will. He had repeated his desire for an interview. Saravia did not yet know what Lipsius had then replied. But he would certainly let them have the latter's third reply to look at before it was sent.[321]

From a number of indications it appears that Saravia was on familiar terms with Lipsius. He greatly admired this professor. Just how well he knew Lipsius emerges from a letter, no less than nine pages in length, which he was to write to Archbishop Bancroft 21 years after leaving the Netherlands.[322] In this he painted a picture of the learned philologist whose stoical attitude to life led him rarely to take sides. He later returned

---

[319] *Ibid.*

[320] GAD, Nr. 112; Doc. XII.

[321] *Ibid.* Coornhert's three letters: *Inv. Lipse,* Nrs. 84.03.18, 84.04.09, 84.04.15.

[322] 20 October 1608. BL. Add. Ms 28571, Nr. 53, fols. 214-219; published by Henri van Crombruggen, "Een brief van Adriaan Saravia over Lipsius en "Het Huis der Liefde," *De vergulden Passer,* (1950), 110-117; Doc. XLV.

to the Roman Catholic church but during Saravia's time in Leiden he had been sympathetic towards the sect known as "The Family of Love". It was at Lipsius' home that Saravia had become acquainted with its leader, Hendrik Barrefelt.[323]

We do not know of any work of Saravia's against Coornhert, whether written in collaboration with others or not. Otherwise the matter continued to occupy him. On 11 March 1590, more than two years after his move to England, he was to ask Cornelisz to send copies of the papers which had been used in the preparations for the disputation.[324] The matter continued to be a subject for discussion in the Netherlands. When in January 1585 the question of the desirability of catechising arose in the Leiden consistory, it was decided to wait "until the case against Coornhert is completed. Therefore Saravia is to be admonished to undertake that this will happen as soon as possible. Christiaan [van de Wouwer] and Platevoet will inform him of this and once this has been done they will discuss the matter together".[325] The States of Holland had little interest in these disputes and checked the exchange of rebuttals and rejoinders. Also, contrary to their express command before the start of the conference, they would not agree to the request from Saravia and the Delft ministers to publish the proceedings of the disputation held at The Hague. Consequently Cornelisz and Donteclock produced their *Wederlegghinghe*.[326] In the preface, dated 14 April 1585, they let it be known that here they speak "for ourselves, in as much as we saw our colleague de Saravia so busy in both the school and church at Leiden, that he could not contribute to this".[327] The desirability of a publication of the proceedings was indeed expressed at the national synod in The Hague,[328] but nothing more came of it until the seventeenth century. These proceedings first appeared in 1617, published by Jasper Tournay at Gouda.[329]

---

[323] It appeared that Lipsius, who rarely passed an opinion on religion in public, and who wrote in such a way that the reader did not know, "num illa quae scripsit profecta sint ab homine Christiano an ab ethnico", said that he had nothing against the Reformed religion, but when asked why then he never took part in the Lord's Supper, answered: "O tu foelix homo es, qui coniugem nactus es tecum in religione consentientem: mea mihi adversatur, quotidianam pacem et domesticam cum uxore colere me oportet, si vivere volo" (*ibid.*, 114) Lipsius maintained relations with the House of Love. See p. 150-152.

[324] GAD, Nr. 112; Doc. XXXVI.

[325] KB, fol. 6; 25 January 1585.

[326] Note 303.

[327] *Wederlegginghe*, 17 f.

[328] Rutgers, *Acta*, 553 f.

[329] *Disputatie over den Catechismus van Heydelberg, openbaarlijck voor den Volcke ghehouden op 't Hof van 's-Gravenhage in Hollandt Anno 1583. Ter Ordonnantie van de Mog. H. H. Staten van Hollandt ende West-Vrieslandt/ende sijne Princelijcke Excell. Wilhelmus van Nassouwen, in 't bywesen ende bestieren van hare Gecommitteerde Tusschen Dirck Volkaersz. Coornhert: ende Saravia D. inde Theologie, gheassisteert met Arent Cornelisz. ende andere Predicanten.* Gouda, 1617.

## 7. IN THE POLITICAL FIELD

### a. *Saravia the Anglophile*

His residence in Leiden offered Saravia the anglophile many opportunities for meeting and getting to know English intellectuals. Some of these visited the town and its university whilst passing through, others stayed for longer or shorter periods. Thus on 1 March 1586 the English poet Geoffrey Whitney paid a visit to the rector magnificus.[330] George Benedicti Werteloo, who lodged with Saravia,[331] was indeed a Dutchman from Haarlem but he had previously studied in Cambridge. George Gilpin, former agent for the Merchant Adventurers in Antwerp, who had been charged by Walsingham in December 1585 to prepare for Leicester's arrival in the Netherlands and for this purpose "to confer with some of the best affected patriots there about some plot to be presented unto him, as well for the removing of the great abuses reigning there as also for the establishing of some well-settled government...",[332] had a conversation with Saravia on 29 August 1586. Was this conversation really concerned exclusively with his signing of the university's album recensionum?[333]

Gilpin became an important personage. At the request of Leicester, whose secretary he had been, and of Saravia he received the privileges of a member of the university.[334] As one of the two English members of the Council of State he was directly involved in Dutch politics. Otherwise he was extremely well acquainted with Dutch culture: in 1587 he had translated the famous anti-Roman Catholic work of Marnix van Sint Aldegonde into English under the title *The Beehive of the Romishe Churche.*[335] When he settled in Leiden,[336] Saravia got the permanent opportunity of gathering up-to-date information about English policy towards the Netherlands. This policy was always of the utmost interest to him. Already in February 1582 he had brought a request from Ghent to the secretary of state, Sir Francis Walsingham, who had tried in vain for years to persuade Queen Elizabeth to lend military support to Orange and the Dutch in their struggle against Spain.[337] He received a letter of introduction from Roland York in which the latter wrote of Saravia: "I find him so well affectioned to her Majesty and her realm, that I desire you to give him credit in that he shall treat with you, and to qualify everything according to your pro-

---

[330] Van Dorsten, *Poets,* 124.

[331] *Ibid.,* 147.

[332] C. Read, *Mr. Secretary Walsingham and the policy of Queen Elizabeth* (3 vols., Oxford, 1925) III, 134.

[333] *Album Recensionum,* 1586.

[334] Van Dorsten, *Poets,* 146 f.

[335] *Ibid.*

[336] *Ibid.,* 146-148.

[337] Read, *Walsingham,* I, 306-422.

ceedings past and that is to come". This utterly unreliable soldier[338] then added: "I and others have spoken with him at large such as are affectioned to the Religion. You may appoint some time of your most leisure to confer with him at large".[339] This recommendation shows that Saravia's sympathies for England and his loyalty to the Queen were well known. He was amongst the advocates of Elizabeth's military intervention in the Netherlands. It is reasonable to suppose that his visit to the secretary of state in February 1582 was of a political nature.

From getting to know each other the two men kept in touch. Saravia acted as liaison officer between the Dutch Calvinists and the Prince of Orange on one hand and Queen Elizabeth's advisers on the other. He corresponded with Walsingham in the summer of 1583. He was the intermediary in the sending of diplomatic communications from Orange to the secretary of state. With these he took the opportunity to inform the latter about political and military developments in the South Netherlands, particularly about the unsuccessful Spanish attack on Ghent which he had witnessed himself.[340] For the time being the Queen remained deaf to such requests for military aid to the Netherlands. When Walsingham received York's letter the remarkable love story of Elizabeth and the French prince, François d'Anjou, brother to the French king, Henry III, to whom the States General had entrusted the sovereignty of the Netherlands in 1581, had just come to an end. Walsingham had witnessed how, on 22 November 1581 in the presence of the French ambassador, Leicester and himself, the Queen had put on "a superb piece of acting" in kissing Anjou and saying to him: "You may write this to the king, that the duke of Anjou shall be my husband".[341] But she quickly changed her mind and her old anti-French phobias reappeared.[342]

---

[338] While serving with the English volunteers in the Netherlands, York took part in a plot whose purpose was to hand over Ghent to Parma. For this he remained imprisoned in Brussels until that city also fell into Parma's hands in 1586. Astonishingly enough this man, who was distrusted in the Netherlands on account of his Roman Catholicism, again acquired opportunities for his dubious practices, after he had returned to the Netherlands with Leicester's troops. In January 1587 he betrayed Zutphen to the Spaniards. Thereafter he remained in Spanish service. *DNB*, LXIII, 337.

[339] *CSPF, January 1581—April 1582*, Nr. 538.

[340] PRO. Sp. 83/17, Nr. 5; Doc. IV. See also p. 46.

[341] J. B. Black *The Reign of Elizabeth 1558-1603* (2nd ed., Oxford, 1959) 355; C. Read, *Lord Burghley and Queen Elizabeth* (pb. ed., London, 1965) 257 f.

[342] Ch. Wilson, *Queen Elizabeth and the Revolt of the Netherlands* (London and Basingstoke, 1970) 74. For Elizabeth's policy towards the Netherlands see further: John Neale, "Elizabeth and the Netherlands 1586-7," in: Id., *Essays in Elizabethan History,* 1958; R. B. Wernham, "English Policy and the Revolt of the Netherlands," in: *Britain and the Netherlands. Papers delivered to the Oxford-Netherlands Conference,* J. S. Bromley and E. H. Kossmann, ed. (London, 1960) 1-40; R. B. Wernham, *Before the Armada. The growth of English Foreign Policy 1485-1588* (London, 1966) 283-405.

Elizabeth had little sympathy for the Dutch revolt in itself.[343] Her efforts were directed towards a balance of power, a situation in which neither Spain nor France would possess a predominant influence in these territories. To engage in a war with Spain was dangerous, there were also internal reasons; until her execution in 1587 the imprisoned Mary Stuart remained the hope of Roman Catholics in England. She hoped for a continuation of Spanish rule in the Netherlands but with a respecting of the religious and political freedoms of the population. However, when, after 1583, the tension mounted between Spain and England and when, after the deaths of Anjou (June 1584) and Orange (July 1584), an embassy from the States General had been sent to the French King, Henry III to offer him the sovereignty over the Netherlands, an offer which the prince declined, Elizabeth changed her policy. The bugbear of French sovereignty over these territories decided her to give military aid. She had no thought of accepting of sovereignty as the Calvinists wanted. Nevertheless the latter continued to cherish the notion and repeatedly showed their longings for this. Saravia was one of their spokesmen.

On 20 August 1585, three days after the fall of Antwerp whose loss sealed that of the South Netherlands[344] the treaty of Nonsuch was signed in which the Queen undertook to send 5000 infantry and 1000 cavalry under the command of "some person of respect and quality", who in the Netherlands would bear the scarcely significant title of Governor General and who would act in consultation with the Council of State. As security England was to receive the strategically important ports of Flushing and The Brill. Philip Sidney, Walsingham's son-in-law and Leicester's nephew, became governor of Flushing, Thomas Cecil, the Lord High Treasurer's son, governor of The Brill.[345] As commander-in-chief of the English forces and governor general, Robert Dudley, Earl of Leicester, landed in Flushing on 20 December 1585.[346]

During his not very successful sojourn in the Netherlands he found one of his most devoted supporters in Saravia. The latter had already corresponded early in the year with the English ambassador William Davison. On 10 January he sent him a letter in which he commended the bearer as someone who was willing and able to be of service to Davison and who, in particular, could inform him about the payment of the troops and the abuses which had crept into this.[347] On 23 January Saravia in-

---

[343] Black, *Reign of Elizabeth*, 333-371; Wilson, *Queen Elizabeth;* Read, *Walsingham;* much source material in: *Relations politiques des Pays-Bas et de l'Angleterre.* J. B. M. C. Kervyn de Lettenhove, ed. 11 vols. Brussels, 1882-1900.

[344] On the question whether and how far Elizabeth's hesitant policy was a cause of Parma's victory: Wilson, *Queen Elizabeth,* 84 f.

[345] R. C. Strong and J. A. van Dorsten, *Leicester's Triumph* (Leiden/London, 1964) 25.

[346] Strong, *Leicester's Triumph,* 35.

[347] PRO. SP. 83/23, fol. 235r; Doc. VIII.

formed the ambassador about the pamphlets of a certain Johan van den Berge, to which Lipsius had drawn his attention. The author of these pamphlets, a Roman Catholic opponent of William of Orange, had let it be known in a letter that the English Queen did not have the means to help the Netherlands. In the time in which van den Berge was financial adviser to Charles V and Philip II, during Queen Mary's reign, he became convinced of England's financial weakness. Since, as a Catholic, the French king would certainly not risk a war with Spain to protect the heretics in the Netherlands, there was only one way left for van den Berge: the conclusion of peace with Spain.[348]

Like other Dutch Calvinists, Saravia was fiercely opposed to peace negotiations with Spain which Elizabeth began secretly and unofficially immediately after the signing of the Treaty of Nonsuch. On 8 June 1585 he wrote a detailed letter to Walsingham. He asked the secretary of state to urge the Queen to assume the rule of the Netherlands. In his opinion a union of the Netherlands and England under the Queen would be better than a military pact. This would serve not only Dutch interests but also England's safety against the "common enemies" Spain and France.[349] In support of the embassy that, under Oldenbarnevelt's leadership, was to arrive in England on 6 July to offer Elizabeth the sovereignty, Saravia declared that earlier offers of the same nature to the French king had been against the popular will, whilst this step was not disapproved of by the best of the people and by the ordinary citizen. Reading between the lines, we can see that at the least Oldenbarnevelt's mission was a controversial affair.[350]

The next day Saravia wrote to the Lord High Treasurer, Burghley, with whom he had had no more contact after his departure from Guernsey. In this plea he again connected England's destiny with the preservation of the United Provinces. "For the destruction of these provinces would lead to the downfall of England; if you protect them you will strengthen your own peace and welfare". An assumption of sovereignty was to be preferred to the conclusion of a treaty. Saravia proposed two measures to Burghley: provision must be made for an equal number of English and Dutch troops in the garrisons and sons of prominent Dutchmen must be brought to England and kept there as hostages until English authority had been permanently established in the Low Countries. He went on to philosophize on this matter that the success or failure of a government's policy depended for the most part on the government itself,

---

[348] In the same letter Saravia reported to the ambassador about Parma's confiscations of the goods of deceased Protestants in the Southern Netherlands. He promised to write later to Davison about the diversity of sects in the country. The letter gives the impression of a regular and serious contact between the two men. *CSPF*, August 1584-August 1585, 237.

[349] Wernham, *English Policy*, 33.

[350] PRO. SP. 84/2, fol. 72, 73, 74; Doc. XIII.

not on the people. A government which put the general welfare above its own interests would discover that the masses needed a firm rule over them. They would easily allow themselves to be ruled if no injustice was done to them and if their rulers permitted them to live according to their own laws. "For as this people is little inclined to do injustices to others, so it will as little tolerate injustice itself. Whoever was to be the ruler of these provinces would have to be moderate in nature. Whoever manages to bear calmly with the rustic and uncouth manners and customs of the people will easily be able to steer and guide them where he wishes". This letter is interesting because it is evident from it that in a period of almost seven years in the Netherlands Saravia observed Dutch people and society with shrewd perception but yet at some distance. He was convinced that the assignment of sovereignty to the wearer of the English crown would be salutary for this unrefined people. He wrote about this, as he indicated at the end of his letter, as though everything he had proposed to Burghley had already been decided and carried out.[351]

According to Saravia the cultural level of the Calvinist ministers was also not very high. When he sent a number of their letters containing requests of the same nature about the transfer of sovereignty to Davison who had in the meantime returned to England, he pointed out in his covering letter that the letters destined to be presented to her majesty for reading were not as finely written as her dignity demanded. He hoped that his apology—the ministers had not wanted to avail themselves of a more learned advocate—would be accepted. Otherwise he left no doubt about his agreement with the contents of the letters: "We desire nothing so much as to live under the rule of your most pious and most gracious queen". His remark on the approaching fall of Antwerp—"a people accustomed to luxury will not be able to endure hunger as this city did",[352] was probably a discreet hint to the queen pointing out English selfinterest in this.

b. *Leicester's supporter*

Attempts were also made in England to use the church to bring about English intervention in the Netherlands. On 19 July, urged by Leicester, Alexander Neville asked the Archbishop of Canterbury, John Whitgift, to use his influence with the queen to promote such a course of action. Whitgift did not accede to the request.[353]

The queen did not consider accepting the sovereignty of the Netherlands. The earlier mentioned despatch of some troops was enough for her. After the small army crossed the North Sea in October 1585, Leicester landed at Flushing on 20 December.[354] On 4 January 1586 the

---

[351] BL. LM. 45. Nr. 21, fol. 49; Doc. XIV. Strype, *Annals,* III; 2, 351-353.

[352] Leiden in 1574.

[353] BL. LM. 45. Nr. 45, fol. 98, 99.

[354] Strong, *Leicester's Triumph,* 35.

senate of Leiden University resolved that Saravia should go to The Hague to welcome the governor.[355] The latter's solemn entry took place there on 6 January.[356] On 12 January Leicester paid a short official visit to Leiden, followed nine days later by a longer and less formal one. He was received by the university on both these occasions. Naturally, as rector magnificus, Saravia played a part in this reception.[357] Shortly after this Leicester made a decision involving Saravia in the latter's reappointment as rector for the year 1586,[358] on the recommendation of the curators. Paulus Buys had previously stated his preference for an appointment by Maurice.[359] Was this already a sign of a certain tension[360] and were the subsequent parties already beginning to emerge?

In his difficult position in the Netherlands Leicester had certainly found one of his most devoted supporters in Saravia. As early as 6 May the rector had to accept a reprimand in the senate: he visited the governor general in his residence at Utrecht too frequently. Significantly it was said: "Saravia did not give all the reasons for his frequent absence, but only that he was summoned from time to time by the Earl of Leicester to report to him on church affairs; also that his excellency had often asked him about the circumstances and revenue of the university and that he had answered what he knew, or rather: that he did not know".[361] John James, the delegate court physician who had been the first English student at Leiden, acted as intermediary between Saravia and Leicester.[362]

From a letter subsequently written to the latter it is clear how greatly Saravia involved himself both with Leicester's internal affairs and with matters concerning church life in Utrecht. We learn that James had asked the advice of the Dutch ministers as to the form of service at Leicester's

---

[355] Molhuysen, *Bronnen*, 42; Van Dorsten, *Poets*, 116.

[356] Strong, *Leicester's Triumph*, 43-49.

[357] Van Dorsten, *Poets*, 116 f.

[358] Molhuysen, *Bronnen*, 43.

[359] *Ibid.*, 42.

[360] Van Dorsten, *Poets*, 128.

[361] Molhuysen, *Bronnen*, 44.

[362] Van Dorsten, *Poets*, 59, 107. The ministers of Leiden had sent their magistrates a detailed report on the preparation for the national synod which had begun in The Hague on 20 June. Saravia promised James to visit him from The Hague and bring him a copy of this report. After several remarks about people of less interest, Saravia asked him for travelling expenses for Jean des Mestres's son-in-law who wanted to quit Antwerp for Leiden with his family. The Des Mestres in question was undoubtedly the elder of the Walloon congregation at Leiden. Hessels, *ELBA*, II, Nr. 223. This letter from Saravia to James was not written between 20 and 23 June, as Hessels supposed, but probably on Saturday, 5 July. Saravia mentioned that he was to leave for The Hague on the next Monday. 5 July was the first Saturday after Monday, 30 June, which was the date of the invitation sent him to take part in the synod. Rutgers, *Acta*, 534. See also his signature, not reproduced by Hessels, *ELBA* 11, Nv. 224, under a letter from Jeremias Bastingius to James, dated 9 July 1586, apparently in support of the commendation which this contained of a refugee and his family from Antwerp. GHL. MS 2478/7; Doc. XVII.

court. Whilst the other ministers had advised the adoption of the form of service customary in the country, Saravia had advised the retention of the Book of Common Prayer. Leicester followed this advice.[363]

It further emerges from the letter that Saravia had been closely concerned with the differences between the congregation of St. Jacob, an independent congregation which had existed since the conversion to Protestantism of the church's pastor, Huibert Duifhuis,[364] and the established Reformed church. The congregation of St. Jacob would not subscribe to the confession. Its existence was a thorn in the flesh to the so-called consistorialists, but the Erasmian town magistrates used to attend its worship.[365] The Utrecht classis asked the Prince of Orange to send deputies to the town to mediate in the long drawn out dispute.[366] In May 1584, the minister Helmichius wrote letters in the same vein to his Delft colleague, Arent Cornelisz. Here, the name of Pierre de Villiers was mentioned amongst others. As court chaplain he as evidently thought to be able to get a favourable hearing from Orange on this matter.[367] In 1585 Saravia became involved in the affair. He also found the schism at Utrecht scandalous.[368] It emerges from a letter to Arent Cornelisz on 7 May 1585 that he considered the Calvinist consistory's proposals for a solution of the problem acceptable but that he thought that the language in which they were expressed was too sharp and insufficiently conciliatory. Furthermore the controversy was protracted because the stadholder of Utrecht, Josse de Zoete, Lord of Villiers, who was to be seriously wounded and captured at the battle of Amerongen a month later, was too much occupied with other matters (the conduct of the war).[369] Probably Pierre de Villiers had joined with Saravia in drawing up a memorandum containing proposals for the restoration of unity in the Reformed church in Utrecht. At any rate he wrote to James about "Villerius'[370] and my proposal to heal the schism in that church, endorsed by both our signatures''. We do not know what this

---

[363] Bodl. Ms Tanner 79, fol. 148, 11 May 1590; Doc. XXXVII.

[364] J. Wiarda, *Huibert Duifhuis, de prediker van St. Jacob.* Amsterdam, 1858; Id., "Huibert Duifhuis," *Kalender voor de Protestanten in Nederland,* II (1857) 199-227; see also: M. G. L. den Boer, "De Unie van Utrecht, Duifhuis en de Utrechtse religievrede," *Jaarboek Oud-Utrecht 1978,* 71-88.

[365] Wtenbogaert, *Kerckelicke Historie,* III, 47 ff., 56 f; Brandt, *Reformatie,* I, 618-621, 669-672; H. J. Royaards, "Proeve eener geschiedenis der Hervorming in de stad en provincie Utrecht," *Ned. A.,* VI (1846) 156-202; VII (1847) 244-261; Kernkamp, *Utrechtse Academie,* 23 f.

[366] J. Hania, *Wernerus Helmichius* (Utrecht, 1895) 103.

[367] *WMV,* III; 4, 47-49.

[368] "Schisma Traiectinae ecclesiae spero brevi componendum", wrote Saravia to Arent Cornelisz. on 15 March 1585. GAD, Nr. 112; Doc. XI.

[369] GAD, Nr. 112; Doc. XII.

[370] "...qui Villerii et meam sententiam de schismate illius ecclesiae curando nostris manibus signatam viderant". The words "Villerii et" are added in the margin. Bodl. Ms Tanner 79, fol. 148; Doc. XXXVII.

proposal contained. No more than Orange, who had worshipped with Duifhuis, did de Villiers have much sympathy for the Calvinist consistory of Utrecht.[371] Thus Orange's court chaplain and his former army chaplain probably proposed a union of the two congregations of a kind less harsh and rigorous than the one that took place a year later. In April 1586 Leicester made Utrecht his court capital. The situation was set fair for the Calvinists. The consistorialists seized the chance to put an end to a ministry which in their eyes was contrary to the confession. With the aid of the stadholder and the English governor the congregation of St. Jacob, quite against its will, was merged with the established Reformed church.[372] On 25 April 1586 the eighteen articles of union[373] were approved by the city council[374] and the following day at the town hall were confirmed and signed in the presence of the stadholder and of James as Leicester's deputy.[375]

Although Saravia did not perhaps entirely agree with the way in which the matter had been settled, he had been very glad that the schism was over. What happened next, however, aroused his horror, for the Calvinists went further. In June 1586 whilst James[376] and Saravia himself were fully occupied in the preparation for the national synod in The Hague, the greater part of the Utrecht city council, not without Leicester's knowledge, was dismissed and replaced by Calvinists. Floris Thin was also forced to leave.[377] From the Calvinist side this development could, not unjustly, be viewed as a freeing of the church from intolerable restriction by the civic authorities. But Saravia had friends among the Utrecht councillors and he correctly regarded the Calvinist coup d'état as an abuse of power. However, his position in the church and as Leicester's supporter led to his being seen as an accomplice by his friends amongst the councillors, including Thin. "Those who were formerly my friends have now become my enemies", he wrote to James. And was this not also the case with Paulus Buys, the difficult and ambitious man, who had been put into

---

[371] Boer, *Hofpredikers,* 144.

[372] On Leicester and the "democraten": J. den Tex, "De Staten in Oldenbarnevelts tijd," in: *Van Standen tot Staten. 600 Jaar Staten van Utrecht 1375-1975* (Utrecht, 1975) 57-64.

[373] P. Bor, *Vervolch vande Neerlandsche Oorloghen,* Book 21, 111v, 112r; D. G. Rengers Hora Siccama, *De geestelijke en kerkelijke goederen onder het canonieke, het gereformeerde en het neutrale recht* (Utrecht, 1905) 245-247.

[374] GA, Nr. 121. Vroedschapresoluties 1582-1590. Fol. 110v.

[375] *Ibid.,* Fol. 111r; Bor, *Vervolch,* 112; Wtenbogaert, *Kerckelicke Historie,* III, 5; Trigland, *Kerckelycke geschiedenissen* (Leiden, 1650) 343.

[376] "Ioannes Iames Doct. Medicus domesticus Excel. ipsius" appears on the list of names of the members of the synod immediately above the consultative member "Adrianus Saravia Doct. et Professor Theologiae Acad. Leid". Rutgers, *Acta,* 538. Along with Adolf van Meetkerken and Adriaan van der Mijle he kept Leicester informed of the synod's decisions and reported these to the States General on behalf of the governor. *Ibid.,* 619, 625 f.

[337] H. M. A. J. van Asch van Wijck, "De Graaf van Leicester in Utrecht," *Tijdschrift voor geschiedenis, Oudheden en Statistiek van Utrecht,* II (1836) 1-28.

prison at Leicester's instigation for quite different reasons?[378] He had
blamed Saravia for this and later, as curator of Leiden University, bore a
grudge against him and that although Saravia had defended and excused
Buys before Leicester, probably on behalf of the same university.[379]
Whether this interpretation does full justice to the facts is hard to determine, but it is clear that Saravia had been put into a paradoxical position
by his pro-English attitude and his support for Leicester.[380] He had great
sympathy for the Church of England, for its liturgy and church government, by Leicester was the strength and stay of the Dutch Calvinists!
Saravia was an advocate of a measure of state authority over the church,
but by his support of Leicester he came into conflict with precisely those
politicians in Holland and Utrecht who were also supporters of such an exercise of authority by the state. That he also in this period was no opponent of the exercise of such authority, is clear from a remarkable letter to
the Utrecht minister, Wernerus Helmichius. Its contents are known to us
because Saravia appended the text to that letter written to Wtenbogaert on
23 April 1612 to which we referred earlier.[381] The letter to Helmichius
must probably be dated in the second half of 1584 because it refers to the
so-called *Black Acts,* by which the royal supremacy over the church in
Scotland was restored in the spring and summer of the same year, against
the wish of the Presbyterians.[382] Saravia thought that the behaviour of the
Reformed churches in the Netherlands invited similar measures from the
authorities: "If we do not give the magistrates what is due to them, they
will take to themselves more than is their due". Helmichius was advised to
exercise a degree of toleration in doctrinal disputes and to consider, "what
is the authority of the civil magistrate in ecclesiastical affairs; whether it
can prescribe laws for the ministers and pastors of the churches in ecclesiastical matters, which the latter ought to obey, etc.".[383] There is still
no evidence from these words of any preference for the supremacy of the
state over the church such as he was later to defend in England. Indeed
Saravia also at this time continued to advocate the proper responsibility of
the church for the judgement of morals as became a good Calvinist. But
already in his Dutch period he ascribed to the state more authority over
the church than the Calvinist consistories wished to allow it.

It appears from the letter written to Walsingham on 24 December 1586

[378] On the relations between Leicester and Buys: L. J. Rogier, *Paulus Buys en Leicester.*
Nijmegen/Utrecht, 1948.
[379] *Ibid.,* 23.
[380] "...nam meum peccatum aliud non erat nisi Domini Comitis observantia et erga
Anglicam gentem amor et studium". BodL. Ms Tanner 79, fol. 148v; Doc. XXXVIII.
[381] p. 15.
[382] G. Donaldson, *The Scottish Reformation* (Cambridge, 1960) 211 ff.; J. H. S. Burgleigh,
*A Church History of Scotland* (repr. London/New York/Toronto, 1961) 202.
[383] *EE,* Nr. 181; Doc. XLVI.

by the diplomat Sir Thomas Wilkes that at the end of that year Saravia had had a conversation with this British statesman who was Killigrew's successor as English member of the Council of State and an advocate of Elizabeth's assumption of sovereignty over the Netherlands.[384] The conversation ranged over political issues concerning the relations between England and the Netherlands. One name that did crop up was that of Herman Moded, the pugnacious Calvinist minister, who on the instructions of the Utrecht magistrates had been to England to plead the Dutch cause there and to effect Leicester's speedy return. Saravia's opinion of Moded, shared by de Villiers, was extraordinarily unfavourable. According to them, he had been "the greatest mutine in all these countries" and "the only occasion of the loss of Ghent", the latter naturally in the period around 1578 when he was a minister in that town. Saravia must have known him as a colleague there and been sickened by his fanatical behaviour.[385]

Just how far from the truth was Saravia's defence against the charges made in the Leiden Senate, emerges from a letter written by him to Leicester on 5 February 1587. This is devoted entirely, not to church affairs, but to political. At that time Leicester was staying in England and Saravia considered it his duty to acquaint him with "all that has happened here", even if the news had long ago reached England by another route. He let him know how appalled they were in Leiden at the treachery of the English commanders, Yorke and Stanley, by which Zutphen and Deventer had fallen into Spanish hands,[386] and at the arrest of the Danish king's ambassador in his attempts to make peace with Parma. All who had the good of land and church at heart hoped for Leicester's speedy return. The latter had began the enterprise so successfully, so said Saravia with an optimism which defied the facts, that he would surely not throw in his hand out of disappointment at the opposition which he encountered? Must the good men, who incessantly prayed that God would incline the English queen to assume the sovereignty over these lands, suffer with the evil? Saravia adjured the governor to return to defend a great multitude of people against the "frenzy of the Roman tyrant".[387]

Leicester returned, but the rumours that Elizabeth was aiming at a peace with Spain continued to persist. Saravia saw in this a great threat from the side of the Roman church. He hoped that the governor would once more visit the towns of Holland to check the evil. For the rest, he

---

[384] For Wilkes see: *DNB*, XXI, 251-253.

[385] *CSP.FS*. June 1586-March 1587, 252 f. *Correspondentie van Robert Dudley graaf van Leycester en andere documenten betreffende zijn gouvernement-generaal in de Nederlanden 1585-1588*, H. Brugmans, ed. (3 vols., Utrecht, 1931) II, 9-12; G. J. Brutel de la Rivière, *Het leven van Hermannus Moded* (Haarlem, 1879) 199.

[386] On 28 January 1587.

[387] BL.CM. Galba, C XI, fol. 278; Doc. XIX.

himself, with the latter's agreement applied to the curators of the university for permission to spend the winter in England.[388] Notwithstanding the answer he received—it was not the first time that he had sought leave for a journey to England[389]—events quickly resulted in his being forced into a hurried departure.

Was he already at this time planning to leave the Netherlands himself? We may virtually conclude this on the basis of his offer to return to the churches in the Channel Islands. Indeed the offer was accepted but nothing ever came of it because the Leiden professor was so soon compelled to flee the Netherlands for other reasons.[390]

### c. *Role in the disturbances involving Leicester at Leiden (October 1587)*

The occasion for this flight were the disturbances involving Leicester in Leiden in October 1587 and Saravia's part in them. In view of W. Bisschof's account, documented as it is with much archival material,[391] we can deal briefly with the events themselves. In short it amounted to this. The Italian colonel, Cosmo de Pescarengis, a member of Leicester's force, had devised a plan to bring Leiden into the latter's hands by military occupation and imprisonment of the leading opponents in the town council among whom were the burgomaster, van der Werff, the town secretary van Hout and the former pensionary, Paulus Buys. In the first instance he had acted in concert with Nicholas de Maulde, son of a French captain who had behaved valiantly in the relief of the town in 1574, Leicester's partisan Hendrik van Zoest, the minister Christiaan van de Wouwer and the elder Jacob Valmaer. Other Leideners were involved in the plot at a later stage. Advice was also sought from the Fleming Adolf van Meetkerke, a member of the Council of State, and from Saravia. The authorities learned of the plans because the town councillor Andries Schot, instead of going to Utrecht to ask Leicester to make his entry into the town on 11 October, reported the matter to the council. After Pescarengis, who had already been arrested on 4 October because of his complicity in a sinister plot of Sonoy's in North Holland, Valmaer and de Maulde were also imprisoned on 11 October. At first the matter was dealt with by a commission of two deputies from the States of Holland and three representatives of the Leiden magistrates. Afterwards the three accused were condemned to death in a trial in which Maurice and Oldenbarnevelt took part and were executed on the scaffold. Eight people, including van der Wouwer, van Meetkerke and Saravia, were excluded from a pardon that was granted to the other accomplices. Accused of taking part in meetings at the house of Pescarengis on 4 October and of van Meetkerke on 9 Oc-

---

[388] Hessels, *ELBA*, II, Nr. 237.

[389] p. 63.

[390] De Schickler, *Les églises du refuge*, II, 438, n. 2.

[391] W. Bisschop, *De woelingen der Leicestersche partij binnen Leiden*. Leiden, 1864.

tober,[392] they were summoned on 16 December.[393] Naturally they did not appear. On 13 January 1588 they were sentenced to death in absence and exiled for life from Rijnland, The Hague and Haagambacht on pain of death should they return. Their possessions were confiscated.[394]

Saravia sought refuge in England, as did van Meetkerke. Bor contrives to let us know the following details about this: "Doctor Adrian Saravia, Professor of Theology in Leyden, being accused here had by now been imprisoned had not his son who was in The Hague and knew of this sent him warning secretly and had cautioned him of it in a letter so that he [Saravia] went immediately to The Hague by coach. There he was crossing the Vijverberg in great confusion but seeing some people whom he knew walking or standing in the square and supposing them to be opposed to him, he thought that they were going to detect him. So in great haste he walked along the lane beside Brunswick House and moreover hid himself and continued in hiding for several days in The Hague but afterwards made his way secretly thence to England".[395] It appears from a letter of 11 November from Leicester to the Leiden magistrates that Saravia did not in fact cross over to England directly, but that he first paid a visit to the governor who was then staying in Alkmaar. On this occasion he swore his innocence of the events at Leiden and handed over to Leicester a written remonstrance intended for the magistrates in which he summarized his arguments. This document was sent on to the magistrates by Leicester.[396]

If Bor's colourful account is in accordance with the facts, Saravia in all innocence knew nothing of the plot. He had returned unsuspectingly to Leiden and, if his son had not warned him, would probably have been arrested there. The town government thought otherwise. On 13 October they sent four deputies, including secretary van Hout, to the consistory, which, not altogether unreasonably, was regarded as a hot-bed of conspiratorial activity. Enquiries were made about the consistory's responsibility for or collaboration in the sending of Valmaer and van de Wouwer to Leicester. Had they not also despatched Saravia with instructions? The brethren naturally answered "no" to the questions,[397] but nevertheless the town government from the outset regarded Saravia as one of the chief accessories.

For his part, the latter vehemently disputed this charge in numerous explanations. In the remonstrance just mentioned he denied the right of the sheriff and bailiff to summon him: as a professor he shared in the privileges of the university and might lawfully only appear before the

[392] GAL, Aflezingsboek E, fol. 251v.
[393] *Ibid.*, fol. 251v, 252r.
[394] Bisschop, *Woelingen*, 71 f.
[395] P. Bor, *Vervolch der Nederlantsche Oorloghen*, 1626. Book 23, fol. 64.
[396] Bisschop, *Woelingen*, 136 f.
[397] KB, fol. 43; 13 October 1587.

Court of Holland.[398] As proof of his innocence he adduced his absence from Leiden on the October days in question. He had been in Utrecht at the time[399] and had there told the governor general about Cosmo's plans with which Leicester would have nothing to do and Saravia had returned to Leiden in the expectation that nothing would come of the coup. He had stayed on there in Leiden for four more days with a clear conscience, despite seeing that various citizens had fled the town for fear of the authorities, and had even lectured undisturbed. Indeed, he had welcomed Maurice and dined with him on the evening of the latter's arrival in Leiden, 25 October. He would not have left the town at all had he not been summoned to The Hague by a member of the Court of Holland—this is a different version from that of Bor's—where he stayed from Wednesday night to Friday morning, from 28 to 30 October. He then left the town to look for Leicester whom he evidently found in Alkmaar. He asked the latter for his protection and mediation with the Leiden magistrates, declaring his exclusion from the general pardon "to be improper and against reason and justice and that the trial which followed it is null since it was not made before his competent judge".[400]

When this was written, Saravia had already been dismissed as professor. The decision to dismiss him was taken by the curators and announced to his wife on 2 November[401] on the grounds of his "having been an accomplice in the conspiracy and mutiny recently planned and put in hand against the government of this town and of the common father land".[402] She answered the university bedels, Claes Buyzer and Loys Elsevier, who informed her, in French, of her husband's dismissal and the reasons for it, that the quitting of his present profession coincided with a desire that they both cherished for a considerable time. On the same day the bedels delivered an order from the curators and burgomasters to Claes Derkxzoon van Montfoort, the university's steward, to make no further payments to Saravia from the day of his dismissal.[403] As regards the latter, we may recall that Saravia had always kept a careful eye on his material interests. He had continually been more exercised in obtaining a pleasant home for himself and his family than he had in meeting the consequent financial obligations. The Leiden court day book reports on 19 May 1588, that he had not paid his rent during his residence in the Faliedebegijnhof.

---

[398] Professors and their widows had indeed to be summoned before the Court, but they themselves had to summon their adversaries before the ordinary judge. Molhuysen, *Voorrechten,* 19.

[399] With van Meetkerke and van de Wouwer, as van den Corput informed Arent Cornelisz on 9 November. *WMV,* II; 2.

[400] Bisschop, *Woelingen,* 137.

[401] Molhuysen, *Bronnen,* 53.

[402] *Ibid.,* Appendices, 159; Witkam, *Dag. zaken,* V, 51; *AC,* 18, fol. 220v, 221r; 2 November 1587.

[403] Text of the official report dated 2 November. *AC,* 39, fol. 220v.

Over against this debt which for a half-year came to 120 guilders, there was an entry of upwards of 106 guilders for the cost of repairs made by him—not a trifling amount for those days. The remaining debt of just over thirteen guilders was entered pro memorie by the regents of the Begijnhof.[404]

On 30 January 1588 Saravia wrote a letter from England to the curators in which he protested at his dismissal and asked to be restored to office. He remarked bitterly that, after the fate that Donellus had suffered—he had been dismissed in April for criticizing the States of Holland and their general van Hohenlo—he had not expected anything else. He held Paulus Buys especially responsible. From the last conversation which he had had with him, the latter was well aware of Saravia's conduct and motives, namely to defeat Pescarengis' violent plans by "pacifica consilia". His departure from The Hague had not been a flight. On the contrary, after consulting with Killigrew, one of the English members of the Council of State, he had, with Buys' knowledge, gone to Leicester to obtain from him a testimony of his goodwill. According to Saravia's version, at the very moment that he had tried to bring about a reconciliation between Buys and the governor,[405] the former had betrayed him. All this is not entirely clear, but it is indeed certain that Saravia played a part in the tensions between the Englishman and the Leiden town authorities. "Cosmo's speech displeased me" said the rector, "I disapproved of his plan and, as seemed proper, reported it to his excellency the earl".[406] Why it seemed proper remains unclear. Would it not have been better if Saravia had reported the plan to the Leiden magistrates if he was really so opposed to it as he made it appear? Curators and magistrates could only conclude from Saravia's defence that he had been involved in the plot as liaison officer between Leicester and the insurgents, or at least that he had known of it and had kept it hidden from the town government.

The letter which the accused wrote to the then rector magnificus, Justus Lipsius, even before his dismissal, namely immediately after his departure from Leiden on 31 October, was in much the same vein.[407] Lipsius, who never in his life took sides in a dispute, had no intention of now being involved in a conflict in which his friend was implicated. He went no further than protestations of warm friendship and continuing association. He held to the law which had been laid down for him by his reason and state of health, "publica numquam tangere", so he wrote.[408] Although this at-

---

[404] GDB A II, fol. 60r; 19 May 1588.

[405] In the summer of 1586 a quarrel had broken out between Leicester and Buys who had previously been strongly pro-English. Buys had been imprisoned in Utrecht for more than six months, not without the governor's knowledge.

[406] Molhuysen, *Bronnen.* Appendices, 161; *AC,* 18, fol. 243.

[407] Burman, *Sylloges,* Nr. 344.

[408] Lipsius, *Epist. Cent.,* II, Nr. 20.

titude was disappointing, Saravia's affection for the great humanist ap-. pears to have remained unshaken.[409] The letters referred to up to now are only some of the briefer examples of a veritable flood of epistles and remonstrances, some very lengthy in which Saravia attempted to prove his innocence in the matter of the Leiden disturbances. They are as follows, an appeal to the Provincial Council of Holland,[410] letters to the Classical Assemblies of Holland and Zeeland[411] and to the churches of South Holland[412] (1 February 1588), to Walsingham,[413] to Amyas Paulet, governor of Jersey (both on 20 September 1588),[414] to Arent Cornelisz (20 July and 9 October 1588)[415] and finally the detailed justification for the magistrates of Leiden (6 October 1588).[416] The most important arguments which Saravia produced against his conviction were these: he had disapproved of Cosmo de Pescarengis' plans from the outset—"pure lunacy and madness", he had called them to Captain Mansart—;[417] he had been absent when, contrary to his expectation and without his knowledge, they had been put into effect; he had not kept his prior knowledge of the plans a secret but had reported them to the nation's highest authority, Leicester; the latter had forbidden his return to Leiden and ordered him to stay in Utrecht or to go to England; if he had known himself to be guilty, he would not have dared to spend another four days in Leiden to lecture and to talk with Buys; as regards the latter, he thought that his attempts at mediation had succeeded and that the rift between Buys and Leicester had been bridged; the competence of the magistrates to pronounce sentence had to be denied on the grounds of the university's privileges.

In his letters to the churches and ministers, Saravia asked whether they would appeal to the States of Holland, the curators of the University and the town government of Leiden for rehabilitation and compensation. The arguments of the loss of his good name, by which "religion had been brought into disrepute",[418] flows too frequently and readily from the pen of someone who had picked the losing side in politics and has not managed to overcome his disappointment at this.

He requested the Provincial Council of Holland that "they would provide him with the proper remedy of justice and mandamente in the form of

[409] Burman, *Sylloges,* Nr. 345. Saravia to Lipsius 26 January (s.v.) 1588; Doc. XXVI.

[410] GAD, Nr. 160; Doc. XXII; *WMV,* III; 5, 299-302.

[411] Amsterdam, Library of the Free University, Department of Manuscripts, Bos Collection, provisional catalogue, Nr. 63; Doc. XXIII.

[412] The Hague, *Arch. Neth. Ref. Church, Ancient Records,* Nr. I, 20; Doc; XXIV.

[413] PRO.SP. 84/26, fol. 327r-328r; Doc. XXXII.

[414] BL.CM. Galba D III, fol. 235-237; Doc. XXXI.

[415] GAD, Nr. 112; Doc. XXVIII and XXXIV.

[416] BL.CM. Galba D III, fol. 240-243; Doc. XXXI.

[417] Amsterdam, Library of the Free University, Bos Collection, Nr. 63, fol. 3v.; Doc. XXIII; The Hague, *Arch. Neth. Ref. Church, Ancient Records.* Nr. I, 20, fol. 6; Doc. XXIV.

[418] GAD, Nr. 160; Doc. XXII; *WMV,* III; 5, 301.

appeal or redress in amplissima forma against the accusation, summons and sentence of those at Leiden''.[419] Paulet was asked to request the English members of the Council of State, Gilpin and Killigrew, to use their influence for a reopening of the affair. In his communication to this old English contact Saravia described the church of Holland as "the church which is moreover (to tell the truth frankly) under the rule of petty tyrants who have thrown off all government in order to govern themselves".[420]

On 6 October 1588, when all these arguments had had no result, Saravia finally wrote the justification which he had always threatened if his attempts to obtain lawful redress should fail. From the beginning of this document we learn something of the activities of Hackius who had intrigued with Buys against Leicester and had been taken to task for this by the consistory, who had also proceeded against the government. Saravia had seen to it that copies of the acta of the consistory meeting in question as well as of the conversation with the magistrates had come into Leicester's possession. He was sternly censored for the latter by the burgomasters.

This apology is the most interesting of all the pieces because it contains several passages from which we can learn Saravia's views on constitutional relations in the Netherlands. The discussion turned on the question of the highest authority in the state. The Leiden magistrates thought that this resided in the States. Leicester was subordinate to them. Saravia, however, denied the sovereignty of the States. For a real sovereign is someone who has nobody over him but God and is answerable only to Him: "un souverain ne recognoit que Dieu par dessus soy, au lieux ou il est souverain, et n'est point accontable de ses actions a autre qua Dieu". The States were nothing more than "procureurs et commissaires" of the towns to whom they were answerable. They cannot limit the power of the governor who is not their lieutenant. After Charles V's abdication the sovereignty is vacant, "and so long as the towns of Holland remain as united as before, sovereignty devolved on all the town-councils together and on one of them in particular, for they constitute one body, one state or county".[421] The extremely complicated constitutional issue of sovereignty became the subject of discussion especially after Orange's death. In this discussion Saravia followed the ideas of the English member of the Council of State, Thomas Wilkes, including the use of the same contradictions which had marked the latter's Remonstrance to the States-General on the matter in March 1587.[422]

---

[419] *WMV*, III; 5, 301.

[420] BL.CM. Galba D III, fol. 237; Doc. XXI.

[421] *Ibid.*, fol. 240-242. There is an English translation of the whole document in: *Texts concerning the Revolt of the Netherlands*, E. H. Kossmann and A. F. Mellink, ed. (London/New York, 1974) 282-285.

[422] *Ibid.*, 49, 272 f.

Amongst the greatest of the disappointments which Saravia had to swallow was the scant willingness of his friends in Dutch church and political life to stand up for his interests after his departure. It was with some apprehension that the Calvinist ministers learned that van Meetkerke, van de Wouwer and Saravia were intending to defend themselves in writing. They distanced themselves in advance from this undertaking because they feared that such apologies would only aggravate the relationship between church and state. They did not wish to become involved in the Leiden affair.[423] Although the Walcheren classis attempted to come to an understanding with Maurice about what they considered the injustice done to Saravia, an attempt which proved unsuccessful because of the stadholder's absence, and although they also roused the ministers of Delft to do something for him who "has fallen into such a great misfortune through no fault of his own (so it seems)" and although they sent a copy of his letter to the ministers of Dordrecht with the declaration that, in their opinion, "the stain is very injurious to the ministry and to our Christian religion, and we all owe it to Dns. Saravia and also especially to the church to do something",[424] the fugitive received real support from no one.[425] On 2 September 1588 de Villiers wrote him a long letter in which he explicitly refrained from a judgement on the question of guilt. Against all the arguments produced by Saravia to prove his innocence, de Villiers cited the counter arguments of the Leiden magistrates in order to demonstate how useless it would be for the convicted man if his case were to be re-opened.[426]

Saravia was very annoyed at this lack of support. Yet before this letter had been written, he let it be known that de Villiers was not a man to help his friends in their need. Do the ministers in Holland realize, so he wrote to Arent Cornelisz, that by allowing the injustice done to him to pass in silence, they are undermining their own standing and prestige with the authorities?[427] For his part, Cornelisz tried to make clear to his friend that he had put them in an awkward position: if they were to come out openly in his defence, for example, in a pamphlet, then the quarrel with the politi-

---

[423] *WMV*, III; 2, 283. Van den Corput to Arent Cornelisz, 9 November 1587.

[424] Walcheren classis to the ministers of Delft, 14 March 1588; Walcheren classis to the ministers of Dordrecht, s.a. Both letters in GAD, Nr. 24.

[425] There is no indication that when Werner Helmichius, minister at Utrecht, with his colleague there, Nicolaas Sopingius, and the Flushing minister, Daniel de Dieu, paid a visit to England in the summer of 1588 to plead the interests of the Reformed Churches in their native land to Queen Elizabeth and to dissuade the monarch from making peace with Spain (Hania, *Helmichius,* 35-40), that he informed Saravia about this before or after his journey. The Dutch agent in London, Joachim Ortell (*NNBW,* V, 406) also made no mention of this, despite the fact that he was well informed about the mission's progress, as emerges from his report to Oldenbarnevelt RA. *Inv. Staten van Holland,* 2629a, fol. 10v.

[426] *WMV*, III, 5, 303-306; Boer, *Hofpredikers,* 138 f.

[427] GAD, Nr. 112; Saravia to Arnold Cornelisz, 20 July 1588; Doc. XXVIII.

ques would blaze up as fiercely as ever; if they kept silent they incurred the suspicion of leaving their brother in the lurch. The ministers considered that Saravia had expressed himself in such a way in his address to the Provincial Court as to provoke the magistrates. They thought that a re-opening of the case would lead to endless disputes which would drag on to his own detriment. They were convinced of his "integritas, fides et bonitas". What he had done wrong had been committed from "im-prudentia", not from "malitia". But the magistrates had now passed sentence once "stricto iure": Saravia had acted against the "salus patriae", so they thought. Consequently it would be regarded as unwar-rantably foolhardy interference if the ministers were now to defend him.[428]

This letter meant the end for Saravia of his efforts. He recorded bitterly that he felt he was abandoned and betrayed by his friends. If they had anything they still wanted to tell him they must write to Regius who would send on their letters. He was so far gone in self-pity that he likened himself to Christ who had been deserted by his disciples.[429]

However, it is evident from a letter that he wrote to Raphelengius at the beginning of 1588 and in which Saravia thanks him for all he had done for him, that not everyone had forgotten him. It emerges from this letter that a part of his confiscated goods had been bought up or preserved in other ways from seizure by the authorities.[430]

On the English side attempts were made for quite a time to obtain rehabilitation both for those at Leiden and others elsewhere who had been condemned for similar reasons.[431] Saravia's name was repeatedly men-tioned in this, the last time on 30 January 1589 by Thomas Bodley to Walsingham.[432] However, all these efforts failed to produce any result.

---

[428] GAD, Nr. 112; Doc. XXX.

[429] Ibid.

[430] Münich, Royal Library, Cod. Mon. Lat. 10359, fol. 44; Doc. XXV.

[431] CSPF July - Dec. 1588, 247 f., 300 f., 339 f., 356, 400; Id. Jan - July 1589, 18, 34, 38, 42, 66 f., 75, 79 f., 121.

[432] Ibid., 80.

CHAPTER THREE

# PILLAR OF THE ELIZABETHAN AND JACOBEAN ESTABLISHMENT IN ENGLAND (1588-1613)

### 1. Rector of Tatenhill (1588-1595)

a. *Office and ordination*

Having fled the Netherlands, Saravia made his way to London where he had many contacts from the past. Later on too, when he had settled elsewhere in the country, he continued to visit the city regularly.[1] We get the impression from his correspondence that he had stored a part of his library there.[2]

One of those well disposed towards him was John Whitgift, Archbishop of Canterbury (1583-1604). Saravia tried, where possible to be of service to him. Thus, in the letter of 2 February 1588 to Franciscus Raphelengius, to which we referred earlier, he conveyed a request from the Archbishop to procure a quarto volume of Pagnini's edition of the Old Testament with an interlinear Latin translation. According to Saravia 700 or 800 copies of this might certainly be sold in England, naturally an attractive prospect for the Leiden publisher.[3] As we shall soon see, Saravia was also to take Whitgift's side in doctrinal disputes. It is evident from the dedication of his *De diversibus gradibus,* published two years later, that he maintained good relations with the ''group of able divines and civil lawyers who can fairly be described as anti-puritans and who were now approaching the height of their powers''.[4]

Indeed it was thanks to his contacts with influential political figures that Saravia quickly obtained the charge of a cure of souls in a well endowed rectory, namely Tatenhill in Staffordshire at the end of January 1588. According to the certificate of the Duke of Lancaster's officials, the annual value of the rectory, which had become vacant in November 1587 on the death of Thomas Pegg,[5] amounted to £26, 20d. On 24 January 1588

---

[1] Saravia to John James, 11 May 1590. BodL. Ms. Tanner, 79, fol. 148; Doc. XXXVII.

[2] ''Librum quem tantopere querebamus inter libros meos qui Londini sunt, hic inveni...''. Saravia to Richard Bancroft, 23 Aug. 1590, BL. Add. Ms, 28571; Nr. 36, fol. 167; Doc. XXXVIII.

[3] Unfortunately it took 25 years before a plan of this nature was carried out by Franciscus Raphelengius Jr. L. and R. Fuks, ''The Hebrew production of the Plantin-Raphelengius Presses in Leyden, 1585-1615'', *Studia Rosenthaliana,* IV (1970) 20 f.

[4] Collinson, *The Elizabethan Puritan Movement,* 387.

[5] PRO. DL. 16/1.

Walsingham signed Saravia's appointment; it was evidently the latter's turn to be selected from the list of potential incumbents kept by the duchy.[6] The question naturally arises as to whether, as a Calvinist minister from the Netherlands, Saravia was reordained in England before being entrusted with a cure of souls.[7] Precisely because he so soon proved himself an advocate of episcopal church government and an opponent of Calvinist views of the office, it is understandable that some have supposed that such a reordination must indeed have taken place.[8] However, we think that it can be established with certainty that this was not the case. To say the least, it must be considered remarkable that Saravia gave no indication of any such reordination in the many autobiographical references in his works. More important, however, than this argument from silence, is the fact that his objections to Calvinist theory and practice of the ministry implied the invalidation of that office in the continental churches as little as his criticism of the papacy and the decadence of the medieval church meant that he held Roman Catholic ordination invalid. Anticipating what we shall be discussing in more detail in the second part of our study, we refer now to a passage in Saravia's *Defensio* which is important for the issue of reordination.[9] Here he opposed Beza's views on a so-called "vocatio extraordinaria", because he feared that this provided no defence against what he termed the "Munsterian insanity". To put it in modern language, he was afraid that a charismatic view of the ministry would open the door to subjective and spiritualistic fanaticisms such as he thought were to be seen among the Anabaptists and which had to be com-

---

[6] *Ibid.* The author is indebted for this explanation to the kindness of Mr. John Walford of the Search Department of the Public Record Office London, who also informed him that the Exchequer First Fruits and Tenth Composition Book mentions, that on 11 March 1587/8 Saravia compounded for all but 52/2d. of the first year's value, his two guarantors being John Holland of Tatenhill and Humphrey Breton of the parish of All Saints, Barking London, generosus. PRO. E. 334/11, p. 33.

[7] On the question of the reordination of clergy who came from the continent: A. J. Mason, *The Church of England and Episcopacy* (Cambridge, 1914) 502-515; B. M. Hamilton Thompson, "The Post-Reformation Episcopate in England," in: K. E. Kirk, ed. *The Apostolic Ministry. Essays on the History and the Doctrine of Episcopacy* (London, 1957) 387-432; Sykes, *Old Priest and New Presbyter* (Cambridge, 1957) 87-117.

[8] Hamilton Thompson, "Post-Reformation Episcopate", 408 f.: "Again, leaving on one side the orthodox Hooker's choice of Saravia as his confessor, it is most improbable that Bancroft would have appointed, or connived at the appointment of a man in presbyterian orders to an English benefice with cure of souls". Apart from the fact that what is here referred to as "most improbable" is based on a petitio principii, it must be noted that Saravia's appointment to the rectory of Great Chart in 1609/10 was by no means his first to an English cure of souls. He had previously received two such appointments, in 1588 as Rector of Tatenhill in the diocese of Coventry and Lichfield, and in 1595 as Vicar of Lewisham in the Rochester diocese. The influence of Bancroft's predecessor must have played a part at least in the first appointment.

[9] *DT,* 23-30.

batted.[10] "If there have been men in France, Germany or the Netherlands who, being neither sent nor ordained by the churches already established in these countries and by their ministries, have dared to assume for themselves the church's office, then I am very far from excusing such indiscretion".[11] It is to be noticed that the Protestant churches on the continent are regarded as established churches in the same way as the Church of England was an established church. Therefore their ordinations were valid. On the other hand a "munus ecclesiasticum" without ordination in an "ecclesia constituta" was invalid. This was alike the case for the ministry in the Roman church: "Whether it be with us or with the Romans, although anyone confesses the doctrine of the church to which he belongs, he cannot, without the legitimate external calling of that church, exercise either the teaching office or the church's ministry if he engages in it".[12] However, once he was ordained there could be no further uncertainty about the validity of his ordination in itself. Only in the event of his being charged with false teaching later, might his calling be declared invalid.[13] In conclusion Saravia wrote: "If there have been any who have had no calling, whether in the Church of Rome or in any other church, then I think that already in this time on that account alone it could be denied that they have any calling".[14] Conversely, on the other hand, as it appears further on from observations upon the Colloquy of Poissy (1561), both Roman Catholic and Reformed theologians might appeal to their lawful ordination: "For although those who met there in Poissy in the King's presence, had not all received the same ordination—some had been ordained by bishops of the Roman church, others by the Reformed churches—, no-one needed to be ashamed of his ordination. So far as I can see, they could, without danger, declare that they had been ordained and called, some by bishops of the Roman church, others by orthodox presbyters, according to the order which has been accepted in the Christian churches, after prior examination of morals and doctrine, on the authority of the magistracy and with the people's consent, with the laying on of hands and

---

[10] He here pursued Beza's views ad absurdum by discussing at length the fanatical actions in May, June and July 1591 of extremists such as Edmund Copinger, Henry Arthington and William Hacket. Collinson, *The Elizabethan Puritan Movement,* 418-425. In fact Saravia knew very well that Beza was just as averse to such phenomena as he was himself.

[11] *DT,* 25.

[12] "Sed sive apud nos, sive apud Romanistas, quantumvis doctrinam quis profiteatur ecclesiae, in qua est, sine externa legitima vocataione illius ecclesiae, non potest officium docendi nec ecclesiae ministerium, si quo fungatur, tueri". *Ibid.,* 30.

[13] "Si postea [after his ordination] ei, qui legitime in aliqua ecclesia vocatus est, moveatur lis de ipsius vocatione, frustra et temere id fit: doctrinae falsitatis prius debet convinci, quam vocatio possit irrita fieri". *Ibid.*

[14] "Qui si nullam, nec ab Ecclesia Romana, nec ab alia habuissent vocationem, repelli potuisse eo solo nomine hoc seculo arbitror, quod vocationem nullam haberent". *Ibid.*

with prayer".[15] After this came sentences which are of decisive importance in answering the question about Saravia's views on the lawfulness of Reformed ordination: "Although I am of the opinion that the ordination of the Church's ministers is properly the work of bishops, yet it is necessary that where these are lacking and cannot be had, orthodox presbyters can in necessity ordain a presbyter. Therefore this ordination, although it is opposed to the order which has been received since the apostles' time, is justified by the unavoidable circumstances. Consequently, in such a situation a presbyter becomes a bishop".[16] In other words, in the circumstances in which the Reformed Churches were situated on the continent, ordination in a presbyterian church had, according to Saravia, the same validity as that in an episcopal church. According to him, there can never be any question of a repetition of ordination. His objection to presbyterian ordination in the Calvinist churches was based, amongst other considerations, on their practice of repeating ordination. "That a minister of the church be ordained more than once was unheard of by the theologians of old".[17]

Three points are clear in this discussion. In the first place it is evident that for Saravia the legitimacy of ordination to and fulfillment of a ministerial office was dependent upon his calling within an "ecclesia constituta", an established church, whether the Roman, the Protestant or the Anglican. Secondly, it is clear, according to him, that the lawfulness of anyone's exercise of ministry could only be called in question if he was accused of error or heresy. Without such an accusation any discussion about the validity of anyone's ordination or ministerial function was senseless. Thirdly, it emerges that presbyterian ordination has the same validity as episcopal because it is the only possibility open to the presbyterian churches. It is not hard to draw the conclusion from all this. If we set aside the suggested possibility of Saravia's earlier ordination in the Roman Catholic Church—and it is in the least impossible that, as a friar in the convent at St. Omer, he had been ordained[18] then it is certain that he regarded or-

---

[15] "Quamvis enim omnes qui ibi convenerant coram rege non eandem haberent ordinationem et alii ab episcopis Romanae Ecclesiae ordinati essent, alii ab ecclesiis reformatis, neminem eorum pudere suae ordinationis debuit. Fateri citra ullum periculum, quod ego videre queam, poterant se ordinatos fuisse et vocatos, alii ab ipsis episcopis Romanae Ecclesiae, alii a presbyteris orthodoxis, ordine recepto in Christi ecclesiis, praecedente examine morum et doctrinae et accedente magistratus authoritate et populi consensu cum impositione manuum et precibus." *Ibid.*, 32.

[16] "Quamvis ordinationes ministrorum ecclesiae proprie ad episcopos pertinere iudicem, necessitas tamen fecit, ub ubi illi desunt nec haberi possunt, orthodoxi presbyteri possunt in necessitate ordinare presbyterum: quae res, tametsi praeter ordinem receptum ab ipsis apostolorum temporibus, necessitate tamen excusatur; quae facit ut in tali rerum statu presbyter fit episcopus." *Ibid.*

[17] "Ecclesiae autem ministrum plusquam semel ordinari, fuit theologis veteribus inauditum." *Ibid.*

[18] Therefore Hamilton Thompson's assertion that "it is very unlikely that he had receiv-

dination as a minister in the Dutch churches as valid and that there can have been no question of a reordination. Hadrianus Saravia was one of the Reformed ministers from the continent who, in the period between Elizabeth's reign and the Civil War, was entrusted with a cure of souls in England without being reordained[19] and to whom is applicable the conclusion that Norman Sykes drew from a number of examples which he described, that "though episcopacy was necessary where it could be had, its absence owing to circumstances of historical necessity did not invalidate the ministry and sacraments of the foreign reformed churches. Accordingly the instances of the admission of such ministers of presbyterian ordination to benefices with cure of souls in England were simply the translation of precept and principle into practice".[20] It is well enough known that Scottish ministers were appointed in large numbers in the Church of England without reordination.[21] This conclusion is not at odds with the passage from the letter which, towards the end of his life in the autumn of 1610 or even later, Saravia wrote to the ministers of Guernsey in the Channel Islands.[22] In this he accused them of having organized their church on the Calvinist model without considering that the Channel Islands formed part of England and that their churches were under the jurisdiction of the Bishop of Winchester. "The example of the *French* churches and of the *Low Countries* doe you no good," he wrote,[23] which was to say that they were in a completely different position from that of those churches and their refugee congregations in England. What he accepted as lawful and valid in France and the Netherlands he considered unlawful and invalid in congregations in the Channel Islands which he regarded as part of the English church. He disputed this conduct on the same grounds

---

ed Roman orders before coming to England, as Bishop Wordsworth assumes" ("The Post-Reformation Episcopate", 408), is as dubious as the rash conclusion: "But the fact that he himself held very definite ideas as to the necessity of episcopal ordination makes it almost incredible that he himself should not have been ordained: the presumption is not to be overthrown by a mere argument from silence." "Presumptions" and such phrases as "unlikely", "almost incredible" and "most improbable" cannot remove the obligation of a serious, independent examination of these "very definite ideas".

[19] Cf. Richard Hooker's Puritan opponent, Walter Travers, lecturer of the Church of the Temple, who had been ordained by the presbytery of Antwerp on 8 May, 1578. For Jean Taffin's evidence on this see: Th. Fuller, *Church History of Britain* (6 vols., Oxford, 1845) V, 179 f. That, in 1586, Whitgift demanded Travers' ordination, does not alter the fact that for nearly five years the latter had exercised his ministry in the Temple Church without there having been any question of reordination. Even more remarkable is the fact that the question of ordination played no part in the controversy between Hooker and Travers. S. J. Knox, *Walter Travers: Paragon of Elizabethan Puritanism* (London, 1962) 44-46, 68, 70-88.

[20] Sykes, *Old Priest*, 94. Against Sykes: A. L. Peck, *Anglicanism and Episcopacy. A. Reexamination of Evidence.* London-New York, 1958.

[21] G. Donaldson, *Making of the Scottish Prayer Book of 1637* (1954), 5, speaks of "thirty Scots who were beneficed in the Elizabethan Church"; quot. Knox, *Travers,* 81.

[22] p. 118, n. 43.

[23] *Clavi Trabales,* 140.

on which, as we shall see, he opposed the Puritans' aspirations in the Church of England. "When your governors shall have a liking to the *English* Reformation, then will they make you leave the *French* Reformation".[24] He went so far as to call these ministers who withdrew from their bishop's authority "excommunicants and schismatics".[25] Saravia's fierce polemic was in no way intended as a fundamental denial of the ministerial office in a Calvinist church but was rather a combatting of what he regarded as disorderly behaviour and the refusal of ecclesiastical authority in the Church of England itself. With this letter he intervened in a controversy which was to result in 1623 in the end of the presbyterian church order in the Channel Islands.[26]

Tatenhill is situated on the left bank of the Trent about 25 miles to the north of Birmingham. The parish, which also included Barton-under-Needwood, Wichnor, Dunstall and Callingwood, was under the jurisdiction of the rural dean of Tutbury. It belonged to the widespread diocese of Coventry and Lichfield. After the dissolution of the monasteries the advowson passed to the crown in right of the Duchy of Lancaster.[27] In 1563 the households numbered 77 in Tatenhill, 86 in Barton-under-Needwood and 21 in Wichnor.[28] In this country parish Saravia got to know the life of the Church of England in all its strengths and weaknesses. He was one of the few university graduates among the local ministers in Staffordshire of whom in 1593 there were only fourteen out of 109, that is to say 12.8%. The position with regard to preachers was not much better; of the 109 only sixteen were licensed as such.[29] Stipends were poor: in 1604 nearly half the clergy had incomes of less than £11 per annum and only three in ten earned more than £27.[30] With an income of £26-20d,[31] Saravia was one of the best paid clergymen in the county. Although on his admission to a cure

---

[24] *Ibid.,* 144.

[25] "I must add one word more which will be hard of digestion. This is it, that you may be upbraided, that as many ministers that are naturall of the countrey, being not made ministers of the church by your bishop, nor by his demissories, nor by any other according to the order of the *English* Church, you are not true and lawfull ministers. Likewise that as many among you as have not taken institution and induction into your parishes from the bishop, nor from his substitute lawfully ordained and authorised so to doe, ye are come in by intrusion and usurpation of cure of souls, which nobody could give you but your bishop, that is, in terms and words Evangelicall, that you are not come into the *Sheep-fold by the door,* but by elsewhere, and that by the ecclesiastical laws you are excommunicants and schismaticks". *Ibid.,* 142 f.

[26] De Schickler, *Les églises du refuge,* II, 463-483.

[27] *The Registers of Tatenhill,* F. J. Wrottesbey, ed. (s.l., 1905) III f.; R. Hardy, *A History of the Parish of Tatenhill* (2 vols., London, 1907) I, 5, 18.

[28] Landor, *Incumbents,* LXXII.

[29] *Ibid.,* XXXVIII. Cf. R. G. Usher, *The Reconstruction of the English Church* (2 vols., London/New York, 1910) 205-243.

[30] *Ibid.,* XXIX f.

[31] PRO. DL. 16/1.

each clergyman had to sign a declaration in which he promised that he would not "openly intermeddle with any artificer's occupation, as covetously to seek a gain thereby", it nonetheless happened that "the Bishop of Lichfield and Coventry made seventy ministers in one day, for money: tailors, shoemakers and other craftsmen. Such men almost certainly continued to exercise their craft: entering the ministry for them was rather like purchasing an annuity".[32]

It is understandable that the learned theologian who had worked in Brussels, Southampton, Ghent and Leiden, scarcely felt at home in the company of his colleagues in Staffordshire and therefore often went to London[33]—Strype is aware that "Dr. Saravia was oftentimes at Lambeth".[34] Moreover his accomodation in Tatenhill left much to be desired. We quickly hear complaints about his house and his material circumstances: the house was so dilapidated that it was on the point of collapsing, so he told Bancroft who at this time was a canon of Westminster Abbey, and even Walsingham was informed. Saravia asked the former to put in a good word for him with the Chancellor of the Duchy of Lancaster; he himself did not dare to. He correctly thought that the rectors of Tatenhill were formerly allowed to take timber from the neighbouring woods for repairs and heating,[35] but that was unfortunately a thing of the past. Moreover, in the first year of his time at Tatenhill, he was much grieved at the death of his son Thomas. The parochial registers record that he was buried on 28 December 1588.[36] In his deep sorrow at the loss of his only son, Saravia evidently wrote to Lipsius who some considerable time later wrote him a letter in which he praised the departed and comforted the father. It was God's eternal decree that we must die. "We all pass this way, my dear Saravia. However, we are not parted from each other, but we quietly precede one another. O blessed ones who have attained the goal of bliss!".[37]

There is little that can be said about the spiritual state of Tatenhill at this period. It is known that only two thirds of the Marian incumbents in Staffordshire conformed to the Elizabethan settlement.[38] On the other hand

---

[32] Chr. Hill, *Economic Problems of the Church from Archbishop Whitgift to the Long Parliament* (repr. Oxford, 1968) 217.

[33] The dedicatory letter of *De Gradibus* is dated from London, that of the *Defensio* from Lambeth.

[34] Strype, *Whitgift*, II, 241.

[35] *A History of Staffordshire* (8 vols., London, 1908-     ), in: *The Victoria History of the Counties of England*, H. A. Doubleday, W. Page, L. F. Salzman, ed. (London, 1900-     ) II, 354; Saravia to Bancroft, 23 Aug. 1590. BL. Add. Ms. 28571, fol. 167; Doc. XXXVIII.

[36] Wrottesbey, *Registers*, 15: "1588. Dec. 28. Thomas, fs Adriani Sarraviae sacrae theologiae professoris rectoris ibidem. sep."

[37] Lipsius to Saravia, 30 July [1589]. *Inv. Lipse*, [88.]08.30. The dating in the inventory is incorrect; Doc. XXXV.

[38] Landor, *Incumbents*, XXIX.

there is no evidence that Puritanism had much influence there. Nevertheless the one known example of an "exercise", a form of meeting which was devised by the Puritan clergy to evade the ban on "prophesyings", took place not far from Tatenhill. This was held in Burton-upon-Trent on Mondays in the last decade of the sixteenth century.[39] In May 1596, six months after Saravia's departure, the Nottinghamshire preacher, John Darrell, who was known for his practice of exorcism, came there and cast the devil out of Thomas Darling.[40] We do not know whether Saravia came across the effects of this Puritan group; its activities would certainly have displeased him.

Saravia served nearly eight years as Rector of Tatenhill. In the latter half of 1588 he still tried, unsuccessfully as we have seen, to prove his innocence in the disturbances involving Leicester at Leiden in an extensive correspondence with various individuals and public bodies in the Netherlands. He was constrained to do this for the restoration of his honour and good name, not because of the possibility of a return to the Netherlands. Having long been attached to England and having had English nationality for twenty years, he felt no desire to return after his experiences in Leiden. There is not the slightest indication that he ever again crossed the North Sea after 1588.

## b. *Theological work*

We know nothing about his pastoral work in Tatenhill but are better informed of his theological activity. It is rather remarkable that the work to which he owes his importance as a theologian was only written after he was 58. His abilities won rapid recognition in England. On 9 July 1590 he was incorporated in the University of Oxford.[41] In the spring of the same year his *De diversis ministrorum Evangelii gradibus* was published in London.[42] The dedication to Archbishop John Whitgift, the Lord Chancellor, Christopher Hatton and the Great Treasurer, William Cecil, Lord Burghley, was dated 29 March.[43] The book is actually a collection of three,

---

[39] Collinson, *The Elizabethan Puritan Movement*, 168.

[40] *Ibid.*, 438.

[41] *Alumni Oxonienses 1500-1714.* J. Forster, ed., IV (London/Oxford, 1892) 1312. The account given ran thus: "Causa est quod honesta conditione vocatus ad ministerium in Ecclesia Anglicana huius universitatis societate cohonestari libenter cupiat." *Register of the University of Oxford*, II: *1571-1622.* A. Clark, ed., I: *Introduction* (Oxford, 1887) 376.

[42] DE/DIVERSIS MINISTRO-/RUM EVANGELII GRA-/DIBUS, SICUT A DOMINO/*fuerunt instituti*, & *traditi ab Aposto-/lis, ac perpetuo omnium Ecclesiarum/usis confirmati, liber unus:*/CUI/Duo alii additi, alter de Honore qui debe-/tur Ecclesiarum Pastoribus, alter de/Sacrilegiis & Sacrilegorum/poenis./Authore HADRIANO SARAVIA/*Belga.*/Iob cap. 8./8 *Inter-roga obsecro aetatem priorem*, & *sollicito animo investiga/patres eorum./9 Hesterni enim sumus*, & *ignari, ut umbra quaedam dies no-/stri super terram./10 An non ipsi docebunt te*, & *dicent tibi, atque ex corde suo/proferent*; *verba?*/LONDINI/*Excudebant*; GEORGIUS; BISHOP/; & RODOLPHUS NEWBERIE./*An. Domini*/MDXC. 4⁰; *STC*, Nr. 21746; *BBHT*, Nr. 2178.

[43] It is inconceivable that it could be supposed that the work was already published in

mutually related, treatises, entitled,: 1. *De diversis ministrorum Evangelii gradibus, sic ut a Domino fuerunt instituti, et traditi ab Apostolis, ac perpetuo omnium Ecclesiarum usu confirmati;* 2. *De honore praesulibus et presbyteris ecclesiarum Christi debito;* 3. *De sacrilegiis et poenis sacrilegorum.* In 1591 a second edition appeared at Frankfurt on the Main[44] and an English translation was also published in London by John Wolf.[45] A further English translation of the third and smallest part of this book appeared in 1629, under the title *Vindiciae sacrae* which strangely enough followed not the second, but the third part of the book, in being entitled, *A Treatise of the Maintenance due to Ec-*

---

1561, as did A. J. van der Aa, *Biografisch Woordenboek der Nederlanden* (repr. in 7 vols., Haarlem, 1969) VI, sub S, 38 and A. A. van Schelven, *NNWB*, IX, 938. Again, the assertion of Russel, *King Edward School*, 43, who dates the book in 1564 as written during Saravia's residence in Guernsey, is without any foundation. The entire content only permits a date after 1587. Not to have detected this is one of the innumerable mistakes in L. B. Smith, *Contribution of Saravia*. On p. 16 he announces that 1561 "may have been the year Saravia's first treatise was published, "De diversis gradibus ministrorum Evangelii". On p. 17 he assures us in note 1: "This edition was published in Frankfurt and as far as is known there are no extant copies of it." But in the same note he says, "The date of 1561 given by both these authors (*NNBW*, for which he makes Molhuysen responsible instead of Van Schelven, and Van der Aa) may be an error." On p. 42 we learn: "If he published a treatise in 1561 in Frankfurt, then it was probably an abbreviated form of the first of these treatises." It is completely unclear how this is now to be reconciled with the contents of the letter to the ministers of the Isle of Guernsey which, following the 1840 translator, Smith took from *Clavi Trabales* (London, 1661) 137-145, and coupled with this treatise. After all this letter must have been written after Saravia's time in Guernsey! The entire argument is on the same level as the fantastic announcement that the treatise *De imperandi authoritate* was written about 1610 (*Ibid.*, p. 163). Smith bases this on a theory according to which Saravia's thought moved in an Erastian direction under James I. Just a glance at the title page of the first edition, to be found in many libraries (*STC*, Nr. 21747!), could have told him that it must be dated in 1593! The biographical section of the book which is grounded on absolutely no original research and which moreover uses inferior and outdated literature, is, for the greater part, based on fiction.

[44] DE/DIVERSIS MINI-/STRORUM EVANGELII/GRADIBUS, SIC UT A DOMINO/Fuerunt instituti, et traditi/ab Apostolis, ac perpetuo omnium Ecclesiarum/usu confirmati, liber unus:/cui/duo alii additi; alter de ho-/nore qui debetur Ecclesiarum Pastoribus; alter de/Sacrilegiis & Sacrilegorum poenis./*Auctore*/HADRIANO SARAVIA/*Belga.*/ Iob cap. 8./8 *Interroga obsecro aetatem priorum, & sollicito animo inve-/stiga patres eorum./9 Hesterni enim sumus, & ignari, ut umbra quaedam dies/nostri super terram./10 An non ipsi docebunt te, & dicent tibi, atque ex corde suo/proferent verba?/*FRANCOFURTI/Apud Ioannem Wechelum & Petrum Fische-/rum consortes./MDLXXXXI. 8°. Not in *STC* and *BBHT*. Copies in Lambeth Palace Libr. G 659; Royal Libr. The Hague; Univ. Libr. Leiden; Univ. Libr. Heidelberg; City Libr. Ulm; Bavarian State Libr. München; State Libr. Nürenberg; Swiss State Libr. Berne.

[45] D./SARAVIA/1./Of the diuerse degrees of the Ministers of the/Gospell./2./Of the honor which is due vnto the Priestes/and Prelates of the Church./3./Of Sacrilege, and the punishment thereof./*The particular Contents of the afore saide Treatises/to be seene in the next Pages./Iob.*8./8. Inquire I pray thee of the former age, and pre-/pare thy selfe to learne of the Fathers,/9. (For we are but of yesterday, and are ignorant.)/10. Shall not they teach thee?/LONDON. *Printed by John Wolfe, and are to be sold* by John Perin at the signe of the Angell/in Paules Church-yard./1592./4°; *STC*, Nr. 21749. Reprinted 1592; *STC*, Nr. 21750.

*clesiasticall Persons.* A translation of the last chapter of part II was added. The book was furnished with a lengthy dedicatory letter from James Martin to the Duchess of Buckingham and an appendix dealing with the arguments of those who rejected the payment of tithes.[46]

The work owes its importance above all to the fact that the author is the first to base episcopal church government on the "ius divinum".[47] It is apparent from the treatise's contents that he particularly directed it against Calvin's successor, Beza. Without mentioning him by name he referred to Beza's distinction between an episcopate willed by God and one founded on human institution.[48] Saravia rightly saw Calvin's successor as the principal inspiration of all who wanted to model the government of the Church of England on the Genevan pattern. The publication of Beza's tract was the culmination of a process, begun in his letter to Grindal in 1566,[49] in which he permitted increasingly serious attacks on the episcopal system in England and Scotland. As regards the latter country, the book was intended in the first place as an answer to the questions of the Scottish Chancellor, Lord Glamis, but after the appearance of the English translation, its "cry for parity" was just as effective in England.[50] Saravia also saw the aspirations of the Presbyterians in the Church of England as due to Beza's influence. "There are three things", so he wrote at the beginning of his defence of the *De Gradibus,* "in which our churches [the Reformed churches on the continent, especially those in France and the Netherlands] without any denial taken from God's Word have differed from early antiquity. The first is the abolition of bishops. The second is the device whereby presbyters and deacons only exercise their ministry temporarily. Thirdly there is the very office and ministry of these two. However, these errors, although new and of recent origin, are already in

---

[46] VINDICIAE SACRAE./A/TREATISE OF THE/Honor and Maintenance due to/*Ecclesiasticall Persons.*/Done out of the Latin, of that famous/Diuine of *Holland,* H. SARAVIA,/sometime Prebend of *Canterbury.*/Ecclesiast. 7. 31./*Feare the Lord, and honour the Priest: and giue him his/Portion, as it is commanded thee.*/L. Coke Reports. B. Winchest. Case. /Ꝛe decay des reuenues de homes de Saint Esglise,/in in le fine serra subuersion del seruice de Dieu, et de/son Religion. /*That is,*/The decay of the Reuenues of men of the holy Church;/will, in the end, be the subuersion of Gods Seruice and/Religion./*In the same Case.*/Dismes sont choses spiritual, et due de iuro Diuino./Tithes are spirituall things, and due by the Law of God./LONDON,/Printed by *T. Cotes* and *R. Cotes* for/*Iames Boler,* 1629. 12°; *STC,* Nr. 21752.

[47] Cargill Thompson, "A Reconsideration of Richard Bancroft's Paul's Cross Sermon of 9 February 1588/9", 265 f.

[48] "...qui reiecto episcoporum ordine, pastoribus adiungunt temporarios presbyteros, quibus omne ecclesiarum regimen et disciplinam ecclesiasticam committunt: et hanc gubernationis formam divinam vocant; alteram quae sub episcopis est, humanum." *De gradibus,* A6 v., a clear reference to Beza's distinction between a divine and human episcopate.

[49] Beza to Grindal, 27 June 1566. *Correspondance de Théodore de Bèze,* VII, 154-166.

[50] Collinson, *The Elizabethan Puritan Movement,* 109 f.; Donaldson, *The Scottish Reformation,* 187 f.; Nijenhuis, *Ecclesia Reformata,* 130-139.

this short time so deeply rooted that I doubt if they can now be eradicated from many hearts, in view of the fact that Beza is their protector and defender. Men usually accord more authority to the fallacies which they have made their own than they do to the truth. For I venture to say this: if Geneva had not chosen to abolish bishops and had not accepted these presbyters and deacons, no-one would ever have discovered or would now discover in Holy Scripture that this was the way it must happen''.[51]

How did a theologian with a distinguished record of service in Calvinist churches[52] come to such a decided rejection of their principles of church order? We must return in detail to this later, but for the present we can affirm that Saravia himself by no means regarded his episcopalian views as a complete break with his Reformed-Presbyterian past. There is a variety of evidence in his writings of a continuing notion of union and fellowship with the churches in the Netherlands. He calls himself Hadrianus Saravia Belga on the titlepage of his *De Gradibus*, a remarkable description for someone who had held English nationality for many years! He continued to talk of the Dutch Calvinists as ''ours''[53] and he called their churches ''our churches''.[54] As we have seen, he recognised their ordination as lawful and valid. His opposition to Geneva had more to do with church order than with doctrine. Although he was critical of minor parts of Reformed teaching, yet it would be hard to say that his theological views in general radically changed after he left the Netherlands.

The ideas Saravia put forward in his treatises did not emerge suddenly but were gradually formed. If we may believe him the difference between presbyterian and episcopal church government was already occupying him early in the 1560's. At that time he discussed it in London with Nicolas des Gallars.[55] As we saw earlier,[56] he had frequently broached the question during the course of his ministry in the Netherlands. During his stay in Ghent he had made known his opinions ''on bishops and on the new kind of elders'' in a confidential conversation with friends. On that occasion he had considered that the present situation of the church, that is to say, a church order without bishops, was acceptable because of the exigencies of the times.[57] He always maintained this view of the presbyterian church order. He also discussed the matter with Leicester's physician and

---

[51] *DT*, 3.

[52] ''Ego 46 annos in ecclesiis reformatis vixi, tam in Anglia quam in Belgio''. *DT*, 113; ''Nam 46 annos novi ecclesias reformatas et ignarus non sum eorum, quae diversis in locis facta sunt fiuntque. Experientiam aeque ac D. Beza pro mea sententia citare possum.'' *Ibid.*, 157; ''Interfui classicis et synodicis omnis generis conventibus, quos equidem non improbo''. *Ibid.*, 198.

[53] *Ibid.*, Preface to the Reader, 2.

[54] *Ibid.*, Prologue, and 3.

[55] *DT*, 113 f.

[56] p. 78.

[57] *RG*, 349.

representative, John James.[58] English theological books were amongst his reading in this period.[59] In the Preface to the reader in his *Defensio*, he mentions that even in a resumé for the benefit of the States of Holland he wrote some chapters, "de necessitate episcoporum". He gives the impression of having discussed the contents of this with his colleagues since, because he could not convince them that his views were right, he did not send the document to the States.[60] He asserted, not without a hint of self-pity, that his preference for an episcopal church order was the reason for his suffering much injustice[61] when he had lived amongst Calvinists and again still later.

Very soon after his arrival in England he decided to give more publicity to his opinions on church government. In the preface to the edition of his theological treatises in 1610 he records that he had been encouraged in this by Whitgift and Bancroft, "duo laudatae memoriae archiepiscopi". That Whitgift, the archbishop, and Bancroft, at that time Canon of Westminster, member of the Ecclesiastical Commission and an ardent opponent of the Puritans as he had shown in his sermon at Paul's Cross on 9 February 1588/9 and was to make even clearer in his *Dangerous Positions* (1593), urged Saravia to write his treatise is to be explained by the fact that opposition to Puritanism stiffened after 1588. England's position in international politics improved remarkably from August of that year. In the same year in which Saravia arrived in Tatenhill the Spanish Armada had been crushingly defeated. There have indeed been different views as to the consequences of this English victory for internal religious affairs. The temporary elimination of the Spanish fleet had made a new invasion attempt in the future no more definitely impossible than had Mary Stuart's execution in 1587 warded off all danger of a restoration of the Pre-Reformation regime—the infiltration especially of Jesuits from France steadily continued.[62] Nonetheless it is understandable that, at least for the time being, the establishment felt itself somewhat safer from Roman assault and so turned against the other danger by which it felt itself threatened, Puritanism.[63] In October and November 1588 this latter had shown its readiness to fight by the publication of the first two *Marprelate Tracts*.[64]

---

[58] "Novi quos habuerimus sermones tum in Hollandia tum hic in Anglia de episcopis et leiturgia Anglicanae Ecclesiae... tu assensus es mihi et meis rationibus celebrataque est coena Domini ritu Anglicanae Ecclesiae." Saravia to John James, 11 May 1590. BodL. Ms. Tanner 79, fol. 148. Doc. XXXVII.

[59] *VV*, 21.

[60] *DT*, 1 f.

[61] *DGM*, 35.

[62] Black, *Elizabeth*, 406 f.

[63] A. A. van Schelven, *Het Calvinisme gedurende zijn bloeitijd* (3 vols., Amsterdam, 1943-[1965]) II, 159 f; Knappen, *Tudor Puritanism*, 295 f; Collinson, *The Elizabethan Puritan Movement*, 391 f.

[64] For the bibliography on this *Ibid.*, 497, n. 13.

Thus a systematic exposition and defence of the established order of church government appeared desirable. Who was more suitable to write such an apology than a capable Reformed theologian who was convinced of the scriptural and historical foundations on which this form of church government had been built?

The establishment's interests largely coincided with Saravia's own desire to give an account of his opinions about the proper government of the church. In a lengthy explanation at the beginning of his *Defensio* he writes about this. "After I had returned here [to England] and talked about these matters with some ministers of this church, it was with amazement that they took note of my views about bishops. And if my supposition is not too rash...., they believed that I chose to talk thus more flatteringly of their honour than I really thought of them in my heart. Moreover I saw that our [the Dutch] churches were suspected of siding with the rebels and schismatics in the English Church and of thus encouraging these to secede from their church and to hold it in contempt. In order to protect our churches against this suspicion I have surveyed the sacred ministry in the English church and published the treatise on the different ranks of ministers so as hereby to bear witness to the union of our hearts in one and the same faith. I was attracted by the example of the bishops of the English Church who not only tolerated and allowed foreigners to maintain rites and ceremonies in their dioceses which differed from their own but also kindly welcomed and aided them. They do wrong, who separate from each other on account of external rites and ceremonies and bring about disunion. When therefore I saw that the best of them did not shrink from maintaining communion with our churches, I thought that I must always maintain communion with the English churches in whatever place I lived. And always when I was present in their churches at the celebration of the Lord's Supper, I received with them the sacred sign of peace and unity between Christians. I thought that I ought to act thus because this is taught and always has been taught by our common faith and by orthodox writers, both ancient and modern. When, because of a difference in external rites, men express abhorrence of communion with this church in which Christ and the grace obtained for us by Christ is purely preached, then they display a very feeble sense of judgement. Such an attitude is surely based on haughtiness, a sign of Pharisaic pride. But, in his answer to my treatise, Beza has once more broken down and completely destroyed what I wanted to build up by my writing and example...".[65]

If we understand Saravia correctly, his intention, both in accepting the ministry in the Church of England and in writing *De Gradibus*, was what we would nowadays describe as "ecumenical". He saw the irenical inclinations of the English episcopate towards the Calvinistic refugee con-

---

[65] *DT*, 2.

gregations and the schismatic tendencies of some presbyterian-minded men striving against each other. Here we can leave aside the question whether this opposition was historically correct. Saravia believed it to be so. As a Reformed theologian from the continent, the community of belief between the Church of England and the continental Reformed churches was more important to him than the difference in liturgal practices. The acceptance of a cure of souls in the Church of England was the consequence of the community of faith with this Church in which he believed. The defense of the episcopate was the consequence of his aversion to schismatic tendencies.[66] We shall see later that other factors were at work in this, especially political opinions.

Other motives than those mentioned here probably indeed played a part in his acceptance of the ministry in the Church of England. Although there is no reason to doubt Saravia's honesty, we may also assume that he was guided not only by theological principle but also by material motives. During his time in Leiden he had already frequently made his financial demands known.[67] In De Gradibus he made it quite clear that he thought ministers' stipends in the Netherlands far too small: for him this was evidence that the church's officers were not shown the respect that was their due. This situation was one reason amongst others for his rejection of the existence of stipends fixed by the government. In evidence he cited the fact that in Flanders salaries of ƒ 200 to a maximum of ƒ 400—at that time that was £5 to £10—were regarded as large incomes. Because of this ministers could not buy books even with two or three year's income.[68] Moreover ministers sometimes had the greatest difficulty in actually getting hold of the money they earned. Saravia told of men who had sometimes to make long and time-consuming journeys and afterwards even then came home without money. All of this was the reason he spoke of the "misera conditio" of ministers in Holland. The government behaved towards them like an employer. He heard a dinner conversation of sheriffs and burgomasters in Ghent who thought that ministers' salaries ought not to be too great so that they should not grow in respect and authority in the eyes of the people.[69] Probably his vision of the ministers' social position, expounded at length in the second part of his treatise,

---

[66] According to Strype, Annals, III, 1, 345 a *Fraternum et amicum de resartienda inter ecclesiae Anglicanae doctores et ministros pace consilium* was written in 1584 or 1585 "by some pious learned foreigner". The text is printed Annals, III, 2, 320-329. In our opinion there are no sound arguments to support P. Milward's suggestion, *Religious Controversies of the Elizabethan Age. A Survey of Printed Sources* (London 1977) 93 f., that Saravia wrote this consilium in 1590. The consilium's author adopted a different position between the opposing parties from that taken by Saravia in his *De Gradibus* published in that same year.

[67] p. 52, 55.

[68] DGM, 79.

[69] Ibid., 81.

"concerning the honour due to prelates and priests",[70] was an important factor in his preferring the English church to the Dutch. The ordinary social situation of the clergy in Staffordshire in Saravia's time, was to be sure, as we have seen, scarcely better than that of his Dutch counterparts which he had denounced as "misera conditio". However, Tatenhill was an exception to this rule[71] and even if this were not the case then, in due course, Saravia was to contrive to procure a larger income in other ways.

The Puritan reaction to *De Gradibus* was naturally a negative one. On 23 August 1590 Saravia reported that a "delirius senex", one of the sort who preached a "sanctior reformatio", had condemned his book in a disgraceful fashion.[72] On 22 July, Jean Castol, minister of the Walloon congregation in London, sent a copy of the book to Beza. He thought he could give the following information about its origin: Beza's *De triplici episcopatu* had come into the possession of Whitgift's and Hatton's chaplains. The latter, at their masters' request, had drawn up the treatise with Saravia. According to Castol it was supposed that the latter had been employed because he had himself been a minister in the Reformed Church. Perhaps, they wanted to appoint him as superintendent of the Reformed refugee congregations, after the death of the then Bishop of London, John Aylmer. He would then have the opportunity of depriving these of their own church organizations.[73] Castol's suspicion was unfounded, Saravia never had any intention of imposing upon these congregations.

On 24 May 1591 Beza let Castol know that he was preparing a reply to Saravia's treatise.[74] Meanwhile Calvin's successor had discovered that Saravia's opinions continued to have some influence in the Netherlands as well. He had received a letter from the Leiden professor, Carolus Gallus,[75] an unstable person and a mediocre theologian and incompetent teacher, in which the latter had raised objections to some of Beza's views on election, creation, the relationship between church and state and church order.[76] On the last of these points he held opinions, especially as regards the ex-

---

[70] *Ibid.*, 39-82.

[71] *Liber Regis,* John Bacon, ed. (London, 1786) 207 gives for Tatenhill: King's Books: 26 1., 1 sh., 8 d., yearly tenths: 2 1., 12 sh., 2d.

[72] Saravia to Bancroft, 23 Aug. 1590. BL. Add. Ms. 28571; Nr. 36, fol. 167. Doc. XXXVIII.

[73] De Schickler, *Églises du refuge,* III, 141 f.

[74] *Ibid.*, III, 146.

[75] *BWPGN,* III, 173-177; *NNBW,* VIII, 582; Witkam, *Dag. zaken,* passim.

[76] When, in May 1587, Gallus was admitted as professor extraordinarius, he declared, "dat hij jegens de leere, zulx die inden landen van Hollandt angenomen es ende openlicken geleert wert, in 't minst poinct geen verschil en heeft, mer daer mede in alles een es". *Ibid.*, I, 192. But he was dismissed as professor ordinarius in 1592, not only on the grounds of his incompetence, but also because of the fact that he, "bij eenige inder leere verdacht gehouden werde". *Ibid.*, III, 117.

egesis of some scriptural passages, which showed a strong affinity with those of Saravia. Gallus also then referred with approval to the latter's treatise, with the reservation that he did not entirely agree with the author. However it must have given Beza food for thought that, on 1 Tim. 5:17, regarded by Calvinists as an important proof text, Gallus had preferred Saravia's exposition to that of the Reformed.[77] Meanwhile the English translation of Saravia's book appeared. On 12 August 1591 Castol, delighted at Beza's plan to write a reply, reported that this translation, ''is even more heinous and harmful than the Latin because it asks nothing else save that the people scorn God's good servants''. Castol repeated his view, ''that these things do not originate from an individual's action but from the authority of those who govern the church''. He therefore advised Beza to include in his preface the letter which he had written to Whitgift in March,[78] advice which Beza did not follow.

His answer was published in 1592 under the title, *Ad tractationem de ministrorum Evangelii gradibus ab H. Saravia editam T. Bezae responsio.*[79] A second edition followed a year later. Although, unlike Matthew Sutcliffe ( ± 1550-1629),[80] the other author who, after the publication of *De Gradibus*, entered the lists to defend episcopacy and combat presbyterian church government, Saravia had not named Beza, the latter well understood that the treatise had concerned him.[81] Beza wanted to preserve silence in the face of Sutcliffe whom he regarded as an ''insolent slanderer''. Saravia probably appeared to him more dangerous because of his possible influence in the Netherlands. So he hoped that there would be resistance to the latter's ideas in that country as well. Was not Saravia better known to them than he and did not the problem he raised affect the Dutch churches no less than Geneva? So wrote Beza to Sibrandus Lubbertus, professor at Franeker, a follower from whom he evidently expected support[82] but who did not react to his suggestion. Episcopacy scarcely ever exercised any power of appeal in the Dutch Reformation. On the other hand, in the

---

[77] Carolus Gallus to Beza, 16 March 1591. H. de Vries [de Heekelingen], *Genève pépinière du Calvinisme hollandais,* I (Fribourg, 1918) 250 f.

[78] Strype, *Whitgift,* II, 105; de Schickler, *Églises du refuge,* III, 146.

[79] AD TRACTATIONEM/DE/MINISTRORUM/EVANGELII GRA-/DIBUS, AB HADRIA-/no Sarauia Belga/editam./THEODORI BEZAE/*responsio.*/Excudebat Ioannes Le Preux./ MDXCII.4⁰.

[80] He published *A Treatise of Ecclesiasticall Discipline.* London, 1591 and *De Presbyterio, eiusque nova in Ecclesia Christiana Politeia, adversus cuiusdam I. B. A. C. de Politeia civili et ecclesiastica... Disputationem.* London, 1591.

[81] ''Etsi abs te non sum nominatim appellatus, ut est ab alio postea non tam certe disputatore quam petulante convitiatore [Matthew Sutcliffe] factum: tamen ista quorsum et in quos dicantur res ipsa demonstrat. Est igitur mihi tecum illa de re necessaria suscepta disceptatio''. *Ad Tract.,* I.

[82] Beza to Sibrandus Lubbertus, 20 Aug. 1592. De Vries de Heekelingen, *Genève pépinière,* II (The Hague, 1924) 42 f. For Lubbertus: C. van der Woude, *Sibrandus Lubbertus.* Kampen, 1963.

English speaking world, the controversy between episcopacy and presbyterianism, begun in the sixteenth century', continued to be of importance. In their debate, Saravia and Beza laid the foundations for a development in which both theological parties thought they could base their views on church order on the ''ius divinum''. After Beza had once done this with great resolution, Saravia followed in his footsteps: in 1594 he took up Beza's challenge in his *Defensio tractationis de diversis ministrorum Evangelii gradibus*.[83] No new arguments were proposed in this lengthy work which also stems from the period of his residence in Tatenhill. But the author repeated and explained at length his view that episcopal church government was founded on Our Lord's institution and was in comformity with the tradition of the early church. Naturally there was much more interest in the debate in England. In 1601 the second edition of the *Defensio* was published in Frankfurt,[84] in 1610 the third appeared in London.[85] The issue of authority was one of the central problems which continually occupied Saravia. This had a bearing not only on the church but on the state also. In this field also the Rector of Tatenhill entered into discussion with his great Genevan opponent, Beza, author of *Du droit des Magistrats*.[86] Indeed he was one of the few in Europe who had realized that this theological justification of the right to rebel was the work of Calvin's successor.[87] Even more clearly than in his ecclesiological works Saravia appeared as a theological defender of the political establishment in England

---

[83] DEFENSIO/TRACTATIONIS/DE DIVERSIS MINI-/STRORUM EVAN-/gelii gradibus, ab HADRIANO/SARAVIA editae/*Contra*/Responsionem Clarissimi viri D./THEODORI BEZAE,/*Eodem*/HADRIANO SARAVIA/authore./LONDINI/Excudebant Reg. Typog./*Anno salutis humanae*./MDXCII. 4⁰. *STC*, Nr. 21748.

[84] DEFENSIO/TRACTATIONIS/DE DIVERSIS MINI-/STRORUM EVANGELII/ GRADIBUS-/Ab HADRIANO SARAVIA editae,/ *Contra*/Responsionem clariss. viri D. THEODORI BEZAE./*Eodem*/HADRIANO SARAVIA AUTORE./*Nunc primum edita in* GERMANIA, *opera* & *studio* ADAMI/HERTZOGAEI: *qui propter moderatissiman suam a* D. BEZE/*opinione, dissensionem, invidiam atque iniuriam passus; hanc praestan-/tissimi* Theologi D. HADRIANI DE SARAVIA *Apologiam,/ magna accessione rerum univer-/sae antiquitatis atque Ecclesiasticarum historiarum consensu diiudican-/ dam committit.*/LIBER VARIA RERUM SCITU DIGNISSIMARUM/cognitione refertus, ac lectu cum Ecclesiasticis tum politicis/utilis atque necessarius./FRANCOFURTI,/*Apud Wolfgangum Richterum, Ann. 1601.* 4⁰. During his research in England, the author found only copies of this second edition in Lambeth Palace and Dr. William's Library, London. But Dr. J. E. Platt (Oxford) informed him that the Bodleian Library has a copy and that, according to the latter's unpublished Inter-Collegiate Catalogue of Books printed before 1641, there are also copies in the libraries of Manchester and Worcester Colleges. ''Surprisingly these are the only copies of any of Saravia's works in our college libraries''. On the continent there are copies in the Niedersachsen State and City Library, Göttingen, and in the State and City Library, Augsburg. It is listed in P. Milward, *Religious Controversies of the Elizabethan Age. A Survey of Printed Sources* (London, 1977) 104, Nr. 393.

[85] Included in *DTT; STC*, Nr. 21751.

[86] Théodore de Bèze, *Du droit des magistrats.* Introduction, edition et notes par R. M. Kingdon. Geneva, 1971.

[87] *Ibid.*, VII.

when in 1593 he published his *De imperandi authoritate et christiana obedientia,*[88] in which he dealt with the question of authority in the state and contested Beza's views. The work evidently had a wide circulation throughout Europe and made a deep impression, even though, according to the preface it was not yet fully complete: three more books were supposed to follow after the four which it already comprised. So far as is known, this never happened. The book was for sale at the Frankfurt Fair. On 14 February 1595 the business man Jacobus Monavius (Monaw) of Breslau asked Ortelianus (Jacob Colius), the learned London merchant, to send him the rest of the book as quickly as possible after publication because he considered it "useful and necessary in these days".[89] In the University Library at Leiden there is a copy once owned by Leonard de Casembroot, a justice in the Court of Holland and a jurist and diplomat who played a part in the negotiations with England in 1587. Although he took Oldenbarnevelt's side in the latter's dispute with Leicester,[90] he appears to have been friendly with Saravia.[91] At any rate, the above mentioned copy of the book has the author's autograph dedication to Casembroot on the titlepage.

It is evident from the correspondence between Monavius and Ortelianus that interest in Saravia's works already existed outside of the limited circle of theologians even during his lifetime. The disturbing effect which these had on his Puritan opponents proves that the latter were thoroughly acquainted with them. In the seventeenth century the work was also a desirable acquisition for scholars and well-to-do members of the merchant class. A copy of the *Defensio*, once owned by Beza and containing his autograph marginal notes, was in the Library of the Dutch historian, Gerardus Johannes Vossius,[92] renowned for its many superb and rare books.[93] Lucas Luce, a merchant in London, who lived in the parish of St. Bennett Finck[94] and was a member of the Dutch Church,[95] owned the col-

---

[88] DE/IMPERANDI/AUTHORITATE,/ET CHRISTIANA/OBEDIENTIA,/Libri Quatuor./*Authore* HADRIANO/SARAVIA./D. Paulus Apost. ad Rom. cap. 13./*Omnis anima potestatibus supereminentibus subiecta esto. Non enim est/potestas nisi a Deo, & quae sunt potestates, sunt a Deo ordinatae./Londini/Excudebant Reg. Typog.*/Anno salutis humanae/MDXCIII. The book was written in 1592. *IA,* 260; *STC,* Nr. 21747.

[89] Hessels, *ELBA* 1, Nr. 266.

[90] *NNBW,* VII, 283.

[91] "D. Cassenbrotus hebb'ick altidt ghehouden voor een from heere", so Saravia wrote in a letter to A. Cornelisz. on 20 July 1588. Doc. XXVIII.

[92] *Catalogus variorum et exquisitissimorum Librorum Gerardi Ioannis Vossii. Quorum Auctio habebitur in aedibus Petri Leffen Bibliopolae sub signo Phoenicis. Die Mercurii 4 Octobris Anno 1656. Prostant Lugduni Batavorum, Apud Petrum Leffen,* Anno MDCLVI, Theologi in Octavo Nr. 95. Cf. Th. de Bèze, *Correspondance,* IX, 9 f.

[93] F. F. Blok, *Contribution to the History of Isaac Vossius's Library* (Amsterdam/London, 1974) 16-33.

[94] Hessels *ELBA,* III, Nr. 3013.

[95] *Ibid.,* Nr. 2500, sub 207-208; Nr. 3013, sub 12; Nr. 3533.

lection of Saravia's *Diversi tractatus theologici* (1611) and presented it to that church's library in 1647.[96] That the works also continued to be read at that time in English Puritan circles is evident from the presence of the *Diversi tractatus theologici* in Richard Baxter's (1615-1691) library.[97] The work's importance may also be gathered to some degree by the fact that it was opposed not only by Beza, but also on the Lutheran side by Johann Gerhard and Jesper Rasmussen Brochmand[98] and on that of the Roman Catholics by Jacob Gretser.[99]

The speed with which Saravia's views were taken up in England, is evident from the fact that in the same year, 1590, Anthony Marten published his *Reconciliation of all the Pastors and Clergy of the Church of England,* a book which displays a knowledge of Saravia's *De Gradibus.*[100]

There was a renewal of interest in Saravia's works in the nineteenth century especially in the circles of the Oxford Movement.[101] In 1840, A. W. Street produced an English translation of *De Gradibus*[102] and the views expressed there on the episcopal office were later seen as a sign of "the Catholic re-birth of the English Church".[103] In 1855, G. A. Denison published the first edition of the original Latin text of Saravia's treatise *De eucharistia* with an English translation.[104] In later historiography this work was regarded, in our view incorrectly, as an example of "Anglo-catholic eucharistic teaching".[105] Finally, we may note that no less a person than John Keble, in the Foreword of his edition of Richard Hooker's works, went into some detail on Saravia's importance for the thought of the great English theologian.[106]

What has just been described must not give the impression that Saravia was only occupied theoretically with the defence of the English establishment and the opposition to those who were regarded as assailants of this establishment. As we have already seen, he had had little contact with Puritan influences in Tatenhill and its neighbourhood, but he was in-

---

[96] Library Dutch Church, Austin Friars, London. Ms. 4 (sign. D5) 51. The author is grateful to Drs. K. Bostoen (Leiden) for information about Luce's benefaction and for the information that Saravia's works are unfortunately no longer present in this library.

[97] G. F. Nuttall, "A Transcript of Richard Baxter's Library Catalogue. A Bibliographical Note", *JEH*, II (1951) 212, sub. 136.

[98] p. 243.

[99] p. 243.

[100] W. D. J. Cargill Thompson, "Anthony Marten and the Elizabethan Debate on Episcopacy", in: G. V. Bennett and J. D. Walsh, ed. *Essays in Modern English Church History, in Memory of Norman Sykes* (London, 1966) 60 f.

[101] The author is grateful to the translator of this study, Dr. J. E. Platt (Oxford), for having pointed this out to him.

[102] See the bibliography.

[103] P. Schaefer, *Die katholische Wiedergeburt der Englischen Kirche* (Munich, 1933) 24.

[104] See the bibliography.

[105] p. 200, n. 56.

[106] Hooker, *Works,* I, LXV-LXVII.

volved in the action against their adherents in London. Saravia was one of the 42 clergy and scholars who were assigned by Archbishop Whitgift in February 1590 to hold talks with 52 separatists (or those regarded as separatists) who were imprisoned in six London gaols. The so-called conferences were to be held twice a week and were intended to convert the prisoners from their errors.[107] Daniel Studley, an elder in the separatist congregation in London, a prisoner "in the Fleete" was assigned to Saravia. The former helped Henry Barrow, who was also later to spend some years in prison,[108] with the publishing of books. The fulfilment of this task, which produced few results, required the Rector of Tatenhill to stay in London at any event in March and April 1590.

### c. *Prebendary of Gloucester (1591-1595)*

At a time in which the practice of pluralism had reached considerable proportions,[109] it was not difficult for a theologian with great abilities and prominent contacts in church and state to increase his income. It is not surprising then that Saravia aspired to a post over and above Tatenhill. It is not clear on what grounds some[110] have thought that he was a canon of Worcester cathedral, but it is now established that their information about this was based on a misunderstanding.[111] The first occasion he obtained an ecclesiastical office after his rectory in Tatenhill, occurred in 1591 when he was appointed as canon of Gloucester cathedral. The diocese was set up as a new foundation carved out of Worcester in 1541. Four years later the crown had drawn up statutes and orders for the cathedral[112] in which it was determined that there should be six canons.[113] Their salary amounted to £7-17s-8d "of lawful money of England".[114] Saravia was appointed on

---

[107] *The Writings of John Greenwood 1587-1590*, L. H. Carlson, ed. Elizabethan Nonconformist Texts, IV (London, 1962) 103.

[108] *Ibid.*, 119, 322; F. J. Powicke, *Henry Barrow Separatist (1550?-1593)* and *The Exiled Church of Amsterdam (1593-1622)* (London, 1900) 38, 43.

[109] Hill, *Economic Problems of the Church*, 224-241. On the practice of pluralism in the diocese of Canterbury in the beginning of Elizabeth's reign: J. I. Daely, "Pluralism in the Diocese of Canterbury during the administration of Matthew Parker, 1559-1575," *JEH*, XVIII (1967) 33-49. See also: S. B. Babbage, *Puritanism and Bancroft*, 294-322.

[110] *DNB*, L, 300; *NNBW*, IX, 937; Russell, *King Edward VI School*, 44; and, of course, Smith, *Contributions of Saravia*, 40.

[111] The cathedral archives at Worcester have convinced the author to the contrary. The Chapter Acts for this period are missing, but there is a reliable list of Bishops, Deans and Prebends (Add. Ms. 56) which gives the names of all the canons in the ten stalls in this period. Saravia's name is not among them.

[112] "Statutes and Orders for the better Rule and Government of the Cathedral Church of Gloucester were appointed and prescribed by the command of King Henry the Eighth, in the thirty-sixth Year of his Reign." R. Atkyns, *Ancient and present state of Gloucestershire*, (2nd ed., Gloucester, 1768) 85-94.

[113] *Ibid.*, 85.

[114] *Ibid.*, 88.

22 October 1591[115] and as was customary[116] was, as the most recent appointment, installed in the sixth stall.[117]

The conduct of dean and canons at Gloucester corresponded to the regulations on residence and pluralism as little as elsewhere.[118] If Saravia's frequent stays in London were not very conducive to the exercise of his ministry in Tatenhill—we know nothing about the deputizing of his duties in his absence—his appointment at Gloucester was even more at odds with all the regulations concerning non-residence. In 1571 it was laid down that two benefices must not be held if they were more than 26 miles from each other.[119] The distance between Tatenhill and Gloucester was more than three times this. Moreover it was prescribed in article 11 of the Statutes and Orders that the canons "shall keep themselves at home and be always resident in our church, except some lawful impediment does prevent". After enumerating these lawful impediments (the service of the king, in the king's court, sickness, the care of the concerns of the church, going and attending in the parliament or convocation etc.) it was stipulated that they might be absent for 80 days "to visit their cures or other benefices, if they have any, and to mind their own private concerns".[120] This was observed as little as the regulation, which was already itself minimizing, that a third of the canons ought always to be present (article 11)[121] and that a meeting of the dean or sub-dean and resident canons must be held every fortnight (article 36).[122]

Although no chapter acts are available for the period in question—the Chapter Acts Books begin with the arrival of William Laud as dean in 1616—the Visitation Book gives a clear picture of the way in which the chapter fulfilled its task. When on Friday 12 April 1594 Bishop John Bullingham arrived to hold a visitation only the sub-dean was present. All the other prebendaries were absent even though the mandates had been

---

[115] PRO.PR. C 66/1375; Patent Rolls 31-37, Eliz. Calendar and Index, 33. Eliz. fol. 25v. Curiously the Register of Crown Presentations BL.LM. 444, fol. 169 dates the royal mandate 23 Oct. 1590; Le Neve, *Fasti,* I, 448; Th. Rudge, *The History and Antiquities of Gloucester* (Gloucester, s.a.) 276; Russell, *King Edward VI School,* 44.

[116] S. Ruder, *A New History of Gloucester* (Cirencester, 1779) 165.

[117] *Ibid.,* 169; Th. Dudley Fosbrooke, *An original History of the City of Gloucester* (London, 1819) 228.

[118] A clear example of this is to be seen in Griffith Lewis who was dean from 1594 to 1607. According to his will he wished to be buried in one of the cathedrals of Gloucester, Worcester or Hereford, or in Westminster Abbey, "in all of which he was a dignitary". This was, of course, contrary to article 9 of the Statutes and Orders in which it was laid down that a dean or canon of Gloucester was not permitted to hold the same office in another cathedral at the same time.

[119] *Select Statutes and other Constitutional Documents illustrative of the reigns of Elizabeth and James I.* G. W. Prothero, ed. (4th ed., Oxford, 1965) 202.

[120] Atkyns, *Gloucestershire,* 85.

[121] *Ibid.,* 86.

[122] *Ibid.,* 93.

fastened to their stalls four weeks before.[123] The absentees were now
"cited as appears in a certificate this day exhibited by the sub-dean and
sealed with capitular seal, called, and not appearing, contumacious and
reserved the penalty of this their contumacy till the next session in this
place".[124] For the same reason the session of 6 June had to be adjourned to
10 July. On this occasion it was said of those who failed then to be present
that "they would then be denounced as excommunicate".[125] Apparently
only two of the prebendaries were there for this third visitation meeting.[126]
The visitation was therefore again postponed, this time to 28 November
when three prebendaries were absent. On all these occasions Saravia was
among the absentees. He made his first appearance on 4 March 1595.
Nothing came of any of the punishments previously threatened. During
this session a discussion took place on the cathedral statutes, to which
Master Pury objected "because they are not confirmed by the king's great
[seal] of England". The majority of those present, including Saravia, did
not share in the objections and "consented to these statutes".[127] This verbal approval of the statutes is the only sign of Saravia's participation in the
Gloucester chapter's deliberations. His name does not again appear in the
books. We do, however, find his signature to an address to the Lord
Treasurer, Burghley, from the deans and prebendaries of the new foundations (which included Gloucester) which asked for measures against the
abuse of the so-called concealments.[128] After taking part in the scandalous
practice of non-residence for four years,[129] he gave up his post in the
Gloucester chapter when he became a prebendary of Canterbury at the
end of 1595.[130]

Before leaving Tatenhill, Saravia made two more excursions into
theological controversy. On the first occasion this was a dispute between
others in which he only played a minor role. The capable but contentious
Hebraist, Hugh Broughton (1549-1612),[131] who was later to become well-
known in Amsterdam, among other things, for his disputation with the
Jew, David Farer,[132] had published his first work in 1588 under the title, *A*

---

[123] GDR, 73, fol. 1.

[124] *Ibid.*

[125] *Ibid.*

[126] GDR, 73, fol. 2.

[127] *Ibid.*, fol. 3.

[128] Strype, *Whitgift*, II, 143-145; text of the address: John Strype, *The life and acts of Matthew Parker*, III, 264 f. At the dissolution of the monasteries, private persons, corporations or
churches had concealed possessions, naturally at the expense of the crown. The recovery of
these concealments gave Elizabeth and James I a great deal of trouble. See Strype, *Annals*,
II, 2, 309 f.

[129] We have not so far been able to find any trace of a dispensation granted to Saravia
either in this instance or in those to be described later.

[130] Ruder, *History*, 169; Rudge, *History*, 276; Fosbrooke, *History*, 228.

[131] *DNB*, II, 1367-1370; *NNBW*, IX, 106-110.

[132] R. B. Evenhuis, *Ook dat was Amsterdam* (5 vols., Amsterdam 1965-    ) II, 179-181;

*concent of Scripture.* In this book, dedicated to the queen, he had tried to reconcile the chronologies of world history and the bible with each other; an attempt which was fiercely attacked at Oxford by John Reynolds. Archbishop Whitgift thought that the book "contained but the curious quirks of a young head", though it is true that he later passed a more favourable judgement on it. However, when Broughton continued the dispute, which especially concerned the interpretation of the 70 weeks in Daniel 9:24-27, by writing a treatise on this, Whitgift prevented its publication. In the discussions which followed this, Saravia acted as an intermediary between the two.[133] When the scholar sent him with the message that the archbishop must be "blamed for hindering the queen's common good", Saravia brough back the reply from Lambeth: "it were better the truth of Daniel were hid, than antiquity so disgraced as in Mr. Br. preface",[134] a view with which the intermediary did not agree. However authoritative Christian antiquity was for Saravia too, it never led him into such inexcusable utterances about the relationship between Scripture and tradition.

The second occasion was a doctrinal dispute, the controversy surrounding William Barrett at Cambridge.[135] On 29 April 1595 the latter[136] preached a sermon before the University there in which he attacked double predestination and especially the doctrine of the perseverance of the elect as a dangerous view which induced people to a security characterized by presumption and arrogance. In this sermon, in which he declared that the believer could really lose God's favour and that in this life he could not be certain of his salvation, he launched sharp attacks on Calvin, Beza, Luther, Peter Martyr and Franciscus Junius. It is true that, under severe pressure from the Calvinistically inclined, he was compelled to recant, but the matter continued to occupy people's attention. Whitgift objected both to the procedure which had been followed in inducing Barrett's recantation and to the contents of the latter's propositions. The disputes in the latter part of the year led to a conference at Lambeth and to the drawing up of the so-called *Lambeth Articles,*[137] a defence of predestination and of the impossibility of losing "vera, viva et justificans fides". Saravia probably

---

M. H. Gans, *Memorboek. Platenatlas van het leven der Joden in Nederland van de Middeleeuwen tot 1940* (4th ed., Baarn, 1974) 36.

[133] "D. Saravia, being a messenger between the Archbishop and him", so wrote Strype, *Whitgift,* II, 118.

[134] *Ibid.,* III, 373.

[135] For the following Strype, *Whitgift,* II, 227-287; III, 317-339; *The Works of John Whitgift.* Parker Soc. (3 vols., Cambridge, 1851-1853) III, 611-615; P. M. Dawley, *John Whitgift and the Reformation* (London, 1955) 209-219; V. J. K. Brook, *Whitgift and the English Church* (repr. London, 1964) 161-165; P. A. Welsby, *Lancelot Andrewes 1555-1626* (repr. London, 1964) 43-45; H. C. Porter, *Reformation and Reaction in Tudor Cambridge* (repr. Cambridge, 1972) 344-363.

[136] C. H. and T. Cooper, *Athenae Cantabrigienses* (Cambridge, 1861) II, 236 f.

[137] Fuller, *Church History,* V, 220 f.

took part in this conference. At the archbishop's request he had previously written a detailed assessment in which he had, on the one hand, agreed with Barrett in making a sharp distinction between the "certitudo" of faith and the "securitas" of presumption, whilst on the other, he defended double predestination with an appeal to Augustine. He wanted to keep the door open to enable various interpretations of this doctrine in the church. He utterly rejected what he considered to be Barrett's unseemly attack "on the pious servants of Christ, John Calvin, Peter Martyr and others".[138] The assessment is interesting because it shows that, just as in comparable disputes in the Reformed church in the Netherlands, Saravia also endeavoured in doctrinal controversies in England to see to it that, within the bounds of the fundamental and necessary acceptance of the essential contents of the faith, room should be allowed for differing interpretations. It was also in accord with his attitude, when Queen Elizabeth forbade the continuation of theological disputes over predestination—which for Sarravia was a matter for interpretation—and the archbishop was therefore compelled to recommend the university "so to use the said propositions [the Lambeth Articles] as there be no publication thereof than in private".[139]

## 2. PREBENDARY OF CANTERBURY

a. *Canon of Canterbury (1595-1612/13) and Vicar of Lewisham (1595-1604)*

About the age of 63, Saravia began a completely new stage in his church career. At the end of 1595 he left Tatenhill to take up residence as one of the members of the chapter of Canterbury cathedral. A year previously he had already been accorded a grant in reverse for the tenure of a canonry in Westminster Abbey.[140] It was to be seven years before he could take up this post.

For more than seventeen years at the end of his long life Saravia remained associated with Canterbury cathedral as a canon. He arrived there on 6 December 1595,[141] as the deceased William Whitaker's successor in the sixth of the twelve stalls[142] which had been established at the new foundation despite Thomas Cranmer's objections to this large number.[143] A pre-

---

[138] Mr. Saravia, Opinion of Barretts Recantation. Trinity College Cambridge, Ms B. 14.9, fol. 169-183; published by J. Strype, *Whitgift*, III, 321-337.

[139] C. Cross, *The royal supremacy in the Elizabethan Church* (London/New York, 1969) 76, 205-207.

[140] PRO.SP. 38/4; SP. 82/1570; PR. C. 66/1414; PR. 31-36 Eliz. Calendar and Index, 36 Eliz., fol. 24v. WA. Reg. BK IX, fol. 1; Advowson 21 Oct. 1594; Mandamus 22 Oct. 1594.

[141] LP. Reg. Whitgift, fol. 298v, 299, 332v; Index. reg. Whitgift, II, 138; Le Neve, *Fasti*, III, 27.

[142] J. Dart, *The History and Antiquities of the Cathedral Church of Canterbury* (London, 1726) 201.

[143] C. E. Woodruff and W. Danks, *Memorial of the Cathedral and Priory of Christ in Canterbury*

bend at Canterbury meant an attractive income. ,According to the Treasurer's Accounts Saravia received in all a daily payment of 15d amounting to £40-2s-11d annually,[144] to which was added a further £6-13s-4d for the year in which he acted as vice-dean.[145]

As we learned earlier, Catherine d'Allez, Saravia's wife, was very attached to a French speaking church service. In Canterbury also she joined the Walloon congregation. She died on 1 February 1605/6 as was mentioned in the death registers of that church.[146] She was buried in the cathedral.[147] At the end of 1606 Saravia married Marguerite, the thirty year old daughter of John Wijts.[148]

At the end of 1595 Saravia was also appointed Vicar of Lewisham,[149] a parish which at that time still came under the jurisdiction of the diocese of Rochester and the deanery of Dartford. According to Hasted "the village of Lewisham consists of one street of more than a mile in length, in which are numbers of neat and handsome houses, inhabited by opulent merchants and traders of the city of London, the vicinity of which makes this place a most agreeable and convenient recess for them".[150] It must be doubted whether the new vicar often preached in the church dedicated to St. Mary the Virgin or undertook much pastoral concern for Lewisham. Because of the lack of parish registers[151] we have no further information. In view of the distance between Canterbury and Lewisham it is certain that Saravia assigned part of his income from this living, valued in the King's Book at £23-19s-2d and the annual tithes at £2-7s-11d,[152] to the payment of a curate. At any rate we know that a certain Abraham Colfe, who had a reputation as a "hot-headed Puritan," "was imprisoned in 1601 for speaking in defense of the Earl of Essex[153] in Christ Church Hall

---

(London, 1912) 290 f.; *The Antiquities of Canterbury in two parts.* The first part by William Somner, 2nd ed. revised and enlarged by Nicolas Battely. The second part by Nicolas Battely (London, 1703) II, 126; also BL. LM. 938, fol. 111-114.

[144] The Treasurer's Accounts are missing between 31-32 and 42-43. Elizabeth. CC. TA. 11-21 (1600/01-1613) mention the same amount.

[145] *Ibid.*

[146] *The registers of the Walloon or Strangers' Church in Canterbury.* R. Hovenden, ed., *PHS,* V (Lyrington, 1891) 576.

[147] Cowper, *Memorial Inscriptions of Canterbury,* 3.

[148] Russell, *King Edward VI School,* 45.

[149] Mandamus 22 Nov. 1595. PRO.SP. C. 82/1587. Induction 15 March 1595/96. BL.LM. 445, fol. 75b.

[150] E. Hasted, *The History and topographical Survey of the County of Kent,* I (new ed. London, 1886) 74.

[151] They were completely destroyed in the fire which the church suffered in December 1830.

[152] Hasted, *Kent,* I, 79.

[153] Robert Devereux, second Earl of Essex, who was condemned to death and executed on 25 February 1601 for attempting a coup d'état. *DNB,* V, 875-890. He had "a fashionable partiality for puritans and poets", thus S. T. Bindoff, *Tudor England* (Penguin Books, repr. 1972) 304, and the Puritans had pinned their hopes on him, so Collinson, *The Elizabethan Puritan Movement,* 444-447.

Oxford: but while under this cloud Colfe was given a curacy at Lewisham by the Vicar".[154] It is interesting to learn that the episcopalian Saravia was willing to install such a convinced Puritan as curate in his parish.

Saravia was neither the first nor last continental theologian to be honoured by becoming a member of the esteemed chapter of Canterbury cathedral. Bernard Ochino[155] and Peter Alexander[156] had been so before him and after him Gerard Vossius,[157] Isaac Casaubon[158] and Pierre du Moulin, father and son,[159] were to be appointed as prebendaries of the cathedral.[160] As regards Pierre du Moulin senior, who returned to France almost immediately after his appointment, he was and continued to be a convinced Calvinist even in his views on church order. The differences between episcopal and presbyterian church government which in England itself gave rise to serious disputes, were considered of minor importance in the relations between the Church of England and the continental churches.[161]

It is not surprising then that Saravia was on good terms with the foreigners' congregations in England. This was first and foremost the case with the Walloon church in Canterbury itself. He preached on various occasions in the cathedral crypt where the Walloons held their services.[162] On one occasion they even arranged an extra service in the week to give him the opportunity to preach.[163] At one of these services a certain Tevelin, who was also at other times a disquieting element in the Walloon congregation,[164] sat laughing during the sermon.[165] Did the Walloons first make enquiries about Saravia from their French-speaking co-religionists in London before giving him the opportunity to preach? There are some points in the acts of the consistory which would appear to indicate that this was so.[166] In any event he won their confidence. He and the congregation

---

[154] D. L. Edwards, *A History of the King's School Canterbury* (London, 1957) 83.

[155] Le Neve, *Fasti,* III, 36.

[156] *Ibid.,* 30.

[157] *Ibid.,* 37.

[158] *Ibid.,* 31.

[159] *Ibid.,* 23.

[160] See also Hasted, *Kent,* I, 606 ff.

[161] L. Rimbault, *Pierre du Moulin 1568-1658. Un pasteur classique à l'age classique* (Paris, 1966) 78 f.

[162] Fr. W. Cross, *History of the Walloon and Huguenot Church at Canterbury, PHS,* XV (London, 1898) 44 f.; B. Magen, *Die Wallonengemeinde in Canterbury von ihrer Gründung, bis zum Jahre 1635.* Bern/Frankfurt (Main), 1973.

[163] CC.FCR. U 47 A 3, fol. 26. 10 April 1596: "On preschera Lundy et Mardy, et on doit saluer Msr Saravia et le prier de precher Lundy". The service did not therefore replace the important one on Tuesdays at which baptisms and the catechizing of confirmation candidates often took place, as Magen supposes, *Wallonengemeinde,* 112.

[164] *Ibid.,* 153.

[165] CC.FCR. U 47 A 3, fol. 53. The fifth of the charges brought against him and described here: "de s'estre esprens a rire au Temple quand Mr Saravia prechoit".

[166] *Ibid.,* fol. 13. 1 Jan. 1595/96: "Dr Sar.", apparently a letter received; *Ibid.,* 16 Jan. 1595/96: "A esté resolu descire aux freres de Londres touchant Sar.".

had verbal[167] and written[168] consultations together. Owing to the loss of
the consistory's acts from the end of 1599 until 1623, we unfortunately only have information on the relations between Saravia and the Walloons for
a limited period, but we may assume that these were good up to the end of
his life. On 14 July he acted as godfather at the baptism of a daughter of
the Walloon minister, Samuel le Chevalier.[169] He again fulfilled this duty
at a baptism on 28 September 1606.[170] His first wife was godmother at
baptisms on 8 February 1599,[171] 8 October 1601—again for the baptism of
one of le Chevalier's daughters[172]—, 27 October and 14 November
1605,[173] the last occasion two and a half months before her death. His second wife, Marguerite appears as a godmother in the baptism registers on
5 March 1609,[174] 2 April 1609,[175] 28 January 1610,[176] 8 July 1610,[177] 13
December 1612[178] and, after her husband's death, on 6 March 1614.[179]

Although his departure from the Netherlands had embittered Saravia
towards the Calvinists in that nation, he was on good terms with their
countrymen in England. He frequently helped them with advice. We
know of several examples of his helpfulness. In 1596 the consistory of
the Dutch congregation at Maidstone asked the consistory of the Dutch
congregation in London to send one of their ministers to mediate in the
case of serious dispute between themselves and a certain Christiaan
Beeckmans.[180] However, London advised that they should arrange the
matter with Saravia. Although there was at first little liking for the suggestion,[181] he eventually received a request a few months later in Canterbury.
He accompanied them to the commissary Dr. Nieuman. The latter undertook to protect them against the English minister Care who was charged
with the supervision of the Dutch congregation at Maidstone and who had
evidently taken Beeckman's part.[182] In 1606 the Dutch congregation at
Sandwich consulted Saravia on a complicated matrimonial problem. Here
again he acted as intermediary with the commissary of the court[183] and

---

[167] *Ibid.*, fol. 44. 6 Aug. 1596: "De parler a Mr Saravia".
[168] *Ibid.*, fol. 119, 19 Aug. 1598: "De Mr Sar".
[169] *Registers Walloon Church Canterbury*, 46.
[170] *Ibid.*, 77.
[171] *Ibid.*, 51.
[172] *Ibid.*, 60.
[173] *Ibid.*, 74.
[174] *Ibid.*, 84.
[175] *Ibid.*, 85.
[176] *Ibid.*, 86.
[177] *Ibid.*, 87.
[178] *Ibid.*, 93.
[179] *Ibid.*, 97.
[180] Hessels, *ELBA*, III, Nr. 1363.
[181] *Ibid.*
[182] *Ibid.*, Nr. 1373.
[183] *Ibid.*, Nr. 1664.

gave advice for a pastorally responsible solution to the problem.[184] A third example of such mediation is Saravia's declaration on the matter of a difference about the ownership of the graveyard next to the Dutch church Austin Friars. On 27 May 1609 he signed a declaration at Westminster which showed that the churchyard was the lawful possession of the Dutch congregation, intended for the burial of their dead. He asked the Town Surveyors to allow the Dutch full possession of their property.[185] He was obviously well disposed to them. Thanks to his position in the Church of England and his knowledge of the language of the foreigners who did not themselves as a rule have much command of English,[186] he was well placed to act as intermediary between the Dutch and the English.

On one occasion Saravia was prepared to lend financial assistance. Thus he promised a sum of twelve[187] or ten[188] pounds to the Leiden student, Jonas Valmaer, whose theological studies had been seriously held up by sickness and who was in financial difficulties. It is true that for reasons well known he was slow in paying this sum,[189] but he did extend twelve days' hospitality to the young man when the latter, on a journey from Sandwich, where his parents lived, to London, where he was going to offer his services to the consistory, in his own words "went to Cantelbergh to Mr. Saravia to amuse myself" and was there taken ill again.[190] Probably he often received visits from Dutchmen. We know that in 1597 he received Jonas van Reigersberch ( ± 1578-1611) who, on completing his theological studies at Leiden, was travelling through England. On this occasion he provided Jonas' Album Amicorum with a verse line from Menander.[191] As we shall see, particularly from his correspondence with Wtenbogaert in 1612, Saravia continued to be interested in events in church and state in the Netherlands, but after his flight in November 1587 he never went there again. He might indeed call himself "Saravia Belga" on the title-page of his De Gradibus, but he regarded England as his real home country.

Whilst Saravia's relations with the Calvinist foreigners' churches was

---

[184] *Ibid.,* Nr. 1671.

[185] *Ibid.,* Nr. 1694; See also Nr. 1722.

[186] This was one of the reasons for the Dutch in Maidstone not agreeing to the commissionary's suggestion that, to prevent further difficulties, they should join the Church of England. *Ibid.,* Nr. 1373.

[187] *Ibid.,* Nr. 1598.

[188] *Ibid.,* 1648.

[189] *Ibid.,* Nr. 1617.

[190] *Ibid.,* Nr. 1648.

[191] Signed: "Hadrianus Saravia Ionae Reigersbergo fraterni amoris hoc testimonium dedit". UBL. Ms B.P.L. 2702, fol. 297. See also P. J. Meertens, "Het album amicorum van Jonas van Reigersberch ( ± 1578-1611)," *Archief; vroegere en latere mededelingen voornamelijk in betrekking tot Zeeland,* 1946-47 (Middelburg, 1947) 30; Id., "De Groot en Heinsius en hun Zeeuwse vrienden," *Archief,* 1949-50 (Middelburg, 1950) 58.

good, those with the Puritans in England were very strained. This is not surprising. Had he not attacked them in his writings as innovators and schismatics? He remained a source of irritation to them long after the publication of his treatises. On 17 June 1599 Henry Paramor, squire of the Isle of Thanet,[192] reported to John Whitgift that there had been unruly scenes in St. Nicholas' church during a service at which Saravia had preached in the presence of the local minister, Peter Simon.[193] After the sermon, "before the people were dismissed, for the latter salme was beginning", two "imprudent fellows", named John Cotton and Roger Pennel, came up to the pulpit to present a piece of writing which, so it appeared later, was dated 20 October 1596. This Puritan propaganda took place on the orders of Lady Hayward. Although Simons tried to calm their feelings, considerable alarm and confusion had arisen amongst the church-goers. Paramor sent the two trouble-makers to prison. He now asked the archbishop what further action he should take.[194] The incident, unimportant in itself, shows just how strained feelings were at the end of the sixteenth-century and the extent to which the Puritans regarded Saravia as their dangerous opponent and therefore the object of their attacks.

On the evidence of the Chapter Acts of Canterbury cathedral, we can establish that, during the first six years of his time there, Saravia took a most active part in the canons' deliberations. It is true that, apart from a few unimportant details,[195] the decisions did not concern him personally, but he was present at 71 out of the 76 meetings. He acted as vice-dean from 30 November 1600 until 25 November 1601.[196] His activity at Canterbury noticeably diminished after this period. From 12 December 1601 up to his death on 15 January 1613 he was, so far as we know,[197] absent from 103 of the 177 meetings. Towards the end of his life sickness was sometimes the reason for his absence. On some occasions despite this, he took part in the making of decisions from his home.[198] His presence was mentioned for the last time at the chapter meeting on 8 July 1612.[199]

---

[192] On the Island of Thanet and St. Nicholas: Hasted, *Kent*, IV, 288 f.

[193] *Ibid.*, 308.

[194] PRO. SP. 12/271.

[195] On 27 March, 1599, it was decided to build a footpath from Saravia's house to Prebendary Richard Wood's "brycke wall"; CC.CA.CA. 1, fol. 218v. On 9 June, 1601, it was resolved that Saravia had to hand over a part of his garden to Nicholas Simpson, his colleague in the eighth stall.

[196] CC.CA. 1, fol. 215, 220v.

[197] The first 28 pages of CC.CA.2, containing the acts from 6 June, 1607 to 8 Dec., 1608, have been lost.

[198] CC.CA. 2, fol. 17r. 6 Nov. 1610: "...quibus D. Saravia in domo sua egrotans litteras suas manu sua signatas assensum suum prebuit"; fol. 19v. 25 Nov. 1610: "...quibus Dr. Saravia prebendarius in domo sua egrotans consensum suum in scriptis manu sua signat. consensum suum prebuit"; fol. 30v. 9 Dec., 1611: "...ad quos Mr. Dr. Saravia in domo sua aegrotans consensum suum prebuit".

[199] *Ibid.*, fol. 36v.

It is not hard to guess the reason for his diminished activity at Canterbury after 1601. At the end of that year, seven years after the grant in reverse had been promised him, he became a member of the chapter of Westminster Abbey, where we first encounter him at the meeting on 3 December 1601.[200] He took his place in the eleventh stall which had become vacant on Lancelot Andrewes' appointment as dean.[201]

b. *Canon of Westminster (1601-1612/13) and Rector of Great Chart (1609/10-1612/13)*

The chapter of St. Peter's Church in Westminster met much less frequently than that of Canterbury; usually two or three, sometimes four, times a year. This was the case during the period in which Saravia was a member. Previously it met more often. Evidently after Andrewes' appointment as dean much of the business was settled outside the meeting. Saravia attended 17 of the 28 meetings between 3 December 1601 and January 1612/13, appearing for the last time on 11 May 1612.[202] A comparison of the Chapter Acts of Canterbury and Westminster shows that throughout this period Saravia was not present in the former town on or about the day on which the Westminster meeting was held. On one occasion he must have moved fast to have been able to attend meetings held in both places one shortly after the other.[203] His absence from chapter meetings at Canterbury in 1608 and 1609 must probably be explained by his participation in the translation of the bible which required his more or less permanent presence in London in those years.[204] Towards the end of his life the number of his absences increased probably because growing physical weakness made the journeys more difficult for him. At any rate there is a striking increase in absence in the last five years of his life.[205] After 1607 he did not go more than once a year to Westminster.[206]

His appointment as prebendary of St. Peter's Church naturally meant another substantial rise in his income. As a canon he enjoyed an annual

---

[200] WA.CA. 1, fol. 267r.

[201] A. à Wood, *Fasti Oxonienses* (Oxford, 1690-1692) 765; Welsby, *L. Andrewes*, 73 f.

[202] Here we are relying on the signatures appended to the acts. It is true that these do not provide completely certain proof of the canon's presence, because it was possible to sign later the acts of a chapter meeting which had not been attended. However, the position of Saravia's signature amongst the rest does not, as things stand, give us any occasion to doubt his honesty.

[203] Cf. CC.CA. 1, fol. 225v. 30 Nov. 1602 and WA.CA. 1, fol. 268v. 3 Dec. 1602.

[204] p. 147-149.

[205] On 7 Dec. 1608 he was absent from Westminster, see WA.CA. 1, fol. 296v. and on 8 Dec. from Canterbury, see CC.CA. 2, fol. 1r. The same was the case on 4 Dec. 1611, see CC. CA. 2, fol. 30r and WA.CA. 2, fol. 8r.

[206] "Non versor in aula, decrepitus senex me in mea domo contineo cum cocleis. Extra meam domum nusquam progredior, nisi ad meam paroechiam et cum magna difficultate semel in anno Londinum". Saravia to Joh. Wtenbogaert, 29 Sept. 1612. Rogge, *Brieven Wtenbogaert*, I, 203.

stipend of £28-5s.[207] To this was added a sum of 28s-6d[208] or 33s-6d[209] to reimburse the costs of removal and the laundry of table linen. In the Steward's Accounts[210] and the Treasurer's Accounts[211] there also appears an extra sum of 8d[212] or 10d.[213] Of more interest is an entry of 60s in the Steward's Accounts for 1602,[214] assigned "pro pupills". The entry, which appears only once in the accounts, possibly indicates that in some way or other he either taught or lodged students for a short time.

It was apparent that Saravia's discharge of the two canonries excluded the possibility of his devoting any attention to Lewisham. After some time he found the situation difficult himself. On 4 June 1599 he at last wrote to the archbishop that he wished either to live in his parish—naturally a purely theoretical wish—or to have a parish in the neighbourhood so that he could easily get to it. The earlier mentioned Simon, Vicar of St. Nicholas on the Isle of Thanet, would be prepared to exchange with him, but he learned "that the people of St. Nicholas were troublesome and ungrateful to their ministers who were only able to maintain their rights after quarrels and a circumstance which, in view of my age, is disagreeable to me".[215] It is apparent from the letter that Whitgift had written to him about the replacement of Master John Worship by Ephraim Pagit,[216] who acted as courier between the archbishop and Saravia. However, the latter had already promised the succession to James Forest. With regard to the proposed exchange between Lewisham and St. Nicholas, Saravia left the decision to Whitgift. However, as we have seen, he had less agreeable experiences when he preached in St. Nicholas two weeks later. Was this the reason why he gave up his plans for the exchange? In any event we hear no more about contacts with that parish.

Almost ten years passed before Saravia's wish was fulfilled for a parish which was nearer to Canterbury than was Lewisham. On 25 February 1609/10 he was appointed Rector of Great Chart in Kent.[217] On 23 March the final formalities (administration of the oath, signing of the articles, etc.), which had been interrupted earlier by a sudden bout of illness, took place at his home in Canterbury. This was further evidence that he had arrived at an age when great physical demands could no longer be expected

---

[207] WA.TA. 33655-33666 (1601-1613).

[208] WA.TA. 33656.

[209] WA.TA. 33655.

[210] WA.SA. 33920-33935.

[211] See Note 207.

[212] In the years 1603-1607, 1609, 1610 and 1612.

[213] In the years 1602, 1605, 1608 and 1611.

[214] WA.SA. 33921.

[215] Univ. Cambridge. Ms. Mm 1, 43, fol. 457 f.; Doc. XL.

[216] *DNB*, XV, 65.

[217] LP. Reg. Bancroft, fol. 297.

of him.[218] Saravia had already given up the vicarage of Lewisham some considerable time before his appointment to Great Chart. According to the Bishop of Rochester's register, Beiston Wolfe was appointed vicar there on 30 August 1604,[219] but it seems that he was never able to take up office there. The same register records that Abraham Colfe, Saravia's curate in Lewisham, was appointed vicar on 18 April 1610[220] after, so we read in the induction mandates, the vicarage had long been vacant following Saravia's "spontanea resignatio".[221] Although Great Chart is closer to Canterbury, this does not mean that Saravia was personally concerned with the cure of souls. According to the parish registers official business was conducted by the curate, Humphrey Everden.[222] The rector could easily afford to pay a deputy from his annual income of £25-6s-0½d.[223]

c. *Defender of the establishment against Roman Catholics and Puritans*[224]

Just as during his time in the Netherlands Saravia had tried to play the part of intermediary between England and the continent, so he regarded it as his duty in England to keep the authorities there informed with what was happening on the continent. It appears from his correspondence that he was especially on the alert and called for vigilance concerning the behaviour of disciples of the Roman church. Members of the foreigners' congregations, particularly the French, provided him with information which he felt he had to pass on to the Archbishop of Canterbury. This is further proof of the close contact which he continued to maintain with these Calvinist circles.

On 27 February 1600 he reported to Whitgift that, during a business journey to Flanders, members of a foreigners' congregation met there inhabitants from the county of Kent who had attended mass under the Jesuits' influence. In St. Omer there were no fewer than 600 Englishmen, mostly young men, who were educated in "bonae litterae" at a school there under the direction of an English prefect. This may well refer to the school which was founded in 1592 by Robert Parsons.[225] According to the information received by Saravia, large sums of money were sent to France from England intended for the Jesuits. Conversely Roman Catholic Englishmen were arriving daily in their native land from Flanders and Spain to convert their countrymen to their faith. They crossed the Chan-

[218] *Ibid.*, fol. 297v, 298r.
[219] KAO, DRC. R8, fol. 195v.
[220] *Ibid.*, fol. 204r; Hasted, *Kent*, I, 79.
[221] KAO, DRa.Ai. 50; 18 April 1610.
[222] CC.CDA. Great Chart. A 80; CC.CDA. V/V/21, fol. 1r, 3v, 3r.
[223] John Bacon, *Liber Regis*, 29.
[224] On James I's religious policy *Constitutional Documents of the Reign of James I A.D. 1603-1625*, with an historical commentary, J. R. Tanner, ed. (Cambridge, 1961) 47-109.
[225] *DNB*, XV, 411-419.

nel "mutatis vestibus" sometimes fifteen at a time. Saravia was also able
to give details of the adventurous ways in which such Roman propagandists managed to come ashore far from any recognised harbours.[226] In the
same vein were two lengthy letters to the archbishop, dated 23 December
1600[227] and 7 January 1601,[228] warning against threats, this time not from
the Jesuits but from the Franciscans. Again in this case the sources of his
information were two "peregrini", this time put in touch with Saravia by
the Walloon minister, le Chevalier. We get the impression that an attempt
on Queen Elizabeth's life was even feared. The central figure was a young
man, John Ellis, son of the innkeeper of the "Three Kings" at Canterbury. After his schooldays there he drifted into a dissolute life. Sent to the
continent by his father with the particular intention of getting to know the
Italian language and culture, he came under the influence in France of a
Franciscan, Antonius, who converted him to the Roman faith. Afterwards
he tried to win to the Roman faith two English presbyters, one of whom
was a captain in the English army serving in the Netherlands. The young
man, who was described by Saravia as completely untrustworthy both
financially and morally, travelled to and fro between England and the continent. He had also aimed at court circles. The archbishop sent on the warning to the queen's secretary, Robert Cecil, along with a description of
Ellis.[229] The information in these letters corroborate what is already
known of the Catholic underground's methods which were aimed at returning England to the Roman obedience.[230] The correspondence is marked
by the degree to which the establishment was alive to and tried to be on its
guard against the dangers of Roman infiltration from the continent. Convinced of the rightness of the "via media" which the ecclesiastical and
political establishment wished to tread between Rome and the Puritans,
Saravia served in its defence whenever he was able.

Puritanism also continued to occupy him. It is true that Beza was silent
after the publication of the *Defensio* in 1594. He might perhaps write
somewhat threateningly to Robert de Macon, Sieur de la Fontaine,
minister of the French congregation in London, and to Jean Castol; "Do
not let it be concluded from my silence that Saravia has stopped my
mouth",[231] but he did not continue the debate. The Reformed in his
native land of France were very put out by the attacks on their church
order which were launched from the episcopalian side. In imitation of

---

[226] Univ. Cambridge. Ms. Mm 1, 43, fol. 458 f.; Doc. XLIII.

[227] Hatfield House. Cecil Papers 82, fol. 82; Doc. XLI.

[228] *Ibid.*, 75, fol. 109, 110r; Doc. XLII.

[229] "A young youth. Of a nyneteene or twentie years of age. Pale faced. Gray eyed.
Flapen heared. Little or no bearde at all, and but sclender of growth." *Ibid.*, 75, fol. 112,
113, 116.

[230] P. McGrath, *Papists and Puritans under Elizabeth I* (London, 1967) 253-299.

[231] Hessels, *ELBA*, II, Nr. 251.

Saravia, Matthew Sutcliffe, dean of Exeter, had published in 1591 his *Treatise of Ecclesiastical Discipline* and *De Presbyterio eiusque nova in Ecclesia Christiana Politeia*. In 1593 the Warden and later Bishop of Winchester, Thomas Bilson, published an apology for the bishop's office entitled, *The Perpetual Government of Christ's Church*, in which the divine institution and apostolic origin of the office were taught most forcibly. All these works were thorns in the flesh to the Huguenots. At length the Reformed Synod of May 1598 decided to ask the English ambassador in France and de la Fontaine in London to take steps to check the spread of the writings of Saravia and his supporter Sutcliffe—these two were named in the synod's decree.[232] It is obvious that this request, which showed little regard for any sense of the political realities, had no effect whatever. It could only strengthen the view in England that, even after Beza had fallen silent on the issue, the Puritans might still count on powerful aid from the continent.

Saravia was certain that the Puritans constituted a great danger for both church and society. A schismatic—so he viewed the Puritan—was as such a sedition-monger in the state and a threat to the establishment. He wrote to the Bishop of London about an unknown Puritan, "He is a schismatic and whoever is the chief instigator of a schism in the church is no different from a rebellious citizen in the state. N's writings, which I have read, are those of a man of utterly false opinions whose dissension from the Roman Catholic Church is prompted not so much by a Christian spirit as by a schismatic. This is a temerity which sets up altar against altar and gathers church against church." Schism in the church and rebellion in the state, these, according to Saravia, were the consequences of the Puritans' behaviour. He saw Beza as the chief culprit behind their machinations, although he was willing to honour the latter as a student of "bonae literae". "But that he alters or renovates something in the churches which the fathers and the early church quite unanimously order that it must remain unchanged, or when, on his own authority he introduces new customs and usages which have never been seen or heard of by anyone anywhere on earth, then I shall not let it pass unremarked. This, however, I shall never concede to Dr. Beza: that he was ever better informed than me about the disputes in the English church, or that he had a clearer insight into its usages. It must not be thought therefore that he has suffered an injustice if I have preferred my considerations to his view".[233] This undated letter shows that Saravia regarded Beza as the continuing inspiration of the aspirations for radical changes in the Church of England. When, a long time after its publication and its translation into English,

---

[232] J. Aymon, *Tous les synodes nationaux des églises réformées de France* (2 vols. The Hague, 1710) I, 232.

[233] BL.Add.Ms. 28571. 51, fol. 207v; Doc. XLIV.

Saravia obtained Beza's *De triplici episcopatu,*[234] intended for the Scottish Chancellor, Lord Glamis, he did not hesitate to attack it in his *Examen tractatus de Episcoporum Triplici Genere,* published in 1610[235] and included in *Diversi Tractatus Theologici* (1611). Beza had then already been dead for five years.

After 1604 he had also written a reply to an unknown Puritan from the continent, addressed by him as "friend and brother", who, in 23 articles, had raised a number of lively objections familiar in his circle against the Church of England's canons established in 1604 and against certain expressions and ideas in the doctrinal utterances of the *Thirty Nine Articles,* the *Book of Common Prayer* and the so-called *Bishop's Bible.*[236] It appears from Saravia's small work[237] that he had personally taken part in the convocation of bishops, deans of cathedral churches, archdeacons, chapters and colleges and proctors of the clergy from each diocese in the province of Canterbury, which had taken place in the spring of 1604 under the chairmanship of Richard Bancroft, then Bishop of London—Archbishop John Whitgift had died on 31 January—and which had established the book of canons which received the royal confirmation on 6 September.[238]

At the same time we must not lose sight of the fact that in theological matters, if the controversial issues of the church's ministry and episcopal church government were not at stake, the defenders of the Elizabethan establishment and the Puritans had generally speaking no cause to oppose each other. The lines of theological division sometimes cut across the parties. This was apparent in 1597 when, for the second time, Saravia was involved in the dispute between the Puritan, Hugh Broughton, and Archbishop Whitgift. On 11 June the former complained in a letter to the Lord Treasurer because Whitgift had prevented his publishing a translation of the bible. Saravia, who was again the intermediary between the two, warned his Lambeth patron of the consequences of his uncompromising attitude: Broughton could go overseas.[239] This did indeed happen.

It is evident from Broughton's divulgences, particularly in the apology which he had included in the above-mentioned letter to Burghley, that Saravia tried to get Whitgift to appreciate the scholarly abilities of the man

---

[234] Text with introduction and translation in Nijenhuis, *Ecclesia Reformata,* 130-187.

[235] On 26 Oct. 1610 when Casaubon read the book and on the next day discussed it with the author, it was only just published, as he twice remarked in his diary, *Ephemerides Isaaci Casauboni,* J. Russell, ed. (2 vols., Oxford, 1850) II, 779.

[236] *Venerabili Viro, mihi multum dilecto & observando fratri N. Hadrianus Saravia salutem. Ubi idem Saravia respondet ad articulos quosdam dicti fratris & amici.* Anno Domini, 1610, in: *DTT.*

[237] *VV,* 21.

[238] On convocation, the book of canons and Puritan reactions: Cardwell, *Synodalia,* I, 165-329; II, 583-586; Usher, *Reconstruction,* I, 334-420; S. B. Babbage, *Puritanism and Richard Bancroft* (London, 1962) 74-146.

[239] Strype, *Whitgift,* II, 356.

for whom he had such a profound dislike.[240] It seems that Saravia had a certain sympathy for the Puritan. Possibly this was connected with the latter's views on the doctrine of Christ's descent into hell. This article of faith was the subject of debate not only on the continent[241] but also in England.[242] Broughton took part in this by developing the striking proposition ''that the hades of the Creed was paradise''.[243] In correspondence with the archbishop he had managed to convince the latter that his viewpoint was correct.[244] In 1597 he thought he could appeal to the English bishops in general. In particular he referred to a sermon of Thomas Bilson, who had been Bishop of Winchester since May of that year.[245] Saravia would no doubt have concurred with both their rejections of the Genevan views. Some years later, however, it emerged that Broughton had wrongly appealed to Bilson. The latter held completely different opinions about the ''descensus ad inferos''. The Puritan then thought that he must strenuously oppose the bishop.[246] As we shall see in a later discussion of the theological aspects of this debate, Saravia took Bilson's line.

In the second part of this study we shall have to keep before us the question as to whether and to what extent there was a connection between Saravia's views and those of such contemporaries as Hooker, Whitgift, Bancroft and others. Saravia was in correspondence with Whitgift and Bancroft. Lambeth was safe ground for him. He maintained friendly relations with Richard Hooker. In July 1595 Hooker became Rector of Bishopsbourne, 4 miles from Canterbury where Saravia took up residence in December of the same year. Thus they lived close to each other for five years. ''And since Saravia was afterwards in familiar intercourse with Hooker, and his confidential adviser when writing on nearly the same subject, we may with reason use the recorded opinions of the one for interpreting what might seem otherwise ambiguous in the other'', so wrote John Keble in his edition of Hooker's works.[247] The latter's biographer, Isaac Walton, reports that when in 1600 at the age of 46, Hooker contracted his fatal illness, Saravia visited him daily. He was ''the chief comfort of his life''.[248] ''About one day before his death, Dr. Saravia, who

---

[240] ''Dr. Saravia told Mr. David Roberts, that he could not beat into my Lord's Grace's head so much as the conceit of my studies: but he would lerne of me, and so bring my Lord Grace to be gracious to my studies.'' *Ibid.*, III, 370.

[241] E. Vogelsang, ''Weltbild und Kreuzestheologie in den Höllenfahrtsstreitigkeiten der Reformationszeit'', *ARG*, XXXVIII (1941) 90-132.

[242] Strype, *Whitgift*, II, 359-367; Knappen, *Tudor Puritanism*, 370 f.

[243] Strype, *Whitgift*, II, 320 f.

[244] *Ibid.*, 220, 222.

[245] *Ibid.*, 366.

[246] *A Collection of scarce and valuable Tracts...*, 2nd ed. W. Scott, ed. (London, 1809) 3-14.

[247] Hooker, *Works*, I, LXVII. Cf. Fr. E. Pamp, ''Walton's Redaction of Hooker,'' *CH*, XVII (1948) 113 f.

[248] *Ibid.*, I, 84.

knew the very secrets of his soul (for they were supposed to be confessors to each other), came to him, and after a conference on the benefit, the necessity and safety of the Church's absolution, it was resolved the doctor should give him both that and the sacrament the day following. To which end, the doctor came and after a short retirement and privacy, they two returned to the company; and then the doctor gave him and some of those friends which were with him, the blessed Sacrament of the body and blood of our Jesus. Which being performed, the doctor thought he saw a reverend gaiety and joy in his face; but it lasted not long; for his bodily infirmities did return suddenly and became more visible, insomuch that the doctor apprehended death ready to seize him; yet, after some amendment, left him at night, with a promise to return early the day following; which he did, and then found him better in appearance, deep in contemplation, and not inclinable to discourse; which gave the doctor occasion to inquire his present thoughts''. The dying man talked with him about ''the number and nature of angels and their blessed obedience and order, without which peace could not be in heaven, and oh that it might be on earth!... I have lived to see this world is made up of perturbations...''.[249] Thus, in his last hours, Hooker was occupied with the realm of ''obedience and order'' before he left ''this world of perturbations''. Were these ideas not the essentials which united both the dying man and his confessor in their theology?

### d. *Theological Work*

After he had written the work on which his reputation chiefly rests during his time at Tatenhill, Saravia continued to be theologically active in the last period of his life. Some years after James I came to the English throne, he wrote a treatise *De sacra eucharistia* dedicated to that prince. In his undated dedication the author relates that he had ''for some years'' considered writing the book and offering it to the King as a token of his gratitude for the latter's reign. We must therefore think of the years 1605 or 1606 as the time when it was written. The manuscript was not published by the author. In 1855 for the first time G. A. Denison produced an edition based on the manuscript he found in the British Museum.[250] Indeed the theologians to whom Saravia had given the text to read had pronounced a favourable verdict on it. Nevertheless he did not venture to publish it because the treatise dealt with a controversy which troubled all Christendom. He was not thinking here of the Roman Catholic Church. This, in his view, had so altered the sacrament into a foul idol that there could be no Christian fellowship with it. He was thinking, however,

---

[249] *Ibid.*, I, 85.

[250] *Saravia on the Holy Eucharist.* The original Latin from the Ms. in the British Museum, now printed for the first time. The translation by G. A. Denison. With notice of the author and appendix. London, 1855. The manuscript in question is: BL. Royal Ms. 8/E/VIII.

especially of the disputes between Protestant theologians on the continent. Starting from the *Concord of Wittenberg* (1536) he wanted to try to produce a view on the eucharist on which all Protestant Christians could agree.[251] Although he thought that this possessed neither influence nor authority, he hoped that it would promote the establishment of peace and reconciliation.[252] In writing this Saravia was therefore not thinking primarily about controversies in England. Doctrinal issues played scarcely any part in the controversy between the Puritans and the Church of England with regard to the Eucharist. They were much more concerned with ceremonies (vestments; standing, sitting or kneeling during the communion, etc.)[253] and the exercise of discipline in connection with admission to Holy Communion which the Puritans regarded as insufficient.[254] Saravia, on the contrary, dealt particularly with the theology of the eucharist. He left aside the problem of discipline and devoted only a brief passage at the end of his treatise to ceremonies. Precisely because of the somewhat pretentious purpose of the treatise it is strange that the author never had it published.

A second important activity was his cooperation in the new translation of the bible the initiative for which had been taken during the Hampton Court Conference in 1604. In July of that year the king sent a letter to Richard Bancroft who was then still Bishop of London but who was soon afterwards to be appointed Archbishop of Canterbury. The monarch informed him that he had appointed "certain learned men to the number of four and fifty for the translation of the Bible".[255] The bishops must seek out "all such learned men within their several dioceses, as having especial skill in the Hebrew and Greek tongues, have taken pains, in their private studies of the Scriptures, for the clearing of any obscurities either in the Hebrew or in the Greek, or touching any difficulties or mistakings in the former English translation". They had to send their comments to Edward Liveby, Hebrew reader at Cambridge (who unfortunately died in May 1605), to John Harding, Hebrew reader at Oxford, or to Lancelot Andrewes, Dean of Westminster[256] who enjoyed a reputation as a Hebrew scholar.[257] At first the project suffered delays. Then came the King's order this time with the names of 47 assistants, divided into six companies, each of which was to take charge of part of the translation.[258] Two of these met

---

[251] *Ibid.*, 4, 6, 16.

[252] *Ibid.*, 14.

[253] See for example: John Field, "A View of Popish Abuses," in: *Puritanism in Tudor England*, H. C. Porter, ed. (London, 1970) 122-138.

[254] Collinson, *The Elizabethan Puritan Movement*, 346-355.

[255] *Documentary Annals of the Reformed Church of England*, E. Cardwell, ed. (2 vols., Oxford, 1844) II, 86.

[256] *Ibid.*

[257] Welsbey, *Andrewes*, 83.

[258] Cardwell, *Annals*, II, 140-144; Fuller, *Church History*, V, 370-374; Pollard, *Records*, 49-53. See note 259.

in Westminster, two in Cambridge, two in Oxford.[259] One of the companies which met in Westminster was presided over by Lancelot Andrewes. They had been allotted the translation of Genesis-II Kings, a not inconsiderable portion of the Old Testament. Saravia was one of its members, amongst whom were several capable linguists, whilst others were less notable. Among others in Andrewes' group was Richard Thomson, nicknamed "Dutch Tomson" because he had been born in the Netherlands of English parents. It is said of him that he "had a reputation both as a drunkard and as a linguist".[260] What is there to say about Saravia's abilities? Although he was not a specialist in Hebrew, he probably taught it at Leiden university until Raphelengius' arrived in 1586 just as he did the exegesis of the Old Testament. It sometimes emerges in his writings that he knew enough to give an opinion on linguistic and exegetical problems relating to the Old Testament. We may recall for example his comments on the translation of Psalm 105:28 and his critical words about some other translations in the King James' Version[261] or his lengthy etymological reflections on the word "episkopos".[262] His linguistic capabilities are also evidenced by the fact that Isaac Casaubon consulted him on problems concerning Arabic and that the latter accorded his advice considerable importance next to that of the famous Scaliger.[263] It has been surmised that his knowledge of modern languages was a reason for his appointment as a translator.[264] It must have been very important for the company's work that one of their members was so well acquainted with the existing Dutch and French translations of the bible. As they declared in their preface, the translators never hesitated, "to consult the Translators or Commentators, Chaldee, Hebrewe, Syrian, Greeke, or Latine, no nor the Spanish, French, Italian, or Dutch".[265]

Little is known of the committees' methods. We only possess a short account from one of the translators.[266] From this it emerges that the task was a very time-consuming occupation which left little opportunity for other activities. The preface also says, with reference to the tradition about the

---

[259] On the translation and translators: *Records of the English Bible. The Documents relating to the translation and publication of the Bible in English, 1525-1611,* edited with an introduction. W. Pollard, ed. (London, 1911) 37-64, 331-377; Ch. C. Butterworth, *The literary Lineage of the King James Bible 1340-1611* (Philadelphia, 1941) 206-243; D. Daiches, *The King James Version of the English Bible of 1611 with special Reference to the Hebrew Tradition* (Chicago, 1941) 148-183; *The Cambridge History of the Bible* (3 vols., pb. Ed. Cambridge, 1976) I: *The West from the Reformation to the present day,* S. J. Greenslade, ed. (Cambridge, 1963) 164-168.

[260] Daiches, *King James Version,* 162.

[261] *VV,* 2.

[262] *ETB,* 3 f.

[263] p. 153.

[264] *Cambridge History of the Bible,* 165.

[265] Pollard, *Records,* 371.

[266] *Ibid.,* 55 f.; Butterworth, *Lineage,* 213 f.

Septuagint: "The worke hath not bene hudled up in 72 dayes, but hath cost the workemen, as light as it seemeth, the paines of twise seven times seventie two dayes and more".[267] This explains why Saravia did not attend any meeting of the chapter of Canterbury cathedral at any rate between 8 December 1608 and 5 August 1609 and probably also for a period before that in 1608.[268] Nothing can be said with any certainty about the remuneration which the translators received for their work, but it is not improbable that they each got about £55.[269]

About the year 1610 Saravia wrote a small work against the Roman Catholic Jesuit controversialist, Jacob Gretser, the defender of Bellarminus.[270] This polemical tract provides some information, in addition to that in Saravia's large works, on his attitude towards the Roman Church and the papacy.

### e. *Saravia and Lipsius*

Saravia kept up his interest in church and theology in the Netherlands until the end of his life. As examples of this we may cite his letter to Bancroft about Lipsius which we shall deal with immediately, his correspondence with Wtenbogaert and, in this connection, his involvement in the Vorstius affair.

The mutual attachment between Lipsius and Saravia was based particularly on respect for each other's scholarly qualities. Psychologically they were the opposites of each other. Despite all the changes which his thinking underwent in the course of the years, Saravia was so resolute in his behaviour in church and state on behalf of nascent Calvinism in the Netherlands and the Anglican establishment in England, rejecting in both stages of his life the decayed Roman church. In contrast the famous jurist, philosopher and philologist, Lipsius' religious and political views were so vague and colourless. Married to a Roman Catholic wife he had quitted Antwerp for Leiden in 1578 not, of course, because of any religious convictions bur from a desire for the liberty and peace which he required for his work. He went to Caspar Coolhaes' church but, to keep the peace with his wife, never took communion in the Calvinist church. Inwardly he remained inclined to Rome and it was not surprising that he returned to that church after he had left the North Netherlands in 1591.[271] We have already seen that Lipsius was not prepared to take sides with Saravia over

---

[267] Pollard, *Records*, 371.

[268] CC.CA. 2, fol. 1-4v.

[269] Pollard, *Records*, 57,

[270] *Responsio Hadriani Saraviae ad quasdam calumnias Iesuiticas nimirum illas Gretzerii in defensione sua Bellarminiana, quas ibi legit inter alias contra ipsum scriptas,* in: *DTT.* It is the answer to *Controversiarum Roberti Bellarmini... Defensio adversus Whitakerum, Junium, Danaeum, alios.* 2 vols., Ingolstadt, 1607-1609.

[271] *NNBW,* III, 778 f.

the consequences of the troubles involving Leicester at Leiden. When, on 26 January 1588, shortly after his flight, Saravia wrote from London inviting him to come to England where he had many readers of his works and admirers and where he could work away without the disturbance of any external pressures,[272] the Leiden scholar thanked him for the invitation on 23 March in a very friendly letter. He reminded him of the good understanding between them during the period in which they had been colleagues at the university. He expressed his dislike of receiving public and political responsibilities. Did he suspect, probably not unjustly, that Saravia wanted to use his visit to England to persuade him to plead his cause in Leiden and to have his rights restored? However that may be, Lipsius would gladly "visit the most beautiful and greatest of islands" in the summer, but at the moment his health prevented him from making such a journey.[273] Nothing ever came of the proposed visit. The last communication we know of between the two men was Lipsius' letter of 30 July 1589 in which he consoled Saravia after the death of his son Thomas. He reported that his *Politica* was almost ready and that he hoped that it would find not superficial but serious readers.[274] Lipsius died on 24 March 1606.

In the light of these facts it is noteworthy that two and a half years later, on 20 October 1608, Saravia wrote a long letter about his Leiden colleague to Archbishop Richard Bancroft which was intended to confirm information previously supplied in a private conversation.[275] The writer of the letter first gave a description of the man whom he admired for his learning and modesty. The degree of friendship which had united them had been apparent from the first edition of Lipsius' letters; in what followed, however, there was no trace of this; the friendship was evidently a thing of the past. Lipsius, who had never been prepared to show his colours or to take sides in any dispute, had returned to the Roman church. After a detailed character sketch of his successor as rector magnificus of Leiden university, Saravia gave Bancroft a number of precise details about Hendrik Niclaes' sect, the "Huis der Liefde",[276] with which he had come into contact at the home of his erstwhile friend. These particulars were the real purpose of the letter. A remarkable feature of the "Huis der Liefde" (Familia Caritatis, House of Love) was that leaders such as Niclaes and

---

[272] *Inv. Lips*, 88.01.26; Doc. XXVI.

[273] Bodl.Ms. Auct. D. 1. 14, fol. 19r; *Inv. Lips*, 88.03.23S; Doc. XXVII.

[274] *Inv. Lipse.*, [88].08.30; Doc. XXXV. It is not clear why the editors of the Inventory place this letter, which is dated 30 July, in August. In any case the year is not 1588 as they suppose, but 1589. Thomas Saravia died at the end of December 1588.

[275] BL. Add.Ms. 28571, fol. 214-218. Published by H. van Crombruggen, "Een brief van Adriaan Saravia over Lipsius en "Het huis der Liefde," *De Vergulden Passer*, XXVIII (1950) 110-117; Doc. XLV.

[276] *NNBW*, V, 367-370; *DNB*, XIV, 427-431; F. Hall, "The Family of Love and the Diocese of Ely", in: D. Baker, ed. *Schism, Heresy and religious protest* (Cambridge, 1972) 213-222. These three give further literature.

Barrefelt and many of their followers were uneducated, but yet the sect had an attraction in certain intellectual circles. Its influence was felt particularly amongst humanists in the Netherlands and far beyond.[277] The common basis was probably provided by a spiritualism and subjectivism which was sceptical of the institutional church and involved a relativizing view of its doctrine.[278] Saravia gives a full and vivid description of an encounter with Hendrik Barrefelt (Jansen), the old man who at that time was acting as the sect's leader,[279] and some of his followers. The famous publisher, Plantin was one such. Although a Roman Catholic, he had sought refuge in Leiden after the fall of Antwerp and was apparently an elder in this community. Saravia accused Plantin of a lack of commitment in the great spiritual struggle of his day: whilst Protestants died under Alva's bloody persecution in the South Netherlands, Plantin had published Niclaes' *The mirror of righteousness* and other works of the sect's founder undisturbed. Saravia had also either received or bought from him a work of Barrefelt's published by him, entitled *The treasure hidden in the field,*[280] a book which to Saravia's mind was more Stoic than Christian. On the basis of this and other writings and of conversations with Lipsius and Plantin, Saravia then outlined in detail the views of this esoteric, spiritualistic, mystical and syncretistic group who, according to his own experiences in the South and North Netherlands, also included ministers and elders of the Reformed church among its disciples. He compared it with David Joris and he reckoned its most important sources of inspiration were the mysticism of Tauler and the *Theologia Germanica* which he had read in his Roman Catholic days. Although both these had been highly regarded by Luther, Saravia would not count Tauler as an orthodox theologian because of his many "scandalous errors" and he rejected the *Theologia Germanica* because of its, in his view, ambiguous speculations. As we are constantly observing both in his correspondence and in his theological works, Saravia shrank from everything that inclined towards spiritualism, sectarianism or any other disparagement of the institutional church. During his time in Leiden he had been displeased at what he considered the great number of sects existing in Holland.[281] All the more admirable then is the objective and precise description which he sent Bancroft of the views of the "Family of Love". This community might have expanded

---

[277] H. de la Fontaine Verwey, "The Family of Love. Radical Spiritualism in the Low Countries", *Quaerendo*, VI (1976) 219-271.

[278] There is an interesting illustration of this in N. Mout, *Bohemen en de Nederlanden in de zestiende eeuw* (Leiden, 1975) 99-117.

[279] *NNBW*, IX, 448 f.; *BWPGN*, IV, 498-501; C. C. de Bruin, "Radicaal Spiritualisme te Leiden," *Rondom het Woord. Theologische Etherleergang*, XVII (1975) 69-73.

[280] *Het Boek der getuygenissen van den verborghen Ackerschat, verklarende de verborghen wonderdaeden Godts...* by Hiël s.l., s.a.

[281] Saravia to Wiliam Davison, 23 January 1585. PRO.SP. 84/1, No. 7; Doc. IX.

hardly at all after 1580—it was also fiercely opposed by the Puritans—yet in 1608 it was evidently still regarded by the English establishment as being such a danger that it was necessary for the church's primate to be informed in detail of its teachings.

## f. *Saravia and Casaubon*

Towards the end of his life Saravia received the gift of a new friendship, that of Isaac Casaubon (1559-1614), a classicist with considerable theological interests,[282] who after King Henry IV's murder in May 1610 was threatened with serious difficulties in his own country, primarily through the actions of Cardinal Du Perron. At Archbishop Bancroft's invitation, Casaubon came to England in October and in January 1611 became Saravia's colleague as a canon of Canterbury cathedral.[283] The two men had already previously become acquainted, for on his journey from Dover to London, Casaubon had stayed in Canterbury for nine days. He spent a whole day visiting the cathedral prebendaries.[284] On 26 October he read and fully approved Saravia's newly published *Examen Tractatus de Episcoporum Triplici Genere*. The next day he visited the author at his home where the book was the topic of conversation.[285] From then on Casaubon cherished a great affection and profound regard for Saravia. In a memorandum of another conversation which he had had with him, he wrote: ''This man is of no little note in England today: a very learned person who is amongst the most zealous for public peace and concord in God's church''. Saravia had complained about Daneau who had unkindly attacked him and had expressed himself harshly on the Genevan church which, with contempt for the early church, had introduced a new form of church government regarded by Saravia as a ''periculosa ἀναρχία''. Evidently Calvin had more authority than all the fathers for the Genevan theologians. Indeed, the former made them out to be asses.[286] As he appears in the memorandum, Saravia here failed to do justice to the predominant trend in Calvin's view of the early church: the fathers, especially Augustine, had a very great authority for him and he frequently appealed to them though their authority had to be regulated according to the Scriptures.[287] Apart from the dispute about church order, in this conversation with Casaubon, Saravia voiced his disagreement with Calvin's views on Christ's ''descensus ad inferos''. For the Genevan reformer the

---

[282] *DNB*, III, 1166-1170; M. Pattison, *Isaac Casaubon 1559-1614*. 2nd ed., Oxford, 1892.

[283] Le Neve, *Fasti*, III, 31.

[284] *Ephemerides Casauboni*, II, 775.

[285] *Ibid.*, 779.

[286] BodL. Casaubon Mss. 28, fol. 6.

[287] J. Koopmans, *Het oudkerkelijk dogma in de Reformatie, bepaaldelijk bij Calvijn*. Wageningen, 1938; L. Smits, *Saint Augustin dans l'œuvre de Jean Calvin*. 2 vols., Assen, 1957; R. J. Mooi, *Het kerk- en dogmahistorische element in de werken van Johannes Calvijn*. Wageningen, 1965.

doctrine was, as it were, the finishing touch to his views on reconciliation by satisfaction.[288] Saravia's objections were so great that he could tell Casaubon that he had devoted a book to them. This was never published and the text is, up to now, unknown to us. Next for discussion, according to the memorandum, was Beza's behaviour during the Colloquy of Poissy (1561). Saravia took great exception to Beza's refusal to sign the Augsburg Confession. In this he apparently disregarded the considerations of church politics which had prompted the Cardinal of Lorraine when he attempted to persuade Beza to sign.[289] Secondly, he rejected Beza's appeal to a "vocatio extraordinaria". In such evasion of the rules of "vocatio ordinaria" he saw the threat of the danger of a revolution in the church, referring in this connection to the "Anabaptismarum furor" and to the behaviour of the Puritans in England.

We have no knowledge of the themes of this conversation from Saravia's works. There had evidently been a substantial exchange of ideas between him and Casaubon, in which a considerable degree of like-mindedness in theological matters emerged. That the two men had become friends is also apparent from an undated writing in which the Frenchman put a number of linguistic problems about Arabic to the elderly prebendary. The letter is evidence not only of the correspondents' erudition but also of the prestige which Saravia enjoyed as a linguist with the French classicist. He evidently accorded a degree of importance to the former's response to his questions next to that of the learned Scaliger.[290]

In May 1612 Saravia paid his last visit to London. On 11 May he attended the meeting of the Westminster chapter for the last time.[291] On 31 May, having first visited the king, Casaubon dined with his friend.[292] Thus in the last year of his life, the former rector magnificus of Leiden university, still maintained indirect relations with the court.

Finally there is the letter which Casaubon wrote to Saravia from London on 13 January 1613, two days before the latter's death. He sympathized with his friend who had told him that he was suffering severe pain. He comforted him with the message of Christ's sufferings and returned Saravia two pieces of writing which the latter had sent him to read.[293]

---

[288] "Ergo si ad inferos descendisse dicitur, nihil mirum est, quum eam mortem pertulerit, quae sceleratis ab irato Deo infligitur". *CO*, II, 376. The suffering of Christ meant "invisibile illud et incomprehensibile iudicium quod coram Deo sustinuit". *Ibid.*, 377.

[289] D. Nugent, *Ecumenism in the Age of the Reformation. The Colloquy of Poissy* (Cambridge, Mass., 1974) 127.

[290] ζητημάτια *Arabica*. BodL. Casaubon. Mss. *Cat. Western MSS.* 3955, fol. 249-252.

[291] WA.CA. 2, fol. 8v.

[292] *Ephemerides Casauboni,* II, 932.

[293] BodL. Casaubon Mss. *Cat. Western Mss.* 3955, fol. 215; *Isaaci Casauboni Epistolae* (Rotterdam, 1709) II, Nr 851; Doc. XLVIII.

### g. *Saravia, Wtenbogaert and Vorstius*

Finally, we must indicate two important letters which Saravia wrote to Johannes Wtenbogaert in 1612 and in which he entered in some depth into problems which were under discussion in the lasting dispute between Remonstrants and Counter-Remonstrants in the Netherlands, a dispute which had ecclesiastical, theological and political aspects.

The first letter, dated 13 April 1612 (o.s.),[294] was a reaction to the sending of Wtenbogaert's *Tract on the office and authority of a higher Christian government in church affairs* (1610).[295] This work advocated the authority of the state within the church, especially with regard to the appointment of ministers, the preservation of sound doctrine, the calling of synods and the fixing of their agendas, as well as representation and decision making at them. The tract voiced the Remonstrants' view on the relationship between church and state and Saravia read it with approval. In his thinking the church was part of society over which the government wielded its authority. This authority is not dependent upon the religious opinions of the individual members of the government. "If an unbelieving government issues a just command on a matter concerning the church, then it must be obeyed; whilst a believing government must not be obeyed if it orders unrighteous acts." Saravia told Wtenbogaert about the oath which holders of ecclesiastical office had to swear in England and in which they acknowledged the king as "the sole and highest governor of this realm...both in all spiritual or ecclesiastical matters as well as in those of the world." As always, he recommended that the English pattern should be followed in the Netherlands. Those who did not recognize the authority of the government in the church must be regarded as rebels. He recalled that the authors of the *Confessio Belgica* (1561) had directed a prefatory piece to this work at the Spanish King and the Dutch States and had thereby acknowledged the government's authority in matters of faith. After some autobiographical information about his own involvement in the creation of the confession he let it be known as his opinion that it ought never to have been ascribed the same authority as God's Word: It was open to revision, it was not intended as a "fidei canon" and not all the articles of faith were of the same importance. Finally Saravia reported that, under the influence of Thomas Bilson and others, he had come to a different view of Christ's "descensus ad inferos" than the Calvinist manuals which he had taught when a minister in the Netherlands. Evidently this doctrinal problem weighed heavily with him. He had previously already told Casaubon of his reflections and had then talked of a book which he

---

[294] *EE*, Nr 181.

[295] *Tractaet Van t'Ampt ende Authoriteyt eener Hoogher Christelicker Overheydt in Kerkelicke Saecken.* Gestelt door Johannem Wtenbogaert, Bedienaer des Heylighen Evangelij, In s'-Graven-Haghe. 's-Gravenhage, 1610.

had written on the issue, but now he informed Wtenbogaert that he had written two books about it which, to be sure, were still not published. So far as we know nothing ever came of this proposed publication. As proof that he already held the same views about the relationship between church and state during the period when he lived in Leiden, he enclosed a copy of a letter written by him at the time to Wernerus Helmichius at Utrecht, in which, amongst other things, he had sided with the then Scottish king, James VI, against the Presbyterians in that land.

In the second letter, written on 29 September,[296] Saravia went at length into a completely different aspect of the dispute between Remonstrants and Counter-Remonstrants, that is the controversy over the appointment of Conradus Vorstius (1569-1622) as successor to the deceased Leiden professor, Arminius. Johannes Wtenbogaert, Arminius' supporter and leader of the Remonstrants and Oldenbarnevelt, Grand Pensionary of Holland, had energetically promoted and defended this appointment. The Counter-Remonstrants, on the other hand, exerted themselves to get it revoked. They accused Vorstius of Arminian heresies and in this they won whole-hearted approval from James I of England. The latter, just as his theologians, did indeed share the Remonstrants' views on the relationship between church and state, but on the doctrinal issue he took their opponents' side. After he had taken note of Vorstius' work and he had to some extent been put up to this by Archbishop Abbot, he had it publicly burned at London, Cambridge and Oxford. He tried to exercise such pressure on the States General by means of his ambassador in The Hague, Ralph Winwood, that the Leiden appointment would be withdrawn. In 1612 James even published a *Declaration*, English, Latin and Dutch translations of which appeared after the original French text. In this he published a number of documents relating to diplomatic actions and he gave vent to his profound aversion to Vorstius' ''abominable heresies'', sometimes in very abusive language. His principal purpose was to prove his own orthodoxy and authentic Catholicity with an eye to his dispute against the pope's exercise of temporal authority.[297] In compiling his writings the king made use of theological advisers who had to provide material for his polemical tracts at his command.[298] The rumour was current both in England and the Netherlands that Saravia had had a hand in the composing of the *Declaration*.[299]

[296] UBA.MsB. 69; Rogge, *Brieven Wtenbogaert*, I, 193-205; Doc. XLVII.

[297] Fr. Shriver, ''Orthodoxy and diplomacy: James I and the Vorstius affair,'' *The English Historical Review*, LXXXV (1970) 449-474.

[298] D. H. Willson, ''James I and his literary Assistants,'' *The Huntington Library Quarterly*, VIII (1944-1945) 35-57.

[299] W. Nijenhuis, ''Saravia en het optreden van Jacobus I tegen de benoeming van Vorstius te Leiden,'' *Ned. AK*, LV (1975) 171-191. Note 8 of this article gives more literature on the dispute.

The letter to Wtenbogaert can be seen as confirming this rumour for it contains a detailed theological refutation of some fundamental aspects of Vorstius' doctrine of God. In particular, Saravia rejected the latter's teaching on God's omnipresence in which a distinction had been made between God's essence and attributes in a way which he found unacceptable. The contents of this very lengthy letter are clearly the same as the opinions which were expressed, albeit in a less systematic fashion, in the *Declaration*. In both the letter and the king's tract an appeal was made to the early church and its belief which had been contravened by Vorstius. Like the king, Saravia thought that Vorstius' theology was as much at odds with that of Rome as with that of the Reformed church and that the potential Leiden professor's attack on Scholasticism was therefore out of order. Saravia went as little as James into the questions of predestination and free will which played such a predominant part in Dutch doctrinal disputes, but confined himself to the issues of the doctrine of God. The similarity in contents between the second part of the *Declaration* and Saravia's letter to Wtenbogaert is so evident that there must surely have been a connection between the two.

It is not therefore surprising that Saravia proposed the same solution of the problem as did the king: Vorstius' appointment must be revoked. He considered that the States' stubbornness was prompted by an unwillingness to give in to the demands of the Counter-Remonstrants who were so resolutely opposed to the government's interference in the church. The letter expressly mentions that the views voiced by the writer were shared by the bishops and academic theologians in the Church of England.

Saravia spoke highly of James' theological ability and of his independent judgement. He evidently wished to create the impression that the rumours that the king had arrived at his opposition to Vorstius' appointment at the instance of others, rumours which were circulating not only in England but also in the Netherlands, were without foundation.[300] He evaded a direct answer to the question of his own role in James' actions by saying: "I do not attend the court. As a decrepit old man I stay in my home like a snail. I never go out of doors except when I visit my parish and once a year, with great difficulty, go to London".[301]

It is, however, certain that Saravia did play a part in the English reaction to the Leiden appointment. Although he may not initially have concerned himself with Dutch political and ecclesiastical disputes, in this case he displayed such a striking interest in the Vorstius affair that he had gone into the latter's work at considerable depth and had consulted others about it to such an extent that he next wrote in great detail to Wtenbogaert who played a leading role in the controversy. Moreover, this letter contained

---

[300] *Ibid.*, p. 190.
[301] Rogge, *Brieven Wtenbogaert*, I, 203.

theological arguments closely akin to those of James' *Declaration*. We know that George Calvert, statesman and later Secretary of State,[302] was the compiler of the *Declaration*, that is to say, that he had assembled the material and put it in order.[303] Saravia was probably one of those who provided this material for the work.[304]

Casaubon was indirectly concerned with the Dutch controversy. On 29 September 1611 in a letter to Petrus Bertius (1565-1624) he rejected Vorstius' opinions. Bertius, regent of the States College at Leiden, was the friend and supporter of Arminius, whose funeral oration he had delivered, and a signatory of the Remonstrance (1610).[305] This funeral oration had given rise to a lengthy pamphlet dispute with the Counter-Remonstrant professor, Gomarus. He wrote about "daily new opinions which have come to such a pass that it is denied that God is infinite, eternal, omnipotent and prescient". He saw that insufficient respect was paid to the fathers and declared of himself: "I am disposed to make much of the early church's judgement".[306] He thus had a similar view to that of Saravia and Vorstius' English opponents. It was not therefore surprising that the theologian at the centre of the dispute felt that he had to justify himself to Casaubon in a lengthy letter written on 13 October.[307] However, the latter's reply on 25 January 1612 left no doubt that, along with James and the English theologians, he thought Vorstius' views must be rejected as heretical and schismatic.[308] In view of his friendship with Saravia it is very possible that Casaubon was the one who conveyed to him the king's wish that he should write a letter to Wtenbogaert with the aim of changing the latter's mind about the Leiden appointment. Considering the way in which James made use of his theological advisers, it is probable that Saravia wrote the letter by order rather than of his own accord. He was the most obvious person for the task since he was better acquainted with the situation in the Netherlands and at Leiden university than anyone else in England. Moreover, he shared Wtenbogaert's views on the relationship between church and state so that he might be presumed to have some authority for Vorstius' promoter. This was perhaps further strengthened by Saravia's ability to appeal to a consensus on the issue amongst English theologians. At the end of his letter he requested Wtenbogaert to treat his

---

[302] *DNB*, III, 722; D. H. Willson, *King James VI & I* (repr. London, 1971) 240.

[303] *CSPD. James I 1611-1618*, III; Willson, "Literary Assistants", 56.

[304] Four "praestantissimi theologi" had been assigned to the public refutation of "Vorstii impia dogmata" in England, so wrote Festus Hommius to Sibrandus Lubbertus on 15 Dec. 1611. BL. Add.Ms. 22961, fol. 218. Probably they had to provide an appendix to the King's work.

[305] *NNBW*, I, 320-323; C. Bangs, *Arminius. A Study in the Dutch Reformation* (Nashville/New York, 1971) 331, 356.

[306] *EE*, Nr. 170.

[307] *Ibid.*, Nr. 175.

[308] *Casauboni Epistolae*, Nr. 770.

writing in confidence.[309] Probably he supposed that the States of Holland had still not forgotten what had happened in Leiden in 1587 and that it would be better that it was not known that he had meddled in this vexed question. Wtenbogaert, however, sent the letter to Vorstius for him to read.[310] Was his favourable opinion really shaken by Saravia's arguments as has indeed been proposed?[311] We doubt it. It was almost a year before any criticism was heard, then on 15 September 1613 Wtenbogaert lamented to his protegé: "Would that these questions had never raised. Would that you had either never handled them in the Treatise on God or that you had expressed your opinion more clearly from the start".[312] However, this criticism appears to have been prompted more by considerations of expediency than by fundamental objections. That Vorstius had to leave Leiden and was never to occupy the chair there was due not to the power of personal persuasion but rather to English diplomatic pressure and internal Dutch political circumstances.

h. *The end*

Hadrianus de Saravia died on 15 January 1612/13 at Canterbury and four days later was buried in the cathedral there with his first wife, Catherine d'Allez. Written on the stone which originally lay on their grave was: "Here lie buried the bodies of Hadrianus de Saravia and his first wife, Catherine d'Allez. He died peacefully in the Lord in the 82nd year of his life on the 15 January in the year of our salvation 1612; she on the 2 February in the year 1605 after 45 years of marriage".[313]

In the north aisle of the nave we can still read the memorial inscription set up on the instructions of Saravia's widow:

"To Hadrianus de Saravia, a beloved husband, Margareta Wiits, surviving to the present, whom he married as his second wife and with whom he lived piously and happily for six years, arranged for this memorial to be set up as an, albeit small, but sincere token of her love. Whilst he lived he was a distinguished Doctor of Theology, a most worthy prebendary of this cathedral church, an outstanding man in all branches of letters, remarkable for the piety, uprightness, sobriety and sweetness of his conduct, renowned for his writings, full of faith and abounding richly in good works. He was a native of

[309] Rogge, *Brieven Wtenbogaert*, I, 205.

[310] *Ibid.*, I, 213.

[311] Chr. Sepp, *Het godgeleerd onderwijs in Nederland gedurende de 16e en 17e eeuw* (2 vols., Leiden, 1873-1874) I, 203.

[312] Rogge, *Brieven Wtenbogaert*, I, 221.

[313] Cowper, *Memorial Inscriptions*, 212. Cowper's copy of the last number: 15to must be due to a misunderstanding: Saravia and Catherine were married for more than 44 years. The date of Catherine's death on the tablet, 2 February 1605, differs from that in the register of the Walloon congregation which gives 1 February 1605. See p. 134, note 146. The year 1605 is of course stilo Angliae and thus actually 1606.

the Netherlands born at Hesdin in Artois. Sometime rector of Leiden, he first came to England at the beginning of the reign of Elizabeth of blessed memory. Doctor, first of Leiden, and afterwards incorporated at Oxford. The righteous man will be remembered for ever. 1612''.[314]

On 1 June 1614 in Canterbury Cathedral the young widow was married to the Rev. Robert Hill, D.D., Rector of St. Bartholomew by the Exchange, London,[315] but she died soon afterwards on 29 June 1615. Her death occasioned a poem from Josuah Sylvester, Saravia's old pupil at Southampton, entitled, "A Funerall Elegie. To My Reverend Friend M[aster] D[octor] Hill: In pious memory of that worthy Matrone, his vertuous and religious Wife, Margarite Wyts (late Widow of the reverend Dr. Hadrianus Saravia) Deceased''.[316]

By the end of his life, Saravia was one of the prosperous members of society. It emerges from his will that he left substantial properties in various dioceses in the Canterbury province.[317] The total value of the household effects which he left in his huge home, were alone estimated at about £1366.[318] In the will a 100 shillings each was bequeathed to the poor of Canterbury town and to the Walloon foreigners' congregation there. £200 was left to a young nephew of Saravia's first wife, Catherine d'Allez, to be paid when he became 25 years old, as well as an annual sum of eighteen pounds for his education. Should the latter die before the age of 25 then the amount set aside for him was set apart to pay for the education of a brother of Marguerite's up to the degree of master of arts. £100 was set aside for another of Catherine's nephews. The Saravia's family's servant and two maids received ten, four and two pounds respectively. The entire residue of the fortune was left to Marguerite.[319]

Saravia's will, made twelve days before his death and witnessed by his colleague as prebendary Richard Colfe and the Walloon minister at Canterbury, Samuel le Chevalier, began, as was customary at the time, with a confession of faith. This is a striking testimony of the ecumenical Christianity to which he had devoted his life. It also shows that Saravia viewed the last fifty years of his life as a unity and did not experience his move to the Church of England as a break in the development of his beliefs. Consequently the Walloon minister could act as a witness. The statement summarizes the guiding purpose of his theological labours:

> "First of all I confess that I die in the faith delivered to the church by the
> apostles of our Lord Jesus Christ and the prophets which form the contents of

---

[314] *Ibid.*, 3.
[315] *Ibid.*, 296.
[316] Russell, *King Edward VI School,* 46.
[317] KAO.PRC. 32/42, fol. 153v; Doc. XLIX.
[318] KAO.PRC. 27/2/67; Doc. XLIX.
[319] KAO.PRC. 32/42, fol. 153v Doc. XLIX.

the canonical books of the Old and New Testament and which is presently accepted in the English Church by public authority. These fifty years, after I had quitted and renounced the errors of tyranny and idolatry which hold sway in the Roman Church, I have taught and professed this faith privately and in public. I accept and greatly esteem the so-called Apostles' Creed, the Creed of Nicea and of the other three ecumenical Councils with that of Athanasius because they are gathered from God's Word. To these I add the Confession of the English Church together with that which the German princes presented to the Emperor at Augsburg in the year of our Lord 1530. I am not aware of any errors which have been condemned by God's Word or by the fathers of the Church's earliest days. I therefore condemn all heresies and teachings which are contrary to the written Word of God and particularly those which were condemned by those four renowned general councils, that of Nicea, of Constantinople, the first of Ephesus and that of Chalcedon. When God shall once summon me out of this life, then, certain of the salvation proclaimed to me by Christ the Lord, I entrust my soul into his hands and I leave my body to my friends to be committed to the earth without an ostentatious funeral''.[320]

---

[320] *Ibid.*, fol. 153-155r.

SECOND PART

THEOLOGY

CHAPTER FOUR

# AUTHORITY

## 1. Crisis of Authority

The religious struggle which went on in the sixteenth century was largely concerned with authority in church and state. The existing organs of authority were attacked. In the sixteenth century papal authority in the church was weighed in the balance and found wanting; in the seventeenth and eighteenth centuries it was the same with the monarch's authority in various countries.

In the corpus christianum which had flourished in the Middle Ages, it was inconceivable that more than one authoritative body could exist in European civilization. In Germany the question as to whether the highest authority rested with emperor or pope was contested with varying results. There were analogous developments elsewhere. In France the conclusion of the Pragmatic Sanction of Bourges (1438) meant that king and parliament received greater powers in church appointments and procedures which, to some degree, fell in with nationalistic Gallican aspirations. In England the *Statutes of Provisors* (1351, 1390) and *of Praemunire* (1353, 1393) expressed growing nationalist feelings. They were directed against the outflow of the proceeds from ecclesiastical sources to the Curia, Roman influence in church appointments and the appeal by English subjects to a foreign, that is, papal court. These and other clashes between the secular and religious power took place within the bounds of the corpus christianum in which the prevalent standard, one emperor, one king, one faith, one church, continued to be upheld. This was the reason that Richard II issued the Letters Patent against the Lollards in 1384 and that John Huss was executed in 1415.

In the three territories just mentioned the sixteenth century Reformation took quite different courses and the crisis of authority was also provisionally resolved in different ways. In Germany the struggle finally resulted in a division between the two religions, Roman Catholic and Lutheran, on the principle, "cuius regio, eius religio". Calvinism had to wait until the Peace of Westphalia (1648) before being recognised as a third religion. In France, the motherland of Calvinism, this movement organized its own church life alongside the Church. After bloody religious wars, Henry IV issued the Edict of Nantes (1598) by which the Reformed who then numbered some ten per cent of the French population, were granted freedom of conscience and a certain measure of freedom of worship and church organization. In this way there arose in France an ec-

clesiastically pluriform society which was something new for Europe, until
Louis XIV brought it to an end by new persecutions and by revoking the
Edict of Nantes (1685). A similar development to that in France occurred
in the Netherlands, with the difference that whilst the Roman Catholic
church remained the embodiment of the official state religion in France,
here the Reformed church became the privileged national church
alongside which other churches were tolerated with varying degrees of
connivance.

Again the situation was quite different in England. Here a national
church arose free of Rome. The king acted as "the only supreme governor...as well in all spiritual or ecclesiastical things or causes, as temporal",
and all ministers of the church had to take an oath to him.[1] The foremost
defender of the Elizabethan settlement, Richard Hooker, thought that the
royal supremacy was the only guarantee of unity and order in both church
and society.[2] This presupposed the existence of "one commonwealth—a
"state" in matters temporal and a "church" in matters spiritual—in
which certain men, the clergy, occupied themselves professionally with
religion". In fact, of course, from the beginning of this settlement, the
liberty or prerogative of the crown had been limited: the monarch was
always thought of as the king-in-parliament,[3] a factor which was to appear
of overwhelming political significance in the pre-history of the Civil War
in the seventeenth century. However, in the final decades of the sixteenth
century England provided an example of the corpus christianum in Constantinian style far more than did Germany or France, to say nothing of
the Netherlands. In England there was neither a territorial partition as in
Luther's native land nor a kind of edict of toleration as in Calvin's, but,
on the contrary, the demand was for "uniformity" and this was urged by
the highest authority.[4] The practical consequences for the two groups of
people who deviated to left and right of the Elizabethan establishment's
"via media", either because they were unwilling in conscience to
acknowledge a higher authority than that of God's Word or because the
Bishop of Rome's authority was supreme for them,[5] is evident from the
long series of measures which culminated in 1593 in the *Act against the*

[1] *Documents illustrative of English Church History*. H. Gee and W. J. Hardy, ed. (repr. New
York, 1972) 448 f.

[2] "...only the king's royal power is of so large compass, that no man commanded by him
according to order of law, can plead himself to be without the bounds and limits of that
authority... And, that kings should be in such sort supreme commanders over all men, we
hold it requisite, as well as for the ordering of spiritual life as of civil affairs; inasmuch as
without universal authority in this kind, they should not be able when need is, to do as vir-
tuous kings have done." Hooker, *Works,* III, 431 f.

[3] G. R. Elton, *The Tudor Constitution* (Cambridge, 1972) 335 f.

[4] Elizabeth's Act of Uniformity (1559). Gee, *Documents,* 458-467.

[5] E. Rose, *Cases of Conscience. Alternatives open to Recusants and Puritans under Elizabeth I and
James I.* Cambridge, 1975.

*Puritans*[6] and the *Act against Recusants*.[7] However, it would not be long before it was discovered too in England that "supremacy" and "uniformity" did not provide adequate answers to the ever more urgent question of true authority. In England too the corpus christianum came to an end.

## 2.   SARAVIA AND CALVINISM

The man with whom this book is concerned was a convinced defender of this supremacy and uniformity. This is the more remarkable because in the earlier periods of his life he had held other convictions. He knew the monastic life from his own experience, probably he was ordained to the priesthood there, he heard scholastic theology taught in Paris and in this period he accepted papal authority. Then came the Calvinist stage. After he had encountered Calvinist preaching in Jacques Taffin's entourage, he moved in Reformed circles for nearly thirty years: in the Dutch refugees' congregations in London, in Antwerp and Brussels, in the Channel Islands and Southampton and then for a further nine years in the Netherlands. He was involved in the creation of the Belgic Confession to which he subscribed to the end of his life. His flight from the Netherlands ushered in the third stage of his long life. He deliberately chose his place in the Church of England and he served his archbishop, his queen and his king faithfully and well, but he never regarded his choice of England as a break with the Reformed churches in France and the Netherlands. He continued to write of them as "our churches" and in Canterbury he preached for the Walloon refugees. He was apparently completely unconscious of differences between the Church of England and the continental Reformed churches which appeared at a later date. This must make us wary of applying to the sixteenth century distinctions and divisions which only played a part in church and theology in the second half of the seventeenth century after the Restoration.

In the sixteenth century the Church of England was entirely dependent upon the continent in her theology. Only Hooker may be considered as the first original thinker, although he also had been profoundly influenced by continental Reformed theology. "The interest therefore in the study of the relations between the English Church and the continental churches during the sixteenth century lies in seeing how and why English minds absorbed continental thought, and why, though so many Englishmen derived their thought from Luther or Calvin or Zwingli, English theology from Hooker onwards was not precisely Lutheran, nor Calvinist, nor Zwinglian".[8] This was the church in which Saravia finally felt most at

---

[6] Gee, *Documents*, 492-498.

[7] *Ibid.*, 498-508.

[8] O. Chadwick, "The sixteenth Century," in: R. R. Darlington, M. D. Knowles, a.o., ed. *The English Church and the Continent* (London, 1959) 61.

home. He was in no way an original thinker. His mind had "absorbed continental thought" to a far greater extent than any of the so-called Marian Exiles. The aspect of his theological work which is mostly discussed is that where he differs from Calvinism, namely in his views of the church's ministry and church government. Must we then conclude from his dispute with Beza and the English Puritans that he abandoned the entire theological thought world in which he had lived for more than 25 years and which, especially during his residence and ministry in the Netherlands from 1578 to 1587, he clearly professed? The answer to this question is important for two reasons, the one historical, the other ecumenical. From the historical point of view Saravia can serve as a concrete example of the actual theological and political relationship between the Church of England and the continental Reformed churches at the end of the sixteenth and the beginning of the seventeenth centuries: there is hardly anyone else who thought and worked so actively in both sorts of church. From the ecumenical standpoint the answer to our question can have an importance for the problems of our own day. Might Saravia act as a model for the bridging of later opposition between episcopalianism and presbyterianism? The answer depends on the reply to another question: did his defence of the bishop's office and his attack on the Reformed elder mean that he had abandoned the fundamental theological tenets of the Calvinist Reformation? If this is not in fact the case, then may we not conclude that in principle a Protestant Calvinist theology allows room for, or at least does not have to be fundamentally opposed to, an episcopal view of the church? The resolution of the latter question will come within the field of ecclesiology.

Before we attempt a provisional answer to the question of the significance of Calvinism for Saravia's thought, it must be pointed out that our sources provide us with little material for such an answer. The great themes in the controversy between Rome and the Reformation, for example, the relationship between Scripture and tradition, the doctrines of justification or the sacraments, only crop up sporadically and incidentally. Saravia's theological thought, in so far as we know it from his treatises and correspondence, revolves like an ellipse around two foci: authority in the church and authority in society. Apart from this there is up to now only one tract known to be written by Saravia which deals with a definite dogmatic topic, that is his *De eucharistra*. We shall return to this. However, we must point out that his attacks on Rome scarcely concerned the above-mentioned subjects, but rather nearly always the pope's pretensions to authority and usurpation of power. Thus in the dispute with Rome too the problem of authority was of prime concern to him.

The limited and one-sided nature of the available material, however, in no way justifies the conclusion that, in England. Saravia repudiated his Calvinist past. On the contrary, it was not a topic of discussion for him simply because it continued silently to be presumed. His discussion with Beza on ministry and hierarchy took place within the bounds of a communion of faith which he shared with Calvin's successor and consequently with Calvinism and of which he was deeply conscious. "Not a single difference exists between us on religion but only on the manner in which it can best be preserved inviolate and expanded." He called his debate with Beza "friendly and brotherly" and could do so because "there is no difference of opinion between us on God's Word and its authority".[9]

There are at least two clear proofs of the fact that Saravia never repudiated his Calvinist past. First, in this connection, we must once more refer to his letter of 13 April (o.s.) 1612 to Wtenbogaert. In this he gave some information on the origins of the *Belgic Confession* and on his part in this. He said of the authors' intention, that they did not want to promulgate a rule of faith but only attempted to prove their beliefs from Scripture.[10] He entirely shared this intention. In modern terms, it could be said that Guido de Brès and his colleagues were not confessionalists. They held a spiritual, not a legalistic, view of their confession. Nevertheless, Saravia declared, "Yet, in my view, there is nothing objectionable in the confession nor anything which I would wish to alter. If, however, there are people who do not agree with everything then they must be given a hearing and instructed from God's Word whether what they are objecting to is in accordance with that Word. No-one who is prepared to allow himself to be instructed ought without reason to be counted an unbeliever. The articles do not all carry the same weight. There may be some of which it can be said that if someone disagrees with them then this is permissible and they must not for this reason be put out of the church. I held the same view of your catechism which I myself taught both in the French[11] and Dutch churches". A Lutheran theologian could never have spoken like this about his confession, only a Calvinist could have expressed its meaning thus. In the confession of the Reformed Church in the Netherlands, Saravia found an adequate expression of Christian belief with which he could associate himself to the end of his life. Like Calvin, however, he held the view that there was a certain order of importance in doctrine: not all articles of faith carried the same weight. In his *Institutes*, the Genevan reformer had drawn the distinction between the "essentials of true doctrine", which were of the essence of religion and the knowledge and acceptance of which were therefore completely necessary, and other articles of Christian doctrine which were of less importance and which consequently ought not to be the

---

[9] "Nulla inter nos est de religione controversia, sed quomodo optime conservari inter homines et propagari possit." *DT*, preface K4. "De verbo Dei aut de eius authoritate nulla inter nos est controversia." *ET*, Epist. Dedic., 4.

[10] "...fidei canonem edere: verum ex canonicis scriptis fidem suam probare." *EE*, Nr. 181; Doc. XLVI.

[11] Walloon.

occasion of division although there might be different views on them. "I say that we are not on account of every minute difference to leave a church in which the sound doctrine of godliness is preserved whole and unimpaired".[12] Both Calvin and Saravia thought that, within the bounds of the confession of "the essentials of true doctrine", there ought to be room for differing views on less important points.

So then it is not at all contrary to his declaration of agreement with the *Belgic Confession* when in the same letter to Wtenbogaert, Saravia reveals his objections to the way in which a particular doctrine, that of Christ's descent into hell, was expressed.[13] After leaving the Netherlands he had changed his mind about this under the influence of the sermons and writings of Thomas Bilson, Bishop of Winchester, and, so he said, of "other learned men who were in no way inferior to Calvin or Beza". He had written two books on this for the Reformed churches which had not yet been published, but he would shortly send Wtenbogaert a manuscript copy by messenger.[14] No copies of such of Saravia's writings have yet been found.

The doctrine he opposed is familiar enough. Calvin had dissociated Christ's descent into hell from the well known scriptural text I Peter 3:19 and understood it as his sense of being forsaken by God on the cross (Matthew 27:46).[15] This view, which was not as new as was supposed,[16] had been adopted in the *Genevan Catechism*,[17] in the *Heidelberg Catechism*,[18] and in the Holy Communion services of the Palatinate and the Netherlands.[19] In England, just as in later Calvinist orthodoxy,[20] there were various opinions on this doctrine. As early as 1562 this gave rise to a sharp dispute

---

[12] *Inst.* (1559), IV, 1, 12; *CO*, II, 755 f.

[13] For the views on the descensus ad inferos in the Reformation and post Reformation periods, see W. Bieder, *Die Vorstellung von der Höllenfahrt Jesu Christi* (Zurich, 1949) 6-32; for the exegesis of 1 Peter 3: 18-20. *Ibid.*, 96-120. Here it may be seen (p. 109 f.) that Hugh Broughton's opinions, which we will consider presently, are not so preposterous as they appear at first sight.

[14] *EE*, Nr. 181; Doc. XLVI.

[15] *Inst.* (1559), II, 16, 8-12; *CO*, II, 375-379.

[16] It contains certain elements of Luther's views and also perhaps of the mystics. Vogelsang, "Weltbild und Kreuzestheologie", 100-104. Calvin himself knew that the doctrine in question had only first been accepted in the church quite late on and that already in the early church different interpretations were current. *Ibid.*, II, 16, 8; *CO*, II, 375. See on this *RGG³*, III, 409 f. s.v. "Höllenfahrt Christi"; F. L. Cross and E. A. Livingstone, ed. *The Oxford Dictionary of the Christian Church* (2nd ed. London/New York/Toronto, 1974) 395, s.v. "The Descent of Christ into Hell."

[17] Questions 65 and 66. *Bekenntnisschriften und Kirchenordnungen der nach Gottes Wort reformierten Kirche*, W. Niesel, ed. (Munich, 1938) 10.

[18] Question 44. *Ibid.*, 159; *De Nederlandsche Belijdenisgeschriften*. J. N. Bakhuizen van den Brink, ed. (2nd ed. Amsterdam, 1976) 174 f.

[19] *Bekenntnisschriften*, 191.

[20] H. Heppe, *Die Dogmatik der evangelisch-reformierten Kirche*. E. Bizer, ed. (Neukirchen, 1958) 394 f.

between those who based their interpretation on I Peter 3:19 and those who followed Calvin's explanation. Both sides naturally appealed to the fathers.[21] As we have already seen, Hugh Broughton entered the controversy by interpreting "inferi" as "the world to come" which he understood as "paradise". In his *Survey of Christ's Sufferings and Descent into Hell* and in shorter writings, Thomas Bilson defended the realistic view of "inferi" as hell. In England, this doctrinal dispute which had gone on in the church for centuries, was tried up with the dispute between the Puritans, who defended Calvin's views, and the representatives of the establishment who found their mouthpiece in Bilson.[22] Perhaps for this reason, Saravia sided with the latter, but it is difficult to see in this any divergence from Calvinism as such. The reformer's disciples themselves held differing opinions on the descent into hell. Moreover, this concerns an article of faith of which Calvin gave the impression that it was not one of the most essential. It is not possible therefore to set Saravia's views against his professed agreement with the *Belgic Confession*.

This agreement is further shown in another way which is closely akin to Calvin's view of a Reformed confession, namely that it did not exclude the Lutheran Augsburg Confession. Although historically he was mistaken,[23] Saravia saw such an exclusivist attitude in Beza's refusal to sign the *Augsburg Confession* during the Colloquy of Poissy (1561).[24] In his will he himself named this Lutheran confession along with the English *Thirty Nine Articles* and the three ecumenical creeds of the early church as the expressions of the Christian faith which he accepted.[25] Here he evinced the same ecumenical conviction which distinguished Calvin who had striven vigorously for communion both with the Lutherans[26] and the Church of England[27] and who had signed the *Augsburg Confession* in both its forms, the *Invariata* (1530) as well as the *Variata* (1541).[28]

Further evidence of Saravia's abiding attachment to the Calvinist tradition is provided by his continual appeal to Calvin himself against Beza's rejection of the bishop's office which the latter called a human invention

---

[21] Strype, *Annals*, I, 519.

[22] Knappen, *Tudor Puritanism*, 371. A detailed description of the history of the doctrinal dispute in England is given by D. D. Wallace, Jr. "Puritan and Anglican: The Interpretation of Christ's Descent Into Hell in Elizabethan Theology", *ARG*, LXIX (1978) 248-287.

[23] He took no account of the fact that the Cardinal of Lorraine raised the question of the Augsburg Confession in connection with the discussion on the Eucharist in the hope of bringing the controversy between Lutherans and Calvinists to light once more. Nugent, *Ecumenism in the Age of the Reformation*, 127, 143, 148 f., 208-218.

[24] Memorandum of a conversation with I. Casaubon (1610). BodL. Casaubon Mss. 28, fol. 6.

[25] KAO.PRC. 32/42, fol. 153r; Doc. XLIX.

[26] W. Nijenhuis, *Calvinus Oecumenicus. Calvijn en de eenheid der kerk in het licht van zijn briefwisseling* (The Hague, 1959) 131-199.

[27] *Ibid.*, 200-219.

[28] Id., "Calvin and the Augsburg Confession", in: *Ecclesia Reformata*, 97-114.

(as opposed to the office given by God and the office used by the devil). There are too many references for us to mention them all; we will cite just a few of them. In order to avoid any misunderstanding, we must note first that Saravia frequently condemned Calvin along with Beza for his share in the conception of the presbyterian church order. For example, Calvin had been the first to use I Tim. 5:17 as a proof text for the scriptural character of the ruling elder who was responsible for the exercise of the "censura morum" but had no authority to teach.[29] Saravia thought that Beza had also taken the exclusion of the deacons from administering the Lord's Supper from Calvin.[30] For the rest he also regarded Peter Martyr, Pierre Viret, Oecolampadius, Luther, Bucer "et alii praeclari Evangelii doctores" as being guilty of limiting the deacon's office to the care of the poor to the exclusion of theological studies and a preaching ministry.[31] When Beza rejected the bishop's office because of the danger of dictatorship in the church. Saravia, not unjustly, observed that Calvin and his successor wielded more authority over their colleagues than even the primate of the Church of England,[32] and he further added: "For my part I would prefer to have Beza as a lawful bishop than as a despotic colleague".[33] He continually harped back to Calvin and Beza as examples of innovators who departed from the "concordia" and "unanimis sententia" of the fathers.[34]

However, setting aside the fact that this criticism of Calvin was restricted to the structure of the Genevan church and never touched on doctrinal matters (with the exception of doctrine of the "descensus ad inferos"), it is much more noteworthy that, especially in his defence of his *De Gradibus*, Saravia frequently appealed to Calvin against Beza if the bishop's office was the topic of discussion. Saravia declared correctly that Calvin was not opposed to episcopacy in principle. He then summed up his entire opposition to Beza's *De triplici genere* thus: "In this exposition, perhaps to the surprise of some, I defend Dr. Calvin's opinion about bishops against Dr. Beza".[35] He appealed to a reference in Calvin's *Harmony of the Gospels*[36] for the application of Exodus 18:21, about the seventy who had to assist Moses. Saravia saw in Calvin's letter to his friend

---

[29] "Dominus Calvinus (ni fallor) fuit primus qui ex hoc loco seniores deduxit, qui non docerent, sed tantum censurae morum praeessent." *DT,* 131.

[30] *Ibid.,* 73.

[31] *Ibid.,* 74.

[32] *Ibid.,* 51 f.

[33] *Ibid.,* 53.

[34] *Ibid.,* 72 f.

[35] "In hac disputatione (quod forsan aliqui mirabuntur) contra D. Bezam D. Calvini sententiam de episcopis progugno." *ETB,* Epist. Dedicat., 2. Cf. another expression: "Nihil aliud in hoc meo tractatu quam quod Calvinus libro quatro suarum Institutionum disseruit, defendo." *DT,* 164.

[36] *DT,* 13. See *CO,* XLV, 309.

Gerard Roussel, who had been consecrated in the Roman church,[37] confirmation of his proposition that the Reformer was not opposed to episcopacy.[38] He thought he could also demonstrate this from certain passages in Calvin's *De necessitate reformandae ecclesiae.*[39]

Saravia was frequently concerned with the exegetical question of the meaning of I Tim. 4:14 where mention is made of the laying on of hands by the πρεσβυτέριον Does this here mean the body of presbyters rather than the "presbyterii ordo", the office, the ministry? In his own exposition of I Tim. Calvin decided on the latter.[40] On various occasions Saravia took the opportunity of pointing out Calvin's view, both in the latter's commentary on I Tim[41] and in his *Institutes,*[42] to Beza who had opted for the other interpretation. It would not be difficult to refer to dozens of other places where Saravia cited Calvin because the latter did not reject the bishop's office as such. Research into church history has confirmed that this is indeed the case.[43]

Must we then conclude, on the grounds of his agreement with the *Belgic Confession* and his frequent appeals to Calvin, that Saravia was a Calvinist and that he remained one? It is certain that he did not wish to be so in an exclusive way, that is in one which was sharply divided from Lutheranism. England was free of the fierce opposition which existed on the continent between Calvinists and Lutherans. Such opposition was foreign to Saravia who liked party names as little as did the great reformers themselves. In his great defence of Bellarmine, the Jesuit, Jacob Gretser, constantly called him a Calvinist, just as he also spoke of "Calviniana Anglia".[44] Where did he get this from? How was it that he labelled the whole "ecclesia anglicana" as "calviniana"?, so a somewhat irritated Saravia wondered. Did Gretzer perhaps think that in England people were more attached to Calvin than to other "doctores nostri temporis" such as Luther, Bucer, Oecolampadius, P. Martyr, Bullinger and Zanchius? "We have drawn the same truth from the same source as they". Did Gretser think, that they were accustomed to swear in the same way by one particular man just as

---

[37] *De christiani hominis officio in sacerdotiis papalis ecclesiae vel administrandis vel abiiciendis* (1537). *CO,* V, 279-312.

[38] *DT,* 36; *ETB,* 52.

[39] *DT,* 160, 164; *ETB;* Prologus, 2, 4; *Ibid.,* 58. See *CO,* VI, 451-534. The quotation in Saravia's *Defensio* is in *CO,* VI, 522 f.

[40] *CO,* LII, 302.

[41] *ETB,* 10, 28.

[42] *DT,* 212, reference to *Inst.* (1559) IV, 3, 16; *CO,* II, 787; *ET,* 58, reference to *Ibid.,* IV, 4, 4; *CO,* II, 790.

[43] J. Pannier, *Calvin et l'épiscopat.* Paris, 1927; Nijenhuis, *Calvinus Oecumenicus,* 304.

[44] *Controversiarum Roberti Bellarmini... Defensio...* Auctore Jacobo Gretsero (2 vols., Ingolstad, 1607-1609) I, 2002; II, 436, 437, 457, 504, 512, 635, 1163, 1165. Gretser repeatedly mentioned the English "Calvinopapistae", by which he meant Sutcliffe, Saravia and other defenders of episcopacy.

he himself did by Ignatius Loyola?[45] "But even suppose that I were first and foremost a follower of Calvin, I would not condemn a hierarchy which submitted to Christ nor would I reject the Church discipline which in former times flourished under bishops, archbishops and patriarchs",[46] thus wrote Saravia with a reference to the place in Calvin's *De necessitate reformandae ecclesiae* which he often[47] cited.[48] He impressed upon Gretser that those who, like the Puritans, rejected episcopacy were at odds with Calvin. The latter was not opposed to the bishop's office as such but only to the Roman form of it which served in defence of the Kingdom of Antichrist.[49] There was no point in quoting "Calvinistam contra Calvinistas".[50]

### 3.  FORMAL AUTHORITY IN THE CHURCH

By the source from which he, together with Calvin and other reformers, had drawn the truth, Saravia meant Holy Scripture. For him this was the only authoritative corpus which Christians had to obey. As he expressed it, in the words of Acts 20:27, in the canonical books of the Bible, "the whole purpose of God had been revealed" in the most reliable way.[51] This does not contradict his frequent appeal to the "consensus patrum": the fathers were the authoritative expositors of Scripture because they lived nearer the apostles' days than do we who are so far removed from them by time, place and culture. "Earlier regulations are not to be judged by those which exist at present. Therefore a knowledge of history is essential. If this is disregarded then people will be borne hither and thither by unsound expositions and will be easily led into error".[52] Consequently he could say that the reform of the church ought to be guided "by the rule of God's Word and the oldest and holiest standards of the ancient fathers".[53] This sounds as though Scripture and tradition were put on a par with each other, but this was not in fact the case. Saravia recognised that the fathers were fallible men and the "consensus patrum" was authoritative for him

---

[45] *RG*, 352.

[46] *Ibid.*

[47] *DT*, 160, 164; *ETB*, Prologus, 2.

[48] See note 39.

[49] "Quam non fuerit episcopis et archiepiscopis adversarius Calvinus, ad illos scriptae testantur epistolae. Quandoque contra episcopos scripsit, istos qui istic apud vos sunt, intellexit; in quibus praeter nomen aut nihil inest episcopi, aut totum, quidquid illud est, convertitur ad regnum defendendum Antichristi".

[50] *RG*, 352.

[51] "...ut in libris illis canonicis omne nos habere Dei consilium expositum certo certius credendum sit". *RG*, 374.

[52] *ET*, Epist. Dedic., 4.

[53] "ad verbi Dei normam et vetustos sanctissimosque veterum patrum canones". *ET*, 102.

so long as it was in accordance with God's Word.[54] The "expressum verbum Dei" could compel reform even if this was contrary to this consensus. "I attribute not the slightest authority to the fathers if they teach anything against the express Word of God. I know that their writings are only a guideline for Christian faith in so far as they are in accordance with it". Saravia thus left no doubt as to his view on the relationship between Scripture and tradition, but this was not by any means to say that the patristic consensus ought to be regarded as of little importance.[55] Although the fathers had their shortcomings, it was a matter of no small importance that they be regarded as "our patrons in the principal articles of Christian religion and external church government".[56] The consensus of the primitive church ought not to be put on a par with God's Word but it was entitled to the highest authority after that Word.[57] Saravia could well say: "The rule of God's people which has been accepted by all churches in the whole world, is an inviolable law", a notion inspired by Vincent of Lérins which he impressed on Beza.[58] However, this idea had to be seen in relation to its starting-point: "it is not likely that a general consensus of all churches at all times could have occurred without God's Word or the apostolic tradition".[59] The fathers' opinions were to be controlled by Scripture which acted as the "norma normans" for church tradition which was itself only the "norma normata". Saravia wanted to further an examination of the Scriptures in his treatise De Gradibus so that it would appear "whether they or we are in error".[60]

On the other hand, it must be pointed out that there is no question here of a free enquiry into the "loca probantia" for episcopal church order, because for him the result was already determined. "The unbroken usage of the fathers in all places and times is an infallible interpreter of the

---

[54] "Contra unanimem et constantem omnium patrum veteris ecclesiae consensum nihil sine expresso Dei verbo est innovandum". DT, Prologus; DGM, Prologus.

[55] "Patribus nihil tribuo, si quid doceant contra expressum Dei verbum. Scio eorum scripta non esse canonem fidei christianae, nisi quatenus cum eo consentiunt; alias universalem consensu patrum in re quapiam contemnere non audeo". DT, 209.

[56] "...ipsos tamen in praecipuis christianae religionis capitibus et externa ecclesiae politia (quae inter nos et pontificios controversa sunt) habere patronos, non parvi momenti res est". Ibid.

[57] "Tametsi populi Dei consensus ab apostolorum temporibus usque ad hanc diem, verbo Dei aequari non debeat; proximum tamen ab eo locum, authoritatis iure sibi vendicat". Ibid.

[58] ETB, 17.

[59] "Mos populi Dei ab omnibus ecclesiis totius orbis receptus, inviolabilis quaedam lex est. Verisimile non est universalem consensum omnium ecclesiarum, et temporum sine verbo Dei aut apostolica traditione potuisse accidere". DGM, Prologus; DT, Prologus.

[60] "Tamen quia nullus consensus, nulla consuetudo, nulla longi temporis praescriptio contra Dei verbum locum in ecclesia Christi retinere debet, ponderandae sunt nobis rationes, et Scripturae loca examinanda, quibus inducti patres illud regimen in ecclesia receperunt, quod hominibus nostrae aetatis minime probatur; ut certo sciamus, illine, an nos erremus". Ibid.

apostolic tradition....Who are we, that, without the express Word of God,
we should dare to alter what has always been observed by all churches?''[61]
Such an utterance sounds like that of the traditionalist and indeed it is.
However, it must be remembered that in his thinking on the question of
the highest authority in the church, Saravia was in a different position
from that of Reformed theologians on the continent. They only fought on
one front, against the Church of Rome. In this struggle new church
organizations had grown up which differed in their beliefs and which quar-
relled fiercely with each other particularly with regard to the doctrine of
the Lord's supper. Saravia however lived, thought and worked in England
in a church which both formally and structurally had maintained a much
greater continuity with the old church and which, in order to preserve its
unity had to fight on two fronts: against the Roman Catholics on the one
side and the Puritans on the other. This battle on two fronts meant that the
authority of God's Word had to be asserted against the Roman Catholics
and the authoritative importance of the early church's tradition against the
Puritans. Thus, when Saravia declared his preference for the ''vetus
mos'', that is episcopal church government, over that of the contemporary
''reformata ecclesia'', the Genevan church order, it was with an eye to the
Roman Catholics that he made it clear that he did not mean the ''mos'' of
the medieval church but exclusively the tradition of the church of the first
five or six Christian centuries.[62] For in this earliest period the church's
faith and order had been in conformity with God's Word. Afterwards the
great decay set in. The ''tyrannis pontificia'' had done so much damage in
the last 600 years that the church had needed a ''magna reformatio''.[63]
Reformation, so Saravia impressed upon the Roman Catholics, is a return
to God's Word and to the model of church life that is in accordance with
God's Word, and thus to the tradition of the early church. However, this
tradition was not independantly normative. Therefore the theologian who
showed such respect towards it could declare against his Jesuit opponent,
Gretser: ''Whenever in the past reform has occurred in God's people both
in faith and practice, this happened not on the basis of the tradition and
usage of previous times but on the basis of God's Word. The Word was
not expounded to sanction existing practices, but on the contrary the practices were accommodated to the Word of God''.[64]

However, as he urged on the Puritans in England and on his former
Reformed colleagues in the Netherlands, we may not repudiate tradition
in our reformation. ''In a true, Christian and free reformation only that

---

[61] *ETB*, 73.

[62] *DT*, 75 f.

[63] *Ibid.*, Prologus, 2.

[64] ''Olim quandocunque in populo Dei aliqua reformatio tam fidei quam morum accidit,
illa non ex usu et moribus praecedentium temporum fiebat, sed ex verbo Dei. Verbum ad
confirmandos mores non trahebatur, sed mores ad verbum Dei''. *RG*, 380.

may be changed where people have departed from the rule prescribed for us in God's Word. Nothing new may be introduced for which no example can be shown from antiquity. Christianity was not born with us. We are neither the only nor the first Christians with whom Christian wisdom was born''.[65]

Saravia's theological views on authority in the church concurred in three respects with those of the continental reformers, including those of Calvin. First, the Reformation meant a return to the absolute authority of God's Word. Secondly, the Reformation meant an attentive harkening to the Fathers as the authoritative expounders of Scripture which on the continent meant especially Augustine. Thirdly, Saravia shared a view of history with the continental theologians which formed the background for them both: the Middle Ages were the period of darkness in which the papal power had denied the authority of God's Word. Luther and Calvin had said exactly the same as Saravia: "At last, God moved by pity for his church, has raised up pious teachers and pastors and caused the light of his Gospel to appear from out of the darkness''.[66]

That Saravia fully shared the formal principle of the continental Reformation according to which Scripture is the only organ of authority and is therefore the norm for all church reform, appeared when he urged on Beza the nine propositions of Hieronymus Zanchi's *De vera reformandarum ecclesiarum reformatorione*. In at least four of these propositions, Zanchi, a Calvinist and an ardent defender of predestination and of the "perseverantia sanctorum", expounded the "sola scriptura" with great clarity. Saravia followed him in this. True religion is only learned in God's Word (proposition 3). The Word of God is contained in the canonical Scriptures (proposition 4). No doctrine is found outside the canonical Scriptures which is necessary for salvation (proposition 6). Whatever conflicts with the Word of God must be expelled from the church. The "adiaphora" can continue to be maintained in so far as they serve "ad aedificationem, ad ordinem aut ad decorem in ecclesia", without, however, binding Christians' consciences. "For the consciences of Christians are bound only by the Word of God" (proposition 8).[67] From this Saravia concluded that the "veteris et apostolicae forma" was to be gathered "liquido et certe" from the Scriptures and "probaliter" from the ancient post-apostolic writers. On account then of the "clearer and more certain" character of the scriptural data the biblical authors ought to be

---

[65] "Ea tantum in vera et christiana liberaque reformatione sunt mutanda, in quibus aberratum fuit a regula, nobis in verbo Dei praescripta. Nihil novi est introducendum, cuius ex antiquitate non possit demonstrari exemplum. Nobiscum non est natus Christianismus, nec soli nos sumus, nec primi Christiani, ut nobiscum sit quoque christiana nata sapientia''. *ET*, 74.

[66] *DT*, Prologus, 3.

[67] *ETB*, 102 f.

consulted, the New Testament first of all, ''inprimis''. Next, ''deinde'', because of the ''acceptable'' character of the ancient writers, their opinions ought to be examined.[68] First Scripture, then the fathers, nothing could be clearer!

However, there are two distinct differences to be observed between Saravia and the continental reformers. First, he undoubtedly appealed to antiquity more frequently than they. In contrast to Calvin, the notion of ''antiquity'' in itself possessed something of an authoritative character for him. His appreciation of the fathers was rather uncritical. The difference emerges if his esteem for Christian antiquity is compared with that of the first and second generation of English reformers who were closer to Luther, Zwingli and Calvin.[69] They, however, were not yet occupied with the theme of Saravia's most important treatises: the defence of the ecclesiastical and political establishment against Puritan criticism. Like the continental Reformation theologians on whom they were also entirely dependent, they were still fighting on one front. It is obvious that, in his battle on two fronts, Saravia needed to defend the structure and government of the Church of England against Genevan influences and therefore reached back to antiquity. There was a great difference in the political and ecclesiastical and consequently in the theological situation in England between the first and second half of the sixteenth century.

The second difference between Saravia and the continental reformers, especially as regards the Reformed, lay in the conclusions which they thought had to be drawn from their common starting point: the church's structure ought to be in accordance with the norm of God's Word. The Dutch Englishman now reached a different conclusion to that of the Genevan fathers. He found the clearest example of a genuine reformation in the Church of England which, with wisdom and moderation in its doctrine, had fully applied the authority of God's Word to its church government and liturgy without departing from the tradition of the early church. Thus the English church had become an example for other churches.[70] However, none of this did anything to disturb the fundamental fellowship between the churches on the continent and that in England: ''There is not

---

[68] *Ibid.*, 104.

[69] S. L. Greenslade, *The English Reformers and the Fathers of the Church* (Oxford, 1960) 6-9.

[70] ''Inter caeteros qui reformarunt ecclesias, saepe miratus sum sapientiam eorum qui Anglicanae Ecclesiae restituerunt verum Dei cultum, et ita se attemperarunt, ut nusquam decesisse ab antiqua et prisca ecclesiae consuetudine reprehendi possint; ea moderatione ubi sint, ut vicinos a reformatione non deterruerint, sed magis suo exemplo invitaverint; quam si alii fuissent secuti, minus bellorum civilium haberemus. Primum ad verbi Dei amussim dogmata et totam fidei doctrinam revocarunt: ecclesiae regimen, ritus et ceremonias ex usu et universali more poluli Dei qui olim fuit, restituerunt; ita ut nullius iure novitatis queant accusari. Quidquid aut reiectum est, aut mutatum, aut retentum fuit, tam authoritate verbi Dei quam usu et traditione Christianorum potest defendi''. *DT,* 4.

the slightest difference of opinion between us on the Word of God and its authority." The formal principle of the Reformation was shared by all.

### 4. MATERIAL AUTHORITY IN THE CHURCH

If, despite a common acceptance of the supreme authority of Scripture in the church, they could come to differing conclusions as to its government and organization, then the question arises as to the position of doctrine, the Gospel as it was understood from Scripture in the Reformation. A comparison between the *Thirty Nine Articles* and various German, French and Dutch confessions reveals that the affinity in doctrine is extremely great although traces of the different Reformation schools, the Lutheran, Zwinglian and Calvinist, cannot easily be found everywhere in the English confession. It is clear that the fundamental doctrine of justification by faith was not in dispute in England. In this respect the Church of England was and is an authentic Protestant church.

There is little to be found in Saravia's writings on the material theological controversy between Rome and the Reformation which came to a head over the doctrine of justification. "I desire to maintain peace and fellowship with all the churches of Christ in which the true doctrine concerning God the Father and His Son Jesus Christ is accepted", he declared.[71] A shorter summary of belief was hardly conceivable. The doctrine of God and Christology, as they had been confessed by the early church, were for him the heart of the Christian faith. Calvin was also able to summarize very briefly the essentials of belief, those articles which must be irrefutably established in the church, namely "that God is one, that Christ is God and God's Son, that our salvation depends on God's mercy, and suchlike".[72] It is striking that, to the two doctrines cited by Saravia, the reformer adds a third: the salvation of mankind by God's grace. The Reformation doctrine of justification was implied in the six words "in Dei misericordia salutem nobis consistere".

The fact that Saravia nowhere dealt with this explicitly and did not imply it in his brief summary of belief, does not mean that it had no value for him. There was no fundamental difference of opinion on the doctrine of justification either between the continental reformers amongst themselves or between them and English theologians. There was an essential consensus on "sola fide" shared by all English reformers from William Tyndale to Richard Hooker,[73] which was expressed thus by John Jewel: "As for those persons whom they upon spite call Zwinglians and

---

[71] *Ibid.*, 3.

[72] *Inst.* (1559), IV, 1, 21; *CO*, II, 756.

[73] E. G. Rupp, *Studies in the making of the English Protestant Tradition* (repr. Cambridge, 1966) 171.

Lutherans, in very deed they of both sides be Christians and good friends and brethren. They vary not betwixt themselves upon the principles and foundations of our religion, nor as touching God, nor Christ, nor the Holy Ghost, nor the nature of justification''.[74] This faith was also presumed by Saravia.[75] It was just at the point where he thought he detected this doctrine with the Roman Catholics that he recognized something of the church in them. He esteemed those canons of the Council of Trent which, rightly or wrongly, he supposed expressed the belief in a way which was acceptable to Reformation Christians. This was the case in Sessio V, cap. 1, 2 and 3 on the Fall of Adam and the "corruptio humanae naturae",[76] which he thought could not be denied by any orthodox theologian, or the end of cap. 8 and the decree "de iustificatione", can. 1 and 2.[77] Whether or not Saravia was correct in reading it in the Reformation sense in these decisions of the Council, the doctrine of justification formed a distinguishing mark of Christ's church for him.[78]

The great themes of Reformation theology did not come into the controversy with the Puritans. How minor were the theological differences between them and the Church of England, is evident from the 23 articles of the "venerabilis vir" to which Saravia wrote a reply. The anonymous Calvinist had made a number of critical remarks about the Canons of the Church of England adopted in 1604, about unimportant parts of its confession, its liturgy and its translation of the bible. These observations concerned the endorsement of the Apocryphal books (art. 1) which for Saravia did not imply that they possessed the same authority as the canonical books.[79] An objection concerned an incidental example of biblical translation (art. 2) on which Saravia made a number of exegetical remarks.[80] More important was an observation on the utter corruption of human nature (art. 3) to which Saravia replied by referring to "quaedam non scripta, sed nobis innata lex", given to all men in their conscience. As we shall see later, this reference to a natural knowledge of God is characteristic of his thought.[81] He denied that the collect for the twelfth Sunday after Trinity could give occasion to "papistica diffidentia" (art. 4).[82] The articles on baptism (art. 5-8) caused him to expound his views on

---

[74] Jewel, *Works.* Parker Soc., I, 69 f. Cit. Rupp, *Ibid.*

[75] "In Epist. ad Rom. disputatur per solam fidem iustificationem accidere homini sine operibus: atque adeo ipsum fidei Patrem Abrahamum diu ante circumcisionem fuisse per fidem iustificatum..." *VV*, 5.

[76] Denzinger, *Enchiridion Symbolorum*, Nr. 788-790.

[77] *Ibid.*, Nr. 811, 812.

[78] *DT*, 327.

[79] *VV*, 1 f.

[80] *Ibid.*, 2 f.

[81] *Ibid.*, 3.

[82] *Ibid.*, 3 f.

this sacrament[83]—we shall return to these later. Further objections were raised to the content of Innocents' Day (art. 8), to the abundance of feast days and holy days (art. 9, 10), to the sacramental character of confirmation (art. 11) and to the role of the bishop in this ceremony (art. 12, 13). Mention was made of the office of deacons (art. 14, 15) and of archdeacons (art. 16), of the adiaphora in the church, liturgical vestments, the names of the days (art. 17, 18, 19) and in general of the demand for uniformity which had been exacted by the canons (art. 20-23). The articles were a symptom of the widespread Puritan displeasure at the canons of 1604.[84]

It is evident that the fundamentals of the Reformation confession did not enter the discussion. The controversy was concerned with church government and especially the ceremonies which were regarded by the Puritans as remnants of superstition surviving from the mediaeval church.[85] If there was a fundamental doctrinal issue which played a background role in all of this then it was that of the church. The ecclesiological concern dominates all Saravia's treatises on church government and ministry. Apart from scattered incidental remarks, other doctrinal topics only come up expressis verbis on four occasions, three times because Saravia had to give advice in theological disputes and once because of his own accord he felt he ought to deal with a very controversial subject in such a way as to make a possible contribution to the bridging of opposing viewpoints. We have in mind his public disputation with the Dutch humanist, Coornhert, in The Hague (1583), the advice he gave at Whitgift's request on the conflict with William Barrett in Cambridge (1595), his opinion of Conrad Vorstius' theology, probably written at the request of Abbott and James I (1612) and his treatise *De sacra eucharistia* (between 1605 and 1610). All these writings were prompted by disputes over the heart of Reformation belief. Precisely because the four publications in question cover a period of nearly 30 years, it is worthwhile to examine them in order to answer the question whether and to what extent the Christian faith, as confessed in the Calvinist tradition, continued to be authoritative for Saravia.

---

[83] *Ibid.*, 5-7.
[84] Babbage, *Puritanism and Bancroft*, 124-146.
[85] *Ibid.*, 138.

# CHAPTER FIVE

# CATHOLIC CALVINISM

## 1. DISPUTATION WITH COORNHERT: JUSTIFICATION (1583)

From 27 October to 4 November and from 28 November to 1 December the public disputation took place in The Hague between Dirck Volckerts-zoon Coornhert and Adrianus Saravia, then still minister at Leiden.[1] This was occasioned by the great humanist's attack on the Reformed doctrinal primer used in the Netherlands, the Heidelberg Catechism.[2] Having already earlier published two writings in which he had attacked the doctrine of original sin,[3] Coornhert produced his *Proeve van de Heydelbergsche Catechismo*[4] in 1582. The 4th and 5th questions and answers of the catechism supplied the starting point for his attack: "What does God's Law require of us? Christ teaches us this in sum, Matth. 22:37-40: Thou shalt love the Lord thy God with all thy heart, and with all thy soul, and with all thy mind and with all thy strength. This is the first and great commandment. And the second is like this, namely: Thou shalt love thy neighbour as thyself. On these two commandments hang all the law and the prophets. Canst thou keep all this perfectly? No, for by nature I am inclined to hate God and my neighbour".[5] Coornhert stated the nature of the question thus: "The catechism and the ministers teach that God's commandment of love cannot be kept perfectly and they answer the fifth question with an open "no". Coornhert, on the other hand, says "yes".[6] Coornhert has rightly been called "the apostle of perfection".[7] Perhaps it is more correct to say: apostle of perfectability. For he saw perfection as the result of a process of growth in which the man who put on Christ finally came to perfect obedience. By Christ's grace and by use of his free will

---

[1] *Disputatie over den Catechismus van Heydelbergh, openbaarlijck voor den Volcke ghehouden op 't Hof van s'Graven-Hage in Hollandt Anno 1583. Ter Ordonnantie van de Mog. H. H. Staten van Hollandt ende West-Vrieslandt ende sijne Princelijcke Excell. Wilhelmus van Nassouwen, in 't bywesen ende bestieren van hare Gecommitteerde. Tusschen Dirck Volckaertsz. Coornhart ende Saravia D. inde Theologie, gheassisteert met Arent Cornelisz. ende andere Predicanten. Gouda, 1617.*

[2] W. Nijenhuis, "Coornhert and the Heidelberg Catechism. Moment in the struggle between Humanism and the Reformation," in: *Ecclesia Reformata*, 188-206.

[3] *Van de Erfzonde, Schulde en Straffe*, in: Coornhert, *Werken*, II, 407-479; *Bootgen... Ibid.*, 393-406.

[4] *Ibid.*, II, 223-236; III, 465-478.

[5] *Belijdenisgeschriften*, 156 f.; *Bekenntnisschriften, 150.*

[6] Coornhert, *Werken*, II, 236.

[7] B. Becker, "Coornhert de zestiende eeuwsche apostel der volmaaktheid", *Ned. AK*, XIX (1926) 59-84.

he arrived at a victory over sin in his life.[8] Coornhert fiercely resisted the reformed doctrine of imputative and forensic justification. He thought that this denigrated the reality of Christ's saving work in man. For him justification was not the declaring righteous but the making righteous. He replaced the idea of imputation with that of the restoration of human nature and the healing of the soul by Christ, the divine physician.[9] The reborn man has been spiritually resurrected. Christ lives in him, God's image has taken shape in his soul, nature's ruin is dead, the inclination to hate God and neighbour is conquered.[10]

Saravia now defended the catechism which taught that man cannot keep God's Law perfectly. On the basis of many biblical passages he argued that the reborn man remains a sinner. "Whenever we look at the holiest men presented to us, we will find that, notwithstanding their piety, according to God's Law they have nonetheless sinned."[11] We may speak of obedience but not of perfect obedience. Saravia was thus also in agreement with answer 62 of the catechism which says: "even our best works in this life are all imperfect and defiled with sin".[12] In summary we may say that he defended Luther's view of the faithful Christian as "simul iustus, simul peccator," which was a common Reformation conviction.

In addition there was his clearly Calvinist view of the purpose of the Law. According to Saravia it had been given, "first so that we should get to know ourselves by its means and, then having resorted to Christ, having found ourselves so imperfect that we are not able to fulfill the least jot of the Law, we are delivered from its curse and henceforth direct our lives according to it".[13] This agreed in content with what the catechism taught about the Law in question and answer 115[14] and also with the famous summary of saving knowledge in question and answer 2, the three things comprise: knowledge of sin, of redemption and of thankfulness.[15] The righteousness which justifies man before God is only to be found in Christ.

---

[8] "Soo nu my in dese vierledighe questie ghevraaght worde, of the mensche in desen leven magh wesen sonder sonde: Ick sal belijden dat hy 't magh wesen, door de genade Godes ende sijnen vryen wille, nyet twijfelende, of de vrye wille self en behoort oock totte ghenade Godes, dat is totte gaven Godes". Disputatie, 6 f.

[9] Coornhert, Werken, III, 229.

[10] Ibid., II, 232a.

[11] Disputatie, 44 f.

[12] Ibid., 58.

[13] Ibid., 55.

[14] "Waarom laat God ons de Tien Geboden zo streng prediken, wanneer toch niemand ze in dit leven kan volbrengen? Allereerst, opdat wij ons leven lang onze zondige aard steeds beter leren kennen en des te meer de vergeving van zonden en de gerechtigheid in Christus begeren te zoeken. In de tweede plaats, opdat wij ons zonder ophouden beijveren en God bidden om de genade van de Heilige Geest, zodat wij steeds meer naar het beeld van God vernieuwd worden tot wij na dit leven de beloofde volmaaktheid bereiken". Belijdenisgeschriften, 214 f.; Bekenntnisschriften, 178.

[15] Belijdenisgeschriften, 154 f.; Bekenntnisschriften, 31 f.

He has covered our unrighteousness with his perfection.[16] For Saravia righteousness was an eschatalogical quality: man does not enter into it in this life but in the future new world spoken of in 2 Peter 3:13.[17] Although Saravia did not get round to treating the imputative character of justification which Coornhert criticized so fiercely—he was so long-winded; the States became tired of the disputation and cut it short—it is clear that he held this view. By grace God holds disobedient and imperfect man as an obedient child.[18] In faith he flees to Christ who is the end of the Law.[19] His works are not judged according to the stern demands of the Law but, according to God's gracious good pleasure, they are held holy and perfect in Christ.[20] Saravia pointed also to the objective character of baptism which was independent of subjective human striving after perfection and by which the Christian had died with Christ: his old human nature had been buried and his new humanity had been raised with Christ (Rom 6:4).[21]

No clear lines were drawn in this disputation. Justification was treated rather one-sidedly by the problems which Coornhert raised. The relationship between justification and sanctification, the pneumatological aspect in fact, remained pretty much in the background. Saravia allowed himself to be pushed by his humanist opponent into the restricted field of defending against the latter's perfectionist claims. However, what he did do, especially in his frequent appeal to Paul, not least to the Epistle to the Romans, was utterly in the spirit of the Reformation. In his view of the Law he stood wholly within the Calvinist tradition with which he was clearly deeply imbued. Later on he correctly wrote to his "very dear and respected friend" who had also come from the continent, that on their arrival in England they had been thoroughly soaked in the customs of the Reformed churches.[22] What he wrote of customs certainly held good also for the content of those churches' confessions.

## 2.   Memorandum on Barrett's Recantation: Predestination (1595)

At issue in the conflict concerning William Barrett at Cambridge was the doctrine of election and reprobation and especially the perserverance of the faithful. Barrett has indeed been called an "anticipator of

---

[16] *Disputatie*, 75.

[17] *Ibid.*, 83.

[18] *Ibid.*, 89.

[19] *Ibid.*

[20] "Want de wercken der geloovigen, die sy doen uyt den gheloove in Christum met een kinderlijcke affectie tot Godt heuren Hemelschen Vader, nyet geexamineert en worden na de rigeure ende strengicheyt der Wet, maar na de ghenadighe opneminghe des welbehagens Gods in Christo, ende alsoo worden sy in hem heyligh ende volmaackt gehouden." *Ibid.*, 91.

[21] *Ibid.*, 96.

[22] "Transmarinarum ecclesiarum moribus imbuti hûc venimus." *VV*, 1.

Arminius".[23] The doctrine that gave rise to prolonged and violent disputes in the Netherlands which were resolved by the Synod of Dordrecht (1618/19) and which gave rise to the existence of the Remonstrant Brotherhood, also aroused dissension in England. As early as the fifteen fifties England had its defenders of Free Will.[24] After the dispute over predestination had been carried on in England, Germany, the Netherlands and Denmark, originally quite independently in different places, it later took on a more international complexion. Thus Peter Baro communicated with the Danish Lutheran, Niels Hemmingson, in opposing the objectionable doctrine. Later the Dutchman, Arminius, turned against the views of the English Puritan, William Perkins.[25]

The doctrine of predestination did not occupy the predominant place in Calvin's theology which it would be ascribed in later Calvinism.[26] Only four chapters are devoted to it in the *Institutes*.[27] The Genevan Catechism and the Heidelberg Catechism attacked by Coornhert are completely silent on the predestinatio gemina and only talk about election to eternal life in the context of ecclesiology.[28] The Reformed confessions also speak very soberly about election. The Belgic Confession of faith summarizes reprobation in a few words whilst the Scottish does not mention it at all.[29]

Remarkably enough the lengthiest treatment is that of Article 17 of the Church of England's *Thirty-Nine Articles*. It treats "of predestination and election" without talking of reprobation. It declares that "the godly consideration of predestination, and our election in Christ, is full of sweet, pleasant, and unspeakable comfort to godly persons...." The lack of mention of reprobation does not mean that this is denied, but is "a recognition of the overwhelming predominance of the doctrine of predestination to life in the treatment of the subject in Scripture".[30] It is clear that, just as in the first decades of the Calvinist Reformation in the Netherlands, there was room in the Church of England for different interpretations of election. Thus in Cambridge Whitaker and Perkins could teach one view of it, Andrewes and Baro another. "The disputes of the 1590's in the university must be interpreted not as a study of reigning and resplendent Calvinism challenged by upstart Arminianism, but as the rear-guard action of one

---

[23] A. G. Dickens, *The English Reformation* (repr. pb., s.l., 1972) 427.

[24] O. T. Hargrave, "The Freewillers in the English Reformation," *CH*, XXXVII (1968) 271-280.

[25] Bangs, *Arminius*, 206-221; *The Work of William Perkins*. I. Breward, ed. (Appleford, 1970) 87 f.

[26] P. Jacobs, *Theologie reformierter Bekenntnisschriften* (Neukirchen, 1959) 94-98.

[27] *Inst.* (1559), III, 21-24; *CO*, II, 678-728.

[28] Gen. Cat., qu. 93 and 96; Heid. Cat., qu. 54. *Belijdenisgeschriften*, 178 f; *Bekenntnisschriften*, 12 f., 161 f.

[29] Confessio Gallicana (1559), art. 12; Confessio Scotica (1560), art. 8; Confessio Belgica (1561), art. 16. *Belijdenisgeschriften*, 96 f.; *Bekenntnisschriften*, 69, 88-91, 125.

[30] D. B. Knox, *Thirty-Nine Articles. The historic basis of Anglican Faith* (London, 1967) 32.

important party on seeing another important party beginning to capture a
little too much territory, upsetting, as it were, the theological balance of
power".[31]

We will not be surprised, when we remember Saravia's behaviour in
similar disputes in the Netherlands, that in the conflict over predestination
in Cambridge, he opted for theological moderation, shunning extreme
standpoints and upholding what he saw as essential in the belief. This attitude implied the toleration of different opinions within the bounds of the
confession.

In his concio ad clerum on 29 April 1595, William Barrett, a disciple of
Baro's, posited six propositions. In the first of these he attacked a "certitudo fidei" which could make men carefree with regard to their salvation
and which degenerated into "securitas". He did not consider that Jesus'
words to Peter, "I have prayed for you that your faith will not fail" (Luke
22:32) were generally applicable (proposition 2). He found the idea of a
"finalis perseverantia" arrogant and impious (proposition 3). No distinctions can be drawn in faith, but only between the faithful. Thus he rejected
the distinction between "fides temporaria, perpetua, simulata" and the
distinguishing of "degrees and measures of true faith", for example,
strong and weak, as taught by Perkins.[32] The proposition which gave most
offence was that in which the certainty of faith in the forgiveness of sins
was denied (proposition 5). It was in connection with this proposition
especially that his opponents accused him of papistical tendencies. Finally
he proposed that the first cause of the reprobation of the damned was their
own sin (proposition 6). In so doing he again took his stand against the
"praedestinatio gemina" in the importance of election and reprobation as
purely decisions of divine will apart from man's belief or unbelief.[33] His
propositions included vehement attacks on Calvin and other continental
reformers. In Barrett's rejection of the absolute decree of reprobation
without regard to man's sin, in his opposition to the "certitudo fidei" and
in his acceptance of the possibility of the loss of faith, we can discern a relationship with Dutch Arminianism.

Here we pass over the recantation wrung from Barrett after lengthy proceedings and the fickle attitude of John Whitgift in the matter[34] and confine ourselves to the contents of the memorandum of Saravia, who was one
of those consulted by the archbishop.[35] The memorandum related to the
text of Barrett's recantation,[36] which had been more or less dictated by his

---

[31] Porter, *Reformation and Reaction,* 287.

[32] Perkins, *Work,* 401.

[33] Strype, *Whitgift,* II, 229 f.

[34] Brook, *Whitgift,* 161-165.

[35] Cambridge, Trin. Coll. Ms. B. 14.9, 169-183; Doc. XXXIX; translation of p. 169
in Strype, *Whitgift,* II, 241-243; printing of the original text *Ibid.,* III, 321-337.

[36] Strype, *Whitgift,* III, 317-320; Doc. XXXIX, 330.

Puritan opponents and expressed their views. Thus Saravia's observations provide us with a good impression of his opinion of the teaching on election of Whitaker, Perkins and other Cambridge Calvinists. The paper is in three parts: a brief observation on the recantation of each of the six propositions,[37] a detailed treatment of the doctrine of election, [38] and a short conclusion.[39] Saravia was glad that Barrett had retracted his impudent abuse of the "names of learned men" but he had no need to withdraw his rejection of "securitas". For, according to Saravia, there was a great difference between the real certainty of faith, "certitudo", and arrogant self assurance, "securitas". His comment on proposition 2 is of minor importance. Here he made a distinction between the "actual believer" who had not been elected and could lose his faith and the elect who would never lose faith.[40] It remained unclear as to who were the "vere credentes" outside election. Otherwise Saravia appeared to accept here some sort of imperishable faith and so came close to the Calvinists. On the other hand, he regretted that Barrett had retracted his third proposition about the "superbia" of "finalis perseverantia". "Securitas" was never free of "arrogantia" and when it was announced in the recantation that the righteous could only increase in faith and persevere to the end, then Saravia thought that this growth in faith did not take place by itself but must be a matter of continuous effort.[41] He agreed with Barrett in so far as the latter had resisted a certain automatic quality in the faith of the believer. This also applied to the forgiveness of sins which was only granted in response to prayer.

Most important is Saravia's opinion on the retraction of the sixth proposition: not God's decree but sin was the proper cause of a man's reprobation. The religious motive here was clear: Barrett wanted to put reprobation outside God's predestination and so to lay the entire responsibility on man. In contrast in the recantation the precise opposite was dictated to him: reprobation proceeded from God's decree. For this he had to refer to Augustine's letter to Simplicianus. However, Saravia observed and later on demonstrated in his more detailed memorandum that the opposite was asserted in this letter. Consequently he did not understand this line of argument.

It is noteworthy that Barrett's recantation concluded with a reference to the seventeenth of the *Thirty-Nine Articles*, but, as we saw, there is nothing

---

[37] Cambridge, Trin. Coll. Ms. 14.9, 169; Doc. XXXIX, 330.

[38] *Ibid.*, 170-182; Doc. XXXIX, 330-342.

[39] *Ibid.*, 182 f.; Doc. XXXIX, 342.

[40] "Quia non omnes vere credentes sunt electi; et vere credentium quorundam fides deserere potest, non electorum."

[41] Strype, *Whitgift*, II, 242, by translating the words in the manuscript "de augmento fidei" by "argument of faith", has evidently read it incorrectly. The text published in *Ibid.*, III, 321-337, contains numerous minor differences from the copy of Saravia's memorandum extant in Trinity College, Cambridge.

at all in this about reprobation! Those who extorted the retraction therefore thought that their views were in agreement with the Church of England's confession to the exclusion of other interpretations. However, there was as yet no attempt to make a change or addition to this confession in the manner of the five canons of Dordrecht (1619). Such a statement would first be given much later, for example in cap. 3 of the Westminster Confession.

The most important part of Saravia's memorandum begins with an explanation of the difference between "certitudo" and "securitas". "Temporaria fides" does not have to be false and "perpetua fides" is not necessarily true. Thus faith is to be judged not by its "duratio" but by its fruits or its cultivator.[42] God has forbidden us "securitas", self assurance, because it reduces the struggle for faith demanded of us and the vigilance which we have to exercise in view of Christ's coming. There can only be certainty of attaining the goal if we use the means which lead to it. "Eternal life has been promised us and in faith we do indeed lay hold of it, but we must keep ourselves on the way which leads to it".[43] "Perseverantia" not "securitas" was the hallmark of the Christian on his way to completion. The New Testament sayings about vigilance and especially that of Jesus: "Whoever perseveres to the end, he shall be saved" (Matth. 10:22) were cited in support.

All of this did not mean that Saravia in any way minimized the Reformation "sola fide". By faith he meant "the one true faith by which we are implanted by Christ and are renewed by the Spirit".[44] Only by faith does a man receive a share in Christ.[45] Apart from faith there is no certainty and no justification.[46] However, Saravia was now concerned with the indissoluble link between justification and sanctification, that is to say a continual renewal. For this "perseverantia" is necessary whilst "securitas" presents a serious threat. True faith cannot be lost.[47] Here we catch strains which are familiar to us from the Calvinist tradition.

In the second part of the memorandum Saravia went into the question of election in some detail. For the most part he based his views on Romans

---

[42] "Est fides natura sua tum ab ipsius effectis, tum ab ipso authore, non a duratione definienda." Cambridge, Trinity Coll. Ms.B. 14.9, 170; Doc. XXXIX, 331.

[43] *Ibid.*, 172, Doc. XXXIX, 332.

[44] "Una tantum est vera fides, qua Christo inserimur et spiritu renovamur." *Ibid.*

[45] "In Christo autem fuisse aut esse nisi per fidem nemo intelligitur." *Ibid.*, 175; Doc. XXXIX, 334.

[46] "Praeterea iustum esse neminem sine fide certum est: iustificamur fide quotquot iustificamur." *Ibid.*

[47] "Scimus renovationem esse propriam fidei iustificanti... Quisquis per penitentiam renovatus est et Spiritus Sancti factus est particeps, gustavitque donum caeleste et bonum Dei verbum et virtutes futuri seculi, verus Christianus est et veram fidem habet: et regnum caelorum ac beatam immortalitatem esset accepturus, si perseveraret... At fides vera non potest amitti." *Ibid.*, 173 ff.; Doc. XXXIX, 333 f.

9 and on Augustine whom he cited frequently. Thus he drew from the same sources which Calvin had used, though the latter was not named in the exposition of election. Saravia evidently did not feel the slightest need to criticize the reformer expressis verbis. The real meaning of the Pauline message about election, as he thought he gathered it in Romans 9, was: to make clear that election and justification depended on God's grace. However, he would not acknowledge a reprobation which proceeded as a logical consequence of election. We do not find in Saravia an analogy between election and reprobation, both based on the decree of predestination, such as exists in Calvin.[48] He did not tire of repeating that the ground of reprobation was different from that of election. Election was founded on God's grace apart from any human merit, reprobation on God's justice and the merits of sin.[49] As regards reprobation Saravia did not venture to go further in his theological convictions than Augustine.[50] To support his argument, he produced numerous proof texts from this Church father from *De praedestinatione et gratia,* the *Confessiones,* letters and sermons, *De dono perseverantiae,* etc.

Next he came to a discussion of the relationship between "praedestinatio" and "praescientia Dei". In common with Augustine, he saw a close connection between the two,[51] which was not in itself at odds with Calvin's views.[52] Saravia, however, went further in regarding predestination as dependent upon "praescientia", not upon God's eternal decree.[53] He appears to diverge from Calvin here, but it is useful to consider the backgrounds at this point. Calvin's opposition to the dependence of

---

[48] *Inst.* (1559), III, 21, 5; *CO,* II, 682 f.

[49] "Paulus in cap. 9 ep. ad Rom. nihil aliud docere vult, quam gratuitam Dei in eligendo et iustificando gratiam; unde alienum est a Pauli intentione, quod pari ratione reprobare et obdurare contenditur cum diversissimae sint causae electionis et reprobationis. Quod allegatur de Jacob et Esau, probat tantum gratuitam fuisse Jacob electionem: nec ad probandum Esau ex pari causa fuisse reprobatum quidquam valet. Nam electio fit ex massa reproba, uterque Jacob et Esau erant filii irae pari damnatione obnoxii, ex qua communi damnatione Jacob Dei gratia servatus est, in qua relictus fuit Esau... sed causa longe diversa mere et sola gratuita gratia miseretur eius, qui conditione sua minime dignus est, cuius misereatur, et obdurat eum qui maxime dignus est illa obduratione, ut hic sit meritum, et illic nullum. Gratia sine ullo merito electionis est causa. Iustitia Dei vero et peccati meritum est causa obdurationis." Cambridge, Trinity Coll. Ms.B.14.9, 175 f.; Doc. XXXIX, 335 f.

[50] "... de reprobatione alia est ratio: in qua ulterius progedi quam Augustinus ex verbo Dei docuit, non audeo." *Ibid.,* 178; Doc. XXXIX, 338.

[51] "Male praedestinationem meo iudicio auspicamur ab aeterno Dei decreto, praeterita praescientia." *Ibid.,* 179; Doc. XXXIX, 339.

[52] On the relationship between predestination and foreknowledge in Calvin, see H. Otten, *Calvins theologische Anschauung von der Prädestination* (Munich, 1938) 113-122.

[53] "Sed neminem prius reprobat, neminem prius obdurat, quam de peccato cognoscat; praecedit decretum scientia, ut iudicium cognitio... In sapiente voluntatem et electionem praecedit plena perfectaque scientia, et cum iudicio et ratione deliberatio." Cambridge, Trinity Coll. Ms.B. 14.9, 180 f.; Doc. XXXIX, 340.

predestination in relation to the "praescientia Dei" had been prompted by his aversion to the way in which the Schoolmen had thus incorporated their views on the importance of human merits into the doctrine of election: God elects people on the basic of his foreknowledge of their merits. There was nothing of this in Saravia. He used the "praescientia Dei" only to explain men's reprobation because of their sins which God foresaw and not their election because of their "praevisa merita". There is no trace of his allowing an attempt to ascribe an independent function to human free will in this fashion as was the case with the later Remonstrants. Saravia did not wish to go further in his views than the Church father to whom Calvin had also frequently appealed in his explanations of election and reprobation.[54] He did not oppose Calvin but rather the latter's disciples in England who went further in drawing logical conclusions from what had been only soberly defined in the confessions. They wrote about the eternal decree as if they had themselves been present at it.[55] No more than Calvin, who warned repeatedly and at length against any speculative thinking about God's decree which went beyond the bounds of what had been revealed in Scripture,[56] did Saravia wish to penetrate by logical thought into the mysteries of election and reprobation.

As regards Barrett's views, he was of the opinion that these were not such that there could be no place for them in the church. Barrett and his supporters did not deviate from the essentials of the doctrine of original sin and human incapacity for good. Least of all were they to be seen as Pelagians.[57] Therefore there must be room for them in the church. Saravia therefore considered the sentence to recant overhasty.[58] Such differing opinions existed amongst ministers who otherwise had deserved well of the church. They ought to tolerate each other in love instead of accusing each other of heresies. At the end of his memorandum, Saravia once more gave his approval that Barrett had had to withdraw his coarse charges against Calvin and others.

His attitude in the dispute with Barrett was quite in accord with his conduct in the Netherlands when he was involved in the synodal verdicts on

---

[54] Smits, *Saint Augustin dans l'œuvre de Jean Calvin,* I, 96-99, 260 f.

[55] "Ita docti quidam viri de aeterno illo Dei decreto scribunt, ac si ipsi divino interfuissent consilio, quando Deus creare homines ab aeterno constituebat." Cambridge, Trinity Coll. Ms.B. 14.9, 179; Doc. XXXIX, 339.

[56] *Inst.* (1559), III, 21, 1; *CO,* II, 678-682.

[57] "Pervenerunt autem isti fratres nostri, pro quibus solicita est pia charitas vestra, ut credant cum ecclesia Christi, peccato primo hominis obnoxium nasci genus humanum nec ab isto malo nisi per iustitiam secundi hominis aliquem liberari. Pervenerunt etiam, ut praeveniri voluntates hominum Dei gratia fateantur: atque ut ad nullum opus bonum vel incipiendum vel perficiendum sibi quemquam sufficere posse consentiant: retenta ergo ista in quae pervenerunt, plurimum eos a Pelagianorum errore discernunt." Cambridge, Trinity Coll. Ms.B. 14.9, 182, Doc. XXXIX, 342.

[58] "Quemobrem nimis praecox fuit illa censura, quae Baretum male recantare coegit, quae bene dixerat." *Ibid.*

the ministers Hortensius and Herberts. Sober as it was on predestination, the Reformed confession permitted such differing interpretations. The ministers of the church must not be asked for more than the basis expressed in the confession. The doctrine of reprobation by God's decree was one of the interpretations which ought not to be coercively imposed. In the wording of the memorandum in 1595, Saravia still took the same standpoint as regards original sin and the associated doctrinal issues as he did during the disputation with Coornhert.

### 3. Objections to Vorstius' Appointment: The Authority of the Early Church (1612)

As early as 1597 Vorstius had been suspected and accused of Socinianism in Germany on account of his writings, *De praedestinatione, De sancta Trinitate* and *De persona et officio Christi.* These charges were repeated in the Netherlands after the publication of his *Tractatus theologicus de Deo* (Steinfurt, 1610); he was supposed to hold heterodox views on God's attributes, the Trinity, Christology and predestination.[59] It is understandable that the Counterremonstrants raised serious opposition when Vorstius was appointed as Arminius' successor in Leiden. The quarrels which flared up over this formed a part of the protracted theological, ecclesiastical and political struggle between Remonstrants and Counterremonstrants which was only resolved at the Synod of Dordrecht (1618/19) with the condemnation of Arminius' disciples. We will here pass over the political aspects of the dispute over Vorstius' appointment[60] and confine ourselves to a description of the theological arguments which Saravia advanced against the professor-elect. In his eyes Vorstius was the originator of the disputes and he thought that he ought to withdraw from the Dutch scene.[61] Thus the prebendary of Canterbury took the side of the Dutch Counterremonstrants. He certainly did not choose this position because he shared their views on predestination about which the dispute was particularly concerned. There is no reason to assume that he thought differently about this than during his involvement with the affairs of Hortensius (1583) and Herberts (1586) and with Barrett's recantation (1595). He certainly did not share the exaggerated views of Gomarus and other theologians in the Netherlands who were moving ever further along the path of a Reformed Scholasticism. Again their dislike of the state's

---

[59] A. Schweizer, "Conradus Vorstius. Vermittlung der reformirten Centraldogmen mit den socianischen Einwendungen," *Theol. Jahrbücher,* XV (1856) 435-486; XVI (1857) 153-184; Sepp, *Het godgeleerd onderwijs in Nederland,* I, 179-214, 264 f.

[60] Nijenhuis, "Saravia en Jacobus I"; G. J. Hoenderdaal, "The Debate about Arminius outside the Netherlands," in: *Leiden University in the seventeenth Century,* 149-152.

[61] "Dr. Vorstius, qui author dissensionum est, amandandus esset," *Brieven Wtenbogaert,* I, 193: Doc. XLVII, 359.

authority in the church greatly displeased him. Yet in his letter of 29
September 1612 to Wtenbogaert he delivered a sharp condemnation of
Vorstius' theology, choosing two places from the latter's work as examples
for his criticism.

The first example was taken from the *Apologetica Oratio* presented to the
States of Holland by Vorstius on 22 March 1612.[62] The topic of discussion
was the doctrine of God's Attributes, in this case particularly His infinity
(infinitas, immensitas) and omnipresence (omnipresentia, ubiquitas).
God is the essence of being. Therefore, so the Schoolmen thought, He is
present as being in the ontological sense.[63] Reformed orthodoxy too
believed that God is not only omnipresent with his "potentia" and "virtus", but also with his "esse". The distinction made by the Socinians between God's "praesentia essentialis" in heaven and his "praesentia
operativa" in the creation and the creature was rejected. Saravia thought,
not without reason, that he found an affinity in Vorstius' work to the latter
opinion. In his *Oratio,* Vorstius declared that he did not wish to deny God's
infinity but only the scholastic view of it. It is apparent from his explanation that he rejected precisely what was essential for Reformed orthodoxy,
the ontological omnipresence: "I declare nothing other than that God is
not infinite in any conceivable sense or in any unlimited way, but that He
has an essence which is distinct and peculiar to Him and that the nature of
this omnipresence is not lightly to be defined beyond Scripture particularly
since several absurd statements about God were bound to follow from that
scholastic double definition; for instance, when He is called infinite in
every way and without any limitation this readily leads to a confusion of
His being with that of other things; thus if He were essentially the All in all
things one might easily think that everything whether good or evil was
directly produced by Him as a consequence of which the Libertines have
formed their opinion that God alone acts on all things thus becoming the
author of all wrong-doing".[64] Vorstius was afraid of a mingling of God's
essence with that of the visible reality of the sinful world by which God
would be regarded as the author of sin. This issue of God's authorship of
sin again always played a fundamental part in the struggle about
predestination.

Saravia upheld the traditional scholastic views on the "infinitas Dei".
He would have nothing to do with Vorstius' distinction between the
"praesentia essentialis" and the "praesentia operativa Dei".[65] He was
not at all impressed by Vorstius' accusations against the Schoolmen, the

---

[62] The speech, which was given in German, is in Schweizer, "Vorstius", 460-478.

[63] "Deus est in omnibus rebus, ut dans eis esse et virtutem et operationem." Thomas
Aquinas, *Summa Theologiae.* I, 8, 2.

[64] Schweizer, "Vorstius", 460.

[65] "Nos in Deo quod potentiam dicimus, nihil aliud esse, quam essentiam credimus, ut
Deo posse sit esse, et esse sit posse." *Brieven Wtenbogaert,* I, 198; Doc. XLVII, 360.

Jesuits and the whole Roman church, for the doctrine which he opposed belonged to the deposit of faith common to all Christian churches. He also appealed to Calvin and Beza, the first of whom had indeed clearly enough attacked the Libertinism feared by Vorstius without ever denying God's infinity and absolute omnipresence. Saravia was willing to follow the Genevan fathers when, as in this case, they were not proclaiming any "new ideas which were unknown to the churches in earlier times".[66] Vorstius' objection that the scholastic view appeared to come close to what we should call pantheism was answered by Saravia with the charge that Vorstius himself held dualistic and gnostic opinions: he excluded God's presence in material, impure reality because he was afraid of mixing the two. However, this mingling was no more possible than that of the sun's rays and the bodies which they penetrated.[67] God can as little be contained ever or anywhere by sinful impure reality, of which Saravia cited some not very tasteful examples, as He can ever or anywhere be excluded from His creation.[68] With an appeal to Paul's sayings on the Areopagus according to which God is not far from each one of us (Acts 17:27), Saravia wrote, "The life and being of all things is in God alone and through Him alone and through His Son and through the Holy Spirit. He is not absent from the created things which he sustains".[69] He spelled out for Vorstius the implications of belief in creation and in this he showed a clear likeness to the early church's defenders of Christian faith against the Gnostics' teaching. In common with the whole tradition of the church—in another example employed by him—he believed in the impurity of the sexual act and procreation, but with an appeal to Job 10: 8-11 and 18 he demonstrated that God worked creatively and was present in this human impurity.[70]

The second example was Vorstius' *Tractatus de Deo*. In Disputatio 3, thesis 9, the latter had written about "varii gradus divinae praesentiae", in heaven and on earth, in the faithful and in unbelievers.[71] In Saravia's view the gradus which existed in the human world was here projected unto God's presence in an objectionable fashion. However, the variety of God's revelations and of the positions of His works did not alter the presence of

---

[66] *Ibid.*, 195 f., Doc. XLVII, 360.

[67] *Ibid.*, 194, 197; Doc. XLVII, 359 f.

[68] *Ibid.*, 196 f.; Doc. XLVII, 361 f.

[69] "In Deo solo, et ab eo solo, illiusque filio et spiritu sancto vita et essentia rerum omnium est." *Ibid.*, 197; Doc. XLVII, 361.

[70] "Sed ubicunque Deus operatur, ibi praesentem ipsius essentiam intelligo." *Ibid.*, 199; Doc. XLVII, 362.

[71] "Varii tamen gradus sunt divinae praesentiae, pro varietate manifestionum atque operationum in rebus creatis. Nam aliter in coelo tamquam in aula regia est Deus; aliter in terra. Matth. 6:9. Aliter in medio eorum est, quos suo praesidio tegit; aliter eorum, quos deserit. Num. 14:42. Aliter denique est in sanctis ac fidelibus; aliter in impiis. 1 Cor. 6:19 et 2 Cor. 6:16. Sic accedit ad nos Deus benefaciendo; recedit a nobis gratiam et auxilium subducendo. Ps. 10:1, 2 et 22:1, 2". Vorstius, *De Deo*, 22.

His essence in reality.[72] Once more he opposed Vorstius' ideas with the belief in creation, this time with a quotation of Ps. 102:26-28.[73]

In his opposition to Vorstius, Saravia confined himself to the doctrine of God particularly to the matter of God's omnipresence. He did not touch upon the disputed issues relating to the doctrine of salvation, especially those of predestination and free will. Otherwise, he never interfered in the disputes between Remonstrants and Counterremonstrants. This letter too did not touch on the heart of this struggle. Saravia was not so much with a defence of the Reformed confession but of the theology of early Christendom. He appealed to the consensus of the ancient church both at the beginning of his long letter[74] and at the end.[75] He explained that Calvin and Beza had no authority for him when they had introduced "innovationes" into the church, but on the issue of the doctrine of God he considered them authoritative and trustworthy theologians who did not dissent from the consensus of the whole church. "And this is the true, ancient and orthodox theology; nothing which is opposed to it may be accepted".[76]

We have seen Saravia involved in doctrinal disputes on three occasions. On the first it appeared that the Reformed belief in the justification of the sinful was unquestionably authoritative for him. It was apparent from the second that he cared nothing for scholastic distinctions which went beyond a fundamental confession of predestination and election as signs of God's gracious saving activity, and that consequently he preferred to confine himself to the elementary and sober confessions of the first generation of Calvinists. For Saravia, as for Calvin, Augustine was the most authoritative source. It was clear from his involvement in the third dispute, how quickly he reacted if he fancied that the consensus of the whole church was being impugned and by this he was thinking especially of that of the early church and patristic theology. This veneration for antiquity was not essentially opposed to his Reformation and fundamentally Calvinistic faith but he did give it a distinct, English, flavour. Along with his theology, which did not differ on any essential point from that of continental Reformed theology, he fitted in best with the church which, with her "via media", claimed to preserve the most continuity with the early church.

---

[72] "Gradus in deitatis praesentia magis et minus nulli sunt, nec absque impietate magis esse in coelo aut minus in terris dici vel cogitari potest. Illa non est in ullo loco magis praesens quam in alio. Pro varietate loci eorumque quae operatur Deus, non mutatur essentiae divinae realis praesentia. Diversitas, quae apparet in creaturis est, non in Deo Deique praesentia." *Brieven Wtenbogaert*, I, 200; Doc. XLVII, 363.

[73] *Ibid.*, 200 f.; Doc. XLVII, 363.

[74] "Huic objectioni tam a priscis veteribus theologis, quam a posteris, qui secuti sunt, fuit olim et est responsum." *Ibid.*, 194; Doc. XLVII, 359.

[75] "Haec est vera, vetus et orthodoxa theologia, cui nulla contraria est recipienda." *Ibid.*, 201; Doc. XLVII, 364.

[76] *Ibid.*, 195, 198; Doc. XLVII, 364.

## CHAPTER SIX

# THE SACRAMENTS

### 1. Treatise on the Eucharist

In contradistinction to the previous three, the fourth example of
Saravia's doctrinal treatises, his *De sacra eucharista*[1] was written not at the
request of others but was drafted on his own initiative. It shows no sign of
entering into the theological debates of the first decade of the seventeenth
century in England. Indeed these debates scarcely touched on eucharistic
doctrine. It emerges from the dedication to the King, opening with the
familiar formal flatteries,[2] that Saravia took the *Wittenberg Concord* (1536)[3]
as his starting point and that, as he informed the reader in the preface, he
read this in the light of the *Augsburg Confession*,[4] thus confirming his esteem
for the historic confession of Lutheranism.

Saravia was thus harking back to an agreement on the eucharist which
had been concluded more than 70 years before between the North and
South Germans as a result of discussions between Luther and Bucer.[5] It is
questionable if he properly understood all the nuances in the dispute which
divided Protestant Germany seriously in the sixteenth century. He saw the
controversy as a dispute over words,[6] supposing that Luther and Bucer
meant to say the same although they used different words.[7] In reality
Bucer held a position midway between that of the Swiss and Luther. He
defended the sacramental unity between the eucharistic elements and
Christ's body and blood against Zurich. On the other hand he had a much
lesser view of this unity than Luther: for him Christ was not the bread, nor
was he in the bread, but with the bread.[8] He laid more stress than Luther
on the subject of faith, on the recipient of the sacrament: Christ's body

---

[1] p. 46, note 250.

[2] His lowly position had at first deterred him from yielding to the wish to visit the king
and to pay his respects. However, friends had convinced him that the monarch would be
agreeable to such a visit. This was indeed the case: the King's graciousness was of the sort
that he disparaged no-one even of the humblest station, etc. *SE*, 2.

[3] *Ibid.*, 4, 16.

[4] *Ibid.*, 16.

[5] Text of the *Concord of Wittenburg: Ibid.*, 122 f.; *Documents illustrative of the Continental Refor-*
*mation*, B. J. Kidd, ed. (Oxford, 1911; repr. 1967) 318 f.; *CR*, III, 75-77. German text:
E. Bizer, *Studien zur Geschichte Abendmahlsstreits im 16. Jahrhundert* (Gütersloh, 1941) 117-119.

[6] "...verborum potius videri potest certamen esse quam rei." *SE*, 34.

[7] *Ibid.*, 32, 120.

[8] Bizer, *Studien*, 122.

was eaten and his blood drunk by the faithful soul. This view is also to be found in the Englishman, Richard Hooker.

The fundamental pronouncement in the first article of the *Concord*: "Itaque sentiunt et docent cum pane et vino vere et substantialiter adesse, exhiberi et consumi corpus Christi et sanguinem", shows that Bucer had to make the greatest concessions in the conversations. He could not arouse any comprehension of this among the Swiss.[9] His changes of front are otherwise not at all clear. In the *Wittenberg Concord,* probably against his inclination, he was induced to declare that Christ's body and blood were even received by the unbelieving. Against this objectivizing statement, however, there was his opinion that the "impii" received only bread and wine, not the body and blood of the Lord, a statement which is difficult to reconcile with the first view. It was left to Calvin to do full justice to both the objectivity of the "praesentia realis" of the "verum corpus Christi"[10] and to the spiritual dimensions by which the subject eats and drinks "with the mouth of faith".

In his treatise on the eucharist Saravia left no doubt that Scripture and the fathers were his sources of authority.[11] As regards the latter, they had lived and guided the church at a time nearest to that of the apostles, therefore he was unwilling to move an inch from their views.[12] He did, however, also maintain here the relative order of two authoritative sources: in one's way of speaking about the sacrament one ought to be in accord with God's Word. Where the theologians of old diverged from the "sacrarum literarum loquendi norma", the theologian must carefully point out their error.[13] He quoted Augustine most frequently, but he interpreted the latter's utterances so that they agreed with his own views, expanding them in a more realistic sense than they had been intended.[14] On the other hand, he attempted to refute the appeal to Ambrose which Roman theologians, correctly from a historical point of view, made in connection with their doctrine of transubstantiation.[15]

Saravia's treatise was in three parts which dealt successively with the "sacramenti natura", the "manducatio impiorum" and the preparation for receiving the sacrament. How he proposed reconciling the opposing parties, emerges from these words: "Why is it that we contend so much over a matter which we both believe? For although we differ in our views yet finally we have to return to the belief that Christ the Lord really gave

---

[9] *Ibid.,* 131-187.

[10] G. P. Hartvelt, *Verum Corpus. Een studie over een centraal hoofdstuk uit de avondmaalsleer van Calvijn.* Delft, 1960.

[11] *SE,* 16, 68, 120.

[12] *Ibid.,* 16.

[13] *Ibid.,* 68.

[14] *Ibid.,* 36 f., 88.

[15] *Ibid.,* 80.

his body and blood to his disciples. However, the way in which this happened is beyond human comprehension; this must be left to God".[16] The faithful must believe that the actual and true body and blood of Christ are present in the eucharist, but the manner of this presence does not lend itself to inquisitive investigation, because it is supernatural and divine in nature.[17]

Along with the *Wittenberg Concord* Saravia chose as his starting point Irenaeus' formulation, "that the eucharist comprises two things, an earthly and a heavenly".[18] With this a third aspect comes in for consideration, the "virtus sacramenti" consisting in the forgiveness of sin and eternal life.[19] Saravia treated the union between the first of the two elements in the spirit of the *Wittenberg Concord.* "For the bread is no more a sacrament without the body of Christ than is the body of Christ without the bread".[20] There is an analogy between the "signa mystica" and the "ipsae res", Christ's suffering and death,[21] so that one sacrament can be made from these two.[22] In company with Augustine, Saravia thought that by God's Word, that is the words of institution, the visible element is made into the sacrament of the invisible grace.[23] Bread and wine act as an image, a "similitudo" of Christ's body and blood, not however an image of things which are absent. The crucified Christ is really present. "Christ's sacraments bestow what they signify".[24] In the likeness of bread and wine the communicant participates in Christ's flesh and blood and in his death.[25] Great stress was laid on the reality and objectivity of Christ's presence. This was independent of men's belief or unbelief. Faith no more bestowed the character of mysteries or of holiness upon the divine signs than unbelief could impair the validity of the sacrament.[26]

The sacramental unity of the two parts was an analogy of the personal

---

[16] *Ibid.,* 18.

[17] "Quod immotum inter fideles esse debet, tantum urgeo, nempe praesentiam realem et veram corporis et sanguinis Domini in coena fidelibus credendum esse. Cuiusmodi autem illa sit, non est curiosius crassiusve inquirendum". *Ibid.,* 34.

[18] "...constare eucharistiam duabus, terrena et coelesti." *Adv. Haer.,* IV, 34.

[19] "Tertium quod notari cupio est peccatorum remissio et vita aeterna, quae virtus est sacramenti distincta ab illis duabus sacramenti partibus. Tria enim in quovis sacramento ab invicem distincta sunt consideranda: externum visibile signum et res invisibilis coelestisque signo sacramentaliter unita, et tertium, quod ab eis manat, sacramenti fructus". *SE,* 22.

[20] *Ibid.,* 22.

[21] *Ibid.,* 54.

[22] *Ibid.,* 56.

[23] "Verbum Dei, id est: mandatum est institutio, accessit ad visibile elementum, et invisibilis gratiae factum est sacramentum". *Ibid.,* 74.

[24] "Fixum enim hoc apud patres erat, Christi sacramenta exhibere quae significant". *Ibid.,* 84.

[25] "Quia tota vita nostra in passione et morte Servatoris nostri sita est, in similitudine cibi et potus caro et sanguis, mors denique Ipsius communicantur". *Ibid.*

[26] *Ibid.,* 78.

unity of Christ's two natures. There could no more be any question in
eucharistic doctrine of a division of the two natures (Nestorius) or of such a
blending that the human nature disappeared into the divine (Eutyches),
than there could be of such a division or blending in Christology. The
analogy between Christology and eucharistic doctrine led to a rejection of
the doctrine of transubstantiation as a form of Eutychianism in respect of
the eucharist: by transubstantiation the bread and wine lost their nature
and attributes after consecration. According to Saravia, whoever reasoned
thus had no defence against Eutychianism in Christology as well.[27] On the
contrary, the bread and wine keep their former nature after the consecration. There is no question of a substantial but rather of a sacramental
"unio" and of the sacramental eating and drinking. Understandably
enough Saravia attacked the doctrine of transubstantiation at many points
in his treatise.[28] He did, however, also deny the Lutheran view on the ubiquity of Christ's body and blood.[29] It is striking that in his repudiation of
Zurich's views he did indeed confess the real presence of Christ's body and
blood in company with the *Wittenberg Concord,* but that the important notion "substantialiter", used in the agreement, was not mentioned by
him.[30] Probably he here differed from Luther on a very essential point
without being conscious of it. Here he came very close to Calvin whom
otherwise he only quoted once.[31]

The second part of the treatise was devoted to the problem of the "manducatio impiorum".[32] If such great stress is laid on the objectivity of the
sacramental act it follows in consequence that the efficacy of the sacrament
is not dependent on either the minister or the recipient. Where the "indigni" follow the Lord's institution they receive his body and blood, but
because they receive without penitence and faith, the act leads to their
judgement. Just as "pii" and "impii" alike can hear the sermon so
they can alike eat and drink at the Lord's table.[33] There are, however,
three sorts of "manducatio" to be distinguished: the "manducatio

---

[27] "Sed hoc fixum apud patres erat, panem et vinum post consecrationem retinere
priorem naturam, et illa nihil priori naturae detrahi; et in Christo duas naturas, divinam et
humanam in una persona sic unitas, ut altera nihil adimeret alteri quod ei esset proprium.
Et quemadmodum panis dicitur caro Christi, et caro Christi panis, vinum sanguis et sanguis
vinum; ita de Christo dicitur: Deus est homo et homo Deus, et Deus natus est de virgine et
virgo Deum peperit, Deus est passus et fudit suum sanguinem. Atque ita nos quoque propter sacramentalem unionem dicimur carnem Christi edere et sanguinem eius bibere,
quotiescumque panem et vinum eucharistiae sumimus. Sacramentum enim sumentibus
propter unionem sacramentalem, panis caro est et vinum sanguis". *Ibid.,* 62.

[28] *Ibid.,* 24, 26, 54, 60 f., 76, 80, etc.

[29] *Ibid.,* 46.

[30] *Ibid.,* 30 f.

[31] *Ibid.,* 44.

[32] The *Concord of Wittenberg* mentions the "indigni" in art. 3.

[33] *SE,* 100.

capernaitica'' or "cyclopica" that is the "manducatio carnalis" which the Jews spoke in their dispute with Jesus in Capernaum (John 6:52); the "manducatio spiritualis" the spiritual eating by faith; and the "manducatio sacramentalis". The "pii" and "impii" have the last form of "manducatio" in common: people participate in the visible tokens without receiving the "pars invisibilis sacramenti" which these tokens signify. However, only these two together make up the sacrament.[34] In the "manducatio spiritualis" people share in the "pars invisibilis sacramenti", in the fruits of the sacrament, in the sacramental grace.[35] This spiritual communion, for which Saravia naturally refers frequently to John 6 and Augustine, was termed by him an initiation in the mysteries.[36] The "impii" eat and drink sacramentally, as did Judas. The "pii" eat and drink spiritually as did the rest of the disciples.[37] The notion of the "manducatio sacramentalis" served as proof of the objective significance of the sacrament for Saravia. He opposed a subjectivizing of the sacrament as well as a purely symbolic view. He encountered the first in antiquity in the Donatists and in his own day in the Anabaptists who made the efficacy of the sacramental gifts dependent upon the faith of the communicant.[38] He thought he found the second in the Swiss view which considered Christ's flesh and blood to be present only "in signo".[39]

Saravia thought he found his own views well reflected in the letter with which in 1536 Bucer dedicated the second edition of his Commentary on the Gospels to Edward Fox, Bishop of Hereford from August of that year.[40] The reference to this letter which Saravia inserted in its entirety in his treatise,[41] is rather remarkable. In it the Strasbourg reformer, on the one hand, defended his retraction of critical remarks on Luther's sacramental doctrine, but, on the other, declared that there was nothing in his views which had not been accepted by Zwingli and Oecolampadius. Bucer would certainly not have satisfied Luther with this letter, written in the same year in which the *Wittenberg Concord* was concluded. The term "vere et substantialiter" was anything but clearly expressed in it. Once more the suspicion arises that, in his zeal for reconciliation, Saravia did not sometimes properly fathom the actual intentions of the conflicting parties and the relevance of some of the terms they used.

---

[34] *Ibid.*, 86 f.

[35] *Ibid.*, 90.

[36] "Postremo sacramenta non tantum habent rationem imaginis, sed etiam testimonii et sirilli quae testantur res divinas et coelestes in terris celebrari, tradi et accipi ab iis qui mysteriis initiantur." *Ibid.*, 94.

[37] *Ibid.*, 116.

[38] *Ibid.*

[39] *Ibid.*, 106.

[40] M. Bucer, *In sacra quatuor Evangelia Enarrationes.* Basel, 1536.

[41] *SE*, 126-150.

Before he discussed the personal preparation of the communicant in the third part of the treatise, he first dealt with the "fructus" and "gratia" of the sacrament, which were received not "ex opere operato" but by faith.[42] The eucharist was instituted for two reasons, on account of the "constitutio humanae naturae" and for the sake of the "externus Dei cultus" without which no religion is possible.[43] The treatise contains some interesting passages on the first aspect. What is the point of the eucharist if we can share in Christ's body and blood by faith apart from it, as Saravia alleged in an unexpected turn which brought him close to Zwingli and Calvin?[44] The answer is: man's bodily nature requires sacraments perceptible to the senses.[45] The fruit of the sacrament consists in this, that man also receives physically that in which he participates spiritually.[46] Our bodies are members of Christ and temples of the Holy Spirit; they no less than our souls share in eternal life. Belief in the resurrection of the dead implies the nourishment of the whole man for eternal life with Christ's body and blood.[47] In the oral manducation the communicant receives by faith a share in the justification and sanctification which is effective for the whole man.[48] Here we encounter a very scriptural aspect in Saravia's eucharistic doctrine which has been too much neglected in the history of the church. For this he quite rightly appeals to Irenaeus in the latter's dispute with the Gnostics. However much affinity the views outlined on the eucharist may show with those of Calvin, the canon of Canterbury was more scriptural in his thought on the importance of the sacrament for man's physical nature than the Genevan reformer who could here scarcely rid himself of a certain dualism.[49] Saravia strongly opposed such a

---

[42] *Ibid.*, 152.

[43] *Ibid.*, 152 f.

[44] "Non enim tantum caro Domini et sanguis percipiuntur quando sacramentis participamus, sed quotiescunque vera fide Christo adglutinamur... Quoties enim fideles fide credunt se passione et morte Domini redemptos, et peccato simul cum Eo sepultos et mortuos, vitae panem edunt. Christi participes fides nos facit... et citra sacramenti usum sola fides suum sortitur effectum." *Ibid.*, 156.

[45] "Prima est humanae naturae constitutio, quae corpore constat et anima. Ambas partes gratia numinis sui Deus replere vult, et dum hic vivimus eam sigillis suis obsignare. Si tantum spiritus essemus, nude spiritualia et coelestia, nullis corporis tecta involucris nobis traderentur. Conditio naturae nostrae sensibilia postulat sacramenta." *Ibid.*, 152.

[46] "Sacramenti haec est virtus, ut suo modo etiam habeas in tuo corpore quod per fidem percipitur mente." *Ibid.*, 156.

[47] "Corpora nostra sunt membra Christi et templa Spiritus Sancti; et sicut anima vitam aeternam habet a Christi carne et sanguine, sic etiam corpus. Male solius animae spiritualis cibus esse Christi caro disputatur, quae est totius hominis, hoc est aminae pariter et corporis. Quando Dominus se vitae panem dixit, futuram resurrectionem corporum respexit... totus homo de Christ carne et sanguine in vitam aeternam saginatur." *Ibid.*, 158.

[48] *Ibid.*, 207.

[49] A classic example of this dualism is to be found in the "Sursum Corda" in the Holy Communion service of the Palatinate, taken up by other Calvinist communion services. "...so lasst uns mit unsern hertzen nicht an dem eusserlichen brodt unnd wein hafften,

dualism. God is the Creator of both body and soul.[50] Rebirth and salvation effect them both.[51] In the eucharist both receive a share in Christ's gifts.[52]

What he wrote at the end of his treatise about a man's self-examination in preparation for his attendance at the eucharist, about faith, hatred of and repentance for sin, as well as love of the neighbour, was nearly identical to what the Dutch churches, following that of the church of the Palatinate, said about preparation in their eucharistic liturgy[53] and what he himself would have read out many times during his residence in the Low Countries. Another aspect of preparation for him was a certain abstinence in sexual intercourse in marriage, a "temporaria ab uxore contentia".[54]

In the final pages he touched on a problem which was continually brought up for discussion by the Puritans. They argued for a celebration of the eucharist in which the communicants were seated at the table instead of receiving the sacrament kneeling which might give occasion to a superstitious veneration of the eucharistic elements. Saravia denied the latter point. Such superstition is no longer present once the doctrine of transubstantiation has been abandoned. He considered the ceremony of kneeling, sitting or standing for communion an "adiaphoron". Any ceremony is acceptable which is intended as an expression of reverence for the mystery of the present Lord.[55]

Two questions must be answered in any attempt to determine the place of Saravia's eucharistic teaching in doctrinal history: what relation did his views have to those of the great continental reformers? How did they relate to ideas current in the Church of England? As regards his relationship with the continent, it has become clear that not only did he on the one hand, reject transubstantiation and the sacrificial character of the eucharist and, on the other, a purely symbolic doctrine of the eucharist, but that also, despite his esteem for the *Augsburg Confession,* it is difficult to

---

sondern hertzen und glauben uber sich in den Himel erheben... unnd nicht zweiffeln, dass wir so warhafftig durch die würckung des heiligen Geists mit seinem leib und blut an unsern seelen gespeist und getrenckt werden..." *Bekenntnisschriften,* 193.

[50] "Quemadmodum Deus Creator est corporis et animi, ita similiter est utriusque Redemptor." *SE,* 172.

[51] "In his locis [John. 3:6; Gal. 5:17] et aliis pluribus caro non accipitur pro corpore et spiritus pro anima, sed pro toto homine corrupto, tam animo quam corpore; eodem enim peccati tenentur reatu. Quorum communis est corruptio, communis est etiam regeneratio et sanctificatio." *Ibid.,* 166.

[52] "Dici etiam potest, sacrae et coelestis rei sacrum visibile signum ab Ipso Domino Jesu Christo institutum quo Seipsum et dona sua toti homini, id est pariter corpori et animae, communicat et tanquam sigillo obsignat." *Ibid.,* 22.

[53] *Bekenntnisschriften,* 190.

[54] *SE,* 190-194.

[55] *Ibid.,* 194-200.

point to many Lutheran influences in him. He rejected the doctrine of ubiquity in so many words, consubstantiation did not arise, "substantialiter" was not mentioned in his paraphrase of the *Wittenberg Concord*.[56] His combination of the "praesentia realis" with the "manducatio spiritualis" is quite close to Calvin's eucharistic teaching. Because he was insufficiently aware of the theological dispute between Wittenberg and Zurich and the terminological nuances which played their part in it, he was sadly mistaken in his estimation of the *Wittenberg Concord*. The Swiss in 1536 had understood better than Saravia that this was not at all an ecumenical confession founded on a theological agreement, but rather a Lutheran article, intended to give Bucer the opportunity to conform to Lutheran orthodoxy by signing it. On the Lutheran side the *Concord* was regarded as being an acceptable interpretation of the *Augsburg Confession* only in the last resort.[57] Consequently Saravia's ecumenical intentions proceeded from a fictitious starting-point.

In comparing the latter's views on the eucharist with those of the *Articles of Religion* in the 1571 version, it must be remembered that the English confession was not concerned with a doctrinal dispute between Protestant theological schools, as was the *Wittenberg Concord,* but that it was intended much more to profess the Reformation belief of the Church of England against the Roman Catholics. In articles 28-31 relating to the eucharist[58] there were none of the nuances encountered above. The eucharist is the sacrament of our redemption by Christ's death. Whoever receives worthily, shares in his body and blood. Transubstantiation is rejected. The reality of the sacramental event is maintained but not polemically emphasised. "The body of Christ is given, taken, and eaten in the supper, only after an heavenly and spiritual manner," by faith. This agrees with what Saravia taught about the "manducatio spiritualis", but he laid more stress on the objective quality of the eucharist than did his church's confession. In article 29 the latter spoke more rigorously than he about the "manducatio impiorum": the "wicked" eat and drink the sacrament only "carnally and visibly" without sharing in Christ's body and blood. By the notion of the "manducatio sacramentalis", Saravia wanted to bar the way to a purely symbolic view.

A comparison with Jewel[59] reveals a considerable affinity between the two. Jewel also thought, "that we do truly and indeed eat the body of Christ and drink his blood. And this shall be the foundation and key of en-

---

[56] Th. Sippell, "Zur Abendmahlslehre des Anglokatholizismus." *Theologische Studien und Kritiken,* CVI (1934/1935) 377-381, considers Saravia's book as "the classical expression" of the eucharistic doctrine of Thomas Cranmer."

[57] H. Grass, *Die Abendmahlslehre bei Luther und Calvin* (Gütersloh, 1954) 148 ff.

[58] Cardwell, *Synodalia,* I, 101 f.

[59] C. W. Dugmore, *Eucharistic Doctrine in England from Hooker to Waterland.* London, 1942. 6 ff.

trance of all the rest".[60] He too wrote about the eucharistic act as a spiritual act, naturally rejecting any idea of transubstantiation,[61] but much more than Saravia he was concerned to distinguish the eucharistic elements from the risen and ascended Christ.[62] For example, in his interpretation of the words of institution, like Origen whom, significantly, he frequently quoted, he wanted to take account of the opposition between letter and spirit, and, like Augustine, to talk of an "allegoria".[63] Jewel's eucharistic teaching was much more spiritualizing than Saravia's, whilst the latter attached much significance to the communicant's physical nature, Jewel would have nothing to do with it here.[64] A similar emphasis on the distinction between the sacramental signs and the reality signified by them is to be found in Edmund Grindal.[65]

Richard Hooker[66] wrote the fifth book of his *Of the Laws of Ecclesiastical Polity* in Bishopsbourne. It was published in 1597.[67] The treatment of eucharistic doctrine in chapters 6 and 7 of this book is clearer and systematically more powerful than Saravia's treatise. Like the latter, Hooker, who was extremely knowledgeable about the eucharistic disputes on the continent,[68] sought for a way between a symbolic view which he found in Zwingli and the Sacramentarians, on the one hand, and the Roman Catholic doctrine of transubstantiation and the Lutheran consubstantiation on the other. He thought of the real presence of Christ's body and blood in man's soul.[69] A true and real self-communication of Christ as the mystical Head occurred by which the communicant was incorporated in Him and united to Him as a mystical member[70] and "a real transmutation of our souls and bodies from sin to righteousness, from death and corruption to immortality and life" was effected.[71] Hooker and Saravia were kindred spirits in many other respects and their views on the eucharist also showed many features in common. However, we must also note here that Saravia had a more stringent view of the relation between

---

[60] Jewell, *Works,* II, 1109 ff.

[61] *Ibid.,* 1117.

[62] *Ibid.,* 1121; C. W. Dugmore, *The Mass and the English Reformers* (London, 1958) 228 f.; a different view in Fr. E. Pamp, Jr., "Walton's Redaction of Hooker," *CH,* XVII (1948) 113-116.

[63] Jewel, *Works,* II, 1112.

[64] "When we speak of the mystery of Christ, and of eating his body, we must shut up and abandon all our bodily senses." *Ibid.,* 1119.

[65] Dugmore, *Eucharistic Doctrine,* 9 f.

[66] J. R. Parris, "Hooker's Doctrine of the Eucharist," *SJT,* XVI (1963) 151-165.

[67] Dugmore, *Eucharistic Doctrine,* 14.

[68] Hooker, *Works,* II, 349-359.

[69] "The real presence of Christ's most blessed body and blood is not therefore to be sought for in the sacrament, but in the worthy receiver of the sacrament." *Ibid.,* 352.

[70] *Ibid.,* 354.

[71] *Ibid.,* 355.

"signum" and "res" than did Hooker. In this way he tried to combine
Augustine with Ambrose by doing justice to both the spiritual and real
character of the eucharist. We shall pass over the question as to whether
his interpretation of both fathers is tenable historically. Hooker, on the
other hand, opted firmly for Augustine against the sort of realism by which
Ambrose became a forerunner of the doctrine of transubstantiation.[72] If
Hooker's opinions are counted as those of one of "the followers of
Calvin"[73] (although the traditionally presumed deep-seated opposition
between Calvin and Luther, has been rendered untenable by modern
research),[74] then there is still more reason to assert that, at many points in
his doctrine of the sacraments, Saravia followed the footsteps of the
Genevan reformer.

## 2. Baptism

Because we do not possess any developed ecclesiology from Saravia, his
treatise on the eucharist—in which he devotes not the slightest attention to
ecclesiological implications—is one of the rare sources for our knowledge
of his views on the sacraments. In this monograph he also made a number
of scattered remarks about baptism, mostly in order to draw an analogy
between the two sacraments. After this we can also draw upon a small
section of his letter *Venerabili Viro.*

He held the same conviction as to the essence of baptism as he did the
eucharist. The sacrament consisted of a "pars visibilis" and a "pars invisibilis". The baptized participated in the latter by faith, but whoever did
not receive the gift of regeneration to a new life, had yet still been baptized
with a "true and complete baptism".[75] Therefore once administered, baptism was unrepeatable, Saravia rejected the view and practice of rebaptism
on conversion which he found in Anabaptism.[76]

The sacrament of baptism, one of the characteristics of the church, is
administered in the church; however, people are not baptized in the name
of the church but in the name of the Triune God. People are not reborn for
the church, but for God.[77] It is as obvious that Saravia thus raised the issue

---

[72] On Augustine and Ambrose: Dugmore, *The Mass and the English Reformers,* 11-22.

[73] Id., *Eucharistic Doctrine,* 19.

[74] Calvin signed the *Augsburg Confession,* not only the Variata (1540), but also the Invariata
(1530). Nijenhuis, "Calvin and the Augsburg Confession," in: *Ecclesia Reformata,* 97-114.

[75] *SE,* 98.

[76] "Par enim est ratio huius sacramenti [the Holy Communion] et baptismi, quem qui
extra veram fidem accipit, nihil accepisse dici non potest, quamvis regenerationis gratiam
non acceperit. Si nihil praeter aquam acciperet malus, ad veram fidem postea conversus
iterum baptizandus esset; sed quia susceptus baptismus in eo integrum et indelibile
sacramentum fuit, postea non iteratur. Iteratio enim cum iniuria prioris illius coniuncta est
sacramenti, tanquam fuerit nullum." *Ibid.,* 110.

[77] *RG,* 380.

of the church's place in the "respublica christiana" as that he thought that he could appeal to Farel, Calvin and Viret for this. The baptized was born into "the Christian people" and made a member of it. In this way he shares in God's covenant and receives the sign of it in baptism. In the same breath one can talk of the life of Christians in the church, the Christian family and the Christian nation.[78]

Whoever is baptized, is baptized into Christ's blood.[79] The gifts bestowed in baptism are: forgiveness of sins, new life, growth in Christian conduct, resurrection from the dead and eternal life.[80] In his view of baptism too, Saravia took account of man's physical nature. For "all promises of eternal and heavenly life apply not only to the soul but also to the body. The fact that we are baptized means the salvation and spiritual rebirth of body and soul alike".[81] Like the eucharist baptism is founded on the divine institution and promise, particularly on Christ's own baptism, which made this act into a sacrament.[82] Here too there can be no question of an action "opere operato": the gifts of grace and salvation are received by faith.[83] The prayer of the baptism service with the words "and by the baptism of thy wellbeloved Son Jesus Christ, didn't sanctify the flood Jordan and all other waters, to the mystical washing away of sin"[84] have nothing in common with the superstition of a prayer of consecration. It adds no quality to the baptismal water but is to be regarded as a thanksgiving.[85] The essential connection between faith and baptism does not involve any chronological order. Faith can precede baptism as with the Ethiopian eunuch (Acts 8:37) and the Roman centurion Cornelius (Acts 10:44f). And was not Abraham justified by faith long before he was circumcised (Rom. 4:10-12)?[86] The baptizandi ought to be regarded as regenerate in whose name the godfathers and godmothers could renounce the devil and profess the faith.[87] Against Puritan opponents Saravia also laid stress on the objective significance, efficacy and validity of the sacrament in his view of baptism.

---

[78] "Quandoquidem infans in christiana familia, vel in christiano populo natus, et ad illum pertinet... unus est, et velut quaedam pars eorum, qui Deo credunt... Qui in Anglia nascitur, Anglus est...". *VV*, 5.

[79] *SE*, 98.

[80] *Ibid.*, 162.

[81] *Ibid.*, 164.

[82] "Nisi divina institutione et dominico baptismo omnes aquae consecratae essent, nullae nostrae preces id efficere quirent." Not the prayers but "verbum expressum et mandati et promissionis" make the act of baptism a sacrament. *VV*, 7.

[83] *SE*, 78.

[84] *Liturgies of Edward VI*, 107.

[85] *VV*, 7.

[86] *Ibid.*, 5.

[87] *Ibid.*, 6.

### 3. Conclusion

After his conversion to the Reformation Saravia was continually occupied with answering the burning question regarding authority in church and state and the bodies which must at once represent and maintain this authority. In company with all the Reformation, the highest and, theologically speaking, the only source of authority for him was Holy Scripture, the Word of God. After this and derived from it, he attached very great authority to the early church. What both these actually meant for him became clear from his standpoint on justification, election, the doctrine of God and the sacraments. The question as to whether and to what extent Christian belief, as confessed in the Calvinist tradition, really exercised a continuing authority over him, must to our mind be answered affirmatively. This was utterly clear in his defence of the Calvinist version of the Reformation doctrine of justification agains the humanist Coornhert, but his view of the eucharist also was inconceivable without the influence of Calvin and Calvinism. The fact that he supported his theological views with arguments borrowed from the fathers more than did the continental reformers merely indicates a difference of emphasis which perhaps displays the influence of his English contemporaries.

What was apparent from his attitude and behaviour both in Ghent and in the North Netherlands also emerged clearly from his later theological work: he disliked theological disputes and he detested the way in which, in the controversies over the eucharist and predestination, speculation ran riot and contradistinctions were pushed to extremes by what he frequently could see were nothing but hair-splitting and verbal differences.

That he took a moderate position in the dispute over Barrett and that he did not involve himself in the predestination controversy between Remonstrants and Counterremonstrants—his main interest, as we saw, concerned the doctrine of God—is not in the least to say that he can no longer be regarded as a Calvinist. Generally speaking we must be increasingly aware that second and third generation Calvinism displayed numerous variants and that the picture of the Reformed tradition as a monolithic unity is based on a misunderstanding.[88] The variants could relate to doctrinal subjects such as the doctrine of election (the Netherlands; England) and the "descensus ad inferos" (both on the continent and in England), but also to the relationship between church and state and in this connection to the view of church discipline (Erastianism in the Palatinate; the influence of Zurich, also in the Netherlands). It was also soon apparent from the attitude of Morély in France with views which tended more to Congregationalism, that there were also differences on questions of church order within the Reformed tradition.

---

[88] W. Nijenhuis, "Varianten binnen het Nederlands Calvinisme in de zestiende eeuw." *Tijdschrift voor geschiedenis*, XXXIX (1976) 358-372.

If, in some of the controversial questions mentioned above, Saravia pursued a course more in line with the moderation in dogmatics prevalent in the Church of England and if his theology with its avoidance of extreme viewpoints appears less clearly outlined on this account, this is certainly not to say that he is not to be counted as a Calvinist. Just because his views are best understood against the background of the Reformed tradition, it is all the more striking that it was in a matter, not of minor, but of fundamental importance, namely the question of church order and government, that he came into conflict with Calvinism. However, he approached this having already acquired a weapon which he received neither from Lutheranism nor the Church of England, but from Calvinism itself. This weapon was the ''ius divinum''.

# CHAPTER SEVEN

# THE CHURCH

## 1. Marks of the Church

No more than his Protestant contemporaries has Saravia left us an ecclesiology. On such issues as the essence of the church, the relation between church and election, church and covenant, Israel and the New Testament community, and the like, we find only a few scattered pronouncements in his treatises. He was primarily interested in the empirical form of the church as he had come to know, love and serve it in the Church of England. To defend this form with biblically theological arguments against other forms of the church was the principal object of his treatises. These were all "livres de circonstance", reactions to actual challenges, first from the Roman quarter but secondly particularly from the Presbyterian and Puritan side. We shall have to bear this historical background in mind.

The church is the multitude of believers,[1] the body of Christ that depends only on Him, not on apostles or bishops.[2] Indeed its glory does not lie in its organization but in the obedience of faith and in the gifts of the Spirit conferred upon it;[3] but this form of government, together with the preaching of God's Word and the administration of the two sacraments, baptism and the eucharist, is among the marks of the church which, instituted by the Lord, handed down by the apostles, confirmed by the fathers, would continue to exist until the end of time.[4] These three "notae ecclesiae" fulfil the threefold commission of the Gospel ministry in the church: preaching, the administration of baptism and eucharist, and church government. To the latter belonged the power of the keys, that of binding and loosing on earth what is bound and loosed in heaven (Matt. 16: 19, 18:18) and in this Saravia included the ordination of ministers and the "censura morum".[5] Under the third mark of the church, "disciplina", he thus understood both church government, "gubernatio ecclesiae" and church discipline, "censura morum".

---

[1] "... ecclesiam hoc est coetum et multitudinem fidelium..." *DT*, 82.

[2] "A capite Christo pendent ecclesiae, non ab ipsis apostolis, minus ab episcopis." *Ibid.*, 87.

[3] "Magnifica ecclesiarum laus et praeclara earum constitutio non ab episcoporum et presbyterorum constitutione pendebat, sed a fidei obedientia, et Spiritus Sancti donis." *Ibid.*, 84.

[4] *DGM*, 16.

[5] *DGM*, 1.

With this third mark of the church, Saravia was in line with Calvinism as we know it from various Reformed confessions. For Calvin himself "disciplina", conceived of as church discipline, was indeed a token of the "properly ordered church" but not a "mark of the church".[6] Just as the *Augsburg Confession* had done,[7] he only called pure preaching and the right administration of the sacraments "notae ecclesiae".[8] However, the *Scottish Confession*[9] and the *Confessio Belgica*[10] named three marks: preaching, administration of the sacraments and "disciplina". The *Articles of Religion* (1571) mention only the two marks, preaching and administration of the sacraments,[11] but already in 1559 in *A Declaration of certain Articles of Religion,* "the authority of the keys duly used"[12] was mentioned besides these two. In the Homily for Whitsunday "the right use of ecclesiastical discipline" was named as a third characteristic.[13]

There was no agreement amongst English theologians of the sixteenth century as to the marks of the church. The two fundamental marks, preaching and administration of the sacraments, were never omitted. Sometimes they confined themselves to these two, sometimes they talked of three or four marks to which love and obedience could also belong subjectively.[14] Saravia followed the tradition of the Reformed confessions, the *Declaration* and the *Homilies*.

It is very important to note that he did not see discipline, which expressed itself in the "censura morum", as a task for the secular authority but as belonging to the church's own commission, thus making it a part of its order. Despite all his objections to the manner in which discipline was exercised by elders in the Reformed churches, he did not follow the path of Zurich which is thought, especially through Rudolf Gualter, to have had great influence upon the Church of England and its archbishop, John Whitgift.[15] Saravia was indeed an advocate of the secular power's authority in the church but he repeatedly and expressis verbis rejected the view according to which the "disciplina morum" was part of this secular

---

[6] J. Plomp, *De kerkelijke tucht bij Calvijn* (Kampen, 1969) 123-128.

[7] *Die Bekenntnisschriften der Evangelisch-Lutherischen Kirche* (Göttingen, 1952) 61.

[8] *Inst.* (1559), IV, 1, 9 and 10; *CO*, II, 753 f.

[9] *Bekenntnisschriften*, 102.

[10] *Ibid.*, 131; *Belijdenisgeschriften*, 124 f.

[11] Cardwell, *Syndolia*, I, 97. The question arises, whether and to what extent does the addition "in al those thynges that of necessitie are requisite to the same", which was added to the 1552 text in 1562, imply the third mark of church-government and discipline.

[12] Cardwell, *Annals*, I, 264.

[13] *Certain Sermons, Appointed by the Queen's Majesty, to be declared and read,* Ed. for the Syndics of the University Press (Cambridge, 1850), 462.

[14] H. F. Woodhouse, *The Doctrine of the Church in Anglican Theology 1547-1603* (London, 1954) 60.

[15] H. Kressner, *Schweizer Ursprünge des anglikanischen Staatskirchentums* (Gütersloh, 1953) 73-133.

jurisdiction so that the commission of the "ministri ecclesiae" was to remain confined to preaching and administering the sacraments. He opted for a joint exercise of discipline by bishops and priests.[16] He considered it absurd if the "ministri ecclesiae" who exercised the "potestas solvendi" in preaching and in baptism, were not to dispose of the "potestas ligandi" in the "disciplina morum". It would be contrary to the duty of a responsible minister, if they were compelled to allow "wolves into the Lord's sheepfold" at celebrations of the Eucharist. The keeping of these wolves from the Lord's table was the task of the church not of the magistrate.[17] Thus he rejected precisely that element in the relationship between church and state about which Thomas Erastus had been concerned in the dispute over church discipline in Heidelberg, namely, the exercise of such discipline by the secular power.[18] Hence it is wrong to call Saravia an Erastian.[19]

According to Saravia there should be room for differences in "adiaphora" within a church which possessed the three above-mentioned marks. This distinction between matters of substance, necessary to salvation, and matters indifferent, accidental, neuter, or "accessary", things which are not obligatory because they are not commanded by Scripture, is also to be encountered in Jewel, Whitgift and Hooker.[20] They played an important part in the dispute with the Puritans because the latter firmly restricted the category of the adiaphora in proportion to that of things commanded or forbidden by God. Among the things indifferent Saravia included: liturgical customs, celibacy, fasting, celebration of the great church festivals such as Christmas, Easter, Whitsun—the reaction to Rome had gone so far in the Calvinist churches that these were no longer kept—, recitation of the Nicene or Athanasian creed in the liturgy, the use of music and musical instruments in worship, sitting, standing or kneeling for communion, the use of vestments, and so on.[21] The rule for deciding

---

[16] "Sunt qui omnem disciplinam morum magistratui committendam opinantur, et sola eaque nuda praedicatione verbi Dei et sacramentorum administratione Evangelii ministerium includunt: quod cum neque verbo Dei, neque ullo maiorum exemplo possit doceri, miror theologis talem opinionem venire in mentem potuisse. Alii sunt, qui censurae ecclesiasticae potestatem tribuunt episcopis et re ac nomine presbyteris, cum ea authoritate quam Deus apostolis et ecclesiae futuris episcopis dedit... Quod me attinet, episcopos ecclesiae necessarios arbitror, et eam disciplinam ac gubernationem ecclesiae esse optimam et divinam, quam pii episcopi, cum veri nominis presbyteris ex praescripto verbi Dei et veterum conciliorum administrant." DGM, preface to the reader, A6v.

[17] Ibid., 1, 2.

[18] Wesel-Roth, Erastus, 90-102.

[19] An example of the English use of the term "Erastianism", in which the crucial question of discipline is disregarded, is to be found in Cross, The royal supremacy, 27, 30-39, 65-67.

[20] Studies in Richard Hooker. Essays preliminary to an Edition of his works. W. Speed Hill, ed. (Cleveland/London, 1972) 16 f., 98 f.

[21] DT, 334.

lay for him in the "aedificatio" of the community. Some aspects of the church's life tend by their nature to this "aedificatio" and are therefore among the completely unalterable elements such as worship, the confession of the Christian faith, the administration of justice and the protection of the innocent. Other aspects, especially liturgical, derive their function of "aedificatio" from their practice. They belong to the things indifferent about which difference of opinion was possible and permissible. He himself was content with liturgical life according to the order of the *Book of Common Prayer* as had already become apparent from his advice to Leicester during his time in the Netherlands.[22] He rejected the Puritans' attempt to make an issue of the "adiaphora" in their struggle for further reform of the church[23] and because of this ambition too he accused them of schismatic tendencies.[24] Saravia's position here did not differ essentially from Calvin's. To be sure the latter had little regard for the Church of England's liturgy but he did not think that it so obscured the essence of the church that it was necessary to wage a fierce struggle over it.[25] During the vestments controversy (1550/1551) the reformer wrote to John Hooper that vestments were not worth such radical opposition.[26] Calvin also acted in a conciliatory manner in the disputes between "Coxians" and "Knoxians" in the English refugee community at Frankfurt.[27] Granted a different valuation of the *Book of Common Prayer,* Saravia shared Calvin's position: it was not worth a schism in the church.

Any sign of division and schism was an abomination to him. "The church is one; it can be neither torn apart or divided".[28] "One God, one Lord Jesus Christ, one church, one baptism, one ministry", so ran his ecumenical confession.[29] Divisions are the work of factious Christians, especially of "teachers who were born for disturbances and quarrels".[30] Israel and Judah remained one after the division because by circumcision they both shared in the covenant of the one God.

Saravia did not believe in the existence of only one true church. Although he found the Church of England the clearest example of a church which had been reformed in accordance with God's Word, yet he was not disposed to compare other churches with it in order to test their ecclesiastical form. They all had their praiseworthy points and their im-

---

[22] p. 97 f.

[23] *VV,* 15.

[24] *Ibid.,* 7 f.

[25] Nijenhuis, *Calvinus Oecumenicus,* 204 f.

[26] J. H. Primus, *The Vestments Controversy. An Historical Study of the earliest tensions within the Church of England in the reigns of Edward VI and Elizabeth* (Kampen, 1960) 63.

[27] Nijenhuis, *Calvinus Oecumenicus,* 212-215.

[28] *DT,* 31.

[29] *Ibid.,* 32.

[30] *Ibid.,* 31.

perfections. Controversy between theological schools could only be harmful since it distracted the churches from their unity in the one "Magister" and "Dominus", Jesus Christ.[31]

In his assessment of the empirical churches Saravia took account of the distinction between the visible and invisible church. The latter was formed by those elected according to Christ's will. It was concealed in the visible church and would remain so until the Last Day when the two would be separated. Saravia used examples for this from the New Testament parables of the wise and foolish virgins and of the tares among the wheat—a classic example also used by Augustine—and, from the *Confessio Belgica*, the famous example of the 7,000 faithful in Elijah's time.[32] For the rest, the relationship between the visible and invisible church and that between church and election—two ecclesiological questions which were treated in various ways in English sixteenth century theology[33]—played no great part in Saravia's ecclesiological reflections. In the discussion in which he engaged the particular concern was with the visible empirical church, its order and its government.

The church is catholic. The marks of its catholicity are the apostolic character of its doctrine and order and its agreement with the universal church.[34] As was the case in his eucharistic teaching, Saravia laid much stress in his ecclesiology on the objective aspects in the church's life. These he found both in the Greek and Latin church of his day.

Finally, we must turn our attention to Saravia's views on the relationship between the local and the universal church and the way in which the ministry functions in this. We saw earlier that he was an advocate of conciliar church government. In his view the universal church ought to have not a monarchical but a collegiate government. It was otherwise with the diocese, as the rule said: not more than one bishop in a diocese. Ignatius and Cyprian[35] were naturally among the many witnesses from antiquity called in support of this. In the light of this principle there could be no objection to the Bishop of Rome if he did not extend his authority outside the bounds of his diocese. What the bishop was for the diocese, the patriarch, archbishop, primate or metropolitan was for the people of the province.

---

[31] "Singulae ecclesiae peculiarem suam habent laudem; habent et suos naevos. Causa nulla est, cur potius reformationis exemplum ab una aliqua peti debeat quam ab alia orthodoxa Christi ecclesia. Habent omnes ecclesiae suas scholas, habent et academias, in quibus nulla in re invenientur theologi eruditione et pietate alii aliis inferiores. Electio peculiaris authorum et praeiudicium plus semper ecclesiae nocuit quam profuit. Unus enim magister noster in coelis: Dominus Jesus Christus." *ET,* Prologus, 2.

[32] *Ibid.,* 65; *DT,* 50.

[33] Woodhouse, *Doctrine of the Church,* 43-58.

[34] "Catholicum illud est, quod inde a temporibus apostolorum ecclesiae fuit traditum, ac usu et moribus post fuit confirmatum, et alios authores non habet quam ipsos apostolos, et consentientem sibi Christi universalem ecclesiam". *Ibid.,* Prologus, 5.

[35] *DGM,* 30-31.

Notably unhistorical is the statement that not only the obedience of the priest to the bishop, but also that of the bishop to his patriarch or metropolitan is based on divine institution to be found in the Old and New Testaments.[36] In theological thinking at the time of the Elizabethan settlement "obedientia" and "subiectio",[37] like the term "conformity", were understood as being pretty well identified with God's eternal will. It is significant that in his attempts to convert the authoritative structures of the early church to a divine institution, Saravia looked for titles in which the authoritative element was pronounced, such as προϊστάμενος (Rom. 12:8) and κυβερνήσεις (1 Cor. 12:28). These were descriptions of the higher pastors, "superiores pastores",[38] who enjoyed great authority in the early church and deserved to also in the present time "in bene constituta christiana republica".[39] It is clear from all this that Saravia thought more of the universal church in relation to the local congregation than vice versa. In this also he differed from his Calvinist opponents.

## 2. ROME

Saravia could speak very paradoxically about the Roman church: although it is not the catholic church in which we believe, nor a sound member of it, yet it cannot be denied the name "church".[40] It is neither orthodox, nor catholic, nor a member of the catholic church, but it was nevertheless our mother in whom and through whom God regenerated us in baptism.[41] For there is something of the church to be discerned where there is the presence of the Scriptures of the Old and New Testaments and baptism in the name of the Triune God as the sign of the covenant.[42] Although Rome is an "adulterous and whorish church" defiled by error, idolatry and superstition, we must nonetheless regard those who are baptized in it and who seek their salvation in Christ as children of God's people and as "our brothers" so long as they do not take up the sins of their adulterous mother. For superstition and abuse cannot undo God's covenant, nor do they invalidate the ministry and sacraments in the Roman church.[43] This also involves the recognition of Roman ordinations.[44]

---

[36] *Ibid.,* 31.

[37] The English translation speaks of "that government, ...in the which the elders are subject to their elder bishops, and the bishops to their higher patriarchs and metropolitanes...". Saravia, *Of the diverse degrees* (London, 1592) 78.

[38] *DGM,* 31 f.

[39] *Ibid.,* 35.

[40] "...et quamvis Romana ecclesia neque catholica ecclesia sit, quam credimus, neque sanum illius membrum, ecclesiae tamen nomen retinere, et esse... non... negari potest...". *ETB,* 62; cf. *DT,* 327.

[41] *DT,* 30.

[42] *Ibid.,* 31.

[43] *Ibid.*

[44] *Ibid.,* 30.

On the one hand, we read the harshest pronouncements about Rome in Saravia. On the other, we see that, against the Puritans who thought that they found objectionable relics of popish superstition in the ministry and liturgy of the Church of England, he was obliged to explain that a custom, an article of belief, a ministry is not sinful just because it is to be found in the Roman church.[45] The ministry, especially the bishop's office, was an important bone of contention in these debates. In Saravia's view, papal tyranny was no argument for the abolition of whole ministry of bishops but only for its reform in accordance with the original Canons. Not abolition but restoration of the former, that is to say, the scriptural and early Christian state of affairs, this was the standard for reformation which he continually applied to church government, especially to the episcopal office. He considered that Anabaptism's radicalism which denied Rome any apostolic and catholic character was the cause of much misunderstanding because it lost sight of the objective foundation of the church in God's mercy and in His covenant.[46] Whoever, like Beza, called the Roman ministry satanic, thus appeared to be giving in to "Anabaptistici furores".[47]

In his assessment of Rome too, Saravia distinguished the elements which were in accord with God's Word or opposed to it and the so-called "media" or "indifferentia". The first included God's Word and baptism, the second, all sorts of idolatry and corruption of sound doctrine. "Media" and "indifferentia" was what had been neither commanded nor forbidden.[48] Rome was recognizable as a church by prayer[49] and by the ministry[50] which last was understood as that of priests and bishops. The pope would not have had the slightest chance of attaining his "objectionable vicariate" if he had not been consecrated bishop. Furthermore, the latter would have been impossible had he not been ordained to the priesthood.[51] The important objective characteristic of the church contained in its hierarchical structure could not be so obscured by superstition and idolatry that Rome was no longer recognizable as a Christian church.

Saravia expressed himself paradoxically as to the Christian character of the Roman church. On the one hand, he could declare that its rites and ceremonies had been so corrupted that in it Christianity had been

---

[45] "Nihil ineptius hac conclusione, qua sic infertur: hoc Antichristus docet, ergo falsum; hoc Antichristus invenit, ergo malum". *DGM*, 34.

[46] "... illi malo [the papal tyranny] hoc unum est remedium, ut eo reiecto, reformentur episcopi ad normam veterum canonum, et regularum ecclesiasticae gubernationis." *DT*, 251; "Huius peccati [of the Anabaptists] prima causa est ignorantia misericordiae Dei erga suam ecclesiam et eos omnes super quos ipsius nomen invocatum est, censenturque in foedere Dei". *ETB*, 47.

[47] *Ibid.*, 49, 66 f.

[48] *Ibid.*, 34.

[49] *Ibid.*, 88.

[50] *Ibid.*, 86, 88.

[51] *ETB*, 65.

transformed not merely into Judaism but into heathenism, but again he hastened to admonish those who therefore wished to abolish all ceremonies. Against this radicalism he advocated the golden mean, the "aurea mediocritas" of the Anglican church which, "sit Deo laus", had been cleansed from Roman "impurities".[52] Impure Christianity is still Christianity. "The papist religion is defiled by superstition and idolatry and is, so to speak, a sort of impure Christianity. For those distinguishing marks of Christianity, the Holy Scriptures of the Old and New Testament, God's covenant, the baptism of Christ, the forgiveness of sins, the name of Christian and most other things which belong to the church, are never found outside the church in heathenism, or Judaism or Mohammedanism. If the heresies which have crept into the Roman church are removed, what remains is Christianity. The papacy too is a sickness of the church, not the church itself. But what leprosy or another deadly infection is to the human body so is the papacy in the body of the catholic church. When, therefore, the papacy is abandoned, the church is not abandoned but corruption is rightly driven out of the church... In the Reformation an adulterous wife becomes a pure bride and is reconciled with Christ her bridegroom; illegitimate and bastard Christians became legitimate".[53] When he addresses Rome on the necessity of such a reformation, he allows no doubt as to what was the authentic norm for this: the Word of God in Scripture.[54]

His criticism of Rome concentrated on two points in particular: its interference with the truth, especially in the doctrine of the sacrifice of the mass and the papal claim to universal authority.[55] Because of its abuse of the truth,[56] the papacy represented the epitome and symbol of heresy for him.[57] Its real sacrilege lay in the doctrine of the sacrificial nature of the mass as a repetition of Christ's sacrifice on the cross and consequently a denial of the latter's unique and unrepeatable character.[58] He mentioned as other deviations from scriptural teaching: communion in one kind in the eucharist, the doctrine of transubstantiation, worship of images,

---

[52] *DT*, 285.

[53] *DGM*, 87 f.

[54] "Nihil enim aliud recipiendum et fide credendum est, quam quod in verbo Dei scripto expresse docetur aut inde deducitur", at the end of a passage which hints at autobiographical references. *RG*, 381.

[55] "Duo enim quaedam execranda sacrilegia totum Romanae ecclesiae ministerium contaminant. Alterum est sacrificandi verum corpus et sanguinem Domini pro vivis et defunctis officium; alterum vicariatus universalis ecclesiae portentum". *ETB*, 65.

[56] *DT*, 3.

[57] "... a papismo, id est: ab haeresi...". *DGM*, 87.

[58] "... qui altare contra altare erexit, et sacerdotium contra Christi sacerdotium, et sacrificium expiatorium pro peccatis vivorum et mortuorum contra illud unum quod iterari non potest a Servatore nostro semel oblatum, instituit". This was contrary to the belief, "praeter unum Dominum Jesum sacerdotum nullum nos agnoscere". *DGM*, 52.

obligatory celibacy of the clergy, justification by works, the doctrine of merits and monasticism.[59] In all of this Saravia voiced the chief themes of Reformation preaching against Rome.

Secondly, he directed his criticism at the papal pretentions tó and usurpation óf authority. He had no objection to the Bishop of Rome being accorded a primacy of honour before that of Constantinople and the other patriarchates;[60] but he considered both the essential primacy which the pope claimed for himself as Peter's successor and his pretentions of authority over secular governments to be utterly unacceptable. At stake in all of this was the issue of authority both in the church and the world.

As regards the primacy, Saravia declared that all the apostles were equal, Peter possessed no essential primacy,[61] at the most a primacy of honour.[62] The power of the keys, which was one of the fundamental distinguishing marks of the church, was given not to Peter but to all the apostles.[63] The pope is not Peter's successor, but the bishops are the apostles' successors.[64] By his pretentions to primacy above other bishops the pope has made his episcopal chair a seat of pride, a "sedes superbiae"[65] and turned his title "servus servorum" into a mark of hypocrisy.[66]

He abhorred the way in which the pope claimed sovereignty over the whole earth and allotted authority to kings as it pleased him.[67] The subjection of governments and the subordinating of secular laws to that of the papal "summum sacerdotium" was a serious error[68] by which the pope profaned both the office of bishop and that of the government.[69] In particular, Saravia was thinking of English history which was not without experience of Rome's claims to secular authority.[70]

This subject recurred frequently in the *Responsio ad Gretzerum.* In his adversary Saravia attacked the Jesuits who he knew acted as shock troops in the battle to reclaim England for Rome; no small threat to the Elizabethan establishment.[71] When Gretser raised the issue of the relation-

---

[59] *DT,* 78.

[60] "Primum ordine et honore inter patriarchas esse episcopum Romanum et secundum Constantinopolitanum patribus non magis contra verbum Dei visum est, quam Petrum dici primum, et Jacobum secundum, et Johannem tertium apostolis". *DT,* 151.

[61] *DGM,* 5.

[62] *DT,* 151.

[63] *DT,* 181.

[64] *ETB,* 40 f.

[65] *DT,* 202.

[66] *DGM,* 74.

[67] *DGM,* 67.

[68] *DT,* 334.

[69] *Ibid.,* 335.

[70] *ETB,* 65.

[71] *RG,* 353.

ship between crown and church and particularly condemned the expression "caput ecclesiae anglicanae"—a title which in fact only Henry VIII had borne; Elizabeth no longer called herself "head" but "supreme governor" of the church,—Saravia compared the sovereign to the Emperor Marcianus and King David.[72] Just like his Jesuit opponent he started from the corpus christianum but his own theocracy was Constantinian in style: the secular authority occupied the top place in the hierarchy which Gretser assigned to the pope. We must bear in mind this theocratic aspect of Saravia's ecclesiological thought if we are presently to understand his defence of the place of bishops and archbishops in Parliament: a national role in the commonwealth as a whole, at the head of which was the king. Saravia was here thinking of a national church in which there was no room for any "principatus universitatis" like that of the pope's.[73] Otherwise, Saravia mockingly supposed, Gretser would have no objection to the king's supremacy over the Church of England if the king were willing to submit to the pope.[74]

The most important part of the *Responsio* is the treatment of the relationship between pope and council. Saravia adduced the spokesmen of fifteenth century conciliarism against Gretser's papal standpoint. He referred to the decrees of the Councils of Constance (6 April 1415) and Basel (16 May 1439) in which the council's authority was set above that of the pope. He quoted at length from the *Considerationes* of Jean Gerson, who had an important part in the Council of Constance's decree, from Nicolaus Cusanus' *De concordantia catholica* and from other conciliar pronouncements[75] to demonstrate that conciliar church government is the most suitable instrument for effecting the reform of the church.

Apart, however, from objections to minor points,[76] Saravia had a typical Reformation difficulty with this fifteenth century conciliarism. In a sermon before the Council of Constance Gerson said: "The church or the general council as its representative is the standard which has been guided by the Holy Spirit and handed down by Christ".[77] Saravia very properly observed that this sort of conciliarism is little changed from papalism: the church itself continues to be regarded as the standard of belief, not now indeed by means of the pope but by that of the council. This, however, makes no essential difference. In opposition to this he set the canonical Scriptures of the Old and New Testament as the only norm commanded

---

[72] *Ibid.*, 354.

[73] *Ibid.*, 356 ff.

[74] *Ibid.*, 372.

[75] *Ibid.*, 360-378.

[76] For example, with regard to Gerson's ideas about the relationship between the monarchical function of the papacy and the aristocratic form of church government by the council: "Eandem potestatem esse aristocraticam et monarchicam, mihi paradoxum est". *Ibid.*, 365.

[77] *Ibid.*, 373.

by the Holy Spirit and handed on by Christ to the churches and their councils. Everything necessary for man's salvation has been delivered to the church in this. Councils may add nothing to it.[78] Thus with regard to conciliarism also, Saravia answered the question of authority with the Reformation "sola scriptura".

His views on the conciliar form of church government were of a piece with his ideas on the church's unity. It is one in Christ. He is its true and only monarchical head. Consequently there can be no human monarchical government in the universal church. The form in which Christ's monarchical sovereignty over the church realizes itself is in that of the aristocracy of the council. This latter type of government can extend over the universal church in a "concilium universale" as its representative. This representative character was very important for Saravia. Only a truly representative church assembly might hope for the Holy Spirit's guidance and, as he was at pains to explain with reference to the limited composition of the Council of Nicea and later councils, such a meeting had never been held after the so-called Apostolic Council of Jerusalem (Acts 15). Anyway it is not the size of the council that is determinative for its authenticity and authority, but Christ's promise (Matth. 18: 19, 20). A universal council can err, a provincial council can be "verum et pium".[79] Monarchical church government only occurs in the local church (the pastor) and in the diocese in which the bishop guarantees unity. However, this is not monarchical church government in the real sense of the word for neither bishop nor archbishop can promulgate canons on their own authority. These must be decided in a provincial or national synod. The authority of all church assemblies at any level depends on the degree to which their decisions are in accord with God's Word.[80]

Altogether it is apparent that Saravia's attitude towards the Roman church scarcely differs from that of the continental reformers; though there are a few differences of emphasis to be noted. Saravia laid greater stress on the objective aspects of the church especially on the objective form of the church's ministry. He stressed the continuity of the ministry between the early, the medieval and the Reformation church in a way which Calvin failed to do. He deliberately refused to go along with Beza when the latter described the Roman ministry as "satanic".[81] The bearer of the office might be so named but not the office itself. These differences of emphasis had little bearing upon the defence that Saravia with his church, the Church of England, conducted against Rome. In fighting on this front, the churches on the continent and the Church of England, the

---

[78] *Ibid.*, 374.
[79] *RG*, 379.
[80] "Ecclesia una est...". *ETB*, 12.
[81] *DT*, 326; *ETB*, 46-67.

reformers and Saravia, acknowledged the same authority: Christ alone, the Scriptures alone, faith alone, God's grace alone.

However, the theologian who is the subject of this study was also, together with his church, engaged on another front. They had to resist those who, on the basis of the above answers, were bent on a thorough-going reformation and wanted to achieve a more radical purge of the church than the Church of England had hitherto displayed, a reformation in the presbyterian fashion. In the struggle between the Church of England and Beza's Puritan followers the question turned on what form the authority of Christ and the Scriptures should assume in the Church. What ought the church's structure to look like if this authority can hold sway?

It was evident that an extremely important and commonly held ec-clesiological proposition became the great point at issue in the dispute. As opposed for example to Lutheranism, both Beza as a representative of the Reformed tradition and Saravia as a theologian in the Church of England, believed that the Church had three distinguishing features: preaching, the administration of the sacraments and "gubernatio" or "disciplina". What, however, did the third mark mean in practice? It was here that the dispute arose. Saravia's historical importance as a theologian lay in the answer he gave to the question. It appeared from this answer that, "where a sufficient and substantial agreement in doctrine seems to exist, problems of church polity and order have presented formidable barriers to union".[82]

### 3. THE THIRD MARK

Saravia's treatises on church government entered into a controversy which arose in the Church of England under continental influences. In-itially episcopacy posed no problems for its theologians.[83] It existed and that was sufficient. So long as there was no demand for its abolition, no one felt the need to defend it. In the view of the first generation of Elizabethan theologians in their church the episcopate had been reformed, that is to say, it had been restored to its original function which was first and foremost pastoral. Thus Jewel wrote, "For we require our bishops to be pastors, labourers, and watchmen. And that this may the more readily be brought to pass, the wealth of the bishops is now diminished and reduc-ed to a reasonable amount, to the end that, being relieved from that royal pomp and courtly bustle, they may with greater ease and diligence employ their leisure in attending to the flock of Christ".[84] If the Bishop of Rome

---

[82] Sykes, *Old Priest*, 1.

[83] *Ibid.*, 1-29.

[84] John Jewel to Josias Simler, 2 Nov. 1559. *The Zürich Letters*, I, 51. For Jewel: C. van der Woude, "John Jewel, apologeet van het Anglicanisme," *Ned. AK*, XLVIII (1967/68) 213-231.

did not fulfill the requirement he ought not to be called a priest, let alone a bishop, for, as Jewel quoted Augustine, "a bishop is a name of labour and not of honour; that the man that seeketh to have pre-eminence, and not to profit, may understand himself to be no bishop".[85] Such an utterance betrays a conception that is highly scriptural but scantly hierarchical. At this point we are still a long way from Saravia's demand for "the honour which is due unto priestes and prelates of the church" as the title of the second part of *De Gradibus* expresses it in the English translation.

In this connection we must take note of an outstanding difference between many Reformed confessions and that of the Church of England's. There was a close relation between faith and order for the Reformed. Calvin inferred the presbyterian Church order with the offices of minister, elder, deacon and possibly doctor, from the New Testament.[86] The French confession (art. 29), the *Confessio Belgica* (art. 30) and the *Confessio Helvetica Posterior* (art. 18)[87] included the threefold ministry, understood in the Calvinist sense, as an object of faith expressis verbis. There is an evident difference here with the *Articles of Religion,* for at the points where these mention the church, its existence (art. 19), its authority (art. 20), councils (art. 21) and the ministry in the congregation (art. 23), nothing is said about the form which church government ought to possess. The offices are not mentioned and we have to make do with the stipulation set out in art. 23 that the local pastor must be "lawfully called and sent", that is to say, "chosen and called to this worke by men who have publique aucthoritie geven unto them in the congregation, to call and sende ministers into the Lordes vineyarde".[88] Anyone wishing to know more about "the consecration of archbishops and bishops", is referred to the Ordinal, but art. 36 smacks more of an announcement than a confession. In contrast to the continental Reformed churches, the Church of England did not regard fundamental principles of church order as objects of faith which must be pronounced on in a confession. This is not to say that these principles were lacking. Among other references we read in the Foreword to the Ordinal: "It is evident unto all men, diligently reading Holy Scripture, and ancient authors, that from the Apostle's time there hath been these orders of ministers in Christ's church: bishops, priests, and deacons". Before being qualified to fulfill these offices a man had to be "called, tried, examined and known to have such qualities as were requisite for the same; and also, by public prayer, with imposition of hands, approved and admitted thereunto".[89] The practice of episcopal succession and ordination was

---

[85] Jewel, *Works,* I, 308.
[86] *Inst.* (1559), IV, 3; *CO,* II, 776-787.
[87] *Bekenntnisschriften,* 73, 131, 253; *Belijdenisgeschriften,* 126 f.
[88] Cardwell, *Synodalia,* I, 97-99.
[89] *Liturgies of Edward VI,* 161.

taken over from the medieval church. They wanted an episcopal ministry which was reformed so that its pastoral nature was restored. There had apparently been no need for the kind of fundamental scriptural and theological revolution of the ministry effected by Calvin and, in his wake, by Calvinism. Neither Jewel, nor Whitgift, nor Hooker taught that episcopal church order was to be gathered from scripture and based on the "ius divinum".[90] Saravia was the first to express this view which indeed he did as a defence against the above-mentioned Puritan arguments in which, inspired by Beza, presbyterian church government was set forth as the only form based on the "ius divinum".

"The responsibility for elevating polity to the rank of a protestant dogma and for anathematizing episcopacy, name and thing, lies with Calvin's successor".[91] It was precisely with regard to England[92] and Scotland[93] that the latter's views became more radical. In his *Confessio christianae fidei* (1560)[94] there was still room for the recognition of forms of church order other than the presbyterian, but from the middle of the sixties Beza was increasingly concerned with the state of affairs in the English church. On 19 December 1564 he dedicated an edition of his *Annotationes in Novum Testamentum* to Queen Elizabeth. In this he expressed the wish that, now that the profession of pure doctrine had been restored in England, this should be followed by a renewal of the "disciplina ecclesiastica". Naturally he meant a church order in line with Reformed principles.[95] He was aware that his involvement in English affairs could aggravate the situation in that country. Whatever came from Geneva was suspect: the queen had not deigned to thank him for his *Annotationes*.[96] Yet he persisted. In a letter on 27 June 1566, he urged Edmund Grindal, then Bishop of London, to associate the Church of England with the *Confessio Helvetica Posterior* in the return to the liturgical simplicity of apostolic times, the reform of discipline and the abolition of the state's authority in the church.[97] His ideas became widely known in England and Scotland through the publication of his correspondence in 1573, through his *De triplici episcopatu* (1576) and especially through the English translation of this work (1580).[98] His views were taken up and spread by Cartwright,

---

[90] Sykes, *Old Priest*, 71 f.; F. Heal and R. O'Day, ed. *Church and Society in England: Henry VIII to James I* (London, 1977) 78-98.

[91] Collinson, *The Elizabethan Puritan Movement*, 109.

[92] *Ibid.*, 109 ff.

[93] Donaldson, *The Scottish Reformation*, 187-191.

[94] Th. Beza, *Confessio christianae fidei et eiusdem collatio cum papisticis haeresibus* (1560) 178 ff.

[95] Th. de Bèze, *Correspondance*, V, 167.

[96] Beza to Bullinger, 19 June 1566. *Ibid.*, VII, 142 f.

[97] *Ibid.*, VII, 154-166.

[98] This translation is included in the edition of the Latin text with a modern English translation in: Nijenhuis, *Ecclesia Reformata*, 130-187.

Travers, Melville and others. To put their principles into practice would mean a radical alteration not only in the organization of the church but also in its relationship to the state. They advocated the equality of the three offices of minister, elder and deacon, the inclusion in the church order of every possible guarantee against any superiority of one office over another (amongst others, by the temporary appointment of elders for only one or two years) and of one local church over another, the division of the church into classes in which the office holders of the local congregations could deliberate over faith and morals in their area without influence from any superior ecclesiastical or secular authority; a strict exercise of discipline by the elders.[99] "Note this suspicious speech of the kind of government," wrote Whitgift in the margin beside these significant sentences from the *Admonition to the Parliament* (1572): "...and hereby he cannot prove that there should be any degrees amongst the ministers and ecclesiastical governors, unless he will say, peradventure, that, as there are under-magistrates and a king above them all, so there should be under-ministers, and one minister above all. But he must remember that it is not necessary in a commonwealth, that there should be one over all; for that there are other good commonwealths, wherein many have like power and authority".[100] In the England of 1572 this sounded like the language of revolution. There were democratizing tendencies involved in Puritan views which, if put into practice, would radically change English society. This society was at this time based on the union of church and state under the supreme authority of the monarch. It is not therefore surprising that the government saw grave political dangers in this movement.[101] The Calvinist inspired revolt in the Netherlands caused Elizabeth quite enough anxiety. The flame of revolution must not spread to England. Saravia was one of the few who knew that Beza, the great inspiration of Puritanism and Presbyterianism, was also the author of the treatise *Du droit des magistrats* (1574).[102] The dispute between Saravia and Beza[103] was more than a theological discussion on church government; it was a struggle between two worlds and two forms of society. The old was sustained by the idea of the "corpus Christianum" whose values were expressed in the terms

---

[99] There are instructive texts which illustrate the Puritan's views in: *Puritan Manifestoes. A Study of the Origin of the Puritan Revolt*, W. F. Frere and C. E. Douglas, ed. London, 1907; H. C. Porter, *Puritanism in Tudor England* (London/Basingstoke, 1970) 80-248; *Elizabethan Puritanism*. L. J. Trinterud, ed. New York, 1971.

[100] Whitgift, *Works*, II, 263.

[101] A. F. Scott Pearson, *Church & State. Political Aspects of sixteenth century Puritanism* (Cambridge, 1928) 61.

[102] Th. de Bèze, *Du droit des Magistrats*, R. M. Kingdon, ed. (Geneva, 1970) VII. The treatise was originally written in Latin, but the French text was published first.

[103] On this struggle also: T. Maruyama, *The Ecclesiology of Theodore Beza. The Reform of the Church* (Genève, 1978) 174-194.

"establishment", "settlement", and "uniformity". The new, perhaps despite itself, was engaged in breaking the harmony of the "corpus Christianum". It pioneered a pluriformity of religious life in which church and state would be critical partners in a society which, for ecclesio-theological, social and political reasons, gradually demanded more scope for "nonconformity". When the establishment was unwilling to allow this scope it had finally to be fought for in a civil war. However things had not yet come to such a pass and for the time being Elizabeth's theologians tried to stem the flood by a vigorous defence of the status quo. When Beza and his disciples appealed to Scripture and the "ius divinum" for their views on church and ministry, "disciplina" and "gubernatio", they challenged the theologians of the Elizabethan settlement to use the same weapons in defence of a position which was summed up by James I in 1604 during the Hampton Court Conference in the aphorism "No bishop, no king".[104] The relations between the Church of England and its Puritan theologians were increasingly polarized by the attacks on the episcopal ministry by men like Cartwright. At the end of 1572 and beginning of 1573, in his *Answer to the Admonition* Whitgift had answered the scriptural pretentions of the Puritans[105] thus: "Yet do I deny that the Scriptures do express particularly everything that is to be done in the church..., or that it doth set down any one certain form and kind of government of the church, to be perpetual for all times, persons, and places, without alteration".[106] He had even weakened the connection between Scripture and church order by deeming "ceremonies, discipline and government, such matters not commanded or prohibited in Scripture"[107] and by roundly declaring: "I find no one certain and perfect kind of government prescribed or commanded in the Scriptures, to the church of Christ". He then voiced a pragmatic opinion on the form of church government, namely "that any one kind of government is so necessary that without it the church cannot be saved, or that it may not be altered into some other kind thought to be more expedient, I utterly deny".[108]

Twenty years later even Richard Hooker still maintained this view. The latter indeed held "Church Polity...the very chiefest" among the "properties common unto all societies Christian",[109] but he rejected the Puritan position according to which an unalterable church government could be reduced from Scripture. He expressly intimated that he did not

---

[104] Cardwell, *History of Conferences* 183 f.

[105] "... that in making orders and ceremonies of the church it is not lawful to do what men list, but they are bound to follow the general rules of the Scripture, that are given to be the squire whereby those should be squared out".

[106] Whitgift, *Works,* I, 191.

[107] *Ibid.,* 363.

[108] *Ibid.,* 184.

[109] Hooker, *Works,* I, 352.

wish to set up another model of church government drawn from the Bible
in opposition to that of the Puritans. He was unwilling to follow their
method, "that in Scripture there must needs be found some particular
form of church polity, which God hath instituted, and which for that very
cause belongeth to all churches to all times".[110] Hooker did indeed, probably under the influence of his friend Saravia,[111] arrive at the view that a
distinction between "greater" and "inferior presbyters" instituted by
Christ himself was to be inferred from Luke 10[112] and that "the ruling
superiority of one bishop over many presbyters in each church is an order
descended from Christ to the apostles",[113] but he never embraced the
aspect essential to Saravia of the immutability of this hierarchical structure
"to the end of time".[114]

In his Paul's Cross Sermon on 9 February 1589, Richard Bancroft, at
that time Canon of Westminster Abbey, went further than Whitgift and
Hooker. He abandoned the viewpoint that discipline and government
were matters which have been neither commanded nor forbidden in Scripture. He attributed the three-fold ministry of bishop, priest and deacon to
the earliest apostolic times. He did not yet claim a divine origin for
episcopacy, but certainly an apostolic one and it would later emerge that
for him the first was a consequence of the second.[115] It was Saravia who, in
De Gradibus, was the first to draw this conclusion and thereby to oppose the
Puritans with their own weapon, that of the "ius divinum".

### 4.   HIERARCHY, ORDER, AUTHORITY

Here, as is often the case, we can get to know the author's motives from
his prefaces, in this case the "epistola dedicatoria" to Archbishop John
Whitgift, Lord Chancellor Christopher Hatton and Lord High Treasurer
William Cecil, Lord Burghley, in the letter to the Dutch ministers and in
the foreword to the reader. In the first of these Saravia wrote that, during
his ten year stay in the Netherlands he had experienced for himself that the
churches there lacked two important things. First, the church's ministers
were not accorded the honour which was their due and this in a country in
which the "ministerium ecclesiae" had been recognised by the secular

---

[110] Hooker, Works, I, 390 f.

[111] W. D. J. Cargill Thompson, "The philosopher of the Politic Society; Richard Hooker
as a Political Thinker", in: Studies in Richard Hooker, 16, 57, 69, 75.

[112] Hooker, Works, II, 473.

[113] Ibid., III, 165.

[114] Sykes, Old Priest, 23, correctly thought that the view that "all good forms of polity civil
as well as ecclesiastical, are established by God" did not imply for Hooker "the claim that it
is the exclusive form of ministry prescribed by the Scriptures".

[115] Thompson, "A Reconsideration of Bancroft's Paul's Cross Sermon," 56 f.; Sykes,
Old Priest, 24-26; Woodhouse, Doctrine of the Church, 85.

power. Secondly they were not paid in accordance with their position in society.[116] This society was thought of as a "societas christiana" and on such a reading questions affecting the ministry and episcopacy concerned not only the church but the whole society. The authority in force in both springs from the same source: God. Consequently they were dependent upon each other; they had much in common and ought to concur with each other in their conduct.[117] Saravia had seen little of such a model of harmonious society in the Netherlands. There were tensions and rivalries between church and state. All this he saw as a consequence of the abolition of episcopacy[118] which was a serious mistake. The bishop ought not to be excluded as an adviser from political activities, nor should the state, as the supreme power, be prevented from exercising its authority in the church.[119] Saravia attributed the troubles in the Netherlands to the fact that the abandonment of the bishop's office there had involved the loss of the harmonious relationship between church and state in the "respublica christiana".[120]

In the letter to the Dutch ministers we encounter several elements which constantly recur in the treatises. The church's unity resides in the bishop. Only he has a care for more than just the interests of the local congregation, a concern for the welfare of the whole church.[121] The new species of "temporary elders", unknown in church tradition, meant an infringement of the authority which was necessary to preserve the church's unity. Moreover the prebyterial-synodal organization worked much too slowly.[122] These elders constituted the constant target of Saravia's

---

[116] *DGM*, Ep. ded., 3r.

[117] "... tamen quando eadem societas ecclesia est et civitas, sicut ab eodem utriusque regiminis authoritas manat; ita ad eundem postremum finem respicit, et eodem se recolligit. Unde fit ut multa habeant communia, quae numquam recte nisi communi consilio ac assensu possunt perfici. Evangelii minister a Domino Servatore regiminis in ecclesia habet authoritatem: magistratus a Domino omnium Creatore in cives, qui quoties simul amice conspirant, et eodem sua consilia referunt, optime cum civitate, optime agitur cum ecclesia". *Ibid.*, 13.

[118] In 1561 an ecclesiastical reorganization, involving a new division of the dioceses and the allocation of new Sees, had been introduced in the Netherlands by Pius IV at the request of the Spanish king, Philip II. From the start there was very considerable opposition to this. Even in 1572, when the revolt began to achieve success, a number of sees were still vacant. Where the Spaniards were driven out, the bishop fled. The establishment of Calvinism in the North Netherlands naturally meant the end of the new hierarchical organization of the Roman church. Restoration, together with a modified division along the lines of the 1561 proposals, first came in 1853. L. J. Rogier, *Geschiedenis van het Katholicisme in Noord-Nederland in de 16e en de 17e eeuw* (2 vols., 2nd ed. Amsterdam, 1957) 201-259; O. J. de Jong, *Nederlandse Kerkgeschiedenis* (Nijkerk, 1972) 114-117, 131 f., 139, 335 f.

[119] *DGM*, Ep. ded., 3v.

[120] *Ibid.*, 42.

[121] *Ibid.*, A4v.

[122] *Ibid.*

criticism, although it is striking that he continued speaking about "our Reformation" and "our churches".[123] However, the secular authorities in the Netherlands had also been guilty of practices in removing ecclesiastical and monastic goods from their intended application: the financing of church work, the training of ministers and literary studies. Whether Henry VIII's Dissolution of the Monasteries fulfilled the requirements which Saravia here set out was a question he left unasked.

More than once in his letter to the Dutch ministers and in the Preface to the reader, he asserted that he was ready to bear with those who differed from him in their view of church order provided that they "correctly maintain the Lord Jesus Christ, that is to say the chief articles of Christian belief without which no-one is a Christian".[124] It was not a question pertaining to salvation that was at issue between Beza and his Calvinist disciples and himself as representative of the English church, rather it was just the question by what "leaders and masters can we be best guided to and kept upon the way to Salvation". In other words, this was in no sense a doctrinal difference but purely one of church order.[125] The acceptance of the bishop's office ought not to alter or diminish any article of faith in the reformed churches.[126] Beza considered the English episcopal ministry as a human institution in contrast to the reformed pastor who held a "divinus episcopatus".[127] Saravia reversed the proposition: the new Calvinist elder was a figure hitherto unknown in the church's history, a human institution which can be tolerated where no other and better elder (that is, one subject to the bishop) can be had. Episcopal church government, on the other hand, is of divine origin and is founded by divine institution both in the Old Testament and the New.[128] The demonstration of this was the main purpose of his writings which were, in effect, so many arguments for a hierarchical order in both church and state in which the bishop was regarded as the guarantor of unity and the maintenance of authority.[129] Whenever he disappeared a "status turbulentus" ensued.[130] The autonomy of local churches not only threatened the unity of the church but also led to the existence of a power vacuum after the abolition of the Roman hierarchy[131] that was dangerous for the whole of society. The man

---

[123] *Ibid.*, A5r.

[124] *Ibid.*, A5v.

[125] "Quaestionis igitur huius nostrae caput non est de tua salute, sed a quibus potissimum ducibus et magistris in viam aeternae salutis deduci et in ea retineri possis". *Ibid.*, A6v.

[126] *Ibid.*

[127] Nijenhuis, *Ecclesia Reformata*, 140-156.

[128] *Ibid.*, Prologus.

[129] *Ibid.*, Preface to the reader.

[130] *Ibid.*, A6r.

[131] *Ibid.*, A4v.

who, in 1568, had wanted to inspire the Dutch revolt with his *Een Hertgron-dighe Begheerte*, now wrote "God has never been the instigator of unrest and confusion but only of order. The men of God were not passionate, racing people but were peaceful and moderate in spirit".[132] The author wanted a restoration or strengthening of authority in both church and state.

According to the first chapter of *De Gradibus*, the ministry consists of three parts: preaching, the administration of the sacraments and church government.[133] All pastors share in one and the same ministry but, as regards the third aspect, there is inequality: there are "diverse degrees of authority".[134] In order to prevent misunderstanding we should note that Saravia uses the terms "gradus" and "ordo" interchangeably.[135] This inequality is founded not only on apostolic tradition but on the institution of the Lord Himself.[136] The New Testament mentions a hierarchical order of 1. apostles, 2. evangelists, 3. prophets, 4. pastors and presbyters, 5. teachers. Within the fourth degree, that of presbyters, there was a distinction between men like Timothy and Titus who were at once presbyters and bishops charged with the "procuratio generalis" for the church as a whole. Their office was superior[137] to that of the ordinary presbyters who only had responsibility for a local church.[138] The aforesaid distinction between these offices forms a theme which extends through all Saravia's treatises. He sought to push this inequality back to an institution of Christ Himself and for this purpose used Luke 10: 1 and 17, the account of the choosing of the "seventy". As the second of the five degrees, these were distinguished from the apostles as evangelists.[139] Of course, this was a false fabrication based on a completely incorrect exegesis which was quite unfit to support the later inequality between bishops and presbyters. The two pairs of hierarchical relationships: that instituted by Christ between apostles and evangelists and that instituted by the apostles between bishops and presbyters continued to be unrelated to each other. Bishops were indeed

---

[132] *DGM*, 37.

[133] *DGM*, 1.

[134] *Ibid.*, 2.

[135] "Dominus duos ministrorum Evangelii ordines creasse imparis dignitatis: quid? Velles me dixisse gradus? Nihil interest, ordo ibi mihi gradus significat. In republica Romana furere tres ordines: senatorius, equestris et plebeius. In hoc Angliae regno tres sunt ordines, sicut et in Gallia. Ubi ordo est, ibi gradus esse nemo sanus diffitebitur. In ecclesia sua si dicam Deum diversos contulisse ordines, vel diversos ministrorum gradus, idem significavero. Nec enim diversi ordines dici possunt, nisi respectu graduum diversorum: et gradus dicitur respectu inferioris aut superioris... Hominum dignitas et honoris locus, gradus et ordo vocatur". *DT*, 150.

[136] "... in hac tertia parte non parva inter eos invenitur inaequalitas, propter diversos authoritatis gradus, quos prima Dominus statim ab initio et postea apostoli constituerunt". *Ibid.*, 2.

[137] *Ibid.*

[138] *Ibid.*, 11 f.

[139] *Ibid.*, 6.

called the apostles' successors but presbyters were not those of the
evangelists. After the latter had joined with the apostles in ordaining the
first presbyters and bishops they played no further part.[140] The account
was only used to prove an inequality founded by Christ.[141] The apostles
and evangelists together shared in what was called the extraordinary
calling, the "vocatio extraordinaria", that is the calling by the Lord
Himself. This is to be distinguished from the ordinary calling, the
"vocatio ordinaria", that is the calling by men, by bishops as the apostles'
successors.[142] The choosing of 70 elders as overseers of the people by
Moses (Num. 11:16) was adduced as an Old Testament parallel of such an
inequality.[143] There was nothing new in what is to us a strange and inade-
quate use of scriptural, especially Old Testament proof texts, in support of
an existing church order. Both the relationship between priests and levites
and the calling of the seventy elders, which constantly recur in Saravia, are
already to be found in the *Constitutiones Apostolorum* (at the end of the fourth
century).[144] The Sarum Ordination Rite had many similar references.[145]

The office of deacon was also involved in this hierarchical structure. Its
institution did indeed precede that of the presbyter (Acts 6) but it was of
less "dignitas".[146] Besides the care of the poor, Saravia also assigned
preaching to deacons as well as the administration of the chalice at the
eucharist, referring to Acts 6:1-15 and 8:26-40. Entirely in line with
church tradition he saw the deacon as the bishop's most important assis-
tant. His liturgical function was such that "the bishop went nowhere and
did nothing without the deacon, yea, that the bishop could sooner miss the
presbyters than the deacon". The diaconate then was almost as important
as the presbyterate and could be seen as a preparation for it.[147] On the one
hand, Saravia rejected the restriction of the deacon's office to the care of
the poor introduced by the reformed. On the other hand he wanted the
care of the poor to be similarly regarded as a real charge upon the church
which ought not to be handed over to the state.[148]

The difference between the pragmatic estimate of the church's ministry
in other English theologians up to 1590 and the principled one of Saravia's

---

[140] *Ibid.,* 11.

[141] "Primum ab ipso Domino duos gradus Evangelii ministrorum institutos videmus:
quorum alter altero fuit superior; et postea ab ipsis apostolis similiter duos: quando
quibusdam ecclesiarum unius civitatis aut provinciae procuratio commissa est, et alii uni
tantum ecclesiae fuerunt praefecti". *Ibid.,* 12.

[142] *Ibid.,* 3.

[143] *Ibid.*

[144] *Didascalia et Constitutiones Apostolorum.* Fr. X. Funk, ed. (2 vols., Paderborn, 1905-1906)
I, 102 f., 522 f., 560 f.; II, 80 f.

[145] E. P. Echlin, *The Story of Anglican Ministry* (Slough, 1974) 6-14.

[146] *Ibid.,* 9.

[147] *Ibid.,* 8.

[148] *Ibid.,* 9.

is strikingly apparent if his views are compared with those, for example, of Jewel. The latter also stated, "that there were different orders of ministers in the church, namely deacons, presbyters and bishops, to whom has been entrusted the instruction of the people and the care for and government over religion".[149] However, there is no trace in this theologian of an attempt to ascribe the inequality of ministerial offices to the "ius divinum" and an institution by Christ.

Characteristic of this difference in estimation is a contrast in the value given to a passage in Jerome's commentary on Titus. In this the church father writes that originally in the New Testament church there was no distinction between bishop and presbyter. The party quarrels in Corinth (1 Cor.: 1:12) had first made it necessary that one member of the presbyters' assembly be charged with the leadership of the congregation. According to Jerome presbyters were distinguished from bishops more by the church's custom than by the Lord's command.[150] For obvious reasons Beza seized on this passage in support of his theory on the equality of ministerial offices.[151] Saravia, for his part, went to great lengths to draw the sting of this patristic proof-text. He devoted a long chapter of *De Gradibus* to it (Ch 23). In his attack Beza went into great detail on this.[152] Saravia rejoined in his *Defensio*[153] and later went still further into the matter in his *Examen*.[154] This passage-of-arms shows us one of the few instances in which Saravia accused a church father of being mistaken: Jerome was led astray because in the early days the words "presbyter" and "episcopus" were interchangeable.[155] But how had the church father got the idea that, before the schisms in question (1 Cor. 3: 1-9), Corinth had been ruled by a "presbyterium" without monarchical leadership?[156] The term "presbyter" was indeed a common description of the office-holder which could also mean the bishop or even the apostle but, from the beginning, it ought really to designate the lowest order in the church.[157] It was not the Corinthian schism but the "dominica institutio" which was the foundation of the monarchical bishop's office.[158]

---

[149] "Varios in ecclesia esse ordines ministrorum, alios esse diaconos, alios presbyteros, alios episcopos, quibus institio populi et religionis cura et procuratio commissa est." Jewel, *Works,* I, 10; English translation: *Ibid.,* 271.

[150] *PL,* XXVI, 597.

[151] Nijenhuis, *Ecclesia Reformata,* 150 f.

[152] Beza, *Ad tractationem responsio,* 135-161. On this treatise and on the controversy between Saravia and Beza, see: T. Maruyama, *The Ecclesiology of Theodore Beza. The Reform of the True Church* (Geneva, 1978) 174-194.

[153] *DT,* 217-257.

[154] *ETB,* 33-36.

[155] *DGM,* 28.

[156] *Ibid.,* 26 f.

[157] "Idem de hoc vocabulo presbyter censendum est, quod generalitate suae significationis omnes pastores complectitur, adeo ut apostoli etiam vocentur presbyteri, cum infimus pastorum ordo hoc particulare nomen habeat." *Ibid.,* 28.

[158] *Ibid.,* 27.

Other English theologians, however, subscribe to the church father's views without criticism. In his controversy with Thomas Harding[159] Jewel quoted Jerome's disputed sentence, "let the bishops know that they stand above the presbyters more by custom than by an actual command of the Lord's" at least twice.[160] The author of the *Apologia Ecclesiae Anglicanae* appealed, not only to Jerome, but also to Chrysostom and Augustine in support of his view "that by the Scriptures of God a bishop and priest are all one".[161] Whitgift avowed that "there was superiority among the ministers of the Word, even in the apostle's time" and twice quoted the said passage from Jerome with approval: this superiority served "to remedy schisms".[162] In company with Saravia, Whitgift saw that the inequality between bishop and presbyter affected church government—their ministry was the same[163]—but he accepted this inequality as a given part of tradition, he did not refer it to the "ius divinum".

In the seventh book of the *Laws of Ecclesiastical Polity*, Hooker went at some length into Jerome's views. The conclusion is sufficiently noteworthy to be quoted here. "The ruling superiority of one bishop over many presbyters in each church, is an order descended from Christ to the apostles, who were themselves bishops at large, and from the apostles to those whom they in their steads appointed bishops over particular countries and cities; and even from those ancient times, universally established, thus many years it hath continued throughout the world... On the other side bishops, albeit they may avouch with conformity of truth that their authority hath thus descended even from the very apostles themselves, yet the absolute and everlasting continuance of it they cannot say that any commandment of the Lord doth enjoin; and therefore must acknowledge that the church hath power by universal consent upon urgent cause to take it away, if thereunto she be constrained through the proud, tyrannical, and unreformable dealings of her bishops...".[164] The bishop's office set up above the elders by the apostles at Christ's command, can be abolished later if it is abused by human lust for power and "unreformable dealings". A remarkable statement!

Neither Jewel, Whitgift or Hooker attacked Jerome in the way that Saravia did. None of them taught the inequality of ministerial offices as an immutable datum as directly and fully as Saravia. This was his answer to Beza and the latter's English disciples who had begun to read off their presbyterian church order directly from Scripture and to base it on God's command.[165]

---

[159] *DNB*, VIII, 1223.

[160] Jewel, *Works*, III, 340, 379.

[161] *Ibid.*, 439.

[162] Whitgift, *Works*, II, 221-226.

[163] *Ibid.*, 265.

[164] Hooker, *Works*, III, 165.

[165] "Episcopatus divinus, sive iure divino institutus, nihil aliud declarat, quam verum

Aërius, known only to us from Epiphanius' attack,[166] was taken up in
the sixteenth century as a prototype of the defence of the equality of
ministerial offices in antiquity by Whitgift[167] and, with an attempt to explain Aërius' intentions, by Hooker.[168] In the latter's view Aërius erred,
not so much in maintaining the same position on the relationship between
bishop and presbyter as Jerome, but because he caused a schism by his
refusal to submit to the church's order. Moreover, in defence of the
equality of ministerial offices, Aërius appealed to God's Word. We might
say that he was an early defender of this equality on the basis of the "ius
divinum". Hooker considered the schismatic dangerous because his ideas
were elaborated by the Puritans in his own day. Right or wrong, this view
continued to be pretty commonly accepted. The Caroline theologian,
Peter Heylin (1600-1662)[169] entitled his history of Presbyterianism *Aërius
Redivivus.*[170]

Because Beza opposed Epiphanius' arguments against the
Aerianians,[171] Saravia naturally regarded him and his followers as allies of
these schismatics. In *De Gradibus* Saravia took over some of Epiphanius'
less relevant arguments, among others, the notable petitio principii: if
there was equality between bishop and presbyter, then not only could the
presbyter be ordained by the bishop but the bishop could be ordained by
the presbyter. Now this is not the case. Therefore there can be no
equality.[172] Calvin's successor did, however, compel Saravia into a serious
line of argument. In his attack on the relevant chapter of *De Gradibus* (Ch.
22), Beza went into Epiphanius' argument that presbyters are as little the
equals of bishops as children are of their father. Fathers beget children,
bishops lay hands on presbyters, not vice versa. Beza now brought up one
of the most disputed texts: 1 Tim. 4:14 which mentions the laying-on of
hands by the πρεσβυτέριον. This text continually recurred in the discussion as a locus probans used by both parties. Beza translated
"presbyterium" as the assembly of presbyters. He thought that even if the
bishop alone performed the laying-on of hands, yet he did so in the name
of the presbyterial college.[173] With this text he defended not only the
equality of all presbyters including the bishop, but, in place of the monar-

---

illorum munus, qui alio peculiari nomine vocantur pastores...''. Nijenhuis, *Ecclesia
Reformata,* 140.

[166] *Realencyklopädie für protestantische Theologie und Kirche,* J. J. Herzog, ed. 3rd ed. A. Hauck
(24 vols., Leipzig, 1896-1913) I, 232 f.

[167] Whitgift, *Works,* II, 200 f.

[168] Hooker, *Works,* III, 200-204.

[169] *DNB,* IX, 770-774.

[170] P. Heylin, *Aërius Redivivus: or the History of the Presbyterians,* London, 1670.

[171] Beza, *Ad tractationem responsio,* 127-135.

[172] *DGM,* 79.

[173] Beza, *Ad tractationem responsio,* 130 f.

chical government of the local church, he put government by the assemblies of office-holders, a very fundamental reformed principle. For his part, Saravia appealed to Calvin who thought that 1 Tim. 4:14 spoke of the office of presbyter, not that of the presbyters' assembly.[174] He advocated the sole right of the bishop to perform the rite of ordination. This led him to such radical expressions as: "so long as the bishop lived or was present the presbyterium could do nothing without him. The bishop was the director and executor of all acts and decisions. The bishops had the presbyters as supporters, helpers and advisers, not as masters who could rule over them".[175]

This statement clearly reflects the desire for a church structure which incorporates a powerful authority. In Saravia's view such an authority was at once ruled out if a place was granted in the church order to the "annus presbyter" or "temporarius presbyter", the elder chosen for only one or two years. This figure was characteristic of the reformed churches. In Geneva the elders had to surrender their mandate each year, after which the Seigneurie, the Little Council, decided on their reelection or replacement. Apart from this, too frequent replacements were not considered desirable.[176] In Scotland the elders and deacons were chosen for one year, "lest of long continuance of such officers men presume upon the liberty of the kirk." It was possible to be reelected. Annual election was also the practice in the English congregation in Geneva.[177] The custom of annual elections was maintained during the seventeenth century in Scotland.[178] Saravia had learned the same rules in the Netherlands.[179] In objecting to this he touched on the heart of the Calvinist view of the ministry. Although the contending parties used the same word, "presbyter", the Reformed meant nothing more by this than the office-holder with whom Saravia was familiar. The duty of the reformed elder was confined to "gubernatio" and "disciplina". He was the visible expression of the third mark of the church.[180] He was denied the right to preach and administer the sacraments. Precisely the opposite was the case with Saravia for whom "gubernatio", "disciplina" and "censura morum" were reserved for the

---

[174] *CO,* II, 302.

[175] *DT,* 216.

[176] *Bekenntnisschriften,* 49.

[177] *The First Book of Discipline,* J. K. Cameron, ed. (Edinburgh, 1972) 175.

[178] Donaldson, *The Scottish Reformation,* 222.

[179] Rutgers, *Acta,* 27, 62 f., 137, 168, 239, 266, 383, 459-462.

[180] On the origin of the Reformed ruling elder in Scotland: G. D. Henderson, *The Scottish ruling elder* (London, 1935) 11-38; W. F. Dankbaar, "Over de voorgeschiedenis van het ouderlingenambt, bepaaldelijk in Oost-Friesland," *Ned. AK,* XLVIII (1967/68) 166-181, has shown that the Reformed office of elder indeed received a scriptural theological foundation from Calvin but that it had had a long prehistory. Already in the Middle Ages, Frisian land and ecclesiastical law acknowledged the laity's part in the church's administrative offices.

bishop. The presbyter, however, had the commission to preach and administer the sacraments. He was a pastor and "verbi divini minister". Together with the bishop, he was the visible expression of the first two marks of the church. For Saravia, any office-holder who was robbed of the two essential tasks of the ministry: preaching and the administration of the sacraments, was no real holder of ministerial office. He knew very well that, in the history of the church, the presbyter whom he had in mind, had functioned as a pastor and minister of God's Word.[181] When Beza spoke of the presbyter, he meant the elder. When Saravia spoke of him, he meant the priest. Beza divided the duties, on the one hand, of preaching the Word and administering the sacraments with pastoral care and, on the other, government and church discipline, between the two. He appealed to 1 Tim. 5:17 ("Let the elders who rule well be counted worthy of double honour, especially those who labour in preaching and teaching") in distinguishing three kinds of ministers: the presbyters, who directed the congregation, the ministers, who preached, and the teachers who gave instruction.[182] On the other hand, this distinction was unacceptable to Saravia because it proposed a sort of minister who took part in the direction of the church but not in preaching. Preaching and the administration of the sacraments were for him the essential ministerial tasks in which bishop and presbyter were entirely equal with each other. "Gubernatio" was the third task for which the bishop was distinct from the presbyter and was superior to him.[183] Bishops could then also be called "superiores presbyteri",[184] whilst they both shared in the one "ministerium Evangelii".[185] He could no more find scriptural warrant for an elder who did not share in this "ministerium"[186] than he could for the temporary nature of some sort of ministerial office.[187] Moreover the government of the church required an ability which was only bestowed as an extraordinary gift of the Holy Spirit. Such capacities were rare and therefore they ought to continue to be reserved for "the highest order of presbyters". The Reformed, however, had entrusted it to the lowest order. They had created a kind of elder who was incapable of instructing the congregation.[188] For Saravia church government was a form of aristocracy. A Reformed church, however, presented a picture which we nowadays would rather call democratic.

---

[181] "Presbyteri apostolici omnes sunt pastores et Verbi Dei ministri". *DGM*, 53; "nemo presbyter ab apostolis fuerit ordinatus, qui ad docendum non esset aptus", *Ibid.*, 14.

[182] *Ad tractationem responsio*, 72 f.

[183] "Aequalitas ministerii inaequalitatem in gubernatione non impedit". *DGM*, 16.

[184] *Ibid.*, 15.

[185] *Ibid.*, 12.

[186] "... in ecclesia vero cum pastoribus ecclesiarum nullos lego, qui pastores non fuerint". *Ibid.*, 13.

[187] "Temporarium nullum ministerium quod fuerit ordinarium". *Ibid.*

[188] *Ibid.*, 12 f.

The background to these ideas lay in a need for order and authority without which neither church nor society could exist.[189] Just as the consul in the Roman senate was equal in his order (ordo) to the other members, but was superior to them in rank (gradus) and authority (auctoritas), so was the archbishop placed in the synod and the bishop among his fellow-presbyters.[190] In particular there ought to be no thought that such relationships would necessarily lead to tyranny. A development from oligarchy to tyranny was to be seen rather in the Calvinist churches. For "the equality of ministerial offices can interfere with the inequality of people no more than inequality can".[191] Once and for all there is a natural inequality between people and so let the best govern church and state!

This need for order and authority was also the background to Saravia's views or ordination. In ordination the person ordained received full power to preach and administer the sacraments.[192] It was reserved to the bishop. Saravia rejected ordination of presbyters by presbyters,[193] but he did not deny its validity. No more than other English theologians of his day did he make the validity of the administration of a sacrament dependent upon the minister's ordination in the apostolic succession.[194] Where, as for example in the Netherlands, there was no bishop such an ordination of one presbyter by another was necessary.[195] However, a general rule should not be made out of exceptional circumstances.[196] The theory of a "vocatio extraordinaria" might lead to Anabaptist fanaticism.[197] Saravia entertained a deep fear of the "Munsteriana insania". It was with horror that he saw the democratizing tendencies advocated by those of the "Genevensis ecclesiae regimen". He would have no truck with the election of office holders by the ordinary members of the church. Such a form of election could only lead to party strife and confusion. When Jean Morély advocated a democratization of church government,[198] he resolved to oppose

---

[189] *DT,* 192.

[190] *Ibid.,* 193.

[191] *Ibid.,* 195.

[192] "Ordinatio est consecratio vel sanctificatio hominis ad Dei et Domini nostri ecclesiae ministerium; in qua per impositionem manuum eorum, quibus talis actio competit, re ipsa actu potestas docendi et sacramenta ministrandi traditur". *ET,* 31.

[193] "Nunquam satis fuit aliquem electum aut expetitum esse ad ecclesiae ministerium vel a plebe vel a presbyterio (si quod fuisset) nisi accessisset apostoli aut viri apostolici ordinatio et institutio". *Ibid.,* 87.

[194] J. Keble, in: Hooker, *Works,* I, LIX ff.; H. F. Woodhouse, "What is meant by succession?" *Theology,* LV (1952) 376-379.

[195] "Ordinatio legitima nulla est sine episcopo, quando haberi potest. Sicut presbyter presbyterum ordinat, ubi orthodoxus episcopus haberi non potest, lex non est, sed necessitas". *ET,* 73.

[196] A detailed discussion of the distinction between "ordinaria ordinatio" and "extraordinaria ordinatio": *Ibid.,* 88.

[197] *DT,* 25.

[198] [J. Morély,] *Traicté De la discipline & police Chrestienne.* Lyon, 1562; R. M. Kingdom,

the Frenchman. He had abandoned the notion when he learned that synods of the French church had condemned Morély's opinions. From a personal meeting with the condemned—in England in the 1570s[199]—he had gained the impression of a pious man who was not maliciously motivated but who was diseased in mind.[200] This qualification is characteristic of Saravia. He regarded all attempts to put church government and jurisdiction into the hands of the people, upon whose will the office-holders would then be dependent, as madness, "fanaticorum hominum delirium".[201] Not only the church but society as a whole was threatened by such attempts. For schism in the church led to rebelliousness in the state.[202] In his great desire for preservation he lumped together, with little distinction, the Puritans who wanted to keep their alterations of church structure in presbyterian fashion within the bounds of the Elizabethan settlement, the Brownist with their plea for the autonomy of the local congregation and the rights of its individual members, and every sort of separatist and spiritualist fanatic. All their opinions were the outcome of dangerous playing with the notion of a "vocatio extraordinaria". They all undermined established authority, denied apostolic church government and disturbed the order in church and society.[203] His chief efforts were aimed at providing this authority with a theological foundation.

Saravia had a great respect for theological learning. Those who devoted their labours to this—so he expounded the verb κοπιᾶν in 1 Tim. 5:17—were those who spent all their energies in the night hours, often at the expense of their health, to writing works by which they served not merely a small part, but the whole of the church. In this they differed from the simply local minister who confined himself to his pastoral work. In intellectual matters therefore he saw a measure of inequality which was fruitfully exploited by the church but this did not lead him to press for a separate ministerial office of teachers. As is well known, Calvin[204] and some Calvinist church orders[205] conceived, in a theoretical structure, of a fourth office next to those of minister, elder and deacon, that of teacher.[206]

---

*Geneva and the Consolidation of the French Protestant Movement 1564-1572: A Contribution to the History of Congregationalism, Presbyterianism, and Calvinist Resistance Theory* (Geneva, 1967) 43-137; W. van 't Spijker, *De democratisering van de kerk anno 1562.* Kampen. s.a.

[199] Kingdon, *Geneva and the Consolidation,* 130 f. on the theory that Morely might have fled to England after St. Bartholemew's Eve (24 August 1572); *Les lettres à Jean Calvin de la collection Sarrau,* R. Peter and J. Rott, éd. (Paris, 1972) 72.

[200] *DT,* 246.

[201] *Ibid.,* 84.

[202] *DMG,* 76 f.

[203] *DT,* 26-28.

[204] *Inst.* (1559), IV, 3, 5; *CO,* 11, 780.

[205] For Geneva: *Bekenntnisschriften,* 48; for the Netherlands: Rutgers, *Acta,* 16 f., 376 f.

[206] Fr. Wendel, *Calvin. Sources et évolution de sa pensée religieuse* (Paris, 1950) 50 f., 230 f.; W. F. Dankbaar, "Het doctorenambt bij Calvijn," *NTT,* XIX (1964/65) 135-165; French translation: "L'office des docteurs chez Calvin," in: *Regards contemporains sur Jean Calvin. Actes du Colloque Calvin Strasbourg 1964* (Paris, 1965) 102-126.

In Calvin's Geneva indeed considerable attention was given to the "ordre des écoles" in which this office took its place. Saravia also attributed great importance to theological study and instruction. He devoted a chapter in his treatise to teachers[207] but wanted to view this function as detached from a ministerial office. For one thing, instruction was the responsibility of presbyter and bishop and for another, the teacher could be ordained presbyter. This indeed had happened in many cases. Without ordination, however, the teacher remained a private individual.[208]

In this connection Saravia reflected at length on the importance of schools and universities, training colleges and seminaries in the promotion of knowledge and virtue. However, in his day he was concerned at the disobedience of some teachers to ecclesiastical authority. The influence of the Puritans in Cambridge must have alarmed him. He warned them to observe their bishop's instructions and not to carry out such ministerial duties as preaching, administering the sacraments, visiting the sick, conducting funerals and leading prayers, without ordination. If we understand Saravia aright, the teacher had a place in the established order and ought not to make the university a hot-bed of subversive actions against church and state.

## 5. THE NORMS

When Beza proclaimed the local minister a bishop by divine law and degraded the episcopal order in the English church to a "humanus episcopatus", Saravia was compelled to prove the opposite from Scripture: the reformed elder was a novelty but the English episcopal order was divine in origin. One scriptural interpretation opposed another. In the dispute in which they engaged, both opponents wrongly thought that they were being obedient to Scripture. At times they arrived at strange interpretations, as for instance, Saravia with his argument from Luke 10:1 and Beza with his exegesis of 1 Tim.: 5:17. The petitio principii which they held in common: church order was founded on divine law, prohibited their drawing the conclusion that no church order at all is to be gathered from Scripture. It required first the rise of historical consciousness in the eighteenth century and then the development of historico-critical biblical research in the nineteenth and twentieth before this conclusion could be reached.

It is not surprising that, in a century in which the historical element, albeit without the modern historical consciousness, played an important role in religious controversies,[209] the two opponents continually appealed

---

[207] *DGM*, 36-38.

[208] *Ibid.*, 37.

[209] P. Polman, *L'élément historique dans la Controverse religieuse du XVIe Siècle*. Gembloux, 1932.

to the fathers and the early Christian councils. Beza did what Calvin had done. From the outset, the Reformed in France attempted to defend their church government with arguments borrowed from antiquity.[210]

Both for Beza and Saravia the fathers were authoritative but not infallible. The former sided with Aërius against Epiphanius, whilst the latter felt he had to convict Jerome of error as regards the equality of bishop and presbyter. Frequently the controversy came to a head over the interpretation of a patristic text.[211] We get the impression that Saravia accorded greater authority to the early church than did Beza. This is obvious enough because he could appeal to antiquity for the church structure which he had in mind with more right than could Calvin's successor for the type of elder that the latter was defending. There are also hundreds of references in Saravia both to the "vetus ecclesia" in general and to individual fathers and councils. The brief conclusion, "haec vetus est theologia", sometimes sounds like a decisive argument.[212] Whatever was old was authoritative as such. For this reason alone "the new kind of elders" could not exist in the light of the "vetus ratio".[213] On the other hand, whatever was new was as such disqualified. A witness was the more reliable the earlier and thus the closer he lived to the apostles' time. Therefore Saravia appealed against Jerome to earlier fathers such as Ignatius, Polycarp, Origen, Tertullian, Cyprian and Irenaeus.[214] The "vetus ordo conservandae disciplinae in ecclesia" was constantly opposed to the "novus ecclesiae regendae modus".[215] The abolition of the old church order could therefore only mean deformation but never reformation.[216] Even the authority of a council like the Nicene was due to this that it had decreed nothing new but had exclusively ordered the maintenance of the "vetus consuetudo".[217]

Antiquity was nearly always adduced as a unity. The appeal was based on the "permanent unanimity of the fathers".[218] The fathers served as examples of piety and learning.[219] Their missionary zeal and their readiness for martyrdom[220] were as exemplary as their views on church structure.[221]

---

[210] A. Dupinet, *La conformité des église réformées de France et de l'église primitive en police et cérémonies, prouvée par l'Ecriture, conciles, docteurs, decrets et canons anciens.* Lyon, 1564.

[211] Such as on Ambrose's exegesis of 1 Tim. 5: 1: *DGM*, 13 f.; Beza, *Ad tractationem responsio*, 69, 72.

[212] *DGM*, 3 f.

[213] *Ibid.*, 16.

[214] *DT*, 233.

[215] *Ibid.*, Prologus.

[216] "Abolere statum aliquem in ecclesia, vel ordinem tantae vetustatis, non est, meo iudicio, reformare sed deformare ecclesiam". *Ibid.*, 196.

[217] *DGM*, 23.

[218] "Contra unanimem et constantem omnium patrum veteris ecclesiae consensum nihil sine expressa Dei verbo est innovandum". *Ibid.*, Prologus; *DT*, Prologus.

[219] *Ibid.*, Prologus.

[220] *DGM*, 19.

[221] *Ibid.*, 31.

In short, it was unthinkable that the churches in the sixteenth century were granted a wisdom which exceeded that of antiquity.[222]

After Scripture and antiquity, however, there was still a third norm for Saravia, namely that of the natural law. It is true that natural law arguments do not occupy as large a place in his treatises on church government as they do in his great work on the state but they are still used repeatedly. Saravia did not appreciate the importance of the natural law in such a systematic way as did Richard Hooker in the first book of his *Laws of Ecclesiastical Polity*,[223] but the relationship between the two is unmistakable. There is a common knowledge of what is right and good which God has planted in men by nature. To this, amongst others, belong piety and religion, the love of one's native country and respect for one's ancestors. The image of God in man has not been completely destroyed by sin. There remains a natural light and with it a natural knowledge of God which is common to all.[224] There is no opposition between Christ's commandments and the natural law,[225] the natural law is not abolished by the Gospel but perfected. Christians are therefore not to despise it as a law invented by men but to respect it as divine law.[226]

Saravia also supposed that he would base his views on the place of the church in society and its hierarchical structure on the natural law. In every commonwealth religion forms an indispensable element,[227] an essential condition for its well-being.[228] For this reason the ''ministri'' were among the highest in society both in Israel and in other nations.[229] They acted as advisers in political matters.[230] This function implied that all peoples held the ministers of their religion in esteem.[231] This is witnessed for example

---

[222] ''Nobiscum natam sapientiam non aestimo, ut aliquid melius constituere possimus, quam factum est a veteribus. Deinde, nihil novi hodie constituendum in ecclesia arbitror ei qui tutus esse vult ab adversariorum calumnia, sine approbato exemplo praecedentium temporum'' *Ibid.,* 81.

[223] Hooker, *Works,* I, 197-285.

[224] ''Commune quoddam naturae lumen semper mansit... Prophanata religio fuit, non sublata... Dei notionem quae omnium mortalium est insculpta mentibus''. *DMG,* 39.

[225] ''Nulla Servatoris nostri praecepta aut legi olim patribus ab ipso datae, aut naturae mortalium mentibus insculptae adversantur''. *Ibid.,* 40.

[226] ''Iura gentium naturaeque legem Evangelii ministerium non tollit, sed usum utriusque in verum finem, qui esse debet, dirigit... Iura gentium, mentis lumen, et illa ipsa cuiusque synteresis, divinae res sunt, etiam in hac universali generis humani corruptione... Quod a Christianis ex illis fontibus hauritur, tanquam humanum inventum non est aspernandum, etiamsi nusquam in sacris codicibus sit scriptum. Est enim vero semper verum quod est consentaneum''. *ET,* 15.

[227] ''Sine sacrorum ministro non potest esse respublica''. *DGM,* 39 f.

[228] ''Nihil prisca antiquitas feliciter posse contingere in republica credidit sine religione''. *Ibid.,* 70.

[229] *Ibid.,* 74.

[230] *Ibid.,* 70.

[231] *Ibid.,* 39.

by Plato, along with the Greeks, the Romans, the Gauls and the Britons.[232] In all these nations there was Saravia's ideal form of society in which priesthood and kingship were closely connected with each other. The first Roman kings were priests, the emperors of the Flavian dynasty (69-96 A.D.) called themselves "pontifex maximus" and claimed the title "dominus et Deus".[233] With this uncritical admiration for antiquity Saravia attempted to give historical examples of what in his view a theocratic polity ought to be. The most useful natural law argument, that of the "dignitas" of the religious leader in all nations,[234] ought naturally to be applied to the "dignitas" due to pastors and bishops in a Christian people, an authority that was based not only on Scripture but also "in iure omnium gentium et in ipsa naturae lege".[235] The hierarchical distinctions between ranks and stations in society also proceeded from the natural law such as that between parents and children and between masters and slaves.[236] On one occasion the natural right reason was joined with an argument from the order of creation in which God created inequality between people. Thus Saravia transformed the variety of spiritual gifts in 1 Cor. 12:12-27 into a defence of inequality in rank between colleagues in the church. He used the parable of the talents (Matthews 25:14-30) in the same way.[237]

## 6.   The Apostolicity of the Church

Saravia's intention was to describe a church which could speak and act with apostolic authority in the "respublica christiana". It could only do this if it was itself fully obedient to this authority and also structured in accordance with it.

The apostles were the founders of the church. They owed their unique authority to the fact that they were eyewitnesses of Christ (1 John 1:1).[238] They were the only ones who had been sent directly by God without human agency to lay the first foundations of the church. By the laying-on of hands as a visible sign they passed on the gift of the Holy Spirit who also Himself guided them infallibly. Their teaching was the guide and rule of faith. All of which served to establish and reinforce the essentials of their apostolicity: the preaching of the Gospel, the administration of the

---

[232] *Ibid.*, 40-42.

[233] *Ibid.*, 42.

[234] "Omnes gentes, illo naturae lumine quod in homine reliquum est, et quo Deo vel deos colendos esse iudicarunt, omni honore et observantia colendos religionis antistites ubique semper arbitrati sunt". DGM, 42.

[235] *Ibid.*, 67.

[236] *DT*, 313.

[237] *ET*, 44.

[238] "testes" αὐτόπται". *Ibid.*, 5.

sacraments and the governing both of the churches and of their subordinate ministers of the Word. All these three functions were to continue to
the end of time.[239] Their "vocatio" was indeed "extraordinaria" but it
was not "temporaria". On the contrary, not only by preaching and
administration of the sacraments, but also by the "ecclesiae gubernatio",
the apostles, in this connection mentioned with the evangelists, provided
an example of perfect church government.[240]

Saravia had to defend this view at length against Beza[241] who thought
that there was no question of any continuing of the work of apostles,
evangelists and prophets from New Testament times. Their function
definitely concluded with the foundation and construction of the Church's
house. What remained to be done afterwards was to maintain the house in
an inhabitable condition and when necessary to repair it. Only the command to preach the Gospel and administer the sacraments remained in
force. For this an "apostolica potestas" was indeed required but not an
"apostolica functio".[242] According to Beza the apostles had no successors.
All apostolic "potestas" had ceased to exist on their death. The apostolic
writings remained as the rule for the church's preaching.[243] The true
apostolic succession was exclusively a succession of teaching. Saravia, on
the other hand, thought—indeed his entire view of church government
was based on this—that a succession of ministerial office was also essential.
The apostles had passed on their "potestas" to the bishops who acted as
their successors. This succession involved the whole apostolic ministry:
preaching, administration of the sacraments and church government.[244]
The example of this succession of apostolic ministerial office which he frequently used was that of Paul's sending of Timothy and Titus as bishops.
In this Saravia made it clear that the one sent spoke and acted with the full
power of the sender: he did not exercise his own jurisdiction, but, as a
deputy, that of the one who sent him. Full apostolic power was transmit-
ted,[245] which in turn was handed on by the bishops to their successors, so
that no church ever existed without a superintendent or bishop with the
same power as the apostles had possessed.[246] This apostolic authority en-

---

[239] *DT*, 177; *ET*, 5.

[240] "... ita etiam apostoli et evangelistae fuerunt exemplum et lex nobis posteris perfecti
regiminis ecclesiastici". *DGM*, 18.

[241] *DT*, 152-171.

[242] Beza, *Ad tractationem responsio*, 88-103.

[243] *Ibid.*, 175.

[244] "Dixi, cuius me non pudet nec piget, episcopos successisse apostolis, et quatenus
episcopatus quidam est, et apostolatus est quidam episcopatus; secundum eam rationem
apostoli, hoc est: episcopi, dici possunt successisse apostolis. Successerunt igitur apostolis
paris et eiusdem cum eis potestatis episcopi in his tribus, viz. in Verbi Dei praedicandi,
sacramenta administrandi et ecclesiam gubernandi authoritate". *DT*, 165.

[245] "... transmissio potestatis apostolicae...". *Ibid.*, 180.

[246] *Ibid.*, 181.

sured the order which was necessary to prevent division and schism in the church. The church still existed thanks to the bishops, those guarantees of unity and brotherhood.[247] The necessary order could continue to be maintained because the bishop gave guidance to the pastors both in their assemblies[248] and outside them. This was in contrast to presbyterian church government in which the president possessed no authority at all between assemblies, where no one exercised any jurisdiction in day events and in which, so Saravia thought on the basis of his experiences in the Netherlands,[249] there was a consequent threat of "anarchia". In the episcopal church order the bishop acted as "episcopus in presbyterio", that is to say, the presbyters could decide nothing without the bishop,[250] whilst the latter had no legislative power outside the synod or presbyterium. There was thus no question of an oligarchy.[251] In defence of this concept of church government, Saravia appealed to such Reformation theologians as Melanchthon, Bucer, Calvin and others.[252]

As we have already remarked on several occasions, Saravia's treatment of the bishop's office as the embodiment of apostolic authority in the church was for him above all a means of promoting its unity. The ministers of the local churches were united "into one body" by the bishops thus counteracting schismatic tendencies.[253] This also served the state's interest since it was important for the government that the church's unity was not threatened by a mass of ministers who were of equal rank. The bishop was therefore also the guarantee of good relations between church and state. Powerful episcopal authority could also lessen the dangers of Puritan rebellion.[254]

### 7. APOSTOLICITY AS MISSION

The first aspect of these ecclesiological reflections which was new in comparison with Saravia's theological contemporaries, was that this was all based on "ius divinum", on "divinia institutio". This principle which

---

[247] "Nam hoc audeo dire, stetisse ecclesiam, tam contra persecutiones adversariorum christianae fidei quam errores haereticorum, secundum divinam protectionem episcoporum virtute; et solam adnuatam sub unis episcopis et archiepiscopis fraternitatem haeresibus et haereticis restitisse". *Ibid.*, 199.

[248] The bishop is "qui praeest alicui pastorum coetui". *Ibid.*, 190.

[249] *ET*, 76.

[250] *DT*, 216.

[251] *ET*, 72.

[252] *DT*, 159 f.

[253] *ET*, 69.

[254] "Communis tum ecclesiae tum reipublicae utilitas haec est: ecclesiae contra schismata et haereses reipublicae in mutua coniunctione et necessaria pastorum ecclesia cum civili magistratu: quae nulla esse cum multitudine aequalium ministrorum ecclesiarum potest". *DT*, Epist. dedic.

he already established at the outset of *De Gradibus*[255] and repeated countless times in that treatise,[256] constantly recurred in the *Defensio* (1594) and the *Examen* (1610). By that time, however, it was no longer new for in 1591, between the publication of *De Gradibus* and the *Defensio*, Matthew Sutcliffe published *A Treatise of Ecclesiastical Discipline*. In 1593 Thomas Bilson published *The Perpetual Government of Christ's Church*. Both these employed similar principles. Later on Lancelot Andrewes, John Overall, Joseph Hall and many others were to continue the developments[257] which had been initiated by a Dutch Calvinist.

There was yet another, second, element in his vision of the apostolate and apostolic succession which was new in his day, new not only for England but for the entire sixteenth century Reformation. We mean his views on apostolicity in the sense of the church's continuing missionary commission.[258] He thought this aspect sufficiently important to devote two chapters of *De Gradibus* to it (Ch. 17 and 18) and to refer to it again at length in the *Defensio*, but we encounter the idea of the church's mission to the nations in other places as well. The development of his ideas is the more striking as the Reformation in general paid scarcely any attention to mission in contrast to the Roman church which, in the Jesuit order, possessed a great missionary force.

Already on the first page of *De Gradibus* we read, "The preaching of the Gospel is Christ's mission to all peoples".[259] The charge for this mission, which is called the most important part of the apostolic office, is valid for

---

[255] *DGM*, 2.

[256] *Ibid.*, 15-17, 21 f. 27, 32 f., 36, etc.

[257] Sykes, *Old Priest*, 65 ff.

[258] *Realencyklopädie für protestantische Theologie und Kirche*, XIII, 127-130; W. Grössel, *Die Mission und die evangelische Kirche im 17. Jahrhundert* (Gotha, 1897) 70-74; P. Drews, "Die Anschauungen reformatorischer Theologen über die Heidenmission," *Zeitschrift fur praktische Theologie*, XIX (1897) 309-315; G. Kawerau, "Adrian Saravia und seine Gedanken über Mission," *Allgemeine Missionszeitschrift*, XXVI (1899) 333-343; G. Warneck, *Abriss einer Geschichte der protestantischen Missionen von der Reformation bis auf die Gegenwart* (Berlin, 1905) 19-21; M. Galm, *Das Erwachen des Missionsgedankes im Protestantismus der Niederlande* (St. Ottilien, 1915) 33-39; J. R. Brütsch, "Le fondement de la mission chez Hadrianus Saravia," *Verbum Caro,* I (1947) 168-171; J. van den Berg, *Constrained by Jesus' Love. An Inquiry into the motives of the Missionary Awaking in Great Britain in the Period between 1698 and 1815* (Kampen, 1956) 16, 23 f.; W. R. Hogg, "The Rise of Protestant Missionary Concern, 1517-1914," in: *The Theology of the Christian Mission.* G. H. Anderson, ed. (New York/Toronto/London, 1961) 101; S. van der Linde, "Het opkomen en de eerste uitwerking van de zendingsgedachte binnen het Nederlandse gereformeerde protestantisme," in: *Opgang en voortgang der Reformatie. Een keuze uit lezingen en artikelen van S. van der Linde* (Amsterdam, 1976) 208; J. M. van der Linde, "Honderd jaar zendingswetenschap in Nederland 1876/77-1975," *NTT,* XXXI (1977) 288; W. F. Dankbaar, "Het apostolaat bij Calvijn," *NTT,* IV (1949/1950) 181; French translation: W. F. Dankbaar, "L'apostolat chez Calvin," *Revue d'histoire et de philosophie religieuses,* XLI (1961) 348.

[259] *DGM*, 1.

unlimited time[260] and knows no boundaries.[261] The apostle is the one who is sent (missus), the envoy (legatus) and the messenger (nuntius).[262] The apostolic mission was no more temporary in nature than apostolic church government. The notions ''extraordinary'' and ''temporary'' must be properly distinguished. The calling of the apostles might have been extraordinary but it was not temporary.[263] After the apostles' death the whole church was placed under the obligation to proclaim the Gospel to all nations until the end of time. Matthew 28:20 applied to the whole church.[264] In this connection Saravia produced the striking statement that the apostolic ministry and authority had been given to the church rather than to individuals. The huge task of proclaiming the Gospel to the whole world could not have been achieved in so short a time by so few. The apostles only began the work of mission and had handed on its continuation and completion to those who came after them. In antiquity the foundation of new churches was carried on with vigour, effort and the shedding of martyrs' blood. ''But today, after 1500 years, the Gospel has not yet reached all nations. I will not now relate how many peoples, who were not visited by the apostles, have accepted Christ as Lord through the preaching of faithful men who were the apostles' successors. I only draw the conclusion that the obligation for this mission and the command concerning the proclamation of the Gospel remains in force in the church so long as there are nations who do not know the Lord. The fact that at the present no one is sent by the churches of Christ to the nations who do not know Him, does not count against the authority for mission but proves a lack of persons fit to be sent, or certainly a want of enthusiasm for the spread of Christ's kingdom... Therefore the church has the authority, denoted by the power of the keys which the Lord gave not only to Peter and his colleagues but to the church so that it can nowadays do what it earlier could, namely, as the opportunity arises, to commit the proclamation of the Gospel with apostolic authority to men who are fit for this mission''.[265]

It is clear from this quotation that the charge for mission was not for Saravia a chance incident but that it was founded on his views about apostolic authority which applied not only to bishops but to the whole church.

The continuing command for mission applied to the preservation and strengthening of existing churches and the planting of new ones. It is apparent from the fact that under the heading of mission our author not only understood the founding of churches where these did not yet exist, but also

---

[260] *Ibid.*, 5.
[261] *Ibid.*, 6.
[262] *Ibid.*, 7.
[263] *Ibid.*, 18.
[264] *Ibid.*
[265] *Ibid.*, 19.

the "restoration of ruined churches",[266] that he hád in mind reclaiming areas for Christianity as well as breaking new ground for the faith. It is not certain where he was thinking of under the former category but he probably meant those territories which had been lost to Islam in the seventh and eighth centuries and those which had been occupied by the Turks in the sixteenth.

He used the Pauline epistles to prove these points. The apostle granted a share in his missionary work to his colleagues Timothy, Titus, Mark, Luke and others and made them "heirs of his apostolic work and authority". These in their turn had successors in their work:[267] the church itself was heir to the apostolic commission and authority. However, just because mission was a task for the whole church a more than local ministerial office was essential. In this way Saravia tied the bishop's apostolic authority to the church's continuing charge to mission.

This was a new vision for the Reformation and it was heard and denied first of all by Beza. In the latter's opinion the command to mission formulated in Matth. 28 applied only to the apostles' time. He no more believed in a succession of the apostolic mission than he did in a succession of apostolic church government.[268] Saravia bound these closely together. The nature of the apostolic church government which he defended had been determined by its goal: mission. He made an essential connection between the permanent apostolic structure and the equally permanent apostolic mission.[269] The apostolic church government guaranteed the authority, given by Christ to the apostles and thereby to the whole church, which was necessary for mission.[270] Beza alas used very unscriptural arguments to elude this continuing charge to mission. He thought that there was so much work for Reformation theologians and their descendants to do in their own house and neighbourhood that the effort of "pilgrimages" to distant lands should be left "to the locusts who have recently risen from the abyss and who abuse the name of Jesus". He meant the Societas Jesu, the Jesuits. He misapplied Matth. 23:15 to dis-

---

[266] *DT,* 157.

[267] "Quemadmodum ipsi successerant apostolis, suos similiter habuere successores; quibus si potestatem acceptam ab apostolis ipsi non contulerunt, ecclesia quae haeres est apostolicae potestatis, contulit". *Ibid.,* 20.

[268] "... quod ad apostolos attinet, aliquid esse in hac praeceptione quod sit illis unis proprium, nempe quod ad omnes gentes docendas mittantur". *Ad tractationem responsio,* 105.

[269] "Nam a fine et natura regiminis apostolici doceo illud regimen esse perpetuum et usque ad consummationem seculi in ecclesia retinendum. Finis enim apostolici regiminis fuit tum aedificatio tum conservatio ecclesiarum; atqui in finem usque seculi ecclesiae aedificandae et conservandae sunt, maneat; igitur necesse est immotum in ecclesiis apostolicum regimen". *DT,* 163.

[270] *Ibid.,* 173; "Mandatum omnibus gentibus praedicandi Evangelium, apostolis in coelum receptis, etiam ecclesiam abligat; ad quam rem apostolica authoritate opus est". *DGM,* 18.

qualify the impressive missionary activities which the Jesuits had displayed from the start of their existence.[271] Saravia rightly replied with some just indignation, "I did not expect such an answer from D. Beza nor from any theologian who has the spread of the Gospel at heart as he should".[272] He too rejected the Jesuits' methods of conversion, but he roundly called the renouncing of the command to mission impious and loveless.[273]

Just how unusual Saravia's views on the Church's charge to mission continued to be for a long time, is shown by the fact that they were still subject to criticism in the seventeenth century, especially in Lutheran orthodoxy. Two representatives of the latter attacked the view of "quidam Calvinianus Hadrianus Saravia". In his *Loci Theologici*, the first edition of which appeared in 1610-22, Johann Gerhard (1582-1637) argued at length against this view. According to him the real command to mission in Matth. 28:16-20 applied only to the apostles, whilst the promise given in this text ("I am with you always..") concerned the whole church. Gerhard, like Beza separated promise and command from each other[274] in a way which, from the point of view of biblical theology, must be considered very dubious. The second Lutheran who opposed Saravia's ideas on mission was the Copenhagen professor, Jesper Rasmussen Brochmand (1585-1652). In his *Universae theologiae systema* (first edition 1633), he also made a distinction between the commands and activities which were limited to the apostles themselves and those which applied to the whole church. He assigned mission to the first category.[275] It is apparent precisely from the opposition of these opponents that, in his ideas about mission, the otherwise so conservatively minded, Saravia was not only in advance of his Reformation contemporaries but also of many theologians in the seventeenth century.

---

[271] In 1539, even before the order had been recognized, Francis Xavier and Simon de Azevedo Rodriguez had been set apart for missionary work.

[272] *DT*, 186.

[273] "Sed ubi verisimile est, nunquam praedicatum esse Evangelium, aut si praedicatum fuit nulla est memoria, delegatione ad illas licet remotissimas gentes ecclesiis Christi magnopere non esse laborandum si oportunitas adsit et spes conversionis adserere, iudico impium et ab omni christiana charitate alienum; modo qui id promovent, eam rationem convertendi ignaros nostrae fidei non sequantur, quam Hispani tenuerunt, sed quam Dominus noster docuit". *Ibid.*, 187.

[274] J. Gerhard, *Loci Theologici* (18 vols., Tübingen, 1767-1779) XIII, 38-42.

[275] Grössel, *Die Mission in der evangelischen Kirche*, 73 f.

# CHAPTER EIGHT

# THE STATE

## 1. HIERARCHICAL ORDER IN SOCIETY

A full two years after Saravia had published his ideas on Church government, that is at the end of 1592,[1] he wrote his *De imperandi authoritate et christiana obedientia.*[2] The treatise was published in 1593, dedicated "to all who love peace and tranquility". This peace he saw threatened by those who called the royal authority in question by making it subordinate to that of the people and Parliament.[3] The epistola dedicatoria left no misunderstanding as to the author's purpose: he wanted to warn against the Monarchomachs and movements akin to them which claimed to oppose tyrants but in reality promoted rebellion and civil war.[4] In opposition to this he stated that "the pious exerted themselves for peace and were more disposed to accept injustice than to cause another injustice and that the most important virtue of Christians lay in patience and submission to God's will".[5] For, "human society is founded on two things, on the royal authority and on obedience". Consequently, nothing was more dangerous than to resist sovereigns with civil war and rebellion, even if they were tyrants.[6] The aim of the work, which was intended to comprise seven books, the last three of which, however, never appeared, was to instruct those whom God had subjected to an alien government in the respect and obedience which they owed to those set over them.[7] Just as in his treatises on the ministry, the author gave the impression that he was working primarily for overseas readers. In this case it was as though he wrote for the Protestants of France or the South Netherlands, but as in his earlier mentioned work, he also definitely had an eye to the English situation and tried, in what he said, to give support to the authorities. The treatise on authority was the companion piece to *De Gradibus.* After making a plea in

---

[1] According to his own account he wrote in 1592, *IA,* 260; and certainly after Queen Elizabeth had ruled for 34 years, *Ibid.,* 201. If Smith, *Contribution of Saravia,* had taken note of these two places he would on their account have left his astonishing theory about the development of Saravia's thought unwritten.

[2] p. 127, n. 88.

[3] *Ibid.,* 109 f.

[4] *Ibid.,* 110 f.

[5] *Ibid.,* 111.

[6] *Ibid.*

[7] *Ibid.,* 112.

the latter for the maintenance of apostolic authority in church government, he now argued for the respecting of the secular government's authority, in this case, the King's authority. Because he thought of society as a theocratic unity, the weakening of one authority at once posed a threat to the other.

Despite all the threats from abroad and despite radical social and economic changes which were beginning to emerge in English society,[8] Elizabeth's government was marked by a certain stability. "Good order and obedience to rulers and magistrates" were virtues for the establishment, but "disobedience and wilful rebellion" counted as sins, as one of the aforesaid topics in the *Book of Homilies* expressed it.[9] However, this was disturbed by the voices of those who proposed certain conditions to obedience. The same John Ponet who wanted to replace the word "bishop" by "superintendent" in the church's usage,[10] had, in his *A shorte treatise of politike power* (1556) considered justified the overthrow of unjust monarchs and, in limited cases, the murder of a tyrant.[11] John Knox's *The first blast of the trumpet against the monstrous regiment of women* (1558) and Christopher Goodman's *How superior powers be obeyed* (1558) were naturally well known in England. After the frightful St. Bartholomew's night in Paris (23/24 Aug. 1572) the Monarchomachs emerged with their writings which defended the people's right of rebellion against a despotic King.[12] François Hotman wrote *Franco-Gallia* (1573) and perhaps the anonymously published *Réveille-matin des François* (1574). In 1574 the *Vindiciae contra tyrannos* was written under the pseudonym Stephanus Junius Brutus Celta, perhaps jointly by Hubert Languet and Philippe du Plessis-Mornay, but more likely by the diplomat Dr Johan Junius de Jonge;[12a] it was published in 1579. Beza's *Du droit des magistrats sur leurs subjects* also came from the press in 1574. On British soil, George Buchanan's *De iure regni apud Scotos Dialogus* was published at Edinburgh in 1579.[13] They were just so many expressions of a Calvinism which was developing in the direction of

[8] L. Stone, *Social Change and Revolution in England 1540-1640.* 4th impr., London, 1970; Chr. Hill, *Society and Puritanism in Pre-Revolutionary England.* Repr. London, 1969.

[9] *Certain Sermons,* 104-117, 551-601.

[10] Strype, *Memorials ecclesiastical of King Edward VI* (Oxford, 1822) 141 f.

[11] W. Nijenhuis, *John Ponet* (± *1514-1556*) *als revolutionair pamflettist.* Assen/Amsterdam, 1976.

[12] A. Elkan, *Die erste Publistik der Bartholomäusnacht.* Heidelberg, 1905.

[12a] D. Visser, "Junius. The Author of the Vindiciae contra Tyrannos?" *TvG,* LXXXIV (1971) 510-525.

[13] On Knox, Goodman and Ponet: J. W. Allen, *A History of Political Thought in the sixteenth Century* (London, 1928) 106-120; on the Monarchomachs Salamonius and Buchanan: *Ibid.,* 302-342; important historical information in the introduction to de Bèze, *Du droit des magistrats,* VII-XLVII; for England: L. Rohlhoff, *Der Kampf um die Staatshoheit in Grossbrittannien. Die britischen Monarchomachen und ihre Beziehungen zum Festlande.* Halle, 1931. On the Monarchomachs in general: K. Wolzendorff, *Staatsrecht und Naturrecht in der Lehre vom Widerstandsrecht des Volkes gegen rechtswidrige Ausübung der Staatsgewalt* (Breslau, 1916) 6-179.

democratization and which, mixed with numerous elements from the sphere of natural law, supplied the spiritual armour which fitted the persecuted Reformed in France as well as the Dutch in their revolt against Spain. Saravia saw it his duty to warn against this kind of seditious literature. At the same time his warning was intended for use at home: as support for the authority of the state as he knew and valued it in the Tudor monarchy.

In the main the treatise is an elaboration and expansion of the principles expressed in the earlier-mentioned *Homilies*: "Almighty God hath created and appointed all things in heaven, earth, and waters, in a most excellent and perfect order. In heaven he hath appointed distinct and several orders and states of archangels and angels. In earth he hath assigned and appointed kings, princes, with other governors under them, in all good and necessary order ... Every degree of people in their vocation, calling, and office, hath appointed to them their duty and order: some are in high degree, some in low; some kings and princes, some inferiors and subjects; priests and laymen, masters and servants, fathers and children, husbands and wives, rich and poor; and every one have need of other: so that in all things is to be lauded and praised the goodly order of God; without the which no house, no city, no commonwealth, can continue and endure, or last. For, where there is no right order, there reigneth all abuse, carnal liberty, enormity, sin, and Babylonical confusion".[14]

This was precisely what Saravia meant by his treatise. It was the thought world to which Richard Hooker had borne witness in the last moments of his life,[15] a world which was governed by a cosmic order, which was hierarchically ruled both in heaven and on earth and in which all things and all men had their own place assigned them by the Creator.[16]

In this world the word "freedom" sounded like a threat. The author of *De imperandi authoritate* began then by rejecting the human craving for freedom which he ascribed to self-love, the desire for knowledge and the lust for power.[17] In contrast to this hankering after freedom he set the submission intended by God in creation in which men were fitted in the cosmic order. God had so arranged the world in His providence "that some give leadership, others are subject". This subjection was not at odds with human dignity[18] nor with Christian freedom which was purely spiritual.[19]

---

[14] *Certain Sermons,* 104.

[15] p. 146.

[16] W. Nijenhuis, "Verstoorde harmonie. De politieke implicaties van de First Admonition to the Parliament (1572)," in: *Geloof en Revolutie. Kerkhistorische kanttekeningen bij een actueel vraagstuk,* aangeboden aan Prof. Dr. W. F. Dankbaar (Amsterdam, 1977) 103 f.

[17] *IA,* 119.

[18] *Ibid.,* 120.

[19] *Ibid.,* 149.

From start to finish of the treatise the author argues from the created order and God's providence. Providence in its wisdom has divided Lordship and subjection between men,[20] it has arranged governments and forms of government upon earth[21] and it rules history.[22] It employs both good and bad rulers[23] and sometimes makes use of tyrants to curb men's lawlessness.[24] Irrespective of the way in which a monarch has come to power, by inheritance or by election, he owes his position to Providence.[25]

Natural law plays a very much more important part in the discourse on the state than in the other treatises. God's command, the natural law and the law of nations are sometimes put on a par with each other.[26] It is folly for Christians to violate natural right (or the law of nature; Saravia uses the notions interchangeably).[27] In practice it is to be used after the most authoritative norm, God's Word.[28] The natural law originates from the same source as Holy Scripture although it is of a lower order. The law of nature is the natural revelation of God's purposes given to every man.[29] Obedience to the authorities issues both from obedience to God's Word and the natural law.[30] The relationships of authority between parents and children,[31] between man and wife[32] and between masters and slaves[33] are

---

[20] "Ille sapiens mundi rector, qui cuncta prudenter disponit, novit, quibus et quando servitus sit libertate utilior". *Ibid.*, 121.

[21] "Deus est qui in sua providentia regna et imperii formas mutas et transfert". *Ibid.*, 158.

[22] "Casus nullus habet in hac re locum; sive sorte, sive suffragiis, regnum alicui obvenerit, a Dei providentia confertur. Sortes quidem mittuntur in sinum, sed a Domino temperantur". *Ibid.*, 160; "Cum mundus hodie eadem providentia regatur, qua olim...". *Ibid.*, 171.

[23] "Deum omnipotentem homines ineffabili sua providentia recte regere et ad eandem rem se bonorum similiter et malorum ministerio uti nosse". *Ibid.*, 161.

[24] *Ibid.*, 190.

[25] "Rex est, quem divina providentia nativitatis aut electionis iure ad regnum nasci voluit". *Ibid.*, 222.

[26] "... in eo quem Deus et naturae lex, gentiumque servire iubent". *Ibid.*, 120; "Ius gentium naturae quaedam lex est..., ius gentium a naturae lege natum est". *Ibid.*, 147.

[27] "Turpe est apud Christianos, quorum pietas illustrior aliarum gentium esse convenit, naturae iura violare". *Ibid.*, 140.

[28] "Nos eam quoque sequemur rationem, quo aut movente Deo aut natura ducimur". *Ibid.*, 243.

[29] "Ius gentium, hoc est naturae lex, mortalium inscripta mentibus, male opponitur divinitus scriptis oraculis, tanquam inferior atque eis imperfectior ex eodem fonte manarint". *Ibid.*, 244.

[30] "...quibus non tantum Deus lege sua obedire mandavit, sed etiam naturae omnes gentes docuit". *Ibid.*, 129.

[31] "naturae lege nati parentibus subiecti sunt". *Ibid.*, 131; "Nati servire et necessaria parentibus ministrare lege Dei et naturae obligantur". *Ibid.*, 139; It is wrong, "aut ordinem naturae perturbari aut reverentiam quae debetur parentibus violare". *Ibid.*, 145.

[32] "...apud omnes gentes ius imperandi dari maritis et subiectionem praecipere feminis". *Ibid.*, 125.

[33] "Quemadmodum naturae lege parentibus subiecti liberi nascuntur, ita servi iure gentium dominis mancipantur... Sed quia est naturae consentaneum in hac mortalitate, et

based on the natural law. In Rom. 13, the most important "locus probans" for the development of Saravia's theory of authority, Paul drew on
the law of nature as well as God's law.[34] What was said of all these relationships of authority applies also to the government's authority; it is
based on "ordinatio divina" and on "ius gentium".[35] The civic legislation
in a Christian society ought also then, with due allowance for the situation,
to be founded on Scripture and the natural law.[36] The King's right is not
dependent upon the will of the people but on God's Word and the law of
nature.[37] The existence of all relationships of authority is founded on the
law of nature whose framer is God.[38] This applies also to forms of government.[39]

We may usefully make a comparison with Calvin. The latter also based
his teaching about governmental authority in the state upon God's Providence.[40] He referred to pagan authors in discussing the government's
function.[41] For him too God's moral law was nothing but the law of nature
and the witness of the conscience given to all men.[42] The continuing influence of humanism is clearly to be traced in the reformer's work and
natural law played an especially important part in his views on the state
and law.[43] With Saravia, however, all this is much more pronounced.
Calvin might not have concealed his admiration for Greek philosophers
and ancient rhetoricians but yet he would not have gone as far as Saravia
who called Aristotle "the most eminent of all philosophers".[44] With this
utterance he took his place on the side of those in Oxford and Cambridge
who took their stand for the teaching of Aristotle as "the ancient and true
philosophy" and who consequently opposed the empirical methods of

---

plerisque utile ac necessarium, fortiter ferendum servilis conditionis onus iis quibus est iure
impositum". *Ibid.*, 146.

[34] "Quicquid de officio virorum, uxorum, parentum, liberorum, dominorum et servorum praecipit apostolus, ex Dei et naturae lege desumpta sunt". *Ibid.*, 205.

[35] *Ibid.*, 195.

[36] "Leges civiles quibus populus christianus regitur, aut ex Verbo Dei scripto, aut ex
naturae lege depromptae sunt, aptanturque moribus, locis et temporibus". *Ibid.*, 244.

[37] *Ibid.*, 278.

[38] "... Deus illius iuris naturae conditor". *Ibid.*, 283.

[39] "... ordinem quem Deis et ipsa naturae lex in hominum gubernatione constituit."
*Ibid.*, 302.

[40] *Inst.* (1559), IV, 20, 4; *CO*, II, 1095.

[41] *Ibid.*, IV, 20, 9; *CO*, II, 1099.

[42] *Ibid.*, IV, 20, 16; *CO*, II, 1106.

[43] Fr. Wendel, *Calvin*, 12-20; J. Neuenhaus, "Calvin als Humanist," in: J. Bohatec, ed.
*Calvinstudien* (Leipzig, 1909) 1-26; Q. Breen, *John Calvin: A Study in French Humanism.* Grand
Rapids, 1931. There is much literature on this subject in R. D. Linder, "Calvinism and
Humanism: The First Generation," *CH,* XLIV (1975) 167-181. The natural law played an
important part in Calvin's thought particularly in his views about law and the state. See
J. Bohatec, *Calvin und das Recht.* Feudingen, 1934.

[44] *IA*, 125, 163. On Calvin and Aristotle: Ch. Partee, *Calvin and Classical Philosophy*
(Leiden, 1977) 97-104.

science and education which made their influence felt with the founding of Gresham College at London in 1575.[45]

No society can exist without government.[46] Relationships of authority are necessary in all its branches. Saravia therefore first wrote at length on the relation between parents and children, husbands and wives in marriage,[47] masters and servants,[48] professors and students[49] and so on, in order to arrive at the highest authority, that of the government. The ruling authority in the churches ought also to be subject to this.[50] The state's well being depends upon the supreme authority which governs by the law of God and of nature and which has been given by God. Irrespective of its form, monarchy, aristocracy or democracy, it is above all laws.[51] Of these three forms of state Saravia's preference was for the first and indeed for absolute monarchy. He was opposed to the role of parliament and to the possibility that the monarch could in any way be called to account for his conduct. Judgement of his deeds must be left to God.[52] This form of government was paternal in nature whether it was hereditary kingship[53] or one which was founded on conquest and enforced recognition.[54] This paternal view implies unreserved obedience; to be a subject means to serve.[55] Order in a nation depends on respect for the supreme authority.

A powerful monarchical authority such as in the Roman Empire—Saravia argued with numerous examples from the philosophy of both Greek and Roman antiquity—meant a guarantee against discord and rebellion.[56] Even if people live under a bad monarch this is still no reason to rebel.[57] There is more danger from the masses than from a monarchical sovereign. Tyranny of the masses is worse than the tyranny of one man.[58] The definition of tyranny as "the absolute rule of one who uses his entire power in his own interest" (Plato, Aristotle) is rejected because such an abuse of power can be as readily seen in a democracy. The term

---

[45] Chr. Hill, *Intellectual Origins of the English Revolution* (pb. ed., London, 1972) 52 ff.

[46] "... nullam societatem consistere posse sine regimine". *IA*, 150.

[47] *Ibid.*, 125-146.

[48] *Ibid.*, 146-150.

[49] *Ibid.*, 150-152.

[50] *Ibid.*, 152-156.

[51] *Ibid.*, 159.

[52] *Ibid.*, 162.

[53] "Princeps optimus ille censetur, qui ita gubernat, ut pater suorum subditorum verius quam dominus dici mereatur. Principes (inquit Philo) sunt publici parentes civitatum ac gentium". *Ibid.*, 168.

[54] "Reges scire convenit se patres esse suorum civium, et eam erga subiectum populum charitatem retinendam, quae est parentum erga liberos". *Ibid.*, 180.

[55] "Regi subiici servire est". *Ibid.*, 179.

[56] *Ibid.*

[57] "... ita nec statim populus, si in malum regem inciderit, iustas causas defectionis aut rebellionis habebit". *Ibid.*, 175 f.

[58] *Ibid.*, 176, 289 f.

"tyranny" originally had no unfavourable significance.[59] Nevertheless
Saravia is prepared to agree with later usage and to define the notion thus:
the violation of law to the detriment of the whole society.[60] Actual political
deeds are at issue here, not intentions.[61] It is of crucial importance for his
discussion with the Monarchomachs that Saravia expressly excluded from
his view of tyranny behaviour of the monarch that conflicted with the
popular will. As far as he was concerned the popular will was in no way a
norm of legitimacy. The latter lay only in the establishment of the government by God.[62]

Any idea of popular sovereignty is constantly criticized throughout the
entire treatise. After Saravia had described the tyrant's vices in detail; lust
for power, contempt for the law, cruelty, extravagance and excess,
bellicosity, greed and, above all, godlessness[63] and had then explained that
such a tyrannical regime is sometimes necessary as a punishment for the
people's sins,[64] he declared that obedience is owed to wicked monarchs so
long as they did not order anything that was contrary to God's commandments. As though all these vices were not opposed to God's commandments! What he meant was that obedience is due so long as the individual
citizen, who in an absolute monarchy naturally bears no responsibility for
such offences, is not himself compelled to be disobedient to God's commandments. According to Saravia, there is no record in the entire history
of the church of Christians resisting a pagan or heretical government.
Only when a tyrant like the Bishop of Rome began to arm subjects against
their sovereigns had resistance been commanded.[65] Here he definitely has
in mind conspiracies against Queen Elizabeth's life,[66] for example, the
Babington plot (1586), and also the murders of William of Orange (1584)
and the French king, Henry III (1589). Rome is the epitome of tyranny.
To subject oneself to her is to share the guilt for her crime and wickedness.
The same applied also to such forms of tyranny as that of the Anabaptists
in Munster (1534/1535). These are the two adversaries who crop up constantly in Saravia's works.

---

[59] Pauly-Wissowa, *Realencyclopädie der classischen Altertumswissenschaft* (repr. Munich,
1958-1974), 2. series, VII, A2, 1821-1842.

[60] "... violatis iuris et detrimentum totius reipublicae ac aliorum civium iniuria". *IA*,
181.

[61] *Ibid.*, 183.

[62] "... tanquam populi voluntas in hac re iuris et aequitatis sit regula, et regna populi sint
beneficia, non solius Dei dona". *Ibid.*

[63] *Ibid.*, 185-189.

[64] *Ibid.*, 190 f.

[65] *Ibid.*, 193.

[66] "Si sacrosanctum majestatis tuae caput, regina Elizabetha, Deus sua providentia
tutatus non esset, iam olim conspiratione malorum periisses. Quis consilia, fraudes, con-
iurationes, quas hoc hominum genus in te, in regnum tuum, machinari non destitit, hos
tringinta quatuor imperii tui annos recenseat?" *Ibid.*, 201.

However, the right and the duty to resistance against such a tyranny does not reside with the individual citizen but exclusively with the sovereigns who have received the sword from God for this purpose.[67] Only the bearer of supreme authority can give the command for the killing of tyrants because he alone can judge the nature and extent of the tyranny better than the individual citizen.[68] The killing of tyrants ought therefore to have a legal foundation. In all this the sovereign was for Saravia the sole representative and executor of the law. This distinguished him from Calvin who, in exceptional circumstances granted the right to rebel to the States General,[69] just as Hotman on the other hand in *Francogallia* and as the author of *Vindiciae,* with an eye to the appreciable following for the Reformation amongst the nobility and town councils, especially in southern France, granted the right to the lower magistrates. Beza took a position midway between these two.[70] The Huguenots tried to create a constitutional basis for the right to resist and rebel. There was no possibility of this for Saravia because there was no place at all for a constitution in his view of the state. Moreover, this never came with his consideration because his idea of the tyrant had only ever been actualized in the papacy and the Anabaptists. In his view, no sovereign of his day qualified for consideration. The Huguenot wars and the Dutch revolt were for him essentially expressions of resistance to the Roman tyrant.

In Saravia's constitutional views a parliament meant nothing more than an assembly of the people's representatives who came to the king as "suppliants" and who themselves ordered nothing.[71] Parliament acted in a purely advisory capacity but had no legislative function.[72] These views were out of touch with political realities in England. Already under Elizabeth parliament's increasing independence was perceptible. The queen had more trouble with them than did her father and there were many conflicts between crown and parliament.[73] Saravia must have observed all this with horror. The monarch was above the law and no

---

[67] *Ibid.,* 194.

[68] "Necare tyrannum privatis non licet, nisi mandet is cui per leges in tyrannum ius est". *Ibid.,* 198.

[69] *Inst.* (1559), IV, 20, 31; *CO,* 1116.

[70] De Bèze, *Du droit des magistrats,* XXXVI-XLI.

[71] "In parlamentis nihil ordines ex imperio iubent; sed supplices accedunt ad suum regem, cui quid fieri ipsius et regni intersit indicant; et authoritas tanti confessus non est alicuius in regem potestatis aut imperii, sed prudentiae et consilii eorum qui novum decretum rogant, eique sese nomine totius regni submittent." *IA,* 276.

[72] "In regno vel optimatum imperio amplissimarum regionum convocantur ordines et conveniunt, qui populum repraesentant; sed ut adsint, non ut praesint, ut consilio suo adiuvent, non ut imperent". *Ibid.,* 282.

[73] Elton, *Tudor Constitution,* 300-317; F. W. Maitland, *The Constitutional History of England* (Cambridge, 1968) 237-280; cf. E. O. Smith, "Crown and Commonwealth. A Study in the official Elizabethan Doctrine of the Prince," *Transactions of the American Philosophical Society,* NS, LXVI, 8 (1976) 30-43.

legislative body could exist above or beside him. He himself was the sole legislator.[74] In his treatise then Saravia opposed George Buchanan who put the king under the law and wanted the laws to apply to the king as to anyone else.[75] Saravia naturally condemned Buchanan's wish to make the king the object of legal proceedings in certain events.[76] The monarch was not only the sole legislator but also the sole judge. Even though he might have deserved the death penalty a thousand times yet there would be no judge competent to punish him.[77]

Here there were two views of the state diametrically opposed to each other. Whilst for Buchanan all governmental authority was derived from the will of the people, Saravia showed the utmost contempt for the same popular will.[78] He regarded the people as a "many-headed monster of which nothing good is to be expected".[79] In opposition to the idea of popular sovereignty and, in his view, on the basis of the Old Testament, he taught the complete state sovereignty and divine right of the king.[80] By its very nature kingship was monarchical and absolute, subject only to God.[81] It is self-evident that the doctrine of the king's divine right and state sovereignty rules out the right to rebel. In the section in which he dealt with the subject, Saravia repeatedly crossed swords with Buchanan, with the author of the *Vindiciae* ("Brutus") and with Guillaume Rossaeus, the name under which hid the Monarchomach and Roman Catholic convert, William Rainolds.[82] There could be no question of killing tyrants.[83] He opposed the theory of the contract between prince and people.[84] He rejected the role which Beza assigned to the lower magistrates as a check on the monarch's power[85] as an infringement of the latter's sovereignty.[86]

---

[74] "Absurdum est adferre, leges latas esse coercendis regibus: leges ac privilegia, quibus accisa est regum potentia, profecta sunt ab ipsis regibus". *Ibid.*, 279.

[75] *Ibid.*, 279; G. Buchanan, *De iure regni apud Scotos, Dialogus* (Edinburgh, 1579) 18 ff.

[76] *Ibid.*, 90.

[77] "Omnis iudicum potestas ac iurisdictio a rege manat, nec in regem tanquam in hominem suae iurisdictioni subiectum possunt ab eo delegati iudices ferre sententiam, non magis quam rex in seipsum. Et quamvis mille mortes esset meritus, in eum animadvertendi non magis potestatem habent, quam rex ipse in seipsum ut sese iugulet, propter aliquod ab eo perpetratum flagitium". *IA*, 274.

[78] Allen, *History of Political Thought*, 337.

[79] *IA*, 281.

[80] "Proïnde populi ego nullam authoritatem supra suos reges agnosco solo naturae iure datam, sine Dei dono speciali, a quo ius gladii datur... saepe fit ut verus ac legitimus rex non placeat seditioso populo; cui si imperare velit vim eis inferat oportet". *Ibid.*, 285.

[81] "Natura regni haec est, ut sit merum et absolutum unius imperium, nulli praeterquam uni Deo subiectum". *Ibid.*, 289.

[82] *DNB*, XVI, 625 f.; Wolzendorff, *Staatsrecht und Naturrecht*, 114 ff.

[83] *IA*, 308-310.

[84] *Ibid.*, 267.

[85] De Bèze, *Du droit des magistrats*, 15 ff.

[86] *IA*, 300 ff.

All this raises the question as to how in 1592 Saravia judged those outbursts of violent resistance, the religious wars in France and the Dutch revolt, in which in 1568 and from 1578 to 1587 he had himself been involved. He devoted a chapter to this at the end of *De imperandi authoritate*. In this he reviewed the political and military events in the countries in which he had spent part of his life. Here he used his norms for the right to rebel as follows. As we have already seen, Rome was for him the epitome of tyranny. The first Huguenot wars were acceptable then because they were waged with the aim of protecting the king from the Roman tyranny embodied in the Guises and the League which had been inspired by the pope and supported by Spain. Catherine de Medici herself had asked help in Germany from the emperor and the Protestant princes on behalf of Condé and his followers who were defending her, her son and her crown. Wars in defence of kingship were naturally entirely legitimate! Saravia passed the following judgement on the current (eighth) religious war (1584-1598). The (still Protestant) Henry IV, son of the pious Jeanne d'Albret, in his fierce attempts to conquer Paris, had not yet spoken the legendary words "Paris vaut bien une messe" (25 July 1593). Saravia therefore still regarded him as a prince, who, supported by England, had taken up the cause of the Huguenots. He consequently rejected Rossaeus' arguments which accused the French Reformed of disloyalty and rebellion. There was no question here of unlawful rebellion, but of a defence of the prince against the assaults of his enemies.[87] Although, in his judgement of the situation in France, Saravia took little account of nuances which did not fit in with his view, for example, Catherine's wayward changes of position, he could pass a favourable judgement in the light of his own standards on the Huguenot wars as resistance led by legitimate princes against unlawful papal tyrants.

It seemed somewhat more difficult to justify the Dutch revolt, because from the beginning this had in fact been directed against Philip II, although the show of acknowledging the Spanish king's authority had been maintained until 1581. Already on 6 October 1588, in his detailed justification against the Leiden magistrates, Saravia had provided a constitutional dissertation from which it was apparent how he saw the revolt.[88] Here he expressed the principle which he later developed at length in *De imperandi authoritate*. The sovereign is he who has no one above him but God to Whom alone he is answerable.[89] After he had first explained why, in his view, the States of Holland was not permitted to lay any claim to sovereign rights,—they were responsible to the towns as their commis-

---

[87] *Ibid.,* 311 f.

[88] BL. CM. Galba, D III, fol. 240-242.

[89] "Un souverain ne recognoit que Dieu par dessus soy, au lieux ou il est souverain et n'est point accontable de ses actions a autre qua Dieu". *Ibid.,* fol. 240v.

sioners and so the definition of sovereign did not apply to them,—he stated
why Philip II possessed no sovereignty over the country. As successor to
his father, Charles V, he could exercise sovereignty over Flanders and Artois, ceded by treaty by France. The formal sovereignty over the other
provinces, Brabant, Gelderland, Holland and Friesland was vested in
Charles' successor as emperor, Ferdinand. Philip II was responsible to
him.[90] In fact, however, neither Ferdinand nor his successor, Maximilian
II, exercised their sovereignty. They had scarcely concerned themselves
with the territories in question so that an interregnum had arisen, a situation which was to be compared to the early days of the Roman republic
(500 B.C.). The sovereignty was provisionally vested in the towns, in so
far as these made up a unity, a republic or a county.[91] It was possible, with
these constitutional artifices, to legitimatize the Dutch revolt: it was not a
rebellion against the lawful sovereign prince, for he simply did not exist.

In *De imperandi authoritate,* however, Saravia followed another line of
reasoning. Flanders and Artois had been ceded by Francis I to Charles V.
William of Orange, however, was the legitimate sovereign over the other
provinces. He could act as sovereign because of his possession of the small
princedom of Orange.[92] Although he had been subordinate to Philip II
and for that reason could not wage war against him, yet he was the real
sovereign who was subject only to God from Whom he had received the
sword. The revolt would never have needed to arise if Alva had not oppressed the true Christian religion, from which he had no political dangers
to fear at all.[93] We already know that Saravia was no admirer of the
fanaticism which was displayed by some Calvinists in the South
Netherlands. The southern part of the country had been lost by the
disorder and dissension issuing from this fanaticism. If people there had
acted with more moderation they could have held out against the enemy.
They had allowed freedom to perish by defending it in an evil, disorderly
fashion.[94]

Saravia could make a positive assessment of the French Huguenots'
rebellion and the Dutch revolt because he regarded it either as defending
the legitimate sovereign or he did not recognize the actual sovereign prince
as such. However, he remained averse to the Monarchomachs' conclusions. The order of the Elizabethan establishment was more preferable to
him than the chaotic situation in France and the Netherlands. It was also

---

[90] *Ibid.,* fol. 241.

[91] ''... la souverainete est tombée en touts les corps des villes ensemble et en nulles delles
en particulier, d'autant qu'elles ne sont qu'un corps, une republique ou conté'', *Ibid.,* fol.
241v.

[92] ''Arausium vulgo Orangia, parva est ditio; princeps tamen in populum illum habet imperium, nemini praeterquam uni Deo subiectum''. *IA,* 163.

[93] *Ibid.,* 312.

[94] *Ibid.,* 174.

to oppose the influence of Calvinist Monarchomach in England that he wrote his treatise.

Saravia was not the only one who tried to support the official policy of the queen and her advisers with an arsenal of theological arguments,[95] but of them all he was perhaps the most radically conservative defender of the divine right of kings and of the state's sovereign power. Thomas Bilson's great work, *The true Difference between christian Subjection and unchristian Rebellion* (1585) would certainly have been familiar to him. Among French authors he may possibly have known the work of Pierre de Belloy, entitled *De l'autorité du roi et crimes de lèsemajesté* (1587), one of the most forceful defences of the divine right of kings and also of their supremacy over the church. We discover many ideas and concepts in Saravia with which we are familiar in Jean Bodin's work, *Six Livres de la République* (1576), such as the notion of the "république bien ordonnée", the direct relation between the state and Providence, the appeal to the natural law and to the Old Testament, the pyramid of examples of authority with the family as the basis and the monarch as the summit, the paternal nature of governmental authority, the exclusive legislative competence of the government, the aversion to revolt and rebellion and the consequent denial of the right to resist.[96] In short there are so many ideas in common that we must conclude that Bodin influenced Saravia.

## 2. CHURCH AND STATE

Saravia clearly outlined the historical-theological connection which suited his views on church and state particularly in the second part of *De Gradibus* which dealt with *De honore praesulibus et presbyteris ecclesiarum Christi debito*. He had in mind a "bene constituta christiana respublica", that is, as he put it in an expression which he used dozens of times, a society in which Christ's Gospel, or the Christian religion "has been accepted by the state's authority".[97] He found examples, not only in Christendom but from outside also, of a social order of which religion was the foundation. He referred frequently to antiquity and to Old Testament Judaism. Kingship and priesthood were closely connected in Egypt and Greece.[98] The Romans connected priesthood with the imperial office and gave the

---

[95] Chr. Morris, *Political Thought in England. Tyndale to Hooker* (London/New York/Toronto, 1953) 68-88, 110-126.

[96] J. W. Allen, "Jean Bodin," in: *The Social and Political Ideas of Some Great Thinkers of the Sixteenth and Seventeenth Centuries* (New York, 1949) 42-61; J. H. Franklin, *Jean Bodin and the Rise of Absolutist Theory.* Cambridge, 1973.

[97] "... recepto publica autoritate Christi Evangelio." *DGM*, 53; "... ubi publica autoritate christiana religio recepta est, et legum ac totius reipublicae facta est fundamentum." *Ibid.*; "... recepta publica autoritate religione christiana." *Ibid.*, 54; etc., etc.

[98] *Ibid.*, 40 f.

Flavian emperors the title pontifex maximus.[99] In his view this all demonstrated that religion was always an integral and indispensable element in society, one of the pillars on which the state was founded, more essential even than armed forces.[100] The Old Testament theocracy was an important model. Eli and Samuel united in themselves the offices of priest and judge.[101] David and Solomon employed Levites and priests as administrators and judges.[102]

Two periods are to be distinguished in the history of Christianity, the pre- and post-Constantinian. This distinction recurs repeatedly in Saravia's writings.[103] Before the Constantinian change the church existed as a part of society or in society. This pre-Constantinian period was to be compared to Israel's life in Egypt and Babylon and that of Christianity under the Mohammedans. After Constantine, however, church and society coincided. It was no longer possible to talk of the church ín society, on the contrary the church wás society.[104] The boundaries of the church and those of society coincided. The whole nation had been baptized, the whole society had become a church.[105] For Saravia the Constantinian and post-Constantinian period was normative. In contrast to those who thought that this ushered in the decline of the church because evangelical poverty was exchanged for worldly power, especially as regards possession—a Dutch theologian in the twentieth century has talked of "the Fall of Christianity"[106]—his view was that Constantine had restored the church and religion to the position which was their due and which benefited them.[107] This emperor's reign was the great turning point in the history of Christianity and culture: the government had changed from an enemy and persecutor into the church's nursing father.[108]

According to Saravia, the papal usurpation of power in the Middle Ages ended this function of the government: it brought the state into a relationship of dependence upon the church. Reformation then also meant a return to the relationships of Constantian times. That is to say that, "after the Roman tyranny has come to an end and the king's authority has been

---

[99] *Ibid.*, 42.

[100] "Sine milite respublica esse potest, sine sacrorum ministro non potest. Usus militis non est perpetuus; quo rarior, eo respublica felicior. Religio numquam intermitti potest." *Ibid.*, 39 f.

[101] *Ibid.*, 68.

[102] *Ibid.*, 69.

[103] *Ibid.*, 76; *DT,* Epist. dedic., 2.

[104] "... ubi ecclesia est respublica et respublica ecclesia." *DGM,* 71.

[105] "Sed ubi totus aliquis populus nomen dedit Christo, et nemo illic est Christi baptismo non sit tinctus, ecclesia est respublica, et respublica est externa et visibilis quaedam ecclesia." *Ibid.*

[106] G. J. Heering, *De zondeval van het Christendom.* 3rd ed. Arnhem, 1933.

[107] *DGM,* 43 ff., 56.

[108] *Ibid.*, 62 f.; *DT,* Epist. dedic., 2.

restored'', the government has the duty of putting in hand the reformation of the church.[109] In England the reformation took place in a way which Saravia considered ideal.[110] Reformation is a task for the government, the king possesses the ''ius reformandi''.[111] Once more France and the Netherlands were Saravia's examples to show what disorder arose if the reformation was taken in hand by the rebel people against the will of the magistrates. God has, to be sure, turned evil into good in those countries, but the rule still holds: God is the creator of order, not of confusion.[112] The church ought to be reformed by the king and the highest magistrates, not by wars and rebellions.[113] Elizabeth served as the shining example of a properly conducted reformation.[114]

These opinions belong to Saravia's picture of the respublica christiana, conceived of as a harmonious unity in which church and state together form an indivisible society. The origin of both lay in God, on the understanding that the state belongs to the order of creation, the church to that of salvation.[115] The supreme authority of the government over the church is presumed because, in this harmonious pattern of society, religion is its first and most important concern.[116] It does not, indeed, have any say in the church's doctrine but it does in the latter's external circumstances, its ''externus status'', which includes the liturgical order of the *Book of Common Prayer*.[117] Stipulations which aimed at resisting uniformity in worship meant unlawful disobedience to the magistrates, in fact a political sin.[118] Individual citizens ought not to oppose liturgical rules

---

[109] *DGM*, 76.

[110] *DT*, 38.

[111] ''Et hodie reges aliique summi magistratus cum illis religionis praesulibus, penes quos est ordinarium apud eos ecclesiae regimen, possunt reformare ecclesiam et purum Dei restituere cultum, sine ullis extraordinariae vocationis Evangelii ministris''. *Ibid.*, 40.

[112] *Ibid.*, 41.

[113] *Ibid.*, 42.

[114] *Ibid.*, 46.

[115] ''Nam etsi duo sint gubernationis genera, alterum civitatis, alterum ecclesiae, tamen utrumque ab eodem profectum est authore. Quod quamvis diversa, fiat ratione, et illud a Deo sit quatenus creator ac moderator rerum humanarum, hoc quatenus redemptor est humani generis, et unumquodque suum habeat finem; tamen quando eadem societas ecclesia est atque civitas, sicut ab eodem utriusque regiminis authoritas manat, ita ad eundem postremum finem respicit et eodem se recolligit. Unde fit ut multa habeant communia, quae nunquam recte nisi communi consilio ac assensu possunt perfici. Evangelii minister a Domino servatore regiminis in ecclesia habet authoritatem; magistratus a Domino omnium creatore in cives, qui quoties simul amice conspirant, et eodem sua consilia referunt, optime cum civitate, optime agitur cum ecclesia''. *DGM*, 1.

[116] *IA*, 158.

[117] ''Quamvis regia potestas doctrinam de filio Dei et de sacramento ac caeteris religionis capitibus innovare non possit (quod nec ipsis concessum est episcopis), tamen de locis ac temporibus, quando et ubi commode habere poterunt pietatis exercitia, constituere valet. Item quo ordine, quo ritu, quo gestu, quo habitu mysteria decentius celebrabuntur''. *Ibid.*, 208.

[118] *Ibid.*, 207 f.

established by the government.[119] Saravia wanted to make clear to the Puritans that their opposition to these rules had political implications.

On the other hand, he left no doubt that the government's authority over the church did not mean that the magistrate might decide as he pleased on church matters. On the contrary, just because religion was based not on human but divine laws, the government ought to consult theologians and interpreters of Scripture in its behaviour towards the church. It could even perhaps summon a synod for this purpose.[120]

Part of his exposition of the relationship between church and state consisted in attacking Roman Catholic opinions on the question. He opposed the view that the king's oath-taking befóre and consecration by the bishop óf the king involved any limitation of royal rights. Against Rossaeus, who cited the investiture of the German emperors, he maintained that kings and emperors possessed complete sovereignty without oath-taking, coronation, or anointing.[121] Coronation by the priest only served to make clear that the king received his "potestas" not from men but from God, namely at the moment of his election, as in the case of the German emperor, or at the moment of his succession. Coronation added nothing to the monarch's rights but sealed the rights which already existed.[122] The Roman Catholic church's arrogant pretention to possess the right, on the grounds of coronation and anointing, to install and depose monarchs was lese-majesty to Saravia.[123] The king's sovereignty was not dependent on his being a Christian as the Anabaptists asserted.[124]

Saravia defended a position similar to that adopted in the Middle Ages by the French Gallicans and which had always had considerable support in England: neither church nor pope had the right to install and depose but the Christian government had the authority to appoint and dismiss bishops and even the pope. Saravia assigned the position which Rome attributed to the pope, to the Christian secular authorities who as God's representatives on earth had to take care of the church and religion as well as of the people and kingdom. This task included the prevention of heresies, schisms, etc. and even possibly, in the event of dereliction of duty, the changing of pastors and bishops for others.[125] In contrast, the church ought to have no power over the state: apostolic authority, that is the authority of Christ's Kingdom, was purely spiritual in nature.[126] The

---

[119] "Quare de his rebus, quod publica authoritate decretum est bona conscientia a privatis reiici aut improbari non debet". *Ibid.,* 208.

[120] *ET,* Ep. dedic., 2.

[121] *IA,* 215.

[122] "Nihil coronatio regi adferat. Ideo enim coronantur reges: quia sunt reges; non autem fiunt reges quia coronantur". *Ibid.,* 220.

[123] *Ibid.,* 222-228.

[124] *Ibid.,* 229.

[125] *Ibid.*

[126] *Ibid.,* 236.

spiritual task of preaching the Word and administering the sacraments ought not to be mixed up with the particularly social and political activities such as the administration of justice, which lay exclusively within the government's province.[127] Saravia made it clear, with many examples from antiquity, that there had never been any question of the church's authority over the state, not even the excommunication of government personnel.[128] For this reason he did not regard Ambrose's action against the emperor Theodosius after the massacre caused by the latter in Thessalonica as excommunication. The emperor was readmitted to the eucharist at Christmas 390 after he had done public penance including the laying down of his imperial insignia.[129]

Saravia argued at length with Bellarmine whose doctrine of the "translatio imperii" assigned a "potestas indirecta" to the pope in secular affairs and thereby maintained the church's superiority over the state. This debate is also interesting because both opponents developed their ideas from the presupposition of the "corpus christianum" in which the two powers, church and state, were so closely united that one could speak of one respublica, one kingdom, one family. Saravia applied what Paul had written about the unity of the church in 1 Cor. 10:16, 17 to this Christian society, "we are one body in Christ".[130] But he rejected Bellarmine's organic view of society in which the church's authority was seen as the soul and that of the government's as the body. He considered it unacceptable to distinquish the state's authority as a purely earthly matter from that of the church conceived of as divine and heavenly.[131] On the other hand, he did see a clear distinction between the two powers, each with its own commission. The church's commission consisted in the proclamation of the Gospel and the administration of the sacraments, that of the government in the maintenance of justice and the punishment of wrong-doing,[132] but the authority of both church and state had the same goal; eternal salvation, "beatitudo aeterna". This is the aim of all legislation, all political actions and all religion and therefore church and state are to strive together in amicable alliance for this single goal.[133] Thus Saravia's thought continued in the medieval pattern. His rejection of Boniface VIII's bull *Unam Sanctam* was merely a difference within the common framework of the "corpus christianum".[134]

---

[127] *Ibid.*, 237 f.

[128] *Ibid.*, 257 ff.

[129] *Ibid.*, 237.

[130] "Primus duas potestates coniungi et convenire inter se, ut unam rempublican, unum regnum, unam familiam, imo atque unum corpus efficiant, quod unum (ut ait apostolus) corpus sumus in Christo, fateor". *Ibid.*, 241.

[131] *Ibid.*, 242 f.

[132] *Ibid.*, 242.

[133] *Ibid.*, 243.

[134] *Ibid.*, 249 f.

It is true that Saravia suggested a certain division between the two powers when he declared that the ecclesiastical power did not govern the political, nor the political the church, but immediately afterwards he made it clear that the church is subordinate to the state in the event of disputes in which legal decisions are necessary. On the other hand, the government is to protect true doctrine and suppress false and it has to look after the "externum ministerium": preaching, administration of the sacraments and church government. Naturally it cannot pronounce judgement on the contents of doctrine and preaching, but, "although kings are not theologians, they do have theologians".[135] James I, even more than Elizabeth, was to make use of his court theologians to give support to his policy.

It is worth recalling in this connection that Saravia expressly assigned the exercise of discipline to the church, not to the government. He was indeed willing to leave open the possibility of an appeal to the secular authority in the event of an unjust ecclesiastical censory measure.[136] On the other hand, he rejected any exemption of the clergy from the state's jurisdiction. Ministers ought to be judged and punished in accordance with the same laws as all other citizens.[137]

However, they ought to have the same rights as all other citizens. This in particular was the tenor of the two smaller treatises which Saravia appended to his *De Gradibus*. As their titles in the English translation indicated, they dealt with "of the honor which is due unto priests and prelates of the Church" and "of sacrilege and the punishment thereof". In the first he argued for a status for the clergy which, so he thought, was to be compared to that of the priests in Old Testament Israel. For this it was proper that they receive reasonable payment. Where this could not be borne by the glebes and the produce of the land, the money ought to come from offerings and tithes. He preferred this form of remuneration to that of the payment of fixed stipends by the government. Besides some remarkable subsidiary arguments for this preference—offerings have a more religious character because their amounts are not determined beforehand, government stipends are more secular because of their guaranteed fixed amounts—he had an interesting motive against the fixed stipend: it would pose a threat to the minister's necessary παρρησία towards the government; whoever pays the piper, calls the tune! In favour of the payment of offerings he argued its character as a continuing form of "pietas" and "cultus Dei". On the other hand, the government ought to see to it that the obligation of paying offerings was fulfilled.[138] In view of the often pitifully low pay of ministers, this was no superfluous admonition.

---

[135] *Ibid.*, 245.
[136] *Ibid.*, 248 f.
[137] *DGM*, 36.
[138] *Ibid.*, 77-82.

The other aspect of the respect due to the clergy was the same right to earthly possessions as any other citizen,[139] a right of which Saravia made good use, as we learn from his will. More important, however, was the right to hold political offices. It seems that Saravia was here going back somewhat from the limitation of the clergy to their spiritual work without meddling in political affairs which he first advocated. Are we then to note a contradiction at this point? We ought to consider the background to the different statements. The warning against interfering in political matters referred to the independent critical speech and action against the government which was characteristic of Puritan circles. The author of *De imperandi authoritate* was utterly opposed to this. However, political action by the clergy in the "respublica christiana" in support of the state's authority and for the promotion of good order in society was quite different. With this in mind the church's pastors could take their place in parliament—which only had an advisory capacity anyway—and could share in the administration of justice in town and country, though naturally as advisers. The involvement in such political duties was not in conflict with their pastoral charge since pastoral care was not just concerned with the soul but also with the body. Moreover the fate of church and state was closely bound up together. They were both "on the same ship and in the same danger".[140]

In the second appendix, dealing with sacrilege, Saravia once more fiercely attacked the seizure of ecclesiastical and monastic goods by the authorities. He understood by "sacrilegium" the profanation of the church and of its ministers' means of support. He found it reprehensible that in Germany and the Netherlands, this had taken place in the name of "reformation". He failed to mention that the Dissolution of the Monasteries by Henry VIII had certainly harmed the church's material circumstances.[141] Perhaps he was referring to this, when he recalled that governments which had confiscated monastic goods had no right to pour the tithes and offerings intended for the poor into the state's coffers.[142] Reformation did not mean the abolition of the distinction between sacred and profane in "externis rebus". Such a removal of the distinction was rather to be seen as an act of atheism. Theft of a sacred thing was a sacrilege,[143] so he contrived to prove from Plato[144] and the Old Testament

---

[139] "Recepto Evangelio autoritate publica, ad eundem modum ministros Evangelii agros et possessiones possidere, aut possidendas ipsis dari, nusquam Servator noster prohibuit". *Ibid.*, 59.

[140] *Ibid.*, 70.

[141] G. W. O. Woodward, *Dissolution of the Monastries.* London, 1969²; J. Youings, *The Dissolution of the Monasteries.* London/New York, 1971.

[142] *DGM*, 87.

[143] *Ibid.*, 84.

[144] *Ibid.*, 88 f.

(Dan. 5:23-28).[145] Saravia apparently failed to see that this sacrilege must necessarily result from that supremacy of the government over the church which he advocated. The argument for the church's spiritual and material independence could not be more than theoretical within the structures of church and society which he defended and the relationships of authority which was inherent in them. The church would only gain its independence when the form of society defended by this theologian of the English establishment was swept away. The answer he gave to the question of authority, was the answer of the past.

---

[145] *Ibid.,* 89 f.

THIRD PART

# DOCUMENTS

## I. SARAVIA TO WILLIAM CECIL
Guernsey, 26 February 1565/66

Eximiae discretionis ac prudentiae viro D. Guilelmo Cecillio
Adrianus Saravius S.P.D.

Singularis illa in Deum pietas atque erga omnes Anglici regni provincias studium, quae nemo in te G.D. non veneratur ac suspicit, facit ut audacter ad te scribam ac familiariter, non ductus alicuius ostentationis gloria, ut solet bona grammaticorum pars, dum favorem et gratiam illustrium virorum ambiunt, argumentum plausibile ut ipsis quidem videtur captantes eos ad tertium usque coelum nimium inepte affectata argutia extollunt. Ego scio quam sit hoc scriptionis genus ingratam viris cordatis, presertim piis qui norunt quae sit nostrae naturae imbecillitas et quam impotenter sui ipsius laudes ferat quodque magis expediat, nostra peccata nobis ob oculis poni atque in mentem revocari, ut eorum agnita turpidine a vitiis et nobis ipsis abhorreamus potius quam nostrarum virtutum preconium; si modo nostras apellare licet quas gratuita Dei liberalitate (et ut ita loquar) commodato quodammodo accepimus, idque tantisper dum Deus illas in nobis fovet. Ideo quicquid merentur laudis, totum debet Deo autori acceptum referri. Ego satius esse duco tacere, quam mortalem in hoc tam fragilis vitae curriculo laudare. Sed cum iusta se mihi offerat scribendi occasio, etsi in me nihil agnoscam quod te movere debeat, ea tamen est tua humanitas, ut non fore ingrata quae scribo confidam. Nam plurimum referre puto tum religioni tum regno et eorum quoque bono qui hic habitant, te omnia quae hic fiunt cognoscere. Tametsi totos tres annos habitaverim in Anglia, nunquam expertus sum id quod vulgo de insularibus dici solet. Sed hic primum id experior adeo ut in istos etiam illud Epimenidis de Cretensibus omnino convenire putem:
            [P. ad Tit.] Haec gens tota ex fraude et mendacio est composita, ipsis Cretensibus mendacior; nulla enim in istorum hominum verbis est fides; peierare nulla est eis religio; sic sibi persuasum habent, satius esse mille se obstringere periuriis quam suis amicis vel minimum ut incommodent. Paucis ab hinc elapsis diebus in pleno magistratus consessu, tribuno huius insulae presente et aliis M. R. legatis, adeo impudenter quidam mentiri nihil est veritus ut obstupescerem hominem quemquam tam impudentem reperiri tamque vecordem qui auderet cum tanta mentiri fiducia atque in contrarium sensum invertere sermonem quem omnes quotquot aderant satis intellexissent. Haec plenius ex D. Decano cognosces, in cuius id fiebat odium; nam res prolixior est quam ut paucis eam possim exponere. Multa alia longe graviora in eodem consessu acciderunt; plena erant omnia turbis et tumultu ut parum abfuerit a seditione.

Porro gens quae sic comparata est ut omnia metiatur suis affectibus et ex ratione privati commodi aut incommodi potius quam ex aequo et bono, vix unquam fieri poterit ut veram non oderit religionem. Quam contemnant Deum et quanto Evangelion prosequantur odio, improborum palam flagitiosa vita et exiguus piorum numerus satis indicat. Exiguum voco, nam si tres tantum aut quatuor ad summum ex hac insula morte aut alia quavis occasione emigrasset, divini verbi ministerium hic apud nos interiret, nisi forte Deus alios suscitaret. Si contingat ecclesiasten ire rui ut illic concionetur, cum risu et cachinnis excipitur nonnunquam tanto murmure undique obstrepunt ut cogatur inceptam concionem deserere; nec hic se continet eorum insolentia sed insuper stercoribus et foetore implent suggestum. Ego a spurcissimo Turca nihil amplius expectarem; nam quod manus continent, id vi fit, metu et formidine R.M.; si paululum suo sinerentur arbitrio, experiremur eos quibusvis Turcis immaniores. Et haec omnia fiunt sciente et connivente magistratu in illis presertim locis ubi habitant. Nam modestiores experimur parœcias ubi nullus senator (quem isti iuratum appellant) habitat. Nulla spes est huic malo occurri posse sub tali magistratu. Omne autem vitiorum genus contempta vel neglecta religione impune regnare minime mirum est; furari, innocentem ledere, hominem interficere hic impune licet. Non dico tamen violari leges, cum nullas habeant: iactant patrias consuetudines quae subinde ad arbitrium imperitorum iudicum mutantur. Multiplex tamen et varium est in hac parva insula forum et iudiciorum omnia sunt plena; nec esse quemquam puto qui in aliquo foro saltem non habeat litem aliquam. Interim sic sunt confusa omnia, ut non putem etiam si conentur id iudices aequam ferri posse sententiam; omitto iudicum imperitiam et iniquitatem et multa quae contra omne ius quotidie ab ipsis fiunt. Miror haec oppresso plebi non displicere modo, sed quod magis est mirum in modum placere: sic in malis suis occalluerunt ut nullum amplius habeant sui mali sensum. Inde fit ut qui iurati vocantur in populum dominentur tanquam in brutas pecudes. Sed omnem flagrare iniuriam ac ex libidine improborum omnia fieri necesse est ubi nullus est Dei metus et omnis religio contemnitur, quae sola cupiditatibus mortalium frenum iniicit. Tanta preterea huic genti socordia et pigrities est innata, ut pauperiem maluit in otio quam iusto labore honestas comparare divitias. Locum habent mercimoniis admodum idoneum nec dubito maximum emolumentum inde posse ad istos redire, si navibus suis securam stationem construere vellent; quod factu satis est facile congestis telluris et lapidum quorum magnam habent copiam aggeribus iam a natura iactis sollidissimis fundamentis; sic posset vis fluctuum et tempestatum a navibus propelli. Nam infida navium statio deterret exteros ab hac insula. Tribunus paratissimus est ad omnia ea quae conducere existimat provinciae cui praefectus est: hortatur et instat ut simul operas iungant ad tutam stationem hac aestate edificandam, atque ad eam rem obtulit quartam suorum proventuum partem, modo tantumdem et ipsi praestent. Quid autem facturi sint γαστέρες ἀργαί nescio. Est et aliud malum quod ipsis tantum non incommodat sed ipsi quoque Angliae regno perniciosum est; nam eorum quae antea dixi, ipsi soli magna ex parte ferunt incommodum. Ego non arbitror te ignorare quantum intersit has insulas sub imperio Angliae retineri: nam si Gallus has occuparet insulas, damni plurimum toti oceano britannico inferre posset, si mari aeque potens esset atque terra. Sed omnia in hoste debent esse suspecta, imbecillitas aeque atque potentia. Vidi tempore belli, cum ad arma fuit concurrendum et suspicio esset magna classe advehi hostes, omnia perturbari ac tumultuosa repleri confusione sine ulla militari disciplina: Tribunus arcem tenebat, sed per insulam designati centuriones ut reliquas partes tueantur suis imperare nesciunt: pars domi delitescit nec adduci potest ut domum exeat, veriti tumultum ac seditionem; pars sine ordine incerta huc atque illuc vagatur spirantes minas contra pios quos ignominoso vocabulo hugnotes vocant, in quos totius mali quod verentur omnem culpam reiiciunt, ita ut magis ab eorum furore nobis sit cavendum quam ab ipsis hostibus si forte vicissent. Ego militiam nunquam sum secutus; tamen longe diversum ordinem memini me vidisse cum in castris Philippi Regis tum in urbibus militum presidio munitis ubi minus erat periculi. Tanta aderat rerum omnium perturbatio, ut non putem hostem ab insula potuisse repelli si advenisset. Res tamen non admodum difficilis in loco natura munito, si fortiter infirmiora quaedam loca ubi descensus hosti patet tueri vellent. Quemadmodum in bello cum resistendum est hosti victi impatientia se ad maledicta et seditionem convertunt, sic pari inconstantia ac levitate (ne quid gravius dicam) in summa omnium leticia eo die quo pax fuit proclamata seditiosus ebriorum concursus duce ex iuratis quopiam pios maledictis lacessebant, parati in proprios cives sua convertere arma si ii qui profitentur Evangelium se obiecissent eorum furori. Inpunitas haec parit ac ad peccandum perversissimorum quorumque accendit libidinem. Sunt praeter haec adhuc multa quae si recenseam modum sum excessurus epistolae; sat est scripsisse praecipua. Nam ad haec scribenda de iis quibus cohabito, rerum quas video indignitate, me compelli vehementer doleo. Si meo silentio eis magis prodesse crederem, malem mihi aut precissam linguam aut mutilatos digitos quam quicquam dicere aut scribere in alicuius infamiam. Sed cogit me studium fidesque erga Dei gloriam et Angliae regnum meum et omnium exulum nomine Christi asylum. Idque fretus tua humanitate ac prudentia, quam non dubito his recte uti posse, ausus sum. Non puto necessarium ut prolixiore oratione apud te instem, ac te rogem ut corruptis huius insulae moribus remedium aliquod adhiberi cures, cum certo sciam ea re te nihil habere antiquius; sufficiet indicasse malum. De schola S.R. Elizabethae D.N. quid dicem nescio nisi re ipsa (tametsi nonnihil videantur promittere) tantum beneficium contemnere. Nihil enim eorum fit quae a legatis R.M. decreta fuerunt: rem quantum possunt protrahunt. Gens barbara omnem literaturam oderunt suisque eam invident. Insulares pueros quos instituam tantum decem habeo; caeteri omnes sunt Angli. Tanto interdum hic conficior taedio ut si Anglici regni municipatum adeptus essem, quamlibet minimam sortem illic preferrem huic meae inter istos conditioni, etiam si mihi triplo auctius stipendium decernerent. Verum haec in malos sic dicta sunto ut probos excepisse me intelligas. Caeterum antequam finiam, te maiorem in modum iterum atque iterum rogabo ut haec eo animo accipias ac scripta sunt et me in imo tuorum clientum catalogi asscribere digneris. Nihil habeo dignum tua D. quod offeram praeter animi gratitudinem et memoriam tuorum in me beneficiorum immortalem, quae tibi libenter et ex animo offero. Vive foelix in Christo. 4. Cal. Martias. Guerenzæa.

PRO SP 15/12, fol. 99, 100

## II. SARAVIA TO WILLIAM CECIL
### Guernsey, 31 January 1566/1567

Ornatissimo viro D. Guilelmo Cecillio
patrono suo Adrianus Saravia S.P.D.

Ne qua forte animi lenitate aut inconstantia, vir ornatissime, factum putes quod ut statueram ad meos Belgas me non contulerim, rationem tibi paucis exponam. Dimissionem a fratribus qui hic sunt impetrare non potui. Abire autem ipsis invitis cum mala ipsorum gratia mihi res prorsus indigna visum est. Preterea ego hic habeo apud me utrumque meum parentem quos Gandavo cum turbae illic inciperent revocavi. At me cum illis, uxore et liberis, in turbulentam precipitare tempestatem, cum quid opis hoc rerum statu patriae meae afferre queam incertus sim, consultum mihi visum non est. Hi sunt trabales clavi qui me hic affixum detinuerunt. Interea, mi domine, si tibi indignus non videor, municeps et civis vester fieri vehementer cupio. De hac gente nihil scribo nisi quod nunquam sibi sit futura dissimilis. Vale. Guerzea. prid. Cal. Februarii.

PRO SP 15/12, fol. 155r
Strype, *Annals,* I; 2, 226

## III. WILLIAM OF ORANGE TO SARAVIA
### Delft, 31 October 1573

A Monsr de Saravia.

Monsr de Saravia, Ayand entendu de Monsr Calvart le debvoir auquel vous vous estes mis pour me laisser escouler *aulcune occasion* au bien de mes affaires, je vous en ay bien voulu faire remerchiement par lettre et aussy vous advertir que de la somme pour laquelle vous aurez respondu j'ay escript a ceulx de Sandwitz quilz ayent a la vous rembourser des deniers qui restoient entre leurs mains, chose que je masseure sera faicte maintenant. Si loccasion se presente de recognoistre ce service que vous mavez faict et a la cause commune, asseure vous que je my employeray de bon coeur. Et pour ce que presentement jescrips encoires a ceulx de Santone et de la Rie comme aussy a toutes aultres eglises dAngleterre de faire une collecte par mois. Je vous prie tenir la main chez vous et a la Rie comme nous nous confions en vous et tellement faire envers eulx quilz monstrent par effect avoir pitie et compassion de leurs freres. Pour toute ayde nont ilz contribue dernierement que dix livres la ou par mois. Ilz pourroient bien contribuer au tant combien que toutesfois de lassistance quilz firent alors par prest je les remerchie comme avant este faict en saison bien necessaire. Et a tant**....
Monsr de Saravia ech. Escript a Delft le dernier doctobre 1573.

** KHA A 11, XIV, 1, 9, fol. 435

KHA XIV, I, 12, fol. 358r

## IV. SARAVIA TO FRANCIS WALSINGHAM
### Gent, 3 September 1582

Grace et Paix par nostre Seigneur Jesu Christ

Mon Seigneur,

Combien que je ne desire rien tant que de pouvoir par toute bonne occasion faire chose, qui vous puisse estre aggreable, et que je ne cognoisse chose, en quoy je me pouroye employer, si ce nest en escrivant quelque fois des affaires de pardeca, toutteffois je ne me puis point acquitter, comme je voudroye, par ce que les postes ne partent point d'icy pour Angleterre, tellement quil fault que le bruict et les courriers previennent mes lettres. Aussi maintenant je ne pense point escriver chose que vostre Seigneurie ignore, mais ce que je fai n'est que pour accompaigner les papiers que je vous envoye de la reception de son Altesse en ceste ville de Gandt. J'ay veu par cy devant comment et avec quelle magnificence le Roy Philippe fut receu, et que ce qui sest faict maintenant est bien peu de chose au pris de ce qui se fit alors, aussi le temps estoit tout autre, la misere et calamite ou le pais est n a point permis den faire davantage. Mais son Altesse a donné un tout aultre contentement au Seigneurs de ceste ville et au peuple, que ne fit alors le Roy dEspaigne, lequel tenoit une Majeste si tres grande, que iamais il ne donna aucune signification davoir pour aggreable les honneurs qu'on luy faisoit. Son Altesse sest monstree en toute chose tant courtoise et populaire qu'on ne sauroit plus, laquelle chose a merveilleusement esté agreable au peuple. Vostre Seigneurie en cognoitra davantage par ce que luy envoye. Je ne doubte point que n'ayez entendu ce qui est advenu a Bruges de la conspiration contre son Altesse et principallement contre son Excellence, comme le jeune Lamoral sest laissé seduire. On avoit grande espoir de luy mais on craindoit sa legerete de jeunesse, et pour ceste causse les quatre membres avoyent esté dadvis quil eut faict un voyage en Angleterre et en Escosse et en Dannemarcke et ailleurs par lespace dun an ou XVI mois pour passer ainsi un peu de temps de sa jeunesse. Il semble que Dieu vueille entierement ruiner la maison Degmont. Au reste nous avons eu devant ceste ville le XXIX d'Aout une chaude escarmouche, lennemy pensoit du tout avoir deffaict nostre camp, et de faict sil se fut hasti dun heure ou de deux plus tost cestoit faict, tout noz gens y fussent demourez, mais Dieu a tellement conduit les affaires, que lennemy ne sen levra point, il y a laisse grand nombre de ses gens tant de cheval comme de piedt. Les Anglois se sont portez fort vaillants et n'y a cestun qui ne leur donne grande louange. son Altesse et son Excellence estoyent au ramparts et ont veu tout le combat, la perte que nous avons receue a esté fort petite au pris de celle de lennemy. Dieu par sa grace vueille mettre fin aux miseres et calamitez de noz gueres et confusions. N'ayant autre chose, après vous avoir baisé les mains. Mon Seigneur, je prieray lEternel vous accroitre en tout bien et apres une longue et heureuse vie vous recevoir au Royaume des cieux. De Gandt ce 3e Septembre.

Vostre humble et tres affectione
serviteur
Adrien de Saravia

PRO SP 83/17, fol. 10

## V. SARAVIA TO ARENT CORNELISZ.
### Leiden, 15 December 1582

D. Arnoldo fratri et symmistae multum dilecto Adrianus Saravia gratiam et pacem a Deo Patre nostro et Domino Jesu optat plurimam.

Quod t.D. mei memor est et mihi per fratrem nostrum Hagium salutem dici iussit, habeo gratiam. Non possum, dilecte frater, non te certiorem facere de nova calamitate quam Sathan rursus contra hanc ecclesiam molitur. Gasparus non potest quiescere et novis libellis nostrum quale quale illud est pacificationis initium perturbare conatur. Excussus est libellus de disciplina ecclesiastica in quo nihil est Gaspari preter epistolam; ipse tantum est interpres opinionis Gualteri. Hackius et ego comitati duobus senioribus heri hominem accessimus, rogantes et obsecrantes ut vellet potiorem habere rationem pacis ecclesiae quam privatae vindictae: homines quibus eius causa nota est non esse tam obesos naris ut non olefaciant quid hoc libello agatur, nempe ministros harum provinciarum diversum sentientes in invidiam vocari; ipsum astute dissimulatis gravioribus et preteritis dogmatibus falsis quod levius est et vulgo gratius arripuisse. Quibus rationibus sese excusaverit ac defenderit et quantum utrumque fuerit fusum verborum prolixum, nimis esset narrare, sed nos nullis rationibus potuimus hominem dimovere a sententia. Ego hodie decrevi de hac iniuria apud magistratum conqueri, nam haec ab eo fieri contra magistratus voluntatem arbitror, a quo ipsi interdictum fuisse scio ne quid moliretur novi aut ederet; quicquid accepero responsi ad te perscribam, sed hac lege ut ulterius meas literas cures mitti ad Corputium ad cuius literas ego nondum respondere potui; tu ei salutem meo nomine dices et rogare me ut quas ad te post haec dabo tanquam ad se quoque scriptas accipere velit; nam mihi certum est una fidelia duos dealbare parietes. Deus te conservet ecclesiae suae incolumem. Lugduno Batavorum 18 Calend. Januari.

1582

GAD, Nr. 112

## VI. SARAVIA TO ARENT CORNELISZ.
### The Hague, 27 December 1583

Genaede ende vrede door Jesum Christum.

De oorsaeke, lieve en werde broeder, dat ick tot uwen brief vande voorgaende weke niet en hebbe gheantwordt is gheweest dat ick dochte selve
binne eenen dach oft twee drie tot Delft te commen ende aldaer een acht of
neghen daghen te blyven. Nu anghesien dat het niet en is ghebuert, so wille ick u mijnen sin ende opinie schriven. Eerst het ware teghen de nature
van een duplicque dat wy souden een synopsin maeken vande replicke ende so daerop dupliceren; naer dat een replicqe groot is de duplicqe moet
grooter vallen, ten ware dat men den viant syn saeke wilde ghewonnen
overgheven. Daeromme hebbe ick begonnen perticulierlick te antwoorden
op alle ende een yeder van syne redenen, bedeelende de replicque in arti-
clen, ghenoteert abcd etc, ende meyne so voort te vaeren. Ick zal u.l. binnen eenen dach of twee sekere quayeren senden. Indien u.l. een deel vande replicke hebben wilt om so voort te vaeren ghelijck ick begonnen hebbe,
ick zal u een deel oversenden. Maer ick en ben gheensins van advise de
verderen te veranderen of onder mynen naem yet hierin te laeten uytgaen
dan met een pertinente antwoorde op alle syne redenen soo wel in perticu-
lier als in general. Waerinne indien u.l. my wilt behulpick zyn, ick zal my
daeraf beloven ende u bedancken. Anders Godt zal my helpen. Vaert wel.
Uytten Hagh desen XXVIIen Decembris, 1583.

U.l. dienstwillighe medebroeder
Adrianus Saravia

GAD, 80, Nr. 7

## VII. SARAVIA TO ARENT CORNELISZ
### Leiden, 23 April 1584

Gratiam et Pacem tibi precor, plurimum dilecte in Christo frater. Petrus Cornelii mihi dixit te scripturum fuisse ad me si domi fuisses quando istac transmet et mirari de rebus nostris quid egeram me nihil scripsisse. Ego certe propter vicinitatem loci non cogitavi potuisse latere te quid in Haga fecerim et id Wolfum tibi ultro esse dicturum. Eius ego sum secutus consilium nec eum ad invidos iudices censui aut ad vos scribendum, quia ab adversario id audieram non esse factum. Interea dum ab hac disputatione Cornhertius feriatur querit alium antagonistam. Scis quem? Lipsium nostrum et iam literis velitatur et in harenam pertrahere conatur hominem ei dissimillimum. Tu vides quo ceca temeritas hominem falsa opinione scientiae inflatum abripeat; pari gloriam hanc aucupetur quod audet cum quibusvis quos fama ab eruditione aliqua singulari commendat congredi. Primis literis petit a D. Lypsio ut cum bona eius gratia librum De Constantia posset in vulgarem sermonem transferre; quibus humaniter respondet librum in vulgus emissum esse in omnisvis potestate, neminem se impedire posse in quamlibet linguam librum transferre, hoc tantum ab interprete postulare ut id fideliter perstetur. Cornhert postea rescribit offensum se quibusdam locis ita ut chartas plures abiecerit et rursus resumpserit; sed cum non iudicaret sine periculo vulgo illa posse proponi abstinere se decrevisse donec cum Lypsio colloquendi erit data opportunitas. Ad has secundas literas respondet se non posse divinare quid eum in scriptis suis offendat; audire se suum librum probari quibus bonis; si quid sit quod ipse plus videat et alicubi erratum sit a se, paratum esse melius discernenti et commonstranti errorem habiturum esse gratiam. Tertio itaque rescribit Cornhert et locos quos consequere non poterat notat, nempe istos de Dei providentia qua Deus mundum regit et de libero arbitrio quod necessario libere in aliquo loco dicet hominem peccare et quod dixerit peccata non fieri nolente aut invito Deo tametsi fiant non volente Deo; indicans se magnopere expetere liberum de hac re cum Lipsio colloquium. Quod his postremis literis D. Lypsius sit responsurus nescio. Communicabit mihi credo suas literas antequam mittat. Hic omnes videre possunt irrequietum hominis ingenium. Non cupio tamen haec ulterius spargi; servabis haec tibi et Regnero, preterea nemini donec res palam aliunde fiat. Vale in Christo, multum observande frater. Lugduno 9 Calend. Maii 1584.

Tuus Saravia

GAD, Nr. 112

## VIII. SARAVIA TO WILLIAM DAVISON
Leiden, 10 January 1585

Grace et Paix par nostre Seigneur Jesu Christ.

Monsieur, combien que je ne face doubte aucune que touts gens de bien et de service ne vous soyent bien venuz et deux mesmes assez recommandez, je nay point toutteffois volu laisser partir d'icy le present porteur sans un mot d'addresse et de recommandation a Vostre Seigneurie. Vous le trouverez homme tres affectionné et fidele a faire touts bons services. Il est controlleur des monstres et vous poura informer de touts les abus qui se commettent au fait de la guere touchant les payements laquelle chose a grand besoin destre redressee sur toutes autres. Mais dautant que Vostre Seigneurie poura par experience cognoitre la vertu et fidelite du personnage, je me deporterai de faire la presente plus longue. Ainsi, Monsieur, je prie l'Eternel vous avoir en sa sainte garde et benir en toutes voz affaires. De Leyde ce Xme de Janvier stilo novo 1585.

Vostre serviteur
Adrien de Saravia

PRO SP 83/23, fol. 235r

## IX. SARAVIA TO WILLIAM DAVISON
Leiden, 23 January 1585

Grace et Paix par nostre Seigneur Jesu Christ.

Monsieur, mes humbles et affectueuses salutations premises. La presente est pour m'acquiter de ma promesse et laisser savoir a v.S., questant de retour en ma maison je me suis enquis du livret qu'on disoit avoir esté semé en ceste ville et ailleurs. Je vous envoye lordonnance et commandement de Messieurs publiee en ceste ville touchant ce fait et attachee a toutes les portes des eglises et autres lieux publiques. Au reste je n'ay sceu recouvrer d aucun des dits livrets, mais Monsieur Lipsius ma raconté tout le contenu dicelui. Le livret nest point nouveau comme on pensoit; il y a pour le moins plus dan et demi que les premiers furent apportez pardeca. Lauteur est un Jehan van den Berghe lequel escrit a un sien amy dAnvers son advis touchant lestat de ce pais, disant beaucoup de mal de feu de la louable memoire le prince dOrange et quant a la Majeste de la Reyne dAngleterre ne touche point lhonneur dicelle. Autrement qu'en discourant quelle n a point le moyen de secourir ces pais cy et, ayant servy par cydevant au finances de l'Empereur Charles et du Roy Philippe du temps de la Reyne Marie, fait un discours des finances dAngleterre, voulant conclure que cest follie desperer aucun secours de ce coste la. Du Roy de France ne fait aucune mention sinon en passant q[ue] veu quil est Roy catholique il ne fault point penser qu'il vueille prendre en sa protection des heretiques et faire la guerre au Roy d'Espagne. La conclusion finale est quon se doibt reconcilier au Roy dEspagne. Quant au propos que j'ai tenu a v.S. des confiscations que le Prince de Parme fait en Flandres des biens de ceux qui sont decede de ce monde en lindignation du Roy, il est ainsi: ceux qui journellement se retirent de Flandres lafferment unaniment. Seulement il fait grace aux enfans qui sont succedez au biens de leur peres et meres, mais ce que freres et soeurs, cousins et autres parens de ligne laterale peuvent avoir herite de leurs freres ou soeurs, oncles ou tantes ou cousins, est remande du fisque. Touchant la diversite des sectes de pardeca je remettrai cela a une autre fois. Et apres avoir tres affectueusement remercie v.S. de lhumanite quil luy a pleu me monstrer, la priant me tenir pour un de ses bien affectionnez serviteurs, ici sera lendroit.

Monsieur, que je prierai lEternel de vous benir en toute choses. De Leyde ce XXIIIe Janvier 1585 stilo novo.

Vostre tres affectionne serviteur
Adrien de Saravia

PRO SP 84/1, No 7

## X. SARAVIA TO ARENT CORNELISZ
### Leiden, 24 January 1585

Genaede ende vrede door Jesum Christum onsen Heere

Eerwerde ende beminde broeder, ick ontvinch ghisteren uwen brief met de copien darin ghesloten ende nopende tgene waertoe U.l. my vermaent, ick hoopet metter eerste ghelegheteyt te doene. So vele Hackii zaeke aengaet, Christiaen met de consistorie hebben sich vromelick ghedreghen ende en verstaen niet dat men teghen de disciplinen predeken zal, vele min dat dese kercke soude sonder discipline wesen. So dat Christianus het teghendeel van tgene Hackius ghepredickt hadde sondachs daernae ghepredicht heeft. Ende Hackius en vindt gheenen troost dar hy wel hopte. De heere magistraten en verstaen oock gheensins dat dese kercke in leere ofte kerckelicke discipline van andere kercken verschillen zal, uytghenomen het bespreck ofte besluyt van het compromis. Ick hebbe gheseyt tot sommeghe van Hackii vrienden die vande gherechte zyn ende burghemeesteren dat indien hy noech meer teghen de kerckelicke discipline uytvart, dat ick my partie teghen hem zal maken. Ick hoope dat hy dese zaeke zal laeten varen ende hem schicken te doen als zyn broederen doen. Indien Christianus doen wilt tgene hy my heeft belooft, ick zoude duncken dat het wel zyn zal met dese kercke. De Heere zy met u. Leyde desen XXIIII ten Januarii 1585.

Uwe dienstwilleghe broeder ende vriendt
Adrianus Saravia

GAD, Nr. 112

## XI. SARAVIA TO ARENT CORNELISZ
### Leiden, 15 March 1585

Salutem per Christum t.P.P. Dilecte in Christo frater, multi veniunt ad me flagitantes ut ea quae cum Cornharto disputata sunt curemus in lucem edi; quid convenerit inter nos de hac re puto vos esse memores. Ego ab eo tempore expecto libellum quem vos composuisse dicebatis ut disputationi annecteretur; quid in mora sit cur eum non miseritis nescio; cuperem scire an sententiam mutaveritis ut ipse sciam quid me facere oporteat et quid fratribus possim respondere.

Cornhartus a magistratu nostro per literas petit ut sibi huc ad academiam cum bona ipsius gratia commigrare liceat ut in literarum otio quod ei reliquum est aetatis transigat, pollicens se deinceps nihil scripturum nisi forte lacessitus cogatur ab adversariorum scriptus se defendere. Petiturus, credo, est magistratus collegii nostri sententiam; responsum quicquid erat a nobis ad te scribam; interim haec tibi servabis donec ab aliis intellexeris similiter; quod uni addo: consulem rectori prohibuisse ne posthac stipendium muneret Colhasio. Schisma Traiectinae ecclesiae spero brevi componendum. Vale multum in Christo dilecte **frater**. Idibus Martiis 1585.

Tuus A. de Saravia

GAD, Nr. 112

## XII. SARAVIA TO ARENT CORNELISZ.
### Leiden, 7 May 1585

Genaede ende vrede door Jesum Christum onsen Heere. Eersaeme en zeer beminde broeder, ick sende U.L. het vertooght onser broederen van Utrecht in het welcke my niet anders en mishaecht dan het belech ende zekere manier van spreken: wat hart voor jeuckende ooren ende rau voor quade maghen, hoe wel ick wel mercke dat men het vertooch heeft willen maken also zoete als moghelick was ende war yet te scherp ende bitter schynt gheseyt te zyne, men versoet het terstont daernaer, maer het en gheeft den vise ende neuswise gheen contenement and daeromme quedam non addita quedam mutata vellem; homines impbrobi ex suo ingenio non ex nostro candore de nobis iudicant. Ten tweeden Myne Heeren hebben voor antwordt gheschreven dat zy zoo ende gheen scholieren in haer stadt en begheren ende daeromme dat hy gheen moyete en doe om hier te commen. Ten derden over twee maende ofte drye is den Rentmeester gheseyt dat hy den goeden heere niet gheven en zoude maer tot myn heeren sende om nieuwe ordinantie. Want wt cracht van de oude ordinantie hy hem niet meer zyn pensioen en consten betaelen. Het termyn expireerde nu den laetsten Aprilis. Myn heeren dyncken dat hy zyn pensioen verbuert heeft doordien dat hy in meer stucken de conditien op de welcke het hem gheaccordeert ende ghegunt was heeft overtreden. Ten IIIIden ick en hoore van Utrecht gans niet. De zaeke die begonnen was staet stille door dat de governeur andere affecten heeft. Van het Vde zal u.l. reets bescheyt hebben. De schryver is wat te lanchsaem in tschryven. Ich verhope dat u.l. tollerabele vinden zal tgene datter gheschreven zal worden. Niet anders hebbende, lieve ende werde broeder, zoo bevele ick u liefde den almoghende Godt, Hem biddende dat Hy u ende uwer arbeyt wilt seghenen. Uyt Leyden desen VIIen Meye 1585.

Uwe dienstwillighe medebroeder<br>
Adrianus Saravia

GAD, Nr. 112

## XIII. SARAVIA TO FRANCIS WALSINGHAM
### Leiden, 8 June 1585

Nobili et Claro viro D. Francisco Walsingamo Domino meo in primis colendo S[alutem].

Tametsi ex D. Davidsono (vir clarissime) plenissime statum harum provinciarum intellecturus sis et si quid preterea erit quod ad communem salutem intersit qui hinc legati sunt suppleturos non dubitem, tamen pro mea erga Christi ecclesiam pietate et ea fide quam quoque R.M$^{ti}$ debeo regnoque Angliae, pauca quaedam ad t.A. scribenda mihi esse iudicavi, quae prudentia tua exactiori examine perpendere poterit. Primum est Regno Angliae honestum utile et necessarium esse harum provinciarum dominium aut saltem defensionem a R.M$^{te}$ suscipi, potius quam ut sinat cum pernicio et interitu tot animarum aut rursus in potestatem Hispanorum eas redigi aut cum periculo (si subsistant donec finis sit aliquis belli gallici) denuo ad Gallos recurrere ut sese eis dedant. Pernicies et periculum non erit tantum harum ecclesiarum et huius gentis sed Angliae nobiscum ac omnium qui puriorem religionem profitentur. Hisce bellis quae tum hic tum in Gallia geruntur certum est regnum et vitam R.M$^{tis}$ atque adeo omnium vestrum peti; nam finis qui hic atque illic erit belli (si voti sui compotes fiant communes adversarii) initium apud vos futurum est. Haec vos videre non dubito. Summa igitur ope huc connitendum est ut vires et copias suas ad iustam sui defensionem omnes evangelii professores coniungant. Nam si nos perierimus, vos diu stare incolumes non poteritis. Hinc in Angliam ad vos legati mittuntur qui a R.M$^{te}$ supplices petant auxilium, quibus conditionibus mitto dicere; luctandum cum regibus non est. Huius rei t.D. certiorem fieri cupio quod quemadmodum legationes ad Gallos invito et reclamante populo ac male sibi ominante susceptae sunt, ita ea quae nunc in Angliam mittitur bonis omnibus probatur nec vulgo displicet et de ea bene ominantur. Nescio quis malus genius rem apud Zelandos remorari conatus est, sed res composita est et quidquid in ea re peccati esse potuit propter communem salutem oblivione delendum est. Cum non putem a R.M$^{te}$ nos esse deserendos in his quibus versamur periculis, duo necessario apud vos in deliberationem venient: utrum defensio tantum harum provinciarum sit suscipienda an potius dominium (nam alterum eligendi in arbitrio R.M$^{tis}$ futurum est), hinc quae commoditates aut incommoditates ex alterutro expectandae sint iudicium erit Reginae et consiliariorum eius, ut quod tutius et utilius pro sua prudentia iudicaverit, obtineat. Tamen, si mihi conceditur libere quod sentio scribere, vereor ne sola societas et ex foedere denfensio sine dominio (uteraque grata et utilis initio his regionibus erit) damnum tandem utrique adferat quod minime metuendum arbitror si hae provinciae sub eiusdem principis imperio cum Regno Angliae coniuncta fuerint! Rationes quibus moveor ex D. Davidsono t.D. poterit cognoscere. Res hodie Deus sua providentia eo deduxit ut Regina tum se suosque defendendi tum vicinos suos servandi ab hostibus infensissimis rara ac precipua quedam potestas deferatur; t.D. officii ac potius pietatis erit consulere quod ad gloriam nominis Dei et ecclesiae Christi defensionem et R.M^tis etRegni salutem conducturum esse intelligis. Si de tua fide ac pietate dubitarem, pluribus verbis de hac re admonendum esse iudicarem, sed cum omnibus nota sit tua virtus, nihil addam sed ipse Deum rogabo ac observabo ut ad letum et foelicem exitum et ecclesiae utilem dirigere sua clementia hanc legationem dignetur. Vale! Deus te quoque servet incolumem. Lugduno Batavorum 8⁰ die Junii 1585.

Tuae amplitudinis observantissimus
Adrianus Saravia

SP 84/2, fol. 39

# XIV. SARAVIA TO WILLIAM CECIL, LORD BURGHLEY
## Leiden, 9 June 1585

Nobilissimo ac clarissimo Domino Magno Thesauriario Regni
Angliae Domini meo S.

Cum non ingratae olim litterae fuerint, quas Guerzia ad T.A. scribere
ausus fui de rebus parvi momenti si conferantur cum harum provinciarum
negotiis, incommitatos nostros legatos meis litteris hinc abire nolui, spe-
rans fore ut consueta humanitate tua accipiantur. Quod officio meo hactenus defuisse merito videri possum, culpam deprecaci malo quam pluribus
excusare; tantum tuam Amplitudinem scire cupio pudore id factum esse,
et quod meis litteris T.A. interpellandam minime iudicaverim. Nunc autem cum iusta scribendi mihi data videatur occasio, continere me diutius
non debui, ut me fide mea cum erga Regiam Maiestatem et Angliae regnum tum imprimis erga Dei ecclesiam liberem. Itaque audaciam scribendi, humanitate tua fretus qua rebus afflictis religionis nomine populi
semper favisti nec favere desinis, sumpsi; quandoquidem hoc tempore
imprimis tuo favore opus est, eoque magis quod salus et vita Serenissimae
D. nostrae Reginae et regni Angliae incolumitas cum periculo nostro coniuncta videatur. Qui nobis inimici sunt, non sunt vobis amici. Consilia
communium hostium quotidie magis et magis patefiunt et quo spectent
videre potestis; ac ex iis quae moliuntur quid vos expectare debeatis iudicare. Expectandum non est donec perierimus, nam casus harum provinciarum trahet secum ruinam Angliae; si eas servabitis pacem et salutem
vestram firmabitis. Quare necessario cum omnibus qui Evangelium
Christi profitentur est ineundi societas nisi certe perire constitutum sit. Et
quo hae provinciae vobis magis sunt vicinae eo arctius vobis sunt coniun-
genda. Quod duobus modis fieri potest, nempe aut arctissimo foedere societatis aut imperii et dominii earum receptione, quorum postremum tum
tutissimum tum utilissimum utrique est futurum. Nam etsi non sit futura
inutilis societas ipsa in hoc perturbato rerum statu, habebit multas difficul-
tates, qui T.D. a Domino Davidsono malo intelligere quam nunc hic re-
censere; tantum videndae erunt commodae rationes et minime odiosae
quibus in fide contineri poterunt. Duas potissimum examinandas tuae
prudentiae proponam. Prima est usus promiscuus militum Anglorum et
indigenarum in praesidiis, quo suspitio diffidentiae tollatur, ut nullus miles aut praeferri se aut contemni prae alio arbitretur; altera obsidum exhi-
bitio ad plures annos donec firmatum hic erit imperium. Optimatum filii
humaniter accepti in Anglia et saepe permutati reddent tandem parentes
et reliquos omnes vobis addictissimos. Haec ratio nulli invidiae est
obnoxia. Facilis est et minus sumptuosa quam sunt futura Anglorum prae-
sidia aut aliorum militum in locis qui carere milite possunt. Omnis miles
civibus gravis est et molestus; unde Julii Caesaris laudanda prudentia est,

qui acceptis obsidibus urbes et provincias non impositis militibus in fide retinebat. Nota T.D. Historia Xenophontis est περὶ τῆς Κύρου παιδείας et quibus rationibus inductus crediderit, ut eius verba utar, πάντων τῶν ἄλλων ζώων εἶναι ῥᾷον ἢ ἀνθρώπων ἄρχειν. At ubi ei mentem venit, Cyri tot homines, tot urbes, tot gentes non invitas paruisse imperio sententiam mutare coactus est; utpote quod hominibus imperare neque impossibile sit neque factu difficile si quis prudenter id agat. Et certe ita est: nam si quis omnia attentus expendere velit, defectiones populorum et rerum publicarum mutationes inveniet non tam vitio plebis accidisse quam eorum qui Reipublicae presunt, quando potiorem suarum libidinum aut cupiditatum habuerunt rationem quam salutis publicae. Nulla est mortalium societas quae se regi non postulet sibique non praeficiat rectorem. Unde cuivis apparet multitudinem imperium facile pati posse et illud ultro expetere ac imperitia et culpa rectorum accidere, si qua imperii dissolutio accidat; violentiam quae ab hoste externo fit excipio. Quod hanc gentem attinet, facile se patietur regi, modo ei nulla fiat iniuria et eam suis legibus vivere rectores patiantur. Quemadmodum enim ad iniuriam inferendam haec gens tarda est, ita est iniuriae maxime impatiens. Quisquis rector harum provinciarum futurus est leni animo sit oportet; qui clementer huius gentis ferre mores rusticos et agrestes possit facile sic flectet et inducet quolibet. Haec familiariter scribo ac si iam omnia facta et transacta essent. Spero enim divinitus hanc vobis oblatam et servandi nos et confirmandi vos non praeterituros esse occasionem. Quod si facitis, sera vereor ne sequatur poenitentia. Nam postquam nos perierimus vos incolumes permanere non poteritis. Quare ego Deum Optimum Maximum precabor ut menti Regiae Maiestatis et consiliariorum eius inspiret quod utile novit futurum et ut incolumem Amplitudinem tuam servet. Vale, et me in numero clientum tuorum habe. Lugduno Batavorum 9 die Mensis Junii 1585.

Tuae Celsitudinis observantissimus<br>Adrianus Saravia

BL LM 45, Nr. 21, fol. 49
Strype, *Annals*, III; 2, 351-353

## XV. SARAVIA TO WILLIAM DAVISON
### Leiden, 18 June 1585

Clarissimo viro D. Davidsono s[alutem] et gratiam per Christum.

Post tuum discessum ex Hollandia nonnulli ex fratribus ministris scripserunt ad me sibi videri ex usu ecclesiarum Hollandiae et vicinarum provinciarum ad M$^{tem}$ R. se supplices literas mittere, quibus rogetur ut defensionem et patrocinium harum provinciarum suscipere velit. Itaque mihi hanc provinciam mandarunt ut scriptas communi omnium nostrum nomine D.t. mitterem tradendas R.M$^{ti}$. Non sunt ita elegantes nec ita scite scripta ut R.M$^{tis}$ dignitas postulat. Sed oratorem me doctiorem aliquem querere fratribus curae non fuit, aut quia non satis fidebant aliis, aut alii ordinis ipsorum non erant presentes quibus has partes imponerent. Meliorem scribam nancisci non potui; utrumque si quo modo honeste excusari posset mihi valde gratum esset. Fuit deliberatum num aliquos ex suo ordine mitterent ad R. in Angliam sed quomodo nostri ordines id essent interpretaturi cum multi dubitarent, literis crediderunt se officio suo in hac re aliqua ex parte posse satisfacere. Nam nihil omnibus nobis magis in votis est quam sub imperio piissimae et clementissimae Reginae posse vivere. Te igitur, Domine Davidsone, maiorem in modum rogo tum meo tum fratrum meorum nomine has S.M$^{ti}$ litteras tradere velis cum summa testificatione amoris et observantiae nostrae erga suam M$^{tem}$. Si ullum unquam officium vestris postulaveris, invenies nos gratos et memores. Nihil hic novi est quod ad me pervenerit a tuo discessu, nisi quod de Antverpia dubitare incipimus num satis tempore auxilia mitti possint antequam sese dedant hosti. Gens assueta delitiis non feret famem quam haec urbs aliquando pertulit. In manu Dei sunt omnia. Ego Deum precor ut Reginae mentem et animum dare velit servandi se regnumque tuum et nos. Vale! Deus sua misericordia servet te tuosque omnes ab omni malo. Lugduno Batavorum 18 die Junii 1585.

T.D. addictus
Adrianus Saravia

SP 84/2, fol. 43

## XVI. SARAVIA TO JOHN JAMES
### Leiden (between 20 and 23) June 1586

Eximio viro et D. doctori Joanni Jacobo Adrianus Saravia s[alutem].

Nisi mihi cras bis concionandum esset, ego ad Celsitudinem D. Comitis misissem actum ultimum inceptae fabulae, sed quia heri primum mihi exemplar actae est redditum et scriptum est satis prolixum, totum describere et transferre non potui, firmos et constantes esse oportet nec cedere improbitati. In convocatione conventus ministrorum qui Hage est erratum puto in nomine, quia creditur esse nationalis synodus. Die Lunae Hagam ire Deo dante constitui. Inde ad vos transcurram et descriptam actam magistratui a ministris oblatam mecum adferam. D. Vulcanius non est domi; ego libros mecum adferam. Salutat te plurimum Arnoldus le clerc. Vale.

Tuus Adrianus Saravia

Bonus et honestus vir D. Joannes des mestres Domino Cilgreo non ignotus generem habet adhuc Antverpiae qui iam confectis negotiis quae illic habebat huc redire ad uxorem et liberos cupit, ad quam rem cum opus habeat comm̄eatu et gratia Celsitud. D., supplicem eius libellum ad te mitto eiusque nomine te vehementer rogo ut Celsitudini offerre velis, re prius communicata cum D. Cilgreo ex quo cognosces hominem esse dignum cui gratificeris. Iterum vale.

GHL Ms. 7428/7, fol. 1027
Hessels, *ELBA,* II, Nr. 223; III, Nr. 1027

# XVII. SARAVIA AND JEREMIAS BASTINGIUS TO JOHN JAMES
## The Hague, 9 July 1586

S. P. Da veniam, Doctor clarissime, quod tam libere ad T.D. scribo; id enim volunt amici quibus difficile est huiusmodi officia recusare. Qui has ad te affert est Carolus Salomons, civis Antverpianus sed exul cum caeteris piis ob Evangelium; de hac nota mihi et notus est et a caeteris amicis commendatur. Is quum coniugem suam adhuc habeat Antverpiae et tres cum ea liberos cupiret ab Illust. principe commeatum sibi impetrari quo tuto illa ad classem nostram pervenire et inde Amsterodamum se conferre possit. Hic ego consilii et auxilii inops cui potius hanc rem commendarem, quam T.D. cuius bonitas ea est ut exposita quibusvis sit piis, auctoritas tanta cuius intercessione apud Excellent. suam sine ullo negotio hoc officiolum obtineri queat. Quod cum ita sit, quaeso T.D. ut bonum hunc virum prompte iuvare digneris ut nactus coniugem suam et liberos ad familiae suae gubernationem capessendam se utiliter conferre possit, de qua tua humanitate cum nihil dubitem verbum non amplius addam. Vale, Doctor clarissime, et da operam ut quam primum tua praesentia frui liceat. Festinantissime Hagae Comitis in coetu nostro 9 Julii 1586. Stylo novo.

> T.D. observantissimus
> Jeremias Bastingius D. et Verbi minister.
> Adrianus Saravia*

* om. Hessels.

GHL. Ms. 7428/7, fol. 1036
Hessels, *ELBA,* II, Nr. 224; III, Nr. 1036

## XVIII. SARAVIA TO JOHN JAMES
### Leiden, 28 October 1586

Clarissimo viro D.D. Joanni Jacobo Adrianus Saravia S.P.D.

Adolescens qui tibi has literas reddet, meus fuit aliquandiu discipulus; probus est et liberaliter institutus tenet flandricam iuxta ac gallicam linguam; magno usui cuivis nobili viro esse posset. Avunculos habet Taffinos qui huic causae fuere semper addictissimi ex quibus est D. Johannes Taffinus Evangelii minister vir tum pietate tum eruditione insignis; ipsis omnibus ob graves et iustas causas plurimum me debere fateor. Quare ego tibi hunc ingenuum adolescentem exulem et profugum quantum possum commendo ut si quem nosti nobilem qui eius famulatu uti velit et honesto habere loco ut eius conditio postulat te (quod polliceri audeo) nunquam tuae commendationis penitebit nec qui receperit in suam familiam admisisse. Sed quod neque adolescenti vitio verti debet neque mihi fraudi esse patrem eum habere inter hostes te celare nolo. Is cupiditate suas possessiones recuperandi non ita se fortiter gessit in pacificatione Antverpiana ut virum constantem decuit sed quicquid in ea re peccatum est magis diffidentia de rebus nostris factum arbitror quam in ecclesiam Christi malevolentia. Quicquid favoris et benevolentiae ei impenderis tanquam meo nato factum in rationes beneficiorum tuorum referam. Vale 5to Calend. Novembris 1586.

Tui amantissimus qui supra
Adr. Saravia

GHL Ms. 7428/7, fol. 1059
Hessels, *ELBA*, II, Nr. 232; III, Nr. 1059

## XIX. SARAVIA TO LEICESTER
Leiden 5 February 1587

Illustrissimo ac vere pio D.D. Roberto Dudlao Comiti Lecestriae et domino meo Gratiam, Salutem et Pacem a Deo Patre et Domino nostro Jesu Christo precor aeternam.

Nisi certo scirem Celsitudinem tuam fidos habere omnium rerum quae hic aguntur scriptores et nuntios, meo officio in hac re non deessem si quid ad meam perveniret notitiam quod scribi dignum esset; sed quum negotiis Reip. non intersim nec ea cura ad me pertineat, nihil ego intelligere potui cuius certior non fueris factus antequam res ad me permanaret. Quod nunc scribo superfluum quoque videri potest, quum ex hoc generoso qui Tuae Celsitudini has literas tradet intellecturus sis quae hic praeter omnium opinionem novissime acciderunt; sed quanta consternatio omnium animos invaserit ob perfidam deditionem Daventriae, T.C. significari a me iudicavi non inutile, simul quanto desiderio reditus tui omnes boni teneantur qui actum de sua salute putant nisi redieris. Ad haec accedit captivitas legati Regis Daniae qui missus ad Parmensem fertur ut cum eo de pace ageret; quod etsi me non moveat, omnes tamen ad quos is rumor pervenit non parum commoventur, et eo malevoli abutuntur; metuunt boni ne offensus ingratitudine quorundam et gentis moribus egregia tua voluntas et studium erga has provincias et imprimis erga Christi Ecclesiam mutatum sit. Tametsi ego quoque in eo fuerim metu, tamen nota Cels. animi tui constantia et magnitudo me semper consolata est et certam spem facit, non futurum ut rem tam praeclaram et tam feliciter inceptam tua sponte deseras: maior T.C. generositas est quam ut malorum improbitati cedat. Regium est quum benefeceris male audire; quod non eo dico quasi Cels. tua male audiat apud bonos sed quod nemo ita feliciter Remp. administrare possit ut omnibus satisfaciat. Tua aequitas nunquam comittet ut quod pauci peccant mali luant omnes boni qui pro incolumitate Regiae Maiestatis vota facere non cessant ad Deum, ut mentem eius inclinet ad suscipiendum harum provinciarum imperium tuamque Celsitudinem huc quamprimum remittat ad componendam hanc Remp. et defendendam Ecclesiam. Tuam igitur Celsitudinem rogabo ac maiorem in modum iterum atque iterum vehementer obsecrabo ut opus feliciter inceptum perficere digneris a Christo Domino nostro, Rege regum et Domino dominantium aeternam accepturus mercedem cui haud dubie militas, non ut cuiquam noceas sed ut innumeram innoxiorum hominum multitudinem defendas adversus Romanae Tyrannidis rabiem. Nihil addam; Deus tuam Celsitudinem conservet et reducat huc incolumem. Lugduno Batavorum quinto die mensis Februarii MDLXXXVII.

Tuae Celsitudinis observantissimus
Adrianus Saravia

BL CM Galba C XI, fol. 278

## XX. SARAVIA TO JOHN JAMES
### Leiden, 1 September 1587

Salutem tibi precor plurimam et alteras mitto literas quibus intelligas rumorem hic spargi de pacificatione qui, tametsi nihil me conturbat, commoventur tamen multi vehementius idque variis de causis ut quisque affectus est. Solis papistis gratus accidit quibus certe ignosco; suadet religionis aut superstitionis potius suae amor pacificationem expetere quae ipsis libertatem adferet; tametsi nulli sit futura tuta. Persuasum tamen habent nihil ipsis in ea fore periculi, aut si quod provident contemnunt et illud subire malunt quam desiderata privari superstitione. Dulce pacis nomen et gratum bello fessis esse deberet; si in pace nullae laterent insidiae iniquissimam pacem iustissimo bello anteferendam, censet Tullius modo illa nihil habeat insidiarum. Quis credat cum pontificiis certam posse pacem iniri? An non nos docent Gallorum toties iteratae pacificationes et per summam perfidiam in ipso pacis pignore violato federis et omnis societatis civilis ruptum esse vinculum? Cum illis hominibus qui in hoc pestilenti versantur errore quod servanda non sit fides hereticis aut episcopum Romanum tantam habere potestatem ut de votis sacramentis promissis pactis iuratis dispensare possit propter maius bonum nulla possunt constare foedera; quis fidere potest eis qui talem authoritatem agnoscunt et ad eam confugiunt quotidies lubitum erit? Tota Romani epscopi Synagoga et quotquot meretricem illam babilonicam adorant sunt ex illo hominum genere quos D. Paulus ad Rom. pr. cap. dicit ἀσπόνδους sed frustra ut tibi hoc persuadeam verba fundo. Hoc tantum volo nulla foedera cum Romanis aut Romanistis iniri posse; ut Rex maxime servare fidem volet, non servabunt ecclesiastici, non servabit papa qui hoc bello in primis petitur. Vereor ne hoc rumor quoque suspiciones et diffidentiam augeat; bene vertat Deus quicquid est. Si scirem Ex. non offensum iri, a nostris curatoribus dimissionem peterem et me ad hyemandum in Anglia pararem. Si Hollandiae civitates sua Ex. visitaverit, multorum simul et oculos et animos recreabit confirmabitque et populi in primis. Calend. Septemb. 1587 stilo Antichristi.

Tui observantissimus
Adrianus Saravia

GHL Ms. 7428/7, fol. 1089
Hessels, *ELBA*, II, Nr. 237; III, Nr. 1089

## XXI. SARAVIA TO JUSTUS LIPSIUS
### 31 October 1587

De tua in me et in meos voluntate ac studio, D. Lipsi, maximas tibi habeo gratias. Pares me relaturum polliceri non audeo; referam quas potero
si unquam se occasio obtulerit. Sed meam innocentiam in dubium vocari
vehementer doleo propter vitae meae conditionem, quae non tantum a
scelere sed ab omni suspicione sceleris integra esse debet. Hoc tamen me
consolatur quod sum extra culpam, ut pote qui semper callida et turbulen-
ta consilia sum aversatus. Cuius rei Deum, meam conscientiam homines-
que testes citare possum. Quotquot me norunt et familiariter mecum de
rebus nostri temporis locuti sunt, sciunt quae sit mea sententia et quis ani-
mus. Quod Leidense negotiam attinet (cuiusmodi sit in medium relinquo,
ut iudicent quorum interest) Tuam Magnitudinem scire cupio quicquid
ad me quocunque modo pervenit: me significasse S. Ex. cuius in primis
interat et simul quid sentirem. Meminisse potes quid reversus Ultraiecto
tibi dixerim, et quam S.Ex. non probaret consilia quae turbas aut seditionem in civitate excitare possunt. Si scilicet qui fuerunt conatus civium, eos
a sua excellentia repressos fuisse arbitror. Nam quod me attinet, consiliis
civium aut aliorum non interfui, nec conscius literarum quas scripserunt,
nec quae cives missi cum sua Ex. sunt locuti. Haec Magn. tuam scire
volui, quo de mea sit certior innocentia. Si D. Busium fueris adlocutus,
salutem ei meis verbis dicito et S. Ex. desiderare ut ad eum veniat, gratum
ipsius adventum futurum sicut ex literis ad eum datis poterit cognoscere:
ego eas ipse attulissem nisi haec intervenisset calamitas. Vale et me, quod
facis, ama. Pridie Calend. Novembris 1587.

Tuae Mag. observantiss,
Adrianus a Saravia

UBL Codices Lipsiani, Ms. Lip. 4
*Inv. Lipse,* 87 10 31
Burman, *Sylloges,* Nr. 344

## XXII. SARAVIA TO THE PROVINCIAL COUNCIL
## OF HOLLAND, 1588

Aen de Edele ende vermogende Heeren, mijne Heeren den President ende Raden van den Provincialen Rade van Hollandt.

Verthoont in aller ootmoet Doctor Adriaen van Saravia, hoe dat hij binnen seer corte dagen heeft connen becommen copie authenticque uut het Register criminel van Leiden, daer bij hij verwitticht is dat den xiij$^{den}$ Januarij xvclxxxviij lestleden Schepenen der Stadt Leiden op sekere voorgaende clachte, citatie ende indaghinge van Foy van Broechoven, Schout derselver stadt, den Remonstrant ongehoort ende uut pure partijdicheit schandelick gecondemneert hebben gebannen te zijn ende gebannen hebben zijn leven lanc geduerende uut der stede ende uut der vrijheit van Leiden mitsgaders uut Rhijnlandt den Hage ende Hageambacht, op lijfstraffe, met confiscatie van alle zijn goeden. Welcke voorss. clachte citatie ende indaghinge niet alleen en zijn notoirlick onwarachtich onrecht ende ongefondeert, soo de Remonstrant hoopt genouchsaemlic te doen blijcken, maer oock ipso iure egeen nul ende van onweerden. Ten eersten, mits dat die niet gebeurt en zijn voor des Remonstrants competenten Rechter, die ten tijde vanden pretensen delicte Professeur was der Universiteit tot Leiden, ende in die qualiteit, achtervolgende de privilegiën derselver universiteit nergens elders betreckelic in prima instantia dan voor u lieder E. ende also ooc ongehouden geweest te compareren voor den Magistraet van Leiden, soo dat de sententie daer naer gevolcht notoirlick ooc te houden is voor gants nul ende van onweerden. Ten tweeden, alsoo de Remonstrant ten tijde de executie tot Leiden geschiede, om sekere ende gewichtige oorsaecken wesende bij den doorluchtigen grave van Leycester, verstont datmen den Remonstrant in dese saecke vermingelt hadde, ende uut den pardoene gesloten, soo heeft hem de Remonstrant gepresenteert aenden Raet van State die bij zijne Ex$^e$ was, ende sich onder hare protectie gestelt tegen de lagen, die hem aen allen canten waren geleit, sich presenterende te rechte te staen voor alle onpartijdige rechters, ofte voor uwe E., zijne competente rechters. Ten welcken einde bijsondere brieven zijn gheschreven van wegen zijne Ex$^e$ ende den raet van State aenden hoochgeboren grave Maurits ende mijne Heeren de Staten van Hollandt ende Magistraet van Leiden: waerop bij niemant van hen lieden geantwoort en is. Ten derden heeft zijne Ex$^e$ noch daernaer die van Leiden met zijne brieven verboden alle ulterieure procedueren ende hen de kennisse ende macht benomen, ten ware dat zij redenen hadden ter contrarie. Waerop zij ooc noyt gerescribeert en hebben: soo dat hen silentie na rechten te houden is voor bewillinge. Ten vierden het is notoir ende kennelick datter bevel gegeven was aen alle de steden van Hollandt ende Zeelandt, om den Remonstrant ende andere ingedaechde te apprehenderen ende vangen, soo dat hij geen vrij acces gehadt en heeft om te mogen verschijnen. Ten vijfden zijne Ex$^e$ als lieutenant van de Coninginne van Engelant ende

Gouverneur generael van de Vereenichde provinciën, die de macht hadde den Remonstrant te bevelen ende verbieden te doen ofte laten dat behoorlick was, heeft den Remonstrant verboden voor die van Leiden te compareren, ende hem bevolen sich te Utrecht te houden ofte naer Engelant te vertrecken., wiens gebot de Remonstrant (dese xxiiij iaren onderdaen geweest hebbende van hare M$^t$ ende van haer Conincrijcke) was meer gehouden te obediëren dan de indaghinge van Foy van Broechove. Ten sesten, die van Leiden, als verbitterde ende partijdige rechters, hadden een preiudicie ende vooroordel laten wtgaen, hoe dat zij de ingedaechde wilden tracteren, te weten met tortuiren, pijnigen ende andere extraordinaire procederen, ende hun proces in het vangenhuis maecken, sonder in vierschare publijckelick tot eenige verantwoordinge toegelaten te zijn, gelijck het gebleken heeft inde drij geëxecuteerde tegen alle rechten, wetten ofte gebruicken vanden lande. Ten sevensten, het gepubliceerde pardoen is oock een openbaer vooroordeel ende sententie condemnatoire, mits dat daer wt hij Remonstrant met andere eerlicke ende godfruchtige mannen wtgesloten zijn, die in dese saecke ofte gants geen schult en hebben, ofte seer weinich daer van geweten. Eindelic de Remonstrant heeft wel geweten hoe verbitterde vianden van zijne persone zijn die van den Magistraet van Leiden, autheurs van dese tragedie, om sekere acte die hij in Engels hadde overgesonden aen zijne Ex$^e$, volgende zijn bevel. Wt alle welcke redenen ende andere in tijden ende wijle tot zijner innocentie te deduceren, hij Remonstrant hem vindende ten ongelijcke beswaert, ende ooc (mits dat hij Dienaer is des goddelicken Woorts) de Religie gescandaliseert, bidt dat uwe E. hem willen voorsien van behoorlicke remedie van iustitie ende mandamente in cas van appellatie ofte reformatie in amplissima forma tegen de clachte, daghingen ende sententie van die van Leiden met datter na gevolcht is, niet tegenstaende eenige laps van tijde, rechten ofte costuimen ter contrarie. Wt crachte van welcken mandamente tot eenen sekeren competenten dage gedachvaert worde de voorss. Foy van Broechove, om die selve te sustineren, ofte sien ende hooren declareren nul ende van onweerde, ten minsten als abusijf retracteren ende reformeren; ten selven einde ende dage oock intimerende die van de Magistraet van Leiden, ende alle andere over deselve sententie gestaen hebbende in forma, met clausulen van inhibitie ende defensie ende andere in materie van appellatie van noode. Ende om promptelick voorsien te zijn op sulck versoeck, als de Remonstrant ten dage dienende sal willen doen, ende sonderlinge om in dese saecke te mogen occuperen bij procureur voor den Remonstrant, absent wesende in den Conincrijcke van Engelandt, ende aldaer Dienaer des Evangelii, niet tegenstaende voorss. daghinge personele, bannissement tegen hem gedecerneert ende alle andere redenen.

Onder stont geschreven,

Adrian van Saravia,
Dienaer des goddelicken Woorts. –

GAD, Nr. 160
WMV, III; 5, 299-302

## XXIII. SARAVIA TO THE CLASSES OF THE CHURCHES
## OF HOLLAND AND ZEELAND
London, 1 February 1587/88[1]

Genade ende vrede door Jesum Christum onsen Heere.

Eerwerde Godfruchtiche ende vorsichteghe broeders, waeras de welstant der gemeene saecke van alle vergaderinge van mensche sy groote ofte cleene, van steden kercken ende collegien verheescht[a] dat een ider zyn naeme ende fame in haer geheel behoede goet ende onghesconden, so is daer toe elck dies te meer verbonden dat hy eenen eerlicken staet ofte ampt bedient. Daeromme eist[b] dat ick, een leeraer ende Ordinaris Professeur in Theologie der Universiteyt tot Leyden ende daer benevens kerkendinaer wesende, niet en mach onverantwoort met stilswygen laeten voorby gaen de schande die myn ampt ende dienst tonrechte gedaen wert van alle de geene die over het feyt van Leyden ende den pardoen gheseten hebben, maer moet my dies beclaegen aen U.l. ende de waerheyt vande saecke te kennen geven, opdat ghy mocht onderrechte zynde myn onooselheyt vooren staen eer ick tot openbare Apologie come. Want ick geensins en mach met sulcke een cladde mynen dienst laten schenden. Het boecsken van verontschuldinghe onlancx uytgegeven raeckt myn stick[c] niet. Want ick van alles dat daer wert genarrert[d] ben onwetende geweest ende absent wanneer het gebeurt is. Ende hoewel ghy liede geen rechters en zyt in dese saeke, nochtans de kennesse compt u toe, tot mynder straffe uyten Worde Godts indien ick schult hebbe, ofte oock verontschuldinghe daer U.l. de waerheyt van dese saecke zult verstaen; dies te meer dat de gene die my dit onghelick doen sich uytgeven voor Christelicke Magistraten ende voorstanders der kercke Christi. Maer door dien het quaelicken mogelick is recht van een saecke te oordelen dander partye onghehoort, ick en zal hier inne niet anders verhalen dan tgene welck niet en can ontkent worden ende ick met levendeghe getuyghen bewysen mach. Ende waer as ick niet en

---

[1] The letter is addressed to "Den Eerwerden seer wisen ende Godfruchtighen mannen de dienaeren des Goddelicken Wordts in haere classike vergaderinghen Walkere, Dordrecht, Delft, den Hage, Rynlandt ende de andere, int ghemeine ende elkeen bysondere der kercken Christi in Hollandt ende Zeelandt". There is a note at the head: "inden Classe ontvangen den viii martij Lxxxviij". Meant is the classis Walcheren. The copy, referred to in Doc. XXIV, is almost verbatim, but it shows many orthographical corrections. We give the original letter, signed by Saravia. Where his secretary, whose native tongue evidently was not Dutch, used a spelling which might make a word uncomprehensible, the correction according to the Hague copy has been given in a footnote. Words like "waeras" ( = whereas) and other Anglicizations have been copied unaltered.

[a] cop.: vereyst
[b] cop.: ist
[c] cop.: stuck
[d] cop.: genarrert

weet wat aenclachte ofte informatie tegen my daef mach wesen, U.l. zal dat door Christelicke vermaen better moghen verneemen van hen over de welcke ick my beclaeghe. Maer wel wetende dat de loghene ende alles wat versiert is voor de waerheyt moet verdwinnen*, soo zal ick alleenlicke eenvoedelick de waerheyt summierlick hier verhaelen van tgene my hervaren is ende presumeere tot kennesse vanden Magistraet van Leyden door torture gecommen te zyne. Daerna hoe quaelick dat zulck gegrondt is om den naem van eenen predicant ende dienaer Christi opentlick tot schande te bringen ende eyndelick wat ick begheere in dese zaecke van U.l. gedaen te zyne.

Eerst en hebbe ick noch daet noch raet gegeven in het stuck waeromme de drye mannen te Leyden gestorven zyn. Ende hoewel ick te Leyden noch was wanneer twee burgeren tot zyn Ex^ce zyn gereyst, en hebbe noch vande reyse noch vande oorsaecke waeromme zy gereyst waeren niet geweten. Ten anderen: al eer die weder thuys ghekeert zyn ben ick nae Utrecht gevaren tot zyn Ex^ce. Al wat ghevolcht is naer de wedercomste vande Burgheren is ghebuert in myn afwesen zonder myn kennesse ofte weten. Insgelicks vande briefve aen zyn Ex^ce en hebbe ick niet eer kennisse gehadt dan Christianus met andere burgeren t Utrecht ghevlucht zynde my hebben geseyt: dat Jacques Valmaer inde Vangnisse was omdat hy by zyn Ex^ce was geweest ende om dat men eenen brief an zyn Ex^ce ghesonden hadde. Men zal niemanden vinden die oynt met my van dese saeke gesproken heeft ofte ick met hem.

Maer het is dat omtrent den derden ofte vierden Octobris Colonel Cosmo zy tweeder tot mynen huyse is comen om my te groeten ende te vragen ofte ick niet nieuwes en hadde. Waerop ick antwoorde dat ick sdaeghs te vooren gehoort hadde vande Burghemeester Willem Jansz. van Hemskercke dat de heeren Staeten hadden geresolveert in alles S.Ex^ce vol contentement te geeven. Ja (seyde hy daerop), ghelick de Staten plegen: sy gecken met S.Ex^ce; de gemeene saecke en stont noynt ergher dan se nu staet, het en zal niet wel gaen tot dat men drie of viere in dese stadt ende alsoo elders byden halse zal grypen ende noemder drye naemelick Pieter Adriaansz., Jan van Haulte ende Paulus Buys.

Daerop soo seyde ick hem: van Pieter Adriaansz. en weet ick niet te seggen, maer soo vele Paulus Buys ende Jan van Haulte belangt, men soude hen groot ongelick doen. Want Paulus Buis is nu met S.Ex^cie gereconciliert ende is bereit S.Ex^cie goeden dienst te doen als ick verhope dat hy doen zal, ende seyde hem waerinne. Ende van de Secretaris Jan van Haulte hebbe ick onlancx zeer heerlicke proposten gehoort van zyn Ex^cie ende is verre van andere opinie dan ghy meint: hij en dinckt niet alleene noodich dat men S.Ex^cie de authoritheyt die men gegeven heeft zal continueren, maer oock dat het goet ware dat men hem de geheele souveraini-

---

* cop.: verdwijnen

teyt vergave om dat de gemeyne zaecke vergaet by gebreke van Authoriteyt, daer uyt besluytende dat men hem ongelick zoude doen ende S.Ex$^{cie}$ zeer quaeden dienst.

Cosmo persisterende in zyn eerste propost antworde dat zy zoo voor my schoon spraecken maer dat contrarie ghenoech een eyder bekent was dat zy nieuwers naer trachteden dan S.Ex$^{cie}$ uyten lande te doen vertrecken om dat de Staten int regiment mochten blyven ende daeromme meer dan tydt was de principale hoofden byden halse te vatten; met diergelycken proposten meer ongefondeert zonder eenige apparente redene van eenege mogelickheyt om te wercke geleyt te zyne, als ick dochte gesproken meer uyt onverduldicheyt om dat hy gecasseert was dan anders.

Vraechde hem nochtans was laste ofte bevel hy daer toe hadde, wat middel om sulcx te executeren ende wat hy met de gevanghenen soude doen, wat goet ofte nutticheyt hy uyt zulck vangen verwachtede. Op het eerste antwoorde my dat hy niet wiste van wien hy last hadde, gevende genoech te verstaen, al en noemde hy niemanden, dat S.Ex$^{cie}$ hem last soude gegeven hebben. Maer seyde hem daerop dat de Schout ofte Procureur generael daer toe bequaemer waren dan hy, ten ware dat se hem wilden tot haerder hulpe gebruicken. Op het tweede dat ick hem ghevraecht hadde antwoorde hy dat Capiteyn Maulde met zyne knechten ende de Witten schout hem souden bystaen. Twelck ick oock debateerde als gans absurdt. Want, seyde ick, wat zullen de borgheren dincken wanneer ghy in de huysen comen sult met soldaten; zy zullen meynen dat ghy de huysen wilt plunderen. Neen, seyde Cosmo, de burghers selve sullen ons daer toe helpen; wy zullen se neemen t'onser assistencie, ghy ende uwes ghelicke sult die daer toe persuaderen. Ick? (seyde ick) die in alle dese stadt geen vyf burgeren met naeme ende toenaeme en kenne? Ghy zyt quaelicken aen my geraeckt om dat te doene, wilt ghy in sulcke een saeke my ende de burgeren ghebruycken, ghy zyt zeer verdolt. Ghy moest daer toe soldaten hebben te peerde ende te voete, ende u meester vander stadt maeken.

Daerop seyde Cosmo noch eens: hier is Capiteyn Maulde ende de Witte schout, de compaignie van Heraugieres die hier voorby de stadt passeren zal; wy zullense in laeten. Ick antwoorde daerop dat de compaignie van Capiteyn Maulde maer van een tsestich hoofden en was ende zoo vande witte schout, ende insgelyck soo ick dochte de compaignie van Heraugieres, de welcke tsaemen niet vele boven twee hondert mannen maeken souden; wat zal dat helpen om een stadt te overweldighen? Dit is wonder dat S.Ex$^{cie}$ die zyne Engelsche heeft gecasseert ende uyt Delfshaven ende Maeslandtsluys doen gaen u soude sulck bevel gegeven hebben; ick en can dat niet verstaen. In somma: ick en sie niet dat eenich goet hier uyt mach verhopt worden; wy sien dat meer quaets uyt het vangen van Paulus Buys gecommen is dan goets. Allegeerde meer andere inconvenienten, als dat andere steden sulcx zeer quaelick zoude neemen ende dat het eenen grooten stanck soude macken al het landt over; dat ick niet en dochte dat het

Zyn Ex<sup>cie</sup> welneemen zoude, met dierghelicken redenen meer. Eyndelick zoo seyde ick: of het schoon geluckte zoo ghy het hebben wilt, waer wilt ghy henen met uwe gevangenen? Eens seyde hy dat hyse naer Utrecht voeren solde, daer nae datmen S.Ex<sup>cie</sup> zoude ontbieden om in de stadt te comen ende order te stellen. Al welcke redenen ick ten besten my moeghelick was wederleyde, vertogende wat groot quaet daer uyt soude volgen ende gans geen goet. Cosmo anders geen troost van my verwervende nam oorlof ende tsedert en hebbe hem noch gesproken noch gesien. Hieraf zyn levende getuyghen, namelick de Capiteyn die met Cosmo ghecommen was.

Daer nae so is de Capiteyn Mansart tot my gecommen, vraegende wat my dochte vande proposten by Cosmo ghehouden. Ick antwoorde dat het pure mallicheyt ende raserie was, hem vermaenende van zulck voorstel te wachten ende hem daartoe niet te laeten ghebruycken. Gaet, seyde ick, ende beraet u met uwen cosin, myn Heere van Meedkercke.

Maer ick voorquaem hem ende was daer voor hem, ende zoo ick verhaelde wat my Cosmo geseyt hadde, so quaem de Capiteyn Maulde. Myn heere van Meetkerke verwonderende van sulcken proposten seyde ten aenhooren van Capiteyn Maulde dat de meeste viandt die syn Ex<sup>cie</sup> hebbe mochte niet erghers en hadde mogen voorstellen dan dat voornemen was om alle dinghen int verwerre te stellen ende zyn Ex<sup>cie</sup> inden haet te bringen van alle die werelt, vermaenende den Capiteyn Mansart hem daermede niet te moyen. Dit is al dat ick vande zake geweeten hebbe, twelck ick niet secreet en hebbe gehouden noch verswegen, maer gecommuniceert met den Dienaer des Goddelicken woorts die tot mynen huyse te dier tyt thuys lach den welcken dese proposten Cosmi alsoo vremt vielen als my.

Tsanders daechs vroech hoorende dat Cosmo gevangen was, dachte dat daerby al dat hy my geseydt hadde doodt bliven soude. Nochtans hebbende oorsaecke tot S.Ex<sup>cie</sup> te reysen, nam voor my al dat ick ghehoort hadde ·hem aen te geven ende wat my daeraf dochte principaelick van het vangen van Paulus Buys. Twelck ick oock gedaen hebbe, biddende zyn Ex<sup>cie</sup> gheheelicken Paulum Buys weder in deerste vriendtschap te willen ontfangen; dat hy een man was om hem noch goeden dienst te moghen doen, vertoogende dat uyt zyn apprehensie meer quaets dan goets ghevolcht was.

Op het eerste van Cosmo hadde ick voor antwoorde dat hy hem geen sulck last gegeven hadde maer hem soude straffen van zulcke vermetenheyt. Had ick, seyde zyn Ex<sup>cie</sup>, in eenige steden willen garnisoen stellen jegen den danck vande burgheren ofte Staten, ick en soude myn volck niet gecasseert hebben noch uyt Delfshaven ende Maeslandtsluys doen vertrecken. Neen, ick en ben daertoe hier niet comen; die ons ende onse hulpe mogen derven, wy moghen se oock noch beter derven.

Van Paulo Buys belastede my dat ick hem van synen wege wel mochte versekeren van zyn vriendtschap ende goede wille, ende dat t'allen tyden hy soulde willen by hem comen, dat hy hem wellecom soude zyn gelick hy

hem noch by andere daer te voren hadde ontboden. Maer omdat somme-
ge boose geesten die nae dat zy gesint zyn van andere oordelen ofte een
quaede conscientie dragende, meynen datmen met hem ende hun saeken
besich is ende spreckt, zeer quaelick hebben beduyt dat ick somwilen by
zyn Ex$^{ce}$ ben gegaen ende daerinne ongerust zyn geweest, soo verclaer ick
voor God den welcken ick tot getuyge neeme, dat ick tot zyne Ex$^{cie}$ om
geen andere oirsaecke en ben gereist dan om oorlof te hebben om met zyn
goede gratie naer Ingelandt te mogen vertrecken met deerste gelegentheyt.
Ende dat hem soude believen een vande joncste soonen des overleden ou-
den heere van Mansart te voorsien met een prebende om zyn studien te
Leyden oft elders te mogen vervolgen, vreesende dat naer myn vertreck by
gebreeke van middelen hy syn studien soude moeten verlaeten.

Alsoo ick dit vervolchde, so is Mre Christiaen de Wouwere mit noch andere burgheren tot Utrecht gearriveert, vanden welcke ick eerst verstaen
hebbe al dat te Leyden in myn afwesen gebuert was waeraf geheel ontwe-
tende zynde vant zeer vremt dat de magistraet van Leyden soo gestoort
ende ontstelt was om dat ettelicke burgeren by S.Ex$^{cie}$ waren geweest ende aen hem hadden geschreven, dies te meer datse haeren raedt van selfs
hadden verandert. Nopende tgene ick wiste vande proposten die de Colonel Cosmo met my gehauden hadde, zoo veele als ick verstaen conste en
wisten sy gans niet. Ende hoewel dat my sommighen ontrieden tot Leyden
weder te keeren, seggende dat ick den Magistraet oock seer suspect was,
soo en wilde ick de suspitie met myn achter bliven niet meerder maeken
noch besteghen maer in myn goede conscientie wel gerust ende getroost
zynde ben weder nae Leyden gekeert.

Onderweghen in een dorp ghenoemt Burgrave, soo ontmoedede ick de
Capiteyn Maude die my verhalde alles wat te Leyden hem ervaren was,
waerop ick hem niet en antworde maer seyde hem wat ick voor synen
broeder hadde ghedaen ende vercreghen. Te Leyden ghearriveert zynde
op eenen sondach vroech ter poort syde, ben daer vier daghen lange ge-
bleven, myn lessen doende na ghewoente sonder van yemanden vanden
Magistraet ghevraecht oft anghesproken te zyne. Ghedurende welcken
tydt myn Heere de Grave Maurits is te Leyden gecommen ende ben
S.Ex$^{cie}$ gaen groeten ende aenspreken om hem te segghen wat my vande
saeke van Leyden dochte, want ick bevroede dat sommighe vande Magistraeten ende van hunne Dienaers maligneerden ende sochten de Ex$^{cie}$
van myn Heere de Grave van Leycester te achterhaelen in dat stuck om
hem te diffameeren ende by den volcke odieux ende leelick te maeken ende
zoo eenider van zyn gouvernement te vervremden.

Daer naer gehoort hebbende dat Paulus Buys thuys gecomen was, ben
tot hem gegaen, hebbe hem de botscap gedaen die my S.Ex$^{cie}$ gelast hadde, ende met meer worden vermaent tot vreede ende eendracht, al dat ge-
passeert was te vergeten, dat hy d'eerste gewest hadde om d Ingelsche te
roepen, dat wy niet en consten bestaen by ons selven, dat de hulpe ende

bystant vanden Ingelsche seker was ende sonder achterdincken ende daeromme noodich met Zyn Ex<sup>cie</sup> t'accorderen, dat hy de eenige heere was in
Engelandt die onse saeke behertichde; waneer wy hem vervremden soude,
dat wy de Coninginne oock van ons souden vervremden; biddende hem
om Gods wille het credit dat hy hadde met de Grave van Hohenloe te doen
dienen om een vreede te maeken tuschen zyn Ex<sup>cie</sup> ende den selven Grave; dat hy daer nae Gode, de kercke Christi ende den lande eenen uytnee-
mende goeden dienst doen soude. Op alles dat ick hem seyde gaf hy my
vol contentement gelyck oock op alle andere tyden wanneer ick hem yet
hebbe vooregedreghen oft iet begeert tot voorderinge vande studien in
Theologie, hoewel datter noyt yet yut is gevolcht dat ick verhopte.

Onder andere proposten riedt ick hem tot zyn Ex<sup>cie</sup> te willen gaen ende
mit hem te willen spreken ende selve mondelinghe tgene hy my verhaelde
tot zynder verschooninge segghen twelck hy seyde niet te dorven doen om
synen vianden willde die op syne scamp yut waren, voor de welcke hy oorsaeke hadde hem te bevreesen, ten ware dat zyn Ecc<sup>ie</sup> hem met eenen spe-
cialen brief ontboode ende in zyn sauvegarde naeme, hem versekerende
dat hy niet en soude gedooghen hem eenich onghelick gedaen te worden,
dat hem niet lievers en soude commen gescieden dan met zyn Ex<sup>cie</sup> te
spreken ende en twyfelde niet hy en soude hem van alles te volle doen.
Item nopende de Grave van Hoenloe dat hy dies versocht zynde van zyn
Ex<sup>cie</sup> om met zyn genaede te spreken, hoe wel hy niet en conde versekeren
wat hy in de saeke souden mogen verwerven, nochtans wilde gaerne daer
toe arbeyden ende zyn uyterste beste doen het geschil te apointeren ende
sien weder tot vriendtscap ende eenicheyt de twee heeren te brengen.
Waerop ick antwoorde ende seyde dat ick gaerne noch eens tot zyn Ex<sup>cie</sup>
soude gaen ende zoo vele doen waert mogelyck een vriendelicken brief
te vercrygen; naer meer worden ben eyndelick soo van Paulo Buis ge-
scheiden.

Thuys commende hebbe noodich gedocht op dese saeke niet te slapen
uyt vreese dat ick hadde dat Cosmo welcken men seyde ghetortureert geweest te hebben ende vele dingen beleden, dat hy onder andere soude
moghen ghekent hebben dat hy vooren hadde Paulum Buys ende andere
te vangen waer uyt meerder diffidentie ende swaericheyt mochte rysen
dan te vooren zoo ben ick nae den Hage gereyst ende hebbe my beraeden
met myn heere de Raetsheere Kilgrewe. Ben daer een geheelen dach geweest toevende naer eenen wagen om naer Harlem te reysen ende zyn
Ex<sup>cie</sup> gaen vinden in Noort Hollandt; tsanderdaechs ben nae Haerlem ende van daer nae Alcmaer gereyst om aldaer de compste van zyn Ex<sup>cie</sup> te
verwachten die op den selven dach dat ick daer quam arriveerde. De welcke gesproken hebbende ende de oorsaecke van myn compste verhaelt hy
beval datmen an Paulum Buys schriven soude twelck oock gedaen wierdt.

Maer op den dach dat ick meynde weder na Leyden te keeren met de
brieven van zyn Ex<sup>cie</sup> so quaemen de tydingen vande executie tot Leyden

ghedaen ende vande pardoene uyt den welcke ick uytgesloten was als een vande geene die niet alleen mede deelachtich soude geweest hebben, maer een hooft ofte beleyder vander zaecke. Daer naer brieven op brieven ende verschoninge op verschoninge zyn tot my geschreven, dat ick my wel wachten soude van zyn Ex^cie te gaen, dat de Magistraeten van Leyden ende de Staten van Hollandt al omme bevel gegeven hadden om my te doen apprehenderen. Ende hadde zy my te Leyden gehadt, dat se my oock metten anderen souden geexecuteert hebben, ja noch meer wiert my aengedregen dat sy alle so op my verbittert waren dat indien ick quaeme met zyn Ex^cie in eenige plaetse daer zy mochten bevelen, dat zy my uyt zyn camer souden doen haelen; wat de waerheyt is mogen zy beter weten als ick.

Daer naer soo hebben de Curateurs vande Universiteyt tot Leyden mynen naem uyt het ghetal der professeurs doen rasseren ofte uytcladden. Ende worde soo ingedaecht vande Schout om te compareren voor den Magistraet van Leiden op peyne van confiscatie van mynen goederen. De welcke indaghinghe achtervolgende de privilegien vande Universiteyt ontwettelick is gheschiet ende niet voor mynen competenten Rechter. Waer af ick my seer verwonderende hebbe myn clachte aenden raedt van Staten gedaen ende myn onooselheyt vertoocht ende daerop brieven vercregen soo an de Ex^cie vanden Grave Maurits als an de gedeputeerde vanden Staten ende aen dien van Leyden, maer daer en is niet op geantwoordt geweest.

Hier hebdy, seer lieve ende werde Broeders, de nackte waerheyt van alles dat my ervaren is in dese saecke van Leyden, waerop ick niet en behoeve vele redenen te allegeeren tot mynder iustificatie; de saecke selve wyst uyt wat ongelick my hierinne wordt gedaen. Nochtans dit wordeken wil ick daer by vougen, dat alle de gene die my dese 27 jaren hebben gekent ende myn predicatie gehoort ofte met my familierelicken gesproken my sullen moeten getuygenisse geven, dat ick noynt en hebbe tegen Magistraeten, overheyden ofte Staten gesproken of met de gemeyne saeke voor den welcke besich geweest of yet anders oproerlick gedaen of gesproken. Maer dat ick altyts alle geweldige proceduren ende aenslagen quaet gevonden hebbe uytgenomen die tegen den viandt gheschieden by bevele vande overheyt, twelck ick soo niet en wille verstaen hebben al of ick door dit myn gevoelen andere preiudiceren wilde of yemanden beswaeren der genen die men te Leyden geexecuteert of uyt het pardoen geslooten zyn, want de procedure tegen my gehouden is sulck dat ick redene hebbe om suspect te houden al dat in die saeke is gehandelt geweest. Christelicke Magistraten en behooren geen besculdinge te ontfangen tegen eenen ouderling dan onder het getuygenisse van twee soo drie wettighe getuygen. Het bevel die Paulus Timotheo geeft is oock alle Christelicke Magistraeten gegeven; nu weet ick wel voor seker dat sy niet eenen hebben gehadt, nochtans hebben my ongehoort veroordeelt. Want Cosmo die zy voor verraeder hebben geexecuteert en con geen wettighe getuyghe tegen my of eenige ander kerckendienaer wesen om tegen my te procederen als men geprocedeert heeft. Laete vaeren dat Cosmo voor zyn doot beclaecht heeft den ouderlingen die by hem waren om hem te troosten, dat hy tonrechte goede luyden beswaert hadde. De Heeren hebben zeer licht gheacht de eere ende goede fame vander Dienaeren Christi, wanneer zy voor de vianden Gods ende zynder kercke hueren naem in verachtingen hebben ghebracht, waeruyt dat sulcks is spruytende ende waertoe dat het tendeert laete ick u alle bedencken. Dat sommighe ghelyck ick gehoort hebbe my besculdigen om dat ick sulcks als ick van Cosmo hadde gehoort den Magistraet niet aengedient te hebben, Antwoorde daerop benevens dat meer ander alsoo wel as ick de proposten Cosmi wel hebben gheweten ende ghehoort de welcke nochtans uyt den pardoen niet uytghesloten en zyn, dat ick uyt menegherleye consideratien dat niet en behoorde te doene. Eerst het soude geweest hebben teghen een hoogher overicheyt dan die van Leyden waren. Ten tweede de boosheyt van sommige was my al te wel bekent die anders niet en sochten dan oorsaeken om zyn Ex^cie te besculdingen ende te lasteren. Ten derde de diffidentie ende wantrouwe waren zoo groot dat ick my grootelick soude mesgrepen hebben hadde ick duer myn aengeven die grooter ghemaeckt uyt de lichverdige worden van eenen soldaet. Ten vierden het sekerste was aen zyn Ex^cie te gaen, Gouverneur Generael vande lande, twelck ick gedaen hebbe. Ten vyfden siende dat Cosmo gevangen was ick en hadde geen oorsaeke meer te vreesen dat hy soude doen tgene ick van hem gehoort hadde. Ten stont my oock niet toe (indien zyn Ex^cie sulck last Cosmo gegeven hadde) te oordelen of hy redene ende oorsaeke hadde soldaten in de stadt te doen comen om hem vande stadt te versekeren, ende daer toe Cosmo zulck last soude gegeven hebben, ick en hadde voor zyn Ex^cie noch niemanden connen verantwoorden; indien ick zynen raet ofte secret kende my vertaut te hebben gheopenbaert. Het vangen van drie ofte vier burgheren by bevele van zyn Ex^cie en mochte van my voor geen verraderie gehouden wesen.

Datmen insereert dat zy souden de stadt gheplundert hebben ende datter groote moort ende blootstortinghe soude gevolcht zyn, en is maer een onsekere collectie, want wy hebben voorgaende exemplen vele ter contrarie datmen al treffelycker persoonen gevangen heeft dan Pieter Adriansz ende Jan van Houte zyn, ende nochtans daer en is noch oproer noch geen bloetstortinge gevolcht als het vangen is geweest vande raedt van Staeten te Bruyssel ende vande Staeten te Ghent ende noch meer andere; daeromme sulcke gaderinge oft van sulcke gevolchden ofte consequentien en sluyten niet daer de herten niet gepassiet en zyn; derhalven segge dat ick my gequeten hebbe als ick schuldich was tegen die daer ick behoorde.

Nu is myn Christelick versoeck ende begeerte aen u.l. dat u believe de gedeputeerde vande Staeten van Hollandt mitsgaeders de Curateurs vande Universiteyt ende de Magistraet van Leyden te willen vermaenen, my myn name ende fame (meer geinteresseert dan ick lyden mach) weder te geven ende my wederomme te stellen in myn geheel gelick ick was voor de maent van Octobris met alle de costen ende schaeden die ick uyt dier oorsaeke hebbe geleden. Of anders ick zal gedwongen zyn myn clachte opentlick te.doene voor Godt ende de menschen. Waertoe nochtans ick niet gaerne en come om den gemeyne vreede wille ende onse gemeyne vianden die sich van onse tweedrachte ende oneenicheden verbliden. Maer wat soude ick doen; zal ick, een dienaar Christi zynde, gedoogen met stille swigen dat mynen naem onder de viande der waerheyt die so vele zyn sal met verraderie besmet bliven? Teghen die over dese saeke gheseten hebben in proces te treden en is my niet ghelegen noch gheraeden; zy connen in dien het hun belieft licht tot kennesse commen van myn onnooselheyt ende huer eyghen rechters wesen in het gene zy nopende mynen persoon hebben verabuseert geweest. Daeromme soo eyst dat ick u.l. ernstelicke wederomme soo vele als het my mogelick is inden naeme des Heeren bidde, soo vele te doene dat de eere myns dienst in haer geheel ghestelt werde; twelck doende so zullen u.l. Gode ende de kercke Christi eenen aengenaemen dienst doen ende mynen persoon tot uwen dienst grootelicks verbinden. Ende zo hier een eynde makende,

Eerwerde, Godvruchteghe ende zeer wise broeders, bevele uwer alle L. de genade des Almoghende Gods dat hy u en uwen dienst in alles wil segghenen. Uyt Londen den xxii Januarii 1588 stilo veteri.

By uwer alle seer dienstwilleghe vriendt ende medebroeder

Adrian van Saravia

Amsterdam, Library of the Free University, Department of Manuscripts, Bos Collection, provisional catalogue, Nr. 63.

The Hague, Archives Synod Netherlands Reformed Church, Ancient Archives, Nr. I, 20 (copy).

## XXIV. SARAVIA TO THE CHURCHES OF SOUTH-HOLLAND
### London, 1 February 1587/88[1]

Copije

Ghenade ende vrede dor Jesum Christum onsen Heere.

Eersame, werde ende lieve broeders. Ick sende aen alle de classen desen ingesloten brief bij den welcken ick van alle de broeders versoecke de eere mijns dienstes te willen voorenstaen in alle billickheijt tegen de valsche calumnie van het feijt van Leyden in het welcke ick ingetrocken ben ende t'onrechte mede beswaert sonder eenighe mijne schult, als U.l.wt den brief beter sullen verstaen. Het en is op mij niet alleen dat de vianden Godes ende Zijner Kercke ghebeten zijn, maer U alle in het ghemeijne, anders niet soeckende dan de kerckendienaers ende heuren dienst stinckende te maken voor den volcke op datse geen credijt en souden hebben, gelijck U.l. niet alleen hier wt, maer oock wt meer andere acten mocht speuren als wt de resolutie der Staten op U.l. vertoech ghenomen ende in printe tlandt deurgestroijt. Indien U.l. dat so laet vorbij gaen, de Heere is rechtveerdich die het oordelen sal. Ick soude een volle apologije hebben laten wtgaen, maer het is mij als noch ontraden ende goet gevonden eerst desen middel te beproeven. Ick schrijve insghelijcken aenden Heeren Staten van Hollandt ten selven fijne om geheel gerestitueert te zyn, twelck vercrijgende wille ten aensien vande ghemeyne vrede d'apologije laten varen. Anders niet en hebbende, seer lieve ende werde broeders, so bevele ick U.l. de ghenade des almachtigen Gods, hem biddende U ende uwen arbeydt te willen seghenen. Wt Londen desen XXVen Januarij 1588 stilo veteri.

Onderstondt Uwer E. dienstwillige vriendt ende medebroeder Adriaen van Saravia. D'opschrift was: Den Eersamen Godtvruchtigen ende seer wijsen heren Hendrick de Corput, Casparus Swerinckhusen, Arnold Cornelij, Libertus Fraxinus dienars des Godlicken Woorts ende een ieder van hen ter plaetsen daer sij zijn residerende Dordrecht, Rotterdam, Delft ende Sgravenhaghe.

[1] On the outside of the letter is written: "Brief D. Adriani Saraviae wt Engelant geschreven, ande kercken van Zuydthollant: tot sijnder defentie in de sake van Leyden. Anno 1588 den 25en Januari".

The Hague, Synod Netherlands Reformed Church, Ancient Archives Nr. I, 20. Record Office.

## XXV. SARAVIA TO FRANCISCUS RAPHELENGIUS
### London, 2 February 1587/88

Grace et Paix par nostre Seigneur Jesu Christ.

Mons$^r$ Raffelin, mon bien bon amy, je vous remercie de lassistance que vous et voz gens ont fait a mon filz, vous asseurant que la ou semblablement je vous pourai faire plaisir ou servir, vous me trouverez prest. Car combien que je voudroye que mes gens eusent laissé faire a Mess$^{rs}$ de Leide ce qu'il leur eut pleu de mes biens, jestime le plaisir de laffection de laquelle il est procedé et non pour suivant ce que je desire avoir este fait; car jespere avec le temps que jaurai la raison du grand tort qu'on ma fait. Quant a ce que je vous doibs, vous recevrez quelque partie du S$^r$ Jan des Mestres et la reste quant mon filz viendra par dela pour aller en Allemagne. Au reste les Theologiens de par deca voir monsieur larchevesque de Cantuerbury voudroyent bien que la bible hebraique avec lexposition interlineaire de Pagnini telle comme elle est avec la grande bible fut imprimee in quarto. Vous en pouriez vendre ici bien 7 ou 8 cent exemplaires; et ce que je vous en ecris est a la requeste du H$^t$ S$^r$ archevesque. N'ayant pour le present autre chose je prierai Dieu de vous avoir en sa garde et benir en toute chose. De Londre ce 23 de janvier 1588 stilo veteri.

Vostre serviable amy
Adrien de Saravia

Royal Library Munich. Cod. Monacensis lat. 10359, fol. 44

## XXVI. SARAVIA TO JUSTUS LIPSIUS
### London, 5 February 1587/88

D. Justo Lipsio Magnifico Rectori Academiae Leidensis, Adrianus Saravia S.D. Leidam

Tametsi, humanissime Lipsi, mihi iucundius esset quam ad te literas dare et vicissim a te accipere, me a scribendo deterret ea quae tibi intercedit cum hominibus mihi infestissimis consuetudo; qui illi sint a te intelligi quam a me nominari malo. De iniuria quae mihi facta est, nihil scribam. Innocentia mea eos latet, qui excaecati odio ita esse rem volunt ut ipsi cupiunt. Sed ego me comprimam; hoc tantum T.D. significatum volo, odium malorum mihi hîc conciliasse amorem bonorem quibus, si huc te venire contigerit, tuus adventus futurus est gratissimus. Scripta tua legunt, admirantur; ingenium coram videre et alloqui si dederis, beabis. Tuam sortem deplorant, te inter eos vivere quos tua familiaritate iudicant indignissimos; a quibus non aliam mercedem te reportaturum arbitrantur quam ego accepi. De D.D. Donello nihil dico, in illum fuere ingrati, sed in me impii; ut meliorem mentem ipsis det Deus, precor. Nihil gravius in eos commisi; ne faciam, in ipsorum adhuc est potestate. Ad te redeo tibique gratias immortales habeo habeboque dum vivam pro singulari tua in me meosque pietate. Me amare perge, et ego te redamare non desinam. Vale. Londino 7 Calend Februarii 1588 stilo veteri.

Plurimam salutem dici meo nomine
opto collegis omnibus et bono
seni d. Nansio[1]

Tuus qui supra
Adrianus a Saravia

---

[1] On him: *NNBW*, III, 902 f.

UBL Codices Lipsiani, Ms. Lip. 4
*Inv. Lipse,* 88 01 26
Burman, *Sylloges,* Nr. 345

## XXVII. JUSTUS LIPSIUS TO SARAVIA
### Leiden, 23 March 1587/88

J. Lipsius Adriano Saraviae Viro Reverendo Salutem Dicit. Certe mihi iucundum fuit litteras tuas et in iis te regustare ex intervallo. Iamdiu cur siluisti? Scire debes me tui et fuisse et esse, ex quo semel te novi peramantem. Collegae fuimus, iuncti sermonibus saepe et consiliis; et ut ut illa nunc non sint (Deo visum aliter), manebimus tamen iuncti animo, optima illa parte nostri. Dissident quidem a te, qui mihi assident. Nihil ad rem. Amare et iudicare possum; *nec probo sane omnia quae fero.* Natura mitis et lenis sum, ut nosti, *nec facile me oppono, praesertim sine spe ulla profectus.* Me et mea quantum possum compono et curo: publica fateor me numquam tangere nisi invitus. Perpetuum hic mihi iudicium est, nec facile ulla Suada aut Sophia eripient mihi hunc errorem. Stoicos illos, quos saepe miror, scio hac in parte esse alios: qui in rem eunt et, ut poëta ait, civilibus undis fortiter se mersant. Sed mihi ingenium meum dictat aliud, et inprimis valitudo, quorum neutrum suadet mihi trahere hoc iugum. Itaque privatim amicus esse didici et fidus amicus; iuvare patriam aut rempublicam animo et voto possum, vix consilio aut facto. Quod autem in ea loca me invitas, agnosco amorem tuum et honesta simul iudicia de me eius gentis, quam ego amare et aestimare semper pro me tuli, semper pro me feram. Quod si Deus vitam aut vim mihi ad menses ailiquot largietur, spondeo audacter, visurum me pulcherrimam et cultissimam eam oram atque una te, quem Deum eundem precor uti ecclesiae suae servet. Vale vir amice. Leidae X Kal. April. MDLXXXVIII.

Tuus J. Lipsius

Salutem dici a me praecipio D. Praesidi
Mekercko ad quem nuper scripsi, D. Doctori James,
D. Hotomanno.

BodL MS Auct. D. 1.14, fol. 19r (copy)
*Inv. Lipse,* 88 03 23 S.

## XXVIII. SARAVIA TO ARENT CORNELISZ
### Tatenhill, 20 July 1588

Genade ende vrede door Jesum Christum onsen Heere.

Eersame ende seer beminde broeder, ick hebbe uw brief ontfanghen vanden 28 Maij die met ons den 18$^{ten}$ is ende dat de 9 July ofte 19 met U.l., waeraf ick U.l. hertelick seer bedancke als ick ooc doe alle de broederen die om mynentwille eenighen arbeit ende moyete hebben ghehadt, hoewel datter als noch niet en is ghevolcht tgene verhopte. Ick ben met hun goede wille ende gunste te vreden ende en vinde niet quaet dat se de bequaemicheyt des tydts waernemen. Want ick oock het selve doe om myn Apologie te laeten uytgaen ofte myn clachte aen hare M$^{teyt}$ ende haren edelen raedt te doene. Want ick een van beide doen moet indien my gheen recht geschiet van myn heeren de Staten. Dat de lust om my te wreken so groot ware als het onghelick twelck my is ghedaen verdient, ick en soude tot nu toe niet hebben ghesweghen. Want my gheen stoffe en ontbreckt om den Godeloosen ter deghen het hooft te wasschen, ick ten laetsten ghecreghen het proces autentiquelick ghecopieert uyt den Registerboeck van Leiden hebbe also extracten uyt den consistorieboeck der kercke tot myne verantwoordinghe dienende, *maer my ontbreckt het accordt ofte protest van ge-lickformicheyt der kercke tot Leide met andere kercken.* Waeraf in dien U.l. my een copie wilde senden my groote vrundschap sult doen. Dat U.l. my schryft van Villerus dat hy my vriendt is en can ick niet ghelooven maer ick hebbe hem een getrauwe vrindt gheweest ende hem verantwordt voor alle menschen groot ende cleyne soo verre dat S.Ex. quade opinie van my creegh om dat ick hem so seere toe stont. Of hy my de selve ghetrauwicheyt heeft bewesen dat weet God ende syn conscientie. Ick en hebbe van hem geen brieven ontfanghen als ick ooc an hem niet en hebbe gheschreven; hoewel hy U heeft belooft an my te schriven hy en meenet niet, hy en is de man niet die kerckelicke saeken seer voorderen zal ofte syne vrienden in den noodt bijstaen. D. Cassenbrotum hebb'ick altidt ghehouden voor een from heere ende het is my seer leet dat ick met hem als hy te Londen was niet en hebbe connen spreken door dien dat ick in een nootsakelicke reyse was ter plaetse daer ick nu ben resideerende om die te siene ende in possessie ghestelt te worden. Ick hopte noch in tydts ghecommen te zyne om hem te spreken maer hy was smorghens vroech van Londen vertrocken als savonts quam. Ick hebbe over twee maende an hem gheschreven ghlyck ic oock doe an Myn heere de President vander Mylen. Nopende hun advis van provisie begeert te hebben vanden hove, het en soude my niet meer gheholpen hebben dan de brieven van S.Ex$^{cie}$ by de welcke hy die van Leide alle ulterieure procedure heeft verboden; dat sy oock gheraeden vinden dat de broeders hun metter saeke niet zullen bemoyen laet ick uwen ordeele ende discretie. Alleenlick segghe dit dat kennende het groot onghelick my is ghedaen ende dat in een vry volck het dissmiluleeren sonder schaet ende wesen can. Ten is my niet onbekent hoe weinick credits de kercke dienaers hebben onder de heeren Staten, maer het en zal door U.l. stille swygen niet meerder werden. Want onder andere consideratien om de kerckendienars stincpende te maeken ende al credit te benemen ende een vreese an te jagen is dit ongheluck my ghedaen. So vele mynen persoon belanght, in portu navigo. Maer siet toe dat tgene an my is begonnen met U.l. niet voorts en gae. Istic impios ecclesiis insidiari certum est; episcoporum et videntium opus est vigilantia; non tam mea quam vestra res agitur. Molitiones et conatus impiorum nulla re facilius retundetis quam si fueritis ita coniuncti ut uni facta iniuria omnium censeatur. Ick sende an den Engelandsche Synodo myn verantwordinghe op den heesch ende clachte by Foy van Broechove teghen my ghedaen, insisterende dat de broederen believe so vele voor my te doene ende voor hun selven als an de Staten myn restitutie te voorderen tgene dat U.l. vreest, te weten de Staten te doen verstaen dat ghylieden allen u myn saeke antreckt is tgene dat u tegen sulcke ongheluck versekeren zal. In dien zy verstaen dat ghy u bevreest uwen broeder in syn gherechticheyt to te staen ende te verantworden, ghy zult alderhande calumnien tallen tyde onderworpen zyn; stantfasticheyt ende getrauwicheyt in uwen dienst crimen dat. Ick begeere alleenlick dit te weten of oock de heeren Staten myn partie zyn, dat is te zeggen of H.E. de procedure ende vonnisse van die van Leiden approberen ende voor goedt houden. Waert saeke dat de Magistraet van Leide ofte de heere Staten sich vande religie niet en roemden, ick en soude op all het gene teghen my is ghedaen niet passen. Maer anghesien dat vianden der religie onder de mantel van de religie willen schulen, reden het is dat hare gheveynstheyt ondeckt worde, dat de werelt erkennen mach wat dat sy zyn. Ick hope dat hier uyt noch groot goet voor de kerckke commen zal. En vreest niet dat ick my overrasschen zal. Sat cito si sat bene. U.E. mach de broeders daeraf versekeren. Want dat ick voor my ghenomen hebbe is to stichtinghe vande kercke ende welvaert vande lande; het sij verre van my dat ick my soude soeken te wreken met achterdeele vande gemeene saeke. Eyndelick U.l. seche noch eens dat D. Vilerus an my schriven zal; ick zalt ghelooven als ick synen brief zal sien maer niet eer. End so, Eerwerde ende seer lieve broeder, ick bevele u ende alle de broeders uwe mededienaers de genaede des Heeren. Uyt Tattenhill in Staffortsher desen 10 Julij stilo veteri 1588.

> Uwe dienstwilleghe broeder
> ende vriendt Adrian de Saravia

GAD, Nr. 112

## XXIX. PIERRE LOYSELEUR DE VILLIERS TO SARAVIA
### The Hague, 2 September 1588

Mons<sup>r</sup>, J'ai entendu par Messieurs Arnoldus et Corputius que vous n'aviez pas receu une lettre que ie vous ai envoiée par un Anglois. Puis qu'ainsi est, ie repeterai ce que ie disoi, et escrirai encores plus amplement, ores que voici la quatriesme sepmaine que le lict me tient malade. Lesdits sieurs m' ont communiqué ce que vous requerez d'eux. Surquoi ie vous prie de considerer, que le meilleur que vous puissiés obtenir des Messieurs les Estats ce sera qu'ils vous feront ouverture de iustice et vous accorderont passe port pour venir, a condition de vous laisser libre, si vous estes innocent, autrement que subirés le iugement, tel qu'il sera donné. Or in quacunque causa eventus iudiciorum sunt dubij: mais en votre fait y a à considerer, premierement que vous avez parlé et écrit au deshonneur des Estats comme en la lettre de Mons<sup>r</sup> de Villers, ou vous approuvez la paix, que vous scavez leur estre tant a contrecoeur, et improuvez leur guerre. Je ne dispute point, si vous avez raison, ou non (vous scavez mon opinion), mais cela vous pourra estre obiecté, ce qui est le moins. En la requeste que vous avez presentée, vous confessez avoir oui parler du fait de Leiden. Ils vous obiecteront, que comme citoien et professeur vous en debuiez advertir le Magistrat du lieu, et que culpa omissionis, ubi de salute civitatis agitur, crimen est. Vous respondés que vous en avez adverti le Seigneur, Conte de Leicestre, superieur Magistrat: ils vous respondront qu'il ne suffit, d'autant que vous ne pouviez ignorer que lors les villes estoient en deffiance dudit Seigneur, à raison de la paix qu'il poursuivoit, et autres raisons, et mesmes qu'on auoit communiqué aux trois consaulx des instructions secretes, qu'on disoit tendre a telles entreprinses, lesquelles quant a moi ie n'ai point veues, mais ie vous di ce qu'on vous obiectera, et qui est le pis, c'est que ledit S<sup>r</sup> Conte a protesté avecq serment solennel en diverses villes et devant divers colleges que iamais il n'en avoit oui parler, ce que sa Maiesté en sa presence à confirmé a nos Ambassadeurs, de quoi ils ont fait raport. Cela estant, non solum excidis probatione, sed etiam alterius criminis, notabene quod viro principi iniuriam feceris. Je ne scai aussi si vous scavés la deposition du S<sup>r</sup> de Maulde, je ne l'ai point veue, mais on m'a asseuré qu'il dit vous en auoir parlé, que vous lui avez desconseillé, parce qu'il n'estoit pas assez fort, d'ont on inferera que vous l'eussiez conseillé, s'il eust esté fort assez de le faire. Je vous represente ce qu'on vous peut obiecter, et de remettre telles choses au iugement des hommes est par trop douteux, tesmoin celui qui disoit, que scai je si ma mere metteroit une febue noire pour une blanche? Ce neantmoins ie scai bien, si vous n'aviez bonnes defenses, que le Procureur Général obtiendroit en cause contre vous sur ces precedentes allegrations. Pour ces raisons et ne sachant que pourriez respondre, j'ai desconseillé qu'ils presentassent votre requeste, et mesmes que le style de la Cour veult que la

partie ou un procureur en Cour presentera les requestes, quanto minus
Dei Ministri. Car ce que vous dites qu'ils doiuent prendre votre cause, les
magistrats diront qu'ils doiuent prendre la leur, et que semper est praesu-
mendum pro sententia, donec contrarium manifeste appareat. Pour la
mesme raison ie leur ai desconseillé de porter votre escrit au Synode, car il
estoit ouvert. Mais quant aux lettres closes, je leur ai donnè conseil de les
porter. Habere ii debent rationem ministerij sui, non minus quam ipse
tui, et vous scavés que les Magistrats pourroient les accuser. Je vous man-
de ces choses simplement, afin que vous y pensiez bien, et le prenez de celui a qui a l'affection vers vous semblable, qu'il a eue tousjours et qui n'a
manqué en rien. Quant à une défense, que vous dites vouloir mettre en lumiere: je pense que la lumiere de prudence n'est pas esteinte en votre
esprit, et qu'il ne vous souuiene des propos, que nous auons eus ensemble de tels escrits, tant y a qu'il n'en arrivera que du mal et pour vous
principallement. Car si vous avez bonne cause, vous trouuerez un fol qui
vous entendra, et si vous avez tort, un sage: et de leur response vour re-
ceuurez double offense. Vint ou trente liront votre defense, qui seront en
danger, et mille liront la cause sans danger. En outre considerez que les affaires de l'estat d'Angleterre est tel, que la conionction de la Hollande lui
est tres utile, et ne vous appuiez point sur une personne, iuxta illud: vanum est etc. Je vous prie prendre de bonne part mon advis, car ie ne vous
puis celer ce que ie crains qui vous peut nuire. On m'a vouln faire croire et
avec le danger de ma vie, que j'estois consentant et conseillant au fait de
Leiden, combien que ie fusse en Zelande, et n'en ouï iamais nouvelle, que
ce ne fust fait. Je voudroi pour l'amour de vous que j'eusse esté plus prest.
Dieu vueille pardonner a ceux, qui ont cerché mon ame, je leur ai rendu le
bien pour le mal, et me garderai bien, Dieu aidant, qu'a l'occasion d'un
ver de terre les gens de bien reçoivent aucun desplaisir. Je vous prie pour
la fin, de vous souuenir de celui du quel la voix n'a point esté ouie ... Je
me recommande a vous, a vostre femme et a vostre fils, et que Dieu
Mons$^r$ vous, (veuille) auoir en sa garde. A la Haie en mon lict, ce 2$^{de}$
Septembre 1588.

                                    Vostre frere ami et serviteur
                                    Villiers.

## XXX. ARENT CORNELISZ. TO SARAVIA
### Delft, 14 September 1588

Gratia et pax a Domino.

Tuae ad me litterae, observande frater ac Symmysta, x Julii datae, xxix demum Augusti redditae mihi sunt, quibus coniunctus erat fasciculus, quem Corputius et ego aperuimus, lectoque tuo libello ad Consiliarios curiae Hollandiae et epistola ad Synodum, expedire judicavimus ante omnia cum Praeside Milio communicare. Diximus ei habere nos abs te litteras ad ipsum et collegas, simul ad Com. Mauritium; quae tua esset petitio, haud dubie ipsum scire ex iis quae privatim ei scripsisses; quum autem nobis apertum misisses libellum, una cum epistola aperta Synodo exhibenda, venisse nos ad eum, ut quae ipsius esset sententia et quod consilium cognosceremus. Depromptas tum ille quas a te habebat litteras nobis praelegit; quum tua causa ad cognitionem ipsius ventura esset, se nulla personae acceptione iudicaturum promittit; de cetero quum iudex sit futurus, consilium se nobis dare posse negat. Exponimus ei in quibus difficultatibus versaremur; si Ministri nomine tuo libellum exhibeant et pro te intercedant, periculum esse ne in nescio quas suspiciones et reprehensiones politicorum incedant; sin autem in tua causa nihil faciant, merito reprehendi posse, quod amicum et fratrem deserant et apologiam tam abs te prodituram quam praevenire praestaret. Ille vero quum persisteret, Villerium adiimus; quod ego quidem eo lubentius feci, ut hac occasione neglecti officii eum monerem. Dicit ille se ad te dedisse litteras per Anglum quendam; me monente et rogante iterum se scripturum spondet; super proposita deliberatione multo sermone demonstrare conatur, nec tibi tutum fore causam tuam iudicio Curiae committere et te hic sistere (quod omnino faciendum esset), nec Ministris apertam tuam epistolam recipere vel libellum supplicem exhibere, qui a procuratore tuo esset exhibendus; esse itaque quam consultissimum ut scripta ista tibi remitterentur et tu paulo penitius rem totam inspiceres; se hoc ipsum tibi significaturum. Haec causa est cur quae ad Synodum scripsisti una cum libello tuo supplice tibi iam remittamus, quibus esse adiunctas vides litteras Villerii, id ipsum complexas, quod nobis coram exposuit; quas cupimus te expendere atque id quod in rem tuam maxime practicum est maturo iudicio praestare. Ampla in illis datur tibi occasio monendi Villerium, si qua in parte amici eum officio defuisse existimas, quod ipse negat; in primis scopulos videbis, qui tibi erunt vitandi. Haud tamen contenti iudicio Villerii, de eo quod a nobis requiris consuluimus advocatum quemdam bonum et profitentem religionem, qui respondit omnibus in eandem sententiam cum Villerio: per procuratorem potius istum libellum exhibendum esse, qui procurator institutam causam persequi posset, id quod Ministris non conveniret. Sed vide quid nobis videatur in tuo illo scripto omittendum. Dicis in tres illos de quibus Leidae supplicium est sumptum, peractum esse contra omnia iura, leges et consuetudines patriae. Sic autem mirifice superiores offendis, et plus tibi probandum sumis quam sit necessum et quam tua causa requirat. Alterum est quod de scripto in Anglicum sermonem abs te translato dicis, quod ipsum etiam non videtur necessarium poni in tali libello quo postulas audiri et sententiam latam rescindi. Plura nam sunt iniqui quod in te conceperant Leidenses argumenta.

Si itaque causam tuam in manus a nobis sumi velis, saltem vide an non ista duo sint omittenda. Sed hoc quoque expendendum videtur. Quantumvis tibi concedatur ut absens per procuratorem causam tuam agas, hoc incommodi metuendum est, ut lis tua in immensum tempus protrahatur et interiectione levissimarum scrupulosarum fortasse oblivione tandem sepeliatur, qualiter evenisse videmus Nicol. Dammio, qui pulsus civitate Leidensi frustra litem adversus eam instituit. Scribis te hoc unum scire cupere an Ordines tui sint adversarii et sententiae Leidensium approbatores. Atqui cognoscere nostro iudicio hoc potuisti ex eo quod diserte scribitur illam esse pronuntiatam ''met advys vanden Staten'', praesentibus Joh. Dousa et Petro Merano, nomine Ordinum. Certum tamen est non omnium civitatum Magistratus in supplicium illud Leidense (cui consentanea est sententia adversum vos lata) consensisse. Nos autem Ministros etsi certum est illam rationem agendi non comprobare, nisi de rectitudine omne constet, ita tu nequaquam opinor a nobis exiges, ut tuam causam defendendam suscipiamus, quae qualis sit nondum satis liquet. Praestat itaque hic suspendere iudicium. Interea quidquid sit, minime certe dubitare nos profitemur de tua integritate, fide et bonitate; si quid abs te est peractum, imprudentia esse peractum non malitia. Negare etiam nolumus, quin odium quorundam privatim adversus tuam personam atque adeo Ecclesiam Dei hanc tibi contumeliam fecerit. Meminimus Hieron. Hortensio parcitum fuisse, quum ille convictus teneretur quod audisset lectionem libelli Cornelii de Hooge, neque indicasset. Nisi odium obstitisset, poterant etiam tibi parcere in leviore delicto (ut demus te deliquisse) propter honorem ministerii. At tamen si placuit magistratibus stricto iure tecum agere, neque conivere ad quidquam eius, quod adversus salutem patriae abs te commissum omissumve statuunt, hoc simpliciter a nobis accusari et te quasi innoxium in ista re defendere velle, temeritatis videretur. Quocirca quod hactenus nihil aliud in tua re praestare potuimus, ne timiditati vel negligentiae in defendendo amico, vel oscitantiae in propugnando nomine ecclesiastico tribuas, sed prudentiae, quae temporum et opportunitatum momenta moretur. Ad Apologiam, de qua item scribis, quod attinet, cupimus te providere, ne plus publice noceas, quam tibi privatim prosis. Digni quidem sunt irreligiosi hi Magistratus qui patiantur id quod tu meditaris; sed vide an tu dignus qui facias, et eorum ulceram coram omnibus detegas. Vitandum ne ista ratione etiam peius Ecclesiae nostrae habeant. Denique quod petis ut tibi curem exemplar protestationis de conformitate Ecclesiae Leidensis cum reliquis, egi de illo cum Ministro Classis Leidensis ante 10 dies, qui dicebat se nescire an exstet adhuc liber in Consistorio Leidensi qui illam protestationem contineret; quaesiturum tamen se, et si inveniret, mihi missurum exemplar. Ubi accepero mittam Datum Delfis, 14 Sept.

T. Arnoldus.

Ad Saraviam.

GAD, Nr. 160
*WMV*, III; 5, 262-265

## XXXI. SARAVIA TO SIR AMYAS PAULET
### Tatenhill, 20 September 1588

Grace et paix par nostre Seigneur Jesus Christ.

Monsieur,

La bonne et singuliere affection que de vostre grace il vous a pleut me tousiours monstrer depuis le temps que m'avez premierement cognu, me donne la hardiesse de vous escrire la presente, en quoy ie resemble au mauvais crediteurs lesquels n'estant point suffisans de s'acquitter de leur vieilles debtes, ne laissent point pourtant d'accroire davantage et en faire des nouvelles. Ainsi est il de moy la ou ie ne vous sauroye suffisament remercier, encore moins par aucun service satisfaire aus grans tesmoinages que i'ay de vostre bonne volonte et encore dernierement quand ie party de Londre me donnant lettres de recommandation au gentilshommes de pardeca. Je ne laisse point pourtant de vous importuner davantage et requerir d'un autre plaisir par lequel s'accroiteront grandement les debtes desquelles ie suis des ia attenu et oblige a vous. Mais la necessité na point de loy et fait oublier touts aultres respects et considerations. Vostre Seig^rie n'ignore point que toute personne apres l'honneur de Dieu et sa bonne conscience doibt sur toute chose avoir son honneur en recommandation, voire iusques a le preferer a sa propre vie. Or est il ainsi que depuis un trois mois en ca, i'ay receu copie Autenticque du proces que ceulx de Leiden ont intenté contre moy en mon absence contre toute loix, droiture et equité me chargeant de choses notoirement fauses dequoy ils ne paeuvent pretendre ignorance si eusmesmes en vouloyent recercher la verité, et or quelles fussent vrayes ne meritent nulle telle infamie et deshonneur comme est celluy qu'ils me font me banissant hors de leur pais et teritoire, confiscant mes biens comme coupable de lese M^te. S'ils m'avoyent volé un cinquante ou soixante mille livres sterlin, on ne trouveroit point estrange de m'en veoir faire mes plaintes ou a sa M^te ou a Messieurs de son conseil. Certes l'integrite de mon nom me vault mieux que nulle chenance quelque grande quelle peut estre non seulement pour le regard de ce que ie doibs a moy mesme mais aussi principallement pour le regard de mon ministere lequel en cecy est deshonoré au deshonneur de Dieu et de son Eglise et grand scandale tant des infirmes que des ennemis de la verité. Le cas est tel que certains tant Colonel que Capitaines accompagnez de certain bon nombre de bourgeois ont mis en deliberation de se saisir d'aucuns personages qui faisoyent mauvaus offices au pais; et entre les estats trois mont esté nommez: Paul Buys pour le premier, le second Pieter Adriansz bourgmestre, le tiers Jan van Haute greffier de la ville de Leyde, et pour ce faire se saisir de la ville et puis apres d'appeller son Ex^ce pour y mettre ordre et ouir les plaintes qu'ils avoyent contre ceux desquels ils s'estoyent saisiz. Or ie suis accusé davoir cognu ceste entreprise sans l'avoir descelé a qui il apparte-

noit. En laquelle accusation il y a deux faultes. La premiere est que ie n'ay
rien sceu de ce qui est mentioné en icelle. Secondement tout ce que ien ay
peu cognoitre par aultre voye que celle qui est mentionée ie lay revelé a
qui il appartenoit a scavoir a son Ex^ce et ne pouvoye faire aultrement que
i'ay fait sans grandement mesprendre et contre le Lieutenant de sa M^te
ma souveraine Princesse il y a XX ans passez et le Gouverneur general des
Provinces. Jay escrit par deux fois a Mons^r le Conte Maurice semblablement aux Estats de Hollande, les suppliant de vouloir mieux et de plus
pres considerer ma cause et me faire desclarer innocent touchant le fait de
Leide, me restituant en mon honneur tel quil estoit auparavant. Car ie ne
juge point du fait de Leide selon ce quil est en sa nature mais comme il est
prins et Intrepreté des malveillans. Finallement i'ay envoye une protestation au conseil provincial de Hollande contre les procedures de ceulx de
Leyde contre moy, remonstrant par sept ou huyt raisons tirées du droit
cognu a tout le monde que toutes lesdites procedures sont abusifves et
auparant non ouies contraires a toute equité et aux loix et usages du païs,
me presentant a le declarer plus amplement si mestier est et qu'il faille en-
trer en proces. Ainsi J'ay envoye une lettre de procuration en Hollande a
Mons^r Guilpin avec pleine et entiere puissance de constituer en mon nom
procureur et advocat pour remonstrer et defendre mon innocence. Car ie
ne puis passer soubs silence que mon nom soit entaché de crime en lEglise
de Dieu. Il souffit que nous soyons calomniez de noz ennemis faus que
ceulx de dedans leur en donnent matiere. Maintenant que la mort m'a privé d'un grand tesmoin et protecteur de mon Innocence, J'ay mon recours
a vostre Seigneurie, la suppliant de me vouloir tendre la main en m'aidant
de vostre faveur te grace pour oster la scandale et reproche qui est donne a
l'eglise par tout le pais Bas et ailleurs ou les copies des sentences imprimées
ont este semées et envoyées afin de denigrer les noms de gens de bien et de
qualité contenus en icelles entre lesquels il leur a pleut d'y mettre aussi le
mien. Maintenant ma requeste seroit qu'il vous pleut me faire ceste grace
que de recommander mon affaire a Monsieur Kilgrewe et a Mons^r Guilpin pour par leur moyen entendre si les Estats me veulent faire droit suivant le contenu de mes lettres, semblablement si par cas daventure Mons^r
Ortel agent pour les Estats se trouvoit en vostre compagnie luy toucher un
mot du tort que mon fait ceulx de Leiden, et quelle est la volonte des Estats
de Hollande. Il m'avyoit promis de leur en escrire ie ne scay s'il la fait tant
y a que ie luy ay envoyé mes lettres pour les addresser a ses Maistres.
Quand i'estoye a Londres voyant qu'on traitoit de la paix, ie me suis de-
porté de beaucoup parler du grand tort que iay receu craindant de nuire a
l'Eglise qui est pardela sous le gouvernement (pour en dire librement la
verité) de petits tyranneaux qui ont secoue tout gouvernement pour gouverner euxmesme a discretion maintenant que le traite de paix est failli ie
parle plus hardiment m'asseurant que la malice des quelques uns ne preiu-
dicera point aux bons qui sont pardela en grande nombre. Esperant don-

ques que de vostre accoustumee bonté ferez plus que ie n'oseroye requerir, Je me deporteray de vous molester davantage ainsi.

Monsieur, Je prie lEternel vous maintenir en sante et longue vie, vous
benissant et tous les vostres en toute choses; de Tattenhill en Stafforshire
ce XX<sup>e</sup> de Septembre 1588.

Le tres affectioné a vostre service
Adrien de Saravia

BL CM Galba D III, fol. 235-236

## XXXII. SARAVIA TO FRANCIS WALSINGHAM
### Tatenhill, 20 September 1588

Monsieur,

La piete et bon zele que tousiours vous avez porte a la religion me donnent la hardiesse de vous molester par ceste presente lettre, suppliant vostre honneur de me vouloir aider de vostre faveur et grace a oster un scandale donné a lEglise sous mon nom par gens qui font servir le nom de religion a leur prouffit particulier, desquels limpieté est si manifeste qu'elle est aisee a cognoitre. Toute personne est tenue apres la bonne conscience quil doibt a Dieu sur toute chose davoir l'integrite de son nom en recommendation, principallement quand il y va de l'honneur de Dieu et du scandale du prochain. Vostre Seigneurie a bien entendu comment Messieurs de Leiden ont publie mon nom avec plusieurs aultres de gens de bien et craindant Dieu comme seditieux et coupable de crime de lesae M.te en une chose ou ie n'ay esté n'ouy ne veu. Touttefois leur mauvaise volonté envers moy (qui n'ai sinon bien merité d'eux) est venue si avant que ma vie n'estoit nulle part asseurée qu'en la suite de feu de haute memoire le Conte de Lecestre et es places ou les Anglois commandoyent, sans savoir en quoy ie pouvois avoir tant offensé Messieurs de Leiden ou les Estats que par coniecture. Finallement par le moyen damis i'ai receu copie Autenticque du proces quon m'a fait en mon absence, et banni hors de leur païs sur peine de la vie et confisqué mes biens comme coupable de trahison pour n'avoir point decelé une certaine entreprise mise en deliberation pour apprehendre trois personnages lesquels on estime faire beaucoup de mauvais offices, a scavoir Paulus Buys, Pieter Adriansz burgmestre et Jan van Haute greffier. Mais il y a deux fautes en leur accusation; la premiere est que le fait ne m'a iamais este communique ainsi qu'il est la narre; secondement ce que i'en ay peu cognoitre par autre voye que celle qui est couchée en l'accusation, ie l'ai declaré a son Ex.ce qui estoit gouverneur general du païs, et luy en ai dit ce qu'il m'en sembloit; en quoy comment qu'on interprete l'affaire, ie me suis fidellement aquitté. Davantage quand le fait tel comme il est couché en l'accusation, sera bien examiné d'un Juge equitable il ne sera point trouvé estre trahison ou crime de lese M.te. Cependant ce deshonneur a este fait a mon Ministere que de m'envelopper au fait d'autruy comme de trahison cognue et non decelée a qui il appartenoit. Or est le fait si cler et si manifeste en ce qui me concerne, que s'il plaisoit a ces Messieurs d'examiner le temps le lieu et autres semblables circumstances, ils trouveroyent la verité de mon innocence. Outre cecy i'ai este cite devant Juges partiaux et incompetens, lesquels n'estoient point mes Juges. Deffenses par deux fois leura esté faite de proceder en ceste affaire. Item i'ay laissé Leide et suis venu en Angleterre par le commandement du Lieutenant de sa Mte ma souveraine Princesse passé XX ans y a et du Gouverneur general du païs, ce non obstant ont procedé en mon absence contre moy iusques a sentence diffinitive. Ainsi J'ai escrit a Mons<sup>r</sup> le Conte Maurice et aux Estats de Hollande par deux fois, les suppliant de mieux examiner mon fait et me faire declarer innocent, me restituant en mon honneur entier tel comme il estoit auparavant. Item i'ay envoyé une protestation au Conseil provincial de Hollande contre les procedures tenues contre moy. Maintenant ma requeste et humble priere est, qu'il plaise a vostre honneur me faire ceste grace que d'escrire a Mons<sup>r</sup> Kilgreve et a Mons<sup>r</sup> Guilpin qui sont pardela, quils vueillent avoir mon affaire pour recommandée et de cognoitre la volonte de Messieurs les Estats afin qu'en cas de refus ie me puisse pourveoir ailleurs comme il sera trouve expedient. Ce temps pendant s'il advenoit que Monsieur Ortel parlat a vous luy en toucher un mot et demander quelle response il a de Messieurs les Estats de Hollande touchant mon affaire. Il me promit devant mon partement de Londres qu'il leur en escriveroit. Je ne puis en bonne conscience dissimuler une telle iniure par laquelle Dieu est deshonore et son Eglise scandalizée entre les ennemis de la verité. J'aimeroye mieux estre mort que d'avoir donné occasion de tel esclandre. Partant, Monsieur, ie vous supplie me vouloir estre si favorable que de m'aider en ce besoin pour oster ceste tache outre ce que m'obligerez infiniment a vostre service. Vous ferez une oeuvre laquelle redondera grandement a l'honneur de Dieu et a ledification de son Eglise ainsi.

Monsieur, Je prierai lEternel vous maintenir en sante et longue vie, vous benissant en toutes voz actions a la gloire de son nom bien et utilité de son Eglise et de sa M<sup>te</sup> et de tout son Royaulme. De Tattenhill en Stafforshere ce XX<sup>e</sup> de Septembre 1588.

Le tres affectione a vostre
Adrien de Saravia

PRO SP 84/26, fol. 329, 330r.

## XXXIII. SARAVIA: JUSTIFICATION BEFORE
## THE MAGISTRATES OF LEYDEN
### 6 October 1588

Les causes pourquoy certains du Magistrat de Leide ont conceu mauvaise opinion de moy et fait que i'ay esté tenu suspect des Etats de Hollande.

Il est ainsi que son Ex^ce estant au camp devant Sutphen, envoya vers moy un gentilhomme nommé Maistre Comdiche avec une lettre de credence, pour cognoistre ce qu'on luy avoit rapporté, que j'auroye ouy dire de Paulus Buys qu'il ne se seroit point porté fidelement en certain affaire que son Ex^ce luy avoit commis mais auroit fait mauvais office, de quoy iestoye du tout ignorant et n'en avoye rien entendu, mais fort bien que peu de iours auparavant certains propos seditieux avoyent esté tenus par un certain Pieter Hack minister, fonde sur le conseil et advertissement, que ledit Hack disoit que Paul Buys avoit donné au Magistrat de Leide, de se donner garde des desseins de son Ex^ce et que le froc ne leur fut ietté par dessus la teste devant qu'ils s'en apperceusent, et autres plusieurs semblables propos seditieux tant contre la religion que la police, dequoy ceux du consistoire (a qui tels propos displaisoyent), estant fort esmerveille, coucherent lesdits propos par escrit et furent dadvis de rappeller ledit Pieter Hack pour ouir s'il les voudroit maintenir, ou bien confesser d'avoir temerairement parlé. Car se disaient ils: nous ne pouvons croire que ce que vous avez dit de Paulus Buys et d'autres notables personnes soit vray. Lequel persistant en ses premiers propos et qu'il n'avoit rien dit que la verité, qu'au besoin il trouveroit bien ses auteurs. Et ainsi il fut resolu d'en advertir les Magistrats, lequel n'en fit point de cas. Afin de n'y rien adiouter du mien, ie fis fixer une copie de tout ce qui estoit enacté au livre du consistoire, et l'envoyai a son Ex^ce, lequel estant de retour du camp la bailla au procureur fiscal du conseil provincial de la Haye pour en prendre plus ample cognoissance et pour proposer le fait au conseil; ce qui a esté empesché par le Magistrat de Leide, lesquels prindrent cela de fort mauvaise part, et voulurent savoir comment et par qui son Ex^ce venoit a avoir la copie de ce qui s'estoit passé, tant au consistoire que pardevant eux. Quant a moy, en estant interrogué, ie ne pouvoye et ne debvoye point nier mon fait cognu a ceux qui m'avoyent livré la copie. Et de cela conceurent un merveilleux grand desplaisir contre moy les Burgmaistres, disant que ie leur avoye fait grand tort. Puis apres environ un demy an on commenca a parler de la souveraineté et ce pour amoindrir l'autorité de son Ex^ce et la faire moindre et inferieure a celle des estats, comme s'il n'eut esté qui leur lieutenant et eux les souverains. Dequoy un iour parlant familierement avec un Burgmaistre, je luy dis ce qu'il m'en sembloit comme i'en iuge en ma conscience et suis certain estre la verité. Premierement que ceux qu'on appelle les Estats n'avoyent iamais esté souverains, qu'ils ne l'estoient point et ne le pouvoyent estre. La raison est toute evidente: un souverain ne recognoit que Dieu par dessus soy au lieux où il est souverain, et n'est point accontable de ses actions a autre qua Dieu, que les Estats avoyent pour maistres les corps des Villes, desquelles il n'estoient que procureurs et commissaires, et avoyent leurs instructions auxquelles leur puissance estoit limitée, estant tenus de faire rapport de leur actions et en rendre conte. Aussi leur titre d'estat representatif demonstroit assez qu'il n'estoient point les vrais Estats mais seulement leur commis, durant le temps de l'assemblée et pour les affaires seulement desquelles ils ont speciale charge, lesquelles points sont du tout contraire a la nature de souveraineté, concluant par la que le Gouverneur general du pais n'estoit point Lieutenant des Estats representatifs, mais de la conté mesme de Hollande qui est le vray estat composé de toute les villes ensemble avec la noblesse et ce non point pour un iour d'assemblée mais iusques a ce que la charge de Gouverneur soit rappellé par le commandement special de toutes les villes et de la noblesse, et qu'il n'estoit en la puissance des Estats de luy oster sa puissance ne de la limiter ny interpreter sans speciale charge et commandement de leur Maistres desquels le Gouverneur tient son autorité et non point d'eux. Et que le serment de son Ex^ce estoit fait a la conté de Hollande et au corps des autres Provinces et non point aux Estats representatifs, qui sont auiourdhuy en autorité et touchant certain cas particulier at demain ne sont plus rien; mais le corps de la Conté demeure tousiour en son autorité, ne se pert point sinon apres quelle est resignée et mise en la main et disposition d'un seul Conte et Seigneur. Au reste que quant a lautorité souveraine ie m'en rapportoye a ce qui en pouvoit estre, mais que le Roy Philippe n'aucun de ses predecesseurs n'avoit onques esté Seigneur souverain de Hollande, Geldre, Frise, Brabant etc excepté lEmpereur Charles en qualité d Empereur. Vrai est que de Flandres et Artois il est Prince souverain par ce que lEmpereur en a aquis la souveraineté par lespee, et que le Roy francois et son successeur le Roy Henri y ont renoncé par plusieurs traites de paix, et ainsi est non seulement Conte de Flandres et Artois mais Prince souverain et vrayement Roy encore qu'il non porte point le titre, ne recognoissant autre que Dieu pour superieur duquel immediatement il tient lesdites contees. Mais quant au Ducez de Brabant, Gueldre, Hollande, Frise il doit homage et service a lempire et est homme ligé de lEmpereur qui est le vrai Prince souverain desdites Ducées et Contées. Et combien que le Roy Philippe ait forfait le droit et titre de Conte de Hollande qu'il ne poeut avoir forfait la souveraineté laquelle il n'avoit onques eu et qu'il y pouvoit bien avoir de l'abus quand on conioindoit l'autorité de lEmpereur Charles avec celle de son filz le Roy Philippe, laquelle est fort differente. Car celle de lEmpereur avoit double respect, cest a savoir dEmpereur et de Conte et ainsi il estoit souverain non point et qualité de Conte mais dEmpereur. Et que combien que le Roy Philippe ait succedé a son Pere, il ne luy a succede qu'en qualité de Conte: tellement que lEmpereur Charles en se deportant de lEmpire et de toutes ses Seigneuries, a eu deux successeurs, l'un a esté Ferdinand son frere qui a succedé a lEmpire et a la souveraineté de toutes les terres et Seigneuries tenues de lEmpire, et le Roy Philippe a lEspaigne et au terres et Seigneuries du païs Bas, a chacune d'icelle selon leur qualité et condition, qui sont diverses les unes aux autres. Que si la souveraineté a esté quittée au Roy Philippe de par lEmpire ce que i'ignore, ou bien si elle est pour le iourdhuy negligée de Lempereur et de lEmpire et abandonnée comme il semble quelle est, si long temps que les villes de Hollande demourent unies ensemble comme elles estoient auparavant, la souveraineté est tombée en touts les corps des villes ensemble et en nulles delles en particulier, d'autant qu'elles ne font qu'un corps vue republique ou Conté. Toutefois et quantes qu'un estat se dissout par la mort du souverain sans successeur ou autrement, la puissance et autorité souveraine ou autre tombe es mains et disposition de toute la republicque, n'est qu'ordre soit prins et estably au paravant pour durant le temps de l'Interregne se gouverner comme on voit en lEmpire Romain et au Royaulmes electifs. Apres que les Rois furent dechasé de Rome, les consuls avec le Senat pensoyent que l'autorité souveraine leur estoit escheue mais le peuple ne lentendit point ainsi, quand il s'appercent que le Senat s'attribuait toute les Royautes et souveraine puissance que les Rois avoyent eus auparavant; ils virent bien qu'on les avoit trompé, leur faisant entendre qu'en deschassant les Rois ils seroyent un peuple libre, mais se trouvants bien esloignez de leur conte quand pour un Roy il en voyoient deux cents. Ils se revolterent du Senat tant que lestat fut estably populaire, auquel combien que le Senat tenoit le premier rang et degré d'honneur et puis apres les Chevaliers, le peuple toutesfois retenoit la principalle autorité en ce qui concernoit la souveraine puissance. Quant a Hollande lestat ne poeut estre que populaire, car les gentilhommes n'ont nulle prerogative de suffraige ne d'autorité en ce qui concerne l'estat, car touts ensemble n'ont qu'une voix non plus que le moindre corps de ville de Hollande. Partant ie ne me puis assez esmerveiller de voz iurisconsultes qui doibvent cognoitre cecy et vous faire entendre quel est vostre estat. Car si long temps que ce point est ignoré vous ne pouvez proceder en voz affaires legitimement comme il appartient, mais faut que commetiez beaucoup de fautes et absurditez en matiere d'estat lequel vous maniez. Or ces propos cy n'aiant este tenu de moy qua deux ou trois, ie ne scai s'ilz ont esté rapportez a Messieurs des estats. Tant y a que depuis ce temps la ils m'ont en suspect et pense de moy que ie faisoye entendre a son Ex<sup>ce</sup> beaucoup de choses au preiudice de leur autorité et du païs. Toutesfois iamais ne luy ai tenu propos aucun de l'estat du païs ny en general ny en particulier, seulement quand il s'est plaind des traversses que les estats luy donnoyent ie l'ai prie que pour l'amour de Dieu et de son Eglise, il luy pleut d'avoir un petit de patience et que finalement les Estats deux mesmes s'accomoderoyent a toute raison. Et que feu de haute memoire le Prince d'Aurenge les avoit gaignez par tels moyens et amené si avant quils ne faisoyent rien sans son congé et conseil, auquel ils estoyent resoluz un petit devant sa mort de mettre entre ses mains tout lestat du païs et le faire Conte de Hollande. Voila le pire conseil que i'ay donné a son Ex<sup>ce</sup>. Il y a un tiers point duquoy Messieurs ont esté fort offensez, c'est qu'un Synode a esté tenu par le commandement de son Ex<sup>ce</sup> et comme ils pensent par mon conseil en quoy aussi ils s'abusent imputant cela plus a moy qu'aux autres ministres, lesquels me prierent de leur tenir compagnie pour requerir son Ex<sup>ce</sup> de vouloir faire establir et autoriser quelque ordre certain pour le gouvernement de lEglise.

BL CM Galba D III, fol. 240-242

## XXXIV. SARAVIA TO ARENT CORNELISZ.
### Tatenhill, 9 October 1588

Per Christum servatorem et Dominum nostrum te et collegas tuos, frater observande, plurimum saluere opto. Literas tuas 11 Julii datas accepi primo die Octobris qui apud vos numeratur ii; quibus mentionem facis literarum quas attulit frater et symmista Helmichius, ad eas satis prolixe iampridem a me responsum est, sed an ultimas meas literas Helmichio ad vos datas receperitis nescio. Miror me nihil intelligere meque a vobis deseri. Quod scribis de morte Georgii mihi maerorem attulit propter summam spem quam singularis eruditionis prebebat. Ego quidem puto merorem causam mortis attulisse animoso iuveni ob rerum necessarium inopiam quae et vestro Samueli, etiam ut audio, Cantabrigiae interitum attulit. Prestaret vestros magistratus nullos alumnos alere quam semel adsumptos tam turpiter negligere. Quod de exemplaribus scribis, illa in Germaniam missa sunt. Christophorus Rafelingius, Plantini nepos, tibi veritatem poterit referre; nulla secum huc attulit meus filius. Quod me nominis mei iacturam sublimi animo contemnere iubes non intelligo; crudeli te dixisse oportuit et ignavo; multo minus quod ecclesiae me dare vis quo ecclesia commaculatur. Sed nec illud, si quid tibi factum est iniuriae, sine contumelia est; sed non mirum mihi esse videri debet fratrem a fratribus deseri et innocentiam sannis et probris impiorum prodi, cum servator a suis fuerit desertus discipulis. De halcyoniis quod tu scribis, vereor ne non diuturni futuri sint. Vale. Die 9 Octobris Tattenhilla. Si quando ad me libet scribere, D. Jacobus Regius minister teutonicae ecclesiae Londini medius est inter nos; ad eum si literas tuas direxeris, ad me eas mitti facile curabit. Iterum vale.

Tui amantiss. Adrianus a Saravia

GAD, Nr. 112

# XXXV. JUSTUS LIPSIUS TO SARAVIA
## 30 July 1589

Quod siluisse me scribis, miror et doleo, cum plene et serio responderim
ad priores omnes litteras tuas. Quas ab aliquo iam intervallo nullas vidi,
praeter has querulas et breves; sed ideo mihi gratas quia tales. Nisi et me
et mea amares, non quereris de officii huius intermissione. Illud gravius, quod de morte filii tui (heu unici) scribis, in quo numquam ex animo
gaudeam, nisi ex animo sum tristatus. Amabam modestissimum ingenium nec ultra laudandum, ne desiderium et caussas dolendi tibi augeamus.
Scis communem legem, dei ab aeterno decretum, et alia quae alii hauriunt
a tuo fonte. Haec ipse tibi nunc instilla. Imus huc omnes, mi Saravia, nec
seiungimur sed leviter alter alterum anteimus. O beati, qui in beata illa
meta! Nam hic etiam in optimo statu quid nisi miseriae? quanto magis in
his publicis Europae ruinis! Nam mutari eam totam et inverti nemo pru-
dens non videt. Censebam Politica nostra posse me mittere sub hoc tempus; trina aut quaterna folia etiamnunc restant. Firmioris attentique iudicii Lectoribus probaturum me id Opus spero, numquam iis qui pervolant
et instar apum scripta saltem delibant. Thomam Heneagium a me salutes
velim, virum Musis et mihi valde carum. III. Kal. Sextil.

*Lipsi Epist. Cent. Duae.* Cent. sec. Nr. 74
*Inv. Lipse* 88 03 23S

## XXXVI. SARAVIA TO ARENT CORNELISZ.
### London, 11 March 1590

Genaede ende Vrede door Jesum Christum onsen Heere.

Eerwerde ende beminde broeders, de oorsaeke deses myn teghenwor-
dich schrivens is om U hertelick te bidden my so vele friendschap te willen
doen als een authentique copie te willen senden beyden van tgene Cornert
in gheschrifte overgaf and dat van onsent weghe daerop wert gheantword
ende dat metten eersten; verstaende wat het schriven sal ghecost hebben
ick en sall niet laeten met hertelicke bedankinghen de costen te doen werden instellen. Varet wel, seer lieve ende weerde broeders, de Heere seghe-
ne U ende Uwen dienst tot synder eere ende opbauwinghe synder gemeente. Uyt Londen den eersten Martii stilo veteri 1590.

Uwer E. dienstwilleghe mededienaer
Adrian van Saravia

GAD, Nr. 112

## XXXVII. SARAVIA [TO JOHN JAMES]
### Tatenhill, 11 May 1590

Gratiam et Pacem a Deo Patre et Domino
Jesu Christo tibi precor aeternam.

Ante meum decessum Londino non perfectum fuisse a me quod cupie-
bas et ipse promiseram, temporis angustiae te rogo, mi Joannes, imputa et
excusa. Nihil enim est in mea situm potestate in quo tibi gratificari paratus non semper fuerim. Tametsi illud non magnopere te adiuvare posse
putem, tibi tamen morem gessissem tuoque iudicio obsecutus fuissem si
tempus habuissem. Apud Reverendissimum Dominum Archiepiscopum
feci quod potui, similiter apud Doctorem Bantcraftium, qui de voluntate
Domini Cancellarii te vult esse securum. Apud Dominum magnum the-
saurarium mentionem de te quod nullam fecerim causa haec est: quod
paucis tantum verbis eum salutaverim et ei familiaris non sum ut aude-
rem. Preterea tu nosti ultronea testimonia haberi suspecta. Opiniones semel conceptas et tempore confirmatas solo depelluntur tempore. Pauci
sunt aequi aestimatores alienarum actionum; quisque prout affectus est
iudicat. Novi quos habuerimus sermones tum in Hollandia tum hîc in
Anglia de Episcopis et leiturgia anglicanae Ecclesiae et cum alii ecclesiarum ministri quos consulueras contra quam ego sentiebam censerent in
publicis precibus familiae Domini Comitis morem sequendum Belgicarum
ecclesiarum, tu adsensus es mihi et meis rationibus celebrataque est coena
Domini ritu Anglicanae Ecclesiae. Quod gravaris odio eorum quae Ultraiecti acciderunt et habitae Synodi factique Leidani, mirarer nisi mihi idem
accidisset apud eos qui Villerii et meam sententiam de schismate illius
ecclesiae curando nostris manibus signatam viderant et probarant de qua
nihil mutaram. Tamen Florus Tinnius et caeteri omnes qui illarum erant
partium et amici fuerant antea, mihi facti sunt inimici. Nemo enim tam
est perditus qui schisma sublatum e civitate possit queri si ulterius qui rebus praeerant non essent progressi; sed sine iudicii forma cives quos ode-
rant dignitate privasse, exilio mulctasse et mandasse custodiae mali res
exempli fuit plenaque odii, cuius rei culpa male in quemquam alium
transfertur quam in ipsos Ultraectinos cives qui potestate sua abusi sunt.
Haec omnia esse facta te et me absentibus et synodo intentis ignarisque
eorum omnium quae Ultraiecti gerebantur scio. Sed quis vis fieri? Ita sunt
comparati homines ut facile suspicionibus indulgeant. Annon me Busius
quem semper defendi et excusavi quantum potui suspicatus est autorem
suae incarcerationis fuisse? De Synodo vero ecquae causa fuit ut cuiquam
ordines hollandici succenserent? An non ipsi in eam concenserant et locum
ubi conveniretur designarant; ipsis inspectantibus convenimus. Si quid inde metuebatur mali, intercedere poterant et ad Dominum Comitem referre. Res nova non erat: quotannis in Hollandia et in ceteris provinciis pro-
vinciales habentur synodi nec generalem convocari inauditum: duae antea

fuerant celebratae. In hac nihil novi fuit constitutûm, nihil innovatum nisi quod quaedam mutata sunt verba quibus minui videri poterat. Magistratuum authoritas ut insigniter impudentes fuerint quos de hac re apud Regiam maiestatem conqueri nihil puduit. Leidanae tragoediae primos authores et consiliarios non novi. Te autem illud consilium nunquam probasse testari audeo. Sed quis ab illo consilio magis abhorruit et magis alienus fuit quam ego? Tamen tanquam author aut fautor in discrimen capitis veni et nisi me Dominus servasset, alienum peccatum luissem. Nam meum peccatum aliud non erat nisi Domini Comitis observantia et erga Anglicam gentem amor et studium. Omnia de quibus quereris mihi leviora meo casu videntur. Nec quicquam habeo consilii quod tibi dem praeter illud quod ipse sequor: ut fortiter feras et contemnas omnes quae sunt huius modi presentis vitae miserias. Regium esse puta cum benefeceris male audire. Tanti est apud me bonae conscientiae testimonium ut nec gemere nec dolere quidem adhuc potuerim ob ea quae contra me homines impii designarunt. Sed illorum vicem vehementer doleo quibus illud consilium aut mortem aut exilium aut bonorum iacturam attulit et in primis Domini Medkerkii ac viduae pupillorumque fortissimi viri Valmarii quos in extremam miseriam haec coniecit calamitas. Quod te puritanum esse arbitrantur facile convinces falsum, qua in re nihil meo consilio tibi opus est. Solidam pietatem retine et in Deo tuam omnem spem atque praesidium colloca. Vale. Tattenhylla Comitatus Stafordiae XI die Maii 1590.

Tuus Hadrianus a Saravia

BodL Ms. Tanner 79, fol. 148

## XXXVIII. SARAVIA TO RICHARD BANCROFT
### Tatenhill, 23 August 1590

Reverendo Viro Domino Richardo Bancraftio theologo
Adrianus a Saravia A.P. in Domino Jesu Christo.

Librum quem tantopere querebamus inter libros meos qui Londini
sunt, hîc inveni, in quo preter theses Erasti tractulus quidam Johannis
Willingi inest, quo de disciplina suam sententiam Electori Palatino 22 Decem............declaravit. Item responsio D. Petri Bocquini et aliorum
doctorum .............ensium quae eidem Principi exhibita fuit 7⁰ die Januarii proxime.............descripta ad te misissem nisi describendi molestus
mihi minus...............quod facilius prestare potui, tibi mitto exemplar
epistolae D. [Bullingeri ad] Erastum, qua videri poteris quod sit ipsius et
aliorum Helvetiorum Theolo[gorum] .....de thesibus Erasti iudicium. Sed
ego vehementer doleo in controversiam vocari apud ecclesias reformatas
rem apud priscos patres minime controversam; quorum etsi severitatem
non probem, non tamen video quomodo ipsam ecclesiasticam censuram
tollendam ab ecclesia aut sublatam possimus defendere. Duos ecclesia habet hostes acerrimos: Anabaptistas et Pontificios, contra quos disputando
quando errorem defendimus veritati aliarum controversiarum deroga-
mus. Arcendos esse a sacris homines prophanos non tantum esse iuris
divini scripti sed ipsius naturae legis quae cum religione nata est arbitror.
Sed de hac re satis.

Si forte contingat te cum Domino Henichio Cancellario Ducatus Lan-
castriae colloqui, vellem de me mentionem faceres ut quae sit ipsius erga
me voluntas et quid de eo sperare possem cognoscam. Caducas et prope-
diem ruituras aedes me habere tibi ni fallor indicavi Vmo D. Walsingamo.
Sperabam ex vicino saltu Newood et vinario Helmle quod in hac mea pa-
roecia situm est, materiam reparandis aedibus et horreis suppeditatum iri.
Id a Domino Henich petere pudor non sinit. Mihi petere rubor, repulsam
pati probrum. Ex veteribus monumentis doceri potes rectoribus huius ecclesiae quondam ad edificandum materiam et ad ignis usum ligna vicinam
sylvam subministrasse. Sed ipsa non est hodie ea quae fuit olim. Hîc cum
finem facerem, famulus meus mihi attulit ex vicino oppido Byrtone sito ad
ripam Trentae librum meum misere laceratum et foedatum censuris ministri cuiusdam ex eorum numero qui sanctiorem reformationem profitentur. Librum tibi mitto, ut videbis quomodo margines laceraverit prius no-
tatos a se, ni fallor, quod aut penituerit aut puduerit censurarum. Si vide-
bitur poteris haec ostendere Reverendiss. D. Archiepiscopo Cantu., cuius
valetudinem precor ut Deus tueatur servetque diu incolumem. Quis sit
bellus meus censor, quae ipsius eruditio, ex notulis poteris cognoscere.
Nomen non adscribo; delyri senis aetati parco. Deumque rogo ut mentem

ei det saniorem. Vale, mihi plurimum amande et observande.....
Tattenhylla 23 die Aug. 1590.

Tui observant. Adrianus [a Saravia]

Vectores ipso Bartholomei die mihi Londino has attulere...........
scriptas; quid a me petant vides. Hardingus.......................
ut filium complector quod mihi fuerit aliqu......................
aedibus, eoque magis quod ab eo tempor[e].......................
semper persecit eius eruditionem et pr...........................
a me commemorari debeant. Itaque ego...........................
cupio mihique factum imputabo quicqui.......edificii contulere Si tibi grave non sit et negotia........maiorem in modum te vehementissimo rogo ut
ei meo nomine [res]pondere digneris. Iterum vale, humanissime D. Ban-
crafte.

BL Add. Ms. 28571. Nr. 36, fol. 167 (manuscript seriously damaged)

## XXXIX. SARAVIA: OPINION OF BARRET'S RECANTATION
### 1595

Palinodia Magistri Bereti eatenus mihi probatur, quod nomina doctorum virorum petulanter insectatus est; ceterum quod salutis securitatem
improbavit, et temporariam fidem quorundam nihil differre a fide iustificante adseruit; meo iudicio non id certe revocari iussus est; nisi forte intel-
lexerit omnem temporariam et historicam fidem nihil differre a fide iustificante.

Et in primo articulo pro ''securus'' vellem positum esse ''certus'': plurimum interest inter securitatem et certitudinem; et in fine ubi legitur
''certos esse et securos'', deleri ''securos'' vellem. In secundo articulo pro
''singulorum credentium fide'' positum vellem ''singulorum electorum fide''; quia non omnes vere credentes sunt electi, et vere credentium quorundam fides deficere potest, non electorum. Tertium articulum non satis
intelligo. Quaevis securitas finalis perseverantiae laudanda non est: interdum fieri potest ut non vacet arrogantiae. Quamvis de salute sua tandiu
quis sit certus quandiu credit, solicitum tamen esse credentem oportet tam
de augmento fidei quam de perseverantia. Quod ait se ingenue profiteri
fidem veram et iustificantem etc., verum non est nisi in electis. De
quarto articulo dico quod Bernardus nunquam dixit in universum omnem
fidem temporariam esse fictam; et si dixit, error est. Quandoque in quibusdam verum est, sed non semper nec in omnibus. In quinto articulo non
adsequor in petitione remissionis peccatorum, quo sensu dicamur ibi potius petere fidei donum vel incrementum quam in caeteris petitionibus.
Quando enim petimus nobis peccata nostra dimitti, id absolute petimus,
quia credimus Deum propter Christum remittere peccata penitentibus.
Remissio peccatorum non datur nisi fide petentibus peccata sibi remitti et
nomen Domini invocantibus: praecedit enim fides invocationem nominis
Dei, et petitionem remissionis peccatorum. In sexto articulo male recanta-
tur peccatum esse veram propriam et primam causam reprobationis.
Quod allegatur ex Augustino ad Simplicianum non ibi invenitur, sed pla-
ne contrarium.

Rationes meae et argumenta quibus ut ita de hac palinodia censeam
haec sunt.[1] Magnum discrimen est inter certitudinem de salute et securitatem. Certitudinem parit fides, securitatem presumptio et arrogantia. Vir-
tutis fidei nomine commendatur certitudo salutis; securitas in vitio est.
Sicubi probati scriptores securitatis vocabulo usi sunt pro certitudine,
catachresis est aut quaedam hyperbole. A securitate fideles ubique Dei
verbum deterret; cum tamen certus esse velit nec quicquam de salute
dubitare, haec certitudo adversus omnes tentationes armat credentes in
Christum, et in rebus desperatis ubique erigit. Securitas vero ignavos red-

---

[1] Here begins the text published by Strype.

dit et in periculis hostibus prodit. Certus fidelis de sua salute esse potest qui de ea non sit securus. Nam fides, quae certitudinem salutis adfert, solicitos de ea retinenda, non securos reddit. Salutis certitudo comitatur fidem; et tamdiu credentes in Christum de sua salute sunt certi quamdiu credunt.

Quaedam est temporaria fides quae tamen vera et minime simulata est eosdemque operatur in homine effectus quos perpetua fides et ab eodem authore proficiscitur. Et sola duratione haec ab illa differt. Vere omnis temporaria fides non dicitur simulata, sicut nec omnis quae perpetua est vera. Accidit enim hypocritarum fidem, qui in externo ecclesiae corpore permixti bonis lacitant, perseverantem esse usque ad finem, et quorundam minime fucatam tantum esse temporariam. Quamvis autem quorundam hypocritarum simulata fides tantum sit temporaria, absit ut propterea credatur esse quaevis temporaria fides simulata. Est fides natura sua tum ab ipsius effectis tum ab ipso authore, non a duratione definienda. Accidere autem ut vera fides in quibusdam temporaria sit et ea quae est aut historica aut simulata in quibusdam perpetua, quod an alicui videatur absurdum, argumenta subiiciam ex verbo Dei desumpta quibus haec docentur, si prius contra securitatem aliquid dixero.

Quod apud Orthodoxos minime est controversum, nempe fidem reddere credentes certos de sua salute, probandum mihi non est; de securitate nostra est questio. Propter multas easque graves causas securos Dominus nos esse prohibuit: et tum de nostra tum de fratrum salute solicitos esse iussit, quando pluribus preceptis et parabolis nos vigilare et orare praecepit. Apud Lucam 18. cap.: Oportet (inquit) semper orare et non fatigari nec segnescere;[2] et alio loco: Cavete vobis, ne quando graventur corda vestra crapula et ebrietate et curis huius vitae: et repente vobis superveniat dies ille (nempe adventus Domini ad iudicium), nam ut laqueus invadet in omnes qui habitant in superficie terrae. Excubate igitur omni tempore, rogantes ut digni habeamini qui effugiatis ista omnia quae futura sunt, et consistatis coram filio hominis.[3] Et apud Marcum: Cavete, vigilate et orate; nescitis enim quando tempus illud sit futurum.[4] A parabola patris familias, qui nescit quando fur venturus sit et perfossurus parietem; similiter et servorum qui, ignari quo tempore Dominus eorum venturus sit, expectant eum vigilantes; Dominus nos quoque vigilare vult. Accedit et alia parabola decem virginum, quarum quinque erant prudentes et quinque fatuae; ex quibus concludit: Vigilate, quia nescitis diem neque horam in qua filius hominis veniet.[5] Haec certe praecepta non sunt eius qui velit nos esse securos.

[2] Luc.18:1.
[3] Luc. 21:34-36.
[4] Marc. 13:33.
[5] Matth. 25:13.

Prima causa est ne Satan nos securos opprimat et in tentationem indu-
cat. Undique hostibus qui in exitium nostrum coniurarunt cingimur; et
nullas machinas non adhibent ad expugnandam nostram fidem. Et inveniuntur Theologi qui securos de salute nos esse volunt? Quomodo securos
esse iubent de salute, quam undique hostes appetunt? Non enim est nobis
lucta adversus carnem et sanguinem, sed adversus imperia et potestates,
adversus mundi dominos et rectores tenebrarum huius seculi, adversus
spirituales malitias quae sunt in sublimi;[6] adversus quas Paulus nos assu-
mere vult universam Dei armaturam. Quomodo securi esse possunt quibus bellum perpetuum est cum hoste pervigili, cui sunt nomina mille et
mille docendi artes? Non ita Dominus quando ait: Orate et vigilate, ne in-
tretis in tentationem.[7] Vitari tentatio sine oratione non potest: ferre insul-
tus daemonum non valemus nisi divino fulciamur auxilio. Quamvis omnis
nostra cura in Deum coniicienda sit certique simus Deo nos esse curae, nihil tamen nostram solicitudinem, id remorari debet. Quaerere et petere
quae daturus est Deus et daturum se promisit, ipse praecepit. Nemo certi-
or de Dei patris benevolentia esse potest quam fuit Dominus noster Jesus
Christus; ipse tamen ut tentatio instabat, ad orandum se cum Apostolis
contulit. Petrus non ignorabat quanta sit Deo de nobis cura quando nos
adhortatur ad sobrietatem et vigilias contra diaboli tentationem. Sobrii
estote (inquit) et vigilate. Nam adversarius vester diabolus tanquam leo
rugiens obambulat, quaerens quem devoret; cui resistite fortes in fide.[8]
David securus in adulterium et parricidium, ut cetera quae in medio acciderunt omittam, sui oblitus cecidit. Et Apostolus Petrus, nimium securus,
turpiter lapsus est.

Altera causa quae nos solicitos tenere debet est incertus dies Domini adventus, ad quem ipse nos semper esse paratos praecipit, ne tanquam laqueus nobis superveniat et eodem involvat cum mundo exitio. Apostolus
Paulus, qui de Dei erga se benevolentia minime dubitabat quam fuerit a
securitate alienus, ipsius verba in priore ad Corinthios testantur quando
ait: Castigo corpus meum et in servitutem redigo, ne quo modo cum aliis
praedicarim ipse reprobus fiam.[9] Et quando Philippenses similiter iubet,
cum timore et tremore suam ipsorum salutem[10] operari, certe securos esse
noluit. Nemo certus de consequendo fine esse potest qui de mediis quae ad
illum finem conducant non est solicitus. Vita aeterna nobis promissa est et
eam quidem fide apprehendimus; sed tenenda est via quae eo ducit.

Quod quaevis fides temporaria non vera sed simulata dicitur, non satis
intelligo quid sit nec quo sensu dicatur. Nam illi fidei nihil deesse videtur,
in qua nihil praeter perseverantiam requiritur. Insimulata fide, ut quis

---

[6] Ef. 6:12.
[7] Marc. 14:38.
[8] 1 Petr. 5:8, 9.
[9] 1 Kor. 9:27.
[10] Phil. 2:12.

maxime perseveraret, nunquam fructum verae fidei consequeretur; una
tantum est vera fides qua Christo inserimur et Spiritu renovamur. At temporaria fides quorundam eos Christo ita inserit et Spiritus sanctificationis
facit participes, ut si perseverarent vitam consequerentur aeternam. Ergo
illa fides vera est. Si quotquot veram habent fidem, perseveraturi sunt in
ea usque in finem et nemo in medio cursu fidem est relicturus, vana est ad
perseverantiam exhortatio, quam habere eum certum est qui fidem amit-
tere non potest. Quando Dominus aerumnas recenset quae a fidelibus
sunt perferendae, ne frangantur animo tolerantia malorum et semel pug-
nasse satis esse putent, nemini aeternam vitae coronam promittit nisi qui
usque ad finem perseveraverit. Unde datur intelligi non omnes perseveraturos qui aliquando bene inceperint.

Nota est parabola satoris et seminis quod in petrosa cecidit: quo signifi-
cantur qui semen verbi Dei accipiunt cum gaudio, sed orta persecutione
offenduntur et verbum Dei abiiciunt.[11] Quod quidam volunt vera fide illud verbum non fuisse susceptum quomodo defendere possint, non video,
cum illud verbum eosdem operetur effectus in eis qui illud suscipiunt quod
in fidelibus qui usque in finem perseverant. Epistola ad Hebraeos tribuit
omnia quae sunt propria verae fidei huic temporariae fidei, nempe quod
verbo Dei illustretur et gustum det doni coelestis, boni Dei verbi ac virtutum futuri seculi et quod faciat participes Spiritus Sancti[12] et per penitentiam hominem renovit; plura his non habent qui vera fide iustificantur. Illa
fides vera esse negari non potest, qua per poenitentiam homo renovatur et
fit particeps Spiritus Sancti; sed plerique qui habent temporariam fidem
per eam haec omnia consequuntur: ergo eorum fidem veram esse oportet.
Nam simulata aut tantum historica fides horum nihil in homine operari
potest. Quando Dominus bis apud Mattheum dixit: Qui perseveraverit in
finem, is salvus erit,[13] idem est ac si diceret: qui non perseveraverit non
servabitur. Quod intelligi non potest de iis qui non eandem habent fidem
non perseverantibus: in qua etiam si perseveraverint non servarentur.
Una enim tantum est fides qua servantur credentes. Ut quis in historica
fide vel simulata maxime perseveret, ut perseverare multos non est
dubium, nihil ad salutem hoc iuvaret. Quando Epistola ad Hebraeos
loquitur de totali apostasia a fide,[14] nisi omnia illi tribuet quae verae fidei
sunt propria et dantur vere crendentibus, ridicula esset apostasia. Quomodo enim a fide quae habetur de Christo, defecisse dici potest qui vere
in eum nunquam credidit sed tantum se credere simulavit? Quomodo
dici potest eum non posse denuo renovari per penitentiam qui nunquam
renovatus fuit? Scimus renovationem esse propriam fidei iustificanti.

---

[11] Matth. 13:5, 20, 21; Marc. 4:5, 16,
 17; Luc. 8:6, 13.
[12] Hebr. 6:4-6.
[13] Matth. 10:22; 24:13.
[14] Hebr. 6:6.

Historica fides neminem renovat nec Spiritus Sancti participem facit.
Gustasse donum coeleste dici non potest cuius conscientia de peccatorum
remissione parta morte Christi persuasa non fuit. Gustus enim verbi Dei
et doni coelestis et virtutum futuri seculi nullus habetur sine fide et appre-
hensione promissionum Dei. Quisquis per penitentiam renovatus est et
Spiritus Sancti factus est particeps gustavitque donum coeleste et bonum
Die verbum et virtutes futuri seculi, verus Christianus est et veram fidem
habet; et regnum coelorum ac beatam immortalitatem esset accepturus si
perseveraret; sola defectio hic indicatur futura causa damnationis: nec ad
salutem quicquam praeter perseverantiam deest.

At fides vera non potest amitti. Sed haec aperte adversantur. Fidem autem qua Christo inserimur non posse amitti, a Paulo in 11. cap. ad Rom.
apertius quam ut tergiversando negari possit, est expositum. Quid hoc sibi
vult: Tu fide stas, noli altum sapere,[15] vel ut alii habent: ne efferaris animo, sed time.[15] Quem nobis hic timorem Paulus inculcat? Non ignoro re-
ligiosum Dei cultum timoris et reverentiae nomine significare Hebraeos.
Sed metus qui a Paulo hoc loco praecipitur, elationi animi et fiduciae secu-
ritatique opponitur, quibus veluti frenum eo iniicit Apostolus. Timor est
mali verisimilis futuri cum dolore expectatio, nisi obviam eatur quando
potest. Malum profecto venturum Apostolus aperte denuntiat totamque
timoris naturam exprimit: nempe fractionem ab oliva cui fideles per fidem
inseruntur; quae quia Iudaeis propter incredulitatem accidit, eam timeri
vult ab iis qui fide stabant et per fidem in locum Iudeorum Christo verae
olivae erant insiti, ne et ipsi defringantur.[16] Hoc est malum quod a fidelibus timeri vult et caveri D. Paulus. Vanus autem esset timor rei quae non
potest accidere. Fieri ergo potest, ut qui sunt Christo per fidem insiti, per
infidelitatem a fide et a Christo excidant. Sed audiamus Domini de hac eadem re sententiam, qui disertis verbis alia similitudine nempe vitis adhuc
in terris agens cum discipulis suis, idem quod per servum suum Paulum
docuit: Ego sum vitis vera(inquit) et Pater meus agricola est. Omnem pal-
mitem in me non ferentem fructum tollit eum, et omnem qui fert fructum
purgat eum, ut fructum plus adferat.[17] Hic palmites in Christo audimus
frugiferos et infrugiferos: quorum alii sunt purgandi, ut abundantiorem
fructum ferant, alii tanquam otiosi et inutiles abscindendi: nimirum qui in
Christo non manent. Quod intelligi non potest de iis qui nunquam fuerunt
in Christo. In Christo autem fuisse aut esse nisi per fidem nemo intelligitur. Sed in eo permanere debet qui fructum Deo ferre desiderat, sine quo
fructum nullum ferre potest. Manete in me (inquit Dominus) et ego in vobis. Nisi quis in me manserit, abiectus foras arescet. Et colligitur et in ig-
nem coniicitur.[18] Quae, obsecro, est horum verborum vis, si quisquis fide

---

[15] Rom. 11:20.
[16] Rom. 11:16-21.
[17] Joh. 15:1, 2.
[18] Joh. 15:4, 6.

Christo semel est insitus, perpetuo in eo est mansurus nec periculum ullum est eis qui semel in Christo vera fide inseruntur; ab eo per incredulitatem discedendi? Eos Dominus adloquitur qui vera fide in eo erant et qui permansuri erunt; quia tamen aliqui esse in Christo possunt praesenti fide qui permansuri non sunt, vult electos esse solicitos de perseverantia et iis omnibus quibus haberi potest, et idcirco haec loquutus est. Praeterea iustum esse neminem sine fide certum est: iustificamur fide quotquot iustificamur. Quomodo enim avertere se iustus a iustitia sua potest? Iustum autem posse a sua iustitia excidere et facere iniquitatem et ita mori, praeter innumera testimonia verbi Dei, Ezechiel duobus in locis perspicuus est testis: tertio cap. 20. vers. et 18. cap. 24. v. Quae autem Scriptura docet de fide eiusque fructibus vera sunt omnia, quamdiu quis in fide perseverat. Quod perseverantiae donum non omnibus fidelibus sed solis electis datum est, illud Servatoris nostri dictum, saepius repetitum: multi vocati, pauci electi,[19] satis evidenter probat.

Ad electionem et obdurationem venio, de qua inter theologos non parva est controversia. Veritatem quisquis capere desiderat, intentionem Pauli sequi et scopum quo colinavit tantum spectare debet nec inde animum aliorsum deflectere. Paulus in 9. cap. ep. ad Rom. nihil aliud docere vult quam gratuitam Dei in eligendo et iustificando gratiam; unde alienum est a Pauli intentione quod pari ratione reprobare et obdurare contenditur, cum diversissimae sint causae electionis et reprobationis. Quod allegatur de Jacob et Esau probat tantum gratuitam fuisse Jacob electionem; nec ad probandum Esau ex pari causa fuisse reprobatum quidquam valet. Nam electio fit ex massa reproba: uterque Jacob et Esau erant filii irae pari damnatione obnoxii, ex qua communi damnatione Jacob Dei gratia servatus est in qua relictus fuit Esau. Quod neque boni quicquam neque mali egisse dicuntur, similiter ad solam electionem referendum est, non autem ad conditionem corruptae naturae, in qua ambo pares erant. Et sensus est nihil fuisse boni in Jacob plus quam in Esau cur praeferretur ei, nec plus mali in Esau quam in Jacob cur non eligeretur. Sed in utroque erat quod iure Deus oderat, nempe peccatum; non enim Deus oderat Esau hominem creaturam suam, sed peccatum quod nec in Jacob amare potuit. Et quod non dicitur odisse Jacob sed dilexisse, accidit quia peccatum sustulit et eius loco gratiam suam substituit ob quam Jacob dilexit. Quam gratiam cur non etiam Esau contulerit, fateor latere nec inquirendum esse. Tamen ut Augustinus de Praedestinatione et Gratia ait,[20] nec iniustus Deus est nec merita singulorum confusa quadam personarum acceptione taxat; nec infirmus ut quicquid voluerit non valuerit explicare, etc. Constat aeternae Dei sapientiae consilii sui ratio cur potius huius misereatur quam illius. Miseretur itaque Deus cuius vult, et quem vult obdurat,[21] sed causa longe

---

[19] Matth. 22:14.
[20] *PL*, VL, 1666f., 1672.
[21] Rom. 9:18.

diversa. Mere et sola gratuita gratia miseretur eius qui conditione sua minime dignus est cuius misereatur, et obdurat eum qui maxime dignus est illa obduratione, ut hic sit meritum et illic nullum. Gratia sine ullo merito electionis est causa. Iustitia Dei vero et peccati meritum est causa obdurationis. Quod similitudinem figuli[22] attinet, non est necesse omni ex parte eam convenire cum re assimulata; satis est si congruat rei propositae quam diximus, hoc est gratuitae electioni. Mens Pauli fuit docere hac similitudine gratiam electionis non esse debitam, sed non reprobationis nullam esse culpam. Communis massa in manu Dei tanquam figuli unde quaedam vasa ad honorem fiunt et quaedam ad contumeliam, non est natura sua media aptaque ad utriumvis, sed tantum ad ignominiam et ad iram meritam. Quando vero ex ea re fiunt vasa fiunt vasa irae ad interitum, iusta merces redditur nec massae perditae ulla fit iniuria. Sed quando ex eadem massa contra ipsius naturam formantur vasa in honorem, sola illic Dei operatur gratia nec ulla inveniri potest meriti causa. Indifferentia ad utrumque nulla potest intelligi in huius materiae natura, in quam iustus et misericors Deus gratiam aut iustitiam suam exercet. Contrarias si quis positiones istis meis constituat, inveniet eas, nisi vehementer fallor, nedum absurdas, sed in Deum et Dei iustitiam et misericordiam impias. In neutram partem peccavit, qui ita peccati meritum obdurationis veram, propriam et iustam causam esse asseruit, ut solam Dei gratiam causam esse electionis sanctorum non negaverit.

Haec et quae a me superius disputata sunt, patrum sententiis et in primis Augustini confirmanda sunt, ut appareat quae a Bareto bene dicta sunt male fuisse retractata. Primo quod securitatem attinet, in libro Confessionum Augustini ita se habet: Nemo securus esse debet qui in ista vita quae tota tentatio nominatur, ut qui fieri potuit ex deteriore melior non fiat etiam ex meliore deterior. Una spes, una fiducia, una firma promissio, misericordia tua.[23] Et inter sententias eiusdem patris ea quae numero est septuagesima octava habet: Sicut praepostera securitas in periculum impellit, ita ordinata solicitudo securitatem parit.[24] Idem pater, recensens tentationes omnis generis quibus oppugnamur, concludit esse difficile ut non ab aliqua quis feriatur. Ubi ergo securitas? (inquit) Hic nusquam; in ista vita nusquam nisi in sola spe promissionum Dei. Ibidem: Cum illuc pervenerimus (coelum intelligit), erit perfecta securitas, cum claudentur portae et confirmabuntur vectes portarum Hierusalem; ibi vere plena iubilatio et magnum gaudium. Et Sermo 39 de verbis Domini: Erunt autem tunc securi qui modo non sunt securi; et tunc timebunt qui modo timere nolunt. Et in tractatu De dono perseverantiae: Deus autem melius iudicavit miscere quosdam non perseveraturos certo numero sanctorum suorum, ut quibus non expedit in huius vitae tentatione securitas non possint

---

[22] Rom. 9:20f.
[23] *Conf.* X, 32.
[24] *MPL,* XLV, 1866.

esse securi.[25] Multos enim a perniciosa elatione reprimit, quod ait Apostolus: Quapropter qui stat, videat ne cadat.[26] Idem pater aperte perseverantiae securitatem damnat fidemque operantem per charitatem et iustificantem temporariam adsumat dari, nec id leniter ut aut aliud agenti aut forte incogitanti excidisse dici potest, sed totis libris De dono perseverantiae et De correptione et gratia hoc accurate disputat et ex verbo Dei docet. Statim initio libri De perseverantia ait: Asserimus ergo Dei donum esse perseverantiam, quae usque in finem perseveratur in Christo. Finem autem dico quo vita ista finitur, in qua tantum modo periculum est, ne cadatur. Itaque utrum quisquam hoc munus acceperit quamdiu hanc vitam ducit, incertum est.[27] Et De correptione et gratia: Si autem iam regeneratus et iustificatus, in malam vitam sua voluntate relabitur, certe iste non potest dicere: non accepi, quia acceptam gratiam Dei suo in malum libero amisit arbitrio, etc. An adhuc et iste nolens concipi potest dicere: quid ego feci qui non accepi; quem constat accepisse, et sua culpa quod acceperat amisisse?[28]

In illa disputatione constitutum ab Augustino discrimen inter donum perseverantiae quod datum fuit primo parenti et illud quod accipiunt per Dei gratiam praedestinati, lucem huic quaestioni potest adferre. Primo itaque homini qui in eo bono quo factus fuerat rectus, acceperat posse non peccare, posse non mori, posse ipsum bonum non deserere, datum est adiutorium perseverantiae, non quo fieret ut perseverarit, sed sine quo per liberum arbitrium perseverare non posset. Nunc vero sanctis in regnum Dei per gratiam Dei praedestinatis, non tantum tale adiutorium perseverantiae datur, sed tale ut eis perseverantia ipsa donetur, non solum ut sine isto dono perseverantes non possint, verum etiam ut per hoc donum non nisi perseverantes sint. Non [solum[a]]enim dixit: Sine me nihil potestis facere;[29] verum etiam dixit: Non vos me elegistis, sed ego elegi vos et posui vos, ut eatis et fructum adferatis et fructus vester maneat;[30] quibus verbis non solum iustitiam verum etiam in illa perseverantiam se dedidisse monstravit.[31] Et ibidem idem pater ait: fortissimo (intellige: Adamo) dimisit atque permisit facere quod volet; infirmis servavit ut ipso donante invictissime quod bonum est vellent et hoc deserere invictissime nollent; dicente ergo Christo: Rogavi pro te ne deficiat fides tua,[32] intelligimus ei dictum, qui aedificatur supra Pet.[33] Haec omnia Augustinus quae

---

[a] Add. August.; om. Saravia.
[25] *Ibid.*, 1003.
[26] 1 Kor. 10:12.
[27] *MPL*, XLV, 993f.
[28] *Ibid.*, XLV, 921.
[29] Joh. 15:5.
[30] Joh. 15:16.
[31] *MPL*, XLV, 937.
[32] Luc. 22:32.
[33] *MPL*, XLV, 940.

quamvis vera et certa sint in eodem tractatu suam hanc orationem idem
pater prosequitur et subdit. Quod autem etiam perseveraturis sanctis sic
ista dicuntur, quasi eos perseveraturos habeatur incertum non aliter hoc
audire debent, quibus expedit non altum sapere sed timere. Quis enim ex
multitudine fidelium, quamdiu in hac mortalitate vivitur, in numero prae-
destinatorum se esse praesumat? Quod id occultari opus est, in hoc loco
ubi cavenda est elatio ut etiam per Satanae angelum ne extolleretur, tan-
tus colaphizaretur Apostolus.[34] Hinc et Apostolis dicebatur: si manseritis
in me, dicente illo qui illos utique sciebat esse mansuros. Et per Prophe-
tam: si volueritis et audiveritis me; cum sciret ipse in quibus operaretur et
velle; et similia multa ita dicuntur propter huius utilitatem secreti, ne forte
quis extollatur; sed omnes etiam qui bene currunt timeant, dum occultum
est quo perveniant. Propter huius ergo utilitatem secreti credendum est
quosdam de filiis perditionis, non accepto dono perseverandi usque in finem, in fide quae per dilectionem operatur incipere vivere et aliquamdiu
fideliter et iuste vivere et postea cadere; neque de hac vita priusquam haec
eis contingat auferri. Quorum si nemini contigisset tamdiu haberent homines istum saluberrimum timorem in quo vitium elationis opprimitur,
donec ad Christi gratiam qua pie vivitur pervenirent, deinceps iam securi
nunquam se ab illo esse casuros. Quae praesumptio in iusto tentationum
loco non expedit, ubi tanta est infirmitas ut superbiam possit generare
securitas. Et haec ex Augustino pro temporaria fide iustificante et dono
perseverantiae adlegata sufficiant.

Ad electionem et reprobationem veniamus. Electionis et praedestinatio-
nis nullam esse causam praeter Dei gratuitam misericordiam, extra controversiam apud omnes orthodoxos semper fuit. De reprobatione alia est
ratio, in qua ulterius progredi quam Augustinus ex verbo Dei docuit non
audeo. Augustinus de hac re ad Sixtum Presbyterum quod modestis qui-
busque satisfacere debet mihi scripsisse videtur. Querimus (inquit) meritum obdurationis et invenimus. Merito namque peccati universa massa
damnata est; nec obdurat Deus impartiendo malitiam sed non impartiendo misericordiam. Quibus enim non impartitur nec digni sunt nec merentur; ac potius ut non impartiatur hoc digni sunt, hoc merentur. Querimus
autem meritum misericordiae et non invenimus, quia nullum est, ne gratia evacuetur si non gratis donatur sed meritis redditur, etc.[35] Postea ibidem: ergo cuius vult miseretur et quem vult obdurat. Hoc facit apud
quem non est iniquitas. Miseretur gratuito dono, obdurat autem iustissimo merito. Et ibidem: Homo, tu quis es qui respondeas Deo? Numquid
dicit figmentum ei qui se finxit: Quare me sic fecisti? An non habet potestatem figulus luti ex eadem massa utique merito recteque damnata facere aliud vas in honorem indebitum propter miseriacordiae gratiam, aliud

---

[34] 2 Kor. 12:7.
[35] *MPL*, XXXIII, 879.

in contumeliam debitam propter irae iustitiam, ut notas faciat divitias glo-
riae suae in vasa misericordiae, sic ostendens quid eis largiatur, cum id
supplicium recipient vasa irae quod pariter omnibus debebatur.[36] Et idem
pater ad Simplicianum:[37] Ergo cuius vult miseretur et quem vult obdurat;
ita sententia superiori posse congruere, ut obduratio Dei sit nolle misereri,
ut non ab illo inrogetur aliquid quo sit homo deterior sed quo sit melior
non erogetur. Haec certius et tutius haec verborum forma mihi videntur
dici quam Deum aeterno suo decreto elegisse quosdam ad vitam aeternam
et alios destinasse ad mortem aeternam nulla habita peccati ratione. Male
praedestinationem meo iudicio auspicamur ab aeterno Dei decreto
praeterita praescientia. Ita docti quidam viri de aeterno illo Dei decreto
scribunt ac si ipsi divino inter fuissent consilio, quando Deus creare homines ab aeterno constituebat. In eorum confutatione immorari hoc tempore
nolo, sed alio ordine ad causas electionis et reprobationis precedendum esse demonstrare nempe a serie ordineque certo causarum quae sub prima
et aeterna illa sunt et ab ea aut aguntur aut diriguntur. Primus omnium
rerum author Deus, ut bonitatem suam communicaret creaturis, eas creavit. Primaque eius intentio fuit creaturae bonum; nihil enim odit eorum
quae fecit. Angelos Deus creavit et hominem bonos et eorum creationis
finis quem intendebat fuit aeterna felicitas. Bonos namque creavit in
bonum ipsis finem. Absurdum et a bonitate summi boni alienum est, ante
peccatum poenam ordinare. Previdet tamen Deus mobilis et inconstantis
voluntatis futuros tam angelos quam hominem, qui non starent in illa per-
fectione in qua eos creaverat; itaque nec consecuturos illius perfectionis finem; sed quod in prorsus contrarium quem suo peccato merebantur, rue-
rent, videlicet in aeternam damnationem, quam ut iustus iudex erat illatu-
rus. Lapsum eorum impedire noluit, quia mala noverat se posse in bonum
convertere et maius quiddam iudicarit esse ex malis bona elicere quam ne
mala fierent impedire. Inde erga homines commiseratio: quorum alios
servare visum est, alios propter impietatem damnare.

Simplex haec mihi videtur veritas ex ipsis rebus ut acciderunt desumpta. Ita Augustinus docuit cum pluribus in locis tum inprimis in Responsio-
ne ad articulos ipsi falso tributos. Omnium quidem hominum (inquit)
Deus creator est, sed nemo ab eo ideo creatus est ut pereat, quia alia causa
est nascendi et alia pereundi. Ut enim nascantur homines est beneficium;
ut autem pereant praevaricationis est vitium. Et nimis ergo impius et in-
doctus est qui vitium naturae non discernit ab authore naturae, a quo
prorsus alienum est quicquid in unoquoque damnandum est. Creantur
enim ut sint homines nec multiplicandis generationum successionibus opi-
ficium suum subtrahit; secundum consilium bonae voluntatis suae repara-
turus in multis quod ipse fecit, puniturus in multis quod ipse non fecit.

---

[36] *Ibid.*, 882.
[37] *CChrSL*, XLIV, 40.

Haec Augustino divina praescientia est tam eorum quae futura sunt quam quae accidere possint respicitque contrarios eventus eorumque fines in contingentibus iisque omnibus quae in hominum reliquit arbitrio, ut faciant aut non faciant et cum nihil lateat divinam praescientiam in causis tantum innumeratur eorum quae Deus ipse facturus est. Prescit enim Deus tam aliena quam sua opera. Sunt in hoc mundo Dei opera, sunt et Diaboli et membrorum ipsius, quae omnia Deus prescivit futura. Suorum operum quae bona sunt ipse est author, et alienorum quae mala sunt moderator et rector, ut illa in bonum vertat aut ex illis bona eliciat. Sed quia ruinam angelorum et Adami lapsum praevidit, id nec angelis nec homini peccandi ullam necessitatem attulit. Hinc Augustino nefas est, Deo ascribere causas ruinarum; qui etsi ex aeterna scientia praecognitum habet, quid uniuscuiusque meritis retributurus sit; nemini tamen per hoc quod falli non potest aut necessitatem aut voluntatem intulit delinquendi. Idem postea. Ad praevaricationem legis, ad neglectum religionis, ad corruptelam disciplinae, ad desertionem fidei, ad perpetrationem qualiscumque peccati, nulla est omnino praedestinatio Dei; nec fieri potest ut per quem a talibus malis surgitur, per eum in talia decidatur. Haec Augustinus. Supplicii peccatis hominum et angelorum debiti ut iustus iudex Deus author est. Sed neminem prius reprobat, neminem prius obdurat quam de peccato cognoscat: precedit decretum scientia et iudicium cognitio. Quamvis Dei voluntas ipsiusque scientia sint ipsa Dei essentia, divinas naturae ordine apud homines, humano more loquimur. In sapiente voluntatem et electionem praecedit plena perfectaque scientia et cum iudicio et ratione deliberatio. Quae non in Deo perfectissima et summa esse negari non possit; male a voluntatis divinae aeterno decreto meo iudicio incipitur. Si quis obiiciat voluntatem divinam esse summam aequitatem et proinde quae voluntate sua ab aeterno decrevit summa aequitate id facere, fatebor quidem; sed voluntas non significat aequitatem. Quare qui hominibus loquuntur si intelligi volunt, substituant pro voluntatis voce aliam, nempe aequitatem; et dicant ab aeterno Deum summa aequitate et iusto iudicio obdurare et reprobare decrevisse quos reprobat quia reprobatione digni sunt, et summa misericordia servare electos qui natura sua indigni sunt; verum loquetur et quod omnes facile intelligent nec erit qui contradicet. Et haec hoc tempore sufficere poterant; sed quia Augustinus ad Simplicianum in recantione adlegatur, in compendium contracta quae ibi disputantur fusius inferam.

Augustinus respondens ad questiones Simpliciani,[38] an quemadmodum nullo merito Jacob fuit a Deo electus, etiam nullo merito improbatus fuit Esau, probat primo electionis nulla merita praecessisse in Jacob; de Esau vero non ita absolute respondere audet; et merito quidem, quia causa dilectionis nulla erat in Jacob, erat odii (quamvis communis) magna in Esau causa. Interrogat igitur his verbis: an forte quemadmodum illud de Jacob

---

[38] *Ibid.*, 32f.

nullis meritis bonae actionis dicitur, ita Esau nullis meritis malae actionis odiosus? Et disputando inquirit quo merito Esau odio haberetur antequam nasceretur. Quod enim (inquit) fecit Deus in Jacob ea quae deligeret, nulla quaestio est. Si autem dicamus fecisse quae odisset, absurdum est, occurrente alia Scriptura et dicente: Neque enim odio habens aliquid constituisses et nihil odisti horum quae fecisti.[39] Ut eruat quo sensu dictum fuerit: Jacob dilexi, Esau odio habui,[40] comparationes adfert creaturarum quas alias aliis Deus praetulit et maiori gloria ornavit, et concludit: sed ille omnia dilexit, quamvis excellentiae diversis gradibus ordinata; quoniam vidit Deus quia omnia bona sunt cum dicto eius instituta; ut autem odisset Esau nisi iniustitiae merito, iniustum est. Etc. Et tandem post acrem disputationem Scripturae huius verum sensum eruit his verbis: Ergo cuius vult miseretur et quem vult obdurat,[41] ita sententiae superiori posse congruere, ut obduratio Dei sit, nolle misereri, ut non ab illo irrogetur aliquid quo sit homo deterior, sed tantum quo melior fiat non erogetur. Quod si fit nulla distinctione meritorum, quis non erumpat in eam vocem quam sibi ipsi subiecit Apostolus[42] et quod si fit (inquit) nihil adfirmans. Tandem sequitur resolutio quaestionis. Sit igitur hoc fixum atque immobile in mente sobria pietate atque stabili fide, quod nulla iniquitas est apud Deum; atque ita tenacissime firmissimeque credatur idipsum quod Deus cuius vult miseretur et cuius vult non miseretur, esse alicuius occulta et humano modo investigabilis aequitatis, quae et in ipsis rebus humanis terrenisque contractibus animadvertenda est. In quibus nisi supernae iustitiae quaedam impressa vestigia teneremus, nunquam in ipsum cubile ac penetrale sanctissimum atque castissimum spiritualium praeceptorum nostra infirmitas inhiaret intentio.

Beati qui esuriunt et sitiunt iustitiam, quoniam ipsi saturabuntur.[43] In ista igitur siccitate vitae conditionisque mortalis, nisi aspergeretur desuper velut tenuissima quaedam aura iustitiae, citius aresceremus quam quod sitiremus. Quapropter cum dando et accipiendo inter se hominum societas convertatur, dentur igitur et accipiantur debita vel non debita, quis non videt iniquitatis argui neminem posse qui quod sibi debetur exegerit, nec eum certe qui quod ei debetur donare voluerit. Hoc autem non est in eorum qui debitores sunt, sed in eius cui debetur arbitrio. Haec imago vel (ut supra dixi) vestigium negotiis hominum de fastigio summo aequitatis impressum est. Sunt igitur omnes homines quandoquidem ut Apostolus ait: in Adam omnes moriuntur,[44] a quo universum genus humanum origo ducitur offensionis Dei, una quaedam massa peccati supplicium debens

---

[39] *Sap.* 11:25.
[40] Rom. 9:13.
[41] Rom. 9:18.
[42] *CChrSL*, 40.
[43] Matth. 5:6.
[44] 1 Kor. 15:22.

divinae summaeque iustitiae; quod sive exigatur sive donetur, nulla est iniquitas. A quibus autem exigendum et quibus donandum sit, superbe iudicant debitores; quemadmodum conducti ad illam vineam iniuste indignati sunt cum tantundem aliis donaretur quantum illis redderetur, etc.[45]

Sequitur et alia quaestio: quo sensu Deus qui nihil odit eorum quae fecit, dicatur odisse Esau.[46] In qua disputatione probat omnem creaturam Dei esse bonam et a Deo amari nec Deum odisse in homine quicquam nisi peccatum. Et concludit: non igitur odit Deus Esau hominem, sed odit Esau peccatorem.[47] Quod quum ita esse negari non possit, non absurde in Esau creditur odii fuisse causam peccatum, quum dilectionis nulla fuit in Jacob nisi gratia, quae non ipsius erat meriti, sed sublata causa odii communi peccato tota divinae gratiae debebatur. Quamobrem nimis preceps illa censura fuit quae Baretum male recantare coegit quae bene dixerat. Longe aequior sanctus pater Augustinus fuit in eos qui per omnia in iis omnibus quae praedestinationem electorum concernunt cum eo non idem sentiebant: de quibus ad Hilarium in libro De praedestinatione sanctorum haec quae hic subiicio respondit: pervenerunt autem isti fratres nostri pro quibus solicita est pia charitas vestra, ut credant cum ecclesia Christi peccato primo hominis obnoxium nasci genus humanum nec ab isto malo nisi per iustitiam secundi hominis aliquem liberari. Pervenerunt etiam ut praeveniri voluntates hominum Dei gratia fateantur atque ut ad nullum opus bonum vel incipiendum vel perficiendum sibi quemquam sufficere posse consentiant; retenta ergo ista in quae pervenerunt plurimum eos a Pelagianorum errore discernunt. Proinde se in eis ambulent et orent eum qui dat intellectum si quid de praedestinatione aliter sapiunt, ipse illis hoc quoque revelabit.

Fuerunt et sunt adhuc hodie in diversis ecclesiis quamplures fideles Christi servi bene de ecclesia meriti qui non idem de praedestinatione sentiunt, qui tamen se mutua charitate fuerunt nec ullius sese mutuo hereseos insimulant. Interea tamen nec convitia nec maledicta Bareti, quae in pios Christi servos Ioannem Calvinum et Petrum Martyrem ac alios acerbius visus est protulisse, ullo modo probo.

---

[45] *CChrSL,* 41f.

[46] *Ibid.,* 44f.

[47] *Ibid.,* 45.

Cambridge, Trinity College, Ms.B.14.9.
Strype. *Whitgift,* III, 321-337 (in accurate transcription).

## XL. SARAVIA TO JOHN WHITGIFT
Canterbury, 4 June 1599

Quod semper in votis habui (Reverendissime in Christo Pater et Domini mihi omni observantia colende) non possum continuo non desiderare, nempe aut ut in parocia mea habitem, aut saltem in loco aliquo vicino, unde facilis et frequens ad eam sit accessus, mihi dari. Tamen nec paroeciam resignare nec permutare nec decedenti curato alium surrogare sine Clementiae voluntate aut consilio aequum censeo. Aut hic magister Simon vicarius S. Nicolai in Tenet, qui mecum per mutuam resignationem permutare paratus est, si modo ita videatur Clem. T. Atque id responsi dedi Ephraim Pagitt, qui mihi tuas literas attulit. Sed ego intelligo populum S. Nicolai durum et in suos pastores ingratum, qui sine lite et mala ipsorum gratia iura sua obtinere nequeant. Quae res quam mihi et meae aetati incommodae, T. Cl. esto iudicium. Tametsi literis tuis parere et Ephraim Pagit surrogare Ioanni Worship paratus sum; significandum tamen tibi iudicavi iam antea successionem fuisse a me promissam mag. Iacobo Forestero si contingeret magistrum Worship discedere, sed hac conditione: si probaret T. Clem. Atque ita tuum erit arbitrium utrum surrogare velis. Iudicavi praeterea mihi esse officii has schedas tibi transmittere, ex quibus aliquo modo ecclesiarum insularium statum cognosces. Possem huius generis plures mittere, sed hoc tempore has paucas sufficere existimavi. Non est meum docere te; quid facto sit opus tua prudentia melius dispiciet. Deus valetudinem tuam conservet incolumen, precor. Cantuaria 4. die Iunii 1599.

Tua Clementiae Observantiss.
Had. Saravia

Cambridge, University Library. Ms. Mm 1, 43, fol. 457f. (copy)

## XLI. SARAVIA TO JOHN WHITGIFT
### Canterbury, 23 December 1600

Reverendiss. in Christo Patri ac Domino
Domino meo Clementiss. S.P.P.

Omnes boni ad suum officium pertinere ducunt, de vita et incolumitate Clementissimae Dominae Reginae magis quam de sua sollicitos esse. Et ita affectos multos tam in Regno quam extra regnum peregrinos novi, qui vitae suae periculum citius subituri sunt quam suppressuri quidquam quod detrimentum ipsius Maiestati esset allaturum. Accidit ut hodie D. Chevalerius venerit ad me duobus comitatus peregrinis, quorum alter non ita pridem a Gallia rediit. Is ait se Ambiani vidisse iuvenem quendam Ioh. Ellis vulgo vocatum, filium civis huius urbis (cui nomen fingerant Ellis) hospitii Trium Regum Domini. Hunc iuvenem aiunt pessimis vixisse moribus, ganeonem, aleatorem, amicis infidum, nullius bonae frugis, nullius denique bonae fidei. Hunc eum primum abduxerunt milites quidem vel generosuli partium D. Austriaci, promittentes patri nihil filio ipsius defuturum ex re fore adolescentis exteras videre regiones et earum edificere linguas et nosse mores. Ubi abiisset adolescens, pater vicinis aiebat se non expectare reditum filii antequam vidisset Italiam et linguam italicam didicisset. Bis tamen paucis intervallis in hanc urbem rediit et cras mane in Aulam proficiscitur. Paucis ab hinc diebus Ambiani visus est ad missam ire, et cum incidisset in quosdam ei notos quod hic vixissent et hodie ibi suam exercent artem, ultro citroque sermone habito eos hortatus est suo exemplo fieri catholicos: quamdiu additi manerent reformatae religioni fore miseros; factus sum (inquit) catholicus et nunc nihil mihi deest. Preterea familiaris admodum ibi erat cuidam franciscano, qui eum Parisios deduxit et postea reduxit et usque ad Abvillam eum est comitatus; ubi et familiare colloquium habuit cum quodem Anglo qui captaneus est et militat sub Austriaco. Abevilla discedens transiecit in Angliam. Nunc secundo ex Gallia redit, pre se ferens se mitti ab iis qui cum imperio sunt. Qui hominem norunt, malum ab eo metuunt; nullum sperant bonum. Dominos Consiliarios nec sapientia nec consilium deficit. Mihi verisimile non est imberberem iuvenem tantae prudentiae et rerum experientiae viris verba dare posse. Sed boni viri suo non esse satisfactum putarunt officio nisi quae viderunt et audiverunt in Gallia ad tuam Clem. transmitterim. Habent enim suspectum adolescentem et ipsius omnes actiones. Ego vero eum non novi; ater an albus sit nescio. De re t.C. utetur pro sua prudentia. Hic Deum precor: ut multos annos Ecclesiae suae tuam vitam servet incolumem. Cantuaria 23 die Decemb. 1600.

Tuae Clementiae Observantiss.
Hadrianus Sarravia

Hatfield House Library. Cecil Papers, 82, fol. 82

## XLII. SARAVIA TO JOHN WHITGIFT
### Canterbury, 7 January 1600/1601

Praeter illa quae ad T.C. scripsi nihil de patre illius adolescentis audio unde commendari aut vituperari magnopere possit. Filium educavit in hac urbe ut potuit. Is puer frequentavit huius ecclesiae scholam, sed postquam grandior factus liberius suo arbitrio vivendi potestatem fuit nactus, alea et comessationibus sese dedidit sui vero et alieni profusus fraude et dolo undecunque et a quibuscunque petuit nummos corradens, unde saepe suos parentes in gravem luctum coniecit. Accidit antequam hinc mare transiret, ut patrem magna pecunia quae apud ipsum deposita erat compilaret cum qua in partes Boreales aufugit. Ibi D. Eirenarchis suspectus propter vitae ipsius dissolutionem et rumorum copiam traditus fuit custodiae. Quod ubi pater ipsius rescivit eo se contulit et partem pecuniae quam nondum decoxerat recepit ac filium reduxit. De iis quae in Gallia facta sunt tres honesti viri peregrini huius Ecclesiae domum reversi narrant quae subiicio; nomina eorum habet pars epistolae quam ex autographo descripsi. Unus eorum cum in Abevilla esset forte fortuna invitatus fuit ad coenam in qua etiam Franciscanus erat qui Iohannem Elis Parrisiis deduxerant Abevillam et ibi tunc ipsius expectabat reditum. Inter coenandum coepit Franciscanus commendare istum Iohannem Elis et adhortari convivam ut exemplo illius relinqueret novam religionem. Nomen Franciscani est Anthonius. Postea alius in eadem urbe Iohannem Elis reversum ex Anglia parantem denuo iter in Angliam habuit obviam et fuit ab eo ad coenam invitatus in hospitio quod Magnum Herculem vocant. Sub coenae tempus cum eo venisset, invenit ipsum cum quodam Anglo qui recens factus erat presbyter et cum Capitaneo Smit, Anglo qui meret in Belgio. Presbyter non ibi mansit nec cum eis coenavit. Ut parem gratiam referret hospes hospiti, ipse similiter Iohannem Elis invitavit qui libenter ab eo quinque aureos solares commodato accepisset. Excusavit se quantum potuit, sed importunitate victus dedit ei duos aureos solares in hac urbe refundendos fratri aut uxori. Paulo post comitatus aliis quatuor Anglis Abevilla secundo in Angliam navigavit et hac transivit illo ipso die quo priorem scripsi epistolam. Ipsius reditus ab aula indies expectatur ab eius patre, qui credit magnum aliquem Dominum opera filii ipsius uti ad magnas res. Hodie rediit ex Gallia Dominus ille qui cum Franciscano coenaverat et a pio adolescente qui Amiani agit cum altero qui etiam in hac urbe natus est literas ad suum patrem scriptas attulit, quas Maior Donoborniae aperuit et latori iussit illas ostendere. Maiori huius urbis illarum literarum partem hic asscripsi. Inde T.Cl. poterit cognoscere consentire inter se omnia et Iohannem Elis esse simulatorem et dissimulatorem improbum. Quo uti ad rem bonam et utilem an quis possit, meum non est iudicium.

> John Elis which came to me and to my companion in the shop wee are won to woorke and weare very glad to see him, but wee weare very sory for to see the

silley abuse in that he did pull off his hat to the Idols and that he did put off his
hat to the preiste and that he did use some wordes which did not like us very
well. This is to let you understand that wee did drinke together one quarte off
wine and no more, for he was very hastie to be gone or elles wee shoulde have
knowne more of his minde. But as wee did drinke together, he did show us some letters which he had in his sleave of his dobblyt and that theare was the di-
vell in them. All this wee did see and heare, but you may enquire of Willyame
Mesman and Peter Dauchine and of Jeames Manschee and you shall heare
more of them ffor they have talked with the fryer which came from Parrys
with thym, and the fryer doeth say that he is a very good Catholicke and doeth
like him very well, and wee do heare by that fryer that he doeth serve a cap-
tayne which doeth serve the ennemy. And this is very true that I have written
on to you and they will certifie you off it that it is true that I have written on to
you this. I commend you on to God.

Hoc est exemplar (Amplissime prosul) quam postridie Calendas Ianuarii scripsi et die sequenti T.Cl. misi, quam tibi non redditam fuisse vehementer doleo. Nihil habeo quod eis addam, nisi adolescentem esse adhuc
imberbem 22 annorum et quatuor illos Anglos in quorum est comitatu pueros pedisequos habere Gallos ex Abevilla assumptos. Literae autem scriptae iussu Cl.T. mihi redditae sunt heri a prandio qui sextus erat huius
mensis. Multos annos ut vivas et valeas, Deum precor. Cantuaria septimo
die Ianuarii.

                                    Tuae Clementiae Observantissimus
                                    Hadrianus Sarravia

Hatfield House Library. Cecil Papers, 75, fol. 109, 110[r]

## XLIII. SARAVIA TO JOHN WHITGIFT
### Canterbury, 27 February 1600/1601

Non possum (Reverendissime in Christo Pater et honorarissime Domine) quae hic intelligo a peregrinis huius ecclesiae Caleto redeuntibus non scribere; quorum alii septem octove menses, alii plus vel minus ibi versati sunt, ut tanquam illic domicilium habentes tuto per Flandriam iter facere possent et sua negotia illic peragere. Hi narrant, diversis in locis notos se vultus Anglorum comitatus Cantii passim obviam habuisse, non qui ibi negotiarentur sed cum Iesuitis et sacrificulis Anglis missas frequentarent eorumque templa audirent et inprimis Duaci. Ibi moneta Anglica frequentior est quavis alia, etiam indigena. In Santo Audomaro esse ultra sexcentos Anglos, quorum maior pars est puerorum et adolescentulorum, qui ibidem instituuntur in bonis literis. Habent enim ibi scholam et collegium, cuius Praefectus vel Rector est Anglus cui nomen est magister Guilelmus Flacbet. Quaedam mulier Caleto ad matrem scripsit, se ab hinc paucis diebus casu fuisse in aedibus cuiusdam ubi ingens pondus pecuniarum missum ex Anglia traditum fuit Syndico Iesuitarum Santaudomari et iumentis impositum deferendum ad magistrum Guilelmum Flacbet. Insulis Iesuitae Angli incipiunt nidificare. Quando agebat Caletii narrant quotidie ex Flandria et Hispania confluxisse Anglos Papistas notos ex superstitione qua advenas caeteros superant. Hi mutatis vestibus mare inde in Angliam ad diversas partes transmittunt, et quodam tempore semel 15 qui recens venerant ex Hispania, huc in diversis navigiis traiecisse. Et ex quodam audivi, quod cum huc navigaret, quinque aut sex Angli cum eo in eadem navi furerint, sed qui in notum portum secum noluerint descendere, advocato piscatorio parvo navigio, dederunt singuli aureum piscatori ut eos exponeret in littore quod ipsi vellent. Haec sunt quae Clem. T. significanda iudicavi. Deus valitudinem vitamque tuam multos annos servet incolumem. Cantuariae 27. die mensis Febr. 1600.

Tuae Clementiae Observantissimus
Hadrianus Sarravia

Cambridge, University Library. Ms. Mm 1, 43, fol. 458f. (copy)

## XLIV. SARAVIA TO THE BISHOP OF LONDON
### Canterbury, 24 October s.a.

Meum de N. et eorum omnium qui cum eo sentiunt iudicium cum primis, reverende Praesul, arbitrabar te pluries ex me audivisse, nempe non alio loco esse apud me quam in republica seditiosi cives habendi sunt schismaticus est, et qui [in] Ecclesia primus author est schismatis, nihil differt a seditioso cive in Republica. N. scripta quae legi mihi visa sunt hominis perversissimi iudicii quique a Romana Ecclesia non tam Christiano Spiritu quam schismatico dissentiret. Quae haec fuit audacia altare contra altare edificare et ecclesiam contra ecclesiam congregare? Exemplum quo ab Ecclesia Romana discessimus, nihil eum iuvat, quia discessum est tantum propter illa in quibus societas salva pietate retineri non potuit quorum, si conciliatio posset obtineri, longe plura publicae paci Christianae danda essent quam schismaticis istis probabitur, qui dum ad suum sensum omnia reformata volunt potius quam ad pacificum totius Christianae gentis communem usum dissipant, non congregant, et infirmorum animos a veritate Christiana avertunt. Isti non cogitant quantum haec dissidia Christianorum noceant in commune universo Christiano nomine. De conciliandis inter se Christianis nullam habent cogitationem, sed alienationem tantam moliuntur a caeteris omnibus Christianis quae nullam unquam conciliationem admittet. Et quod schismaticorum omnium semper fuit proprium, in istis hominibus invenies: seorsim Ecclesias sibi colligere, sibi de singularitate placere et omnes alias prae se despicere ecclesias. Quod non pergant in suo schismate quod inchoarant non fit quod schismatis eos poeniteat, sed quia fautores potentes nullos habent; quos ubi nacti fuerint redibunt ad ingenium. Quid aliud nunc hac disputatione queritur? Schismatis nomen habet crimen et infamiam, quod fateri nec se ullam habuisse causam allegare posse grave nimis est. Labe huius turpitudinis aspergenda est Leitourgia Anglicanae Ecclesiae cum Antistitum nimia severtitate. Haec honesta ratio visa est abstergendae omnis foeditatis suscitati in Ecclesia discidii. Quam facile est ostendere malum utinam tam facile esset afferre remedium. De bono Rege non nisi bona expectanda sunt; hinc nullum nisi bonum expecto exitum. Si in me esset audacia quam video in istis hominibus, ego iam olim ad Regem scripsissem. Si Dominus Beza viveret, haud dubie ultro ad Regem suam sententiam scripsisset de rebus Ecclesiasticis in hoc regno controversis, quas non nisi aliorum relatione, vera falsane nil dico, didicisse oportuerit, nihil tamen quicquam ab officio suo indignum se facere credidisset. Quia cum una sit tantum Ecclesia Catholica, quicquid in aliqua una peccatur illius parte ad omnes alias pertinet. Ipse tamen tam remotus ab Anglia parte tantum altera audita non potuit non falli, quod saepe ei evenit; quod quamvis ignorare non posset, nihilominus scripsisset. Quid vero aliud quam illud ipsum quod ante scripsit de triplici Episcoporum genere? Ego me cum D. Beza non comparo: primas partes quod me attinet in omni bonarum literarum genere ei lubens concedo, sed non ut quicquam in Ecclesiis mutet aut innovet quae Patrum et priscarum Ecclesiarum generalis consensus esse firma et immota iubet, aut ut ipsius authoritas novos mores et ritus nusquam terrarum alicubi visos aut auditos invehat, non dissimulabo. Sed hoc D. Bezae non concedam: quod unquam Anglicanae Ecclesiae controversias melius me noverit aut illius mores propius inspexerit, quare si meas rationes ipsius iudicio praefero, nullam ipsi censeri debeo facere iniuriam. Scribam igitur atque temeritatis et audaciae subibo potius nomen quam neglecti in hac parte officii, et ostendam Regi facilem viam et liberandi sese ab omnibus importunis petitionibus reformatorum adeo honestam et piam ut nemini bono quisquis erit displicere queat. In una tantum re laborabo: ut inveniam nobilem per quem Regi tradatur mea Epistola. Vale, Praesul Amplissime. Cantuaria 24 die Octobris.

Tuae Reverentiae addictissimus
Had. Saravia

BL Add. Ms. 28571. Nr. 51, fol. 207

## XLV. SARAVIA TO RICHARD BANCROFT
### Canterbury, 20 October 1608

Amplissimo Presuli Reverendissimo in Christo Patri ac Domino hono-
ratissimo D. Richardo, Dei Providentia Cantuariensi Archiepiscopo et
Ecclesiae Anglicanae Primati et Regiae Maiestati a sacratioribus consiliis,
Domino meo S.P.P.

Quae aliquando Cl. T. in familiari colloquio de Iusto Lypsio narravi,
D. Pashiefieldus hortatur ut in epistola illa eadem retexam; tibi gratum id
futurum ait. Exordiar igitur ab amicitia quae quondam inter nos non vul-
garis intercessit: cuius rei ipsius ad me literae testes fuerunt, quas in prima
earum editione cum aliis pluribus evulgavit; sed in secunda praeterivit,
nulla a me affectus iniuria. Simul cum coelo mutavit animum quando ad
Romanistas transiit, apud quos male nomen meum audit hereticus. Ipse
ille idem sibi similis non permansit constans qui de constantia scripsit; nisi
forte insignis dissimulator fuerit qui aliud in pectore clausum tenuerit, aliud foris simulaverit; cuius rei tametsi non parva ediderit signa cum apud
nos viveret; nostri candoris non erat male facta dictave amici interpretari.
Dilexi hominem et colui quantum alius quivis ex Leydanae Academiae
professoribus, tum propter ipsius raram eruditionem tum etiam propter
singularem morum mansuetudinem ac modestiam qua se omnibus amabi-
lem praebebat. Et cum ipsius scripta nescio quid tumidi et inflati spirare
videantur, in moribus nihil erat huiusmodi. Doctrinam evangelicam nunquam professus est, illi tamen aperte quod sciam (quamdiu nobiscum
vixit) nunquam adversatus est. In controversiis quas nebulones illic move-
rant, meliori parti favere et assentiri, pacem et concordiam amare, et odisse seditiosos nobis videbatur. Sed familiae H. N. mos est, publica authoritate constitutae religioni palam non adversari: illius observantes videri et
haberi volunt. A crassa Romanae Ecclesiae idololatria abhorrere sese pro-
fitebatur, quam tamen suo libro de Halensi idolo confirmavit. Ab illa vero
quam nos profitemur non alienum habere animum, ex ipsius tum dictis
tum factis mihi persuadebam. Sed in hoc generali et magno religionis dis-
sidio quod nulli parti se adiungeret, propter amicos quos multos habebat
non idem de religione sentientes, ne forte illorum quemquam offenderet
fieri credebam. Omnia sua scripta tunc ita attemperabat, ut religionem
non tangeret et lector nesciat num illa quae scripsit profecta sint ab homine Christiano an ab ethnico. Hoc quidem et a me, et ab aliis animadver-
sum fuit, sed dissimulandum duximus, quia magnorum virorum se tueri
poterat exemplo qui, cum Christiani essent, philosophica argumenta ita
tractarunt ut in illis nihil appareat Christiani. Levinus Torrentius, qui
summus illi fuit amicus, in epistola quadam id notavit, et hominem ita
philosophos admirari ut Christi doctrina pennas teneat, graviter admo-
nuit. Inter varios sermones quos familiariter habuimus, incidit mentio antiquitatis morum priscae Ecclesiae super illo apophthegmate, quo pro

symbolo utitur: moribus antiquis stat res romana virisque; quod quum non minus recessum sit Romae a moribus et doctrina Ecclesiae quae ab Apostolis ibi plantata fuit et viguit aliquot seculis, quam in rebus civilibus quae fuerunt olim sub regibus vel consulibus vel imperatoribus, me plurimum mirari Iesuitas, qui propter variam eruditionem hoc ignorare non possunt, defendere tamen immensam illam potestatem quam hodie sibi arrogat Romanus Episcopus in omnes tum Reges eorumque Regna tum episcopos omnes et eorum episcopatus, quae ignorata fuit priscis temporibus; similiter imaginum usum in Ecclesiis, qui nullus erat antiquitus, et alia id genus quam plurima, tanquam ab apostolis tradita tam impudenter audere. Desperatae cuiusdam esset impudentiae ex praesenti rerum statu civili aut qui ab his mille annis fuit, de illo iudicium facere velle qui fuit olim sub Tullio aut sub Augusto primisve Regibus. Lypsius a puero fuit a Iesuitis institutus in omni disciplinarum genere et eorum mores apprime noverat. Is mihi ita respondit. primum parem non esse omnium eruditionem plerosque antiquitatis esse ignaros, et illos qui ceteros eruditione et iudicio excellunt (qui pauci sunt) dissimulare quod sciunt. Quia eorum iudicio rudiores Christiani non inutiliter illa nesciant et vulgus Christianorum in officio non male superstitione contineatur; a qua si illos liberes, aut in heresim aut in impietatem prolabentur; doctioribus illa nihil noceant. Alio tempore cum ex ipso audirem nihil in nostra religione eum improbare, quaesivi ab eo, cur non se nobis in coenae Dominicae communione adiungeret. O, (inquiebat) tu foelix homo es, qui coniugem nactus es tecum in religione consentientem; mea mihi adversatur; quotidianam pacem et domesticam cum uxore colere me oportet, si vivere volo. Plantini similiter uxor et ipsius domestici ac familiares, uno Raphelingio seniore excepto, qui gener ipsius erat, papistae erant: eam autem religionem rudioribus animis aptiorem mihi credere visus est. Cum tempore quodam ruri spatiaremur Lypsius, Plantinus et ego, nobis de religione multus variusque fuit sermo; tunc Plantinus: religiones, inquit, sunt et semper fuerunt plurimae et variae sibique invicem inimicae. Habent enim omnes simulationis et dissimulationis plurimum; contemnendae tamen non sunt, quamdiu nullum scelus habent admixtum, propter imbeciliores animos. Vulgus hominum rudimentis huiusmodi habet opus: celestia et divina aliter capere non potest. Una tantum pietas est, quae simplex est nec habet quicquam simulati. Multos religiosos mundus semper habuit, pios vere perpaucos. Abruptus ab iis qui supervenerunt amicis hic fuit sermo nec eundem resumendi post se obtulit occasio. Accidit quodam tempore cum in Lypsii essem aedibus, advenire quendam senem incessu et habitu externo gravem, cana et promissa barba, cum comitatu quatuor aut quinque virorum; ipse Antverpiae aliquando eundem hominem videram cum pari comitatu, et tunc eum notaveram ut de facie mihi notus esset, quippe quem mihi amici et fratres iudicassent esse patriarcham familiae charitatis et successisse H. N. Hic non vulgari salutatione complexus est Lypsium;

idem fecerunt ipsius comites. Ego tacitus mirabar unde haec tanta notitia et familiaritas esset Lypsio cum illo homine. Itaque cum post salutationem alloquerentur sese, erat in illo comitatu quidam mihi antea notus, quocum de religione multa fueram pluries Cortraci collocutus, ubi tunc diversabatur mercimoniorum causa. Illum ego salutavi et quo modo se res ipsius haberent interrogavi: num nihil damni accepisset ex capto ab hostibus Cortraco. Postquam illi omnes discessissent, quaesivit ex me Lypsius num homines illos nossem; respondi fieri posse ut illos viderim, sed praeter illum unum quem salutaveram esse pariter ignotos. Plantinum autem fuisse illius sectae presbyterum a pluribus accepi; et cum Leydae ageret, bibliopola quidem (qui ipsius fuerat famulus) hoc ei palam exprobravit; de quo tamen apud amicos conquestus non est nec probri loco duxit. Istius patriarchae librum quendam, cui titulus est ,,Thesaurus in agro absconditus'', domi suae impressum teutonice et gallice ab eo accepi, pretio an dono non memini. Totius libri summa huc redit, homines in sese habere thesaurum illum absconditum, et perverso errore homines extra se quaerere quod in eis latet ipsisque est intimum. Et haec opinio a Stoicorum sententia non multum abhorrere videtur, quae hominis faelicitatem et summum bonum contendit mortales habere in semetipsis si vellent uti: et per ipsos stare quod non sunt beati. Ad stoicam quandam philosophiam mihi traducere videntur omnia quae in sacris continentur literis. Illo libro quamvis author aliud agere videatur et Christi mentionem faciat, omne Christi evertit meritum, et quod in Christo Christique meritis quaerimus, intra nos ipsos nos habere disputat. Quum in Belgio flagraret persecutio Ducis Albani, Speculum iustitiae H. N. aliaque ipsius opuscula Plantinus excudebat. Ubi Christi fideles variis modis affligebantur, istius farinae homines nihil metuebant; cum omnes pii fugerent et in exilium abibant, isti securi in pace et otio domi suae manebant. Quando istorum hominum libros lego, in labyrintho versari mihi videor. Per ambages lectorem deducunt et suspensum tenent; identidem alia sermonis forma idem inculcant; novis confictis vocabulis utuntur, quae in verbo Dei nusquam inveniuntur nec veteres theologi illis sunt usi. Illa quidem videntur magnifica et nescio quid exotici sonare. Sed ut dicam paucis quod sentio: defectionem veram docent a Christianismo; Christum enim nullum habent nisi typicum. Sacras literas veteris testamenti et novi suis allegoriis trahunt quo libet. Quidquid in novo testamento de Christo legitur, allegoria est, quae veritatem tollit historiae et ad virtutes trahit quas in quovis Christiano inveniri oportet. Ego pluries cum Plantino egi, quem sciebam illius doctrinae fumo infuscatum, ut aliquid ab eo discerem. Sed verbis assentiebatur nobis in omnibus, excepto ceremoniarum usu et externo Dei cultu. Quem ut necessarium hominum vulgo fatebatur, ita superfluum eum esse perfectioribus aiebat. Ab illis tamen contemni non oportere, propter infirmorum scandalum. Quo quis illis minus eget, magis illis utetur, ne quemquam offendat eorum qui externo illo cultu veluti manu ducuntur ad meliorem et prestantiorem sta-

tum, quem vocant Christi. Id autem fit per regenerationem spiritus sancti
in novum hominem, in qua homo fit Deus et Deus homo. Et magnifice
novis suis nominibus efferunt haec, quae imperitis speciosa videntur, cum
sub ipsis lateant magnae blasphemiae. Illud quod de Christo legimus,
quod Deus sit factus homo et homo Deus, idem fieri oportere in quovis
perfecto homine novaque creatura docent. Et illam novam creaturam vocant in suo idiomate ,,vergodet mensche'', quem latine diceres ,,hominem
Deificatum''. In cultu vero externo, qui hominem ducit ad Deum et ad
perfectiorem statum, missam aliasque papisticas ceremonias numerant.
Huius familiae author H. N. commentariolum edidit in Missam, expo-
nens quae ibi sunt mysteria, quae divinarum et celestium rerum imagines,
quas sibi ob oculos praeponere debent missophili; gradus enim ipsis est ad
praestantiorem Dei cognitionem. Invitant omnes alias sectas ad se, non ut
illas relinquant sed ut istam suae addant tamquam colophonem; nimirum
quod omnes deficiantur vera pietate nisi haec accesserit. Mahumetista,
Judeus, papista cuiusvis ordinis, Episcopus, presbyter, monachus, Franciscanus, Dominicanus, Iesuita, et quivis alius hypocrita, immo ipsimet
Cardinales et alia pecora campi, in hac familia stabulari possunt. Quapropter ego nihil miror hominem qui in hac fuit heresi, laudare potuisse
idolum Halense. Invenere procul dubio acumine sui ingenii isti homines
in imagine Virginis Mariae mysterium laude et commendatione dignum.
Alias Lypsius ad laudandum mutum idolum pertractus nunquam fuisset.
Missam commendat H. N.; quidni Lypsius imaginem virginis Mariae
laudet? Utrobique latet mysterium, quod non omnes intelligunt. In com-
mentariolo suo H. N. de mysteriis septem sacramentorum et de praecipuis
ceremoniis ecclesiae Catholicae ac in primis de Missa, ad quam colendam
suam cohortatur familiam, illos omnes reprehendit qui ab Ecclesia Catholica defecerunt et contra tum septem sacramentorum tum ipsius missae
mysteria scribere ausi sunt. Fuerunt meo tempore in Flandria et similiter
in Holandia huius farinae ministri et seniores qui nobiscum eandem profi-
tebantur doctrinam et eadem sacramenta ministrabant. Quidam ex illis
mihi sua communicavit arcana et libros, praefatus se negaturum omnia si
proderem. Sed nihil opus fuit: post ipse tandem satis seipsum prodidit editione cuiusdam sui libri simul cum Davidis Georgii precipuo volumine,
quod typis mandaverat. De hac re convictus in Synodo, Magistratus urbis
in qua ministerio fungebatur, hominem defendit et in suo munere ut antea
perseverare iussit. Qua in re dissentiant David Georgius ab H. N. ego
nescio: uterque deificationem docet; sed nihil Davidis ad meas manus pervenit. Ex sermonibus Tauleri et Theologia Germanica, quam in latinum
sermonem Castallio transtulit, suae doctrinae fundamenta isti desumere
videri volunt. Utrumque tamen in suis scriptis commendat, ubi vero nescio,
D. Lutherus; et ego cum in papatu vivebam illos libros legi et omnia can-
dide interpretabar: quod mihi viderentur homines ab externis et superfluis
ceremoniis, quibus Dei cultus obruitur, transferre ad spiritualem et verum

Dei cultum. Nunc vero quamvis in Taulero nihil quod tam foedis erroribus patrocinetur, inveniam, inter orthodoxos illum non habeo. Sed Theologia Germanica tota referta est theorematibus ambiguis quae Doctrinam
H. N. confirmare videntur. Liber brevis est et facilis comparatu. Horum
omnium T. C. iudicium esto. Haec pluribus forsan describo quam necesse
est, ut melius quid de Do. Lypsio suspicer intelligas; quibus non plus fidei
adhiberi desidero quam res ipsa evincit. Hic igitur finiam, Deumque precabor ut Cl. tuam multos annos servet Ecclesiae suae incolumem Cantuariae 20 die Octobris 1608.

Tuae Clementiae observantissimus
Had. de Saravia.

BL Add. Ms. 28571. Nr. 53, fol. 214r-218r
H. van Crombruggen, ''Een brief van Adriaan Saravia over Lipsius en 'Het Huis der Liefde' ''. *De vergulden Passer,* XXVIII (1950) 112-117

## XLVI. SARAVIA TO JOHANNES WTENBOGAERT
### Canterbury, 23 April 1612

Docto pioque mihique multum dilecto fratri ac Domino
Iohanni Uytenbogard Hadrianus Saravia S.P.P.

Mihi plurimum in Domino dilecte Frater, tuus ad meas manus de summi imperii in rebus Ecclesiasticis authoritate tractatus pervenit, unde tantam percepi laetitiam quantum tristitiae de altercationibus Leydanis. Deo
gratias ago, qui tibi hanc mentem et animum dedit quod publico scripto à
tam pernicioso errore vestros homines deterrere ausus es. Vereor enim ne
Ecclesiis Christi plus mali sit allaturus, quam illi cogitent qui obstinate
eum defendunt. Propter hanc controversiam miserorum Papistarum hic in
Anglia divexantur conscientiae. Discrimen tantum est in subiecto summi
imperii, quod hic in uno residet Monarcha, apud vos est in multitudine
vel Optimatum vel populi. Quae res auget difficultatem. Quia vestri Ordines de Religione non sunt eiusdem sententiae, vestrorum ministrorum
nonnulli, si non omnes, pro veris Christianis quibus tuto fidere possint, illos in rebus Ecclesiasticis admittere non audent iudices. Haec speciosa videtur oratio. Sed non vident eadem ratione probaturos, illos penes quos
est summum imperium, potestatem nullam habere iudicandi de tela et la-
nificio, de textoribus et fullonibus, de re navali et aliis artificiis quorum
non tenent scientiam. Ignorare videntur, Magistratus quae non intelligit
discere à peritis: quae textorum sunt à textoribus, quae fabrorum à fabris,
et nautarum à nautis, ad quos causa quae controvertitur non pertinet.
Quare potestas in rebus Ecclesiasticis ad summum imperium aeque pertinet, etiamsi penes quos illud est, sint infideles aut mali Christiani sicut ad
fideles et pios. Personarum in hac re non est spectanda fides et Religio sed
data divinitus potestas. Si iusta in negotio Ecclesiastico imperaverit infide-
lis Magistratus, parendum est; cum fideli si iubeat iniqua, non sit obe-
diendum. Quos alieno subesse imperio Deus voluit si pii sunt, praecepti
tantum et potestatis à Deo institutae habebunt rationem. Nos vero et quotquot Ecclesiae hic in Anglia ministerio fungimur, solemni iuramento profitemur nos agnoscere Regem summum habere imperium, non tantum in
causis civilibus sed etiam Ecclesiasticis. Sacramentum ego hic subiicio, ut
videas quam in summum imperium vestri homines sint iniqui. Forma
iuramenti haec est. Ego N. palam testor et ex conscientia mea declaro, quod
Maiestas Regia unicus est supremus gubernator huius Regni, omniumque
aliorum suae Maiestatis Dominiorum ac territoriorum, tam in omnibus
spiritualibus sive Ecclesiasticis rebus aut causis quam in temporalibus, et
quod nullus extraneus Princeps, persona, status aut potentatus habet aut
habere debet ullam iurisdictionem, potestatem, superioritatem intra hoc
Regnum; et proinde renuncio et penitus reiicio omnes extraneas iurisdictiones, potestates, superioritates, authoritates. Et promitto me deinceps
fidem et veram obedientiam Regiae Maiestati eiusque haeredibus et legiti-

mis successoribus praestiturum, et pro virili mea adiuturum ac propugna-
turum omnes iurisdictiones, privilegia, praeminentias et authoritates Regiae Maiestati, haeredibus suis et successoribus concessas vel debitas, sive
imperiali huius Regni coronae unitas et annexas. Ita me Deus amet! et per
huius libri contenta. Haec Sacramenti forma aut similis aliqua esset
optanda in usu esse apud vos, ad omnem suspicionem tollendam de
Ministris et Ecclesiarum vestrarum Pastoribus quos, cum isthic essem,
memini non detulisse Magistratibus quantum debebant, quando illorum
potestatem in causis Ecclesiasticis nullam agnoscunt. Quae de hac re disputata sunt à probatissimis Theologis, miror vestros hominas aut non legisse
aut lecta contemnere. Non enim alio loco habendi sunt quam seditioso-
rum, qui summi imperii summam authoritatem, in causis etiam Ecclesiasticis, non agnoscunt, et suae aristocratiae tribuunt illam authoritatem in
rebus Ecclesiasticis quam Papa tribuit suae Monarchiae. Sed iudicii im-
probitatem istorum hominum specta. Oppressi tyrannide Papae Romani
ad Magistratus civilis, qualis qualis erat, authoritatem et defensionem
provocavimus et audiri in causa mere Ecclesiastica postulavimus; et tunc
nihil non potestatis civili Magistratui tribuebamus, quisquis ille esset.
Huius rei testis est epistola ad Hispaniarum Regem et Ordines Belgicarum Provinciarum, quae olim praefixa fuit fidei Confessioni Ecclesiarum
et tecum reputa cuius Religionis illi fuerint, quantum tamen illis tribueri-
mus in fidei negotio. Ego tunc temporis Minister eram Ecclesiae Gallica-
nae Antverpiae, et exemplaria illius Confessionis Principi Auriaco et Comiti Egmondano offerenda curavi. Frater uxoris meae erat Comiti Ludo-
vico à cubiculis, qui me ad dominum suum adduxit, ut illi innotescerem et
exemplaria recens editae Confessionis darem ulterius principibus distribu-
enda. Congregavi primum tunc temporis Ecclesiam Bruxellis auxilio Domini de Tolossa, fratris Domini sanctae Aldegundae, ex aulicis et paucis
quibusdam civibus Gallici sermonis. In altercationibus Leidanis illam fidei Confessionem et Catechismum allegari et urgeri video, ac si ipsum esset Dei verbum. Homines improbi Confessionem Augustanam audacter
despiciunt; et qui modestiores haberi volunt, in illa esse aliquid, quod mutatum vellent, desiderant; in sua vero Confessione, ac si fidei Canon esset,
nihil mutari patiuntur. Ego me illius Confessionis ex primis unum suisse
authoribus profiteor, sicut atque Hermanus Modetus; nescio an plures
sint superstites. Illa primo fuit conscripta Gallico sermone à Christi servo
et martyre Guidone de Bres. Sed antequam ederetur, Ministris verbi Dei
quos potuit nancisci, illam communicavit et emendandum, si quid displi-
ceret, addendum, detrahendum proposuit: ut unius opus censeri non debeat. Sed nemo eorum qui manum apposuerunt, unquam cogitavit fidei
canonem edere, verum ex Canonicis scriptis fidem suam probare. Nihil
tamen meo iudicio in illa est quod reprehendam aut mutare velim. Quod si
sint aliqui quibus non omnia probentur, audiendos censeo et ex verbo Dei
docendos si quod reprehendunt secundum Dei verbum. Nemo temere in-

ter impios censendus est qui doceri paratus est. Articulorum non idem omnium est pondus; esse possunt nonnulli à quibus si dissentiant sunt ferendi, non ab Ecclesia idcirco alienandi. Idem censeo de Catechismis vestris, quos ipse aliquando tam in Gallicis quam Teutonicis Ecclesiis docui. Ab illis tamen dissentio ex expositione descensus Christi ad inferos; postquam à vestris eiectus huc sum reversus, mutavi sententiam, melius hic in Anglia edoctus concionibus et scriptis tum doctissimi viri Reverendi Episcopi Vintoniensis tum aliorum doctorum hominum, qui nulla in parte aut Calvino aut Bezae cedunt. De qua re ad Ecclesias quae Reformatae dicuntur duos conscripsi libros, qui nondum viderunt lucem. Sunt hic plures de hoc argumento hinc inde scripti libri sermone Anglico. Tibi per vestrum tabellarium brevi mittam descriptum exemplar; interea iubeo te salvare et pro veritate fortiter stare. Cantuariae die 13 Aprilis stilo Angliae 1612.

Mitto tibi hic exemplar epistolae, quam cum Leydae habitabam scripsi D. Helmichio, et opportune, cum schedas alias evolverem, se mihi obtulit; non enim nunc primum vestri hanc movent camarinam, verum est error qui ex otio natus est, ut primum pax dari coepit Ecclesiis.

Observande in Christo frater. Reversus Middelburgo domum xvi die Aprilis stilo novo, inveni dilectionis tuae literas xxv Martii stilo veteri datas, quibus studium tuum et animum erga pacem et concordiam intellexi; de quo nunquam dubitavi. Scio enim omnem te movisse lapidem ad tollendum quod natum est in vestra urbe scisma. Sed enim non quaeritur causa et author sed finis, et quomodo suspicionem quam de vobis et ordine Ecclesiastico concepit Magistratus, amovere possitis; iure an iniuria, nec hoc quaeritur. Suspectam censuram nostrarum Ecclesiarum passim esse video Magistratibus, tanquam sub illa tyrannis aliqua lateat quae tandem successu temporis aucta viribus, Magistratus authoritatem sibi subiiciet. Quam sit humanum ingenium imperii illegitimi impatiens, notum est; odit enim omnes, qui potestatem aliquam sibi vendicare volunt. Haec opinio nisi tollitur, frustra laboratis. Fratrum nostrorum in Scotia recens exemplum nos commovere et commonere debet, ut prudenter nos in hac re geramus: erant enim illic per totum regnum Ecclesiae constitutae ea forma regiminis quae hic est; sed eam edicto publico Rex abrogavit et aliam sua authoritate constituit; nec video nos aliquid melius posse sperare. Quantum prudentia tua Magistratui Christiano authoritatis in rebus Ecclesiasticis tribuat, nescio. Vereor ne aliqua in re Magistratui negatum sit quod concedendum oportuit; ut dubitem, facit huius Ecclesiae exemplum et aliarum quarum audivi et legi sententiam; temere tamen nihil iudico, tantum aio me id vereri. Sed ut quid ego sentiam et quid sequendum ac tenendum ab omnibus tuto iudicem, paucis exponam. Non minus in Ecclesiasticis rebus authoritatis Magistratus Christianos habere arbitror quam olim habuere Reges et Duces populi Dei, quorum mandatis Sacerdotes et

Levitas, in iis quae sui muneris erant, parere Deus voluit, quamdiu intra divinae legis cancellos se continuerunt. Moses Dux populi Dei et Josua caeterique iudices mandata dederunt Sacerdotibus et Levitis. David templi structuram et ordinem quem tenerent Sacerdotes et Levitae in eius ministerio constituit; nihil opus plura commemorem, cum copiosissime hanc quaestionem disputatam habeamus à nostris Theologis, quos vestros homines legisse non dubito. Nisi quod Magistratui debetur dederimus, ipse plus quam debet ad se rapiet. Si Anglicam aut Scoticam linguam intelligeres, ego ad te mitterem Regis Scotorum Apologiam, in qua rationem reddit abrogatae, aut verius mutatae, Ecclesiasticae politiae quam Ministri constituerant et aliam ipse praescripserit. Vester Magistratus vobis contrarios Ministros, quibus vestros conatus frangant, semper opponent. Quid peccatum sit in hac re à Scotis iudicem, nihil attinet scribere; ne idem vobis usu veniat, tempori prospiciendum et videndum est, quantum et quatenus dissentientes etiam in nonnullis doctrinae capitibus sint tolerandi. Deinde quae sit Magistratus civilis authoritas in politia Ecclesiastica; an possit leges praescribere politicas Ministris et Pastoribus Ecclesiarum in rebus Ecclesiasticis, quibus parere debeant, etc.

Quam mihi in hac re consentiam videre potes. Hermanus Modetus erat in alia sententia, et ad eum si scripsissem, laterem lavissem. Mihi insignis facta est iniuria, sed Deo sit gratia, nihil mihi illa nocuit. Si quid mali inde secutum est, ipsi authores detrimentum acceperunt; fui enim pacis et Magistratuum authoritatis semper studiosissimus, si quis Minister verbi Dei alius. Iterum vale Frater omni studio et amore colende.

*EE*, 294-296 (Ep. 181)

# XLVII. SARAVIA TO JOHANNES WTENBOGAERT
## Canterbury, 29 September 1612

Literas tuas (mihi plurimum dilecte et observande frater) non sine la-
chrymis et magno animi maerore perlegi, quia turbarum quas istic Satan
suscitavit, nullum bonum video finem. Do. Vorstius, qui author dissensionum est, amandandus esset; quod Do. Ordines non puto esse facturos.
Infensi sunt ministris, qui summo civili imperio debitam authoritatem in
rebus Ecclesiasticis non agnoscunt nisi tantum in suis decretis synodalibus
exequendis. Si idem tecum in hac re sentirent, benigniores Do. Ordines
invenirent. Vestrae synodi non mihi videntur malum posse sanare; irrita-
bunt et schisma maius reddent suorumque sectatorum Vorstius auxerit
numerum. Quod si omnes cum Vorstio consenserint et conciliatio fiat,
quamdiu scripta sua defendet, quod facit, sui erroris infamia vestras Ecclesias asperget. Inter vos quidem si forte pacem qualem qualem estis ad
tempus habituri, aliae Ecclesiae sententiam Vorstii de Deo nunquam pro-
babunt. De Anglicana Ecclesia certo scio, idem de Gallicana et Lutherana
dico. Legi ipsius Apologetica scripta de Deo, sed ubique errorem suum
palliat et defendit. Verbis ludit et idem cum Ecclesiis sentire videri vult;
sed passim fucum suum ipse satis aperte detegit. Blanditur suo lectori, sed
ego te meminisse velim distichi Catonis: Noli homines blando nimium sermone probare, Fistula dulce canit volucrem dum decipit auceps. Unum de
multis adferam ipsius argumentum ad fallendum ita eleganter et populari-
ter concinnatum ut nihil desit. Illud ex 18 et 19 pag. Apologeticae Oratio-
nis ad D. Ordinis sumpsi et tibi hic examinandum propono. Cum Deus
(inquit) omni modo et prorsus indiscrete dicitur infinitus esse etc. Hinc videre licet, quo sensu Deum infinitum esse credat. Idem invenies in aliis ipsius scriptis, quibus aperte prodit se credere Deum aliquo modo non esse
infinitum. Distingui vult inter infinitatem essentiae Dei et absolutam infinitatem quam Deo non credit competere. Quod si ita esset, consequu-
turum putat ut aliarum rerum Dei essentia permisceatur essentiis. Huic
obiectioni tam a priscis veteribus Theologis quam a posteris qui secuti
sunt, fuit olim et est responsum. Excusationem nullam ipsius tergiversatio
in hoc errore admittit; vanum est quod metuit, cum solis radios permeare
per diaphana omnia corpora videamus, nec tamen illis permisceri. Si ratio
illa valeret, tunc Deus misceri illis corporibus quibus praesens adest sua
essentia, nempe in coelis, sole et astris, ubi nullae sunt latrinae, nulla sterquilinia, quibus tanta maiestas inquinetur, sequeretur. Sed suo more
respondebit, haec verba esse disputantis non affirmantis. Si lumini solis
quod translucet solida corpora pellucida praesensque illis est intime nemo
sanus illorum corporum actiones tribuet, quo modo poterit Deo malum
quod creatura perpetrat imputari? Quod si terreni orbis universa moles
perlucida esset, solis lumen illam totam transluceret sine ulla sui cum corporibus concretione. Quanto lux illa aeterna, per quam omnia facta sunt

et [quae] quovis corporeo lumine longe purior et simplicior est, magis per
omnia diffundere se sine ulla cum rebus mixtione aut iniuria quae possit a
creatura procedere credenda est? Opacitas terrae solis lumini officit et te-
nebras facit. Aeternae luci nihil est quod obstare queat, quin ubique praesens adsit. Cogitemus lucem sine corpore solis (erat enim ante creatum so-
lem), in illa exemplum habemus aeternae lucis, id est deitatis essentiae
qua veluti manu ducimur ad praesentiam realem divini numinis in omnibus locis intelligendam. Quod homines fanatici inde trahunt, insania est
quae rerum veritati nihil derogat. Cavendum imprimis, ne qui homines
fanaticos vitare vult, ipse fanaticus fiat. Non bene insania sanatur alia insania, nec error est errore confutandus. Si ex vero principio praesentiae
essentiae divinae rebus in omnibus infert humana ignorantia absurda,
quantas blasphemias inferre licebit, si realiter praesentem divinam essentiam ubique esse negemus? Non ex alio principio primus Gentilium error
de minutulis deis et inferioribus numinibus natus est. Quod Aldegundum
attinet, nimium crassus ipsius fuit error, cuius certe me puduit; qui cur
magis Vorstio placeat quam docta D. Bezae responsio, satis demirari nequeo. Nihil me movet Bezae nomen, sed rationes et argumenta magni fa-
cio, quamvis illa sint ipsi cum aliis Theologis communia. D. Calvinus contra Libertinos docte scripsit, sed Deum simpliciter et absolute ubique
praesentem nusquam negavit. Si Do. Bezam et Calvinum de hac re
Vorstius sequeretur, Ecclesias turbare non pergeret. Non haec noto, quod
homines probem Calvini et Bezae scriptis addictos. Libere ab ipsis dissentire me profiteor quotiescunque novas opiniones ante ipsorum tempora ecclesia incognitas invexerunt. Scholasticos tantum quosdam doctores culpa-
re et unum quendam Iesuitam videri vult, cum omnes tam scholasticos
quam Iesuitas adversarios habeat, totamque Romanam Ecclesiam, cum
qua nos non satis scilicet controversiarum habemus, nisi etiam haec adda-
tur, ad omnium Ecclesiarum vere Christianarum infamiam. Quid de illis
Christi dicam Ecclesiis, quibus a Luthero nomen vulgo datur? Quibus
maledicendi maior causa data erit, quam hic bonus pacis conciliator cogitare potest. Hoc tamen ipsius constituto errore, cessabit omnis de praesentia corporis Christi omnibus in locis disputatio. Magnum hujus Theologi
acumen ingenii, qui rationem nobis se invenisse credit qua et Libertinos et
Lutheranos, Papistas denique omnes ad unum iugulaverit. Multi iam hos
nonaginta annos et amplius scriptores contra Libertinos, contra Lutheranos et contra Papistas depugnarunt, quibus in mentem non venit praesentiam essentiae divinae in omnibus rebus aut negare aut distinguere. Hanc
novam Theologiam omnes ignorarunt, qua tam facile Papistae, Luthera-
ni, ipsi denique Libertini foedi erroris possent convinci. Nam isti omnes
argumenta ducunt ab essentiae Dei infinitate, ut probent suos errores.
Quae si non est aut si ubique simpliciter et indistincte non est, corruit
quicquid magnis voluminibus hactenus disputatum fuit. Ut suum errorem
probet, adfert omnia illa argumenta, quae mihi quondam ab illis qui in eo-

dem erant errore fuerunt obiecta: nempe consequens fore ut (sicut doctores Scholastici tradunt) tota Dei essentia sit in omnibus et singulis foedis latrinis et sterquiliniis, imo in singulis ipsis diabolis sit. Popularis haec est oratio, quae facile apud rudem plebeculam inveniet fidem, et citius recipietur, quantumvis sit falsa, quam crassis ingeniis paradoxum de Dei presentia in foedis illis locis quae commemorat; sed non apud rerum divinarum et humanarum peritos, qui sciunt latrinas et sterquilinia et siquid sit illis magis foedum sensibus nostris sordere et faetere, non Deo nec rerum naturae. Sunt sterquilinia et latrinae nobis sterquilinia et latrinae, non Deo. Quamvis non probem haec et quicquid est huius generis rudi et indocto populo proponi, qui lacte potius quam solido cibo alendus est, minus tamen ferendum est haec a Theologo negari. Deus enim ut nullis locis includitur, ita nec ullis excluditur. Qui illis faedis locis Dei praesentiam essentialem excludit, quantam distantiam inter Dei essentialem praesentiam et illa loca constituet? Noster Theologus Deum Deique essentiam templo suo Hierosolymitano et ab altari suo propter foetes et stercora victimarum quae ibi immolabantur excludet, et coelo empyreo ipsi Deo coaeterno ipsum recludet. Sed cum Dei Maiestatem revereri se vult videri, illam nimis impie violat. Nullis enim corporeis nostris sordibus foedari inquinarique potest Deus, qui non illis, sed impiis de tanta sua Maiestate iudiciis offenditur. Qui cloacas nostras et sordes et foeditates Deo et naturae esse, quod sunt nostris sensibus, credit, ille nec Theologus nec Philosophus est. Qui puriorem et sinceriorem Dei Maiestatem, ubi ubi illa esse cogitetur, non credit quam ut loci foeditate possit contaminari, impius est. Si mundis omnia munda fides reddit, quid potest Deo esse immundum? In lege animalia munda et immunda leguntur; sed illis quibus illa lex lata fuit, non Deo qui tam immunda creavit animalia quam munda, et cum ipse mundus esset, creavit omnia munda; nihil enim quod ipsi immundum esset, creare potuit. De diabolis quid dicemus? Dei creaturae sunt, et de nobis quod Paulus asseruit: quod in ipso movemur, vivimus et sumus, de diabolis et aliis quibusvis rebus quae subsistunt, est intelligendum, per quem habent quod sunt, vivunt et moventur diaboli. Num ab ipsis remotior est Deus quam ab hominibus impiis et caeteris rebus creatis? Paulus apud Athenienses ait quod non longe absit ab unoquoque nostrum. In Deo solo et ab eo solo illiusque filio et spiritu sancto vita et essentia rerum omnium est, nec rebus creatis abes quas sustinet. De verbo Dei aeterno dicitur: sine ipso factum est nihil quod factum est; in ipso vita erat et illa lux lucet in tenebris. Nec tamen misceri rebus nemini magis videri debet mirum quam lucem solis non misceri corporibus, quae irradiat et penetrat. Sed ridebit has rationes Vorstius, qui potentiam virtutemque Dei ab essentia separat. Nos in Deo quod potentiam dicimus nihil aliud esse quam essentiam credimus, ut Deo posse sit esse et esse sit posse. Abripior quo nolo; mihi enim propositum non est contra Vorstium disputare; tantum te admonitum cupio, ut ab homine tibi caveas. Quod in plerisque a Calvino et a Beza non

temere dissentit, ubi sine verbo Dei contra verbum Dei novas opiniones
nunquam ante in Ecclesia Dei auditas ex solis suis cogitationibus et coniec-
turis fallacibus fabricarunt, non improbo; sed ipsi videndum est ne in illud
ipsum crimen incidat, ne et ipse novum dogma et infame contra omnium
Theologorum sententiam et Philosophorum, qui veram de Dei essentia tenent sententiam, invehat. Quod nobis non recipere tam fas esse debet
quam ipsi, non dicam a Calvino et Beza sed ab omnibus Theologis
Christianis dissentire. Aldegundus omnem suam Theologiam labefactas-
set suo illo foedo errore, nisi cessisset. Suum errorem Vorstius extenuat et
defendit odiosis et popularibus rationibus, et ignorantiam de hac re prae-
fert scientiae, et sterquilinia, atomos et aquae guttas similesque nugas nobis allegat, in quibus praesentiam Dei essentiam definire prophanum censet. Quae nisi ipse prophanus esset, numquam allegasset nec illis Dei
simplicitatem et immensitatem obscurari asseruisset. Indigna sunt quibus
responderetur nisi a Vorstio ipsique similibus moverentur et olim mota essent. Facit de rebus divinis crassum et hebes iudicium pravorum hominum, ut ad illas etiam sensui humano sordidas et profanas obiectiones
respondendum sit; quia sicut sine impietate Dei immensitas includi ullo
loco non potest dici, ita nec excludi. In utroque errore quantae sint tene-
brae, quot errorum et haeresium monstra nascantur, vellem D. Vorstium
cogitare. Quo loco abesse intelligi potest qui se coelum et terram implere
dixit, et quem coeli coelorum non capiunt? Quis de Dei simplicitate et pu-
ritate melius sentit obsecro an ille qui illam tantam esse credit (ut est) quae
nullis nostris sterquiliniis, nullis nostris sordibus, possit contaminari, an
ille qui foedari et inquinari illis opinatur, si praesens dicatur rebus, quae-
cunque illae sint, sive sensibus nostris blandiantur, sive illis adversentur.
Non omnium animalium excrementa (si Vorstius malit stercora) sensus
humani aversantur. Quaedam sunt, quae sensibus placent et gustui et ol-
factui grata sunt. Expendat omnium rerum procreationem, si vult, et ex
corruptione generari omnia inveniet, et hominem imprimis. Videat quid
sit semen ex quo gignitur homo et in quam cloacam et sentinam decidat ad
generationem hominis. Num ab illo loco, utpote qui vera sit latrina et ster-
quilinium, Dei essentialem praesentiam excludet? Dei templa corpora
sunt Christianorum. Ecquid illa sunt aliud quam cloacae et sterquilinia?
Deus tamen in uteris matrum format humana corpora, ut cum Jobo mortales omnes dicere possint: manus tuae fecerunt me, et plasmaverunt me
totum in circuitu etc. Memento quod sicut lutum feceris me, et in pulve-
rem reduces me. Nonne sicut lac mulsisti me et sicut caseum me coagu-
lasti? Pelle et carnibus vestisti me, ossibus et nervis compegisti me. Quare
de vulva eduxisti me? etc. Sed haec omnia Deus absens a foedis istis locis
ubi haec facta sunt et quotidie fiunt, perfecerit scilicet; sed ubicunque
Deus operatur, ibi praesentem ipsius essentiam esse intelligo. Forte Dei
potentiam allegabit et praesentiam essentialem excludet. Et hoc est effu-
gium quo receptum se habere credit, sicuti et in praesentiae modo et

praesentiam se non negare dicet, sed modum se ignorare. Hic nobis verba dari a Theologo, ut sic suum tegat errorem, indignum est, quia de modo non est haec nostra controversia. Nemo negat praesentem et absentem Deum variis modis dici. Deus alio modo praesens in Christo, alio modo in Sanctis suis praesens intelligitur. In Christo per unionem personalem verbi aeterni cum humana natura, in Sanctis per gratiarum collationem. Alio modo praeterea praesens adest protegens et conservans, alio modo puniens et castigans. Sed de essentiae deitatis in omnibus locis praesentia nostra quaestio est, quae unius tantum modi est. Et quamvis illa sit incomprehensibilis, sicut est et ipsa essentia, negari absque impietate non potest. Nec alio modo in coelis, alio modo in terris esse in se ipsa intelligenda est, quamvis alio modo illic quam hic in suis creaturis se manifestet. Illa una est et eadem ubicunque est sibique similis. Maior tamen gloria, maior maiestas in coelestibus creaturis relucet quam in terrenis. Sed illa quae in ipso Deo nunc est, una et eadem semper et ubique fuit et immensa est, ut fuit ab aeterno. Idem valet quod varios gradus divinae essentiali praesentiae constituit disput. 3 thesi 9; ubi pro varietate Dei manifestationum et operationum in rebus creatis impie quod in creaturis est aut sit ipsi essentiali Deitatis praesentiae tribuit. Gradus in deitatis praesentia magis et minus nulli sunt, nec absque impietate magis esse in coelo aut minus in terris dici vel cogitari potest. Illa non est in ullo loco magis praesens quam in alio. Pro varietate loci eorumque quae operatur Deus, non mutatur essentiae divinae realis praesentia. Diversitas quae apparet, in creaturis est, non in Deo Deique praesentia. Alia est gloria coelorum et coelestium creaturarum et alia rerum huius inferioris orbis. A diversitate operationum Dei demonstrare velle diversitatem graduum praesentiae divinae essentiae inepta et indigna Theologo est ratiocinatio, ut magis vel minus esse in coelis aut alicubi quam in terris intelligatur. Fixum hoc et immotum omnibus Theologis est, quod in Psalmis legimus: Initio Domine terram fundasti et opera manuum tuarum sunt coeli. Ipsi peribunt, tu autem permanes, et omnes sicut vestimentum veterascent. Veluti pallium mutabis eos et mutabuntur. Tu autem idem ipse es et anni tui non deficient. Deum nunc esse in coelis praesentem inficias non ibit (ni fallor) D. Vorstius. Sed quando Deus mutabit coelos tanquam pallium et mutabuntur, num tunc Deitatis praesentia illic minus erit quam nunc est aut postea futura postquam fecerit coelum novum et terram novam? Quae nunc sunt, caduca sunt; restituta vero erunt aeterna. Admiranda illa futura est omnium rerum mutatio, sed in Deo Deique in rebus praesentia nulla. Ipse idem permanebit, apud quem nulla est transmutatio nec vicissitudinis obumbratio. Quando Deus in principio creavit coelum et terram et simul cum temporibus locorum spacia et rerum intervalla, fuit ubi erat antea, non includi excludive potuit locis rebusve creatis. Omnia in ipso verius erant quam ipse in illis. Et cum ex partibus heterogeneis Deus non componatur, non magis in coelo esse potuit quam in terris, vel aliter non magis in Deo erat aut esse potuit coe-

lum quam terra. Deus Deique praesentia permanet et in aeternum permanebit ubi fuit, est et erat ante conditum mundum, sibi similis et eadem.
Quod Deus dicitur proprius aut remotius adesse aut abesse, advenire et
decedere, adsumere et abiicere, deitatis reali praesentiae nemo Theologus
orthodoxus attribuit, sed gratiae et auxilio Dei hominibus dato aut negato.
Quando Deus sua clementia hominibus benefacit, illis dicitur adesse, et illi
qui Dei iustis iudiciis affliguntur, deserti a Deo dicuntur ab illis qui Dei
providentia res humanas administrari credunt. Sed haec nihil addunt nec
adimunt deitatis essentiali praesentiae. Et haec est vera, vetus et orthodoxa Theologia cui nulla contraria est recipienda. Ut vestrarum Ecclesiarum pastores merito D. Vorstio se opposuisse videri debeant; possunt tamen in modo et agendi ratione nonnihil errasse. Videri enim possunt multitudine accusationum voluisse hominem opprimere, atque ita miscuerint
vereor vera falsis et suspiciones incertas cum iis quibus ipse non contradi-
cit; quasi in illis non satis sit, unde hominem redarguere potuerint et demonstrare ineptum esse ad illam functionem ad quam vocatus est. In qua
re fidem sibi in veris et necessariis accusationibus derogarunt. Ad malum
hoc accedit etiam quod ministros ministrorumque authoritatem D. Ordines habent suspectam, utpote quibus ab illis in rebus Ecclesiasticis debita
denegetur potestas. Quod D. Ordinibus non potest non movere stoma-
chum, ut magis illis faveant qui civilis magistratus integram defendunt authoritatem. Si tecum sentirent, maior esset apud illos ipsorum gratia.
Nam istic quicquid fit, quantum ego iudicare possum, invidia et stomacho
fit, ut sic D. Ordines ulciscantur ministros et suam authoritatem supra illos in rebus Ecclesiasticis ostendant. Quae res exitium tum Ecclesiae tum
Reip. aliquando vereor ne allatura sit. Nam summum illud imperium non
est a Deo ordinatum, ut illi, penes quos Deus illud esse voluit, per se de
omnibus rebus iudicent quas Deus illorum subiecit imperio, nisi illarum
rerum habeant notitiam. Gratia exempli: si inter nautas de re navali, inter
textores de tela et lana, inter sartores de re vestiaria, inter medicos et phar-
macopolas de re medica et de pharmacis oriatur controversia unde respub.
detrimentum sit acceptura, non puto quempiam ita insanire, qui de his rebus iudicium sibi sumere velit si illarum sit imperitus, et non potius in iudicium adhibiturus sit illarum artium magistros. Idem de rebus Theologicis est iudicium. Si D. Ordines suos Theologos suspectos habent, habet
Germania, habet Gallia, habet Anglia et habet Scotia, habet etiam Helve-
tia suos Theologos, quibus nihil unquam cum Vorstio fuit commercii. Illos accersant et iudicium de Vorstii scriptis audiant. Quos omnes si contemnant Do. Ordines et unum Vorstium cum paucis quibusdam qui ipsi
favent, inducti forte potius dominorum authoritate quam veritate defen-
dant, se contemptum iri vicissim ab illis expectent oportet, qui patrocinari
Vorstii adversariis tam fas sibi esse credent in bona causa et veritate pro-
pugnanda quam Dominis ordinibus in mala haeresibusque defendendis.
Quod allegabitur Vorstii innocentia, nihil est quamdiu Theologis illa non

apparet. Dicam de me, qui ab omni odio et invidia D. Vorstii sum alienus, quando primum ipsius librum De Deo legi, ignorans an eundem Theologi nostrarum Academiarum et Episcopi legerent, idem quod illi de libro iudicavi; et mirabar in Ecclesiis Christi inveniri Theologum qui adeo impias et absurdas de Dei essentia haberet opiniones; neque mihi mirum fuit a D. nostro Rege improbari. Do. Vorstius in suis defensionibus ubique ad memoriam Regiae Maiestatis assurgit, et credit alieno impulsu ipsius damnasse scripta; sed errat. Cordatior Rex noster est et inter Theologos non postremus. Si Do. Ordines in illa facultate tantum profecissent, D. Vorstium defendere non pergerent. Regia Maiestas in hac re nihil habet opus alio monitore; ab aliorum iudicio non pendet; ipse per se sapit et totam rem intelligit. Cui cum Vorstius non cedat et sua defendere pergat, nescio quomodo illud accipiat. Non versor in Aula; decrepitus senex me in mea domo contineo cum cocleis. Extra meam domum nusquam progredior, nisi ad meam paroeciam et cum magna difficultate semel in anno Londinum. Omnes quos illic convenire potui Theologi, tam Episcopi quam alii viri bene in Theologicis scriptis versati D. Vorstii de Deo damnant opiniones. Liberi sunt, nec inter illos censendi qui in verba iurarunt Calvini. Quorum iudicia Dominos Ordines contemnere et tuum Vorstium praeferre valde miror. Ego duos composui libros de merito mortis corporeae Christi. Primus est contra Calvinum, Bezam, Pareum, Nicholaum de Cusa, Johannem Ferum *et contra meipsum*, qui aliquando catechismum Calvini in Ecclesiis Gallicis et Heidelbergensem in Teutonicis docui. Alter est contra sectatores Calvini, qui ulterius in illo errore progressi sunt quam Calvinus. Controversia hic in Anglia patrio sermone tractata sunt, sed sine ullo motu publico. Disputationes quidem ............[a] irrequietis hominibus motae contra doctissimas Reverendissimi Wintoniensis Bilsoni .........[a] Christi ad inferos, sed silentium fuit illis impositum. Illis concionibus iussu Reverendi .......[a] Archiepiscopi, in cuius tunc aedibus vivebam interfui, sunt anni octodecim. Quamvis ........[a] essem sententia, non potui tamen non cedere veritati, quam contra Calvinum propugn......[a] verendissimus Wintoniensis. Occasione illarum concionum et calumniarum contra pias illas et doctas conciones, hos libros conscripsi; sed veritus lites hactenus apud me retinui. Undique enim in me scholae Genevensis Ecclesiarum Ministri turmatim irruent, et illi maxime, qui in religionis statu, qui nunc istic est apud vos, piaculum censent quidquam immutare. Ego contra testor et *in vestris catechismis doctrinam de descensu Christi ad inferos, quae ibi ex Calvino docetur, corrigendam, et in regimine Ecclesiastico Episcopos esse supra Ministrorum multitudinem constituendos,* et Hagae Comitis aut alibi *erigendum Senatum Ecclesiasticum,* qui de causis et controversiis Ecclesiasticis iudicet et ad quem sit a Consistoriis et Synodis provincialibus, siquis se illarum iudiciis offensum iudicet, libera provocatio; et illum Senatum com-

---

[a] Manuscript damaged.

ponendum ex *urbium Episcopis* et *Iurisconsultis*. Turbarum apud vos aliâs nullus unquam futurus est finis. Quanta (mi frater) putas ex scriptis hinc inde in hac causa Vorstii et illa quae fuit Arminii esse nata et quotidie nasci scandala? Quae, si causae fuissent sine scriptis disceptatae apud Senatum Ecclesiasticum, nulla essent. Quae acta sunt, non sunt firma, quia non creduntur a legitimis iudicibus profecta. Traditionem Apostolicam ab omnibus Christi Ecclesiis, quae per orbem universum terrarum fuerunt, usque ad Calvini tempora receptam ego longe praefero unius Genevae novae inventioni. Quod illum eundem ordinem apud Gallos et istic apud vos video, nihil me movet, quia stulta quaedam est imitatio, non certa ratio. Ego Dominis Ordinibus, quamvis de me pessime meritis, bene cupio, et sarto-tectam suam authoritatem in rebus Ecclesiasticis manere, similiter et Ecclesiarum Ministris omnibus suam. Sed in omnibus rebus alicuius momenti nollem illos quicquam moliri nisi de consilio et assensu aut etiam iussu Dominorum Ordinum aut *Magistratuum oppidi* in quo vivunt. Nam illi sunt veri seniores populi, quorum tam crebra in verbo Dei fit mentio. Nuper qui sunt asciti tantum nomen et umbram habent seniorum, non rem, et plus obesse quam prodesse possunt. Haec scribo, ut noris quam sim alienus a *Genevensium moribus, qui tandem Ecclesias evertent,* nisi Deus sua gratia malum avertat. Libros meos perlegendos et probandos summis, quos hic habemus, Theologis misi, quos cum accepero ad te transmittam. Si moram ferre non potes, pollicere mihi non in vulgum prodituros dum vivam, et ego exemplaria tibi mittam. Quam dolem D. Vorstium maculare, quae bene scripsit, istis crassis de Deo erroribus eloqui nequeo. Vere ab Ecclesiaste cap. 10 v. 1 dictum: musca mortua fetere facit unguentum aromatarii; sic qui pretiosus est propter sapientiam et gloriam stultitia parva. In omnibus suis Apologeticis scriptis seipsum magis accusat quam ab erroribus purgat. Sed hic finem faciam. Et memineris me epistolam tibi soli scribere, de cuius fide et taciturnitate nihil dubito; nisi forte amicum habes, qui sit tibi veluti alter tu. Vale. Cantuaria 3$^{tio}$ Calendae Octobris 1612.

Tua amantissimus,
Had. de Saravia.

Clarissimo ornatissimoque viro D. Johanni Wtenbogaert, Theologo amico et fratri integerrimo dentur. In Haga Comitis Hollandiae. Cantuaria pridie calendas Decembris 1612.

UBA Ms. B 69
Rogge, *Brieven Wtenbogaert,* I, 193-206 (Nr. 134)

## XLVIII. ISAACUS CASAUBONUS TO SARAVIA
### London, 13 January 1613

Venerande pater,

Cognoveram de tuo morbo etiam prius quam tuae literae mihi redderentur. Eramus igitur ego et uxor de tua valetudine admodum solliciti; et quum aliud nihil possemus, supplicibus precibus a Deo Opt. Max. subinde petebamus ut te sublevaret et priori ἐυεξία, si ita esset ipsi gratum, brevi restitueret. Sed didici a tuis, quas modo accepi, nondum remisisse dolores illos acerrimos, quibus exerceri patientiam tuam magno illi rerum omnium arbitrio placet. Non hortabor te, pater venerande, ut non solum aequo sed etiam forti et generoso animo hoc quicquid est cruciatuum feras. Scio ea virtute ac pietate esse te instructum ut monitore opus non habeas. Nemo te melius novit, levia esse quaecumque huic misero corpori adversa possunt contingere, prae illis quae vicem nostram passus est Servator mundi, Dominus noster, ὁ θεάνθρωπος, Jesus Christus; levia etiam esse prae illis bonis quae pios manent. Haec et similia his pauci Christiani ignorant; sed harum rerum notitia sese consolari, proprium est illorum quorum nomina in libro Vitae sunt inscripta. Te eorum ex numero esse, observande pater, et vita tua omnis fecit fidem hactenus, et scripta etiam tua luculente demonstrant, cum caetera tum etiam illa quae nunc tibi remitto. Legi illa pari cum fructu et voluptate. Longam epistolam super ea re ad te scripseram, quae errore nescio quo non Cantuariam sed Cantabrigiam delata est ad D. Duportum. Ne te morer diutius, ego atque uxor Deum supplices veneramur per Filium ipsius Jesum Christum, ut te doloribus hisce liberatum praestet valentem, et Ecclesiae suae lectissimaeque foeminae uxori tuae ac nobis amicis tuis te adhuc conservet. Nos si quid tua causa vel Dominae coniugis tuae possemus, scito et confide, *ad omnia obsequia* esse paratos. Londini, die Ianuarii 13.1613.

Tui observanitissimus
Is. Casaubonus

BodL Western Ms. Nr. 3955, fol. 215
I. Casaubonus, *Epistolae* (Roterodami, 1709) II, 514 (Ep. 851)

## XLIX. SARAVIA'S LAST WILL
Canterbury, 3 January 1612/1613

In nomine Dei patris en filii et spiritus sancti. Ego, Hadrianus De Saravia Cantuariensis Cathedralis metropoliticae ecclesiae presbyter prebendarius, meum testamentum in hunc qui sequitur modum condidi. Primum in illa fide me mori profiteor, quam Apostoli Domini nostri Jesu Christi et Prophetae tradiderunt ecclesiis et in libris canonicis veteris et novi testamenti continetur, ac in Anglicana ecclesia hodie publica auchoritate est recepta. Quam hos quinquaginta annos, relictis et abiuratis Romanae ecclesiae quae nunc est tyrannidis et idolatriae erroribus, in Angliae regni et in ultramarinis ecclesiis privatim et publice docui et professus sum. Symbolum quod dicitur Apostolorum similiter et Nycenum aliorumque trium generalium Conciliorum cum illo quod est Athanasii, recipio et amplector: ut pote quae ex verbo Dei sint deducta. Quibus adiungo Anglicanae ecclesiae confessionem cum illa quam Augustae Germaniae principes Caesari Carolo quinto anno Domini 1530 obtulerunt. Nullius erroris aut a verbo Dei aut a patribus primorum temporum ecclesiae damnati mihi conscius sum. Damno itaque omnes haereses et doctrinas alienas a verbo Dei scripto, et illas imprimis quas quatuor illa celeberrima concilia generalia: Nicenum, Constantinopolitanum et Ephesinum primum et Chalcedonense damnarunt. Quandocumque me ex hac vita Deus evocabit, de salute mihi praedicta per Christum Dominum certus, in ipsius manibus commendo spiritum meum, corpus meum amicis sepeliendum sine funebri pompa.

Relinquo substantiam omnem quam mihi Deus dedit, dilectae meae coniugi domicillae Margaritae de Wyttis ut de illa disponat, sicut hic subiicio: *primo* centum pauperibus urbis Cantuariensis; do legoque totidem peregrinorum ecclesiae pauperibus, ibidem exulantium, similiter centum pauperibus parochiae meae Greate Charte, a die tricesimo sepulturae meae solvendus. *Item* ducentas Anglicas libras dedi et do Gerardo de Vairier, Catharinae d'Allez defunctae meae uxoris nepotulo, tum demum ipsi tradendas quando ad maturam aetatem pervenerit; quam definio viginti quatuor completis annis. Interea temporis ad studia ipsius in literis prosequenda decem et octo libras Anglicas quotannis in illo sumptus ei suppeditabit. Quod si alieno animo fiat a literis, uxor mea praefata aut tutores apud mercatorem aut alium quempiam a quo vivendi recte et christiane rationem discere potuerit, illum collocabunt. *Item* Guilelmo d'Allez, Anthonii filio, Leland defunctae coniugis meae nepoti lego centum libras Anglicas. Si Gerardio Vairier mori ante dictam adultam aetatem contigerit, ducenta illae librae quas illi legavi, erunt uxoris meae. Gerardo a Mettkerke fratri suo singulis annis viginti marcas pendes, ut sua studia sequatur, in quatuor partes divisas, quinque marcas singulis trimestibus, donec gradum magistri artium erit adeptus aut per tempus potuerit adeptus. Famulo meo Willemo Tompson ultra stipendium quod ei debebit die sepulturae meae, si in meo servitio perseveraverit do legoque decem libras. Ancillae meae Rebeccae quatuor libras et Dorotheae duas, si tunc fuerint in meo servitio. *Caetera* omnia in arbitrio sunto domicillae Margaritae Wytis uxoris meae quem huius mei testamenti executricem nuncupo, cui omnia non prius legata do legoque. Et haec est nunc mea suprema voluntas cuius mutandae ut ius tempusque dabunt mihi potestatem retineo. *In cuius rei testimonium* haec propria manu signavi et apposito sigillo confirmavi tertia die Ianuarii Anno Domini 1612 stilo Angliae. Hadrianus de Saravia, testibus Richardo Colfe Samuel Cevaglerius.

Concordat cum testamento originale
dicti Domini Adriani Saravia defuncti
facta diligente collacione per nos
Robertum Lawse, notarium publicum
et Rich. Inge.

*Probatum* fuit huiusmodi testamentum suprascriptum Hadriani de Saravia clerici, sacrae theologiae doctoris, prebendarii ecclesiae Cathedralis et metropoliticae Christi Cantuariensis defuncti, habentis dum vixit ac mortis suae tempore bona notabilia in diversis diocesibus sive iurisdictionibus Cantuariae provinciae vicesimo primo die Ianuarii Anno Domini iuxta computationem ecclesiae Anglicanae millesimo sexcentesimi duodecimo coram magistro Iacobo Vistell clerico, verbi Dei predicatore licentiato substituto venerablilis viri magistri Georgii Neesman legum doctoris civitatis et diocesis Cantuariensis commissarii pro predicto Roberto Lawse notario publico iuramento Margarite Wyttis relictae et executricis in eodem testamento nominatae ac approbatae et insinuatae personae. Ac commissa fuit et est administratio bonorum iure et creditore predicti defuncti personae praefatae executrici primitus ad gratiam Dei Evangelia iuratae salve iure cuiuscumque.

(Added are some documents, among which a caveat and the exact inventory of goods up to a total amount of £1366, sh. 03, d. 01 and also ''all the books with the shelves whereon they stand: £100 en ''upon bonds and bils, is it shalbe received: £914)

PRC 32.32/42, fol. 153-155r.
PRC 27/2/67

# BIBLIOGRAPHY

## 1. MANUSCRIPTS

*Amsterdam,* Library of the University of Amsterdam
Ms. B 69.
*Amsterdam,* Library of the Free University
Collection Bos; provisional inventory, Ms. 63.
*Brussels,* Public Record Office (Rijksarchief)
Papiers d'État, Nr. 27.
*Cambridge,* Trinity College
Ms. B 14.9.
*Cambridge,* University Library
Ms. Mm 1, 43.
*Canterbury,* Cathedral Archives and Library
Chapter Acts 1581-1607.
Chapter Acts 1608-1628.
Accounts Treasurer Nrs. 11-21 (1600-1612).
Accounts Steward.
French Church Records: Actes du consistoire de l'église wallonne de Canterbury 1595-1599.
*Delft,* City Archives Office
Archives Reformed Church, Mss. Nrs. 24, 80, 112, 160.
*Dordrecht,* City Archives Office
Archives Reformed Church, Ms. Nr. 10.
*Gloucester,* City Library
Gloucester Diocesan Records, Nr. 73: Visitation Book 1594.
*The Hague,* Archives Offices of the Netherlands Reformed Church
Ancient Records, Nr. I, 20.
*Hatfield House*
Cecil Papers, Nrs. 75, 82, 93, 95.
*Leiden,* City Archives Office
Afleesingboek der Stadt Leyden, E.
Gerechtsdagboek, A 1.
Missivenboek, A.
Accounts Lodewycx van Treslongue, stewart of the Chapter of Hogeland, 1582, 1583, 1584.
1e Stadsdienaarsaanneemboek.
Vroedschapsboek, KL.
Archives Dutch Reformed Church, Nr. 001: Consistory Book.
Archives Walloon Church, Nr. 40: First Consistory Book (1584-1611).
*Leiden,* University Library
Codices Lipsiani, Ms. Lip. 4.
Ms. B.P.L. 2702: Album amicorum Jonas van Reigersberch.
*London,* British Library
Additional Manuscripts, Nrs. 22960, 22961, 22962, 28571.
Lansdowne Manuscripts, Nr. 45: Burghley Papers 1585.
Lansdowne Manuscripts, Nr. 444: Register of Crown Presentations, II.
Cotton Manuscripts, Galba C XI, D III, D IV.
Royal Manuscripts, 8 E VIII.
*London,* Guildhall Library

L 19.92: Dutch Church, Austin Friars.
  Ms. 7428/7: Archivum, VII.
  Ms. 7396/1: Bills and receipts, I: 1565-1600.
  Ms. 7397/5: Acta Books of the Consistory, V: 1572-1573, 1578-1585.
*London,* Lambeth Palace
  Register Ab. Whitgift.
  Register Ab. Bancroft.
  Muniment Book B.
  Register Ab. Abbot.
*London,* Public Record Office
  SP 12, 15, 38, 83, 84.
  PR.
  LD 16/1.
*London,* Westminster Abbey Archives
  CA: Chapter Acts, I and II.
  SA: Stewart's Accounts.
  TA: Treasurer's Accounts.
  Reg. BK, IX.
*Maidstone,* Kent Archives Office
  PRC 32/42.
  PRC 27/2/67.
  Rochester Episcopalis Register, V: 1543-1637.
  Induction Mandates Lewisham.
*Munich,* Royal Library
  Codex Monacensis Lat. 10359.
*Oxford,* Bodleyan Library
  Ms. Tanner, 79.
  Ms. Auct. D, 1.14.
  Ms. Add. C 69.
  Casaubon Mss.
*Saint-Omer,* City Library
  Ms. 799: Annales par Jean Ballin.
  Ms. 809: Annales de la ville de St. Omer et l'établissement des maisons religieuses,
    I: jusqu' en l'an 1554.
*Utrecht,* City Archives Office
  Vroedschapsresoluties 1582-1590.
*Worcester,* Cathedral Library
  Add. Ms., 56: Lists of Bishops, Deans and Prebends.

## 2. PRINTED WORKS OF SARAVIA

Zaraphya, Hadrianus, *Een hertgrondighe Begheerte, vanden Edelen, Lanckmoedighen, Hoochgeboren Prince van Oraengien, mitsgaders alle syne Christelijcke, edele, vrome Bontghenooten, op
alle menschen begheert, van wat condicie oft qualiteit sy zijn, die den Heere lief hebben ende vreesen,
ende ooc beminnende zijn de welvaert van onsen ghenadigen, hoochgeboren Coninck Philips van
Spaengien Nederlanden, mitsgaders oock dat Keyserlijcke Rijcke: Welcke landen nu soeckt te beder-
ven ende heel te ruineeren, onder tschijn van bescherminghe, eenen ghenaemt Duca de Alba: In wiens
herte noch verborgen ligt een onwtsprekelijcke bloetdorstige tyrannije, die hy volbrengen sal, soo verre
hy d'overhant crijght, so ghy in dit cleen Boecxken wel sult bevinden dat het warachtich is. 2 Tessal.
5. Proevet al: en dat goet is, behout.* s.l., 1568, den 21. Septemb. New edition in:
  M. G. Schenk, ed. *Verantwoordinge, Verklaringhe ende Waerschouwinghe mitsgaders eene Hertgrondighe Begheerte...* (Amsterdam, 1933) 129-155.
*Disputatie over den Catechismus van Heydelbergh, openbaarlijck voor den Volcke ghehouden op 't*

*Hof van s'Graven-Hage in Hollandt ende West-Vrieslandt ende sijne Princelijcke Excell. Wilhelmus van Nassouwen, in 't bywesen ende bestieren van hare Gecomitteerde. Tusschen Dirck Volckaertsz. Coornhart ende Saravia D. inde Theologie, gheassisteert met Arent Cornelisz. ende andere Predicanten.* Gouda, 1617.

Saravia, H. *De diversis ministrorum Evangelii gradibus, sicut a Domino fuerunt instituti, et traditi ab apostolis, ac perpetua omnium ecclesiarum usis confirmati,* liber unus, cui duo alii additi, alter *De honore qui debetur ecclesiarum pastoribus,* alter *De sacrilegiis et sacrilegorum poenis.* London, 1590; Frankfurt, 1591.

Saravia, H. *Of the diverse degrees of the Ministers of the Gospell. 2. Of the honor which is due unto the Priestes and Prelates of the Church. 3. Of Sacrilege and the punishment thereof.* London, 1592.

Saravia, H. *De imperandi authoritate et christiana obedientia.* Libri quatuor. London, 1593.

Saravia, H. *Defensio tractationis De diversis ministrorum Evangelii gradibus...Contra Responsionem Clarissimi viri D. Theodori Bezae.* London, 1594; nunc primum edita in Germania....Frankfurt, 1601.

Saravia, H. *De sacra eucharistia tractatus,* G. A. Denison, ed. London, 1855.

"Een brief van Adriaan Saravia over Lipsius en 'Het Huis der Liefde' ". H. van Crombruggen, ed. *De vergulden Passer,* XXVIII (1950) 110-117.

*The Holy Bible, conteyning the Old Testament, and the New: Newly Translated out of the Originall tongues: & with the former Translations (Tyndale's, Matthew's, Coverdale's, Cranmer's, Parker's, and the Genevan) diligently compared and reuised by his Maiesties speciall Comandement. Appointed to be read in Churches. (Genesis-2 Kings revised at Westminster by Lancelot Andrewes Bishop of Ely, John Overal, Hadrianus Saravia, Richard Clarke, John Layfield, Robert Teigh, Francis Burleigh, Geoffrey King, Richard Thomson, William Bedwell;.....)* London, 1611.

Saravia, H. *Diversi tractatus theologici.* London, 1611.

"A Letter of Dr. Hadrianus Saravia to the Ministers of the Isle of Garnsay; written in French and translated into English," in: *Clavi Trabales; or Nailes fastened by some Great Masters of Assemblyes. Confirming the Kings Supremacy, the Subjects Duty, Church Government by Bishops...* Nic. Bernard, ed. (London, 1661) 137-146.

Translation:

Saravia, Hadrianus. *A Treatise on the different degrees of Christian Priesthood.* Translated from the Latin by A.W.S[treet] Oxford, 1840.

## 3. PRINTED SOURCES

*Actes du Consistoire de l'Église Française de Threadneedle Street, Londres,* II: *1571-1577,* A. M. Oakley, ed. *PubHS,* XLVIII. London, 1969.

*Acta van de Nederlandsche synoden der zestiende eeuw,* F. L. Rutgers, ed. The Hague, 1889. *WMV,* I, 4.

*Acta der provinciale en particuliere synoden, gehouden in de Noordelijke Nederlanden, gedurende de jaren 1572-1620,* J. Reitsma en S. D. van Veen, ed. 8 vols., Groningen, 1892-1899.

*Album Studiosorum Academiae Lugduno Batavae 1575-1875,* G. du Rieu, ed. The Hague, 1875.

*Alumni Oxoniensis 1500-1714,* J. Forster, ed., IV. London/Oxford, 1892.

*Documentary Annals of the Reformed Church of England: being a Collection of Injunctions, Declarations, Orders, Articles of Inquiry, &c. from the year 1546 to the year 1716,* E. Cardwell, ed. New ed. 2 vols., Oxford, 1844.

*Archives ou correspondance de la maison d'Orange-Nassau,* G. Groen van Prinsterer, ed. 1. série: *1552-1584.* 8 vols., Leiden, 1837-1847.

*Ioannis Meursi Athenae Batavae. Sive, De Urbe Leidensi, & Academia, Virisque claris; qui utramque ingenio suo, atque scriptis illustrarunt:* Libri duo. Leiden, 1625.

*Bekenntnisschriften der Evangelisch-Lutherischen Kirche.* Göttingen, 1952.

*Bekenntnisschriften und Kirchenordnungen der nach Gottes Wort reformierten Kirche,* W. Niesel, ed. Munich, 1938.

*De Nederlandse Belijdenisgeschriften,* J. N. Bakhuizen van den Brink, ed. 2nd ed. Amsterdam, 1976.

*Bescheiden aangaande de Kerkhervorming in Vlaanderen,* H. Q. Janssen, ed. *WMV,* III; 3.

Beza, Th. *Confessio christianae fidei et eiusdem collatio cum papisticis haeresibus* (s.l., 1560).

Bèze, Th. de. *Correspondance,* recueillie par H. Aubert; publiée par H. Meylan, A. Dufour, C. Chimelli et M. Turchetti. Vol. 1- . Geneva, 1960-

Bèze, Th. de. *Du droit des magistrats,* R. M. Kingdon, ed. Geneva, 1971.

Beza, Th. *Ad tractationem de ministrorum Evangelii gradibus, ab Hadriano Saravia Belga editam.* [Geneva] 1592.

*The First Book of Discipline,* J. K. Cameron, ed. Edinburgh, 1972.

*The Third Book of Remembrance of Southampton 1514-1602,* III: *1573-1589,* A. L. Merson, ed. Southampton, 1965.

*Bronnen tot de geschiedenis der Leidsche universiteit,* P. C. Molhuysen, ed. 7 vols., The Hague, 1913-1924.

Buchanan, G. *De iure regni apud Scotos, Dialogus.* Edinburgh, 1579.

*Calendar of State Papers. Domestic Series, preserved in the State Paper Department of her Majesty's Public Record Office.* London, 1856.

*Calendar of State Papers. Foreign Series, preserved in the State Paper Department of Her Majesty's Public Record Office,* 25 vols., *London, 1861-1950.* Continued as *List and Analysis of State Papers. Foreign Series.* London, 1964.

*Lettres de Calvin,* J. Bonnet, ed. 2 vols., Paris, 1854.

*Ioannis Calvini Opera quae supersunt omnia,* G. Baum, E. Cunitz, E. Reuss, ed. 59 vols., *CR,* XXIX-LXXXVII. Brunswick, 1863-1900.

Casaubonus, I. *Ephemerides,* J. Russel, ed. 2 vols., Oxford, 1850.

Casaubonus, I. *Epistolae.* Rotterdam, 1709.

*Clavi Trabales; or Nailes fastened by some great Masters of Assemblyes. Confirming the Kings Supremacy. The Subjects Duty. Church Government by Bishops,* N. Bernard, ed. London, 1661.

*A Collection of scarce and valuable Tracts,* W. Scott, ed. 2nd ed. London, 1809.

Coornhert, D. V. *Wercken,* C. Bomgaert, ed. 3 vols., Amsterdam, 1630.

*Corpus Documentorum Inquisitionis,* P. Fredericq, ed. 5 vols., Ghent, 1889-1906.

*Correspondentie van Robert Dudley graaf van Leycester en andere documenten betreffende zijn gouvernement-generaal in de Nederlanden 1585-1588,* H. Brugmans, uitg. 3 vols., Utrecht, 193.

*Didascalia et Constitutiones Apostolorum,* Fr. X. Funk, ed. 2 vols., Paderborn, 1905-1906.

*Documents illustrative of the Continental Reformation,* B. J. Kidd, ed. Oxford, 1911; repr. 1967.

*Documents illustrative of English Church History,* H. Gee and W. J. Hardy, ed. Repr. New York, 1972.

*Constitutional Documents of the Reign of James I. A.D. 1603-1625,* J. R. Tanner, ed. Cambridge, 1961.

Denzinger, H. *Enchiridion Symbolorum,* A. Schönmetzer, ed. 35th ed. Friburgi Brisgoviae Romae Neo-Eboraci, 1973.

*Ecclesiae Londino-Batavae Archivum. Epistulae et tractatus ecclesiae Londino-Batavae historiam illustrantes,* J. H. Hessels, ed. 3 vols., Cambridge, 1887-1897.

*Epistolae Tigurinae de rebus potissimum ad ecclesiae Anglicanae reformationem pertinentibus conscriptae,* Parker Society. 2 vols., Cambridge, 1848.

*Opus Epistolarum Erasmi.* P.S., H. M. Allen and H. W. Garrod, ed. 11 vols., Oxford, 1906-1947.

Gerhard, J. *Loci Theologici.* 18 vols., Tübingen, 1767-1779 XIII.

Gretserus, J. *Controversiarum Roberti Bellarmini S. R. E. Cardinalis amplissimi Defensio...adversus Junium, Danaeum, Sibrandum, Sutlivium, Witackerum, Chamierum, Abbatam, Povelum, Dresserum, aliosque Sectarios.* 2 vols., Ingolstadt, 1607-1609.

*A History of Conferences and other Proceedings connected with the Revision of the Book of Common Prayer; from the Year 1558 to the Year 1690,* E. Cardwell, ed. Oxford, 1849.

Hooker, R. *Works,* J. Keble, ed. 4th ed. 3 vols., Oxford, 1863.

*The Works of John Jewel,* Parker Society. 4 vols., Cambridge, 1845-1850.

Junius, Fr. *Opuscula Theologica Selecta,* A. Kuyperus, ed. Amsterdam, 1882.

*Kerkeraadsprotocollen der Nederduitsche vluchtelingenkerken te London 1560-1563,* A. A. van Schelven, ed. Amsterdam, 1921.

*Oude kerkordeningen der Nederlandsche Hervormde gemeenten (1563-1638) en het concept-reglement op de organisatie van het Hervormd Kerkgenootschap in het Koninkrijk Holland,* C. Hooyer, ed. Zaltbommel, 1865.

*De Kroniek van Godevaert van Haecht over de troebelen van 1565 tot 1574 te Antwerpen en elders,* R. Roosbroeck, ed. 2 vols., Antwerp, 1929-1930.

Lettenhove, J. B. M. C. Kervyn de. *Relations politiques des Pays-Bas et de l'Angleterre,* 11 vols., Brussels, 1882-1900.

*Letters of Denization and Acts of Naturalisation for Aliens in England 1509-1603, PubHS,* VIII, 1893.

*Original Letters relative to the English Reformation, written during the Reigns of King Henri VIII, King Edward VI, and Queen Mary: chiefly from the Archives of Zürich,* Parker Society, Cambridge, 1847.

*The Zürich Letters, comprising the Correspondance of several Bishops and Others with some of the Helvetian Reformers during the Reign of Queen Elizabeth,* Parker Society. 2 vols., Cambridge, 1842-1845.

*Liber Regis,* John Bacon, ed. London, 1786.

Lipsius, J. *Epistolarum selectarum centuria prima [-quinta] miscellanea.* 4 vols., Antwerp, 1611-1614.

*Iusti Lipsi Epistolarum Centuriae Duae.* Frankfurt, 1591.

*Two Liturgies, A.D. 1549 and A.D. 1552; with other Documents set forth by Authority in the Reign of King Edward VI,* J. Kelley, ed. Parker Society. Cambridge, 1844.

*Livre Synodal contenant les articles résolus dans les Synodes des Églises Wallonnes des Pays-Bas,* I: *1563-1685.* The Hague, 1896.

*Puritan Manifestoes. A Study of the Origin of the Puritan Revolt,* W. H. Frere and C. E. Douglas, ed. London, 1907.

*Philippi Melanchthonis Opera quae sunt omnia,* C. G. Bretschneider, H. E. Bindseil, ed. CR, I-XXVIII. Halle Brunswick, 1834-1860.

*Mémoires pour servir à l'histoire des dix-sept provinces des Pays-Bas, de la principauté te Liège, et de quelques contrées voisines,* J. N. Paquot, ed. 3 vols., Louvain, 1765-1770.

*Memorieboek der Stad Ghent van 't jaer 1301 tot 1795,* 4 vols., Ghent, 1852-1861.

Micron, M. *De christelicke ordinancien der Nederlantscher ghemeinten te Londen (1554),* W. F. Dankbaar, ed. The Hague, 1956.

[Morély, J.] *Traicté De la discipline et police Chrestienne.* Lyon, 1562.

Neve, J. le, *'Fasti Ecclesiae Anglicanae 1541-1857.* III: *Canterbury, Rochester and Winchester Dioceses,* J. M. Horne, ed. London, 1974.

Neve, J. le, *Fasti Ecclesiae Anglicanae,* T. D. Hardy, ed. 3 vols., Oxford, 1854.

*Patrologiae cursus completus. Series Graeca,* J. P. Migne, ed. 161 vols., Paris, 1857-1866.

*Patrologiae cursus completus. Series Latina,* J. P. Migne, ed. 221 vols., Paris, 1844-1864.

*The Work of William Perkins,* I. Breward, ed. Appleford, 1970.

*Puritanism in England,* H. C. Porter, ed. London/Basingstoke, 1970.

*Elizabethan Puritanism,* L. J. Trinterud, ed. New York, 1971.

*Record of the English Bible. The Documents relating to the translation and publication of the Bible in English and publication in English, 1525-1611,* W. Pollard, ed. London, 1911.

*Register of the University of Oxford,* II: *1571-1622,* A. Clark, ed., I: *Introduction.* Oxford, 1887.

*The Register of the Walloon or Strangers' Church in Canterbury,* I, R. Hovenden, ed.

*PubHS,* V. Lyrington, 1891.

*The Registers of Tatenhill,* F. J. Wrotesbey, ed. s.l., 1905.

*Registre de l'église wallonne de Southampton,* H. M. Godfray, ed. *PubHS* IV s.l. 1890.

*Resolutiën van de Heeren Staten van Holland en West-Vriesland 31 Jan. 1524-22 Jan. 1795.* 231 vols., The Hague, ± 1750-1798.

*Returns of Aliens dwelling in the City and Suburbs of London from the Reign of Henry VIII to that of James I,* R. E. G. and E. F. Kirk, ed. 3 vols., Aberdeen, 1900-1908.

Schoockius, M. *De bonis vulgo ecclesiasticis dictis.* Groningen, 1651.

*Select Statutes and other Constitutional Documents illustrative of the reigns of Elizabeth and James I,* G. W. Prothero, ed. 4th ed. Oxford, 1965.

*Certain Sermons, Appointed by the Queen's Majesty, to be declared and read.* Syndics of the University Press. Cambridge, 1850.

*Staffordshire Incumbents and Parochial Records (1530-1680).* W. Noble, ed. London, 1916.

*Sylloges epistolarum a viris illustribus scriptarum.* Tomi quinque, collecti et digesti per Petrum Burmannum (Leiden, 1727) I.

*Synodalia. A Collection of Articles of Religion, Canons, and Proceedings of Convocations in the Province of Canterbury from the year 1547 to the year 1717,* E. Caldwell, ed. 2 vols., Oxford, 1942.

*Tous les synodes nationaux des églises réformées de France,* J. Aymon, ed. 2 vols., The Hague, 1710.

*Texts concerning the Revolt of the Netherlands,* E. H. Kossmann and A. F. Mellink, ed. London/New York, 1974.

*Troubles religieux de XVIe siècle dans la Flandre maritime,* Ed. de Cousemaker, ed. 4 vols., Bruges, 1877.

*Praestantium ac eruditorum virorum Epistolae Ecclesiasticae et Theologicae varii argumenti.* Editio tertia [Ph. van Limborch, ed.] Amsterdam, 1704.

Vorstius, C. *Tractatus theologicus de Deo sive de Natura et Attributis Dei...* Steinfurt, 1610.

Vries [de Heekelingen], H. de. *Genève pépinière du Calvinisme hollandais.* I: *Les étudiants des Pays-Bas à Genève au temps de Théodore de Bèze.* Fribourg, 1918; II: *Correspondance des élèves de Théodore de Bèze après leur départ de Genève.* The Hague, 1924.

*Werken der Marnix-Vereeniging.* 11 vols., Utrecht, 1870-1889.

*The Works of John Whitgift,* Parker Society. 3 vols., Cambridge, 1851-1853.

*The Writings of John Greenwood 1887-1590,* L. H. Carlson, ed. *Elizabethan Nonconformist Texts,* IV. London, 1962.

Wtenbogaert, J. *Brieven en onuitgegeven stukken,* H. C. Rogge, ed. 3 vols., Utrecht, 1868-1874.

Wtenbogaert, J. *Tractaet Van 't Ampt ende Authoriteyt eener Hoogher Christelicker Overheydt in Kerckelicke Saecken.* The Hague, 1610.

## 4. REFERENCE WORKS

*Bibliography of British History Tudor Period, 1485-1603,* C. Read, ed. 2nd ed. Oxford, 1959.

*Bibliography of British History Stuart Period, 1603-1714,* C. Read, G. Davies and M. F. Keeler, ed. 2nd ed. Oxford, 1970.

*Bibliographie nationale. Dictionnaire des écrivains belges et catalogue de leurs publications 1830-1880.* 4 vols., Brussels/Weissenbruch, 1886-1910.

*Catalogue de la Bibliothèque Wallonne déposée à Leide,* 2e Suppl. Leiden, 1865.

*A Short-title Catalogue of Books Printed in England, Scotland, & Ireland and of English Books Printed Abroad 1475-1640,* 2nd ed. W. A. Jackson, F. S. Ferguson & F. Pantzer, ed. II: *I-Z.* London, 1976.

*Catalogus van de tractaten, pamfletten, enz. over de geschiedenis van Nederland, aanwezig in de bibliotheek van Isaac Meulman.* 3 vols., Amsterdam, 1866-1868.

*The Oxford Dictionary of the Christian Church,* F. L. Cross and E. A. Livingstone, ed. 2nd ed. London, 1974.

*Dictionary of National Biography.* 63 vols., London, 1885-1900; repr. 22 vols., Oxford, 1968.

Doorninck, J. I. van. *Vermomde en naamlooze schrijvers opgespoord op het gebied der Nederlandsche en Vlaamsche letteren.* 2 vols., Leiden, 1883-1885; repr. 1970.

Elton, G. R. *Modern Historians on British History 1485-1945. A critical bibliography 1945-1969.* London, 1970.

*La France protestante,* Eugène and Emile Haag, ed. 2nd ed. 6 vols., Paris, 1877-1888.

*Inventaire de la correspondance de Juste Lipse 1564-1606,* A. Gerlo and H. D. L. Vervliet, ed. Antwerp, 1968.

Glasius, B. *Godgeleerd Nederland. Biografisch Woordenboek van Nederlandsche godgeleerden* 3 vols., 's-Hertogenbosch, 1851-1856.

*Realencyclopädie der classischen Altertumswissenschaft.* Repr. München, 1958-1974.

*Realencyklopädie für protestantische Theologie und Kirche,* 3rd ed. (Leipzig, 1896-1913) XIII, 127.130.

*Die Religion in Geschichte und Gegenwart,* 3rd. ed. K. Galling, H. von Campenhausen, E. Dinkler, G. Gloege and E. Løgstrup, ed. 7 vols., Tübingen, 1957-1965.

Somner, W. and Battely, N. ed. *The Antiquities of Canterbury,* 2nd ed. London, s.a.

Witkam, H. J. ed. *De dagelijkse zaken van de Leidse universiteit van 1581 tot 1596.* Introduction and 10 vols., Priv. pr. Leiden, 1969-1975.

Wood, A. à. *Fasti Oxonienses.* New ed. with additions by Ph. Bliss. London, 1721.

Woodruff, C. E. and Danks, W. *Memorials of the Cathedral and Priory of Christ in Canterbury* London, 1912.

*Biografisch Woordenboek der Nederlanden,* A. J. van der AA, ed. 7 vols., Haarlem, 1969.

*Nieuw Nederlandsch Biografisch Woordenboek,* P. C. Molhuysen and P. J. Blok, ed. 10 vols., Leiden, 1911-1937.

*Biografisch Woordenboek van Protestantse Godgeleerden in Nederland,* J. P. de Bie en J. Loosjes, ed. 5 vols. and 1 number. The Hague, 1907-1949.

*Biografisch Lexicon voor de Geschiedenis van het Nederlandse Protestantisme,* D. Nauta, A. de Groot, O. J. de Jong, S. van der Linde and G. H. M. Posthumus Meyjes, ed. (5 vols., Kampen, 1978-    ) I.

## 5. LITERATURE

Abel, D. "The Elizabethan Archbishop," *History Today,* VI (1956) 686-694.

Allen, J. W. "Jean Bodin," in: *The Social and Political Ideas of Some great Thinkers of the sixteenth and seventeenth Centuries* (New York, 1949) 42-61.

Allen, J. W. *A History of Political Thought in the sixteenth Century.* London, 1928.

Asch van Wijck, H. M. A. J. "De Graaf van Leicester in Utrecht," *Tijdschrift voor Geschiedenis, Oudheden en Statistiek van Utrecht,* II (1836) 1-28.

Atkyns, R. *Ancient and present state of Gloucestershire,* 2nd ed. Gloucester, 1768.

Babbage, S. B. *Puritanism and Richard Bancroft.* London, 1962.

Bakhuizen van den Brink, J. N. "La Confession de Foi des Églises Réformées de France de 1559 et la Confession des Pays-Bas de 1561," in: Id., *Ecclesia,* II (The Hague, 1966) 309-335.

Bangs, C. *Arminius. A Study in the Dutch Reformation.* Nashville/New York, 1971.

Becker, B. *Bronnen tot de kennis van het leven en de werken van D. V. Coornhert.* The Hague, 1928.

Becker, B. "Coornhert, de 16de eeuwsche apostel der volmaakbaarheid," *Ned.AK,* XIX (1926) 59-84.

Benham, W. *Diocesan Histories: Winchester.* London, 1884.

Berg, J. van den. *Constrained by Jesus' Love. An Inquiry into the Motives of the Missionary Awakening in Great-Britain in the Period between 1698 and 1815.* Kampen, 1956.

Berkelbach van der Sprenkel, J. W. *Oranje en de vestiging van de Nederlandse staat,* 2nd ed. Amsterdam, 1960.

Besant, W. *London.* London, 1898.

Bieder, W. *Die Vorstellung von der Höllenfahrt Jesu Christi.* Zürich, 1949.

Bindoff, S. T. *Tudor England.* The Pelican History of England, V. Repr. Penguin. Harmondsworth, 1972.

Bisschop, W. *De woelingen der Leicestersche partij binnen Leiden.* Leiden, 1864.

Bizer, E. *Studien zur Geschichte des Abendmahlsstreites im 16. Jahrhundert.* Gütersloh, 1941.

Black, J. B. *The Reign of Elizabeth 1558-1603.* The Oxford History of England, VIII. 2nd ed. Oxford, 1959.

Blok, P. J. "Aanteekeningen over 'de Zwijger' en over het Wilhelmus," *Bijdragen voor Vaderlandsche Geschiedenis en Oudheidkunde,* 4e reeks, VIII (1910) 443-447.

Blok, P. J. *Geschiedenis eener Hollandsche stad.* (4 vols., The Hague, 1910-1918) III.

Blok, P. J. *Willem de Eerste, Prins van Oranje.* 2 vols., Amsterdam, 1919-1920.

Boer, C. *Hofpredikers van Prins Willem van Oranje. Jean Taffin en Pierre Loyseleur de Villiers* The Hague, 1952.

Boer, M. G. L. den. "De Unie van Utrecht, Duifhuis en de Utrechtse religievrede," *Jaar-Boek Oud-Utrecht 1978,* 71-88.

Bohatec, J. *Calvin und das Recht.* Feudingen, 1934.

Bonger, H. *Leven en werk van D. V. Coornhert.* Amsterdam, 1978.

Bonger, H. *De motivering van de godsdienstvrijheid bij Dirck Volckertszoon Coornhert.* Arnhem, s.a.

Bor, P. *Historie der Nederlandtsche Oorloghen.* Amsterdam, 1670.

Bor, P. Chrz. *Oorspronck, begin en vervolgh der Nederlandsche oorlogen, beroerten, en borgerlycke oneenigheden.* 4 vols., Amsterdam, 1679-1684.

Bor, P. *Vervolch der Nederlantsche Oorloghen.* Derden-deels, tweede stuck. Leyden/Amsterdam, 1626.

Brandi, K. *Deutsche Geschichte im Zeitalter der Reformation und Gegenreformation.* Repr. Darmstadt, 1960.

Brandt, G. *Historie der Reformatie en andere Kerkelycke geschiedenissen in en omtrent de Nederlanden* 4 vols., Amsterdam/Rotterdam, 1671-1704.

Breen, Q. *John Calvin: A Study in French Humanism.* Grand Rapids, 1931.

Bromiley, G. W. "Anglicanism and the Ministry," *SJT,* VII (1954) 73-82.

Brook, V. J. K. *Whitgift and the English Church.* Repr. London, 1964.

Bruch, H. *Slaat op den trommele. Het Wilhelmus en de Geuzenliederen.* Leiden, 1971.

Brütsch, J. R. "Le fondement de la mission chez Hadrianus Saravia," *Verbum Caro,* I (1947) 168-171.

Bruin, C. C. de. "Radicaal Spiritualisme te Leiden," *Rondom het Woord. Theologische Etherleergang,* XVII (1975) 66-81.

Brutel de la Rivière, G. J. *Het leven van Hermannus Moded.* Haarlem, 1879.

Busscher, E. de. *Recherches sur les peintres et sculpteurs à Gand aux XVIe, XVIIe et XVIIIe siècles.* Ghent, 1866.

Butterworth, Ch. C. *The literary Lineage of the King James Bible 1340-1611.* Philadelphia, 1941.

*The Cambridge History of the Bible,* II: *The West from the Reformation to the present day,* S. L. Greenslade, ed. Cambridge, 1963.

Cargill Thompson, W. D. J. "Anthony Marten and the Elizabethan Debate on Episcopacy," in: *Essays in Modern English Church History, in memory of Norman Sykes,* G. V. Bennet and J. D. Walsh, ed. London, 1966.

Cargill Thompson, W. D. J. "A Reconsideration of Richard Bancroft's Paul's Cross Sermon of 9 February 1588/9," *JEH,* XX (1969) 253-266.

Chairie, Ch. de la. *Hesdin. Ses origines, ses monuments, ses promenades.* Hesdin, s.a.

Cohen, G. *Écrivains français en Hollande.* Paris, 1920.

Collinson, P. "The Elizabethan Puritans and the Foreign Reformed Churches in London," *ProHS,* XX (1958-1964) 528-555.

Collinson, P. *The Elizabethan Puritan Movement.* London, 1967.

Coolen, G. "Fragment d'obituaire et réforme des Cordeliers de St. Omer," *Bulletin de la Société Académique des Antiquaires de la Morinie,* XX, 1963.

Cooper, C. H. and T. *Athenae Cantabrigienses.* Cambridge, 1861.

Cowper, J. M. *The Memorial Inscriptions of the Cathedral Church of Canterbury.* Canterbury, 1897.

Crew, Ph. M. *Calvinist Preaching and Iconoclasm in the Netherlands 1544-1569.* Cambridge/London/New York/Melbourne, 1978.

Crombruggen, H. van. "Een brief van Adriaan Saravia over Lipsius en 'Het huis der Liefde'." *De vergulden Passer,* XXVIII (1950) 110-117.

Cross, C. *The royal supremacy in the Elizabethan Church.* London/New York, 1969.

Cross, Fr. W. *History of the Walloon and Huguenot Church at Canterbury.* London, 1898.

Cuno, W. *Franciscus Junius der Ältere, Professor der Theologie und Pastor (1545-1602). Sein Leben und Wirken, seine Schriften und Briefe.* Amsterdam, 1891.

Daiches, D. *The King James Version of the English Bible with special Reference to the Hebrew Tradition.* Chicago, 1941.

Dale, J. H. van. "Geheime verkondiging der hervormde leer te Vlissingen ten jare 1558," in: H. Q. Janssen en J. H. van Dale, ed. *Bijdragen tot de Oudheidkunde inzonderheid van Zeeuws-Vlaanderen,* I (1856) 352-358.

Dankbaar, W. F. "Het apostolaat bij Calvijn," *NTT,* IV (1949/1950) 177-192; French translation: "L'apostdat chez Calvin," *Revue d'histoire et de philosophie religieuses,* XLI (1961), 345-354.

Dankbaar, W. F. "Het doctorenambt bij Calvijn,"*NTT* IV (1964/1965) 135-165; French translation: "L'office des docteurs chez Calvin," in: *Regards contemporains sur Jean Calvin. Actes du colloque Calvin, Strasbourg 1964* (Paris, 1965) 102-126.

Dankbaar, W. F. *Hoogtepunten uit het Nederlandsche Calvinisme in de zestiende eeuw.* Haarlem, 1946.

Danvin, J. *Vicissitudes, heur et malheur du Vieil-Hesdin.* Saint-Pol, 1866.

Darlington, R. R., Knowles, M.D. and others, *The English Church and the Continent.* London, 1959.

Dart, J. *The History and Antiquities of the Cathedral Church of Canterbury.* London, 1726.

Davies, D. W. *Dutch Influences on English Culture 1558-1625.* Ithaca, N.Y., 1964.

Dawley, P. M. *John Whitgift and the Reformation.* London, 1955.

Decavele, J. *De dageraad van de Reformatie in Vlaanderen (1520-1565).* 2 vols., Brussels, 1975.

Denis, Ph. *Les églises d'étrangers à Londres jusqu'à la mort de Calvin.* Mémoire Université de Liège, 1973-1974.

Derheims, *Histoire de la ville de Saint-Omer.* St. Omer, 1843.

Deschamps de Pas, L. *Histoire de la ville de Saint-Omer jusqu'à 1870.* Arras, 1880.

Despretz, A. "De instauratie der Gentse Calvinistische Republiek (1577-1579)," *Handelingen der Maatschappij voor Geschiedenis en Oudheidkunde te Gent,* N.R., XVII (1963) 119-229.

Dickens, A. G. *The English Reformation.* Repr. pb. s.l., 1972.

Donaldson, G. *The Scottish Reformation.* Cambridge, 1960.

Dorsten, J. A. van. *Poets, Patrons and Professors. Sir Philip Sydney, Daniel Rogers and the Leiden Humanists.* Leiden/London, 1962.

Drews, P. "Die Anschauungen reformatorischer Theologen über die Heidenmission," *Zeitschrift für praktische Theologie,* XIX (1897) 309-315.

Dugmore, C. W. *Eucharistic Doctrine in England from Hooker to Waterland.* London, 1942.

Dugmore, C. W. *The Mass and the English Reformers.* London, 1958.

Eagleston, A. J. "The Quarrel between the Ministers and the Civil Power, 1581-5," *Société guerniaise. Reports and Transactions,* XII, 480-490.

Echlin, E. P. *The Story of Anglican Ministry.* Slough, 1974.

Edwards, D. L. *A History of the King's School Canterbury.* London, 1957.

Elkan, A. *Philipp Marnix von St. Aldegunde.* I: *Die Jugend Johanns und Philips van Marnix.* Leipzig, 1910.

Elkan, A. *Die erste Publistik der Bartholomäusnacht.* Heidelberg, 1905.

Elton, G. R. *The Tudor Constitution.* Cambridge, 1972.

Essen, L. van der. *Alexandre Farnèse. Prince de Parma. Gouverneur général des Pays-Bas (1545-1592).* 5 vols., Brussels, 1933-1937.

Evenhuis, R. B. *Ook dat was Amsterdam.* 5 vols., Amsterdam, 1965.

Fatio, O. *Nihil pulchrius ordine. Contribution à l'étude de la discipline ecclésiastique aux Pays-Bas. Ou Lambert Daneau aux Pays-Bas (1581-1583).* Leiden, 1971.

Faye, W. E. de. "Huguenots in the Channel Islands," *ProHS,* XIX (1952-1958) 28-40.

Fockema Andreae, S. J. "Uit de geschiedenis van de Waals-hervormde Kerk," *Jaarboekje voor geschiedenis en oudheidkunde van Leiden,* XLVII (1955) 108-130.

Fontaine Verwey, H. de la. "The Family of Love. Radical Spiritualism in the Low Countries," *Quaerendo,* VI (1976) 219-271.

Fosbrooke, Th. D. *An original History of the City of Gloucester.* London, 1819.

Franklin, J. H. *Jean Bodin and the Rise of Absolutist Theory.* Cambridge, 1973.

Fredericq, P. *Note sur l'université de Gand (1578-1584).* Ghent, 1878.

Fuks, L. and R. "The Hebrew production of the Plantin-Raphelengius Presses in Leyden, 1585-1615," *Studia Rosenthaliana,* IV (1970) 1-24.

Fuller, Th. *The Church History of Britain; from the birth of Jesus Christ until the year 1648.* 6 vols., Oxford, 1845.

Galm, M. *Das Erwachen des Missionsgedankens im Protestantismus der Niederlande.* St. Ottilien, 1915.

Garret, Chr. *The Marian Exiles.* Repr. Cambridge, 1966.

Gaudentius, P. *Bedeutung und Verdienst des Franziskaner-Ordens im Kampfe gegen den Protestantismus,* I. Bozen, 1880.

Guerts, P. A. M. *De Nederlandse opstand in de pamfletten 1566-1584.* Nijmegen, 1956.

Geyl, P. *Geschiedenis van de Nederlandse stam,* I-III. Amsterdam/Antwerp, 1949-1959.

Godin, A. *Spiritualité franciscaine en Flandre au XVIe siècle. L'homéliaire de Jean Vitrier.* Geneva, 1971.

Grass, H. *Die Abendmahlslehre bei Luther und Calvin.* Gütersloh, 1954.

Gratien, P. "Le grand schisme et la réforme des Cordeliers à Saint-Omer (1408-1409). Notes et documents," *Franciscana,* V (1922) 5-15, 143-180.

Grave, J. W. de. "Notes on the Register of the Walloon Church of Southampton and the Church of the Channel Islands," *PHS,* V (1894-1896) 125-178.

Greenslade, S. L. *The English Reformers and the Fathers of the Church.* Oxford, 1960.

Groenhuis, G. *De Predikanten. De sociale positie van de gereformeerde predikanten in de Republiek der Verenigde Nederlanden voor ± 1700.* Groningen, 1977.

Grössel, W. *Die Mission und die evangelische Kirche im 17. Jahrhundert.* Gotha, 1897.

Haeghen, V. van der. "Bijdragen tot de geschiedenis der Hervormde Kerk te Gent, gedurende de jaren 1578-1584 (Bloeitijd der Gentsche Reformatie)," *BMHG,* XII (1889) 182-280.

Hall, F. "The Family of Love and the Diocese of Ely," in: *Schism, Heresy and Religious Protest.* D. Bakker, ed. (Cambridge, 1972) 213-222.

Hania, J. *Wernerus Helmichius.* Utrecht, 1895.

Hardenberg, H. *Het archief van curatoren der Leidsche universiteit.* 2 vols., Zaltbommel, 1935.

Hardenberg, H. *De archieven van senaat en faculteiten benevens het archief van de academische vierschaar der Leidsche universiteit.* Zaltbommel, 1935.

Hardy, R. *A History of the Parish of Tatenhill.* 2 vols., London, 1907.

Hargrave, O. T. "The Freewillers in the English Reformation," *CH,* XXXVII (1968) 271-280.

Hartvelt, G. P. *Verum Corpus. Een studie over een centraal hoofdstuk uit de avondmaalsleer van Calvijn.* Delft, 1960.

Hasted, E. *The History and topographical Survey of the County of Kent.* 4 vols., Canterbury, 1778-1799; New Ed. London, 1886.

Hauben, P. J. *Three Spanish Heretics and the Reformation.* Geneva, 1967.

Heal, F. and O'Day, R. ed. *Church and Society in England: Henry VIII to James I.* London, 1977.

Heering, G. J. *De zondeval van het Christendom,* 3rd ed. Arnhem, 1933.

Heeroma, K. " " 'tSal hier haest zijn ghedaen'," *Verslagen en Mededelingen van de Koninklijke Vlaamse Academie voor Taal- en Letterkunde.* New Series (Ghent, 1970) 526-542.

Henderson, G. D. *The Scottish ruling elder.* London, 1935.

Heppe, H. *Die Dogmatik der evangelisch-reformierten Kirche,* 2nd ed. Neukirchen, 1958.

Heylin, P. *Aërius Redivivus: or the History of the Presbyterians.* London, 1670.

Higham, F. *Lancelot Andrewes.* London, 1952.

Hill, Chr. *Intellectual Origins of the English Revolution.* Pb. ed. London, 1972.

Hill, Chr. *Economic Problems of the Church from Archbishop Whitgift to the Long Parliament.* Repr. Oxford, 1968.

Hill, Chr. *Society and Puritanism in Pre-Revolutionary England.* Repr. London, 1969.

Hodges, G. F. "Adrian Saravia. Headmaster of Elizabeth College," *Société guerniaise. Reports and Transactions,* XII (1933) 57-72.

Hoenderdaal, G. J. "The Debate about Arminius outside the Netherlands," in: Th. H. Lunsingh Scheurleer and G. H. M. Posthumus Meyjes, ed. *Leiden University in the Seventeenth Century. An Exchange of Learning* (Leiden, 1975) 137-159.

Hogg, W. R. "The Rise of Protestant Missionary Concern, 1517-1914," in: *The Theology of the Christian Mission,* G. H. Anderson, ed. New York, 1961.

Hooft, P. C. *Nederlandtsche Histoorien.* Amsterdam, 1642.

Houtte, J. A. van, Niermeyer, J. F. Presser, J. Romein, J. Werveke, H. van. ed. *Algemene Geschiedenis der Nederlanden.* 12 vols., Utrecht/Antwerpen/Brussel/Ghent/Leuven, 1949-1958.

Huizinga, J. *Verzamelde Werken.* 9 vols., Haarlem, 1948-1953.

Itterzon, G. P. van. *Franciscus Gomarus.* The Hague, 1930.

Jacobs, P. *Theologie reformierter Bekenntnisschriften.* Neukirchen, 1959.

Janssen, H. Q. *De kerkhervorming te Brugge.* 2 vols., Rotterdam, 1856.

Janssen, H. Q. *De kerkhervorming in Vlaanderen, historisch geschetst naar onuitgegeven bescheiden.* 2 vols., Arnhem, 1868.

Jones, W. M. "Foreign Teachers in Sixteenth Century England," *The Historian,* XXI (1958/1959) 162-175.

Jong, O. J. de. *Beeldenstorm in de Nederlanden.* Groningen, 1964.

Jong, O. J. de. *Nederlandse Kerkgeschiedenis.* Nijkerk, 1972.

Jongkees, A. G. *Staat en kerk in Holland en Zeeland onder de Bourgondische hertogen 1425-1477.* Groningen/Batavia, 1942.

Kawerau, "Adrian Saravia und seine Gedanken über Mission," *Allgemeine Missionszeitschrift,* XXVI (1899) 333-343.

Kernkamp, G. W. *De Utrechtsche Academie 1636-1936.* 3 vols., Utrecht, 1936.

Kingdon, R. M. *Geneva and the Consolidation of the French Protestant Movement 1564-1572. A Contribution to the History of Congregationalism, Presbyterianism, and Calvinist Resistance Theory.* Geneva, 1967.

Kirk, K. E. ed. *The Apostolic Ministry. Essays on the History and the Doctrine of Episcopacy.* London, 1957.

Kist, N. C. "Het allereerste begin der Fransche Evangelie-prediking en der Waalsche gemeente te Leiden in 1581," *Ned.A.,* VII (1847) 309-313.

Kleyn, H. G. "Adrianus Saravia en de Confessio Belgica," *Kerkelijke Courant,* 7 March 1896.

Knappen, M. M. *Tudor Puritanism,* 3rd ed. Chicago/London, 1970.

Knox, D. B. *Thirty-Nine Articles. The historic basis of Anglican Faith.* London, 1967.

Knox, S. J. *Walter Travers: Paragon of Elizabethan Puritanism.* London, 1962.

Koopmans, J. *Het oudkerkelijk dogma in de Reformatie, bepaaldelijk bij Calvijn.* Wageningen, 1938; German transl. *Das altkirchliche Dogma in der Reformation.* Munich, 1955.

Kressner, H. *Schweizer Ursprünge des anglikanischen Staatskirchentums.* Gütersloh, 1953.

Lambley, K. *The Teaching and Cultivation of the French Language in England during Tudor and Stuart Times.* Manchester, 1920.

Langeraad, L. A. van. *Guido de Bray. Zijn leven en werken. Bijdragen tot de geschiedenis van het Zuid-Nederlandsche Protestantisme.* Zierikzee, 1884.

Langeraad, L. A. van. "Adrianus Saravia te Leiden," *Kerkelijke Courant,* 20 February 1897.

Lenselink, S. J. "De dichter van het Wilhelmus," *Levende talen,* Nr. 146 (October 1948) 147-151.

Lenselink, S. J. "Maker van het Wilhelmus sprak in Dordt voor de Staten-Vergadering 1572," *Trouw*, 11 November 1948.

Lenselink, S. J. "Marnix en het Wilhelmus," *Tijdschrift voor Nederlandsche Taal- en Letterkunde*, LXVII (1950) 241-263.

Lenselink, S. J. "Het Wilhelmus, een andere interpretatie," *De Nieuwe Taalgids*, LVIII (1964) 140-148.

Linde, J. M. van der. "Honderd jaar zendingswetenschap in Nederland 1876/77-1975," *NTT* (1977) 226-242.

Linde, S. van der. "Het opkomen en de eerste uitwerking van de zendingsgedachte binnen het Nederlandse gereformeerde protestantisme," in: Id., *Opgang en voortgang der Reformatie* (Amsterdam, 1976) 201-216.

Lindeboom, J. *Austin Friars. Geschiedenis van de Nederlandsche Hervormde Gemeente te Londen 1550-1950.* The Hague, 1950.

Linder, R. D. "Calvinism and Humanism," *CH*, XLIV (1975) 167-181.

McGrath, P. *Papists and Puritans under Elizabeth I.* London, 1967.

Magen, B. *Die Wallonengemeinde in Canterbury von ihrer Gründung bis zum Jahre 1635.* Bern/ Frankfurt, 1973.

Maitland, F. W. *The Constitutional History of England.* Cambridge, 1968.

Maruyama, T. *The Ecclesiology of Theodore Beza. The Reform of the True Church.* Geneva, 1978.

Mason, A. J. *The Church of England and Episcopacy.* Cambridge, 1914.

Meertens, P. J. "Het album amicorum van Jonas Reigersberch ( ± 1578-1611)," *Archief; vroegere en latere mededelingen voornamelijk in betrekking tot Zeeland*, 1946-47 (Middelburg, 1947) 1-39.

Meertens, P. J. "De Groot en Heinsius en hun Zeeuwse vrienden," *Archief; vroegere en latere mededelingen voornamelijk in betrekking tot Zeeland, 1949-50* (Middelburg, 1950) 53-99.

Meiklejohn, M. J. C. *London. A short History.* London, 1908.

Meunier, P. *Histoire d'Hesdin.* I: *La paroisse. Depuis la fondation de la ville en 1554 jusqu'à la révolution française.* Montreuil-sur-Mer, 1896.

Meyhoffer, J. "Adrien Saravia," *BSHPB*, II, 2 (1921) 68-74.

Mieris, Fr. van. *Beschryving der stad Leyden.* 3 vols., Leiden, 1762.

Milward, P. *Religious Controversies of the Elizabethan Age. A Survey of Printed Sources.* London, 1977.

Moens, W. J. C. "The Walloon Settlement and the French Church at Southampton," *ProHS*, III (1888-1889) 51-76.

Molhuysen, P. C. "De voorrechten der Leidsche universiteit," *Mededeelingen der Koninklijke Academie van Wetenschappen*, Afdeling Letterkunde, 58, B, 1. Amsterdam, 1924.

Mooi, R. J. *Het kerk- en dogmahistorisch element in de werken van Johannes Calvijn.* Wageningen, 1965.

Moreau, G. *Histoire du Protestantisme à Tournai jusqu'à la veille de la Révolution des Pays-Bas.* Paris, 1962.

Morris, Chr. *Political Thought in England. Tyndale to Hooker.* London, 1953.

Motley, J. L. *History of the Netherlands.* 6 vols., New York, s.a.

Mout, N. *Bohemen en de Nederlanden in de zestiende eeuw.* Leiden, 1975.

Neal, D. *The History of the Puritans or Protestant Nonconformists.* 5 vols., London, 1837. Repr., 1970.

Neale, J. E. *The Age of Catherine de Medici and Essays in Elizabethan History.* Repr. pb. London, 1970.

Neale, J. E. *Essays in Elizabethan History.* London, 1958.

Neale, J. E. *Queen Elizabeth I.* Repr. pb. Harmondsworth, 1973.

Neuenhaus, J. "Calvin als Humanist," in: J. Bohatec, ed. *Calvinstudien.* Leipzig, 1909.

Neve, J. le. *Monumenta Anglicana; being inscriptions on the monuments of eminent persons deceased in or since 1600 (to the end of 1718).* 5 vols., London, 1719.

Nugent, D. *Ecumenism in the Age of the Reformation. The Colloquy of Poissy.* Cambridge, Mass., 1974.

Nuttall, G. F. "A Transcript of Richard Baxter's Library Catalogue. A Bibliographical Note," *JEH*, II (1951) 207-221; III (1952) 74-100.

Nijenhuis, W. *Calvinus Oecumenicus. Calvijn en de eenheid der kerk in het licht van zijn briefwisseling.* The Hague, 1959.

Nijenhuis, W. *Ecclesia Reformata. Studies on the Reformation.* Leiden, 1972.

Nijenhuis, W. *John Ponet ( ± 1514-1556) als revolutionair pamflettist.* Assen/Amsterdam, 1976.

Nijenhuis, W. "Saravia en het optreden van Jacobus I tegen de benoeming van Vorstius te Leiden," *Ned.AK,* LV (1975) 171-191.

Nijenhuis, W. "Varianten binnen het Nederlands Calvinisme in de zestiende eeuw," *Tijdschrift voor Geschiedenis,* LXXXIX (1976) 358-372.

Nijenhuis, W. "Verstoorde harmonie. De politieke implicaties van de First Admonition to the Parliament (1572)," in: *Geloof en Revolutie. Kerkhistorische kanttekeningen bij een actueel vraagstuk,* aangeboden aan Prof. Dr. W. F. Dankbaar op zijn zeventigste verjaardag (Amsterdam, 1977) 103-124.

Oppenraay, Th. van. *La doctrine de la prédestination dans l'église réformée des Pays-Bas depuis l'origine jusqu'au synode national de Dordrecht en 1618 et 1619.* Louvain, 1906.

Otten, H. *Calvins theologische Anschauung von der Prädestination.* Munich, 1938.

Paillard, Ch. "Les grands prêches calvinistes de Valenciennes," *BSHPB,* XXVI (1877).

Pamp, Fr. E. Jr., "Walton's redaction of Hooker," *CH,* XVII (1948) 95-116.

Pannier, J. *Calvin et l'épiscopat.* Paris, 1927.

Pannier, J. *Les origines de la Confession de Foi et de la Discipline des églises réformées de France.* Paris, 1936.

Parris, J. R. "Hooker's Doctrine of the Eucharist," *SJT,* XVI (1963) 151-165.

Partee, Ch. *Calvin and Classical Philosophy.* Leiden, 1977.

Pattison, M. *Isaac Casaubon 1559-1614,* 2nd ed. Oxford, 1892.

Peck, A. L. *Anglicanism and Episcopacy. A Re-examination of Evidence. With special reference to Professor Norman Sykes' Old Priest and New Presbyter. Together with an essay on Validity.* London/New York, 1958.

Plomp, J. *De kerkelijke tucht bij Calvijn.* Kampen, 1969.

Polman, P. *L'élément historique dans la Controverse religieuse du XVIe siècle.* Gembloux, 1932.

Pollard, A. W. ed. *Records of the English Bible.* London, 1911.

Porter, H. C. *Puritanism in Tudor England.* London, 1970.

Porter, H. C. *Reformation and Reaction in Tudor Cambridge.* Repr. Cambridge, 1972.

Post, R. R. *Kerkgeschiedenis van Nederland in de Middeleeuwen.* 2 vols., Utrecht/Antwerp, 1957.

Posthumus Meyjes, G. H. M. "Le Collège Wallon," in: Th. Lunsingh Scheurleer and G. H. M. Posthumus Meyjes, ed. *Leiden University in the seventeenth Century. An exchange of Learning* (Leiden, 1975) 111-135.

Powicke, F. J. *Henry Barrow Separatist (1550?-1593) and The Exiled Church of Amsterdam. 1593-1622)* (London, 1900.

Prims, Fl. *Geschiedenis van Antwerpen.* 29 vols., Brussels, 1927-1949.

Primus, J. H. *The Vestments Controversy. An Historical Study of the earliest Tensions within the Church of England in the Reigns of Edward VI and Elizabeth.* Kampen, 1960.

Rahlenbeck, Ch. A. "Quelques notes sur les réformés flamands et wallons du 16e siècle refugiés en Angleterre," *PHS,* IV (1891-1893) 22-44.

Rahlenbeck, Ch. A. "Les réfugiés belges du seizième siècle en Angleterre," *Revue trimestrielle,* XII (1865), 4, 5-48.

Read, C. *Lord Burghley and Queen Elizabeth.* Pb. ed. London, 1965.

Read, C. *Mr Secretary Cecil and Queen Elizabeth.* Pb. ed. London, 1965.

Read, C. *Mr Secretary Walsingham and the policy of Queen Elizabeth.* 3 vols., Oxford, 1925.

Reitsma, J. *Franciscus Junius. Een levensbeeld uit den eersten tijd der kerkhervorming.* Groningen, 1864.

Renaudet, A. *Érasme, sa pensée religieuse et son action d'après sa correspondance (1518-1521).* Paris, 1926.

Renaudet, A. "Érasme, sa vie et son oeuvre jusqu'en 1517 d'après sa correspondance," *Revue Historique*, III (1912) 253-255.

Renaudet, A. "Paris de 1494 à 1517," in: *Courants religieux et Humanisme à la fin du XVIe siècle. Colloque de Strasbourg 9-11 mai 1975*. Paris, 1959.

Renaudet, A. *Préréforme et Humanisme*. Paris, 1953.

Rengers Hora Siccama, D. G. *De geestelijke en kerkelijke goederen onder het canonieke, het gereformeerde en het neutrale recht*, I. Utrecht, 1905.

Rieu, W. N. du. "Lambert Daneau à Leyde. Fondation de la communauté wallonne à Leyde le 26 mars 1581," *BHEW*, I (1885) 69-90.

Rimbault, L. *Pierre du Moulin 1568-1658. Un Pasteur classique à l'age classique*. Paris, 1966.

Rogge, H. C. "Het beroep van Vorstius tot hoogleeraar te Leiden," *De Gids*, XXXVII (1873) 31-70, 449-558.

Rogge, H. C. *Caspar Janszoon Coolhaes. De voorlooper van Arminius en de Remonstranten*. 2 vols., Amsterdam, 1856-1858.

Rogge, H. C. *Johannes Wtenbogaert en zijn tijd*. 2 vols., Amsterdam, 1874-1875.

Rogier, L. J. *Paulus Buys en Leicester*. Nijmegen/Utrecht, 1948.

Rogier, L. J. *Geschiedenis van het Katholicisme in Noord-Nederland in de 16e en 17e eeuw*. 3 vols., 2nd ed. Amsterdam, 1957; repr. Pb. ed. 5th ed.; Amsterdam/Brussels, 1964.

Rohloff, L. *Der Kampf um die Staatshoheit in Grossbritannien. Die britischen Monarchomachen und ihre Beziehungen zum Festlande*. Halle, 1931.

Romein, J. and A. *Erflaters van onze beschaving. Nederlandse gestalten uit zes eeuwen*. 9 vols., Amsterdam, 1971.

Rose, E. *Cases of Conscience. Alternatives open to Recusants and Puritans under Elizabeth I and James I*. Cambridge, 1975.

Ruder, S. *A New History of Gloucester*. Cirencester, 1779.

Rudge, Th. *The History and Antiquities of Gloucester*. Gloucester, s.a.

Rupp, E. G. *Studies in the making of the English Protestant Tradition*. Repr. Cambridge, 1966.

Russell, Ch. Fr. *A History of King Edward VI School*. Priv. pr., 1940.

Ruys, Th. Jr. *Petrus Dathenus*. Utrecht, 1919.

Schaefer, P. *Die katholische Wiedergeburt der Englischen Kirche*. Munich, 1933.

Schelven, A. A. van. *Het Calvinisme gedurende zijn bloeitijd* (3 vols., Amsterdam, 1943-[1965]) II.

Schelven, A. A. van. *Willem van Oranje*. Amsterdam, 1948.

Schickler, F. de. *Les églises du refuge en Angleterre*. 3 vols., Paris, 1892.

Schilling, N. *Niederländische Exulanten im 16-Jahrhundert. Ihre Stellung im Sozialgefüge und im religiösen Leben deutscher und englischer Städte*. Gütersloh, 1972.

Schotel, G. D. J. *Kerkelijk Dordrecht, eene bijdrage tot de geschiedenis der vaderlandsche Hervormde Kerk, sedert het jaar 1572*. 2 vols., Utrecht, 1841-1845.

Schweizer, A. "Conradus Vorstius. Vermittlung der reformirten Centraldogmen mit den socianischen Einwendungen," *Theol. Jahrbücher*, XV (1856) 435-486; XVI (1857) 153-184.

Scott Pearson, A. F. *Church and State. Political Aspects of sixteenth century Puritanism*. Cambridge, 1928.

Sepp, Chr. *Drie Evangeliedienaren uit den tijd der Hervorming*. Leiden, 1879.

Sepp, Chr. *Het godgeleerd onderwijs in Nederland gedurende de 16e en 17e eeuw*. 2 vols., Leiden, 1873-1874.

Sepp, Chr. *Polemische en irenische theologie*. Leiden, 1881.

Servais Dirks, P. F. *Histoire litéraire et bibliographique des Frères Mineurs de l'Observance de St.-Francois en Belgique et dans les Pays-Bas*. Antwerp, 1885.

Shriver, Fr. "Orthodoxy and diplomacy: James I and the Vorstius affair". *The English Historical Review*, LXXXV (1970) 449-474.

Siegenbeek, M. *Geschiedenis der Leidsche Hoogeschool van hare oprichting in den jare 1575 tot het jaar 1825*. 2 vols., Leiden, 1829-1832.

Silvester Davies, J. *History of Southampton*. Southampton, 1833.

Simon, J. *Education and Society in Tudor England.* Cambridge, 1967.

Sippell, Th. "Zur Abendmahlslehre des Anglokatholizismus," *Theologische Studien und Kritiken,* CVI (1934/1935) 376-391.

Smit, J. *Den Haag in den geuzentijd.* s.l., 1922.

Smit, J. "De vestiging van het Protestantisme in Den Haag en zijn eerste voorgangers," *Ned.AK,* XIX (1926) 205-264.

Smith, E. O. *Crown and Commonwealth. A Study in the official Elizabethan Doctrine of the Prince. Transactions of the American Philosophical Society held at Philadelphia for promoting useful knowledge.* New Series, LXVI, 8. Philadelphia, 1976.

Smith, L. B. *The Contribution of Hadrian à Saravia to the Doctrine of the Nature of the Church and its Mission: an Examination of his Doctrine as related to that of his Anglican Contemporaries,* Typewr. doct. diss. Edinburgh, 1965.

Smits, L. *Saint Augustin dans l'oeuvre de Jean Calvin.* 2 vols., Assen, 1957.

Speed Hill, W. ed. *Studies in Richard Hooker. Essays preliminary to an Edition of his Works.* Cleveland/London, 1972.

Spijker, W. van 't. *Democratisering van de kerk anno 1562.* Kampen, s.a.

Stone, L. *Social Change and Revolution in England 1540-1640.* 4th ed. London, 1970.

Strype, J. *Annals of the Reformation and Establishment of Religion and other various Occurrences in the Church of England during Queen Elizabeth's happy Reign.* 4 vols., Oxford, 1824.

Strype, J. *The Life and Acts of Matthew Parker.* 3 vols., Oxford, 1821.

Strype, J. *The Life and Acts of John Whitgift.* 3 vols., Oxford, 1822.

Strype, J. *Ecclesiastical memorials relating chiefly to religion, and the reformation of it, and the emergencies of the Church of England under King Henry VIII, King Edward VI, and Queen Mary the First.* (3 vols., Oxford, 1822) II.

Sykes, N. "The Church of England and non-episcopal churches in the sixteenth and seventeenth centuries," *Theology.* Occasional Paper, N.S. XI, 1948. 2nd ed. 1949.

Sykes, N. *Old Priest and New Presbyter. The Anglican attitude to Episcopacy, Presbyterianism and Papacy since the Reformation.* Cambridge, 1957.

Tex, J. den, *Oldenbarnevelt.* 3 vols., Haarlem, 1960-1966.

Tex, J. den. "De Staten in Oldenbarnevelts tijd" in: *Van Standen tot Staten. 600 Jaar Staten van Utrecht 1375-1975.* Stichtse Historische Reeks, I (Utrecht, 1975) 51-89.

Triglandius, J. *Kerkelycke geschiedenissen begrypende de swaere en bekommerlijcke geschillen, in de Vereenigde Nederlanden voorgevallen, met derselver beslissinge ende aenmerckingen op de kerkelycke Historie van Johannes Wtenbogaert.* Leiden, 1650.

Tukker, C. A. *De classis Dordrecht van 1573 tot 1609. Bijdrage tot de kennis van in- en extern leven van de Gereformeerde Kerk in de periode van haar organisering.* Leiden, 1965.

Usher, R. G. *The Reconstruction of the English Church.* 2 vols., London/New York, 1910.

Venemans, B. A. *Franciscus Junius en zijn Eirenicum de pace ecclesiae catholicae.* Leiden, s.a.

Verheyden, A. L. E. *De Hervorming in de Zuidelijke Nederlanden in de XVIe eeuw.* Brussel, 1949.

Doubleday, H. A. Page, W. Salman, L. F. ed. *The Victoria History of the Counties of England.* London, 1900.

Visser, D. "Junius. The Author of the Vindiciae contra Tyrannos?" *TvG,* LXXXIV (1971) 510-525.

Vogelsang, E. "Weltbild und Kreuzestheologie in den Höllenfahrtsstreitigkeiten der Reformationszeit," *ARG,* XXXVIII (1941) 90-132.

Wallace, D. D. Jr. "Puritan and Anglican: The Interpretation of Christ's Descent Into Hell in Elizabethan Theology," *ARG,* LXIX (1978) 248-287.

Wansink, H. *Politieke wetenschappen aan de Leidse universiteit 1575- ± 1650.* Utrecht, 1975.

Warneck, G. *Abriss einer Geschichte der protestantischen Missionen von der Reformation bis auf die Gegenwart.* Berlin, 1905.

Water, J. W. te. *Historie der Hervormde Kerk en doorluchtige schoole te Gent.* Utrecht, 1794.

Water, J. W. te. *Kort verhaal der Reformatie van Zeeland.* Middelburg, 1766.

Welsby, P. A. *Lancelot Andrewes 1555-1626.* London, 1964.

Wendel, Fr. *Calvin. Sources et évolution de sa pensée religieuse.* Paris, 1950.

Wernham, R. B. *Before the Armada. The growth of English Foreign Policy 1485-1588.* London, 1966.

Wernham, R. B. "English Policy and the Revolt of the Netherlands," in: J. S. Bromley and E. H. Kossmann, ed. *Britain and the Netherlands. Papers delivered to the Oxford-Netherlands Conference* (London, 1960) 11-40.

Wesel-Roth, R. *Thomas Erastus. Ein Beitrag zur Geschichte der reformierten Kirche und zur Lehre von der Staatssouveränität.* Lahr/Baden, 1954.

White, B. R. *The English Separatist Tradition. From the Marian Martyrs to the Pilgrim Fathers.* London, 1971.

Wiarda, J. *Huibert Duifhuis, de prediker van St. Jacob.* Amsterdam, 1858.

Wiarda, J. "Huibert Duifhuis," *Kalender voor de Protestanten in Nederland,* II (1857) 199-227.

Willson, D. H. "James I and his literary Assistents," *The Huntington Library Quarterly,* VIII (1944-1945) 35-57.

Willson, D. H. *King James VI & I.* Repr. London, 1971.

Wilson, Ch. *Queen Elizabeth and the Revolt of the Netherlands.* London, 1970.

Woltjer, J. J. *De Leidse universiteit in verleden en heden.* Leiden, 1965.

Wolzendorff, E. *Staatsrecht und Naturrecht in der Lehre vom Widerstandsrecht des Volkes gegen rechtswidrige Ausübung der Staatsgewalt.* Breslau, 1916; repr. Aalen, 1968.

Woodhouse, H. F. *The Doctrine of the Church in Anglican Theology 1547-1603.* London, 1954.

Woodhouse, H. F. "What is Meant by Succession?" *Theology,* LV (1952) 376-379.

Woodward, G. W. O. *Dissolution of the Monasteries.* 2nd ed. London, 1969.

Woude, C. van der. "John Jewel, apologeet van het Anglicanisme," *Ned.AK,* XLVIII. (1967) 213-231.

Woude, C. van der. *Sibrandus Lubbertus.* Kampen, 1963.

[Wtenbogaert, J.] *De Kerckelicke Historie, Vervatende verscheyden Ghedenckwaerdige saken, in de Christenheyt voor-gevallen. Van het Iaer Vierhondert af, tot in het Iaer Sesthien-hondert ende Negenthien. Voornamentlijck in dese Geunieerde Provintien.* 5 vols., s.l., 1647.

Youings, J. *The Dissolution of the Monasteries.* London/New York, 1971.

# INDICES

Numbers printed in italics refer to the footnotes.

## INDEX OF PERSONAL NAMES

# INDEX OF SUBJECTS

# INDEX OF MODERN AUTHORS